D1028497

MUMMIES & MAGIC

The
Funerary Arts
of
Ancient Egypt

MUMMIES & MAGIC

The Funerary Arts of Ancient Egypt

Sue D'Auria   Peter Lacovara   Catharine H. Roehrig

MUSEUM OF FINE ARTS, BOSTON
DALLAS MUSEUM OF ART

Reprinted with the support of The Edward and Betty Marcus Foundation

Copyright 1988 by the Museum of Fine Arts, Boston

The 1988 exhibition and catalogue were supported by grants from the National Endowment for the Humanities, a federal agency.

Designed by Janet O'Donoghue and Cynthia Rockwell Randall

Library of Congress Catalogue Card No. 88-61493

Reprinted with changes 1992 by the Dallas Museum of Art with the permission of the Museum of Fine Arts, Boston

This catalogue was reprinted on the occasion of a long-term loan of Egyptian art from the Museum of Fine Arts, Boston to the Dallas Museum of Art, from September 1990 to September 2000.

ISBN 0-87846-303-8

Printed in Hong Kong

Photography Credits

Unless otherwise noted, all photography was done by the Department of Photographic Services at the Museum of Fine Arts, Boston.

Cover and all color plate photography by Tom Jenkins, DMA, courtesy the Museum of Fine Arts, Boston.

Department of Egyptian and Ancient Near Eastern Art: frontispiece; cats. 22, 23, 46; figs. 2, 4, 7, 10, 13, 14, 23, 36, 44, 47, 49-52, 55, 58, 73, 76, 83.

Lacovara, Peter: cat. 171, fig. 90.

Marx, Myron: figs. 91-93.

Metropolitan Museum of Art: cat. 115 (all photographs).

Oriental Institute of the University of Chicago: fig. 86.

Peabody Museum of Natural History, Yale University: fig. 3.

Drawing Credits

Bruyère, B., Deir el-Medineh (1922-1923), pl. 19: fig. 12.

Davies, Nina M., Journal of Egyptian Archaeology 34 (1938), fig. 9, p. 30: fig. 15.

Erman, A., Die Religion der Ägypter, 1934, fig. 85, p. 216: fig. 20.

Griffin, Barbara Arsenault: cats. 38, 65, 66; fig. 11.

Harvey, Stephen P.: figs. 31-33.

Hornung, E., Tal der Könige, 1982, pp. 137, 138: figs. 19, 21.

Kendall, Timothy: cat. 55 (inscription).

Manuelian, Peter Der: cats. 24, 49, 61, 85, 101, 109, 110, 186, 204; figs. 17 (after pl. VII in te Velde, Seth, God of Confusion, 1967), 18 (after E. Hornung, Aegyptiaca Helvetica 8, 1980), 89.

Markowitz, Yvonne: cats. 1, 3, 4, 12, 29, 59, 68-70, 76, 105, 111, 113, 129, 180, 183, 187, 201, 209; figs. 5, 31-33 (design), 45, 46, 56, 57, 74, 79, 81, 87.

Metropolitan Museum of Art: cat. 86 (all drawings).

de Morgan, John, Recherches sur les Origines de l'Egypte 1, 1896, p. 85, vol. 1: fig. 8; Recherches sur les Origines de l'Egypte 2, 1897, p. 157, vol. 2: fig. 9.

Naville, E., Das Ägyptischer Totenbuch der XVIII. bis XX. Dynastie, 1 (1971), pl. 2: fig. 24; pl. 4: fig. 26; pl. 3: fig. 27.

Piankoff, A., The Tomb of Ramesses VI, 1 (1954), fig. 77: fig. 25.

Roth, Ann Macy: cats. 38 (inscription), 55, 80, 90, 173, 177; figs. 28, 29, 37-43, 77, 78, 88.

Schenck, William P.: figs. 30, 34, 35, 48, 53, 54, 80, 82, 85.

Frontispiece: False door from the tomb of Idu (G 7102).

Cover: Coffin panel of Satmeket, full view and detail (pp. 109-117).

Contents

Preface

In 1988, the Museum of Fine Arts, Boston presented the exhibition *Mummies and Magic: The Funerary Arts of Ancient Egypt.* The Museum conceived the exhibition in response to the wide public interest generated by the collaboration between Sue D'Auria of the Museum of Fine Arts, Boston and Myron Marx of Brigham and Women's Hospital to study the Museum's mummies with CT-scan technology. This fascinating application of a new technology to the study of ancient objects led to the idea for a sequel to the exhibition *Egypt's Golden Age: The Art of Living in the New Kingdom, 1558-1085 B.C.,* shown by the Museum in 1982. This new exhibition, *Mummies and Magic,* would focus on funerary arts and rituals as they affected the average ancient Egyptian. The exhibit drew on the Museum of Fine Arts, Boston's vast collection, much of which had never been publicly displayed.

In 1990, we, the Director of the Museum of Fine Arts, Boston, and the Director of the Dallas Museum of Art, reached a remarkable and groundbreaking agreement. Realizing that the Boston Museum had far more Egyptian material than it could effectively display, and that the Dallas Museum would like to display the kind of antiquities that it would be impossible to acquire on the market today, the Boston Museum agreed to loan Dallas over 350 Egyptian artworks for a ten-year period. In return, the Dallas Museum would underwrite all shipping and installation costs for the pieces and would supply a conservator to Boston's Egyptian Department to conserve Egyptian antiquities. In a time of rising museum costs and escalating art market prices, this arrangement would benefit both institutions. The proposed collaboration became a reality thanks to the very generous support of The Edward and Betty Marcus Foundation, a Dallas-based foundation administering the estate of two people who supported the arts throughout their lives.

The Boston loan to Dallas is threefold: funerary arts, based on the *Mummies and Magic* exhibit; the arts of daily life, based on the *Egypt's Golden Age* exhibit; and a selection of Nubian material, much of it the result of George W. Reisner's excavations in ancient Nubia. The funerary arts loan pieces went on display in Dallas in fall 1990 to great public acclaim. It continues to be one of the most heavily attended exhibits in the Museum. The objects illustrating the arts of daily life will go on display in 1992, and the Nubian material is scheduled for the following year. As part of a general reorganization of the Dallas Museum's collections, prompted by the new Nancy and Jake Hamon Wing, the Museum will display the Egyptian loan exhibit in relation to its noted African art collection in a new Museum of Africa and Asia, on the Museum's Third Level.

In addition to their farseeing support of this long-term loan of Egyptian art, the trustees of The Edward and Betty Marcus Foundation also agreed to fund this reprint of the *Mummies and Magic* catalogue. The original Boston printing consisted of only 2,000 copies and soon went out of print. It is a major scholarly contribution to the study of ancient Egyptian religion and society which well merits reprinting. The Boston Museum agreed that the reprint could include color illustrations of pieces in the loan to Dallas because some of these works were not in the original exhibition. A new edition of this catalogue will serve an invaluable educational purpose, which was a major concern of The Edward and Betty Marcus Foundation in underwriting the loan exhibits and their associated programs.

The *Mummies and Magic* exhibition resulted from the joint efforts of many Boston Museum staff members. Especially significant were the curatorial personnel: Peter Lacovara, Sue D'Auria, and Catharine H. Roehrig of the Department of Egyptian and Ancient Near Eastern Art. Arthur Beale, Susanne Gänsicke, Pamela Hatchfield, Jean-Louis Lachevre, Margaret Leveque, Richard Newmann, Merville Nichols, Leslie Ransick, and Carol Warner all worked on the conservation and restoration of the funerary objects. Tom Wong, Judith G. Downes, and the Exhibition Design Department were responsible for the original installation. Other staff members involved in the Boston exhibition were Ross W. Farrar, Deputy Director; Linda Thomas, Registrar; John E. Morrison, Superintendent; and J. Clifford Theriault, Assistant Superintendent. Janet Spitz and Lisa Harris of the Development Office, and Exhibition Program Manager Désirée Caldwell provided invaluable assistance. The Boston exhibition was made possible by two grants from the National Endowment for the Humanities, a federal agency: one for planning the project, and a second for its implementation and the publications that accompanied it.

At the Dallas Museum, a number of staff members worked to make *Eternal Egypt,* the installation of the Boston loan material, a success. These include Emily Sano, Deputy Director and Senior Curator of Non-Western Art; Anne Bromberg, Research Curator/Associate Curator of Ancient Art; Mark Snedegar, Associate Designer; Phil Angell, Carpenter; Greg Dittmar, Graphic Designer; Queta Moore Watson, Editor; Kimberly Bush, Registrar; Robert Rozelle, Director of Publications; Nancy Berry, Director of Public Programs; Gail Davitt, Manager of Docent Programs; Aileen Horan, Manager of Gateway Gallery/Go Van Gogh; and Melissa Berry, Director of Special Programs. Dallas Museum of Art photographer Tom Jenkins created superb photographs of the art. Rita Freed, Curator of Egyptian Art, and the staff of the Egyptian Department at the Museum of Fine Arts, Boston greatly assisted the Dallas loan. Susanne Gänsicke and Jean-Louis Lachevre, of the Museum of Fine Arts, Boston Research Laboratory, conserved the loan pieces for their display in Dallas.

In a period when most American museums have serious problems in funding their operations, acquiring new works of art, and displaying their permanent collections, the cooperation between the Dallas Museum of Art and the Museum of Fine Arts, Boston for the *Eternal Egypt* exhibit is a model for one creative way in which museums can approach the 21st century.

RICHARD R. BRETTELL
Director, Dallas Museum of Art

ALAN SHESTACK
Director, Museum of Fine Arts, Boston

Foreword

From the ordinary patterns of daily life to speculation on the origin of the universe, the creation of man, and his relations to the gods, all our knowledge of ancient Egypt is derived from three types of evidence. The first is the written word. The Egyptians composed texts of all sorts, including personal letters, economic texts dealing with matters as mundane as the deliveries of dried fish, and philosophical speculation. The second source is two- and three-dimensional representation: painted scenes and reliefs cut in stone on the walls of temples and offering chapels of tombs and statues made for a variety of specific functions. These two aspects of communication – language and representation – are closely related. They are supplemented by the third aspect: the artifactual, which includes the actual implements used by the ancient Egyptians, objects of daily use as well as the objects used in religious and funerary cults.

Curiously, language and representation can be profitably analyzed in terms of each other. For example, in a scene often repeated in the decoration of the above-ground chapels of tombs, the deceased is shown contemplating rows of family members, associates, and servants, who are bringing provisions and animals to him. This scene can be read as a sentence, with the deceased as its subject, the contemplation as its main verb, and the offering bearers as the object. The tense of this sentence, however is ambiguous: is the action taking place in the past, present, or future? Otherwise stated, is the deceased reviewing his life on earth in the past, or is he watching the on-going activities on his estate from a vantage point in the hereafter? As if to reinforce and complement the message, the scene is usually accompanied by a text that serves as a caption or label, "viewing the produce of the fields," or the like. The use of the infinitive "viewing" is similarly non-committal in terms of past, present, or future reference. Thus the scene and the text reinforce one another in their expressions of tense and the important elements of the idea to be communicated, while the details are complementary. The scene supplies additional visual information, such as the color of the animals' hides and the number of offering bearers, while the text provides social details that are impossible to render in the representation, such as the name and official titles of the deceased, and the relationship to him of the other figures – mother, father, sister, brother, steward, butcher, and so forth.

Some aspects of Egyptian life – political administration (from titles), economics (from inventories), jurisprudence (from lawsuits), literature, and wisdom – are known almost entirely from texts. Much of what we know, however, can only be reconstructed from the archaeological remains, the bulk of which come from tombs. Paradoxically, we know more of Egyptian life from cemeteries than from cities, villages, and farms. In their tomb chapels, the Egyptians recorded scenes of daily life, and in their burial chambers were placed the objects they had used in life, to sustain them and make pleasant their journey and stay in the realm of the dead.

The topic "mummies and magic" thus embraces a broad spectrum of Egyptian life, as well as the Egyptians' beliefs about death and the dead. Through the study of actual mummies we can learn their ages at death, their medical and dental histories, and the diseases from which they suffered. By extension, the study of burials and tomb chapels, the art and architecture of tombs, and the accompanying burial equipment provide the scholar with a rich and rewarding trove of information, ranging from the contents of the pots left in the tomb as gifts to the techniques of jewelry manufacture.

We think of Egyptian magic mainly in terms of spells against scorpions and poisonous serpents. But spells of a higher order, the Pyramid Texts, the Coffin Texts, and the Book of the Dead, bring us into the realm of the highest and most advanced Egyptian thoughts about the life to come. These spells were created to enable the king, and later his officials, to ascend to the celestial regions, to ward off the enemies who beset travelers to the other world, and to join the imperishable stars. It is not surprising that one of the main archives of Egyptian literary texts was found in the tomb equipment of an Egyptian "magician" of the Middle Kingdom, texts including the Story of Sinuhe and the Complaints of the Eloquent Peasant.

"Mummies & Magic: The Funerary Arts of Ancient Egypt" encompasses Egyptian life and Egyptian thought, as illustrated by the artifactual and artistic production of an extraordinary civilization.

WILLIAM KELLY SIMPSON
Consultative Curator,
Department of Egyptian and
Ancient Near Eastern Art

Acknowledgments

The "Mummies & Magic" exhibition is the result of nearly four years of preparation and cooperation by many different departments of the Museum, particularly the junior staff.

Our thanks to the scholars throughout the world who contributed to the catalogue; to Cynthia Purvis, editor in the Office of Publications, who, with great skill and humor, integrated more than forty authors' diverse styles; and to Carolyn Wojcik, volunteer in the Department of Egyptian and Ancient Near Eastern Art, whose tireless effort has been an inspiration to us all. Edith Bundy, Rima Bulos, and Stephen Harvey of the Department spent long hours assisting with the editing, and line drawings were provided by Yvonne Markowitz, William P. Schenck, Barbara Arsenault Griffin, and Peter Der Manuelian. We are grateful to Ann Macy Roth for her preparation of the index and her valuable editorial suggestions. We would also like to thank Carl Zahn, Director of the Office of Publications, and Janet O'Donoghue and Cynthia Rockwell Randall, designers of the catalogue.

This catalogue would not have been possible without the excellent photographs, most of which have been taken over the last two years by the Museum's photography staff. We would like to thank Janice Sorkow, Director of Photographic Services, and her staff: William R. Buckley, Thomas P. Lang, Joe Logue, John C. Lutsch, Gary Ruuska, Marty Wolfand, and John D. Woolf in the Photo Studio; Pamela Baldwin, Susan Dackerman, Sandra Mongeon, and Ann Petrone in Photographic Services.

For valuable help in supplying information and research materials we are indebted to Marsha Hill, Christine Lilyquist, Ann Russmann, Dorothea Arnold, Larry Berman, Peter Dorman, and William P. Schenck of the Department of Egyptian Art of the Metropolitan Museum of Art; Dr. C. N. Reeves of the Department of Egyptian Antiquities at the British Museum; and Dr. Gerry Scott of the Yale University Art Gallery.

For loans of important objects to the collection we are deeply indebted to Kathryn L. Maxson and Myles Silberstein, Miles Collier, Christos Bastis, Peter Diem, The Field Museum of Natural History in Chicago, and the Peabody Museum of Natural History at Yale University.

We would also like to thank the National Endowment for the Humanities for underwriting this project, in particular Marsha Semmel, Assistant Director for the Humanities Project in Museums and Historical Organizations, and Thomas H. Wilson and Elizabeth H. Turner, Program Officers, museums. For their help and expertise we are most grateful to Janet Spitz and Lisa Harris of the Museum's Development Office.

Many members and friends of the Egyptian Department contributed long hours of work on this project including Tara Wyman, Karen Kennedy, Timothy Kendall, Brian Curran, Ellen Woolf, Anne Noonan, Millicent Jick, Lilliane LeBel, and Joseph Fury.

For contributing their valuable skills to the project we would also like to thank Madeleine Hinkes, Blyth Hazen, Myron Marx, Douglas Hansen, Brigham and Women's Hospital, and the CEMAX company.

Finally, we would like to thank the Museum's administration and staff for their support and input, including Alan Shestack, Ross Farrar and Jan Fontein. Special thanks to Tom Wong, Judith G. Downes, Masumi Nagatomi, Susan D. Wong, and Janie Driscoll in the Design Department; Linda Thomas, Kim Pashko, Patricia Loiko, and Galen Martin Mott in the Registrar's Office; Cliff Theriault, Jack Morrison, Steve Malachowski, Herb Johnson, Peter Johnson, Henry Clifford Philbrook III, Raymond W. Burke, and Ralph LaVoie in Buildings and Grounds; Richard M. Newman and Susan Mulski in the Research Laboratory; furniture conservators Robert G. Walker and Susan Odell; Jane Hutchins and Leslie Smith; and Lorri Berenberg, Nancy McCallie, and William J. Burback in the Department of Education.

SD'A, PL, CHR

8

Chronology

Predynastic Period (Upper Egypt)

Badarian	4800-4200 B.C.
Naqada I (Amratian)	4200-3700 B.C.
Naqada II (Gerzean)	3700-3250 B.C.
Naqada III (Late Gerzean-Dyn. 0)	3250-3100 B.C.

Archaic Period

Dynasty 1	3100-2857 B.C.
Dynasty 2	2857-2705 B.C.
Dynasty 3	2705-2630 B.C.

Old Kingdom

Dynasty 4	2630-2524 B.C.
Dynasty 5	2524-2400 B.C.
Dynasty 6	2400-2250? B.C.

First Intermediate Period

Dynasty 7	2250-2230 B.C.
Dynasty 8	2230-2213 B.C.
Dynasty 9	2213-2175 B.C.
Dynasty 10	2175-ca. 2035 B.C.
Dynasty 11 (Pre-Conquest)	2134-2061 B.C.

Middle Kingdom

Dynasty 11 (Post-Conquest)	2061-1991 B.C.
Dynasty 12	1991-1784 B.C.

Second Intermediate Period

Dynasty 13	1784-1668 B.C.
Dynasty 14	1720-1665 B.C.
Dynasty 15	1668-1560 B.C.
Dynasty 16	1665-1565 B.C.
Dynasty 17	1668-1570 B.C.

New Kingdom

Dynasty 18	1570-1293 B.C.
Dynasty 19	1293-1185 B.C.
Dynasty 20	1185-1070 B.C.

Third Intermediate Period

Dynasty 21	1070-946 B.C.
Dynasty 22	946-712 B.C.
Dynasty 23	828-765? B.C.
Dynasty 24	760-712 B.C.
Dynasty 25	767-656 B.C.

Saite Period

Dynasty 26	685-525 B.C.

Late Period

Dynasties 27-30	525-343 B.C.

Persian Reconquest 343-332 B.C.

Ptolemaic Period 332-31 B.C.

Roman Period 31 B.C. - A.D. 395

Coptic Period late 2nd century A. D. to A.D. 641

Arab Conquest A.D. 641

This chronology is used with the kind permission of the late Klaus Baer.

Authors

LA-M	Laila Abdel-Malek, Boston
JPA	James P. Allen, New Haven
MB	Martha Bell, Chicago
RB	Robert Bianchi, Brooklyn
MLB	Morris L. Bierbrier, London
JB	Janine Bourriau, Cambridge, England
AB	Andrew Boyce, Cambridge, England
EB	Edward Brovarski, Boston
LHC	Lorelei H. Corcoran, Chicago
SD'A	Sue D'Auria, Boston
SD	Susan Doll, Vienna
DF	Detlef Franke, Munich
RF	Rita Freed, Memphis
SPH	Stephen P. Harvey, Boston
PH	Pamela Hatchfield, Boston
JLH	Joyce L. Haynes, Sunderland
JH	John Herrmann, Jr., Boston
MJ	Millicent Jick, Boston
SJ	Sally Johnson, Princeton
TK	Timothy Kendall, Boston
PL	Peter Lacovara, Boston
MEL	Mary Ellen Lane, Washington, D.C.
RJL	Ronald J. Leprohon, Toronto
ML	Margaret Leveque, Boston
YJM	Yvonne J. Markowitz, Boston
MM	Myron Marx, San Francisco
NN	Nancy Netzer, Boston
LP	Laure Pantalacci, Paris
BAP	Barbara A. Porter, New York
SQ	Stephen Quirke, Cambridge, England
MJR	Maarten J. Raven, Leiden
CNR	C.N. Reeves, London
RKR	Robert K. Ritner, Chicago
CHR	Catharine H. Roehrig, Boston
ER	Eva Rogge, Vienna
AMR	Ann Macy Roth, Boston
ERR	Edna R. Russmann, New York
WKS	William Kelly Simpson, New Haven
DS	Donald Spanel, Brooklyn
AJS	A.J. Spencer, London
NS	Nigel Strudwick, Los Angeles
JHT	John H. Taylor, Birmingham, England
HtV	Herman te Velde, Groningen
JY	Janice Yellin, Wellesley
A-PZ	Alain-Pierre Zivie, Paris

Introduction

Fig. 1. View of the Way Collection on display in the old Museum of Fine Arts in Copley Square, about 1890.

The galleries of ancient Egyptian art are among the most popular in the Museum with young and old visitors alike. There has always been a keen interest in the mummies, coffins, and funerary objects. Due to accidents of preservation and the preferences of early archaeologists and collectors, much of the surviving material culture of ancient Egypt is of a funerary nature. There is relatively little information available to the general public on this aspect of Egyptian culture and many misconceptions have arisen about ancient Egypt and its funerary practices. These have been fueled by the media's creation of the "mummy's curse," by innumerable horror movies, and by wild imagination.

The exhibition "Mummies & Magic: The Funerary Arts of Ancient Egypt" is intended to explain what is known about the funerary beliefs of the Egyptians and to reveal how their burial practices developed over a period of more than 3000 years, incorporating influences from the outside world while retaining a remarkable continuity. Part of its purpose is to explain the symbolism and ritual that formed the basis of the Egyptian belief in a material afterlife.

The core of the Egyptian collection was formed in 1872, when the newly incorporated Museum was given the Egyptian collection of C. Granville Way. Way's father had purchased part of the collection that Robert Hay, a Scottish antiquarian, had acquired on a number of expeditions he conducted to Egypt between 1824 and 1838. The Way collection includes the bulk of the Museum's holdings of late period funerary art, including a series of cartonnage and wooden coffins of the Third Intermediate Period, *shawabti*s, animal mummies, and canopic jars.

In 1875, Francis Cabot Lowell presented the Museum with a number of pieces collected in Egypt by his brother John in the mid 1830s. Even more important than the objects was the loan of Lowell's copious diaries and accompanying watercolors and sketches by his companion Charles Gleyre.

The Museum was an early supporter of the excavations of the Egypt Exploration Fund (now Egypt Exploration Society), a British society founded in 1882. For many years it maintained an American branch in which the Museum was quite active, and from 1885 to 1909, objects excavated and contributed by the

Fund enriched the collection. These include material from the Delta sites excavated by Petrie and Naville, and objects discovered by Petrie and others at sites throughout Egypt, including Abydos, Dendera, and Hawara.

In 1902, the Museum established a department of Egyptian art, with Albert M. Lythgoe as its first curator. Almost at once Lythgoe went to Egypt, where he learned the archaeological excavation techniques developed by the American Egyptologist George Andrew Reisner. Reisner was excavating at that time for the University of California under the sponsorship of Phoebe A. Hearst. In 1905, the Museum and Harvard University assumed the sponsorship of Reisner's expedition, which was known thereafter as the Harvard University-Museum of Fine Arts Expedition. For nearly forty years Reisner continued his excavations, training a whole generation of archaeologists. Reisner was the first archaeologist to use extensive photographic documentation in fieldwork; he established a thorough system of recording, and his techniques were adopted by many other American and foreign expeditions. He systematically excavated dozens of Predynastic Period, Old Kingdom, First Intermediate Period, Middle Kingdom, and Late Period sites. He concentrated particularly on the great Old Kingdom necropolis at Giza. In addition to uncovering the monuments of Mycerinus, he cleared more than 429 mastaba tombs of Dynasties 4 to 6.

The corpus of Old Kingdom art that was added to the Museum's collection through Reisner's work, including the extraordinary collection of sculpture and relief, and particularly the mysterious reserve heads, is without equal outside of Cairo. In addition to these masterpieces there are many unique examples of funerary equipment, including a plaster mask and body cover, a Dynasty 4 mummy and coffin, and a faience bead dress restored for this exhibition.

Reisner also uncovered a vast amount of material of the First Intermediate Period and Middle Kingdom at Naga ed-Dêr, including a number of provincial grave stelae and coffins and a magnificent jewelry group from an undisturbed mummy. At Deir el-Bersha, the expedition recovered objects of the early Middle Kingdom, including the almost complete tomb equipment of the nomarch Djehuty-nakht. Among the objects from this tomb were spectacular painted coffins and a lovely wooden procession of offering bearers.

Fig. 2. Old Kingdom sarcophagi and the sarcophagus of Kheper-re after excavation at Giza, about 1930.

From 1924 to 1932, the Museum expedition excavated five of the Egyptian forts placed near the second cataract of the Nile, in what is now the Sudan. The forts were active from the late Middle Kingdom through the New Kingdom, and the material retrieved from their excavation has contributed to the Museum's collection of Second Intermediate Period and early New Kingdom objects.

After Reisner's death in 1942 he was succeeded by Dows Dunham and William Stevenson Smith, who concerned themselves with publishing the vast body of material already discovered, rather than conducting new excavations. The collection was enriched through gifts, purchases, and exchanges, notably the Roman mummy shrouds and the coffins of Hennetawy acquired through exchange with the Metropolitan Museum of Art.

In more recent years, the Museum has been fortunate to obtain a great number of fine objects in areas that had been poorly represented. As the Department of Egyptian and Ancient Near Eastern Art approaches its second century, we look forward with renewed commitment to the care and publication of this magnificent archaeological collection.

SD'A, PL, CHR

Mummification in Ancient Egypt

Egyptian mummies have been a source of fascination for hundreds of years. Textual references to mummies appear as early as the twelfth century, and the resins used in the mummification process were thought to be related to the bituminous matter flowing from the "Mummy Mountain" in Persia, which possessed medicinal qualities.[1] By the sixteenth century, powdered mummy was prescribed routinely to combat all sorts of ailments, from wounds and bruises to stomach disorders. Because of its supposed efficacy as a medicine, Egyptian mummies were much in demand in Europe, and a great number of them were destroyed for this purpose. In fact, the demand was so great that it could not be met by the transport of authentic mummies from Egypt, and it is said that modern "mummies" were produced by charlatans to satisfy the market.[2] The use of mummies as medicine ended in the eighteenth century, but the destruction of Egyptian mummies continued into the nineteenth century, when they were not only used as fuel for Egyptian locomotives, but were brought into the U.S. during the Civil War by a paper manufacturer, who used the bandages in the manufacture of brown wrapping paper.[3] European travelers brought back mummies from their voyages to Egypt, and some were sold on the antiquities market. The unwrapping and autopsy of mummies became a popular form of parlor entertainment, although there was some scholarly interest in the proceedings.[4] The end result of this experimentation and destruction was the depletion of the number of mummies. Fortunately, today mummies can be studied using noninvasive techniques, and a great deal can be learned about them without unwrapping or autopsying them (see "Modern Radiographic Evaluation of Egyptian Mummies," p. 246).

The image of the mummy that has resulted from the Hollywood movies of the past forty years has been that of a mysterious being. The mummification process is often thought of as one known only to the ancients. This is not the case, for a great deal is known about the methods used by the Egyptian embalmers.

In very early times, the Egyptians buried their dead without coffins in simple pit graves dug into the desert sands (fig. 3). The hot, dry, sand, which came into direct contact with the bodies, desiccated them and acted as a natural preservative. The remarkable preservation of the natural "mummies" must have been observed by the ancient Egyptians, and may have contributed to early religious beliefs in survival after death. With the rise of the Egyptian state, and the attendant accumulation of wealth, some Egyptians began to be buried in coffins, at first of reed and later of wood, and tombs were lined with brick or wood (see "Funerary Architecture" p. 20). Ironically, the more elaborate burials contributed directly to the decay of the bodies within, because the desiccating desert sand no longer came in contact with the bodies. Since religious beliefs dictated that the body be preserved (see "Funerary Texts and their Meaning," p. 38) the ancient Egyptians began to experiment with methods of artificial preservation. At first, the body, in a contracted position, was simply wrapped with linen bandages that had been soaked in resin. Bodies treated in this way have been excavated from Archaic Period mastabas at Sakkara.[5] In Dynasty 3, attempts were made to render the body's appearance more lifelike by padding it and adding details in linen. Such was the case with human remains, possibly of the king himself, found in the burial chamber of the Step Pyramid of Djoser.[6] This process continued into the later Old Kingdom (fig. 4 [cat. 6]). In late Dynasties 5 and 6, the desire to simulate the appearance of the deceased was carried one step further; a layer of plaster was applied to the body, and the features were molded (see cat. 23).

The more complex treatment of the outer wrappings contributed nothing to the preservation of the body, except to mask the inward decay, and thus the ancient embalmers began to experiment with chemical treatments. The advent of true mummification was in Dynasty 4, when a procedure was developed that

Fig. 3. Predynastic burial.

Fig. 4. Old Kingdom mummy from Giza tomb G 2220.

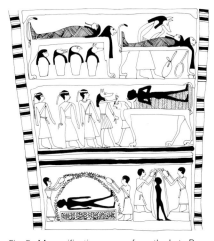

Fig. 5. Mummification scenes from the Late Period coffin of Djed-bast-iuef-ankh, Hildesheim Museum. *Lower register,* purification of the body with streams of water; *middle register,* the body attended by priests and treated; *upper register,* the wrapped mummy with canopic jars, and attended by Anubis.

was to be used with some variation for the next two thousand years. Though the Egyptians left no texts describing the actual process, the accounts of the Greek writers Herodotus,[7] writing in the fifth century B.C., and Diodorus,[8] who lived 400 years later, provide a great deal of information that probably applies to earlier periods as well. The employment of the basic processes that they describe has been confirmed by the examination of the mummies themselves. Different stages of the process were also depicted on coffins[9] (fig. 5), which illustrate the purifying ceremonies accompanying mummification, as well as showing the body on the embalming bed (see cat. 171), attended by priests.

The most elaborate, and expensive, technique described by Herodotus and Diodorus involved the removal of four internal organs, which would have been subject to rapid decay. The lungs, liver, stomach, and intestines were removed through an incision in the left flank. The kidneys were generally left in place. The heart was never intentionally removed, as it, rather than the brain, was seen as the seat of intelligence. If removed accidentally, it sometimes was sewn back into place.[10] The viscera were embalmed separately and placed in four canopic jars that were stored in a chest in the tomb (see cat. 10). This method was practiced in Dynasty 4, if not earlier, as evidenced by the discovery in the tomb of Queen Hetep-heres (the mother of Khufu, builder of the Great Pyramid) of an alabaster canopic box containing mummified viscera. Amazingly, when the box was opened, the wrapped viscera were found to be resting in a solution of 3% natron, still in liquid form after more than 4,000 years.[11]

Called *netjery* in ancient Egyptian, natron (from which the chemical symbol for sodium, Na, derives) was the basic element employed in mummification. A combination of sodium carbonate and sodium bicarbonate (with impurities of sodium chloride and sodium sulphate), it was found in several places in Egypt, most notably in the Wadi en-Natrun, approximately forty miles northwest of Cairo.[12] Natron was valued not only for its properties as a desiccant; it was also a purifying and cleansing agent used in ceremonies of purification.[13] During mummification, the eviscerated body would be packed with natron, which would also be heaped around the exterior. In later times, the length of time it took to totally desiccate the body was about forty days, but in the Old Kingdom, when much experimentation was taking place, natron was probably used in solution, necessitating more time. This may account for an inscription from the tomb of Meres-ankh at Giza, which states that 273 or 274 days elapsed between her death and burial.[14] This is an inordinately long time when compared to the seventy days that is known from the New Kingdom and later. The body cavity was packed with linen that had been soaked in resin, and then the final layer was probably soaked in resin and molded. On the male mummies, the sexual organs were reproduced in linen. The features of the face were detailed in paint.[15] The mummy was placed in its coffin in an extended position (rather than the contracted one used in earlier times) on its left side. It is possible that an extended position was used because of the new method of mummification, which required access to the abdominal cavity.[16]

Very few mummies have survived from the Old Kingdom. This is due not only to the experimental nature of the mummification process, but also to the fact that mummification was limited to members of the royal family for religious reasons (see "Funerary Texts and their Meaning," p. 48). This was probably the case in the early Middle Kingdom as well. The mummies of several princesses of Dynasty 11 have been excavated beneath the temple complex of King Mentuhotep II at Deir el-Bahri.[17] Surprisingly, the viscera had not been removed through an incision, but a new technique was employed. This was the second, less expensive one discussed by Herodotus, who says that "oil of cedar" was injected through the anus and the body "pickled" in natron,[18] which effectively purged the body of its internal organs. This method was probably used on the Dynasty 11 mummies, though "oil of cedar" has no purging qualities, and some other substance, such as oil of turpentine, was probably the substance employed.[19] It has been recently suggested that this technique was not less expensive, but simply a regional variation used in Upper Egypt.[20] We know that some early Dynasty 11 mummies did have their viscera removed through incisions, since the tomb of Djehuty-nakht (cat. 43) contained canopic jars, one of which was recovered. This seems to have been the practice in the succeeding dynasty as well, as evidenced, for example, by the mummy of Senebtisi found at Lisht.[21] The preservation of these mummies was much better than those of the Old Kingdom, presumably because the embalmers had discovered the advantages of using natron in dry rather than liquid form. Modern experiments with pigeons, mice, and dry natron have indicated that the desiccation process takes a much shorter period (closer to the thirty-five or forty days known from the New Kingdom), and results in a well-preserved mummy.[22]

Another apparent innovation of the early Middle Kingdom was the removal of the brain. This has been documented in the head of Djehuty-nakht (fig. 6 and cat. 43), though the technique was obviously experimental at this stage, and was not refined until the New Kingdom. Removal of the brain using methods similar to that performed on Djehuty-nakht has been observed in Dynasty 12 mummies as well.[23] To the ancient Egyptians, the brain had no special significance, and thus it was discarded. The face of Djehuty-nakht was well modeled with linen, and the eyebrows painted to enhance realism, continuing the trend set in the Old Kingdom.

The mummification process was further refined in the New Kingdom, as evidenced by the royal mummies discovered in two caches at Thebes, where priests placed them after many of the royal tombs were robbed at the end of the New Kingdom.[24] Most of these mummies were very well preserved. The brains had been removed through the nose, which was the technique that became standard.[25] Molten resin was poured into the body cavities, which were then packed with linen. The resin would have inhibited the growth of bacteria and had disinfecting and deodorizing qualities.[26]

The art of mummification reached its zenith in Dynasty 21. The priests who restored the desecrated mummies of the New Kingdom kings must have noted that the bodies were not as lifelike as desired, and the mummification process was further developed. The process, which was used with minor variations through the Late Period, was quite complex. The body was brought to one of the embalming centers that must have been distributed up and down the Nile. This was known as the *per nefer* (literally, "good house"). The brain was re-

Fig. 6. Head of Djehuty-nakht from Deir el-Bersha (cat. 43).

Fig. 7. Mummy of the Saite period from Giza G 7757 A, room IV.

moved, and linen was sometimes packed into the cranial cavity (see cat. 170). The four viscera were extracted through the embalming incision, and the body cavities washed with, according to Herodotus, palm wine and spices.[27] The viscera were mummified separately in natron. In Dynasty 21, they were not placed in canopic jars, but were wrapped in four linen packages, each accompanied by a wax figure of one of the four protective canopic deities, the Four Sons of Horus (see cat. 172), and replaced in the body. Canopic jars had become such a standard element of funerary equipment, however, that full sets of ''dummy'' canopic jars were still provided (cat. 117). In Dynasty 26, canopic jars made a brief reappearance, as the viscera were again placed within them, but in the Late Period, the general practice was to wrap the organs in a parcel placed between the legs of the mummy.

The body was packed with linen and other materials[28] and heaped with dry natron for about forty days. (It is interesting to note that in modern-day Egypt, a funerary ceremony is carried out forty days after a death.[29]) At the end of this period of desiccation, the temporary packing material was removed. The body was then washed and packed with a variety of materials, including resin-soaked linen, sawdust, and even lichen and onions.[30] This packing compensated for the effects of desiccation, which left the body shrunken and weighing up to 75 percent less[31], and restored the body to its original contours. In Dynasty 22 and later, greater reliance was placed on the use of molten resin, which was poured liberally into the body cavities (see cat. 170). The embalming incision was closed, and a metal plate decorated with the protective *wedjat* eye (cat. 173) was placed over it. In Dynasty 21, subcutaneous packing with pads of linen, sand, or even sawdust restored a lifelike appearance. Such packing beneath the skin via a series of small incisions is first attested in the Dynasty 18 mummy of King Amenhotep III.[32] The desiccated eyes were left in place, and covered with linen pads, over which the eyelids were drawn. Artificial eyes of stone were sometimes inserted (see cat. 120). The entire surface of the body was then treated with molten resin in order to toughen and waterproof it.[33]

The final stage of the process, the wrapping of the mummy, now began. Protective amulets or jewelry would be inserted between layers of the wrappings (cat. 129). The body was wrapped in hundreds of yards of linen. Usually layers of coarse linen were placed closest to the body, while fine layers completed the wrapping, sometimes in elaborate patterns (fig. 7). Some of the linen used for mummies was purchased especially for this purpose, but the coarser layers could include household linens saved by the deceased for burial. Wealthier patrons might be buried in linens that had been used to dress temple statues of the gods.[34] The bandaging took approximately fifteen days, and was accompanied by great ceremony, including the recitation of the texts known as the "Ritual of Embalming," copies of which date from the Roman period[35] (see "Funerary Texts and their Meaning," p. 43). The mummy was placed in its coffin and carried in procession to the tomb.

Religious beliefs prescribed that refuse embalming material be placed in jars and buried near the tomb. A cache of embalming equipment, dating to the Late Period, was discovered by Reisner at Giza (see cat. 182), and contained nearly thirty pottery jars of various types, approximately seventeen bowls and dishes, and faience amulets representing Nefertum, Ptah, Taweret, and *wedjat* eyes.[36] Similar caches have been excavated, the best known being that belonging to the tomb of Tutankhamen, which comprised not only embalming equipment, but also the remains of the meal eaten at the king's funeral.[37]

In the Ptolemaic and Roman periods, the mummification process suffered a great decline. Though many people were mummified (mummy tags were used for identification during the transportation and embalming processes; see cat. 184), much less attention was paid to the chemical procedures. The brain was no longer removed, and the embalmers relied on the use of molten resin poured into the body cavities and the cranium. The focus was now upon cosmetic touches such as the application of gold leaf to the skin and nails (cat. 175). Mummies were now elaborately wrapped in linen strips forming geometric patterns, and surmounted by portrait panels (cats. 155 and 156). This detailed treatment, however, belies the condition of the bodies within the wrappings, as X-rays show that many of them are almost totally disarticulated. Some bodies have been found to be incomplete, and the embalmers occasionally made restorations of limbs in wood, pottery, mud, or linen.[38]

With the rise of Christianity in the Coptic period, religious beliefs no longer required preserving the body. Though some Coptic period bodies were treated with natron,[39] little attempt was made to use other methods, and the process soon was eliminated from Egyptian funerary practices.

The preservation of most of the mummies in the Museum's collection, revealed through X-rays and CT scans, is excellent. As one would expect, those dating to Dynasty 22, when the mummification process was at its height, are especially well preserved. Even such delicate structures as the optic nerve and aorta were identified. It appears that the Egyptians' desire to enter eternity with a well-preserved body has been fulfilled.

SUE D'AURIA

1. Abd Allatif, quoted in Pettigrew 1834, p. 3.
2. See the discussion in Pettigrew 1834, pp. 6-12.
3. Slugett 1980, p. 163.
4. Dawson 1934.
5. Quibell 1923, pp. 11, 19, 28, 32, pl. XXIX.
6. Lauer and Derry 1935, pp. 28-29.
7. Herodotus 1972, pp. 160-162.
8. Diodorus 1985, pp. 118-119.
9. Capart 1943b.
10. Andrews 1984, p. 16.
11. Reisner and Smith 1955, pp. 21-22, pl. 44.
12. Iskander 1980, p. 8.
13. Lucas 1962, p. 281.
14. Dunham and Simpson 1974, p. 8.
15. See the examples cited in Iskander 1980, pp. 11-12.
16. Reisner 1932a, p. 13.
17. Engelbach and Derry 1942, pp. 246-256.
18. Herodotus 1972, p. 161.
19. Lucas 1962, p. 309; Andrews 1984, p. 17.
20. Adams 1984, p. 21.
21. Mace and Winlock 1916.
22. Garner 1979. See also Lucas 1932, pp. 133-134.
23. Strouhal 1986.
24. Adams 1984, pp. 45-46. For recent studies of the royal mummies, see Harris and Wente 1980.
25. Leek 1969.
26. Iskander 1980, p. 16.
27. Herodotus 1972, p. 160.
28. Iskander and Shaheen 1964.
29. Iskander 1980, p. 22.
30. Iskander 1980, p. 23. For plant products used in mummification, see Baumann 1960.
31. Andrews 1984, p. 21.
32. David and Tapp 1984, p. 14.
33. Andrews 1984, p. 23.
34. Andrews 1984, p. 25.
35. Sauneron 1952. Little is known about the embalmers themselves. For a discussion, see Shore and Smith 1956.
36. Field nos. 25-2-317 to 25-2-368.
37. Winlock 1941.
38. Spencer 1982, p. 125.
39. Prominska 1986.

Funerary Architecture

For no other culture is our knowledge so dependent on mortuary remains as it is for ancient Egypt. This distorted view of the civilization of the Nile Valley has resulted, in part, from the genesis of Egyptian archaeology in the antiquarian interests of the Enlightenment. It was then nurtured by the great museums of Europe, which engaged in securing the well-preserved and mysterious objects cached in the sepulchers of the pharaohs. The relative ease and great reward in excavating cemetery sites as opposed to habitations continues to tempt Egyptologists to concentrate on the mortuary as opposed to the mundane.[1]

Yet in spite of nearly two centuries of concentrated study and publication, and the innumerable coffins, *shawabti*s, canopic jars, amulets, and other funerary objects in thousands of museum collections the world over, relatively little has been explained about the function, significance, and history of these pieces in the context of Egyptian society and beliefs.

Only within the last few years has any scholarly investigation been done on the "anthropology of death" in ancient Egypt. Interesting studies have been undertaken by Merrillees on the role of sexual dimorphism in burial practices[2] and by O'Connor on paleodemography[3] and social hierarchy in burial ground layout.[4] Many questions, however, remain, and re-analysis of previously excavated material and careful new excavations of cemetery sites are needed to answer them.

The tomb was not only the great repository for most of the material remains of ancient Egypt, but as Reisner pointed out, the structure itself is an artifact and should be subject to the same sorts of analysis as any pot or scarab.[5] The Egyptian tomb served two essential functions: to house the body and to provide a place for offerings to be given and the cult of the deceased to be carried out. These functions were relegated to two separate, but usually connected, areas: the substructure and the superstructure.

Discussions of tomb architecture generally focus on royal monuments, which follow a different, though related, line of development than do private tombs. While elaborate built tombs, cliff tombs, and catacombs are found in various periods, the simple pit tomb was the standard type of Egyptian grave for the common man. The following brief overview of private tomb development in Egypt provides a context for material discussed in the exhibition.

The earliest graves known from the Nile Valley appear in Nubia and date to the end of the Paleolithic Period (about 12,000-10,000 B.C.). These graves were flat-bottomed ovals covered with sandstone slabs. They were usually about one meter long and 50 centimeters wide and contained one to four bodies each. The bodies were tightly contracted and usually positioned on the left side with the head to the east; no artifacts appear to have been intentionally interred with them.[6]

The advent of the Neolithic or Predynastic Period (4800-3100 B.C.) in Egypt is still shrouded in mystery, but the peoples of Upper Egypt do not appear to be directly descended from the Paleolithic occupants of the area.[7] The earliest phase of the Neolithic in Middle and Upper Egypt is known as the Badarian Period (4800-4200 B.C.), after the site of Badari in Middle Egypt. For the first time, artifacts are buried with the deceased, usually near the hands or the head. The bodies were tightly contracted and oriented to the west in roughly circular graves, usually about 135 centimeters in diameter.[8] Some tombs at Badari had matting or sticks lining the walls of the graves,[9] but no evidence of superstructures was visible to the excavators.[10]

The succeeding phase of the Neolithic or Predynastic Period is the Naqada I, or Amratian (4200-3700 B.C.). Badarian traditions continue, but the graves tend to be larger and oval.[11] The burials become concomitantly richer with more grave goods, including stone vessels and ornaments (fig. 8). More of this material ap-

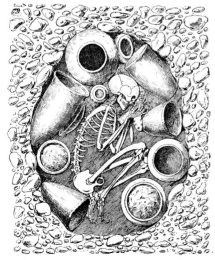

Fig. 8. Predynastic burial from el-Amrah.

Fig. 9. Niched brick facade from the tomb of Neithhotep at Naqada.

pears to have been produced specifically for burial, including decorated pottery,[12] "costume" jewelry and funerary figurines (see cat. 1).

Grave size continues to increase in the later phases of the Predynastic, the Naqada II (3700-3250 B.C.) and Naqada III (3250-3100 B.C.). The oval burial pits gradually evolve into larger rectangular chambers, roughly 175 centimeters long and 110 centimeters wide.[13] Some of these graves were lined with wooden planks or brickwork. In one grave at Mesaeed the wood panels were painted red,[14] and at Hierakonpolis the walls of a large tomb of the period were painted with scenes of ships and animals such as those found on contemporary pottery decoration.[15]

A very different culture occupied northern or Lower Egypt in the Predynastic Period. Although early excavators suggested that these people buried their dead in the village rather than in a separate cemetery, we now know that this was not the case and that, instead, the habitation gradually grew over a disused earlier cemetery.[16] With the gradual unification of Egypt, many of the northern cultural traditions were superseded by those of Upper Egypt. The end of the Predynastic Period in Egypt saw a much greater disparity in tomb size and concentration of wealth, a trend that continued through the Old Kingdom.

In the Archaic Period (3100-2630 B.C.) there were great advances in tomb architecture that included elaborate niched mudbrick facades (fig. 9) derived from Mesopotamian architecture[17] and the earliest use of masonry.[18] The tombs of the kings and queens of Dynasties 1 and 2 at Abydos, as well as those of some high officials, were surrounded by graves of servants (see cat. 4). Less elaborate graves of the period were sometimes lined with wood, brick, or matting beneath a low, mounded superstructure (see cat. 5).

Later in the period, stairways were introduced to permit access to the substructures of the tombs, and stone portcullis slabs to block the entry of tomb robbers. The niched facade was eventually simplified, with one niche at the northern end and one at the southern emphasized as offering places. This eventually led to the development of the "false door," through which the spirit of the deceased could return to the world of the living and receive sustenance (see frontispiece).

Offering niches were eventually incorporated into the body of the tomb superstructure to allow the cult to be carried out in a protected area. They also provided an additional surface to be decorated with painted plaster or carved wooden panels, as in the tomb of Hesy-Re,[19] or with stone relief, as in the tomb of Kha-bau-Sokar.[20]

Dynasty 4 (2630-2524 B.C.) saw the development of the classic Old Kingdom "mastaba," tomb, which takes its name from the Arabic word for a slant-sided, rectangular mud bench, which it resembles. These mastabas had stone or mud-

Fig. 10. Section of the western mastaba field at Giza looking down from the top of the pyramid of Khufu.

brick superstructures with flat tops and battered sides (fig. 10). The earliest of these at Giza had small chapels appended to the exterior and a stela showing the deceased seated at a table of offerings (cat. 27).[21]

These chapels eventually evolved into a complex series of offering chambers decorated with scenes of daily life, images of the deceased and his family, and funerary themes. Sealed statue niches, or *serdabs*, were also included within the superstructure of the tomb to house sculptures of the deceased, which would serve as substitute bodies for the habitation of the spirit (cats. 16-18).

The stairway entrance to the burial chamber was replaced in Dynasty 4 by a straight shaft cutting through the superstructure and into the bedrock below. These shafts were usually situated behind the false door. A multiplicity of shafts, false doors, and chapels are found in the family tombs of the later Old Kingdom. The walls of the chapels were covered with carved and painted decoration depicting the tomb owners, scenes of daily life, or offerings for the next world (cat. 14).

In the Mycerinus quarry cemetery at Giza, the mastabas were sculpted out of the limestone of the plateau. Elsewhere at Giza, and at Deshasha, Sheik Said, Aswan, and other sites, tomb chapels and burial chambers were cut directly into bedrock with no built superstructures.[22]

The first major breakdown in Egyptian civilization, the First Intermediate Period, saw a rapid decline in all aspects of society, funerary art and architecture among them. The tombs of even the most important personages of the time are remarkably crude and provincial.[23] By and large, elaborately sculpted rock-cut tomb chapels and masonry superstructures disappear. Typical funerary monuments of the period at such sites as Naga ed-Dêr consist of simple brick superstructures fronted by small chapels housing roughly carved limestone stelae (see cat. 37), which was all that remained of the elaborate decoration of Old Kingdom mastaba chapels.

Grave goods consisted mainly of pottery and small stone vessels, jewelry, and wooden model boats and figures. These objects are descendants of more elegant Old Kingdom prototypes and constitute what has been called the "Herakleopolitan" burial type.[24] These burials contain a great many models, which replaced the relief scenes of daily life on Old Kingdom tomb chapels.

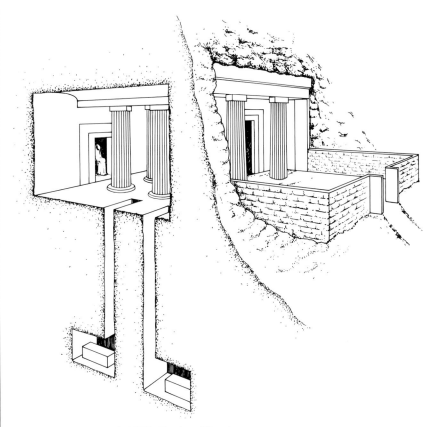

Fig. 11. Reconstruction of a Middle Kingdom cliff tomb.

The reunification of Egypt in the Middle Kingdom (2061-1782 B.C.), is reflected in a dramatic change in the funerary arts. Large and impressive rock-cut tombs appear at Thebes,[25] Bersha[26] and other sites in Middle and Upper Egypt.[27] These are based on the rock-cut tombs of the Old Kingdom with pillared exterior porticos and chapels with false doors.[28] Burials of the period were furnished with elaborate grave goods, including massive cedar coffins (cat. 43), wooden sculpture (cat. 32), and sumptuous jewelry (cat. 44).

The reign of Sesostris I (1943-1899 B.C.) saw a return to the old Memphite artistic traditions. While some features of the old ''Herakleopolitan type'' burials continued well into Dynasty 12 (1991-1784 B.C.),[29] objects such as the wooden models became fewer and more finely crafted and decorated. Additional types of funerary offerings and apotropaic objects, such as faience model food and animals (cat. 58), appear.

Elaborately decorated rock-cut tombs with pillared porticos (fig. 11) and columned halls dating to Dynasty 12 are found at Beni Hasan, Bersha, Asyut, Meir and elsewhere.[30] Relief carving (cat. 47), sculpture, and painted decoration show such scenes of daily life as wrestling, military conquest, hunting, fishing, and trapping, and such funerary motifs as offering bearers, *ka* priests and the voyage to Abydos.[31]

Mastaba tombs, too, continue, although few superstructures survive. The tomb chapel of Sesostris-ankh at Lisht was decorated with finely carved stone relief with scenes evocative of Old Kingdom chapel decoration. The burial chamber was protected with a series of portcullis blocking stones.[32]

Simpler mudbrick tombs and cenotaphs are found at Abydos in the Middle Kingdom (2061-1787 B.C.) and Second Intermediate Period (1782-1570 B.C.).[33] The cenotaphs were situated between the early Osiris temple and Umm el-Ga'ab. They consisted of small mudbrick structures that contained stelae or statues

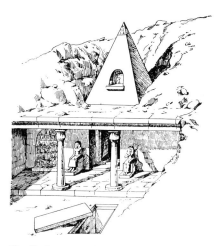

Fig. 12. Reconstruction of a Deir el-Medina tomb chapel.

and were dedicated by individuals buried elsewhere who wished to share in the offerings brought to Osiris.[34]

The effects of a weakening state are visible in the arts of the late Middle Kingdom, just as they had been in the First Intermediate Period. Elaborately decorated tombs again disappear, while funerary monuments and grave goods become simple and poorly executed (cats. 62-64). Most of these burials appear to have been in simple pit tombs.[35]

With the expulsion of the Hyksos and the foundation of the New Kingdom (1570-1070 B.C.), elaborate tombs reappear. The tombs of early Dynasty 18 (1570-1293 B.C.) hark back to Middle Kingdom traditions, and the classic Theban "T" shaped tomb of the New Kingdom may be seen as a combination of the pillared portico and rectangular chapel of the Theban "saf" tombs of Dynasty 11.

Tombs of the New Kingdom were decorated both with relief carving and painting. Decoration was generally limited to the tomb chapel, although in rare instances the burial chamber, too, was decorated (cat. 86). The decoration, like that on the tombs of Dynasty 12, consisted both of funereal themes and scenes of daily life.[36]

With the Thutmoside Period (1524-1450 B.C.), tomb decoration became even more elaborate with new scenes of official duties, and representations of the king and the gods. The tombs themselves become more complex, with pillared corridors and hypostyle halls.[37]

With the abandonment of the pyramidal form for royal burials as a safeguard to hide the pharaoh's tombs from robbers at the beginning of Dynasty 18, the pyramidal form was taken over in a vastly scaled-down version by non-royal people. The superstructures of some of the private tombs of the New Kingdom incorporated a mudbrick pyramid. The best-preserved of these are at the workmen's village of Deir el-Medina, dating chiefly to the Ramesside Period.[38] Here they cap painted, arched-roofed tomb chapels with niches for stelae or statues. The pyramid itself often had a niche for a statue (cat. 89) and a stone pyramidion at the apex. They were also often fronted by a pillared portico and courtyard (fig. 12).

Many of the burial chambers in the Deir el-Medina tombs also had painted decoration. Unlike the tombs of the Theban officials of Dynasty 18, these chambers were decorated almost exclusively with funereal subjects, including depictions of the deceased in the afterlife, and of Osiris and Anubis. This more somber aspect of tomb decoration was to dominate the monuments of the later New Kingdom.

The Third Intermediate Period (1070-712 B.C.) marks a sharp break with the sumptuous tombs of the New Kingdom. The coffin itself becomes the sole focus of all the artistic and mythological expression formerly lavished on the tomb (cats. 115, 120-122). Burials of the period were often mass interments in family tombs (cat. 115) or great caches in rough, rock-hewn chambers[39] or mudbrick vaults.

It was not until the revival of Egyptian culture during Dynasty 25 (757-656 B.C.) that tomb architecture and decoration returned to a semblance of their former glories. The deliberate revivalism of the period is seen in the careful copying of motifs and styles from all previous periods in Egyptian history. Massive tomb complexes were built at Thebes along the causeway of the Hatshepsut mortuary temple at Deir el-Bahri.[40] Painted tombs and relief-decorated rock-cut tombs also reappear.[41] These elaborate tombs continue into the Saite Period, along with great shaft tombs containing massive stone sarcophagi (cat. 127) and great rock-cut catacombs (fig. 13).

Fig. 13. Catacomb burials of the Saite Period from Giza G 7757 A, room IV.

Fig. 14. Coptic cemetery at Naga ed-Dêr (ca. 1905).

The end of the dynastic period saw the development of the tomb chapel in imitation of houses or temples as illustrated in the tombs at Tuna el-Gebel.[42] In the area of Alexandria there were great catacombs at Kom el Shukafa with painted and relief decoration of Egyptian motifs done in classical style.

The beautifully wrapped portrait mummies of the Roman Period from the Fayum seem to have been buried in simple pit graves in the earth,[43] while the tombs at Kom Abu Billou were rectangular mudbrick structures with barrel vaulted roofs and a niche in the eastern end containing a limestone stela (cat. 163).[44] Although the vast cemeteries of the Coptic Period (A.D. 395-641) have been extensively plundered for their elaborately embroidered burial tunics (cats. 166 and 167), few have ever been carefully excavated and published. The burials in a Coptic cemetery excavated by Reisner at Naga ed-Dêr consisted of bodies placed in simple pit graves with few objects other than jewelry (cat. 169). Many modern Coptic tombs have brick vaulted burial chambers much like those of the private tombs of the Archaic Period five thousand years ago (fig. 14).

PETER LACOVARA

1. Cf. Bietak 1979, pp. 97.
2. Merrillees 1974, pp. 14-141.
3. O'Connor 1972, pp. 78-100.
4. O'Connor 1974, pp. 15-37.
5. Lacovara and Wojcik (forthcoming).
6. Wendorf 1968, pp. 954-995.
7. Butzer 1976, pp. 9-11.
8. Brunton and Caton-Thompson 1928, p. 18.
9. Brunton and Caton-Thompson 1928, p. 18.
10. Brunton and Caton-Thompson 1928, p. 20.
11. Kaiser 1957, pp. 69-77.
12. Cf. Needler 1984, p. 232; while Needler points out that many decorated types do occasionally turn up in settlement contexts, the incidence of these vessels is far more rare than in mortuary assemblages.
13. Cf. Kaiser 1957, p. 73.
14. Mesaeed tomb no. 18, Stephen Harvey, personal communication.
15. Ridley 1973, pp. 22-24.
16. Kemp 1968, pp. 22-33.
17. Frankfort 1941, pp. 329-358.
18. Saad 1945-1947.
19. Firth 1913.
20. Terrace and Fischer 1970. pp. 37-44.
21. Reisner 1932b.
22. Cf. Simpson 1976a.
23. Vandier 1950.
24. Williams 1976.
25. Winlock 1942, p. 18ff.
26. Badawy 1966, p. 127ff.
27. Badawy 1966, p. 127ff.
28. Badawy 1966, p. 127ff.
29. Mace and Winlock 1916.
30. Badawy 1966, pp. 143.
31. Newberry 1893a.
32. Metropolitan Museum of Art 1933, pp. 9-28.
33. Badawy 1966, pp. 181-185.
34. O'Connor 1979, pp. 48-49.
35. Petrie 1909, pp. 6-10.
36. Cf. Davies 1943.
37. Badawy 1968, pp. 411-414.
38. Bruyère 1926, pp. 2-28.
39. Winlock 1942, pp. 93-99.
40. Bietak and Reiser-Haslauer 1978, pp. 30-40.
41. Winlock 1942, pp. 81-83; Fazzini 1975, p. 115.
42. Gabra 1941.
43. Cf. Wildung and Grimm 1978, p. 31.
44. Hawass 1979, pp. 75-88.

Funerary Mythology

The Egyptian View of Death

The experience of death is universal, but mankind has seldom accepted this fact without protest. To a certain degree all religion can be considered a great monument to this protest against death.[1] The protest against death that the ancient Egyptians expressed in their religion is imposing to all who have studied the monuments in Egypt itself or in museums with Egyptian collections all over the world. Most of what remains of ancient Egyptian culture, whether it is material (pyramids, mummies, statuary, and other remains) or literary (texts on stone and papyrus and other inscriptions), is funerary. Although our knowledge of ancient Egyptian culture is doubtless one-sided, since most of its non-funerary aspects are lost forever, it must be said that the ancient Egyptians focused on questions of life and death to a degree unsurpassed, before or since. In the millennia of their history they developed an imposing, extensive, and intricate funerary mythology to answer the riddle of death and to make its prospect more acceptable.

In Egypt, death was not considered shameful and forbidden as it has been until quite recently in much of modern Western culture,[2] but was accepted instead as part of creation.[3] It was considered not just the end of life, but also the entrance to a new mode of being. The Egyptians believed that, although life is transitory,[4] it could be preserved through renewal. In ritual this mythical truth was reversed, and life renewed by preservation. Death might be viewed as an enemy[5] or as a friend,[6] but it was inevitable. The underlying idea was that life can only exist, be renewed, and be regained through death. Not only human beings, but also such gods as Re and Osiris were mortal: They had life in the sense that they had died and arisen from the dead. The renewal, that mysterious process that Kristensen[7] called life from death, came about outside the created world in the unfathomable depth and darkness of the primeval waters (Nun) that surround this world. It is in that mysterious space that the deceased could live again. One sun-hymn reads:

> How beautiful is thy shining forth in the horizon
> We are in renewal of life. We have entered into Nun
> He has renovated (us) to one who is young for the first time
> The (one) has been stripped off, the other put on.[8]

The last sentence has been interpreted to mean, "The old man is cast off and the new man is put on."[9] It may also call to mind the mummy-bandages that are thrown off in the decisive moment of resurrection[10] and the white garments that the glorified dead wear in depictions of the Underworld. The dead bodies sink after death in the chaotic, lightless, and endless primeval waters. Here the sun-god, after having shone upon earth, descends in the evening and gives light and life in the Underworld and orders at least part of it with time and space into life-times[11] and abodes in which the resurrected dead can live. The Underworld is created or divided into twelve hours, according to the Book of Amduat, and into twelve portals, according to the Book of Gates. The dead do not all sink back into the uncreated non-being like the enemies of the gods. They are preserved, and arise from the dead in a mysterious space, a realm of the dead that man on earth can reach only in his imagination and through his knowledge about the mysterious course that the sun daily makes around this world.

Egyptian Funerary Mythology and Ritual

The Pyramid Texts, mankind's oldest corpus of written religious texts, dating from the first half of the third millennium B.C., or even earlier, already represent an intricate funerary mythology. Here it is stated that the king survives after death among the gods in heaven. Many passages appear at first sight to be rather unmythological protests against death.

> Oho! Oho! Raise yourself, O King; receive your head, collect your bones, gather your limbs together, throw off the earth from your flesh, receive your bread which does not grow moldy and your beer which does not grow sour.[12]

> O my father, the King, raise yourself upon your left side, place yourself upon your right side for this fresh water which I have given to you. O my father, the King, raise yourself upon your left side, place yourself upon your right side for this warm bread which I have made for you.[13]

This utterance seems to begin with a very naturalistic, flat denial of death with no mythological detour. It seems to suggest that the deceased king is not dead but only asleep, and can raise himself, eat, and drink. It is, however, not simply an emotional outcry denying the reality of death, but a traditional ritual text written in several pyramids and recited at the occasion of offering. Food was offered to the dead, not so much with the expectation that they would really eat it, but with the aim of including them in the community. The dead were not expelled from the community, but given a special status as the blessed dead to whom food was offered on certain occasions. As every human being knows, the personality does not simply disappear on the day of burial. In Egypt, it would be dangerous to neglect the traditional obligations of alimentation. One should not take this text to mean the Egyptians of the third millennium B.C. believed that the dead king would rise to eat and drink on earth. This would, at best, happen in an imaginary or mythological abode.

The Pyramid Text goes on with words, names, and sentences that we would, without any hesitation, call mythological:

> O my father, the King, the doors of the sky are opened for you, the doors of the celestial expanses are thrown open for you. The gods of Pe are full of sorrow and they come to Osiris at the sound of the wails of Isis and Nephthys. The souls of Pe clash (sticks) for you, they smite their flesh for you, they clap their hands for you, they tug their side-locks for you and they say to Osiris: "Go and come, wake up and sleep, for you are enduring in life! Stand up and see this, stand up and hear this which your son has done for you, which Horus has done for you. He smites him who smote you, he binds him who bound you. . . . You shall ascend to the sky, you shall become Wepwawet, your son Horus will lead you on the celestial ways; the sky is given to you, the earth is given to you, the Field of Rushes is given to you in company with these two great gods who come out of Heliopolis."

Without here giving a detailed explanation of all the mythological features in this funerary text, one can remark that the burial of the king in his pyramid represents his resurrection and ascension to heaven, whose doors are said to be open for him.

We might easily mistake mythological texts like those cited above for mere emotional exaggeration. What did the Egyptians really believe? A prominent early twentieth-century Egyptologist, evaluating the following mythological text from the middle of the second millennium B.C., wrote: "But looking behind all the make believe we discern clearly enough, a radical skepticism as to man's fate in the hereafter. The emotions conjured up a brightly colored picture, but the reason, had it been consulted, would have told another tale."[14]

> You come in, you go out,
> Your heart in joy at the praise of the lord of the gods;
> A good burial after revered old age,
> After old age has come.
> You take your place in the lord-of-life (coffin),
> You come to the earth in the tomb of the west.
> To become indeed a living *ba*,
> It shall thrive on bread, water and air;
> To assume the form of phoenix, swallow,
> Or falcon or heron, as you wish.
> You cross in the ferry without being hindered,
> You fare on the water's flowing flood.
> You come to life a second time,
> Your *ba* shall not forsake your corpse.
> Your *ba* is divine among the spirits,
> The worthy *bas* converse with you.
> You join them to receive what is given on earth,
> You thrive on water, you breathe air,
> You drink as your heart desires,

Your eyes are given you to see,
Your ears to hear what is spoken;
Your mouth speaks, your feet walk,
Your hands, your arms have motion.
Your flesh is firm, your muscles are smooth,
You delight in all your limbs;
You count your members; all these, sound,
There is no fault in what is yours.
Your heart is yours in very truth,
You have your own, your former heart.
You rise to heaven, you open *duat* (Netherworld)
In any shape that you desire.
You are summoned daily to Wen-nefer's altar.
You receive the bread that comes before (him)
The offering to the lord of the sacred land.[15]

A modern Westerner might indeed see this example of Egyptian funerary mythology as "make believe," but within the context of Egyptian cosmographical and anthropological beliefs it is not unreasonable. Funerary texts, like this one from the tomb of Paheri in el-Kab, assure the deceased that he can and, indeed, will make use of the possibilities of a new life that are available, according to the traditional Egyptian knowledge and conception of the universe.

Funerary texts are often called magical texts.[16] But the distinction between the magical and the religious is one of definition. The word *magic* is often used simply to label actions, sayings, and ideas that do not seem reasonable from a Western positivistic or Christian point of view.

Souls of the Dead

According to the text cited above, the deceased comes into the earth after burial. The earth is here another expression for that mysterious region outside the world of the living that in a foregoing text was called Nun or primeval waters. We have already suggested that the personality is not annihilated at death. The deceased becomes a living *ba*. In older Egyptological literature, the *ba*, represented as a bird, sometimes with a human head, was often incorrectly translated as soul; one might instead call the *ba* the alter ego, the embodiment of psychic and physical forces.[17] The *ba* travels far in the cosmic circuit in the course of the sun-god. It may, as well, visit well-known spots on earth. The mummy remains motionless in the tomb or Underworld. The tomb is identified with the Underworld in the funerary texts and representations on the walls of the tomb or coffin and in papyri close to and around the mummy. The corporeal resurrection of the deceased comes about when the *ba* visits the tomb and unites itself with the mummy. The *ba* united with the mummy is an *akh*.[18] *Akh* is usually translated as "spirit" but its corporeal aspect should not be neglected. A bodily spirit or spiritual body may seem a contradiction in terms, but it is not unknown in religious, or at least Christian, terminology: If there is a physical body, there is also a spiritual body.[19]

The inevitable process of aging – the decay of sight, hearing, speech and mobility – that culminates in the complete bodily impotence that we call death seems to be thought reversible. Life arises from death: "You come to a life a second time." But it is also said, "You have your own, your former heart." The heart was believed to be the center of man's personality,[20] and provided continuity in the identity of the old and that of the new resurrected person. For this reason the heart was carefully left in the body during mummification and, as an extra precaution, a heart-scarab was added to the mummy. A spell was added in the Book of the Dead to give the heart back to the owner in the hereafter, in case the heart was lost in spite of all precautions.[21]

In the last lines of our quotation the deceased is reassured that he will be summoned to the altar of Osiris and receive the offerings. In the later texts it is said

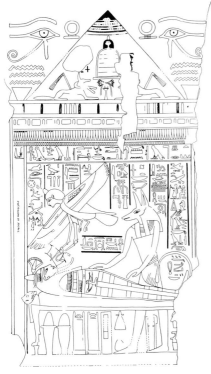

Fig. 15. The *ba* bird gives the hieroglyphic signs of the breath of life to the deceased, who is prepared by Anubis for resurrection. Relief in Theban tomb 106.

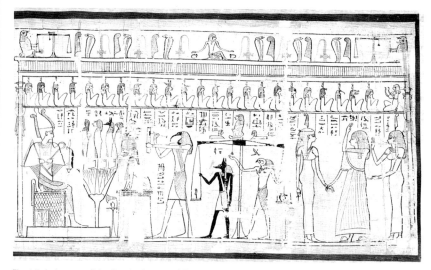

Fig. 16. Judgment of the Dead, vignette of Spell 125 in the Book of the Dead (cat. 134).

that he eats bread beside the god, that the gate opens for him; the bolts slide back automatically and he reaches the Hall of the Two Truths.

Judgment of the Dead

In this so-called Hall of the Two Truths, (or the two Maat goddesses), the judgment of the dead[22] takes place, as is well known from the texts and representations of the New Kingdom, especially from text and vignette of Spell 125 of the Book of the Dead. This judgment is represented largely as a solemn pro-forma session. Indeed the Egyptian hereafter is not described in Egyptian funerary literature solely in terms of unearthly bliss. Sinners and criminals, called the nameless enemies of the gods, were punished in the hereafter; but nowhere is the punishment known to have struck a well-known Egyptian whose name was written in a tomb, in a funerary papyrus, or on a coffin and who was admitted to the final judgment. Enemies of the gods were doubtless not allowed entry into the Hall of the Two Truths. This ceremonial judgment was apparently not believed to be a serious examination that the person in question could possibly fail. Although it is out of the question that the judgment would result in condemnation to die a second death, the examination could be painful because its aim, as is explained in Spell 125 of the Book of the Dead, was to separate the deceased from his sins.

Already resurrected, the deceased was ushered into the Hall of Judgment, usually by Anubis, who had presided over his mummification and had protected him so far. He greeted the lords of the judgment, who could be Re and his nine gods or Osiris and his forty-two messengers, assuring them, "I know you, I know your names." A balance stood in the hall. The heart of the deceased, as the seat of identity and memory of the details of life on earth, was put in one of the scales. In the other was a feather of Maat, the symbol of truth, justice and order. The well-prepared resurrected person did not wait for a painful interrogation to begin, but recited a formula, the so-called Negative Confession, in which he denied all sorts of ethical or cultic sins:

> I have not done falsehood against men.
> I have not impoverished my associates.
> I have done no wrong in the Place of Truth.
> I have not learnt that which is not.
> I have done no evil.
> I have not made people labor daily in excess of what was due to be done for me. . .[23]

He might also have recited a second formula, another declaration of innocence, that addressed the forty-two judges of Osiris:

O Far-strider who came forth from Heliopolis, I have done no falsehood.
O Fire-embracer who came forth from Kher-aha, I have not robbed. O Long-nosed
[Thoth] who came forth from Hermopolis, I have not been rapacious.
O Swallower of shades who came forth from the cavern, I have not stolen. . .[24]

The scales of the balance remained in equilibrium as long as the deceased
spoke the truth. But every deviation from truth made the heart heavy, and the
balancing pan holding the feather would rise. Anubis, sometimes together with
Horus, verified the results and brought the scales in balance again. The presence of Anubis reassured those who were mummified; having performed the
mummification, the god already had an intimate knowledge of the deceased.
The god Thoth made a written record and reported the outcome, usually
favorable. In case of doubt the personal circumstances and fate of the deceased
were taken into consideration as mitigating factors. Moreover a well-prepared
person should have spoken to his heart with the words of Spell 30B of the Book
of the Dead:

O my heart which I had from my mother!
O my heart which I had from my mother!
O my heart of my different ages!
Do not stand up as a witness against me,
do not be opposed to me in the tribunal,
do not be hostile to me in the presence of the Keeper of the Balance. . .[25]

At this point a general verdict would be given like that written in the Papyrus
of Ani:

Words spoken by the Great Ennead to Thoth who dwells in Hermopolis: What you
have said is true. The Osiris scribe Ani, justified is righteous. He has committed no
crime nor has he acted against us. Ammit shall not be permitted to prevail over
him. Let there be given to him of the bread-offerings which go before Osiris and a
permanent grant of land in the Field of Offerings as for the followers of Horus.[26]

Ammit, whose name may mean "Devourer of the (condemned) Dead," is a hybrid monster with the head of a crocodile, forepart of a lion, and hindquarters of
a hippopotamus. She would sit very near the balance, but she is never shown
devouring a deceased who had entered the Hall of Judgment.

This does not mean that the Egyptian did not believe in punishment in the hereafter, but the punished were always the others, the enemies of the gods. They
were beheaded, chopped into pieces, cooked in a cauldron, roasted in fire and
burned until nothing was left. They were not only tortured, but annihilated, and
died a second death so that they could not come to life again.

Perils of the Underworld

In funerary literature one may discern a certain fear that the deceased might in-
advertently be drawn into the terrible punishments of the enemies. For this reason he is provided with many spells to prevent and ward off the dangers in the
hereafter. These spells contain information and prescriptions as to what to do
and say at the right moment. Even the deceased who is not mixed up with enemies and is himself not guilty of criminal or sinful acts fears that his *ba* may be
caught in a net between heaven and earth, that unpleasant doorkeepers may be
reluctant, or even refuse, to open gates that one necessarily has to pass. He
may be caught, he may be bound, he may be tortured and thrown into pits and
prisons. A ferry-man may ask difficult questions.

One typically dangerous situation was the lake of fire[27] that one had to pass and
in which the enemies were burned. It stank. Birds flew away from it. As soon as
the justified approached this horrifying lake of fire, which could not be evaded, it
would turn into a pond with cool refreshing water from which he could drink and
through which he could easily wade.

These dangers could be overcome by knowledge written in books of funerary
mythology and by calling on mighty gods, especially Osiris, the lord of the Underworld, or the sun-god Re, who travels in his boat through the mysterious re-

gions of the Underworld. Hymns to these gods are included in the Book of the Dead to provide a religious attitude in the hereafter. Better than such a last-minute, post-mortem religion in the hereafter is the religious attitude on earth:

> Those who used to worship Re on earth, who charmed Apophis, who offered their oblations, who censed their gods they indeed, after they have gone to rest, they dispose of their libations, they receive their food offerings. . . .Those who spoke the truth on earth, who were not in the proximity of sins, they are invited unto this gate. They live in righteousness. Their libations come from their pools.[28]

It was not only knowledge or religion that counted, but also ethical behavior, as this later text suggests:

> He who is beneficent on earth, to him one is beneficent in the Netherworld. And he who is evil, to him one is evil. It is so decreed (and will remain so) forever.[29]

The deceased who has overcome all dangers on the road to the hereafter is admitted to the Hall of Judgment, where he is purified or separated from all his sins.

The Realm of the Dead

In the Pyramid Texts the deceased pharaoh is assured that he will be accepted as a living god among the gods in heaven. In later funerary literature – the Coffin Texts, the Book of the Dead, and such New Kingdom compositions as the Amduat, the Book of Gates, the Book of Caverns, and the Book of the Earth – the hereafter is more often described as being under or in the earth. The knowledge of the hereafter was closely connected with Egyptian theological and cosmological speculations about the course of the sun, which disappears at night in the west and supposedly travels under the earth, reappearing in the morning in the east. Egyptian funerary mythology seems largely to be derived from the mythology and cult of the sun-god Re. In the earliest funerary texts, the Pyramid Texts, funerary mythology centered on Osiris, the god who died and arose from the dead. This mythology was influenced by the theology of the sun-god Re venerated in Heliopolis.

According to Egyptian conceptions, the abode of the dead is indeed a mysterious region. The dead may be called "those whose place is hidden or mysterious" and the abode itself the "mysterious space." It is a mythical place that can be reached only in the imagination. Courageous explorers cannot visit this mysterious place as they might visit far countries. The knowledge of the abode of the dead does not seem to be based on ecstatic experiences or reports of human visitors who had made a temporary visit to that mysterious region. The late story of Khaemwase in which such a visit is described is a rather exceptional phenomenon in Egyptian culture.[30]

The hereafter can only be incompletely indicated with symbols, words, and pictures, derived from this world. It may be called the West because the sun sets in the west and was thought to descend into the hereafter or Underworld (*duat*), because it was thought that the sun travelled under the earth from west to east during the night. Sometimes it is called "the Great City" but it is often stressed in word and image that it is a region with water and vegetation of plants and trees, sometimes called Ealu-fields, although a desert may also be found there. It is separated from the world of the living by a broad stream. A great river is also in the hereafter along which the sun-god Re proceeds in his boat. One can imagine that a sandbank is in this river as sandbanks are in the Nile. This is the sandbank of Apophis, the enemy of Re. Apophis does not succeed, however, in his attempt to shipwreck Re's boat.

The battle of Re with Apophis in the Underworld in the evening, at dawn, or in the middle of the night is often mentioned in sun-hymns and funerary literature. The dead watch as Re and the gods in his boat ward off this threatening monster of chaos in the shape of a huge serpent. Apophis is conjured with words, bound, attacked with knives, and subdued to nothingness. All occupants of the

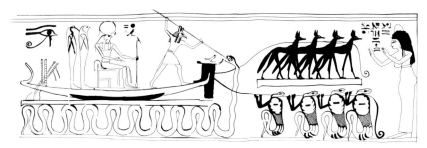

Fig. 17. Seth harpoons Apophis, the monster of chaos, from the prow of the sun barque, on the funerary papyrus of Her-Weben, Cairo.

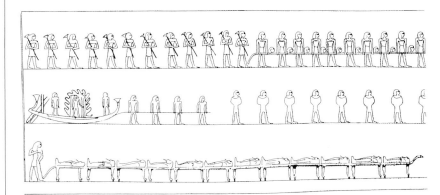

Fig. 18. Book of Gates. Part of the sixth hour. In the lower register, mummified dead rest on couches and are about to arise from death on the arrival of the sun-god (middle register).

sunboat may take part in this glorious battle: Sia (the personification of wisdom), Hu (the creative Word), Heka (creative energy or magic), and greater gods and goddesses such as Hathor, Isis, Maat, Horus, Thoth and Seth. Especially the mischievous, murderous and violent thunder-god Seth may be represented as standing with his huge spear in the prow of the sun-boat, and repelling with word and deed the monster of chaos.

As mentioned above, the Egyptians divided the day and night into twelve hours each, hence the Underworld is divided in twelve departments or hours. The sun-god remains one hour in each department of the Underworld.

But time in the hereafter is different from time on earth. One hour in the Underworld is the equivalent of a lifetime ($^ch^cw$) during which the resurrected live their life and cultivate the fields that are allotted to them, and enjoy the light of the sun. As soon as the sun-bark approaches a portal of the Underworld, the gates open automatically. When the sun-god shines in the darkness and speaks his creative word the sarcophagi or shrines are opened and the mummies arise from their sleep of death. They throw off the mummy-bandages that had protected them and take food and clothing and all that was necessary in the new life. According to the Book of Gates the sun-god in the Underworld speaks:

> O gods (i.e., deceased) who are in the Underworld,
> who are behind the ruler of the West (i.e., Osiris),
> who are stretched on their side,
> who are sleeping on their supports,
> raise your flesh,
> pull together your bones,
> collect your limbs,
> unite your flesh.
> May there be sweet breath to your noses,
> Loosing for your mummy-wrappings.
> May your head-masks be uncovered.
> May there be light for your divine eyes
> in order that you may see the light by means of them.
> Stand up from your weariness.[31]

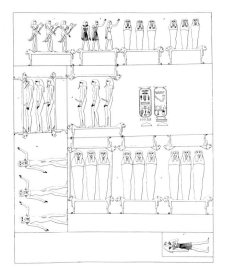

Fig. 19. The process of resurrection, during which the mummy-bindings are thrown off and new clothes put on. Painting on the ceiling of the tomb of Ramesses IX.

Resurrection

Mummy-bindings had to be removed at the moment of resurrection. Mummification prepared the body for resurrection in the Underworld and protected it in its journey to that mysterious space. Mummy-bindings were both protective attire for the "space traveler" and, at the same time, the bonds of death. They may be called the bonds of Seth, because Seth was the god of death, who brought death into the world by murdering Osiris. The thoroughness with which the Egyptians are wrapped makes understandable such special prayers as the one written on a coffin in the Metropolitan Museum of Art in New York, directing the goddess Isis to free the mummy from its wrappings at the moment of resurrection: "Ho my mother Isis, come that you may remove the bindings which are on me."[32]

Representations of the process of resurrection are depicted on ceilings of royal tombs in the Valley of the Kings:[33] some of the dead are still in mummy-shrouds. Others have arisen and are standing upright, clearly visible as nude males and females. Still others move their arms, while a few already wear their new garments of the hereafter. The Egyptians did not cherish an idea of paradisical nudity. On earth, not only food and drink, but also linen cloth was offered to the dead and in the Underworld the dead receive, among other offerings from the sun-god, food, drink, and clothing.

During the one nocturnal hour that the sun-god visits a department of the Underworld, the dead in that department come to life again and live a lifetime. The resurrected see the sun-god face to face. They jubilate and adore him. They behold the glorious sun-boat and all its divine occupants. They repeat life also in other respects, as may be gathered from the typical scenes of daily life in Theban tombs. Cultivation of the fields, fishing and fowling, playing games, music-making and dancing, banquets together with wife and children and other members of the family and friends and many other scenes of daily life are repeated. Repeating a life-time in such a nocturnal hour, flooded by the light of the sun, was diverting and recreative. The old people, with their new bodies in the bloom of life, enjoy doing once again what they did on earth. This life in the Underworld does not seem to have the toils and faults of earthly life. And, even if some of these appear, it remains an idyllic life on the whole.

In the same space and at the same time, however, enemies are punished, as one may conclude from the texts and representations of the Books of the Underworld. There is no clear-cut spatial division between "heaven" and "hell" as in some other religions. One might discern a tendency to depict the punishment of the enemies in the lower register of the three registers of Amduat and Book of Gates, at the right side of the sun-boat, which would mean the left side, since everything in the Underworld is reversed. At our present state of knowledge, however, it is hazardous to conclude that on the left side of the river the enemies are punished to death and on the right side the justified dead enjoy life as one might expect. One should also take into consideration that the Underworld is a mysterious region that is not ordered spatially like the earth. The sun, which gives light and life to the justified, gives burning heat and death to the enemies. A lake may give life and refreshment to the one and death and fire to the other. King Merikare is warned on earth:

> The Court that judges the wretch
> You know they are not lenient
> On the day of judging the miserable
> In the hour of doing their task.
> It is painful when the accuser has knowledge.
> Do not trust in length of years:
> They view a life-time in an hour
> When a man remains over after death.
> His deeds are set beside him as a treasure
> And being yonder lasts forever.

Fig. 20. Drawing of Papyrus Berlin 3008 showing life of the resurrected in the Ealu-fields. Ploughing, sowing, reaping, and threshing in the middle register. Vignette of Spell 110, of the Book of the Dead.

> A fool is he who does what they reprove.
> He who reaches them without having done wrong
> Will exist there like a god,
> Free-striding like the lords forever![34]

Some of the deceased, or rather, their *bas*, are not admitted at the entrance-gate of the hereafter or do not get a place in the sun-boat that is said to be the ship of millions (of occupants). Others arrive in the hereafter only to be punished for a life-time. The judges "view a life-time in an hour." But for the justified, "His deeds are set beside him as treasure." But what about those who have no treasure to set beside them? Repeating life or living anew (*wḥm ꜥnḫ*) may also mean to bring life to completeness and fulfillment in a new way. The one who starved to death on earth may now cultivate the fruitful fields and bring in rich harvests. The woman who was barren, or died too young on earth, may bear a child in the Underworld, as statuettes of a woman with child found in women's tombs suggest. Those who are separated from their sins and have some blank spots may repeat their life in a somewhat different way. Men may enjoy life in an ideal way, a life-time long like a nightmovie of one hour.

At the end of a nocturnal hour, the sun-boat goes on with its occupants and followers, gods and *bas*, to the next department. The dead lament after Re has passed them by. The gates close automatically and the dead sink back in the sleep of death after having returned into their protective mummy-wrappings. Their life is over, only to be renewed after twenty-three hours in the next night.

Preparations for Death

In hieroglyphic writing the mummy sign is used to denote words signifying not only mummy, but also statue, image, form or shape. According to Egyptian conception, a human being living on earth is already an image of the sun-god. An aim of mummification was to stylize the human corpse into a divine image. The ideal body of the resurrected in the hereafter was prefabricated in the work of the mummification on earth. A fine-looking mummy was a persuasive symbol of resurrection. While mummification was highly desirable, there is no certain evidence that mummification was ever a necessary precondition for corporeal resurrection. The Egyptians were certainly aware of the fact that the bodies of some of their loved ones were irreparably lost and could not be mummified, not to mention all the bodies of the poor that were not mummified. Corporeal resurrection was not restricted to the privileged members of the elite who were buried with all the ritual pomp and circumstance on earth and who were mummified. In several places in the Books of the Underworld[35] a special concern is

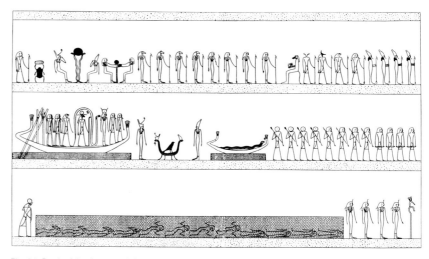

Fig. 21. Book of Amduat, tenth hour. In the lower register, non-mummified dead float disorderedly in the water before resurrection.

shown for all those deceased who had not undergone special additional preparations to make the "space-travel" to the Underworld, been provided with mummy-shrouds, coffins and so on. In texts and representations attention was paid to human remains floating in the Nun or primeval waters. A divine rescue party was at work at the command of the sun-god to pull those aimlessly floating corpses out of the endless space of the depth of the primeval waters. The bodies were brought ashore in the Underworld. It is written, "Stand up weary ones, behold, Re takes measures on your behalf."[36] This and other textual evidence indicates that those who were not mummified on earth could also repeat life in the Underworld. At the word of the sun-god they also arose bodily from the dead. It seems that these texts and representations concerning those who are in Nun refer, not only to those who were accidentally drowned in the waters of the Nile, but to the general situation of the departed. Men who die return to the non-being, to the primeval waters prior to and outside the created world of the living. It would be natural that the corpses decay in the endless darkness and depth of nothingness. The sun-god, however, creates and recreates the endless and the deep, dividing it into time and space, into an Underworld in which people, under certain conditions, are allowed to live anew. People were drawn from the primeval waters to receive another life in the hereafter.

A life in the hereafter was prefabricated by words, deeds and gifts. These extensive preparations evince an impressive prayer to draw life from death. In Egypt the human protest against death was turned into a persuasive prayer or, as some would have it, into magic, to preserve and renew life.

Skepticism

Even in Egyptian culture, some remained skeptical as to the funerary mythology of the hereafter that mortal man on earth can only reach by imagination and speculation. The skeptical words of Intef are also human:

> None comes from there
> To tell of their state
> To tell of their needs
> To calm our hearts
> Until we go where they have gone.[37]

HERMAN TE VELDE

1. Van Baaren 1964, p. 164.
2. Ariès 1974, p. 85ff.
3. Rössler-Köhler 1980, cols. 252f., e.g. Pyr. § 1466, here and henceforth according to the text-edition of Sethe 1908-1910 and the English translation of Faulkner 1969.
4. Wirz 1982.

5. Zandee 1960.
6. Kristensen 1926.
7. cf. n.6.
8. Pap. Ch. Beatty IV rt 11, 8-10, cf. Gardiner 1935a and Assmann 1975b, nr. 195, 274-278.
9. Gardiner 1935a, p. 34, n. 10; and De Buck 1939, p.6.
10. Zandee 1960, p. 78.
11. Hornung 1978, p. 281ff.
12. Pyr. § 654-655.
13. Pyr. § 1002-1003; 1004-1010.
14. Gardiner 1935b, p. 30ff.
15. Tomb of Paheri in el-Kab: Lichtheim 1976, p. 17.
16. E.g. Morenz 1964, p.140; Morenz 1965, pp. 399-445.
17. Žabkar 1973, pp. 588-590; Žabkar 1968, pp. 106-114.
18. Hornung 1983, p. 173; Hornung 1984, p. 494ff. On *akh* in general: Englund 1978; Demarée 1983, p. 189ff.
19. 1 Corinthians 15:44.
20. Brunner 1977, col. 1159.
21. Spell 26 cf. the translation of the Book of the Dead: Faulkner 1985, p. 37. See Pyr. § 1640.
22. Seeber 1976.
23. Cf. Faulkner 1985, p.29.
24. Cf. Faulkner 1985, p.31.
25. Cf. Faulkner 1985, p.27.
26. Faulkner 1985, p. 14; Spencer 1982, p.145.
27. On punishments: Hornung 1968. On the lake of fire: Hornung 1968, p. 22f.; Seeber 1976, pp. 184-186.
28. Book of Gates, 2nd scene 5th and 6th Hour: Hornung 1979, pp. 15-21; 1980, pp.47, 50; cf. English translation. Zandee 1969, p. 284.
29. Lichtheim 1980, p. 141.
30. Lichtheim 1980, p. 138-142; cf. Gressmann 1918.
31. Book of Gates, 6th Hour, scene 40: Hornung 1979, pp. 236-239; Hornung 1980, p. 168; cf. English translation Zandee 1969, p. 301.
32. Hayes 1959, p. 71; cf. Hornung 1983, p. 170.
33. Hornung 1982, p. 137 and 146 (pl.117); Hornung 1983, p. 170ff.
34. Lichtheim 1973, p. 101.
35. Book of Gates, 9th Hour, scene 58: Hornung 1979, pp. 312-317; 1980, pp. 214-219; English translation Zandee 1969, pp. 310-311. Amduat, 10th Hour: Hornung 1963, I, pp. 176-177; II, pp. 169-171. For the rescue-party see: Amduat, 5th Hour, nos. 339-343.
36. Zandee 1969, p. 310.
37. Lichtheim 1973, p. 196. cf. Wirz 1982, pp. 73-77.

Funerary Texts and their Meaning

Mummies and tombs attest to more than just an ancient solution to the problem of burying the dead. Egyptian burials, like those of every culture, also reflect uniquely human thoughts and emotions in the face of death. Objects buried with Neanderthal bodies show that this is an experience as old as human culture itself.[1] What sets ancient Egypt apart, in the history of human culture, is the extraordinarily detailed testimony to that experience that has been preserved for us. More than any other ancient civilization, the Egyptians have left us not just the bodies and the memory of their dead but also a record of the profoundly human feelings that lie behind these remains.

That record is preserved in the vast collection of ancient Egyptian funerary texts. From the advent of writing to the end of pharaonic civilization, these texts bear witness to the Egyptians' attempts to answer the questions that have troubled every human being: Why do we die? And what awaits us after death?

The Texts

The Pyramid Texts

The oldest and most carefully structured funerary texts are those found in the pyramids of nine kings and queens of the late Old Kingdom (Dynasties 6-8, ca. 2500-2200 B.C.). On internal evidence, these Pyramid Texts date to at least a century before the earliest preserved copy.[2] Some reflect traditions of burial, in the ground or in mud-brick mastabas, that predate even the earliest pyramids:

> Stand up! Remove your earth!
> Throw off your dust! (Pyr. 747b)
>
> Pull down his mastaba!
> Make his brick crumble! (Pyr. *1942c)

The texts are carved in vertical columns on the walls of the chambers and corridors inside the pyramid (fig. 22). They are divided into spells (or "Utterances") varying in length from one sentence to several pages in modern translation. The spells usually begin with the words *ḏd-mdw* ("recitation" or "utterance") and end with a dividing line or a sign derived from the hieroglyph for *ḥwt* ("section" or, literally, "enclosure"). In all, there are some 800 spells, though no one source contains them all. The number varies with the size of each pyramid, from 228 in that of Unis, the smallest, to more than 675 in that of Pepi II.

The Pyramid Texts are not a haphazard collection of "magical" spells, but three different genres, each with a specific function and relationship to the architecture of the pyramid chambers in which they are inscribed. The most transparently "magical" are the spells directed against such harmful creatures as a poisonous snake that might crawl from beneath the (mudbrick) walls of the tomb.

> Wall-spit! Brick-vomit!
> That which comes out of your mouth has been turned back against you yourself!
> (Pyr. 246 a-b)

This genre may contain some of the most ancient Pyramid Texts. Many words and phrases are still impossible to translate – some perhaps the equivalents of our "abracadabra:"

> *kbbhititibitiš̌s* son of *hifgt* –
> that is your name! (Pyr. 240)

These "Incantations" complement the protective function of the pyramid itself. They are inscribed on the wall overlooking the entrance to the room in which the grave goods were stored (the *serdab*) and – in Unis's pyramid – on the wall above the king's sarcophagus.

The second genre is that of ritual texts, containing the "script" of various funerary rituals that were performed on behalf of the deceased. In them, the dead king or queen is addressed as Osiris (king of the dead). The speaker is usually the king's son and successor in the role of Horus (king of the living). The Pyramid Texts contain two major groups of such texts, Offering and "Resurrection"

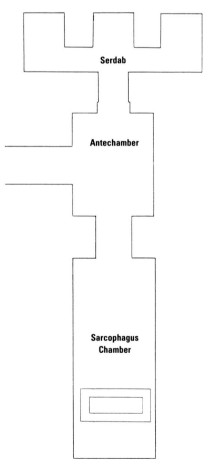

Fig. 22. Plan of the burial chambers in the pyramid of Unis.

Serdab

Antechamber

Sarcophagus Chamber

Rituals, both traditionally inscribed in the sarcophagus chamber, the innermost room of the pyramid.

The Offering Ritual, which is always found on the north side of the chamber, consists of mostly short spells accompanying the presentation of food and other offerings. Each offering is called the "Eye of Horus," and the spell often contains a word-play on the offering itself. For example:

> Osiris King (name), receive the Eye of Horus:
> it cannot be cut (šᶜ) away from you.
> Two pieces (šᶜt) of bread. (Pyr. 87a-b).

Besides the usual introductory recitation, these spells also contain such "stage directions" as "Recite 4 times for King (name); lift up 4 times," (Pyr. 87b) or "Set at his left side" (Pyr. 65a).

The ritual itself begins with purification and the mouth-opening ceremony, designed to restore the deceased's faculties. Then follows the presentation of food and drink – all the major items of the Egyptian diet – in the Great Offering (dbḥt-ḥtp, "Necessary Offering"); the largest pyramids add spells for offerings of objects and statues as well. The ritual concludes with the formal Reversion of Offerings to the deceased's use, a final purification, and the smashing of the ritual vessels.

The south side of the sarcophagus chamber is devoted to the text of the "Resurrection" Ritual, a separate sequence of longer spells whose theme is the deceased's departure from this world to the next. This ritual opens with the words, "You have not gone away dead, you have gone away alive" (Pyr. 134a), and ends with the assurance, "Your name shall endure among men even as it comes into being among the gods" (Pyr. 256d).

Spells of the third genre are for use by the deceased himself. Originally in the first person, most have been "personalized" by inserting the name of the king or queen in place of the first-person pronoun. This collection of "personal" spells is the largest and most varied group of Pyramid Texts, lining the walls of the antechamber and the corridor that leads out of the tomb. Unlike the ritual texts, the spells do not occur in a fixed sequence, but vary from pyramid to pyramid. Occasionally, groups of three or more spells deal with a common theme – often metaphors for the passage from this life to the next, such as ladders to the sky or the crossing of a waterway.

In addition to Old Kingdom royal tombs, Pyramid Texts also occur in non-royal burials, possibly from as early as Dynasty 6, through the Roman period. Although the oldest copies are all royal, there is evidence that the same texts enjoyed a much wider use even before their first preserved appearance in a non-royal burial. Private tombs from the earliest dynasties have lists of offerings whose content and sequence are the same as those presented in the Offering Ritual (see cat. 24).[3] The Pyramid Texts themselves were probably inscribed from a generic "master copy" in which either the deceased spoke in the first person or the space for his name was represented by the word mn ("so-and-so").[4] In some cases, the deceased clearly speaks as someone other than a king:

> I will not deny the Sun,
> I will not reject the King. (Pyr. 891d-92a)

> I will not be accused,
> I will not be seized for the King,
> I will not be taken to the officials. (Pyr. 1042a-d)

Coffin Texts

The first attested uses of funerary texts by people other than the king or queen, however, date from the First Intermediate Period and the Middle Kingdom. These are known as Coffin Texts, because they are most often found on

Fig. 23. Map of the Underworld from the Book of Two Ways on the inner coffin of Djehuty-nakht (cat. 43).

Fig. 24. The opening of the mouth ritual performed on a mummy outside the tomb.

wooden coffins, although examples also occur in papyri and on the walls of some tombs. Each coffin is, in effect, a contracted version of the pyramid chambers of the Old Kingdom,[5] and the texts once inscribed on the walls inside the pyramid are now written in ink on the sides of the coffin. Many of these coffins reproduce the ritual texts from the Pyramid Texts – the "Resurrection" Ritual appears in full, and the Offering Ritual is usually represented by an offering-list and a "frieze of objects."

Most of the Coffin Texts belong to the genre of "personal" spells, and are the direct descendants of those that line the antechamber and corridor of Old Kingdom pyramids. Some 1185 spells have been identified, though the typical coffin has fewer than 200. In some cases the spell is identical to, or a new version of, one already known from the Pyramid Texts,[6] and a few once thought to be new to the Coffin Texts are now known to have been part of the Pyramid Texts as well (e.g., CT 516-519). For such reasons it is not easy to draw a hard and fast line between Pyramid Texts and Coffin Texts; for the most part they form a single, continuous tradition of funerary literature.

The Coffin Texts do contain one new genre not found in the Pyramid Texts (although its beginnings can be detected there). This is the "Guide to the Hereafter," a series of spells, often illustrated with a map (fig. 23), describing the obstacles and inhabitants of the next world and providing instruction and appropriate words for safe passage. The most important of these guides is the Book of Two Ways (essentially, CT 1029-1185), which appears in Middle Kingdom coffins from el-Bersha.[7]

Mouth-Opening Ritual

The Pyramid Texts and Coffin Texts remained the standard for Egyptian funerary literature throughout the Middle Kingdom. With the disruption of the Second Intermediate Period, a new tradition made its appearance. Though Pyramid Texts continued to be copied for some royal and private burials, the majority of funerary literature after the Second Intermediate Period is contained in a series of new collections, or "books," descended from the different genres of the older tradition.

From the Offering Ritual of the Pyramid Texts comes the New Kingdom Mouth-Opening Ritual, now codified into 75 separate "scenes," often illustrated with accompanying vignettes (fig. 24). The new ritual is performed on the statue or the mummy of the deceased. After an initial purification, the ritual proceeds to the sacrifice of a bull; the mouth-opening ceremony itself; and offerings of food, clothing, oils, and other goods. It ends with an invocation to the gods as the statue or mummy is installed in the tomb. Some copies ascribe this ritual to the time of Amenhotep I (Dynasty 18, ca. 1550 B.C.), but the earliest full copy is found in the tomb of Rekh-mi-re, vizier under Thutmose III and Amenhotep II (Dynasty 18, ca. 1450 B.C.). Classic examples appear on the walls of New Kingdom private and royal tombs, and the ritual itself survives to the Roman period.

Netherworld Books

The Coffin Texts' "Guides to the Hereafter" generate a new series of separate "Netherworld Books" in the New Kingdom. Known collectively to the Egyptians as "Amduat" (im-dwȝt, or "What is in the Netherworld"),[8] these include, among others, the Book of Gates, Book of Caverns, and the collection that we call Amduat (whose actual Egyptian title is "Writing of the Hidden Chamber"). All have as a common theme the sun's travel through the world of darkness during the hours of the night. They describe the inhabitants of the Netherworld and the process of the sun's journey through it to rebirth at dawn, usually with elaborate illustrations (fig. 25). During the New Kingdom, they are found almost exclusively in the royal tombs in the Valley of the Kings; later copies occur in private papyri and sarcophagi. The oldest such "book" is the Amduat, which first appears in the tomb of Thutmose I (Dynasty 18, ca. 1520 B.C.). The Book of Gates occurs first under Horemheb (Dynasty 18, ca. 1300 B.C.), and the others date from the time of Seti I to Merneptah (Dynasty 19, ca. 1290-1200 B.C.).[9]

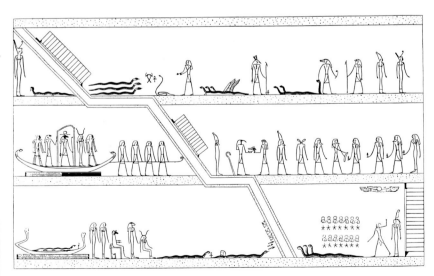

Fig. 25. The journey through the Underworld from the Book of Amduat.

Book of the Dead

The Mouth-Opening Ritual and the "Netherworld Books" are specialized descendants of the Pyramid Texts and Coffin Texts. The most direct descendant of the older tradition, however, is the Book of the Dead, known to the Egyptians as "The Spell(s) for Coming Forth into (or by) Day" (*prt m hrw*). This is a collection of some 200 spells, sixty percent of which go back to spells in the Pyramid Texts or Coffin Texts, or both. It was usually written on papyri, though individual spells from it appear elsewhere as well – for example, Spell 6 ("Spell for making a *shawabti* work for a person in the necropolis") on *shawabti*s and Spell 30 ("Spell for preventing the heart of a person from being barred from him in the necropolis") on heart scarabs. The number and sequence of Book of the Dead spells vary from papyrus to papyrus; standardized collections do not appear until near the end of the pharaonic period.[10]

Nearly all of the spells in the Book of the Dead are "personal" spells. Most are illustrated and many, like the following, have titles and instructions for their use:

> Spell of a *tyet*-amulet of red jasper put at the deceased's throat.
> To be said by (name):
> "You have your blood, Isis.
> You have your effectiveness, Isis.
> You have your magic, Isis.
> The amulet is a protection of this great one,
> guarding against the one who would do him harm."
> This spell should be said over a *tyet*-amulet of red jasper moistened with liquid from Life-containing plants, strung on sycamore fiber, and put at the deceased's throat. (BD 156)

In spells that go back to the Pyramid Texts or Coffin Texts, the ancient editors sometimes added explanations of particular passages – for example, in Book of the Dead Spell 17, descended from Spell 335 of the Coffin Texts:

> I am the great phoenix that is in Heliopolis, the accountant of that which exists.
> *Who then is it? It is Osiris.*
> *As for "that which exists," it is the great god.*
>
> Variant: *it is Continuity and Everlastingness.*
> *As for Continuity, it is Day. As for Everlastingness, it is Night.*

Of the new spells in the Book of the Dead, the most important is Spell 125, dealing with the final judgment. Illustrations of this spell show the deceased being led by Anubis into the Hall of Double Order (see cat. 83a), named after the forty-two gods who represent the various aspects of Order (Maat) and sit in two rows, one on either side of the hall. In the presence of these judges the deceased's heart (the seat of thought and emotion) is weighed in the scales against a feather (the hieroglyph for Maat), while Thoth, the god of writing, records the procedure. The text of Spell 125 contains words that the deceased needs to say to help in his judgment. Part of his case is the Negative Confession (Spell 125b), with a denial addressed to each of the forty-two judges. For example:

> O Strayer from Bubastis – I have not eavesdropped.
> O Pale One from Heliopolis – I have not been talkative.
> O Viper from Busiris – I have not litigated except as concerns my own property.

The hoped-for outcome of this judgment is that the deceased is declared "justified" (*m3ᶜ ḫrw* "true of voice") in his behavior during life, and is introduced by Horus (king of the living) to Osiris (king of the next world). But justification is not automatic: a monster called "The Gobbler" waits by the scales to devour those found not "true of voice."

The Book of the Dead first appears in its classic form in Dynasty 18, though early versions of it are known from the late Middle Kingdom and the Second Intermediate Period.[11] From Dynasty 18 on, it became the standard for funerary literature until the end of Egyptian civilization. The final centuries of Egyptian history gave rise to only a few new funerary texts, most written on papyri.

The Book of Spending Eternity (this is the Egyptian title) belongs to the genre of "Netherworld Books," and dates to the Ptolemaic Period (after 332 B.C.).[12] The Book of Breathing (also the Egyptian title) is a linear descendant of the Book of the Dead, divided into two sections. The first was said to have been discovered at Thebes during Dynasty 26, but its earliest copies date from the Ptolemaic Period.[13] It consists of prayers and a Negative Confession recited for the deceased, as Osiris, by the goddess Isis, his wife, "to make his *ba* live, to make his body live, to rejoin each of his parts, so that he might join the horizon with his father the Sun."[14] The second section, much longer than the first, consists mostly of "personal" spells, including a long litany for the preservation of the deceased's name. It dates from the first or second century A.D.[15] From the same period comes the Ritual of Embalming, on the same pattern as the New Kingdom Mouth-Opening Ritual. Eleven "scenes" are preserved, each with instructions to the embalmers along with appropriate spells to be recited. Such a ritual undoubtedly accompanied the process of mummification throughout Egyptian history, and it is possible that this late text goes back at least to a New Kingdom original.[16]

The Meaning of the Texts

In spite of differences in age, form, and content, all Egyptian funerary texts belong to one of only three basic genres of funerary literature, each with a specific function. *Protective spells*, or "Incantations," are designed to guard the tomb and its contents on earth. The best examples occur in the Pyramid Texts, but others appear in the Coffin Texts and Book of the Dead. *Ritual texts* accompany the various funerary rites that the living perform on behalf of the dead. These include the Offering and "Resurrection" Rituals of the Pyramid Texts as well as the later Mouth-Opening Ritual and the Ritual of Embalming. *Personal spells*, the largest and most varied of the three genres, are intended to aid the deceased in making a successful transition from this world to eternal life in the next. Their focus is entirely on the hereafter: guides to its topography, charms for changing into whatever form may be needed to overcome its obstacles, spells to secure assistance or protection from its inhabitants, the correct words to help in passing its final judgment, and prayers to its gods for acceptance into their company.

The function of each of these genres is related to the Egyptian understanding of what happens to a human being at death. To the Egyptians, each person was composed of three essential elements: body, *ba*, and *ka*. The body is the physical element, unique to each individual. It changes throughout life – the Egyptian idiom for "growing up" is *irt ḫprw* ("making changes") – with death the last such change. Unlike the body, the *ba* (Egyptian *b₃*) is not a physical element, but it is individual to each human being. In essence, the *ba* is the sum total of all the non-physical things that make each human being unique – a concept not too dissimilar from our own terms "personality" or "character." Even inanimate things, such as doors and villages, have *bas*[17] – unique "personalities" that set them apart from others of the same kind. Looked at another way, the *ba* is the impression that a person or a thing makes on others (the abstract *b₃w* means "impressiveness"). It is therefore the means by which an individual makes himself known: the wind, for example, is the *ba* of Shu (god of the atmosphere).[18] Although it is not a physical element, the *ba* does have a physical connection, in the same way that it is impossible to think of someone's personality without also picturing that person's body – the physical elements that contribute to our impression of the individual.

The *ka* (*k₃*) is an individual's life-force – what makes the difference between a living person and a dead one. Like the *ba*, it is not a physical element, although it too has a physical connection. The Egyptians recognized that food was somehow associated with the life-force – since people can die from lack of it – and they used the abstract term "sustenance" (*k₃w*) as a synonym for "food," as we still do. The presentation of food offerings is based on this recognition. The offerings are meant not as a presentation of food to be physically eaten, but as a means of offering the life-preserving force in food (the *k₃w*) to the deceased. The same applies in the world of the living: when Egyptians presented food or drink to one another, it was often with the words *n k₃·k* ("for your ka").

Life-force (*ka*) is not individual, but common to all living people and the gods. It was made in the beginning by the creator, and its transmission to the body is part of the process of birth. Egyptian texts make clear that the *ka* is passed from parents to offspring – from the creator to other gods and to the king:

> Atum . . .
> You sneezed Shu, you spat out Tefnut.
> You put your arms around them . . .
> so that your *ka* might be in them.
> Atum, put your arms around King (name) . . .
> so that the *ka* of King (name) might be in him. (Pyr. 1652-1653)

and from the king to man:

> The King is *ka*.
> His mouth is abundance.
> The one who is to exist is the one whom
> he has brought into being.
> He is the Uniter of every limb,
> the begetter who brings people into being.
> (Sehetep-ib-re stela: C 20538 II 15-16)

During life, the *ka* belongs with the body as part of a living human being – the Pyramid Texts refer to "my *ka* of my body" (Pyr. 372d/373b). At death, it separates from the body; the death of Queen Meresankh III, for example, is described as "her *ka* going to rest, her (body's) proceeding to the embalming-house."[19] The *ka* itself does not die: "As for my dying, my *ka* gains control thereby" (Pyr. 1054a-b). Instead, it goes to the next world (Pyr. 615c, N 1055 + 44, Nt 692), from where it needs to be summoned (Pyr. 63b, 2051a-b) to return to the deceased (Pyr. 375b) and recognize him (Pyr. 1614c). The deceased's goal is to "live with his *ka*" (Pyr. 338a, 908b, 2028c; cf. 17c, 1275a/1276a, *1821a-b), to be reunited with it: "I have come to you, father; I have come to you, Osiris, bringing you that *ka* of yours that has been away" (Pyr. 1328a-b Nt).

After death, the deceased journeys to his *ka* (Pyr. 826b, 832b, 1431b) – a synonym for "the dead" is "those who go/have gone to their *ka*" (Pyr. 598c, 829d, 836d-e, 948a-b, 975b-c, 1165b). Since the body remains behind in the tomb, what makes this journey is the *ba*. It too separates from the body:

> How a person sends his *ba*:
> Go, go, *ba* of mine,
> so that yonder person, wherever he is, may see you in your living appearance,
> so that he may stand and sit with you in his presence . . .
> The god of grain, who lives after death, is the one who will receive you at that door of sunshine
> from which you emerge when you leave the fluid of my flesh and the sweat of my head. (CT II 98a-101a)

The Pyramid Texts assure the deceased that the gods "shall take you to the sky in your *ba*" (Pyr. 799c) and "shall make you a way on which you may go forth into the company of the gods, alive in your *ba*" (Pyr. *1946e). Although the *ba* is encouraged to leave the body, there is still a need to preserve this physical part of the individual, because it is part of an entire human being. The body serves as an "anchor" for the *ba* in this world, and can be revisited by it in the tomb (fig. 26). So essential was this "anchor" that, in the Old Kingdom, "spare" bodies in the form of statues were often placed in the tomb along with the mummy.

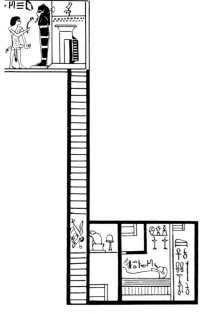

Fig. 26. The *ba* returning to the tomb.

The Egyptian hope for life after death is expressed most concisely in the words of Paheri's stela:

A perfect burial after old age . . .
your joining your place in the sarcophagus,
your joining the earth in the western cliff [*the body's destiny*].
Becoming also a living *ba* –
its having control of bread, water, and air [*the means of life*];
its changing into whatever (form) you wish [*in order to overcome the obstacles of the next world*];
your proceeding in the ferryboat [*to the next world*] without being turned back;
your sailing on the Primeval Waters [*with the sun*].
Your life happening again,
without your *ba* forsaking your body,
while your *ba* becomes divine with the *akh*s.[20]

The *akh* is the form that allows the deceased to live in the hereafter, eternal and unchanging, without "dying again."[21] *Akh*s are one of three kinds of beings that inhabit the hereafter: gods, *akh*s, and the dead (cf. CT IV 32a-b). The Pyramid Texts assure the dead king:

You shall lead those in the Primeval Waters
[*the dead*], you shall direct the affairs of the gods,
you shall place (each) *akh* in his *akh*.
(Pyr. 1166b-c)

The gods (*ntrw*) are the original inhabitants of the next world, the superhuman elements and forces of nature that make up the universe. The *akh*s (*3hiw*) and the dead (*mwtw*) are human beings who have lived, died, and gone on to the next world. The *akh*s have made a successful transition to new life with the gods in the next world. The Pyramid Texts call them *3hiw ntriw* ("*akh*s who have become divine," [Pyr. 969b MN]; compare Paheri's "your *ba* becomes divine with the *akh*s"), or *ntrw ntriw* ("gods who have become divine," [Pyr. 969b P]; that is, who have acquired their divinity secondarily). The dead are those who have failed to make the transition and have therefore "died again," this time without hope of new life.

Akh is a state acquired after death, when the *ba* successfully reunites with its life-force, the *ka*. The deceased is called "one who has gone to become *akh*" (Pyr. 62a):

You have gone away to live.
You have not gone away to die.
You have gone away to become *akh* among the *akh*s. (Pyr. 833a-b)

The ultimate hope of every Egyptian who dies is to go "to the sky . . . among the gods and the *akh*s. He shall see how they become *akh*, so that he may become *akh* in the same way" (Pyr. 1566d-67a). The process is not automatic: there is always the danger of "dying again." The entire purpose of Egyptian funerary literature is to aid the deceased in avoiding this disaster and achieving the goal of becoming *akh*. In Egyptian, the generic term for all funerary texts is *s3hw* ("what makes an *akh*").[22]

The process begins with mummification: "the evening is set aside for you with oils and wrapping in the arms of the Weaving-Goddess" (Sinuhe B 191-92). The Ritual of Embalming, though it appears late in the history of funerary texts, shows the kind of rites that must have accompanied this procedure throughout Egyptian history. On the day of burial, the mummy is taken in procession, along with its burial offerings, to the tomb (fig. 27), a scene vividly described in the "Story of Sinuhe."

A procession is made for you on the day of joining earth,
the mummy-case of gold, the head of lapis-lazuli,
the sky above you as you lie in the bier,
oxen drawing you, chanters preceding you.
Funerary dances are done for you at the mouth of your tomb.

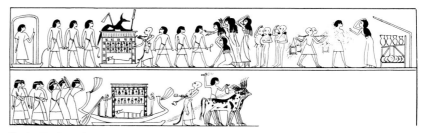

Fig. 27. The funeral procession.

> The Necessary Offering is invoked for you,
> sacrifice is made at your offering-stone. (Sinuhe B 192-196)

The funerary texts proper begin with the Offering Ritual ("the Necessary Offering is invoked for you, sacrifice is made at your offering-stone"). The purpose of this ritual is twofold. It is meant to restore to the deceased the faculties he had during life, "so that he may claim his body" (Pyr. 14c) – a function later specialized in the Mouth-Opening Ritual of the New Kingdom. It is also designed to release the *ba* from the body to begin its journey to the next world. The offerings are made "so that you may become *ba* through it" (Pyr. 578c-79a, 859a-c, 2075a-b), and the end of the ritual proclaims: "You are come to your *ba*, Osiris" (Pyr. 215b). In the Pyramid Texts, the "Resurrection" Ritual then follows,[23] encouraging the *ba* to sever its attachment to this world:

> Go after your Sun . . .that you may be beside your god,
> and leave your estate to your son of your begetting [Pyr. 137a-d]

and announcing to the gods,

> This King (name) has come to you . . . having left (his son) Horus behind him . . . his *ba* having brought him. (Pyr. 250a-d)

In the Old Kingdom pyramids, these ritual texts are inscribed in the innermost room of the substructure, the sarcophagus chamber containing the king's body (fig. 22). Conceptually, this room is analogous to the *dwȝt* ("Netherworld"), in which the body of the sun passes the night awaiting his rebirth into new life at dawn.[24] The king's *ba* is envisioned as rising from the sarcophagus as a result of these rituals and proceeding out of the Netherworld. In the earliest inscribed pyramid (that of Unis) the first spell of the next room (the antechamber) addresses the king "as you come forth from the Netherworld" (Pyr. 257c).

Once released from the body, the deceased's *ba* must make its own way through the hazards of the next world to rejoin the *ka*. The personal spells of Egyptian funerary literature, including the Guides to the Hereafter, are designed to aid in this transition. Unlike the initial stages of the process, however, this final journey must be made by the deceased alone. Most of the "personal" spells are written in the first person, to be spoken by the deceased rather than by a survivor on earth. After the rituals of the sarcophagus chamber are concluded, the first words in the antechamber are: "Your son Horus has acted for you" (Pyr. 257a) – as if to say, "the living have done all they can for you: you are now on your own."

Among the many obstacles that can prevent the *ba*'s successful reunion with the *ka*, the most formidable is the final judgment. The spells surrounding this trial are some of the longest in the Book of the Dead, and form the focal point in many copies. The idea of a final judgment, however, is much older than these New Kingdom manuscripts. In the Pyramid Texts, the deceased declares "I shall not sit in the judgment-hall of the god" (Pyr. 309d) and "I have taken myself from the judgment-hall" (Pyr. 1174c), but has to undergo the trial nonetheless.

I am one who goes and returns . . .
wishing to be justified in what I have done.
The male and female gods have made judgment for me,
the Double Order listened,
Shu was a witness,
and the Double Order decreed . . .
that I raise myself to what I wanted. (Pyr. 316b-17c = CT VI 185d-86d)

This is essentially the same process described in detail in the Book of the Dead. In the Pyramid Texts, Anubis is already called "the official of the judgment-hall" (Pyr. 1713c), and the Coffin Texts mention "those scales . . . in which Order is weighed" (CT V 321c-d).

It is important to realize that the Egyptian concept of final judgment is not a "religious" one, in which the deceased is called by God to answer for his sins, but a social judgment. The deeds denied in the Negative Confession are not sins against the commandments of a god. Rather, they are social evils — acts that disturb the natural order (Maat) that makes happy and peaceful life possible on earth.

I have not added to nor diminished the measure of volume.
I have not diminished the measure of length.
I have not encroached on cultivated land.
I have not added to the balance-weights.
I have not tampered with the balance-plumb.
I have not taken milk from a child's mouth.
I have not driven animals from their pasturage . . .
I have not barred the water in its seasons.
I have not built a dam against the free flow of water. (BD 125b)

Like the virtuous biographies inscribed in private tombs, such denials are meant to convince the gods that the deceased is a citizen worthy of the next world by his behavior in this life. When he passes the trial, the deceased is formally transferred by the king responsible for maintaining order among the living (Horus) to the king responsible for the same task in the next world (Osiris). Only then is he finally assured of new life.

In the Egyptian mind, the reunion of the *ba* with the *ka* and its transformation into new life as an *akh* was equivalent to the process that the sun goes through each morning as it rises from the Netherworld. The sun's transformation takes place in the horizon, the boundary between the Netherworld and the day sky — the Egyptian term is *akhet* (ȝḫt, literally "place of becoming *akh*"). So too, say the Pyramid Texts, "King (name) has not died dead — he has become *akh* in the *akhet*" (Pyr. 350b-c, 1385b-c; cf. 152d ff., 1046b, 1261b).

Conceptually, the *akhet* is identical with the antechamber of the Old Kingdom pyramids.[25] The final spell of the ritual texts in the sarcophagus chamber encourages the deceased to "stand at the door of the *akhet*" (Pyr. 255a). Once transformed into an *akh*, the deceased is free to rise into new life — to "come forth into day." The final spell in Unis's antechamber tells the king, "You are full of your *akh*, you are come from the *akhet*" (Pyr. 455b), and the first words in the corridor leading to daylight urge him to "Pull back the (doorbolt) — open the door of the sky" (Pyr. 502a).

*   *   *   *   *

In spite of their uniformity of purpose, funerary texts do reflect changes in the Egyptians' concepts of human life and destiny. The earliest texts occur in royal tombs, and only later are they inscribed in private tombs as well. This development is paralleled by the fact that at first only a deceased king is called "Osiris" — identifying him with the king of the next world, as befits his rank — while in the Coffin Texts and afterwards, all deceased receive this title. The process has been called the "democratization of the hereafter,"[26] and in one sense this is an accurate description of the change that took place in funerary customs between the Old and Middle Kingdoms.

In the Old Kingdom, the Egyptians' destiny was linked to that of their king – as illustrated concretely by the complex of officials' tombs that lie near the royal pyramids of the time. Assurance of the king's final destiny seems to have been of primary importance. If his successful transition to the next life, as Osiris, was assured, his subjects could be confident that they would find the same tranquility and order in the next world that their king made possible on earth. This was undoubtedly the spirit that built the great pyramids of the Old Kingdom, much like that which erected the great Gothic cathedrals of the Middle Ages. In laboring to assure the king's successful transition to new life, the Egyptians were assuring their own destiny as well.

The keystone of this attitude is the analogy of this world to the next. As long as the Egyptian state was stable – which it was throughout most of the Old Kingdom – there was every reason to believe that prosperity and order depended on the king. The breakdown of social order at the end of the Old Kingdom destroyed that illusion, and had a profound psychological effect on the ancient Egyptians – visible in their literature as well as in their funerary texts. This in turn is the key to the so-called process of "democratization." When people could no longer depend on the king for security in this world, they could not do so in the next world either. Each person had to become responsible for his own afterlife – hence, the use of funerary texts in private as well as royal tombs. Each person became his own "Osiris."

In actuality, the conceptual leap from king to commoner was not as great as it might seem. There are plenty of indications that already in the Old Kingdom the commoner's destiny was viewed in much the same terms as that of his king. The Pyramid Texts themselves may have been composed with private as well as royal use in mind, and private tombs contain scenes in which priests perform the Mouth-Opening Ritual and recite *sꜣḥw* for the deceased.[27] The appearance of Pyramid Texts, Coffin Texts, and their descendants in private burials is no more than the writing out of what was implicit much earlier in Old Kingdom tombs.

The notion of what happens to human beings after they die, however, did not change. Throughout Egyptian history, funerary rituals and their texts were designed to complement that notion – to preserve the body and to release the *ba* so that it could make a successful passage to rejoin the *ka* and be reborn into a new, eternal life as an *akh*. These texts reflect not a morbid fixation with death, but a firm hope and practical concern for the continuation of life:

> What my *ba* said to me: . . .
> You should adhere to life, as you have said.
> Desire me here and ignore the West –
> but desire that you may reach the West, that your body may touch the earth,
> and I will alight after you have become weary.
> Then we shall make harbor together.[28]

JAMES P. ALLEN

1. Wenke 1980, p. 184.
2. Schott 1945, pp. 2-6; Allen 1984, § 723.
3. Barta 1963, pp. 5-90.
4. Cf. Pyr. 147a, in which Unis's copy has *mn* where others have the deceased's name.
5. An intermediate stage in this process is preserved in the pyramids of Pepi II's three queens and that of the Dynasty 8 pharaoh Ibi, where the substructure has been simplified to a single room. See Allen 1986, p. 1.
6. Allen 1950, pp. 110-137.
7. Lesko 1972. See also Lesko 1971-72, pp. 89-101; Mueller 1972, pp. 99-125.
8. Piankoff 1964, pp. 147-49.
9. Hornung 1972, pp.17-23.
10. Allen 1974, p. 1.
11. Capart 1934, pp. 243-251; Budge 1910 (BM 10553).

12. Goyon 1972b, p. 76; Assmann 1975, pp. 54-55.
13. Goyon 1972a, p. 194.
14. Goyon 1972a, pp. 216, 224-226.
15. Goyon 1972a, p. 194.
16. Goyon 1972a, p. 22 n. 5.
17. Žabkar 1968, pp. 48-50.
18. Žabkar 1968, pp. 11-15.
19. Dunham and Simpson 1974, p. 8 and fig. 2.
20. Tyler and Griffith 1894, pl. 9, 5-6.
21. See Englund 1978. Also Friedman 1984, pp. 39-46; Friedman 1985, pp. 82-97; Friedman 1986, pp. 99-106.
22. Barta 1981, pp. 62-63.
23. Confirmed by the title of its first spell, PT 213, in the Middle Kingdom copy of M1C: "Spell of making *akh* after the Reversion of Offerings."
24. Spiegel 1971, p. 25 and fig. 2. The beginning of the offering ritual in the Dynasty 26 copy of TT 33 is entitled: "The House of the Netherworld (*pr dw3t*), the Necessary Offering, purifying the offering-table." The Mouth-Opening Ritual is also located in the "House of the Netherworld," (Kitchen 1969, p. 371, 4).
25. Spiegel 1971, p. 25 and fig. 2.
26. Breasted 1912, p. 257.
27. For a convenient collection, see Lapp 1986, §§ 258-323.
28. From the "Dispute of a Man with his *Ba*," Erman 1896, pp. 73-75 and pl. 10, 147-154. The West is the direction of the next world, and "become weary" is a synonym for "died."

Egyptian Funerary Texts in Translation: Allen 1974, Faulkner 1969, Faulkner 1973-1978, Goyon 1972, Hornung 1972, Hornung 1979-80, Otto 1980, Piankoff 1954, Piankoff 1955, Piankoff 1968.

Osiris

Generally known as the Egyptian god who ruled in the afterlife, Osiris was not solely a funerary god, but also part of the Heliopolitan cosmogony. This was only one of three theories explaining the creation of the world that developed in the formative period of Egyptian religious thought and that were based on the traditions of the great cult centers at Heliopolis, Hermopolis, and Memphis.

According to the Heliopolitan tradition, the world began as a watery chaos called Nun, out of which emerged a mound supporting the sun god Atum (later identified with Re). Using his own powers of generation, Atum created air and moisture in the forms of the god Shu and the goddess Tefnut. These two deities produced earth and sky, the god Geb and the goddess Nut, who in turn bore the gods Osiris and Seth, and the goddesses Isis and Nephthys. Together these deities were known as the Great Ennead, or group of nine, which was often referred to as a single divine entity.

The name "Osiris" is an ancient Greek rendering of the god's Egyptian name. The usual hieroglyphic writing of the name, a throne over an eye, probably has the phonetic value *wsir*; its etymology remains unclear, though many different theories have been put forward.[1]

Osiris was a central figure in the development of funerary ritual from the late Old Kingdom on. This is reflected in the cycle of myths that developed to explain his death and resurrection. The most coherent record of the story dates from the second century A.D., when the Greek biographer Plutarch included Osiris among the famous people whose biographies he recorded. While there is no complete version of the cycle in ancient Egyptian texts, references to various events in the cycle in the Pyramid Texts and other sources suggest that Plutarch's story was based on very ancient Egyptian tradition.

This cycle incorporated elements of earlier myths, such as the dispute between the gods Seth and Horus, which is also closely connected with funerary ritual. In this early myth, Horus was a god of the heavens whose eyes were equated with the sun and the moon. Seth was a somewhat malevolent god of the desert who stole the lunar eye of Horus, called the *wedjat* eye. A violent struggle between the two gods ensued, and before Horus could retrieve the eye, Seth cast it away. It was later discovered by Thoth, who found it in pieces and made it whole again; this may be the origin of the name "*wedjat*," which means "that which is whole." The *wedjat* eye was a powerful magical symbol frequently used as an amulet in funerary art (see cats. 129 and 173).

Another episode in this myth concerns the trial that was held to decide which of the gods, Horus or Seth, would triumph. The eventual justification of Horus in this trial is a prototype for the judgment of the deceased before Osiris in the afterlife (see cat. 83).

The myth of Osiris, as later told by Plutarch, describes Osiris as a living king of Egypt whose brother Seth was jealous of his power. According to the myth, Seth organized a feast at which Osiris was guest of honor. At the feast, Seth presented a large box to the guest who could fit inside it. When Osiris lay in the box, Seth closed the lid and threw it in the Nile, drowning Osiris. The body of Osiris was later retrieved by his wife Isis (see cat. 128), but it was taken from her by Seth who cut it into pieces that were taken to different parts of Egypt and as far away as Byblos. Isis and her sister Nephthys recovered the pieces and Isis brought Osiris back to life long enough to conceive a child by him (see cat. 202). The child born of this union was Horus, whom Isis hid until he was old enough to avenge his father's murder, overcoming Seth and retaking the throne of Egypt.

In its earliest recognizable form, the cult of Osiris was closely linked with royalty, Osiris representing the dead king and Horus his living counterpart. Though some scholars have attempted to date the rise of Osiris as a funerary deity to

Dynasty 1, there is no firm evidence for an Osirian cult before Dynasty 5, when the god's name occurs sporadically in mastaba tombs and prominently in texts in the pyramid of Unis, the last king of the dynasty.[2] In these texts, comprised of spells intended to safeguard the deceased king in the afterlife, the dead pharaoh is identified with Osiris. During Dynasty 6, Osiris achieved an importance in royal funerary texts that far surpassed his significance in the texts found in the non-royal mastaba tombs of the same period.[3] From the late First Intermediate Period on, however, first the nobility and later less exalted people, women as well as men, could be identified with Osiris after death, a process often referred to by modern scholars as the "democratization" of the afterlife.

One of the principal cult centers of Osiris, from at least the late Old Kingdom, was the Upper Egyptian city of Abydos, though he also had a connection with Busiris in the Delta and with Heliopolis through his association with the Great Ennead. The earliest kings of dynastic Egypt had been buried at Abydos and the principal god, whose identity Osiris absorbed, was the jackal divinity Khentiamentiu, "Foremost of Westerners" (Westerners being the dead). As "Osiris, Foremost of Westerners," Osiris was seen as ruling over the dead in the afterlife. From the Old Kingdom on, the voyage of the deceased to Abydos was an important part of funerary ritual depicted in tomb paintings and provided for in the wooden model boats of the First Intermediate Period and early Middle Kingdom (see cats. 34 and 43).

The figure of Osiris is almost always represented in the form of a mummy enveloped in a tight shroud from which the hands protrude (see cats. 197 and 200), usually holding the crook and flail (see cat. 201). He usually wears either the white crown of Upper Egypt or the *atef* crown and a false beard. All of these were used as symbols of kingship from the time of Narmer. The god's face and hands are often painted green, probably to reflect his association with the flooding of the Nile and by extension with vegetation and the fertility of the land (see cats. 211 and 212). Many of these same iconographic features appear in funerary art in an attempt to identify the deceased with Osiris by representing him with the attributes of the god. This is especially true in the anthropoid coffins that begin to appear in the Middle Kingdom.

CATHARINE H. ROEHRIG

1. For a discussion of these, see Griffiths 1980, pp. 87-99; summarized in Griffiths 1981, cols. 623-625.
2. Griffiths 1980, p. 41.
3. Griffiths 1980, p. 5.

Bibliography: Griffiths 1980, te Velde 1967.

The Social Aspects of Death

To deal with their uncertainties about the nature of death, the ancient Egyptians developed a number of complicated rituals and institutions. Since they hoped to live forever in the realm of the dead, the buildings, equipment, and supplies they provided for their afterlife were generally more durable than those required for a comparatively brief life on earth. Because these eternal goods have survived better, death often overshadows life in our view of Egyptian culture. And yet, the very elaborateness of these preparations emphasizes the Egyptians' attachment to life and their desire to remain a part of the human community even after death.

The Egyptians viewed death not as the end of life, but as the gateway to an eternal existence. The afterlife could only be attained, however, by those who had made the proper material and magical preparations and had lived a virtuous life on earth. To ensure eternal life, it was customary for all who could afford it to build and equip tombs well before death, and to arrange for the services of priests and the provision of offerings in their mortuary cults.

As a result of these beliefs, a large part of Egypt's wealth was involved in the preparation for death and the maintenance of the cults of the dead. Such cults were an integral part of the economy: during most periods of Egyptian history they helped to organize the cultivation of a good proportion of the arable land, gave employment to much of the population, and provided a market for both necessities and luxury goods.

Preparations for death were made even by people who questioned their usefulness. Among these skeptics were those who enjoyed the pessimistic "Song of the Harpist," which suggested that the pyramids and other great monuments of the past had not guaranteed their builders eternal life: "See, no one has been allowed to take his property with him, and there is no one who has gone who has come back."[1] This song, ironically, was recorded on the walls of several well-equipped tombs of the type that its verses claim to be futile. The owners of these tombs must have carried out the elaborate and expensive preparations for death dictated by Egyptian custom primarily in order to maintain their social status.

Endowing a Mortuary Cult

In addition to preparing a tomb and its contents (for the words of the poet notwithstanding, it was widely believed that a person could "take his property with him"), the tomb owner had to institute a perpetual mortuary cult, with employees who could ensure that offerings were provided and the proper rituals of the mortuary cult were carried out. This living memorial, like the monument to which it was attached, helped to give life to the dead person by perpetuating the memory of his name in the thoughts of the living.

One of the principal prerequisites for a proper mortuary cult was the establishment of an endowment, usually a parcel of farmland called a mortuary estate, the produce of which would both pay the personnel of the cult and supply offerings of food, drink, and other necessities. These mortuary estates, which were often named after the deceased, were sometimes represented on the walls of tomb chapels of the Old Kingdom as women (since the word for estate was feminine) bringing produce of all sorts to the tomb owner.

One of the earliest surviving literary texts, the instructions of Prince Hardjedef for his son, emphasizes the importance of these arrangements:

> When you prosper, found your household,
> Take a hearty wife, a son will be born you
> It is for the son you build a house.
> When you make a place for yourself,
> Make good your dwelling in the graveyard
> Make worthy your station in the West.[2]

The text then goes on to advise that land be set aside to endow a mortuary cult, and that the priest who was to perform the necessary rituals be well provided for, since, "He profits you more than your own son. Prefer him even to your [heir]."[3]

In many cases, however, the principal mortuary priest *was* the son of the tomb owner. Since the mortuary endowment of a private cult, like that of a king, was a perpetual one, with the produce of certain fields going to the maintenance of the cult and its priest, such priesthoods were a good way to provide security for one's children and at the same time enforce the filial piety that was the ideal according to the Osirian mythology. Just as Horus performed the funerary ritual for his dead father Osiris, a son was responsible for the proper burial of his father and for performing the funeral rites. The fulfillment of these responsibilities was, in fact, a necessary legal condition for inheritance of property: to neglect them implied that one was not truly a son.

Several kinds of priests were needed to perform the necessary rituals. A lector priest, the *ḫry-ḥ3bt*, took part in the offering ritual, and is often depicted reading the formulas of a ritual from a scroll. The *wt* priest, an embalmer, was present at the funeral, and may have taken part in rituals at other times as well. These two priests were not permanently attached to the cult, however. The full-time priest, who received the largest part of the endowment, was the *ḥm-k3*, or servant of the *ka* (the soul of the dead person). This office could be performed by several people, sometimes serving in rotation.

Mortuary cults were funded with the resources at hand: a carefully arranged system of rotating priestly service is recorded in the late Old Kingdom tomb of Ni-ka-ankh at Tehne.[4] The tomb owner, whose principal asset appears to have been his office as sole priest in the local cult of the goddess Hathor, divided the annual proceeds of that office into twelve parts, grafted onto the duties it entailed a requirement of service in his own mortuary cult, and divided the office among members of his family, with each share being paid out in return for a month of service in each cult. The fact that service in yet another cult, that of a man named Khenu-ka, was also required suggests that this idea was not original with Ni-ka-ankh.

Hapy-djefai, a nomarch (district governor) of the 13th nome of Upper Egypt, also grafted his own cult onto an existing one, that of the god Wepwawet, of which he was high priest. Contracts with various officials in Wepwawet's cult (including himself and his successors as high priest), specify that funds from Hapi-djefai's patrimony were added to the Wepwawet endowment to pay for the extra service.[5] In this case, it was not the revenues of an existing cult that were appropriated, but its administrative structure, which was made responsible for the fulfillment of these contracts. Involving the temple administration in these contracts increased the probability that the cult would be maintained.

A simpler, and probably more common, system is hinted at in a series of letters from a man named Heka-nakht to his son giving instructions as to agricultural and family matters.[6] He seems to have been a mortuary priest of the vizier Ipy, who died in late Dynasty 11, and the endowment that paid for his services was presumably the land his family farmed. Heka-nakht's son apparently performed the required offering rituals when his father was away, since the cache of letters was found near Ipy's chapel.

Building a Tomb

In addition to establishing an endowment to support priestly service, it was necessary to provide a place where that service could take place. Building and equipping a tomb was one of the main occupations of adult Egyptians of the upper classes. The tomb required frequent supervisory visits, and was no doubt the object of family excursions, during which the owner could show off its beauties.

The tomb also enabled a grateful king to reward his servants: a lintel, doorway, or other architectural element, clearly stated to be a gift of the king in its inscriptions, conferred both status and higher-quality artwork upon the tomb owner.[7]

The structure of Egyptian tombs varied over time, but it always included two areas, the actual place of burial and the chapel. These parts were usually united in a single building or complex, although this was not strictly necessary.

The burial chamber was always inaccessible, usually built below ground or cut deep into a rock cliff. In it were placed equipment for the burial and the afterlife, including such special funerary objects as the coffin, canopic jars, and *shawabtis*, as well as the amulets and magical texts that would smooth the path of the dead soul to the other world. Here also were placed the ordinary utensils of daily life needed in the afterlife: furniture, tools, games, clothing, hunting equipment, perfume bottles – in short, anything that the tomb owner felt unable to live without. These were often objects that had been used by the deceased during his lifetime, although some were specially manufactured for the tomb.

The burial chamber was often undecorated, but sometimes had painted scenes of offerings and daily life, similar to those in the chapel. These scenes were occasionally replaced with models of wood or stone, treating the same subjects. In both cases, the intention was to ensure by magic that the provisions and activities depicted would continue in the other world.

The chapel was the public part of the tomb, and was accessible to the priests and passersby who came to make offerings. The spirit of the deceased could also enter and leave the chapel, by means of a "false door" in one of its western walls, which theoretically communicated directly with the burial chamber. The spirit could inhabit statues in the chapel or in an inaccessible chamber called a *serdab* (see cats. 16-18), from which he could look into the chapel through a slit. In this way, the deceased could partake of the offerings placed on his offering table, which was set up before the false door or a statue for this purpose.

The tomb chapel could be a complicated warren of rooms, with several false doors and many *serdab* statues, or it could be a simple niche in the side of the mound covering the burial chamber, which would hold only a stela or small false door. Similarly, it could be decorated with abundant carved and painted relief, or with only a single ink inscription. Whatever the economic level of the tomb owner, however, the same principles of decoration applied.

The Egyptians believed that saying a thing would make it so, at least in the shadowy world of the afterlife. The name or a picture of something would also make it real (the name was doubly valuable, since in hieroglyphic writing a picture of an object was usually included in its name). The Egyptians made use of all possible methods to ensure a constant supply of offerings. A priest was hired to bring real offerings and to say the requisite formulas, but these offerings were also illustrated on the wall (in piles, being carried, or in compartmental lists) and the formulas were inscribed on the false door. Models and scenes showing a happy life in the afterworld had a similar magical function, and helped to make the events pictured a reality.

These lively decorations had another purpose: they helped to lure passersby into the tomb where, if the decorations pleased and entertained them, they might say an offering formula for the benefit of the deceased, which would supplement the prayers of the paid priests. There were no doubt many such tourists. In ancient times, Egyptian cemeteries were far from the desolate places they are today: workmen and artists were employed on neighboring tombs, families would visit the tombs of dead relatives or those they were preparing for themselves, and mortuary priests attached to the tombs made frequent visits to perform their duties.

Aware of these potential visitors, tomb owners often included amusing scenes and jokes in their tomb decoration. Some also placed inscriptions outside their chapels, inviting passersby to come in and make an offering, extolling the beauty of the decoration and the high place the deceased owner no doubt held in the other world (as evidenced by the high titles he had held in this one).

The most important element of the decoration was, however, the owner's name. Since the name was viewed as a part of the personality, its presence in the memories of the living was thought to help keep the soul alive, and many children who erected monuments to a parent claimed to have "caused his name to live." For this reason, the name was usually carved on the most enduring elements of the tomb, such as stone lintels, columns, and doorways, which were often made of better-quality hard stone for structural reasons. It was also attached to all images of the deceased in the tomb, wall decoration as well as statuary, so that, if necessary, each image could function as a temporary residence for the soul.

Ex Voto Statues and Stelae

Offerings to the dead were not limited to those made in their tomb chapels. Since the dead soul could be invoked simply by speaking its owner's name, it was considered wise to erect secondary memorials outside the tomb. As early as the Middle Kingdom, it became popular to ask for funerary offerings in temples and places of pilgrimage, by means of stelae and statues set up in courtyards or along processional routes that would be seen by large numbers of people.

The earliest examples of such monuments are small stelae that essentially duplicated the scene on the tablet of the tomb's false door, where the deceased and his family were shown in front of a table of offerings and a brief offering formula is given. Statues were also inscribed with the offering formula, which in a tomb chapel could be omitted since it would be present nearby on a lintel or false door. The important features were the name and image of the deceased, which allowed him to partake of the results of any offering formula that might be recited for him.

In the Middle Kingdom these memorials tended to be set up in such special parts of a holy precinct as the "terrace of the great god" at Abydos[8] and the shrine of the deified official Heka-ib on Elephantine Island.[9] Although these monuments were clearly funerary, they also enabled the people depicted on them to share in all the periodic festivals of the gods and partake of the incense and offerings attached to such celebrations.

Although the excavation of such an area has never been recorded and published in full detail, there is sufficient evidence to suggest that these monuments were not isolated, but formed part of the decoration of small mud-brick chapels. These chapels served as cenotaphs, secondary to the chapels near the actual burials of the owners. These small "offering chapels" are comparable to the royal cenotaphs set up at Abydos by the kings of the New Kingdom, which have the same form as the mortuary temples of these kings, with a few modifications to increase the role of Osiris in the decoration.

In later periods, the practice of erecting secondary funerary monuments was elaborated, by showing the deceased with an image or shrine of the god in whose temple the monument was placed. This had the two-fold effect of demonstrating the piety of the deceased and his worthiness to receive offerings while putting the deceased under the protection of the god so honored. In the Late Period it became common to inscribe statues with the entire autobiography of the deceased, which covered most of the body with the exception of the face and hands, and was invariably laudatory in tone.

The sites of these later monuments were either the major cult centers of a state god, such as Amen-Re of Thebes or Ptah of Memphis, or places of pilgrimage. Among the latter, the animal cemeteries of the Late Period were particularly popular: the catacomb-like Serapeum at Sakkara, the tombs of the sacred ibises of Thoth at Tuna el-Gebel, and other animal cemeteries have hundreds of depressions in their walls, all of which originally held stelae commemorating the visits of pilgrims and asking for the protection of the god and the prayers of visitors.

The most popular site for *ex voto* memorials during all periods was Abydos, the cult center of the god of the dead, Osiris. Here, where the tomb of one of the Dynasty 1 kings was later mistaken for the tomb of Osiris himself, was an ideal place to call upon the god's protection and to set up one's own mortuary monument. Many of the chapels had a number of stelae of varying quality and style.[10] Since space in the prime locations along processional routes must have been expensive, it seems likely that each chapel had stelae set up over several generations of a family. Even within the individual stelae, more family members were shown than was usual in tomb stelae.

Pilgrimage to Abydos

The extent to which *ex voto* monuments were connected to the ritual pilgrimage to Abydos, known from the iconographic evidence, remains unclear. The representations of this ritual, which are most common in the Middle Kingdom, show the deceased as a mummiform figure reposing on a bier. It is unclear whether this figure was the actual mummy or a mummiform statue; whether the destination of the voyage was actually Abydos or simply a nearby area (perhaps a part of the cemetery) that served as a symbolic site of the tomb of Osiris; and whether this journey took place before death, as part of the funeral, or even later. The ritual seems to have derived from a royal ritual, which was presumably carried out in actuality, in part to inform and convince the populace of the death of the king. In a nonroyal context, the ritual voyage to Abydos may have been enacted in differing ways depending on the customs of the period and the wealth of the deceased.

If the pilgrimage was actually made to the Osiris temple at Abydos rather than to a place that had been equated with it for ritual purposes, it seems likely that this was the time at which memorial stelae were set up in the family chapels there.

The Funeral

Having completed his tomb, collected its furnishings, arranged for service in perpetuity in his mortuary cult, and perhaps erected some secondary monuments at Abydos or other shrines, a wealthy Egyptian could die happy. In spite of his sanguine hopes of a well-supplied afterlife, mourning was customary (fig. 28). The attitude of mourning is clear from the phrase used for it: at the death of Amenemhat I, the royal court was said to be "in head-upon-knee."[11] Scenes in tombs of all periods show both men and women weeping, tearing their hair and clothing, casting dirt upon their heads, and collapsing on the ground. Old Kingdom representations[12] clearly show that men and women mourned in separate places, the women inside the house and the men outside, a separation that still occurs in modern Egyptian funerals. In some New Kingdom wall paintings, the mourning women wear strips of blue cloth tied around their heads, a custom that survived into modern times to mark the immediate household of the deceased.[13]

The coffin of the deceased left his house, either carried by his retainers or drawn on a sledge, usually by friends. At least two mourning women normally accompanied the procession. In later periods, these mourners represented Isis and Nephthys (the role of Isis normally being taken by the wife of the de-

Fig. 28. Mourning women from the tomb chapel of Mereruka.

ceased). Also present were the embalmer (*wt*), who carried a tall staff in some cases and in others clapped two sticks together, and the lector priest, who wore a sash across his shoulder and carried a rolled scroll. In the New Kingdom and later, other priests, such as the *stm* and the *imy-ḥnt*, also took part in the funeral. When the procession reached the river it carried the coffin of the deceased onto a funerary barge, which was towed by boats of rowers and in some cases by people standing on the riverbank. The two women stood at the prow and stern of the barge, flanking the coffin, which was placed under a canopy in the middle of the deck. In the procession recorded in the tomb of Mereruka, several men cast themselves into the river as the boats depart.[14]

After crossing the river, the boat arrived at the *w ᶜbt*, the place of purification. This building on the riverbank may have been the place where the deceased was mummified. In any event, it was the site of purifying rituals. From here the mummy was taken in procession to the necropolis, often on a sledge drawn by oxen. At the tomb, the deceased was greeted by *muu* dancers, who wore distinctive high openwork crowns, apparently made of vegetation. In the Old Kingdom, the arrival was followed directly by the beginning of the offering ritual; however the later representations include a number of other rituals at this point, perhaps rituals that were taken over from the royal sphere at the end of the Old Kingdom.[15] These include processions to various places representing different cult centers in Egypt, the enigmatic rites involving the *tekhenu*, an amorphous crouching figure drawn on a sledge, and the procession of the canopic box or shrine that contained the internal organs of the deceased.

The most important of these new rituals was the ritual of the opening of the mouth. This ritual was derived from a rite originally performed on statues of gods, where the mouth was ritually "opened" with a chisel to allow the god to partake of offerings made to him. By the time of the Pyramid Texts, this ritual was also performed on the mummy of the king, and later it was included in the funeral services of commoners as well. It was a complicated ritual, perhaps a combination of similar rituals from traditions in different parts of Egypt. It was thought to revitalize the dead person, allowing him to eat, breathe, and otherwise participate in his environment.

The true centerpiece of the funeral, however, was the offering ritual. Made up of many smaller rituals, it involved making offerings of food and drink, libations, incense, and other goods before the false door of the tomb, accompanied by the proper words and gestures. This ritual sustained and strengthened the *ka* of the deceased so that it could be glorified, becoming an effective spirit, or *akh* (see "Funerary Texts and their Meaning," p. 45). Unlike the other rituals, the offering ritual, discussed below, continued to be performed after the funeral.

The offering ritual was followed by the actual burial, the introduction of the body and the grave goods into the burial chamber. Cattle were butchered at this point, partly for use in the ritual, but also no doubt for the feast that followed the funeral. In some cases, a statue was also interred, which had made a pilgrimage to Abydos, at least symbolically. This part of the rite was omitted from most funerals, and the voyage to Abydos was undertaken as a separate ritual.[16] The formal funeral rites, as recorded in the wall representations, concluded with protective rituals intended to keep the tomb intact and its contents safe.

The Offering Ritual

The funeral was, of course, the occasion when the most concentrated collection of rites was carried out, but its central element, the offering ritual, had to be repeated frequently to keep the dead soul well-fed and well-equipped. This ritual consisted of making a real offering on the offering table of the tomb chapel, and reciting the offering formula. Even if no real offering were made, the recitation of the formula was sufficient to give the dead soul nourishment.

The offering formula is known as the *htp-di-nswt* ("hetep di nesut") formula for its first three words, ⧫ (the signs can be arranged in different orders or accompanied by other signs), which can be translated "an offering which the king gives." This phrase can be seen on many of the walls of Egyptian tombs and also on objects that were placed in tombs and on *ex voto* statues and stelae.

Theoretically, according to the formula, an ordinary person could not make an offering, but only the king or a god. To make the offering acceptable, the ordinary person said the formula, which claimed that either the offering was given by the king to a god to be passed along to the deceased or that it was given directly to the deceased from the king and a god jointly (the formula was apparently differently interpreted in different periods).[17] Osiris and Anubis are the gods most frequently mentioned in such formulas, but other gods and goddesses occur as well, especially in later periods. The offering itself was called an invocation offering, literally a "going forth at the voice" or *peret-er-kheru*, which referred to the fact that it was the spoken part of the offering that made it effective nourishment for the *ka*.

This invocation offering consisted of a list of standard commodities offered in thousands to the deceased, normally "a thousand loaves of bread, a thousand jugs of beer, a thousand oxen, a thousand birds, a thousand bolts of cloth, a thousand vessels of alabaster, and a thousand of every good and pure thing on which gods live. . . ." Of course it was not necessary (nor was it possible) for such quantities of offerings to be brought into the chapel or placed on the altar; the words themselves supplied the missing goods. After the list of commodities, the formula concluded with the phrase, "to the *ka* of," followed by the titles and name of the deceased. The formula could be recited by a *ka* priest, or one of the other priests in attendance on special occasions, or by a casual visitor to the tomb chapel.

The offering ritual was frequently depicted in Old Kingdom tomb chapels (fig. 29).[18] The formula was spoken by a man standing in front of the false door with an arm outstretched. The man making the offering was also shown kneeling before an offering table. In most depictions of this ritual, the priest who made the offering was preceded or followed by other priests, who poured libations and burned incense.

The full ritual then continued with three or four lector priests, each kneeling with one fist held against the chest and the other raised behind the head. These priests were usually captioned "*s3ḫt*," a word perhaps best translated as "causing to become an *akh*." This transformation is the aim of the entire ritual: to feed and supply the *ka* of the dead man so that it becomes an *akh*, or transfigured spirit. Other lector priests held scrolls unrolled before them, and pre-

Fig. 29. The offering ritual from the tomb chapel of Princess Watetkhethor.

sumably read ritual texts. In the final stage of the ritual, the last priest left the chapel, dragging a broom behind him to obliterate any traces of footprints.

Festivals

In addition to the funeral, the full offering ritual was also carried out on special occasions, primarily festivals. Since the dead were not thought to have left the community, it was necessary to include them in feasting and other community festivities. On their false doors, tomb owners often listed the festivals at which they hoped to receive offerings. These included such religious feasts as those of the gods Sokar and Thoth, and such secular festivals as the beginning of the civil year.

Perhaps the most popular feast in the Egyptian calendar was the New Kingdom "Feast of the Valley," known from the area around Luxor.[19] On that day, in conjunction with a visit of the god Amen of Karnak to the mortuary temples of the kings on the West Bank, families also crossed the river to the cemeteries of Thebes to picnic in the tomb chapels of their ancestors. This feast, in which the dead were thought to join, helped the living to continue their relationships with their dead relatives, and enabled the dead to continue to participate in the festivals of the community.

Such festive occasions, seen as reunions, are likely to have been part of the festival calendar in other parts of Egypt as well. Even in modern times, the custom of visiting the family tomb in cemeteries during important festivals has persisted in Egypt,[20] a remnant of the ancient Egyptians' communal view of the afterlife and the important role given to the dead in ancient Egyptian society.

ANN MACY ROTH

1. Müller 1932, pls. 14-15, lines 2-3.
2. Lichtheim 1973, p. 58.
3. Lichtheim 1973, p. 59.
4. Fraser 1902, pl. 4.
5. Griffith 1889, lines 269-324; Theodorides 1971, p. 303.
6. James 1962, pp. 1-2.
7. For example, the inscriptions in Sethe 1933, pp. 38-40 and Reisner unpublished.
8. Simpson 1974a.
9. Habachi 1985.
10. Simpson 1974a.
11. Lichtheim 1973, p. 224.
12. Wilson 1944, pp. 201-218, includes copies of many of the relevant scenes. Figure 28 is taken from the mastaba of Mereruka, after Duell et al. 1938, pl. 131.
13. Lane 1871, p. 257.
14. Sakkara 1938, pl. 130.
15. Altenmüller 1975, p. 757.
16. Settgast 1963, p. 80.
17. For a summary of the various interpretations that have been suggested for the initial words of this formula, see Gardiner 1957, pp. 170-173, and more recently Lapp 1986, pp. 35-36.
18. This figure is taken from an unpublished scene in room B3 of the mastaba of Mereruka.
19. Graefe 1985, pp. 187-189.
20. Lane 1871, pp. 211-212.

Bibliography: Sakkara 1938, p. 130.

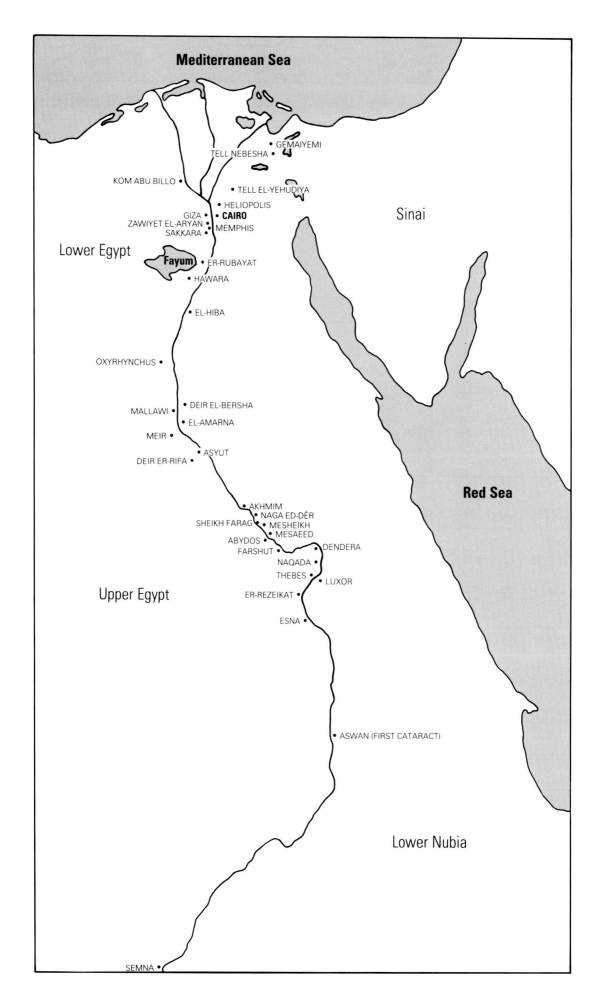

Mediterranean Sea

• GEMAIYEMI

TELL NEBESHA •

KOM ABU BILLO •

• TELL EL-YEHUDIYA

Sinai

• HELIOPOLIS

GIZA • • **CAIRO**

ZAWIYET EL-ARYAN • • MEMPHIS

SAKKARA •

Lower Egypt

Fayum • • ER-RUBAYAT

• HAWARA

• EL-HIBA

OXYRHYNCHUS •

• DEIR EL-BERSHA

MALLAWI •

• EL-AMARNA

MEIR •

• ASYUT

DEIR ER-RIFA •

• AKHMIM

• NAGA ED-DÊR

SHEIKH FARAG • • MESHEIKH

• MESAEED

ABYDOS • • DENDERA

FARSHUT •

NAQADA •

THEBES • • LUXOR

Upper Egypt

ER-REZEIKAT •

ESNA •

Red Sea

• ASWAN (FIRST CATARACT)

Lower Nubia

SEMNA •

Color Plates

I.
∧ **False door of Sat-in-teti**
Old Kingdom
On loan to the Dallas Museum of Art

II.
> **Seated statue of a man**
Old Kingdom
On loan to the Dallas Museum of Art

III.
< **Cartonnage of Ankhpefhor**
Third Intermediate Kingdom
On loan to the Dallas Museum of Art

IV.

△ **Mummy mask**
Greco-Roman Period
On loan to the Dallas Museum of Art

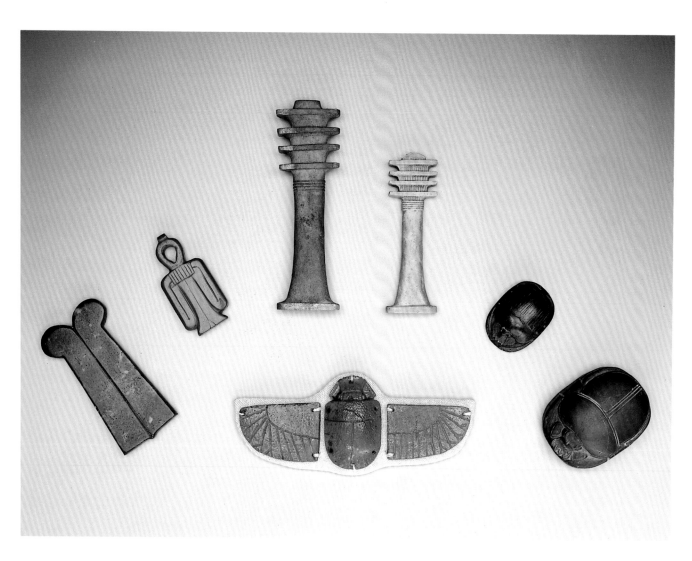

V.
∧ **Group of amulets**
Late Period
On loan to the Dallas Museum of Art

VI.
∨ **Four canopic jars**
Late Period
On loan to the Dallas Museum of Art

VII.
< **Canopic chest with Horus falcon**
Greco-Roman Period
On loan to the Dallas Museum of Art

VIII.
> **Ptah-Sokar-Osiris figure with falcon**
Greco-Roman Period
On loan to the Dallas Museum of Art

Predynastic Period

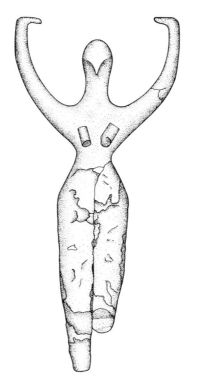

1

1
Figurine

Possibly from Naqada
Predynastic, Naqada II (Gerzean)
Pottery
Height 18.6 cm., width 9 cm., depth 6.3 cm.
Emily Esther Sears Fund, 1904 (04.1803)

This figurine is paralleled by several excavated clay human figures dated to the beginning of the Naqada II stage of the
Predynastic Period.[1] This particular example
is hand modeled of five separate clay cylin-
ders welded with clay to form the body,
legs, and arms. It is composed of a low-
fired fine Nile silt and is seriously salt
damaged.

The figure represents a female with a narrow waist and broad hips. The legs are indicated by an incised line dividing the tapering
lower half of the piece. Breasts were suggested by lumps of applied clay, one of
which is now lost. The head is indicated by
a pinched, rolled-over extrusion of the upper
body; the arms curve up and in.

The upraised arms, suggesting an attitude
of mourning, also appear on decorated ware
(Petrie's "D-Ware" pottery),[2] again suggesting a funerary connotation. The beaked
head can probably be explained as a simple
abstraction[3] as indicated by the similar treatment given the hands of the figure. Such
figurines are not common and those of females outnumber representations of males.
This example, which is said to be from

Naqada, most closely resembles a group of
excavated figurines found at el-Ma'mariya,
Hierakonpolis, and Khozam.[4] It is possible
that, like most of the others, the lower half
of this figurine had a white coating of plaster, indicating a garment; however the surface is so badly decayed it is now impossible to tell.

While they have been compared with the
later, so-called "concubine" (see cat. 74) or
servant figures,[5] we have so little information on the background of most of the
known figurines, that their exact purpose
can only remain an object of speculation.[6]

PL

1. Needler 1984, pp. 335-344.
2. Cf. Mellink and Filip 1974, fig. 202.
3. Kantor 1974, pp. 227-256.
4. Ucko 1968, pp. 429-434.
5. Ucko and Hodges 1963, pp. 205-222, esp. pp.
   205-213.
6. Needler 1984, pp. 335-336.

0   50   100   cm.

Fig. 30

2
Tomb group

From Mesaeed tomb 102
Predynastic, Naqada IIc (Early Gerzean)
Harvard University-Museum of Fine Arts
Expedition, 1910

a. Pottery
Height 4-19.1 cm., diam. 8.1-13.1 cm. (11.301, 308, 326)
b. Palettes
Stone
Height 7.1 and 8.9 cm., width 16 and 14.2 cm. (11.210-211)
c. Rubbing stone
Stone
Height 4 cm., diam 4 cm. (11.263)
d. Necklace
Pottery, stone, and shell
Length (restrung): 34 cm. (11.3120)

Predynastic Egyptian burials provide some of our most important information on early cultures of the Nile valley. Although some settlements of this period have been found and partially excavated,[1] the bulk of our knowledge of prehistoric Egypt derives from the excavation of cemeteries. We know from the often lavish quantity and quality of goods buried in Predynastic graves that the Egyptians already had a developed belief in life after death in an era prior to the first attempts at mummification.

Cemeteries composed of several hundred graves are first known from the Badarian and Amratian periods.[2] Many Amratian graves are little more than ovals dug in the sand; into these the body was placed, knees bent and drawn to the chest, along with one or two simple pottery vases, a stone palette and some flint tools. The body

was sometimes covered with an animal hide, and occasionally both body and grave goods were covered by reed matting. Large cemeteries were begun in the Naqada I (Amratian) period, probably as a result of the increase in the size and number of agriculturally based settlements.[3]

From the beginning of the Amratian period into the Early Dynastic era, the amount and diversity of material interred with the dead increased fairly steadily, as did the size of graves.[4] In the Gerzean period, burials changed from mere depressions in the sand to square pits with wooden sides. The addition of wood and reed supports to the walls of the tomb eventually led to the creation of actual wooden coffins in the Archaic period.[5] Red-on-white decorated pottery vases are fairly common in graves of the Gerzean period, as are zoomorphic slate palettes, ivory objects, ceramic figurines (see cat. 1) and finely wrought stone tools (see cat. 3). There appears to be some relation between the social standing of the tomb owner and the size and wealth of his or her tomb.[6] However, the statistics are open to question, as the great majority of Predynastic graves were plundered prior to systematic excavation.

The Predynastic cemetery at Mesaeed is located on the east bank of the Nile, opposite the modern village of Girga, and was excavated by George A. Reisner in four weeks during two separate seasons in 1910 and 1913. Mesaeed is the Predynastic portion of the vast burial region that includes Naga ed-Dêr, Mesheikh, and Sheikh Farag.[7] The site was composed of about 700 graves, most of which were Predynastic, the remainder dating to the early Archaic period. As a result of the speed with which Reisner's workmen cleared the cemetery (an average of forty graves a day were excavated), the records on each tomb lack detailed information. Nonetheless, the records and material that he brought to Boston constitute a major source of information on prehistoric Egypt.

Tomb 102 had been plundered when Reisner uncovered it, and contained a disturbed skeleton of an adult whose gender was not determined at the time of discovery. Near the body and on the sides of the grave lay the pottery, stone, and copper offerings that the plunderers had left behind (fig. 30). The two slate palettes in the form of fish and the rubbing stone fashioned from a desert pebble stone were found together on one side of the tomb, most likely in their original position. Such stone palettes, often carved in the shape of birds, fish, or other animals, are standard grave offerings of this period, and were used to grind cosmetic pigment. Small cloth bags containing malachite, from which green eye paint is produced, have been found in many Predynastic graves.[8] The fish on these slate cosmetic palettes represented may be the *bulti* fish, which was a symbol of rebirth and regeneration in Dynastic times.[9]

Black and white beads that probably once composed a necklace were found in the tomb, although their findspot was not recorded. The long cylindrical beads are of black polished ceramic,[10] a rare example at this early date of the use of fired fine Nile silt for jewelry, although unbaked mud beads are common. Each bead was probably rolled by hand and pierced with an awl before being fired in a reducing atmosphere, in the same process by which black-topped redware vases were produced. Another small cylindrical bead of hollow shell, possibly from a dentalia shell, as well as a drop pendant fashioned from a piece of banded calcite, were also found.[11] In addition to these beads, a ''hollow cylindrical object''[12] of copper was discovered in the grave, which was unfortunately neither drawn, photographed, nor brought to Boston. Although not common in the Predynastic era, copper objects were produced at this period from naturally occurring nuggets.[13] It was probably a bead or similar adornment, and may well represent the original wealth of the grave.

The vases found in the tomb are uniformly small, a fact which implies that larger vessels used to contain food offerings or scented oils usually seen in graves of this period may have been removed.[14] This hypothesis would account for the vast empty areas at the western end of the tomb. The two decorated vases are of particular interest as examples of decorated marl ceramics, which are almost always found in funerary contexts. Marl wares, first produced in the early Gerzean period, are made from white or green desert clay. The banks of the Nile provided a source of brown alluvial silt, which was used from the Badarian period on to produce rougher utilitarian vessels. The lug-handled ovoid vase decorated on each side with a boat is an example of one of the most common Predynastic ceramics (fig. 31). The boats most likely represent some aspect of funerary rites, and they may relate to later traditions involving the ritual voyage to Abydos, which was clearly a religious center from very early times. These boats commonly bear a symbolic device on a raised pole at one end of the ship. The ''standards'' are variously interpreted as symbols of deities, flags of the port of origin, and tribal ensigns.[15] The standard depicted on both boats on the Mesaeed pot, a horizontal *Z*, is the most common one. Although the resemblance of some of these standards to hieroglyphs of the Dynastic period has often been mentioned, the relationship between these single designs and a developed system of writing has yet to be understood. In addition to the boat motif, fan-shaped plants are depicted,

as are groups of painted lines resembling our letter *Z* (fig. 32). The base is decorated with a single spiral, and the rim bears four groups of four vertical strokes.

The squat lug-handled vase from this tomb is also decorated with ocher paint on a buff vase; spirals cover its entire surface (fig. 33). Full-sized versions of this form were suspended from cords run through the handles. Such suspended vases are assumed to be ceramic imitations of stone prototypes, and the spirals suggest the irregularities of the stone surface.[16] The small black-topped redware vase is a fine example of its variety; its small mouth and pointed base indicate its place near the end of the production of black-topped redware vases. Another carefully made dish of fine redware was polished only on the inside and exterior rim, while most of the outside was left rough. The remaining eight jars found in the grave are dishes and flasks of varying degrees of roughly finished Nile silt. They probably contained the offerings of food and drink thought to be necessary for the deceased in the next life.

SPH

1. The Predynastic burial practices and chronology discussed in this entry pertain only to the Upper Egyptian prehistoric sequence. Lower Egypt maintained a cultural identity distinct from, but in contact with, the Amratian and Gerzean cultures of the South. For Lower Egyptian Predynastic sites, see Hoffman 1979. For the settlements at Badari, Armant, Abydos, and Hierakonpolis, see Baumgartel 1960, pp. 122-139; Hoffman 1979, pp. 145-164; Trigger 1986, pp. 27-40.
2. Brunton and Caton-Thompson 1928.
3. Trigger 1986, p. 32.
4. See Castillos 1977, 1978, 1979.
5. Baumgartel 1960, p. 125.
6. Castillos 1977, 1978, 1979.
7. Brovarski 1980.
8. Lythgoe and Dunham 1965; Needler 1984, p. 319.
9. Gamer-Wallert 1975, pp. 232-233; Needler 1984 no. 138, pp. 250-251.
10. R. Newman, Research Laboratory of the Museum of Fine Arts, Boston, personal communication.
11. For similar beads of the same date, see Needler 1984, el 'Adaima no. 39, p. 81, and no. 239, p. 312.
12. Mesaeed tomb 102 record, on file in the Museum of Fine Arts, Boston.
13. Baumgartel 1960, p. 1-3; Trigger 1986, pp. 29-30.
14. Petrie 1896, pp. 11, 38-40; Mond and Myers 1937, pp. 60-61.
15. Newberry 1913, pp.132-142.
16. Bourriau 1981, cat. 36 a and b, p. 29; Harvey 1987, p. 47, Yale Peabody Museum 6815 for traces of cord.

Fig. 31

Fig. 32

Fig. 33

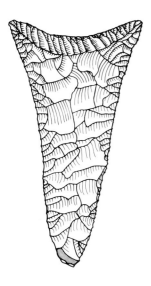

3

3
Fish-tail knife

From Mesaeed tomb 825
Predynastic, Naqada IIa (Early Gerzean)
Flint
Height 13.5 cm., width 7.5 cm.
Harvard University-Museum of Fine Arts
Expedition, 1913 (13.3915)

Few Egyptian objects from the historical era have known antecedents in the Predynastic Period. One of the most interesting such carryovers into Dynastic burial practice is the so-called "fish-tail" flint knife, which closely resembles the Archaic and Old Kingdom *pesesh-kef* wand (cat. 11).[1] Although the function of the Predynastic bifurcated knife is not known, its significance in burial ritual is clear as early as the beginning of the Naqada I (Amratian) Period, when it first occurs in significant numbers as a grave offering. The flint knife is imitated in such materials as clay and copper as early as the Predynastic Period, which implies that the purpose of the tool was largely ritualistic even at this date.[2] By Dynasty 4, the *pesesh-kef* wand appears to have transformed entirely into a model of the earlier flint tool, and although the wands were still sometimes produced of flint or obsidian, they usually had dull or rounded edges.[3]

This knife is made of grayish-brown flint, and was discovered at the Predynastic cemetery of Mesaeed in a disturbed wood-lined burial in which were found only this flint tool and a fragment of a slate palette. The rough finishing of this example and its shape correspond to van Walsem's Type 1.[4] Such flints were usually carefully pressure-flaked from a large piece of tabular flint,[5] and a portion of rough cortex remains on the lower point of this knife. This example was less painstakingly finished than others along the sides and top and lacks denticulation. The more crudely worked lower portion was covered by a short wooden or ivory haft.

In addition, the maker of this knife notched rough protrusions into the sides to better hold the haft in place. An example of a wooden haft originally 9 cm. long was found covering 4.5 cm. of the lower end of a fish-tail knife in a tomb at Naga ed-Dêr.[6] A Predynastic knife hafted with a gold handle[7] appears to be of questionable authenticity, particularly as the handle more closely resembles a dagger pommel, and the use of rivets through flint represents an unknown practice.[8] It seems clear that the implement was never intended to be used as a lance, but was rather held in the hand. Several individuals were buried clutching other varieties of finely worked flint tools,[9] and fish-tail flints are often found near the hands and forearms of intact burials.[10] The Predynastic knife, with its deeply indented sides and top, evolved gradually into a streamlined rectangle that more closely resembles the Old Kingdom *pesesh-kef* models.

The function of these knives cannot be deduced from their form alone. On the basis of the fine denticulations along the "cutting edge," several scholars have described them as prehistoric "table knives."[11] However, these "teeth" are rarely worn or broken, a fact that has led one scholar to conclude that they were produced primarily for ritual use.[12] Moreover, the seeming majority display breakage into two or more fragments, damage that was more than likely intentionally carried out at the time of burial. Fragments of such broken fish-tail knives have often been found scattered across the floors of undisturbed graves, probably as part of the burial rites.[13] An example in the Metropolitan Museum is covered on the upper bifurcated "cutting edge" with a non-reusable envelope made of "reeds and grass."[14] Such a protective cover is not to be expected in the case of an object of everyday use.

If the significance of the fish-tail knife is primarily ritual, to what sort of rite could its use be ascribed? There is no consensus as to the exact place of the historically known *pesesh-kef* in funerary ritual, despite the appearance of that tool in funerary texts and scenes from the Old Kingdom to Dynasty 26.[15] Van Walsem has recently attempted to prove that the *pesesh-kef* was used to support the chin of the deceased during mummification.[16] However, the knifelike nature of the flint predecessor, as well as the entire lack of mummification practices in the Predynastic Period indicate that this is unlikely, and the supporting textual and logical evidence for such an explanation is not convincing. It seems most likely that the Predynastic object played a magical role in funerary rites, and was subsequently ritually broken and interred with the body. Such a rite would give the deceased the appearance and mobility of the jaws that he or she had in life, in preparation for the "opening of

the mouth" ceremony that awakened the deceased's faculties of speech.[17] There is an apparent association of fish-tail flints with male burials in the Predynastic era, although they are known from women's graves as well.[18] Perhaps such differential distribution of grave goods implies that fish-tail knives were buried only with individuals of a particular social status.

SPH

1. The most exhaustive treatments of the Prehistoric tool and its dynastic counterpart are Massoulard 1936 and van Walsem 1978.
2. Painted clay examples: Petrie 1920, pl. XXVIII nos. 14, 15, 16, 18; copper: Ayrton and Loat 1911, pl. XIX no. 5, el-Mahasna tomb H 85, which is serrated along the edges in imitation of the flint implement.
3. See van Walsem 1978, pp. 227-229 and fig. 1 for several examples.
4. Van Walsem 1978, pp. 237-239.
5. Baumgartel 1960, p. 24.
6. Lythgoe and Dunham 1965, Naga ed-Dêr tomb N7625, p. 409, fig. 184, f and h; see also Baumgartel 1970, pl. XL, a fish-tail flint with traces of hafting still adhering from Naqada, tomb 1388, Ashmolean 1895.1001.
7. Saleh and Sourouzian 1987, cat. 5, C.G. 64868.
8. Baumgartel 1960, pp. 5-6.
9. Lythgoe and Dunham 1965, Naga ed-Dêr tomb 7491, pp. 309-310, fig. 138, d-f.
10. Lythgoe and Dunham 1965, tomb N7625, see note 6 above.
11. Needler 1984, no. 162, p. 267; Schäfer 1906, p. 67 n. 1; Scharff 1931, pp. 86-87.
12. Hester 1976, pp. 348-349.
13. Naga ed-Dêr tomb N 7491, see note 9 above; Brunton 1937, Mostagedda tombs 1803, 1847, 1854, pp. 90-91.
14. Myers 1933, p. 55 and pl. XI.
15. Van Walsem 1978, pp. 233-234.
16. Van Walsem 1978.
17. Otto 1960, pp. 16-17, 97-98.
18. exx: tomb B109 at Diospolis Parva, Petrie 1898, p. 33; tomb H 140, Ayrton and Loat 1911, p. 15 and pl. XXII, 4.

Archaic Period

4
Stela

From Abydos, Umm el-Ga'ab
Archaic Period, Dynasty 1
Limestone
Height 21 cm., length 31 cm., depth 7.5 cm.
Gift of Egypt Exploration Fund, 1901
(01.7294)

This crudely carved limestone stela of a woman comes from Sir Flinders Petrie's excavations of the Abydos site of Umm el-Ga'ab. Much of it is now destroyed, but the original rounded top would have shown the woman seated with her legs drawn up in the common hieroglyphic determinative for females.[1] In front of the figure is the *ka* hieroglyph of two upraised arms and, below it the wave-shaped *n* hieroglyph. The rough raised relief is very carelessly carved; most of the features are only roughly blocked out. Like most such early stelae, this one is awkwardly proportioned; the ear size is exaggerated, while the chin is far too small.

The inscription to the right of the figure has been read as "kai ny;" this may be the individual's name[2] or may simply record that the stela belonged to the "soul of [ ]." Many of the names on similar stelae are compounded with the *ka* hieroglyph, suggesting that the latter interpretation may be the correct one.[3] This particular stela comes from one of more than 300 subsidiary burials beside the tomb of King Djer, whose tomb was later venerated as the tomb of Osiris.[4]

More than 250 such stelae are known; on some, figures and inscriptions are merely scratched into the stone, while the quality of the finest is only slightly higher than that of this example. These stelae stood over the subsidiary graves that surrounded the tombs of the Dynasty 1 and 2 kings at Abydos. The majority of these burials belonged to women, possibly members of the court, judging from their elaborate dress, fine grave goods and such titles as "the Beholder of Horus" or the "Favorite of Horus (i.e., the king)."[5] Others belonged to males and even favorite dogs.[6]

Despite the wealth and status of the owners of some of the stelae, these burials are generally believed to be *sati*, or sacrificial burials. Petrie records that in the tomb of Ka'a "the bricks were mostly used too new, probably less than a week after having been made. Hence the walls have seriously collapsed . . . [upon the subsidiary burials, which] . . . must therefore have taken place all at once, immediately the king's tomb was built, and hence they must have been sacrificed at the funeral."[7] In other instances the subsidiary graves were outside the superstructure of the royal tomb and there was no reason that the interments could not have taken place at a later date. Such burials also occur around the great "funerary palaces" associated with the royal tombs at Abydos,[8] and in conjunction with the large tombs of officials at Sakkara,[9] Abu Roash, and Giza, but none are as numerous or as lavish as those at Abydos.[10]

The number of these subsidiary burials appears to fall off after the middle of Dynasty 1, and the practice totally disappears with the end of the Archaic Period.[11]

PL

1. Cf. Fischer 1979a, p. 18.
2. Leprohon 1985, pp. 43-44.
3. Petrie 1901, pls. XXVI, XXVII.
4. Petrie 1901, p. 8.
5. Kemp 1967, pp. 22-32, esp. p. 26.
6. Petrie 1900b, pl. 32, nos. 10-12.
7. Petrie 1900b, p. 14.
8. Petrie 1925a, p. 4.
9. Emery 1961, pp. 137-139.
10. Kemp 1967.
11. David 1982, p. 35.

Bibliography: Petrie 1901a, pl. 27 no. 112; Leprohon 1985, pp. 43-44.

4

5
Tomb group

From Zawiyet el-Aryan tomb Z 122
Archaic Period, Dynasty 2
Harvard University-Museum of Fine Arts
Expedition, 1911

a. Dish
    Calcite (Egyptian alabaster)
    Height 27 cm., diam. 17.7 cm. (11.2313)
b. Bowl
    Calcite (Egyptian alabaster)
    Height 4.5 cm., diam. 13.5 cm. (11.2369)
c. Pottery
    Height 23.4-28 cm., diam. 13.1-13.8 cm.
    (11.2896, 11.2965, 11.2983)

In the winter of 1910-1911 the Harvard University-Museum of Fine Arts Expedition excavated a cemetery at Zawiyet el-Ayran, approximately six kilometers south of the Giza Pyramids. Many of the 300 graves excavated belonged to the Archaic Period.[1]

Nothing remained of the superstructure of tomb Z 122 or the others thereabouts, but they were most probably low, domed rectangular mounds of stones plastered with mud or gypsum,[2] as opposed to the elaborate, niched superstructures of the burials of court members and high officials of the period.[3]

The burial chamber was sunk below the surface and would have been covered with a roof of wooden planks supported on round wooden beams running sideways across the burial chamber and resting on a shelf cut into the rock above the actual grave. The burial itself took place in a rectangular pit, 155 cm. long and about 90 cm. wide, cut into the limestone bedrock. The walls of the pit had been lined with wood approximately 15 cm. thick. Such wood panelling must have eventually led to the development of wooden coffins. Indeed, some wooden coffins were found at this site, although they were of a plain box type,[4] without the panelled facade of many other Archaic coffins.[5] The development of the two types of coffin, plain box and niched, continued throughout the Old Kingdom (see cat. 6).

Buried in Z 122 was the body of an elderly male,[6] with his knees drawn to his chest and his upper back leaning forward (fig. 34). While it has been suggested that this fetal position symbolizes rebirth,[7] a more prosaic and more likely interpretation could be that it was a means to avoid the construction of a larger tomb. In this context, it is interesting to note that the practice of contracted burials disappeared with the advent of larger coffins during the Old Kingdom.

On top of the coffin in Z 122 were the remains of a wooden litter roughly 100 cm. long and 30 cm. wide. The litter was made up of two long poles with papyrus umbel ends and two short ones acting as cross braces at the head and foot. Slots were cut every 3 cm. for a leather or rope lattice. A similar litter was found in a neighboring tomb;[8] they likely served to carry the body of the deceased to the grave, as did the wooden beds frequently found in graves of this period.[9] Throughout later periods, whatever was used to carry the body and funerary material to the grave was considered unclean and abandoned at or near the graveside.[10]

The grave goods from this tomb were comparatively simple; the knowledge that this was a poor burial may have protected it from being plundered.[11] The objects, placed in the burial chamber around the body, consisted of four reddish-orange marl clay jars, one of which contained grain. The jars are typical of Dynasty 1, with applied turned rims and covered with a burnished red wash,[12] much of which has since decayed. A broken pottery bowl or tray on a base was in front of the body's legs, and a stack of pottery and finely made calcite (Egyptian alabaster) bowls was at the head end of the grave.

The type of grave belonged to Reisner's Type i, small tombs dating from Dynasty 0 to about the middle of Dynasty 1;[13] quite a few of these were found at Zawiyet along with a few larger ones that also dated to the early Archaic Period. There appears to have been little activity at the site until Dynasty 3, when a number of larger tombs were built in connection with the step pyramid of Khaba.[14]

PL

1. Dunham 1978, p. 17.
2. Reisner 1936, p. 3.
3. Cf. Emery 1961, pp. 182-191.
4. Dunham 1978, pp. 14, 16, 18.
5. Hayes 1953, p. 42, fig. 30.
6. Dr. Douglas Hansen, personal communication 1988.
7. Baumgartel 1960, p. 124.
8. Dunham 1978, pp. 18-19.
9. Cf. Killen 1980, pp. 23-26.
10. Cf. Lehner and Lacovara 1985, pp. 169-174.
11. Cf. Spencer 1982, p. 74.
12. Kaiser 1964, pp. 86-125, fig. 3.
13. Cf. Reisner 1936.
14. Cf. Dunham 1978, pp. 29-34.

Bibliography: Reisner 1936, p. 380, fig. 190; Dunham 1978, p. 17.

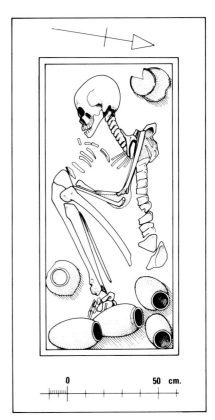

Fig. 34

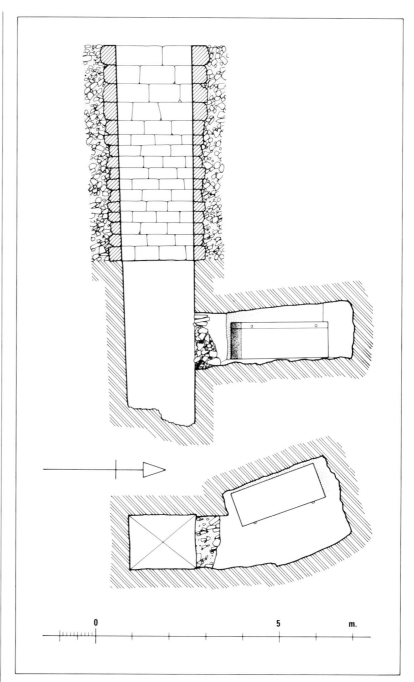

Fig. 35

6
Tomb group of a woman

From Giza tomb G 2220 B
Old Kingdom, Dynasty 4, about 2548-
2526 B.C.
Cedar
Coffin length 240 cm., width 98 cm., depth
83.5 cm.
Harvard University-Museum of Fine Arts
Expedition, 1933 (33.1016, 1017)

Shaft B in mastaba G 2220 at Giza was excavated in January 1933 by the Harvard University-Museum of Fine Arts Expedition
under the direction of G.A. Reisner. Located
at the northern edge of the cemetery to the
west of the Great Pyramid of Khufu, the es-

pecially large mastaba was equipped with a
small chapel lined in fine white limestone
casing blocks, though only a small part of
the decoration of the east wall was begun.
Like shaft C, which was apparently the mastaba's chief shaft, shaft B was left unfinished; but a chamber had been cut into the
side of the shaft before its bottom had been
reached. In this chamber, behind a wall of
rubble and mud brick, was the intact burial
of a woman, perhaps the wife of the anonymous tomb owner. Apart from her coffin
and mummy, the burial chamber was entirely empty (fig. 35).

The outer surfaces of the coffin were per-
fectly flat and uninscribed, though the
whole was beautifully crafted of cedar

boards fitted together with round wooden pegs; knotholes were carefully patched with better wood. The interior was equally unadorned, as was the lid, which was recessed to fit the top edge of the coffin. Two small hand knobs were visible along the east side of the lid (its head was oriented to the north). The base of the coffin is of a single piece of wood, and the lid two pieces joined. Each of the sides is made up of three planks.

Inside the coffin, the mummy of a woman was covered by a large sheet, in which regular folds were still visible; it had presumably been taken from a storage chest and spread over the body just before burial, and then become slightly crumpled and disarranged as the body was put into the coffin.

The mummy itself was lying against the west side of the coffin, partially on the left side, fully extended with arms at the sides and feet together (fig. 36). The mummy was very carefully wrapped: fingers and toes were individually wrapped, arms and legs were wrapped with ten-centimeter-wide linen tapes to a thickness of one centimeter, and the body and upper legs were wrapped with thirty-seven layers of linen bands, into which were inserted wads and pads of linen to give a more lifelike appearance. (Two of the pads bore ink inscriptions, reading ''fine royal linen.'') The breasts were made of layers of narrow bandages wrapped in a criss-cross pattern and molded using wet resin, with small wads of linen attached as nipples. The neck and face were similarly sculpted, and the head wrapped with linen ending in a twist to form a pigtail. Finally a mid-calf-length tunic with a V-neck was placed over the body, so that the body appears to be dressed in the narrow V-necked sheath we know from contemporary tomb decoration.

The name of the principal owner of this mastaba is not known. The unfinished reliefs begun in the chapel indicate that it was built for a man and his family, but neither names nor titles are preserved. Shaft C was incomplete, and contained neither a body nor grave goods; Reisner records it as having been completely plundered, but it may simply not have been used. (A third shaft, A, which was assumed by the excavators, proved not to exist.)

The mastaba itself surpasses in size all but a few of the largest mastabas in the western cemetery, and compares well with all but the largest in the eastern cemetery (most of which belonged to members of the royal family). Reisner speculated from the location that the owner was closely related to the owner of the nearby mastaba G2210 and probably also to the owner of G2130. The name and titles of the former have been lost, but the latter holds the title King's Son.

The two-niched chapel is most common after the beginning of the reign of Menkaure, although for very large mastabas such as this one the date could be somewhat earlier. Reisner dates the principal burial to the reign of Shepseskaf and the burial in shaft B to Dynasty 5, presuming that the fortunes of the owner fell with the death of Menkaure.[1] It is also possible that the owner's fortunes improved at this or another period, and work on the large mastaba ceased only to allow the building of an even more impressive monument elsewhere. If that was the case, the burial in shaft B may belong to a first wife or a daughter, who died before the tomb owner decided to relocate his tomb. If the mummy is indeed that of the tomb owner's wife, we have one other record of her appearance: one of the partially carved scenes in the mastaba chapel shows her with her husband and small son.

AMR

1. Reisner unpublished, app. C, p. 55.

Bibliography: Reisner 1942, pp. 451-453 pl. 42.

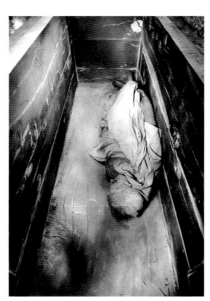

Fig. 36

7
Set of eighty model vessels

From Giza tomb G 7440 Z
Old Kingdom, Dynasty 4
Calcite (Egyptian alabaster)
Height 1.7-6.4 cm., diam. 2.1-6.3 cm.
Harvard University-Museum of Fine Arts Expedition, 1927 (27.1483-1591)

Eighty miniature vessels and a miniature table in fine banded calcite were found in G 7440 Z. They were scattered on the floor of the burial chamber beside the sarcophagus of an unnamed woman (see cat. 9).

Fig. 37

Fig. 38

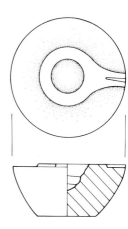

Fig. 39

Fig. 40

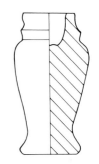

Fig. 41

Fig. 42   Fig. 43

These models developed from full-sized vessels familiar from the Archaic Period (see cat. 5) and Old Kingdom. Such miniatures were cheap substitutes for actual vessels and presumably served just as well in the afterlife. Indeed, some are not even hollowed out, since it was the outward form that was apparently important.

Among the standard types represented in this group was a *khnum* jug (fig. 37)[1] probably derived from a one-handled jug used originally for sacred oils.[2] The cylinder jars with splayed bases (type OK I d, [fig. 38]), are descended from an Old Kingdom type that remained popular through most of Egyptian history (see cat. 79). The wide-shouldered jar with a flat collar (fig. 39), derived from metal vases of the Archaic period known as *nmst* jars, was represented by five models.[3] A model ewer and basin (fig. 40)[4] were carved together as the actual examples would have been used. Also included were five tall jars with concave collars,[5] a type that may have evolved from a jar with a rope-tied seal around the neck, giving its unique appearance (fig. 41).

There were also six deep bowls (fig. 42)[6] and fifty-nine dishes (fig. 43).[7] The miniature offering table[8] copies the circular table with a squat cylindrical base that appears in the reign of Khasekhemwy (see cat. 19)[9] and continues throughout the Old Kingdom, and on false doors and offering scenes well into the Late Period.

Already by Dynasty 4 model pottery, limestone, calcite, and copper vessels and offerings are substituted for their actual counterparts.[10] Large sets like this become rare by the end of the Old Kingdom and limestone is frequently substituted for the finer calcite. The large set of model and actual copper vessels from the tomb of Impy is a unique exception to this trend.[11]

PL

1. 27.1480, Reisner type OK XIV b.
2. Brovarski 1982, p. 7.
3. 27.1475-1479, type OK V d.
4. 27.1481 type OK V e.
5. 27.1470-1474, type OK XVI a.
6. 27.1484-1489, types OK IX a/OK X b.
7. 27.1490-1541, type OK X a.
8. 27.1469, type OK XII b
9. Reisner and Smith 1955, p. 101.
10. Reisner and Smith 1955, p. 91.
11. Reisner 1913, pp. 53-66.

Bibliography: Reisner and Smith 1955, pp. 90-102.

8
Headrest

From Giza tomb G 7440 Z
Old Kingdom
Limestone
Height 29 cm., width 19.5 cm.,
depth 9.5 cm.
Harvard University-Museum of Fine Arts
Expedition, 1927 (27.1547)

This headrest was found inside the limestone sarcophagus of mastaba G 7440 Z. Originally, it supported the head of the wrapped body, which was placed on its left side. The burial was undisturbed by robbers, but at some point the body fell onto its back and the headrest separated into three

parts: a curved top with a square abacus, a fluted stem, and a rectangular base with a low round torus.[1] This form, with its fluted stem and abacus, are characteristic of the Old Kingdom. The pieces were held together by round tenons on either end of the stem that fit into mortices in the top and base. These were secured with a fine lime plaster. The tenon holding the stem to the base was broken when the headrest fell over and the broken piece remains securely plastered to the base (fig. 44).

Headrests are mentioned in the Coffin Texts (CT III, 300, Spell 232) and there is a spell for them in the Book of the Dead (Chap. 166).[2] From Dynasty 3 on headrests are frequently depicted on tomb walls, coffins, stelae, and other funerary art showing burial equipment. It is not surprising therefore that headrests were common components of burials, especially in the Old Kingdom. Though none were found in the earliest mastabas at Giza, they are mentioned on early slab stelae and were probably included in burials.[3]

Since the earliest headrests seem to have been made of wood, their absence in early burials may be due to decay. Thirty-five wooden examples, in varying states of preservation, were found at Giza, usually in smaller or earlier graves. The importance of the headrest is emphasized by the fact that even the poorest burials at Giza usually had brick or rough stone blocks beneath the head of the deceased.[4]

Later Old Kingdom examples found in the larger Dynasty 5 and 6 mastabas at Giza were frequently made of Egyptian alabaster and, less often, of limestone.[5] In later periods, though headrests were still made from stone, wood was more commonly used. From Dynasty 18 on, the headrest form was also used as an amulet, usually made from haematite or faience (see cat. 179) and often inscribed with the spell from the Book of the Dead.

Similar headrests from Giza in the Museum's collection include two carved from single pieces of stone,[6] and one constructed, like this one, in three pieces.[7] A fourth was made in three pieces, but instead of being joined by tenons, the surfaces were slightly roughened, and seem to have balanced on one another, with no plaster to secure them.[8] A fifth headrest, now on exhibition in the Egyptian galleries,[9] was constructed in the same way as the current example and inscribed in a column down the stem for a man named Ibi.

CHR

1. Unpublished photograph *in situ*, NS B6189.
2. Fischer 1979, cols. 688-689.
3. Reisner unpublished, p. 596.
4. Reisner unpublished, p. 579. Stones were placed beneath the head of the deceased as early as Predynastic times.
5. Reisner unpublished, p. 576.

6. MFA 21.2790 (G 4520 A, alabaster), found in the coffin, see Reisner 1942, p. 506; fig.310 (p. 504); pls. 67b (*in situ*), 69d; Reisner unpublished, p 583. MFA 31.800 (G 7753 A, limestone), found in the coffin, see Reisner unpublished, p. 587. Photographed at Giza, NS B7920.
7. MFA 21.2792 (G 1360, limestone), found in the burial pit, see Reisner unpublished, p. 587. Inscribed with the name *Rw-n-Pth*. Photographed *in situ*, NS B13005. No longer in the Museum's collection.
8. MFA 37.1334 (G 4811 B, alabaster), found in pieces in the burial chamber. Photographed *in situ*, NS C6964, C6988.
9. MFA 13.2925 (G 2381 A, alabaster), found supporting the head of the deceased, see Museum of Fine Arts 1913, p. 59; Reisner unpublished, p. 585. Photographed at Giza, NS C3350.

Bibliography: Reisner unpublished, pp. 586-587.

Literature: Fischer 1979, cols. 686-693; Reisner 1923, pp. 229-241; Reisner unpublished, pp. 575-598.

Fig. 44

9
Bead-net dress

From Giza tomb G 7440 Z
Old Kingdom, Dynasty 4, reign of Khufu
Faience
Length 113 cm., width 44 cm. (as reconstructed)
Harvard University-Museum of Fine Arts
Expedition, 1927 (27.1548)

Works of art from all periods of ancient Egyptian history show women wearing dresses with an overall lozenge-pattern. They are most numerous in later periods, but there are several examples of the dress on Old Kingdom private statue-groups and painted tomb-reliefs.[1] To date, very few patterned garments of any kind have been found in Egyptian tombs; most of what is known about them has therefore been based largely on these representations. Traditionally, it has been assumed that these multicolored patterns on women's dresses depict beadwork of some kind, but the conventions of Egyptian draughtsmanship, which often preclude the representation of perceptual reality, make it difficult to establish with certainty whether the beads were sewn on or woven into a cloth dress, or if the pattern was created by a netting of beads made entirely or partially separate from the garment underneath. On the works of art cited above the beaded pattern covers the entire dress and appears to be integrated either by weaving or embroidery into a conventional linen garment; on others, a netting is clearly depicted as a separate overgarment[2] comparable to the fish-net dresses worn by Snefru's female rowers after they removed their existing garments.[3] Material remains for comparison are few and fragmentary, providing only meager evidence of two types of ancient Egyptian beadwork: the weaving of a bead-net unattached to any cloth[4] and the stringing of beads on the weft threads of woven cloth.[5]

The bead-net dress, the first to have come from an undisturbed burial, is a very important addition to the existing information regarding these patterned dresses. The excavation diary[6] and the photographs of the body *in situ* (see fig. 44) provided the essential information for the reconstruction of this, the only complete bead-net dress found to date. On and about the unidentified body, bead groups unattached to any cloth and still containing their original threading were preserved in the exact configuration of the lozenge pattern. Across the chest, vertically grouped large, dark blue cylinder-beads remained, marking the division between bodice and skirt. In the area of the lower edge of the garment, forty-two light and dark blue floral beads were scattered, many of them containing the original threading, which also passed through the tiny ring bead that forms the stamen of the flower. Obvious parallels have been drawn with the configuration of the lozenge patterned dresses painted on the Old Kingdom statues and reliefs already cited: generally, these works exhibit a garment with a high-waisted bodice line topped by a striped halter and often marked at the hemline by a fringe of floral pendants. Although there were no separate faience breast caps[7] among the beads of the halter of the dress, the cloth fragments of the wrappings did include separate breast covers made of molded linen. On a number of Old Kingdom statues, breast caps are indicated by concentric circles of alternating light and dark colors,[8] a configuration that could also indicate beadwork created specifically to cover

the linen breast covers. Other than a Dynasty 5 fragment from Qau, which can be identified by the breast caps as part of a dress, all other extant specimens of bead-netting are shroudlike coverings on post–Dynasty 21 mummies.[9]

Faience beads have been strung into an open lozenge pattern for the main body of a long fitted dress. The light-colored cylinder-beads (probably pale green originally) have been arranged diagonally and the join between them is composed of three tiny ring-beads, a light-colored one centered between two darker blue ones (fig. 45). A row of large dark blue cylinder-beads spans the entire width of the dress at the high-waisted join of the skirt and the halter. The halter is made of alternating rows of vertically placed dark blue cylinder-beads and a half-lozenge patterned netting. On the bottom edge of the garment a double row of alternating cylinder and ring beads forms a horizontal band from which the floral beads hang freely.

The dress is the first complete example of the narrow, form-fitting, bead-net dress indicated by painted lozenge pattern of the dresses on the Old Kingdom statuary and relief (fig. 46). It is also evidence that such a dress was, at least sometimes, made entirely separate from any cloth garment, because the only pieces of cloth preserved in the burial were the fragmentary wrappings adhering to the bones and the separate breast covers of molded linen. In Dynasty 4, because traditional mummification practices had not yet fully developed, bodies were wrapped, each limb individually, in many layers of linen molded with resin to simulate a lifelike appearance.[10] The Giza 7440 Z burial is an example of this phenomenon and it follows logically that a bead-net placed over such a lifelike mummy would simulate a garment of life.

MJ

1. Statue groups: Louvre A102, Leiden L125, Cairo 6, Cairo 22, Cairo 55. Tomb reliefs: Princess Hemetre, Hassan 1950, fig. 41, Pl.XXVIc. Female villagers in Sahure's Valley Temple, Borchardt 1913, Blatt 48. Wife of Ti, Steindorff 1913, Tafel 130; Staehelin 1966, p. 169. Meres-ankh III, Dunham and Simpson 1974, fig.4. Wife of tomb owner, Moussa and Junge 1975, pl.3. Wife of tomb owner, Moussa and Altenmüller 1971, pl.7. Wife of tomb owner, Giza mastaba G2185, Akhmeret-nesut (cat. 14).
2. In particular, Middle Kingdom statues of offering bearers: Cairo CG 36290, Berlin VÄGM 10-80, Louvre E 12029.
3. Papyrus Westcar V, 11-13, Wente and Simpson 1972, p. 20. Lichtheim 1973, p. 216.
4. University College London, UC 17743. The bead-net is from a plundered Dynasty 5 tomb at Qau and measures 51 x 57 cm. There are also two small boxes of unstrung beads. Brunton 1927, pp. 23, 64, Pl.XXIX, 19.
5. Reisner 1923, pp. 103-104.
6. The diary was written by Noel Wheeler of the

Harvard-MFA Expedition team. On March 19, 1927, he uncovered pit Z, which was cut in the rock against the casing of the mastaba of Min-khaf. A week later, after opening the lid of an uninscribed limestone sarcophagus, he wrote that in it he found "a limestone head-rest in three separate pieces....and bead-work in confusion over the full length of the body." The clearance of the burial and the recording were completed on May 26, 1927, when the contents were packed for shipment to Boston.

7. Hall 1981, p. 39. Faience breast caps, 4.3 cm. in diameter, are a noteworthy feature of the Petrie Museum dress.
8. Louvre A102, Leiden L125, Cairo CG55, CG101, and CG89.
9. British Museum BM 6697, BM 6669, BM 6692, BM 20745, and MFA 95.1407 (cat. 125).
10. It is noteworthy that the mummy from tomb G 2220 (cat. 6) was also covered with a narrow halter-topped dress, though in this case it was only the front half and it was made of plain linen.

Literature: Riefstahl 1944; Hall 1986; Staehelin 1966, p. 169, no. 4; Hall 1981, pp. 37-43; Museum of Fine Arts 1982, pp. 170-172, 180-181.

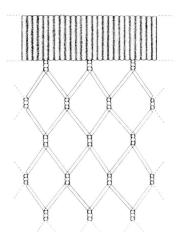

Fig. 45

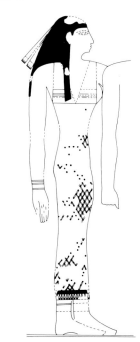

Fig. 46

10

10
Set of canopic jars

From Giza tomb G 4733 E
Old Kingdom
Limestone
Height 28-28.8 cm., diam. 16.5-17.3 cm.
Harvard University-Museum of Fine Arts
Expedition, 1914 (20.1943a-d)

This set of rough limestone jars with convex disk lids is typical of the earliest form of canopic jars from the Old Kingdom. When the viscera, or internal organs, were first removed from the body in the process of mummification, they were wrapped with linen in four separate parcels and deposited in a recess or pit in the tomb at the southern end of the burial chamber. These recesses are first observed in tombs at Medum from early Dynasty 4.[1] The tomb of Hetep-heres, mother of Khufu (Cheops), from Giza, about 2600 B.C., provides the earliest example of a canopic chest divided into four compartments, each containing a canopic parcel.[2] The earliest canopic jars are found in the tomb of Queen Meres-ankh III at Giza, probably from the reign of Menkaure (Mycerinus), about 2548 B.C.[3] Jars with convex disk lids, made of limestone or Egyptian alabaster, appear regularly thereafter in Old Kingdom tombs. They are usually uninscribed, but one set is known to have been incised with the name of the vizier Ka-gemni.[4] There are jars similar to these in collections at Boston,[5] New York,[6] and London.[7]

Early Egyptologists called these jars "canopic," an allusion to the Greek myth of a sailor named Canopus who died in Egypt, and was worshipped there in the form of a jar. Many canopic jars from later periods have human-headed lids (see cats. 53, 54, 91, 92), thus evoking the myth.

MLB

1. Reisner 1936, pp. 220-221.
2. Reisner and Smith 1955, pp. 21-22.
3. Reisner 1942, p 159; Dunham and Simpson 1974, pp. 8.21, 23, pl., fig. 16.
4. Firth and Gunn 1926a, pl. 12 a-b.
5. MFA 13.3104-3106, 13.3108-3110; Brovarski 1978.
6. Hayes 1953, p. 118.
7. British Museum EA 35083.

Bibliography: Brovarski 1978, pp. 83-84.

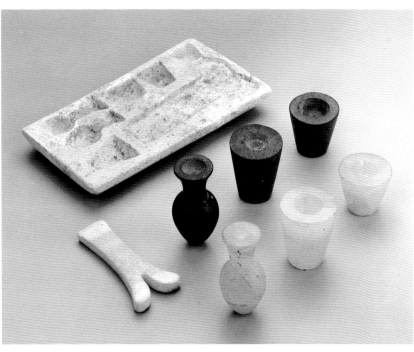

11

11

Model equipment with a *pesesh-kef*

Old Kingdom, Dynasty 6
Havard University-Museum of Fine Arts
Expedition

a. Plate
   From Giza tomb G 2382
   Alabaster
   Length 17.5 cm., width 9.6 cm. (13.3144)
b. Stone vessels
   From Giza tomb G 2381 A
   Height 3.6 cm., diam. 3.7 cm. (13.3252, 3257,
   3263)
c. Quartz vessels
   From Giza tomb G 2381 A
   Height 3.2 cm., diam. 3 cm. (13.3265, 3266,
   3269)
d. *Pesesh-kef* wand
   From Giza tomb G 7550 B
   Alabaster
   Length 5 cm. (28.1148)

One of the oldest and most mysterious rituals in the Egyptian mortuary cult involves the *pesesh-kef* wand, a long flint flake, split at one end. Sometimes referred to as "fishtail knives,"[1] these implements are known from Predynastic burials and settlements. In the New Kingdom they are depicted in representations of the "opening of the mouth" ritual,[2] and the reference to a *pesesh-kef* in the Pyramid Texts shows that they were already used in Old Kingdom rituals.[3] Other Old Kingdom evidence for these implements includes a number of amulets which are clearly related by their shape,[4] and the presence of model *pesesh-kef* wands as the central element of sets of model equipment such as the one exhibited here.

These sets have been found at several Old Kingdom sites, including Giza, Sakkara, Dendera, Abydos, and Zawiyet el-Amwat (Zawiyet el-Maiytan).[5] The tools and vessels they contain were set into limestone platters, which have recesses carved to hold each piece of the set. In addition to the *pesesh-kef*, usually of limestone or alabaster, the sets most often contain two small narrow-necked jars, one of light-colored stone, the other of dark stone; four small open cups with angled sides, two each of dark and light stone. Such sets usually, though not in this case, contain a pair of flat implements in the shape of a quarter oval, most often of dark stone, called *ntrty* or *sb3*.[6]

The group shown here is a composite of pieces from three different mastaba tombs in the Giza necropolis. The quartz crystal and basalt vessels were selected from a much greater number (which probably originally comprised several sets) from shaft A of G 2381. The platter was discovered in the courtyard of nearby mastaba G 2382, and the provenance of the alabaster *pesesh-kef* wand is recorded only as mastaba G 7550 B. The upper and lower left corners of the platter have been restored.

The function of the *pesesh-kef* and the associated objects has been the subject of considerable speculation. It has been suggested that the shape was that of an ordinary table knife during the Predynastic Period.[7] Meyers pointed out that the shape of the blade is remarkably similar to the instrument used in the Jewish ritual of circumcision,[8] but rejects this possibility because the *pesesh-kef* is found in graves. The fact that models of the implement have also been found in tombs of women,[9] and the *pesesh-kef* amulets exclusively so,[10] is perhaps a more disturbing problem. Most recently, van Walsem has used textual sources to argue that the implement was used to prevent the jaw from falling open during mummification.[11]

The name of the instrument has clearly been shown to have had two parts, the word *kf*, which sometimes begins the name, referring to its material, either flint in general or a special type of flint.[12] The remaining word, *psš*, is a participial form of the verb "to divide," and refers to either the instrument's shape ("that which has been divided") or its purpose ("the splitter").

The earliest reference to the *pesesh-kef* is in Pyramid Texts Spell 37, where it is said to make firm (*smn*) the jawbones of the deceased.[13] This spell endures as a part of the funeral ritual through the New Kingdom. In the Pyramid Texts, it is followed by a reference to the *ntrty* instruments, which are said to open the mouth of the king.[14] These implements also normally follow the *pesesh-kef* in Old Kingdom offering lists,[15] and hence were presumably used in the same ritual. These blades, said to be made of meteoric iron or some other metal,[16] always occur in pairs in the offering lists, one described as Upper and the other as Lower Egyptian.

It has been suggested by Massoulard that the color of the vessels in this set indicates a division of the ritual into Upper and Lower Egyptian parts, the white vessels being used for the former and the black for the latter.[17] Another explanation is closer at hand: a few spells after those mentioning the *pesesh-kef*, Spell 43 equates the two eyes of Horus, the black and the white, with two jars, one black and one white.[18] In the pyramid of Unis, these jars are determined with signs identical to the jars used in these sets, and there can be no doubt that these are meant. Later in the ritual, in Spells 54 through 57,[19] four short pots occur together; although their colors are not clearly indicated, they likely corresponded to the two black and two white pots that normally occur in these sets.

Whatever their exact function, these "tool kits" found in Old Kingdom tombs were obviously thought to be of some use in the afterlife. It is to be hoped that examples will someday come to light in a well-preserved archaeological context that will clarify the way they were used.

AMR

1. Myers 1937, p. 37.
2. Otto 1960, pp. 97-98.
3. Pyr. 30a.
4. Brunton 1935, pp. 213-217.
5. For a list of the 27 known sets giving publication information (where possible), see Van Walsem 1978-1979, pp. 224-225.
6. Helck 1967, pp. 39-40, discusses the widely varying names for these instruments and a possible explanation for their evolution.
7. Schäfer 1906, p. 67, no. 1.
8. Myers 1937, p. 37.
9. Massoulard 1936, p. 152.
10. Brunton 1935, p. 216.
11. Van Walsem 1978-1979, pp. 193-249.
12. Helck 1967, p. 38; and Harris 1961, p. 228, citing a personal communication by J. Černy. These discussions are based on the occurrences of the instrument in the Abu Sir papyri from the mortuary temple of Neferirkare, where *kf* is clearly a material. The relevant papyri are published in Posener-Kriéger and de Cenival 1968, pls. XX-XXII and discussed in Posener-Kriéger 1976, pp. 164 and 174.
13. Pyr. 30a.
14. Pyr. 30b.
15. Barta 1963, pp. 94-95 and fig. 5.
16. Harris 1961, pp. 166-168, has *bi3* may have been iron ore from Sinai and the haematite of Aswan.
17. Massoulard 1936, p. 154.
18. Sethe 1934, Pyr. 33ab.
19. Sethe 1934, Pyr. 39abc, 40a,b.

12

Oil tablet

From Giza tomb 4733 E
Old Kingdom
Calcite
Length 19.5 cm., width 9.2 cm., depth 2.2 cm.
Harvard University-Museum of Fine Arts Expedition, 1914 (24.599)

This small Egyptian alabaster tablet is divided into seven sections by a series of vertical lines. At the bottom of each division, above a small depression, is a lightly engraved column of hieroglyphs naming the seven sacred oils: *seti-heb*, *heknu*, *sefeti*, *ni-chenem*, *tewat*, *best ash*, *best tiehenu*. Below each name is the hieroglyph of a sealed oil jar lying on its side.

These seven sacred oils are an important element in the Egyptian burial and offering rituals. Their names first occur on jar labels from the royal tombs of Dynasty 1 at Abydos. Although we do not know their modern names, there is little doubt that they were used for anointing the body at particular points in the funerary rituals. It was very important that they be present in the tomb, either in reality or magically, and they are found in offering lists elsewhere in this catalogue. In Dynasty 5, these seven oils are sometimes shown in their own spe-

12

cial offering list on the false door, as in the famous tomb of Ti at Sakkara.[1]

Several similar oil tablets have been found in the course of excavations; they have always been located in the burial chambers. The depressions in the surface were intended as repositories for small quantities of each oil, where each would be associated with its name and available for ritual use. Jars containing larger quantities of the oils would probably also be placed among the burial equipment. Seven oil jars are shown in the paintings on the walls of the burial chamber of Kaiemankh at Giza.[2] They would thus be readily available for the use of the deceased.

NS

1. Wild 1966, pl. CLXXXII.
2. Junker 1940, pl. XIV.

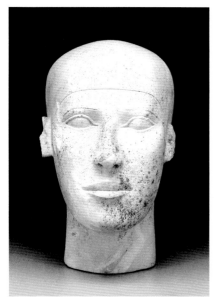

13

13
Reserve head

From Giza tomb G 4140
Old Kingdom, mid to late Dynasty 4
Limestone
Height 26.5 cm.
Harvard University-Museum of Fine Arts
Expedition, 1914 (14.717)

Although most reserve heads date to the Dynasty 4 reigns of Khufu, Khafre, and Menkaure, a small number belong to Dynasty 5. Possibly the earliest is the one found by de Morgan in Dahshur mastaba 5, if that mastaba is dated to the reign of Snefru (2630-2606 B.C.).[1] Very few heads have been found outside that cemetery, and still fewer at sites other than Giza, specifically Dahshur and Abusir. All told some thirty-one reserve heads are known.[2]

By and large, the heads represent the great people of the court of Dynasty 4. In many instances we do not know their names or identity, and in others their names and what we imagine we can read in lineaments of their faces are all we know about them.

This head of a prince with characteristic Old Kingdom features rather more delicate than usual was found in a tomb at Giza with that of the Princess Meret-ites, a daughter of Khufu.[3] Presumably the prince was her husband. William Stevenson Smith felt that the head of the prince belonged to a somewhat idealized group of reserve heads bearing a strong resemblance to the relief portraits in chapels of the later reign of Khufu, with their straight noses, lightly rounded or flattish, and delicately worked eyes and mouth. Although the delicate rimming of the eye apparent in the head of Princess Meret-ites is also seen in the head of the prince, in the latter, the lower edge of the eyebrow is indicated by a clean-cut line.[4] The surface modeling of both heads shows a smooth gradation from plane to plane. The hair of both is short and cropped close to the skull, like a close-fitting cap.

Like the Ankh-haf bust, the heads are not parts of statues, and at first glance they seem to contradict many of our suppositions about the nature and function of Egyptian funerary sculpture.[5] The traditional explanation, first advanced by Ludwig Borchardt, and also subscribed to by Junker and Reisner, is that the reserve heads were made as substitutes for the mummies' vulnerable heads and faces, the chief embodiment of personal character.[6]

The circumstances surrounding the discovery of the heads found by Reisner have never been adequately published, and it is not surprising that a number of recent articles address the significance of the reserve heads. A statement that the reserve heads seem to have been buried in the bottom of the tomb shaft, at or near the entrance to the burial chamber rather than within it,[7] does not take into account other evidence that these heads were originally placed within the burial chamber as Reisner opined, and were associated with the original burial.[8] While many of the heads, perhaps fifteen or sixteen all told, were found in the tomb shaft, generally at the bottom,[9] at least six – including those of Princess Meret-ites and of Kanofer from G 1203, now in Berkeley – were found within the burial chamber.[10] The tombs to which all these heads belonged were grievously plundered and the majority of the heads found by Reisner rested on debris in the shafts thrown out from the burial chamber by thieves. The present example was actually found in such debris in shaft G 4140 A near the top of the portcullis stone, while the head of the princess was found in the burial chamber buried under water-washed sand of later date. It seemed obvious to Reisner that the reserve heads were indeed placed in the chamber, in spite of the fact that no evidence existed of their original position. The heads are all cut off at the base of the neck and a smooth, flat surface enables them to stand upright. Perhaps they were placed on the sarcophagus itself, on the slab cover of the sarcophagus pit, or simply on the floor of the chamber.[11] Junker's view that they were set up in the space between the tomb shaft and the burial chamber has been effectively disposed of by Allyn Kelley, who points out that the reconstruction contradicts what is known about the method of burial-chamber masonry blocking.[12]

A recent hypothesis identifies the reserve heads as sculptor's prototypes and postulates that molds were taken from at least some of the heads and used to produce replicas in plaster or mud at other work sites, perhaps at the tomb site for workers on relief portraits or in the sculptors' workshop.[13] This theory attempts to explain several puzzling features of the reserve heads. Except for one of the heads in Boston,[14] the ears of the heads are invariably damaged. In addition, many of the heads show a vertical scoring from the top of the head down the back of the skull. In another head in Boston, this one from tomb G 4440,[15] the cranial groove represents a prominent rough cutting with secondary chipping of limestone at the sides.

In theory, when the linen or plaster had dried, the sculptor would remove the mask by cutting from the top of the cranium down to the base of the neck with an adze, knife, or chisel, leaving in some instances the cranial groove. The ears would often break off while the mold was being wrenched from the head. In cases like that of the Ankh-haf bust, the ears were made separately and doweled to the head, so that they might come off more easily and be replaced on the original.[16] The use of plaster is suggested by the large quantity of plaster still adhering to the left cheek of the reserve head from G 4940, which apparently stuck too firmly to the stone to come off when the mask was removed.

The damage to the ears, however, can be better attributed to the rough handling the heads received at the hands of the thieves who plundered the burial chambers and threw the reserve heads into the shafts along with other debris. Moreover, it is difficult to understand how a plaster or linen mask, once dried, could be removed without causing serious damage. It might be removed in halves, but one would expect the mold to be divided front and back, so as not to damage the features of the face, in which case the groove should run ear to ear instead of beginning near the crown and ending at the base of the neck. This is the case, for example, with the "death mask" from the Teti Pyramid Cemetery at Sakkara found by Quibell.[17]

The large patch of plaster adhering to the cheek of the reserve head from G 4940 is usually explained as a correction layer added by a sculptor dissatisfied with the treatment of the left side of the face.[18] Plaster was often used in ancient Egypt to correct defects in stone or shoddy workmanship,[19] and several other heads show a coating of plaster over the limestone to correct defects in the cutting.[20] The head from G 4940 is crudely executed and it is possible the head represents the clumsy efforts of an apprentice, who never finished his work.

Smith thought that when the practice of placing reserve heads in the tomb fell into disuse, its place was taken frequently by the covering of the actual face and body with modeled plaster (see cat. 23). Even though most known plaster masks appear to postdate the reserve heads, the suggestion has been made that the latter were used as a base for the plaster mold, then applied over the linen-molded features of the deceased.[21] However, the plaster coatings appear to have been formed directly over the linen wrappings of the deceased

and still show imprints from the original linen bandages. What is more, neither of the masks in Boston, for example, exhibits the negative impression to be expected on the inside, if they were indeed modeled over the reserve heads.[22]

The traditional interpretation of the heads leaves unexplained the cranial groove that appears in about half the heads. Reisner was so puzzled by them he surmised the grooves were made by plunderers in search of gold to ascertain if the heads were hollow.[23]

It is a little-recognized fact that at least some of the reserve heads were once painted. Thus, a black-painted reserve head was found by the Austrian Expedition in the burial chamber of G 4560.[24] An examination of the head of Kanofer revealed traces of both black and yellow pigments.[25] Considerable red paint is visible on the surface of the male head from G 4440, and since the color overlaps the sideburns, it is likely the entire head was painted a uniform red.

EB

1. de Morgan 1895, p. 5; Smith 1949, p. 27 [29].
2. Smith 1949, p. 23.
3. Cairo JE 46217.
4. Smith 1949, p. 29.
5. Millet 1981, p. 129.
6. Borchardt 1907, p. 133.
7. Kelley 1974, p. 5; Millet p. 129.
8. Reisner unpublished, pp. 231-236.
9. Kelley 1974, p. 7 and n. 11.
10. Smith 1949, pp. 25-27, nos. 2, 15, 21, 28, 29, 30.
11. Reisner unpublished, p. 239.
12. Kelley 1974, pp. 7-8.
13. Kelley 1974, p. 9; Millet 1981, p. 130.
14. MFA 14.719.
15. MFA 14.718.
16. As in the head from G 4940 MFA 21.329.
17. Quibell 1909, pl. 55, pp. 20, 112-113.
18. Cf. Millet 1981, p. 130.
19. Lucas and Harris 1962, p. 77.
20. Smith 1949, pp. 29-30.
21. Kelley 1974, p. 9.
22. MFA 37.644 (Smith 1949, p. 28 [3]), 39.828 (cat. 23).
23. Reisner unpublished, p. 238.
24. Eaton-Krauss 1976, p. 24 n. 23.
25. Knudsen 1987.

Bibliography: Reisner unpublished, pp. 231-239; Smith 1949, pp. 23-30.

Fig. 47

14

Mastaba chapel of Akh-Meret-Nesut and his family

From Giza tomb G 2184
Old Kingdom, late Dynasty 5 or Dynasty 6
Harvard University-Museum of Fine Arts Expedition, 1912

a. Seated statue of Akh-meret-nesut
Limestone
Height 69 cm., width 24.5 cm., depth 44.5 cm. (12.1482)

b. Offering slab
Limestone and alabaster
Block length 54.5 cm., width 53.5 cm.; basin length 27.2, width 19.2 cm. (12.1481)

c. Lintel
Limestone
Length 10.5 cm., width 23 cm., depth 30 cm.

One of the more interesting mastabas in the Old Kingdom necropolis at Giza is the tomb of the official Akh-meret-nesut. Decorated with finely executed and innovative reliefs and paintings, the tomb was twice altered in both plan and decoration. The second version of the chapel has been reconstructed in the exhibition, as a backdrop for the fine statue of the tomb owner and the offering basin found in the tomb.

The seated statue of Akh-meret-nesut is carved in the rounded, chunky style typical of late Dynasty 5 and early Dynasty 6. His left hand is flat upon his knee, and his right is closed in a fist. He wears a simple kilt with a pleated section wrapped across the front to close it, and the handle of a dagger extends above his belt. His wig is simple, with a center part and strands of roughly equal length. The damage to the nose somewhat obscures the delicacy of

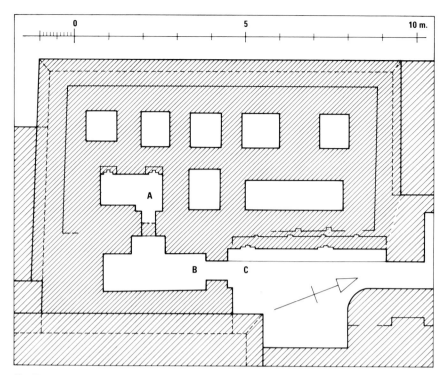

Fig. 48

Fig. 49

his features, but the carving is very fine. Around his feet are given his name and titles: King's Acquaintance, Venerated Before his Lord, Overseer of the Place of Palace Retainers (ẖntyw-š), and Inspector, Akh-meret-nesut.

The statue was originally set into the floor of Akh-meret-nesut's mastaba chapel (fig. 47). This chapel was built into the east side of the mastaba, a flat-topped mound that was built to mark the burial shafts of officials during the Old Kingdom period. Beside the statue, also set into the floor, was an offering basin with three compartments. Each compartment was presumably fitted with an alabaster basin or tablet, but only the smaller dish at the front, inscribed with the name of Akh-meret-nesut, is preserved.

Both the statue and the offering table were placed in the blocked doorway to the innermost room of Akh-meret-nesut's chapel, and thus presumably belong to the second version of the mastaba, when this door was blocked off. The pieces are exhibited in their original position in the reconstruction of the second stage of Akh-meret-nesut's mastaba chapel.

The excavation of the mastaba was begun on Tuesday, February 13, 1912, by Clarence Fisher, an assistant to Reisner working with the Harvard University-Museum of Fine Arts Expedition. The quality and the interesting features of its decoration were immediately apparent. According to the preliminary report, Fisher considered this mastaba "in many respects the finest small mastaba ever found by the Expedition."[1] The unusual content and style of the paintings in the room with the statue so impressed Reisner that he asked Mrs. Firth, the wife of a British archaeologist working nearby, to make watercolor drawings of the scenes. These watercolors have become an important record, since the scenes were almost entirely effaced by water damage in a shipboard fire during their transport to Boston. The present reconstruction is based on Mrs. Firth's copies, supplemented by Reisner's excavation photographs and some additional watercolors by Fisher.

Not until 1935 were the seven shafts in the body of the mastaba excavated. Four of them contained features of interest. Shaft B contained a skeleton and a limestone coffin lid; shaft C contained another skeleton, while shaft E held a wooden coffin in which were the bones of two later burials. Although no burial remained in shaft G, a rectangular pit had been cut in its stone floor and fitted with a lid to form a built-in coffin.[2]

Three different versions of the mastaba chapel were built. In each version, Akh-meret-nesut devoted the principal southern niche to his own and his wife's cult, while providing a cult place for his parents at the lesser northern niche.

First Version

The earliest form of the mastaba had a simple one-room chapel, chamber A (see fig. 48), cut into the southern end of the east face of the stone-encased mastaba and itself lined with stone. This chapel had two false doors: a southern one for Akh-meret-nesut himself and a northern one shared with his wife (for a discussion of the false door, see essay on funerary customs). The room had been entered prior to Reisner's excavations and the tablet of the northern false door removed. It is now in the Smith Collection of Egyptian Antiquities at the Linköping Museum in Sweden.[3] These doors formed the entire west wall of the chapel, separated only by an area painted in red to imitate patterned hangings. A figure of Akh-meret-nesut was painted on the south wall of the chapel.

The only other decoration at this period was outside the chapel, on the eastern face of the mastaba. At the northern half of this face, balancing the entrance to the chapel at the southern end of the same face, a small stone false door with only a single pair of jambs was set into the mastaba. Its tablet depicts Akh-meret-nesut's parents at an offering table; while the lintel below gives the name of his father and its drum bears the name of his mother. To the left (south) of it was an even tinier door, one course of masonry high. It consisted only of a lintel and drum with the name of Akh-meret-nesut's father.

Second Version

The version of the chapel reconstructed in the exhibition represented a major change in the architecture of the tomb. The mastaba itself was considerably enlarged, and the earlier chapel blocked off by a false door. (This closed-off room may have served as a *serdab* [see p. 16], though no statue was found in it at the time of the excavation.) The south face of the mastaba was extended to the east, blocking the "street" between G 2184 and the large mastaba to the east of it, G 5090. In the space thus appropriated, another small stone-lined chapel, chamber B (see fig. 48), was created. It opened at the north into a courtyard in front of the false doors of Akh-meret-nesut's parents. This courtyard (C) was also constructed by blocking off the areas between existing buildings with mud brick walls. In one corner of the courtyard, the northwest corner of mastaba G 5080 intruded, making the space somewhat irregular.

The decoration of these areas was far more elaborate than that of the previous version. In the niche formed by blocking the door to chamber A, a false door was erected. The lintel and side pillars from the first version of the door were left intact, and the doorway was partially blocked. Above the niched face on the blocking stones was a tablet showing Akh-meret-nesut at a table of offerings. (This tablet was briefly described in the earliest accounts of the excavations,[4] but has since disappeared.)

In front of the false door was the square limestone offering-table and the seated statue of Akh-meret-nesut. A slightly smaller space to the right of the table might have contained a smaller statue of either Akh-meret-nesut or his wife. The round offering dish found broken in the courtyard may also have originally been put in this area. On each side of this niche several registers of scenes were painted directly on the stone.

On the left (southern) face of the niche are five registers: in the bottom register, three men wrestle a bull to the earth in order to butcher him; above this, three men bring bundles of papyrus from the marshes. In the third register, a cow is being milked; her head turned with concern to her bleating calf, who looks longingly at the pot of milk from which he is held back by another herdsman. In the fourth, a spotted cow gives birth to a calf, to the intense interest of a passing dog; a herdsman crouches behind ready to beat off the dog if it attempts to interfere. The top register shows a larger scene. Akh-meret-nesut, who wears a handful of marsh flowers draped over one shoulder, stands in a papyrus skiff spearing fish (the artist has extended the water up in front of the prow of the boat to show the skewered fish more clearly). Next to him in the skiff sits his wife, steadying his leg with one hand and grasping a blossom in the other. Behind them is a papyrus thicket, full of birds of every kind and two oversized dragonflies; while in the water below the skiff, two hippos are attacking a crocodile, whose tail lashes out above the water and seems likely to upset the placid domestic vignette above.

To the right of the false door, in the lower two registers, men lead a bull and an oryx to be slaughtered. Above this a scene labeled "crossing the canal [by] the herdsmen," shows two men in a boat and another in the water, assisting cattle to ford a canal. In the water below are two crocodiles; one is shown entire, the other only as a head abruptly appearing above the surface of the water. One of the men in the boat holds out his hand in a gesture meant to ward off danger. Two registers above show boats and the top register contains two men who wear yokes with loaded baskets at each end.

Painted scenes also decorate the two walls flanking the niche. To the left a narrow panel shows animals and other offerings. In the lowest register, an unidentifiable animal is led in, and above this are scenes of butchers at work. The third register shows men leading in two hyenas, which were domesticated and raised for meat by the ancient Egyptians. The hyenas were drawn on a much larger scale than the men, which is quite common in this tomb. In most of these scenes, both animals and men were drawn as large as the height of the register allowed, so their relative proportions are distorted. The register above this shows piles of offerings, including bread in various shapes and sizes. Above it is a register showing cuts of meat on little platforms, and at the top, two more registers of offerings.

The wall to the right (north) of the niche is longer, but unfortunately only four registers of its interesting decoration are preserved. The lowest register is a conventional one, showing three men leading cattle in for slaughter. The second register shows goats at their various activities. To the right, four goats nibble at the vegetation on two trees, two of them climbing right up into the branches to nibble at the tender top branches. To the left one goat gives birth and two others copulate, while a baby goat and a rather malevolent-looking cat look on. The male goat's horns extend up into the register above, lending him an impetuous appearance. To the far right of the third register the goat theme concludes in a rather macabre reflection of the tree-climbing scene just below: a tanner skins a goat that hangs by its heels from the upper branch of a tree.

In the winnowing scene in the center of this register, a man tosses wheat into the air with a pitchfork so that the lighter chaff will blow away. To the left of this a very unusual scene shows men loading grain into granaries by leaning down from the upper part of the domed building and lifting baskets of grain from the heads of the men below. The register above contains still more grain-processing scenes: the threshing of the wheat by donkeys is the comic centerpiece, in which a man raises a stick to discourage the tired donkeys from stopping in their tracks to nibble the grain at their feet. To the left are the feet of the tomb owner, who leans lazily on his staff, his faithful dog at his feet, watching the activity in this register as well as several lost registers above.

The south wall of this chapel also seems to have been painted, but only small areas have been preserved.[5] Reisner saw on this wall only bands of geometric patterns; these bands are actually part of a patterned mat upon which Akh-meret-nesut and his wife are seated. Their feet and lower legs are faintly visible, and there is enough detail visible to establish that the woman is wearing a dress of net beads forming a diamond pattern on the white sheath she wears beneath it (see cat. 9 for a similar dress). There are also traces of the wooden seat on which the couple is sitting, which, like the seat on the tablet of the false door, seems to have crossed in front of the wife's legs.

In front of the pair is an offering table upon which a round loaf of bread was painted; another round object was part of a pile below it.

Only three registers of decoration on the east wall can be reconstructed. The top register shows a fishing expedition, in which the men at left are pulling in either end of a large net full of fish, straining at their ropes while the overseer and his dog look on. To the right some of the same fishermen carry home their catch in a large round basket. The lower two registers probably represent a banquet. In the upper one are entertainers, dancers, clapping women, a man playing the transverse flute and a singer (so labeled in the text) at the far right. In the lowest register sit the guests: several of Akh-meret-nesut's male dependents at right (one named Inkhi), and to the left, five women, including three of his sisters, one of whom is named after Khufu. Akh-meret-nesut would probably have stood at the south end of the wall enjoying the party.

No further decoration is recorded in this room; however the courtyard, which seems to have been open to the sky, was also decorated with painted scenes that probably date to the same phase of the renovation. The doorway between the painted chapel and the courtyard, which was put in during this phase, was finely carved stone; the eastern reveal shows Akh-meret-nesut and his wife, and the western reveal shows his parents. The lintel, drum and jambs are inscribed with his names and titles. (This section of the second phase is on exhibition in the second Egyptian gallery.)

On the west side of the courtyard, against the battered stone wall of the original face of the mastaba, a niched facade was built up with mud bricks. This facade contained four niches, all plastered and brightly painted with patterns in imitation of woven mats or cloth hangings. In the third panel from the south end, the top part of the niched facade was cut back to reveal the original false-door tablet of Akh-meret-nesut's mother and father that had formed part of the first phase of the mastaba's decoration, and continued to serve as a cult place in the second version.

The remainder of the decoration in the courtyard was painted on plaster, and because of its fragility was preserved only to the height of the middle of the first register, which seems to have contained primarily herds of animals and their herdsmen. One vignette has been copied from this area, showing two dogs attacking a wounded oryx, perhaps part of a hunting scene. This band of scenes began at the eastern edge of the stone door jamb and wrapped around the corner of mastaba G 5090 which jutted into the courtyard at its southeast corner, continuing on the east wall. It cannot be de-

termined whether the curved wall at the north end of the courtyard was built during this phase or belonged to the final stage of modification, nor can it be said whether this wall or the angled wall beneath it were originally plastered and painted.

Third Version

The final change in mastaba G 2184 was less extensive than the previous one, though it may have been more expensive. It probably included narrowing the entrance to the courtyard by adding the rounded wall described above, but the major change was to cover the west wall of the courtyard with a stone facade decorated with painted sunk relief texts and scenes (fig. 49). (This addition is currently on exhibition in the second Egyptian gallery on the second floor of the Museum.) The stone facade includes two false doors, the southern one dedicated to Akh-meret-nesut, and the northern one – almost directly over the original northern niche on the mastaba face – again dedicated to his parents. Between the false doors is a scene of Akh-meret-nesut receiving a foreigner and recalcitrant tax-payers who are led in by his brothers, all in attitudes of submission.

To the north of the northern false door is an unusual scene of Akh-meret-nesut swinging back his lasso. As elsewhere in the tomb, the artist here used an off-balance stance to depict a single frozen moment of action. Akh-meret-nesut's lasso is swung back over the panelling of the false door, as though the hunt were taking place in front of the stone facade rather than on its surface. This scene is made especially intriguing by the fact that there was no animal depicted to make a target for the lasso, and there is no place on the west wall where an animal of this scale could be restored. One possibility that has been suggested[6] is that the target animal was depicted on the curved wall just opposite this scene; a very unusual conceit, and one that would have made the entering visitor feel as though he had just walked into the middle of a rodeo ring.

In spite of the different phases in which the mastaba was decorated, all of the scenes in this tomb chapel and courtyard share a liveliness and verisimilitude that is unknown from other Giza mastabas of this period. The pose of an overseer or even a tomb owner slouching against his staff is not common in the Old Kingdom; it occurs four times in this tomb, once on the stone facade of version three. The frequent jokes, the graphic innovations such as the crocodile shown only as a head that has suddenly appeared from the water, and the cases in which a part of the scene is extended beyond the register boundaries point to artists who were unusually inventive in their portrayal of movement and of such emotions as surprise, fear, and lust. It is tempting to

suggest that the same artist directed both the paintings of the second version and the carving of the final addition.

The way Akh-meret-nesut decorated his tomb tell us a good deal about him and his family. His father, Ka-nefer, has only the common title *iry-ḫt nswt*; usually translated "King's Acquaintance," the title's exact meaning is not known, but it apparently did not imply great significance or power. His mother seems to have come from a better family. In the earliest phase of the chapel decoration, she is given the title *mitrt*, a title that went back to the earliest periods of Egyptian history, and probably implied a prominent family, though its exact meaning is also unknown. In later texts she also holds the title King's Acquaintance, but she is also called a priestess of the goddesses Neith and Hathor, priesthoods held by many of the great ladies of her day.

Neferet-sedjem, the wife of Akh-meret-nesut, was given no titles in the tomb. Their son, who was also named Akh-meret-nesut, is shown as a small boy in the latest stage of the decoration. Four brothers of Akh-meret-nesut are also depicted in this stage: Seneb, Peshes, Nefer-netjer, and the steward Ka-heb.

Because the tomb was decorated in three different stages, it is possible to say something about the course of Akh-meret-nesut's career. In the earliest stage he bears his father's title, King's Acquaintance, but he already has a higher title, Overseer of the Place of *ḫnty-šs* of the Palace. It is not certain exactly who the people called *ḫnty-š* were but it seems probable that they were personal servants of the king.[7] In one text Akh-meret-nesut is given the title Inspector (*sḥd*) of the same place, a step below his final rank, so apparently he had already had a promotion by the time he began to decorate his small tomb.

In the second phase of building, Akh-meret-nesut has added the title Overseer of the Royal *ḥry-ˁ* of the *š* of the Palace. The *ḥry-ˁ* were apparently craftsmen of some sort, while the *š* likely has the same meaning as it has in the title *ḫnty-š*, so probably this was simply an extension of his previous responsibilities. An inscription in the newer part of the tomb, however, notes that "His majesty made this for him, in order that he might be venerated." The modification of his mastaba chapel was thus a mark of royal favor.

The final modification of the mastaba chapel was also a royal gift: a text states: "It is his lord who made this." In this part of the chapel, Akh-meret-nesut has added his latest title, "wab-priest of the king," to his earlier titles. This was his first priestly office, and probably records his attendance upon the king at some religious ceremony.

The like-named son of Akhet-meret-nesut

may have continued in his father's position. In mastaba G 2421, a lintel was found bearing the name Akhet-meret-nesut and the title overseer of ẖnty-šš, reused there to fill up a doorway. If this lintel was not taken from the tomb of the elder Akhet-meret-nesut (there is no obvious place in that tomb to restore it), it may have been taken from a lost chapel built by his son.

AMR

1. Fisher 1913, p. 20.
2. Reisner unpublished, p. 95.
3. Björkman 1971, pp. 52-53 and pl. 16(4) (cat. 100).
4. Giza Field Diaries, February 16, 1912, and February 20, 1912 (in the Museum of Fine Arts).
5. No watercolors were done of this wall. The scene has been reconstructed from photographs and from a similar scene on the tablet of the false door in the Linköping Museum. There is no record of the colors, although it seems likely that the wall was painted from the same palette used on other walls.
6. Smith 1947, p. 198.
7. For discussions of this enigmatic title, see Stadelmann 1981, pp. 153-164 and Roth forthcoming.

15
Pair statue of Ptah-khenui and wife

From Giza G 2004
Old Kingdom, mid to late Dynasty 5
Limestone
Height 70.1 cm.
Harvard University-Museum of Fine Arts
Expedition, 1905-06 (06.1876)

Ptah-khenui adopts the classic attitude for men, striding forward with his left leg advanced, arms pressed tightly against the body, handkerchiefs grasped in his closed hands. He wears a short wig of overlapping rows of curls, and a broad collar around his neck. His short skirt is stiffly starched or otherwise reinforced to form a flaring front panel. The upper edge of the skirt is tucked in behind the bow of the girdle that holds the skirt in place.[1]

Ptah-khenui's wife is assigned the traditional position on the left of her husband. She stands with feet together and places her right arm around his waist, her left hand on his arm in a gesture of affection. She wears a full, shoulder-length wig, broad collar and shift, bracelets, and anklets. Her natural hair shows in the horizontal strands directly over her forehead. Her form-fitting shift with the neck cut into a deep V leaves the arms and the tips of the shoulders bare.

The colors of the statue are almost as fresh as on the day the statue chamber was sealed. The deeply tanned skin of Ptah-khenui is brick red, and his wife's is ocher yellow. The wigs are black, as are the rims and irises of the eyes and the eyebrows. Skirt and shift are white, as are the rounded

15

edges of the folded cloths in Ptah-khenui's hand. His broad collar is painted alternately blue and green in imitation of a beaded prototype. The black parallel lines over the green paint undoubtedly represent the slender, tubular beads strung longitudinally in actual collars, while the plain blue rows perhaps represent the same beads placed horizontally. Ptah-khenui's wife's collar is identical to her husband's except for an outer row of drop beads. The color is largely gone from the bracelet on her left arm but traces of blue remain. Red and green are preserved on her anklets.

The support at the back of the statue reaches to the shoulders of the figures but extends outward only as far as Ptah-khenui's right leg. It is painted gray along with the base, on whose upper surface Ptah-khenui's name and title, Supervisor of the Tenants of the Palace, is inscribed in

black. His spouse is called ''his wife whom he loves,'' but her name is faded. Strangely, the areas of negative space between the arms of the figures are painted black.

When Reisner found the statue in the *serdab* of G 2004, the head of the woman was separated from the body and was lying in the sand under the right hand of the man. The break is visible in the photograph. A model of bread pots on a fire, carved in painted limestone, suggests there was a servant statue of wood along with this statue, and the *serdab* is big enough to have allowed for a number of wooden figures.[2]

EB

1. Erman 1971, pp. 202; Riefstahl 1944, p. 3.
2. Smith 1949, pp. 68-69.

Bibliography: Smith 1949, pp. 68-69; Porter and Moss 1974, p. 67.

Serdabs

To ensure the safety of the statues essential to his eternal well-being, the ancient Egyptian walled them up in enclosed chambers, known to Egyptologists as *serdabs*, after a modern Arabic word meaning "cellar." The ancient term for *serdab* was *pr-twt* ("statue chamber").[1] The *serdab* was often connected to the chapel or offering place either by a slot with a horizontal aperture in the false door or by a slot with a vertical aperture in the walls of the offering room. The Egyptians called this slot or "*serdab* squint" the *ptr·ty nt hwt-k₃* ("eyes of the *ka*-mansion").[2] When the slot was in the false door, all offerings were laid before it by the priests and their recitations were spoken at about the level of aperture over or under the drum.[3] When the slot was in the north or south walls of the chapel, it usually opened on a table or offering scene, where the same ceremonies were carried out.[4] When the *serdab* was outside the chapel, the aperture of the squint faced either the offering corridor or visitors approaching the chapel.[5]

The earliest dated example of the practice of placing statues in a *serdab* is provided by the pyramid temple of Djoser. Just east of the temple north of the Step Pyramid stands an exterior *serdab* built of fine limestone against the casing of the lowest stage. This contained the famous statue of Djoser now in Cairo and had in its outer wall two circular holes opposite the eyes.[6] In private tombs also, the *serdab* first appears in the reign of Djoser in the twin mastaba of Kha-bau-Sokar and his wife Hathor-nefer-hetep.[7] The tomb of Metjen at Sakkara, datable to the reign of Sneferu, had a *serdab* on the south of its cruciform chapel connected by a squint with the offering chamber.[8] In the *serdab* was found the red granite statue of Metjen in Berlin.[9] The stone-lined and decorated cruciform chapel of Re-hetep at Medum was later blocked up with brick and converted into a *serdab* with the lifelike statues of Re-hetep and Nofret standing in the deep recess of the false door.[10] Only one mastaba at Giza finished in the reign of Khufu was equipped with a *serdab*; G 4000, the mastaba of Hemiunu, in fact had two *serdabs*, one behind each of the offering niches of the interior corridor chapel.[11] The northern *serdab* contained the portrait statue of the corpulent prince, now in Hildesheim.[12] Only two mastabas with *serdabs* at Giza can be dated to the reign of Khafre.[13] The use of *serdabs* began to increase at Giza in the reign of Menkaure,[14] and became frequent in large mastabas at Giza and Sakkara from the end of the reign of Menkaure to the end of the reign of Neferirkare. The *serdab* was in general use in large mastabas at Giza and Sakkara after Neferirkare.

The statues found in intact *serdabs* almost

Fig. 50

invariably faced the *serdab* squint and thus the offering room, where periodic services were performed to provide the spirit of the deceased with the necessities of life after death.[15] It was particularly important for the incense smoke to envelop the statue, since to the ancient Egyptians incense had both purifying and revivifying properties.[16] Figures in relief are actually depicted elevating censers and burning incense beside *serdab* squints in the tombs of Ti and Sakkara and Senedjem-ib Inti at Giza.[17]

About the middle of Dynasty 5, statues of the owner and his family were supplemented in *serdabs* by figures of servants engaged in domestic activities.[18] Later, statues were placed in the burial chamber; in Dynasty 6 these included servant statues and other models.[19] This practice eventually led to the discontinuance of *serdabs*; during the First Intermediate Period and Middle Kingdom, groups of servant statues in wood were placed in the burial chamber with the coffin and other burial equipment (see cats. 35, 36, and 43).

EB

1. Blackman 1916, pp. 250-254; Junker 1938, pp. 119-122; Brovarski 1984, p. 874.
2. Blackman 1916, p. 251.
3. E.g., G 2184 (Akh-meret-nesut, cat. 14), G 4940 (Seshem-nefer [I]), G 4970 (Nesut-nefer).
4. E.g., G 1029 (Sekhem-ka), G 2415 (Weri), G 4611 (Niuty).
5. E.g., G 5270 (Rawer [I]), G 5470 (Rawer [II]). Cf. Lythgoe and Ransom 1916, p. 9, fig. 4.
6. Firth and Quibell 1935, pp. 50-51, pl. 28.
7. Reisner 1936, pp. 267-269, fig. 158. Cf. FS 3070, 3078: ibid., p. 202 [1], fig. 157; 204 [5], fig. 164; Smith 1949, p. 151, n. 1, pl. 34; Smith 1958, p. 41, pl. 27 [B]. For the date of the mastaba of Kha-bau-Sokar, see Cherpion 1980: pp. 79-90.
8. See Goedicke 1966, pp. 1-71.
9. Berlin 1106: Kaiser 1967, pp. 23-24, cat. no. 222.
10. Petrie 1892, pl. 7.
11. Junker 1929, pp. 132 ff, figs. 18-20, pl. 16.
12. Junker 1929, pp. 153-157, pls. 18-23.
13. Junker 1929, pp. 234-242, fig. 55 (G 4750, Akhi); Reisner unpublished, p. 41, fig. 8 (G 7510, Ankh-haf).
14. G 5110 (Duaen-re), G 7070 (Snefru-khaf), G 7350 (Hetep-heres [II]), MQ 1 (Khuen-re).7.
15. E.g., G 1020 (Hetepi), G 1039, G 1104 (Messa), G 1206 (Ikhetneb), G 1608 (Senenu), G 2009 (Mesi).
16. Blackman 1912, pp. 69-75.
17. Wild 1966, pls. 169, 172; Naville 1913, pl. 22b (incomplete).
18. E.g., G 1213, G 2004 (Ptah-khenui), G 2185 (Nefer-sefen-khufu), G 2415 (Weri), G 2420 (Nedjemu), G 5411; Hassan 1932, p. 115, pl. 71 (Meres-ankh); pp. 95ff.
19. Smith 1949, pp. 90ff.

Literature: Reisner unpublished, chap. IX

Serdab group (16-20)

In winter of 1905-1906, the first season he worked for the Harvard University-Museum of Fine Arts Expedition, Reisner found a group of painted limestone figures (cats. 16-18) in an intact *serdab* or statue chamber in cemetery G 2000 at Giza. Many of the people buried in the minor mastabas of the cemetery were tenant farmers of the palace or mortuary priests who served the cults of the Dynasty 4 kings Khufu, Khafre, and Menkaure. The workmanship of all the statues is good, and that of the standing pair statue of Mesi and Senenu (fig. 50) is well above average for ''middle-class'' work.

G 2009 was a mastaba of irregular form with a retaining wall of different sorts of masonry. The chapel was entered from the east by a doorway in the north end of the east wall. The false door stood in a deep alcove at the south end of the west wall. The *serdab* was behind the false door and connected with the chapel by a slot or ''serdab squint'' opening in the door above the drum. The statues all faced the slot.

Fig. 50 shows the placement of the statues within the unroofed and cleared *serdab*. The standing pair statue went to Cairo, and the Museum received the standing pair from an adjacent tomb (cat. 15). While subsequent excavation campaigns would bring to the Museum its magnificent series of works of art of Dynasty 4, the arrival in Boston of the figures from G 2000 generated considerable interest, in part because of their well preserved painted surfaces.

In an adjacent corridor of the tomb two offering basins were found. One was still in place before an uninscribed false door; the other was overturned nearby (cat. 20). The inscriptions on the basins are identical sign for sign, except for the names of the deceased, Khnemu and Semer-ka, and indicate that they were probably produced at the same time. Strangely, although ten individuals are named on the objects found in G 2009, we are largely ignorant of their relationships, since few details are provided.

EB

1. Porter and Moss 1974, pp. 66-70.
2. Smith 1949, pp. 68-69.

Bibliography: Bates 1907, pp. 20-21; Smith 1949, pp. 68-69.

16
Statuette of a naked boy

From Giza 2009
Old Kingdom, mid to late Dynasty 5
Limestone
Height 18 cm.
Harvard University-Museum of Fine
Arts Expedition (06.1881)

All the conventions employed by the Egyptian artist to depict young boys are represented in this small figure. The boy stands with his left leg forward and his left arm hanging at his side. His right hand is raised with the forefinger placed on his lower lip in a gesture that is probably indicative of shyness. It is more common in portrayals of boys than girls. He wears his own hair cropped close but with a plaited lock, an-

other insignia of childhood, hanging down on his right breast. Egypt's climate was warm most of the year and children often went about naked, as does our young subject. Since he has not yet reached puberty, he is uncircumcised.

In front of his right foot is inscribed: ''the craftsman, Ptah-nefer-ti.'' The presence of the title certainly suggests the statue's owner was already grown when this portrait of him was made.

As Smith has remarked, the portrayal hardly suggests the forms of childhood except in the small size and the dressing of the hair. Indeed, the rather stocky proportions are similar to those of the seated pair (cat. 18) and the standing triad (cat. 17) from G 2009.

16

17
Triad of standing male figures

From Giza 2009
Old Kingdom, mid to late Dynasty 5
Limestone
Height 25 cm.
Harvard University-Museum of Fine Arts
Expedition, 1906 (06.1882)

Three male figures are portrayed side by side. Khu-Ptah in the middle holds the hanging hands of Hes to his right and Ni-kau-Khufu to his left. The latter grasp handkerchiefs in the hands clenched at their sides. All three men wear short kilts and broad collars with rows of green and blue beads, but the sculptor has differentiated their wigs. Hes wears a full, striated wig that almost entirely covers his ears. By contrast, Ni-kau-Khufu wears his own wavy hair

17

cropped close to his head. The three figures are supported by a broad back slab rising to just above their heads. The top of the base and the slab are painted black, but the rest of the base and support are red. On the front of the base the title of each individual is inscribed along with his name; each is ''Tenant Farmer of the Palace.''

EB

18
Seated pair

From Giza 2009
Old Kingdom, mid to late Dynasty 5
Limestone
Height 35.5 cm.
Harvard University-Museum of Fine Arts
Expedition, 1906 (06.1885)

Bau and Baru sit on a simple cubic seat with feet close together. Her right arm is around his waist and her left hand is open, palm down, on her thigh. Bau has his right hand on his thigh, holding a handkerchief, while his left hand is also open palm down. He wears a short curled wig, a beaded broad collar painted alternately green and blue, and a short kilt. The overlapping outer end of his kilt is sketched in black on his lap. Baru has a full wig, whose locks are indicated by parallel lines. The wigs are painted black and their garments white, while his skin is brick red and hers ocher yellow. The paint on her upper body has spalled away along with the shoulder straps of her V-necked dress and a broad collar. But both figures have elaborate beaded counterweights hanging down at the back of their necklaces. The blocklike seat is painted red, and speckled black in imitation of granite. The negative space between arms and legs is black, as is the upper surface of the base. On the right of his legs is written, ''the Tenant Farmer, Bau.'' The same inscription was

18, front

18, back

repeated in paint to the left of his legs but is now barely visible. To the left of Baru's legs is inscribed "Priestess of Neith, Opener-of-the-ways, and Tenant Farmer, Baru."

EB

19
Offering table

From Giza 2009
Old Kingdom, mid to late Dynasty 5
Alabaster
Height 5.7 cm., diam. 16.5 cm.
Harvard University-Museum of Fine Arts
Expedition, 1906 (06.1883)

A round alabaster offering table was discovered in the *serdab* chamber of G 2009. Normally such a table would be placed outside

the *serdab*, in the offering chapel so that offerings could be made upon it by visitors. In this case, however, the table was inaccessible; hence it seems likely that it was piled with food offerings and other organic material when the *serdab* was closed, and that this material had decayed and was not recovered in the excavation. Originally found in two pieces, the table seems to have become dislodged from its cylindrical base — which was found at the foot of the large pair statue now in Cairo — and fallen, breaking against the same statue base (see fig. 50).

EB

20
Offering basin

From Giza 2009
Old Kingdom, mid to late Dynasty 5
Limestone
Height 12.2 cm, width 21.6 cm, depth 36.7 cm.
Harvard University-Museum of Fine Arts
Expedition, 1906 (06.1884)

Rectangular basins with flat tops and rectangular rims (see fig. 51), below which the sides slope to a flat bottom, were called by the ancient Egyptians *s n kbh* ("basins for libation").[1] The interior of the basin follows the lines of the outer contours, and clearly it served as a receptacle for liquid offerings – primarily water but also beer, wine, and milk – made during the periodic mortuary services.[2] Already in the Old Kingdom, however, this sort of basin was sometimes conceived as a miniature pool or lake; the spirit of the deceased could sit beside it under shade trees or row in its waters.[3]

Offering basins were ordinarily sunk flush with the ground in front of the false door, with only the hieroglyphs on the rim showing. The incised inscription on the present basin reads, "May the Tenant Farmer Khnemu be handsomely buried in the necropolis, a possessor of honor with the Great God. May offerings of bread, beer, cakes, fowl, and oxen be invoked [for] him every day and [on] the monthly and bimonthly feasts, (namely) the Tenant Farmer Khnemu."

Other forms of offering basins include double-ledge basins, which have a second rim inside. Numerous examples have more than one basin. The basin depression in offering stones is, of course, quite common.[4]

EB

1. Fischer 1978a, p. 51.
2. Fischer 1978a, pp. 51-52; Moret 1978, pp. 21-22 (CG 57016); Ghazi 1980, pp. 29 (CG 57026), 30-31 (CG 57028).
3. Fischer 1978a, pp. 51-52.
4. See Moret 1978; Mostafa 1982.

Fig. 51

21
Statuette of a woman grinding grain

From Giza tomb 2185
Old Kingdom, Dynasty 5
Limestone
Height 19.5 cm., length 30.9 cm., width 8.2 cm.
Harvard University-Museum of Fine Arts
Expedition, 1912 (12.1486)

Limestone statuettes depicting servants were first placed in tombs in late Dynasty 4, becoming quite numerous in Dynasty 5. These small figures generally depict people performing necessary tasks usually, though not always, related to food preparation. They were believed to provide services to the deceased in case offerings of food and other necessities ceased. The most common varieties show women grinding grain and men or women straining mash to make beer. Less common types represent potters, butchers, people tending fires, and other workers.[1] Most of these statuettes were found in tombs at Giza or Sakkara.

Stone servant statuettes had almost disappeared by the end of the Old Kingdom; they were replaced in the First Intermediate Period and early Middle Kingdom by wooden models (see cats. 35 and 43). Though the stone figures were relatively common in Dynasty 5, they seldom appeared in large numbers in individual tombs as did their later wooden counterparts.

This statuette was found, along with a pair statuette of standing men, in a small *serdab* connected with mastaba G 2185 at Giza. It depicts a kneeling woman grinding some sort of grain. The figure is well carved, with some indication of the musculature in the arms and legs, but the legs are not completely disengaged from the base. The woman wears a kilt tied at her right side. A cloth knotted at the back of her head covers most of the hair, except around the brow and in front of the ears. The facial features, though somewhat heavy, are carefully carved with special attention paid to the details around the eyes. The hands and feet include fingernails and toenails. The quern and grinder are well defined, with the ground flour shown spilling over the front of the quern and a partially emptied grain sack at the back. Several very similar examples are now in Boston[2] and the Egyptian Museum.[3]

The statuette was covered with a fine layer of plaster before it was painted. The woman's skin was originally yellow, traces of which may be seen on her face, hands, and feet. Her hair was black as was the base. The quern and grinder were red. The kilt, headcloth, grain sack, and flour were probably white.

CHR

1. For examples of these types, see Breasted 1948.
2. MFA 21.1601 (with legs disengaged), in Breasted 1948 p. 18, pl. 16b.
3. CG 114 and CG 115 (legs disengaged), in Borchardt 1911, pp. 88 and 89, pl. 25.

Bibliography: Smith 1947, p. 74; Breasted 1948, p. 20 (3), pl. 19 (b).

Literature: Smith 1947, pp. 95ff; Borchardt 1897, pp. 119-134.

21

22
Offering table of Ny-ka-nesut

From Giza, on the surface east of tomb G 2156
Old Kingdom, mid Dynasty 5
Limestone
Length 52 cm., width 39 cm., depth 5 cm.
Harvard University-Museum of Fine Arts Expedition, 1912 (12.1513)

The top of this limestone offering table was cut in the shape of a large *hetep* hieroglyph, which represents a loaf of bread placed on a table and means "offering" or "to offer." The surface was smoothed, but the rest of the stone was left rough. The excavator of the piece, G.A. Reisner, suggested that the left side of the piece was cut to fit in the corner of a room.[1] On the right and left two lines of hieroglyphs, carved in good sunk relief, give the titles and name of the owner: on the right, "the Priest of Khufu, the Keeper of the Secrets, Ny-ka-nesut," and on the left, "the Great One of the Tens of Upper Egypt, the One Belonging to the Foremost Seat, Ny-ka-nesut." These titles show that the owner, usually called Ny-ka-nesut II to distinguish him from his similarly named father,[2] was concerned with the legal administration, and was the recipient of largesse from the temples of Khufu. Although the offering table was not found in tomb 2156, there can be little doubt that it belonged to that tomb.

Such tables were indispensable parts of the

22

funerary cult in the Old Kingdom and were placed in front of false doors (cat. 28). Together these two elements formed the central offering place in the tomb-chapel. Those maintaining the cult placed the offerings of food and drink on the table, where they could be magically consumed by the spirit of the dead man, which would gain access to the chapel through the false door.

The design of this offering table is very simple; others contain basins for the offerings (cat. 14), more elaborate texts, and, in some cases, carved representations (cat. 61), intended to magically replace the real offerings, should they fail to materialize.

NS

1. Reisner 1942, p. 447, fig. 269.
2. Porter and Moss 1974, pp. 78-80.

Bibliography: Reisner 1942, p. 447, fig. 269; Junker 1955, pp. 147-148, fig. 17.

Literature: Mostafa 1982.

23
Mummy covering

From Giza tomb G 2037 b
Old Kingdom, possibly Dynasty 6
Plaster
Mask height 21 cm.
Harvard University-Museum of Fine Arts Expedition, 1939 (39.828)

Careful wrapping of the mummy in linen to simulate the appearance of the deceased in life was the rule in the Old Kingdom. At Giza the Harvard University-Museum of Fine Arts Expedition and Hermann Junker found evidence of a different treatment of the body. In more than a dozen instances, the ancient embalmers applied a layer of white plaster over the linen wrappings of the mummy.[1] Sometimes only the head was covered with plaster but in a number of cases the rest of the body was covered as well. Of these the present plaster coating is the best preserved.[2] The plaster-coated mummy lay on its back with a wooden headrest under the neck that raised the upper body at an angle of twenty or thirty degrees. The plaster evidently was applied when the mummy was already in the coffin, for it covers only the top and sides of the body, not the back, and conforms to its contours. The general as-

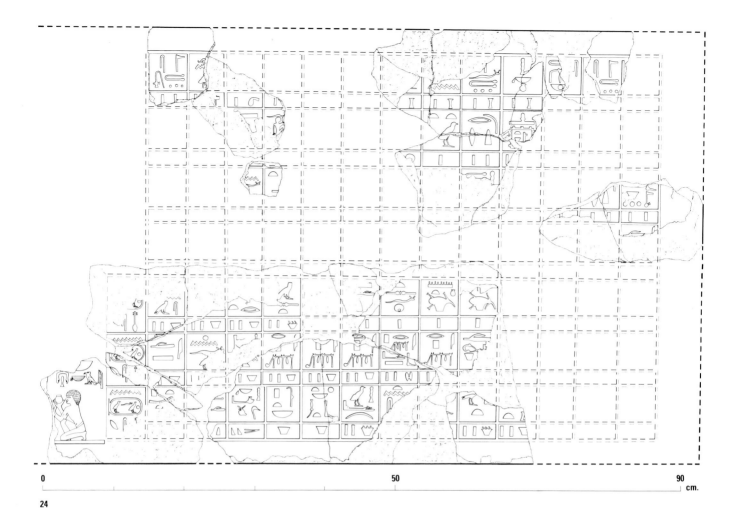

0   50   90

cm.

24

pect of the man represented is modeled in the plaster, the features of the head and torso, arms and legs are all carefully delineated. The top of his short kilt is also indicated.

While the face is delicately modeled and gives the impression of portraiture, it is important to remember that the plaster coating is applied over the linen wrappings on the head of the mummy; this is not an ordinary death mask taken from an actual face such as that found in the Teti pyramid temple by Quibell.[3]

Reisner dated the majority of the plaster masks or body coverings from late Dynasty 5 to the end of Dynasty 6, and it is clear that they were common in Dynasty 6.[4] G 2037b may belong to Dynasty 6 and is certainly no earlier than the second half of the preceding dynasty.[5] The plaster covering was found in the main shaft, inside a decayed wooden coffin; no traces of the skeleton remained.

EB

1. Smith 1949, pp. 27-28.
2. Cf. Junker 1944, pl. 24, pp. 113-116, with position on fig. 38.
3. Quibell 1909, pl. 55, pp. 20, 112-113; Smith 1949, p. 27.
4. Reisner unpublished, p. 702.
5. Reisner unpublished, Appendix L.

Bibliography: Smith 1949, pp. 25-28.

23

24
Offering list of Nefer-sef-Khufu

From Giza tomb G 2185
Old Kingdom, late Dynasty 5 or Dynasty 6
Limestone
Length 57.8 cm., width 83.8 cm., depth 6.3 cm.
Harvard University-Museum of Fine Arts Expedition, 1912 (12.1491-1503)

Thirteen fragments of two approximately equal-size slabs comprise just under half of a typical offering list of the second half of the Old Kingdom. The list consists of a series of square compartments. In the upper part of each compartment hieroglyphs give the name of the individual item; vertical strokes below indicate the number of portions of the item required by the ritual. The largest fragments show parts of the beginning and end of the list. At the end of each row of the list a compartment contained the words "for Nefer-sef-Khufu," for whose tomb the list was made. To the left of this is the figure of a kneeling soul-priest making the ritual offering. With the exception of this figure, which is in raised relief, the list is cut in sunk relief. Such contrasting use of relief is common; perhaps because it was more resistant to damage, sunk relief was used for important lists and texts in place of the more aesthetically satisfying raised relief.

The offering list was one of the principal elements of tomb decoration, not just in the Old Kingdom, but for all periods. It usually accompanied a scene of the deceased at table, partaking of a funerary meal, and was generally near the false door. Its function was principally magical: while the ancient Egyptians expected their relatives, dependents, or priests to bring regular food offerings to sustain the spirit of the deceased, they recognized the possibility that these offerings might one day cease. In this event, the objects represented on the tomb walls would come magically into being.

Thus the offering list in its fullest form contained all that was thought to be necessary for the well-being of the deceased. Egyptian offering lists are quite consistent in content, and this list likely contained ninety-one elements, made up of seven rows of thirteen compartments.[1] It begins with the libation and the seven sacred oils, and moves through breads, meat, fowl, drinks, and fruit. The last few elements are usually rather generalized, such as "offerings of all the year," "all sweet things," and "choice things" – in other words, anything not covered by the other components of the list.

NS

1. Barta 1963.

Bibliography: Heritage Plantation 1979, cat. 18.

Literature: Barta 1963.

25
Model offerings

From Giza tomb G 4733 E
Old Kingdom, late Dynasty 5
Calcite (Egyptian alabaster)
Harvard University-Museum of Fine Arts
Expedition, 1914 (21.2430; 21.2816-2826;
21.2829, 2830; 21.2832-2834; 21.2904; 14-
2-41; 14-2-42; 14-2-44; 14-2-48; 14-2-49;
14-2-54; 14-2-55; 14-2-57; 14-2-59; 14-2-
60; 14-2-61; 14-2-64)

The large limestone offering cases of early Dynasty 6 representing dressed fowl and meat pieces (cat. 26) were the approximate size of the items represented. In the private tombs of the end of the same dynasty around the pyramid of Pepi II at South Sakkara, Jéquier found two sets of large solid models on a similar scale. In the tomb of Heneni there were ten models, five representing trussed birds painted yellow with black beaks and eyes and five representing meat pieces, painted red. The tomb of Wash-Ptah contained a similar set of models but only four meat pieces and two dressed birds were preserved.[1] Reisner thought the large models developed from the offering cases.

25

On the other hand, Reisner found at Giza a set of ninety-five small models of food offerings in the burial chamber of a tomb dated by a box sealing to the reign of Djedkare Isesi, penultimate king of Dynasty 5.[2] These alabaster models represent many of the same offerings known from the limestone cases: dressed birds, meat pieces, breads, and cakes. Numerous forms occur that are not paralleled in the larger offering cases, however, including cone and bullet shaped loaves, rounded cakes with rounded edges, rounded cakes with cones rising in the middle of the upper surface, spherical cake balls, and trefoil cakes. Fancy forms include a cake in the form of a winged bird and perhaps another in the shape of a haunch of beef. A peculiar biconical loaf with truncated ends is probably the *kemehu*-bread known from offering lists.[3] A number of the models cannot be identified; some may represent vegetables or fruits.

Like the offering list (see cat. 24), the model offerings were intended to substitute through magical means actual offerings should those cease to be supplied by the mortuary priests or descendants of the deceased.

EB

1. Jéquier 1929, pp. 26, 28, fig. 29.
2. Reisner and Smith 1955, p. 53.
3. Barta 1963, pp. 49, 74, 124; Borchardt 1907, fig. 103.

Bibliography: Reisner unpublished, pp. 623-626.

26
Food cases

Senedjem-ib Complex at Giza
Old Kingdom, early Dynasty 6
Limestone
Harvard University-Museum of Fine Arts
Expedition, 1912

a. Case in the shape of a goose
   From Giza tomb G 2385 A
   Length 38 cm. (13.3480, 3487)
b. Case in the shape of a pigeon or dove
   From tomb G 2381 Z
   Length 24 cm. (13.4313, 4315)
c. Case in the shape of a joint of beef
   From Giza tomb G 2385 A
   Length 55 cm., width 23.5 cm., height 10.5 cm.
   (13.4307, 4311)
d. Case in the shape of ribs
   From Giza tomb G 2385 A
   Length 55.9 cm. (13.4324, 4326)
e. Case in the shape of a round cake
   From Giza tomb G 2385 A
   Diam. 29.2 (13.3489, 3491)
f. Case in the shape of a shoulder piece or thigh
   From Giza, tomb G 2381 Z
   Length 44 cm., width 23 cm., height 5.5 cm.
   (13.4323)
g. Case for unidentified meat piece
   From Giza tomb G 2385 A
   Length 31 cm., width 23.5 cm., height 11.3 cm.
   (13.3476)

The ancient Egyptians believed the deceased required offerings of food and drink for survival in the beyond. The presence of bird and animal bones and of limestone food cases to contain pieces of meat, trussed birds, and breads or cakes of various kinds proves food was deposited in the burial chambers of the mastabas at Giza. The pottery vessels found in the burial chambers were obviously containers for wine, beer, milk, or water. Table vessels, bowls, basins, and beakers used in serving food were also found.

In two burial chambers of the Senedjem-ib Complex at Giza (G 2381 Z, 2385 A) the Harvard University-Museum of Fine Arts Expedition found a number of limestone food cases. The cases were originally painted yellow inside and out, and consisted of two parts, a lower case or receptacle and a fitting upper case or cover. The edges of the cases had no rebate or groove but the upper case lay edge to edge on the lower case with no evidence of fastening. This is also true of later food cases, which appear to have been tied together with cloth strips or string (see cat. 81).[1]

The hollows of the cases are large enough to have contained food offerings, and Reisner assumed they did. Even though none actually held such remains, seventeen lots of bones were found jumbled together along the east wall of the burial chamber of G 2381 Z. They comprised four skeletons of birds, apparently two geese and two smaller birds, and thirteen meat pieces, including rib-pieces and legs and shoulders of oxen, along with legs of calves. Abundant remains of linen indicate the offerings were once wrapped up.

The most common meat offering seen in Old Kingdom reliefs, a foreleg or haunch of beef, is not represented among the food cases, although smaller pieces are. Meat pieces on a long bone with a joint exposed at each end recur in the scenes and in the longer list of offerings inscribed on tomb walls. They are apparently from a leg of beef but exhibit two different forms hard to distinguish, but called in Egyptian iw^c and

26a

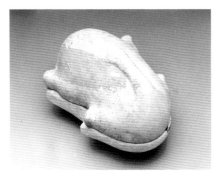

26b

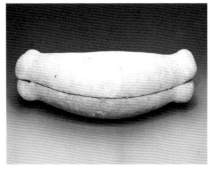

26c

26d

26e

swt. Both forms are included among the food cases and one of the two pieces certainly represents the second or upper joint of the leg of an ox, possibly the piece exhibited here (26c). Found in G 2381 Z but not preserved in G 2385 A was a case in the shape of a shoulder piece or thigh from one end of which a single large bone protrudes. A model offering of identical form is known (see cat. 25). Another case represents a cut of meat containing several ribs. On the cover four ribs are shown in relief, and in the bottom of the receptacle four grooves are hollowed in the stone (26d). In both burial chambers two ovoid cases were discovered. Reisner thought they were intended to contain a piece of meat stripped from the bone. A very similar form occurs among the model offerings (cat. 25).

All told, eleven complete and four incom-

plete cases for trussed birds were found in G 2385 A and G 2381 Z. Cases of eight varying sizes were discovered in the former and of four varying sizes in the latter. Considering their dimensions, the larger cases (26a) probably contained geese or large ducks, the medium cases ducks, and the smaller cases pigeons or doves (26b).

It is difficult to identify the form of a round or circular case (26e) with any known meat piece, and it is possible that a flat cake or bread was intended. There are more than fifteen words for bread or cake in the Old Kingdom offering list, which probably reflect differences in flour or other ingredients, shape, or method of baking.[2]

EB

1. Lansing 1920, pp. 7-8, fig. 3.
2. Montet 1981, pp. 85-86.

Bibliography: Reisner unpublished, pp. 619-622, 626-631; Hayes 1953, p. 119, fig. 73.

27
Slab stela of Meret-ites II

From Giza tomb G 4140
Old Kingdom, Dynasty 4
Limestone
Height 51 cm., width 82.5 cm.
Harvard University-Museum of Fine Arts
Expedition, 1912 (12.1510)

In the reign of Khufu during Dynasty 4, high officials began to build stone mastaba tombs in a cemetery west of the pyramid of their king. Perhaps because of the expense of stone (earlier non-royal tombs were built largely of mud brick) and the limited space allowed by the regular plan of the cemetery, these tombs were simpler in plan and decoration than the earlier tombs at Meydum, Sakkara, and Dahshur. Each of the early stone mastabas at Giza had two niches in its eastern face, the largest to the south, marking the site where offerings were to be made. A slab stela was set into the niche at about chest height,[1] depicting the deceased seated before a table of bread loaves. The fineness of their carving and painting suggests that the stelae were made by the craftsmen of the king. The owners apparently found these tombs too modest: in many cases chapels were added to the original mastabas, covering and protecting the slab stelae and preserving their brilliant colors in almost pristine condition. The tradition of the slab stela survived, however, in the rectangular tablet set above the central niche of the "false door," a shallow but elaborately-paneled niche that developed out of the deep niches in the early mastabas (see cat. 28). These tablets were sometimes painted white, to imitate a slab stela of fine white limestone inserted into the false door, while the door itself was painted red to imitate granite.[2]

The slab stela exhibited here belonged to a woman, whose name and title, "king's daughter of his body, Meret-ites," are written in the damaged register above her head. Although the surface of her stela has weathered, the carving is of the finest Dynasty 4 quality, with figures and hieroglyphs alike rendered in exquisitely detailed low relief. Feathers are shown on the birds, the tiny rectangular pools are filled with zig-zag lines representing water, and the features of the princess are beautifully modeled. She wears a long wig, and a simple sheath dress. The knot at her shoulder is usually part of the leopard skin worn by *setem* priests; it occurs on most stelae of this type, including those women who claim to be daughters of kings. The chair on which she is seated has the legs of a calf (in later periods, lions' feet were more common), and her feet demonstrate the unrealistic convention in which the heel of the back foot is visible through the arch of the foot in front.

27

A list of offerings begins in the upper register with hieroglyphs that have been turned to face the hieroglyphs of the name and title, so that the names of the offerings appear to march towards the name of their recipient. The offerings listed are those standard on such stelae: incense, green and black eye-paint, oil, wine, *ished*-fruit, figs, and *w*c*ah*-fruit. These, and the more extensive offerings listed in the lower registers, are the prototype of the compartmental offering list of the later Old Kingdom (see cat. 24). Below them, to the right and under the table are shown the bread, beer, meat, and poultry offerings required for the standard offering ritual, each supplemented by the tall papyrus-plant sign, indicating the quantity 1000.

On the right part of the stela is a compartmental list of linen and grain that occurs on earlier stelae, but which seems to have died out not long after these stelae were made.[3] Four different types of linen are listed; below them are the numbers thought to represent the surface area of the pieces,[4] and below this the quantity 1000. The seven round-topped buildings under the linen list represent granaries, each labeled with a different type of grain.

The slab stelae thus contained, in compact form, all the elements necessary for the maintenance of the dead spirit, elements which the more extensive tomb decoration of later periods could only elaborate and repeat.

AMR

1. Reisner 1932b, p. 326.
2. Reisner 1932b, p. 326.
3. Smith 1935, p. 135.
4. Posener-Kriéger 1977, pp. 86-96.

Literature: Leprohon 1985, pp. 82-85; Reisner 1942, fig. 280 and pls. 46, 57a.

28
False door of Kha

From Giza tomb 7211 B
Old Kingdom, probably late Dynasty 6
Limestone
Height 104 cm., width 88 cm., depth 11.5 cm.
Harvard University-Museum of Fine Arts Expedition, 1925 (25.1514)

This false door was cut for the "Nobleman of the King, the Overseer of Craftsmen, Kha." A rectangular panel at the top shows the deceased seated in front of a table of bread, depicted as a series of vertical loaves; below is a lintel with his name and titles. On the left outer jamb, beneath a prayer to the god Anubis for offerings, is a standing figure of Kha; the right outer jamb bears an exhortation to visitors to recite a wish for offerings for the deceased, and a seated figure of the deceased. The left inner jamb shows Kha standing with a short prayer above, while that on the right shows him, arms raised, below the text "the one who adores Djedef-hor, the honored one, Kha." Djedef-hor was a son of King Khufu of Dynasty 4, and was clearly regarded as something of a sage; a cult developed around him in the later Old Kingdom. The find/spot of this false door was almost next to the tomb of Djedef-hor.

All the carving is executed in sunk relief. The figures have the elongated forms common from the middle of Dynasty 6 on, and the carving is less skillful than that on the major monuments of the dynasty.

The false door is a form of stela, or gravestone. In its classic form, as here, it developed out of the simple rectangular slab-stela (see cat. 27) of Dynasties 2 to 4, which

28

broadly resemble the panel of this piece. These stelae were set in niches, and the sides of the niche gradually came to be decorated.[1] Our term "false door" is derived from its similarity to the architecture of a real door, with its jambs and architraves.

The false door was the focus of the Old Kingdom tomb. It was the principal place at which cult activity was undertaken for the spirit of the deceased. The particular function of the door was to allow the spirit to pass between the hidden chambers where the body was buried and the unconcealed offering chapel. Certain Old Kingdom examples underscore this connection by representing the two panels of a double door in the central niche together with a series of bolts.[2] In front of the door was usually a table (cat. 22) on which the offerings for the spirit were placed. The spirit passed through the door to gain sustenance from these. Some examples dating to Dynasty 6 suggest that the false door also functioned as a type of statue shrine.

The false door never went completely out of fashion during the Pharaonic period, but from the First Intermediate Period on it declined in popularity and was largely replaced by the common rectangular, round-topped stela.

NS

1. Reisner 1942, pls. 17-18.
2. E.g., that of Semdent, Kanawati 1984, pls. 5 and 6.
3. E.g., MFA 21.961.

Bibliography: Goedicke 1958, pp. 35-55, pl. I.

Literature: Wiebach 1981; Strudwick 1981.

First Intermediate Period

29
Seal-amulets

a. From Giza
   Late Old Kingdom
   Limestone
   Diam. 2.2 cm., height 1.5 cm.
   Harvard University-Museum of Fine Arts Expedition, 1913 (13.3412)
b. From Sheikh Farag tomb SF 5006
   First Intermediate Period
   Faience
   Length 1.8 cm., width 1.6 cm., height .9 cm.
   Harvard University-Museum of Fine Arts Expedition, 1924 (24.1592)
c. From the Mycerinus Valley Temple, Giza
   Late Old Kingdom
   Steatite
   Diam. 2 cm., height .7 cm.
   Harvard University-Museum of Fine Arts Expedition, 1911 (11.957)
d. From Giza tomb G 2320 A
   Late Old Kingdom
   Bone
   Length 1.6 cm., width 1.5 cm., height .7 cm.
   Harvard University-Museum of Fine Arts Expedition, 1913 (13.3408)
e. From Sheikh Farag tomb SF 42
   First Intermediate Period
   Steatite
   Length 1.7 cm., width .9 cm., height .8 cm
   Harvard University-Museum of Fine Arts Expedition, 1913 (13.3807)
f. From Giza G 2381
   First Intermediate Period
   Black steatite
   Diam. 1.2 cm., height .9 cm.
   Harvard University-Museum of Fine Arts Expedition, 1913 (13.3397)
g. Provenance unknown
   First Intermediate Period
   Black steatite
   Diam. 2 cm., height 1.1 cm.
   Hay Collection, Gift of C. Granville Way, 1872 (72.1265)
h. Provenance unknown
   First Intermediate Period
   Glazed steatite
   Length 1.3 cm., width 1 cm., height .7 cm.
   Hay Collection, Gift of C. Granville Way, 1872 (72.3830)
i. From Deir el-Bahri
   First Intermediate Period
   Glazed steatite
   Length 1.1 cm., width .7 cm., height .6 cm.
   Gift of Egypt Exploration Fund, 1897 (97.975)
j. From Semna S 552
   First Intermediate Period
   Glazed steatite
   Length 1.1 cm., width .8 cm., height .5 cm.
   Harvard University-Museum of Fine Arts Expedition, 1924 (24.1550)
k. From Deir el-Bahri
   First Intermediate Period
   Glazed steatite
   Length 1.6 cm., width 1.2 cm., height .6 cm.
   Gift of Egypt Exploration Fund, 1897 (97.956)
l. From Mesheikh Mes 2109
   First Intermediate Period
   Steatite
   Length 1.3 cm., width .8 cm., height .5 cm.
   Harvard University-Museum of Fine Arts Expedition, 1912 (12.1302)

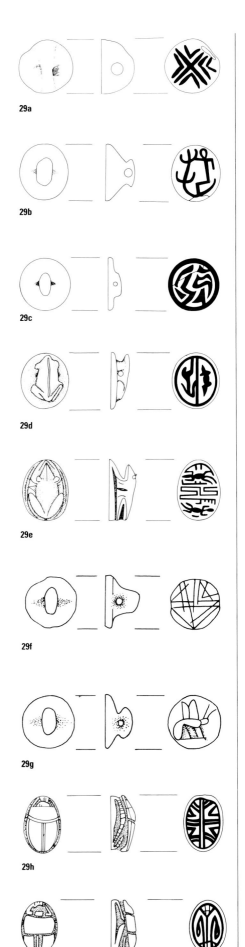

29a

29b

29c

29d

29e

29f

29g

29h

29i

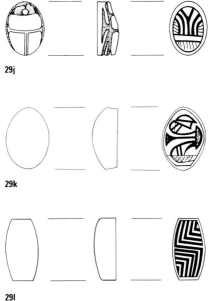

29j

29k

29l

Perhaps the most easily recognized Egyptian artifacts, scarabs may be seen by the thousand in major and minor museums throughout the world. Hundreds more have found their way into private collections. Their small size and the ease with which they can be copied have also made scarab jewelry very popular.

It is often forgotten that the scarab as an art form did not exist before the First Intermediate Period and that it developed out of the earlier seal-amulets that appeared during the late Old Kingdom. These objects are called seal-amulets since they seem to have developed from the amulets that are found in great abundance in graves from the late Predynastic Period through the Old Kingdom. Seal-amulets have been discovered most often in the graves of women and children.[1] They are usually of a size and construction that argues against their having been used as actual seals, though scarabs of later periods were clearly used as such.[2]

The initial form of the seal-amulet was the disk-shaped "button seal" found in small numbers at late Old Kingdom and early First Intermediate Period sites throughout Egypt. Button seals were often made of ivory, a material seldom used for later forms, and had either a pierced ridge (29a) or shank (29b,c) on their backs. The designs carved on the bases were sometimes merely crude lines (29a), but more often consisted of stick-figure animals or people (29b) or combinations of the two (29c). Both types of button seal disappear by the late First Intermediate Period.

A third type of early seal-amulet has the body or head of an animal carved on the back, rather than a shank or ridge. The most commonly used animals were the beetle[3] and the frog (29d,e). Crouching lions and dogs, seated apes, hippopotamus heads,

human heads, and double hawk heads have also been found.[4] As with the shank- and ridge-backed seal-amulets, the flat bottoms of animal-backed seal-amulets were decorated with stick-figure people and animals (29d), but these designs often deteriorate into the maze pattern that is common on the scarabs of the First Intermediate Period (29e where two lizard or crocodile figures form part of the maze pattern).

The diversity among animal-backed seal-amulets was undoubtedly due to the newness of the art form which had not become standardized during the Old Kingdom. Eventually experimentation by the Egyptian artists led to the development of the true scarab, which began to appear in the early First Intermediate Period and dominated the art form from the late First Intermediate Period on, though other back forms are found in small numbers during other periods.

The earliest scarabs are often very simple with the wing cases and heads barely indicated on the backs, and the legs shown with rough incised lines on the sides, if at all.[5] Though this simple form continues, the later scarabs are often more elaborately treated, with some attempt made to distinguish types of beetles and with more attention paid to the details of the legs (29h-j). Some of the late First Intermediate Period examples have the legs carved completely in the round.

While the earliest scarabs sometimes retain the stick-figure designs of their button-seal precursors (29f), more often they are decorated with maze, floral (29i), and geometric patterns (29h), or combinations of these. Frequently the floral and geometric patterns include cross-hatched lozenge shapes (29i,j).

During the First Intermediate Period other shapes, such as the cowroid (29k), hemisphere, hemi-cylinder, ovoid (29l), rectangle, and dome, were also used for seal-amulets. While they never became as prevalent as the scarab, these non-animal shapes may be found in small numbers in later periods as well. In the First Intermediate Period, they were usually decorated with the same types of designs as the scarabs using maze (29l) and floral (29k) patterns most commonly.

The seal-amulet was in its infancy during the late Old Kingdom and early First Intermediate Period. When one examines the various back types that were being used, it is not surprising that the Egyptian artists finally settled for the scarab (see cat. 129b). First of all, the scarab is a powerful amulet since the beetle hieroglyph means "to exist" or "come into being." It is also possible to carve a recognizable three-dimensional representation of a beetle with a minimum of effort. Many of the earliest scarabs are merely ovoids with lines scratched on the back to represent the wings and shoulders. The ovoid shape was an ideal choice, having no rough edges to break off, but with ample room for a design or inscription on the flat bottom.

CHR

1. The vast majority of excavated examples come from the sites of Qau, Mostagedda, and Matmar in Middle Egypt. See Brunton 1927, pp. 55-59, XXXII-XXXVII; Brunton 1937, pp. 107-108, pl. LX; Brunton 1948, pp. 49-50, pl. XXXIII.
2. Small oval-shaped sealings dating from the Middle Kingdom and later have been found at several sites. See Reisner 1923a, pls. 2-3.
3. These are not true scarabs since the insect seems to have been plastered onto a disk rather than forming an integral part of the whole composition.
4. See Brunton 1927, pls. 109-136.
5. See Brunton 1927, pl. XXXIII, 138-154.

Bibliography: Reisner 1932, fig. 48.13 (29c); Reisner 1932a, fig. 50.11 (29e); Reisner 1932a, fig. 49.16 (29l, not to scale).

Literature: Brunton 1927, pp. 55-59, XXXII-XXXVII; Brunton 1937, pp. 107-108, pl. LX; Brunton 1948, pp. 49-50, pl. XXXIII; Reisner 1932a, pp. 108-120; Roehrig 1976; Petrie 1925a; Tufnell and Ward 1966; Ward 1970; Ward 1978.

30
Chapel of Sat-in-teti

From Sakkara, near the pyramid of Teti
Late Dynasty 6 or First Intermediate Period
Stela height 117.5 cm, width 80 cm., depth 10 cm.
Right wall height 118 cm., width 55.5 cm., depth 80 cm.
Left wall height 83.5 cm., width 55 cm., depth 70 cm.
Purchased from the Egyptian Antiquities Service, 1924 (24.593)

The false door of the small offering chapel of Sat-in-teti is typical of the late Old Kingdom: quite small, with three pairs of jambs, two architraves, and one lintel, each decorated with one line or column of text. At the bottom of the middle and outer jambs the deceased is shown holding a staff or smelling a lotus. The central panel, bearing a representation of the deceased at table, flares outwards at the top, a feature appearing from the middle of Dynasty 6 on. The outside is framed by a torus molding with a cavetto cornice on top. Both features make their first appearance in later Dynasty 5. The decoration on the false door, except for the central panel, is in sunk relief.

On the upper half of the right panel, below an offering list of ninety-seven elements, are three small registers. The top one shows Sat-in-teti seated before a table of bread, around which are arranged other offerings. Behind her chair is a harp with a human head at the top and that of a lion at

30, false door

the bottom. The second register shows two men trying to control a bull on a rope, with the caption "Control him, he is a sturdy bull." This is clearly preparatory to slaughter, since a man follows with a knife and bowl for catching the blood. The bottom register shows four women carrying offerings and birds and leading animals. The offering list is cut in sunk relief, the remainder

The top of the left panel, now missing, clearly bore a similar offering list. Below are two registers. Sat-in-teti again is shown seated before offerings; above her head is a large and elaborate bowl of lotus flowers. The flat, undetailed state of the upper part of this scene shows that it was not finished. In the lower register are two butchers at work, one of whom says, "Let me go; this is an excellent choice piece," while to the right two men carry away ribs and a haunch

of beef. The caption reads, "Carrying the choice parts of the bull for the spirit of the honored one, Sat-in-teti."

This small chapel also contained an offering table (not in the Museum's collection) re-carved from a block from the funerary chapel of the wife of Mereruka, owner of an early Dynasty 6 mastaba at Sakkara. Parallel examples suggest that the chapel would have been roofed over, although no traces of roofing blocks survived.

The three panels display the basic elements of an Old Kingdom tomb chapel, the component parts of which are also to be found separately in this exhibition. Central to it is the false door, the principal offering place, while of only slightly less importance are the offering lists and the depiction of the deceased partaking of the food. This chapel also features the two most common other scenes found in the Old Kingdom, those of

30, right panel

30, left panel

butchers and offering bearers. Meat was clearly a very important part of the offering ritual, and most decorated tombs have a scene showing its production.

A very wide range of scenes is known from tombs of this period. The particular choice must have depended on the owner's preferences and means. Very elaborate tombs were not often constructed in the late Old Kingdom, but during this period many individuals who previously would not have had a tomb chapel were able to construct some form of funerary monument. While not elab-

orate, Sat-in-teti's tomb chapel fulfilled all the basic functions. Should the daily offerings and rituals not be performed, their magical equivalents would satisfy her requirements.

NS

Bibliography: Firth and Gunn 1926a, pp. 4, 38, 185-186, 203-204; Firth and Gunn 1926b, pls. 20C, D; 21, A-C; Simpson 1972i, pp. 8-11.

31
Coffin of Menkabu

From Farshut
First Intermediate Period, probably
Dynasty 11
Wood
Length 195 cm., width 42 cm., height 57 cm.
Emily Esther Sears Fund (03.1631a,b)

The rectangular wooden coffin was covered with stucco and painted a dark red in imitation of cedar wood. A band of polychrome hieroglyphs on a white ground extends around the rim of the box and another runs lengthwise on the cover. The two sacred eyes on the left, or east, side of the coffin are surrounded by a simple, yellow painted frame. They adopt the form of the *wedjat*, a human eye with the markings of a falcon head. The eye and brow are black but the markings are green and yellow. According to Egyptian tradition, Horus's eye was ripped out by the wicked god Seth but miraculously restored by the ibis-god Thoth. The *wedjat* eye was considered a potent amulet (see cat. 129). In later times, the twin *wedjats* were thought to represent the sun and the moon. The eyes on the sides of Middle Kingdom coffins, however, allowed the soul of the deceased to look out and view the sun. Undoubtedly, they also allowed the deceased to view the funerary ceremonies conducted on his behalf.

Anubis – Lord of Sepa, ''He who is before the Divine Booth'' – on the lid of the coffin, and Osiris – Lord of Busiris, ''He who presides over the Westerners,'' Lord of Abydos – on the left side cause Menkabu to receive funerary offerings. On the right side, Anubis – ''He who is Upon His Mountain,'' ''Who is in the Bandages,'' Lord of the Cemetery – assures a proper burial. On the foot end a short prayer for funerary offering is twice repeated, while the inscription on the east side terminates on the foot end.

The hieroglyphs of the coffin are notable for their bold outlines, bright colors, and lively detail. Bright yellow, dark red, and pale green (along with a somber gray) are boldly combined with a decorative intent.[1]

In the vignette that determines the word for burial, the mummified deceased on a bed is attended by mourners who express their grief in agitated gestures.[2] Similar groupings occur in the coffin of Henuy from Gebelein[3]

31

and the stela of Sobek-aa from Moalla.[4] In the coffin painting, the deceased lies on a bed with the figure of a woman held over him by two female attendants standing at the ends of the bed. In the stela, Sobek-aa embraces the female figure and pulls her to him. The three vignettes probably allude to death and revivification by means of sexual intercourse.[5]

What interests us here are the chronological implications, since the parallelism confirms the paleographic evidence that the two coffins and the stela belong to the reign of Mentuhotep II. Specific features that reveal Theban influence include the extensive use of the expletive stroke after alphabetic signs, biliterals, triliterals, ideograms, and determinatives, and the tendency to set horizontal signs on end.

The hieroglyph of the horned viper (*Cerastes cornutus*) is shown decapitated to prevent it from magically coming to life in the tomb and harming the owner. [6]

EB

1. Terrace 1968a, p. 267.
2. Terrace 1968a, p. 267.
3. Steindorff 1901, pl. 3.
4. Michalowski 1968, fig. 265.
5. Desroches-Noblecourt 1953, p. 20.
6. Lacau 1914, pp. 1-64.

Bibliography: Smith 1960, p. 82, fig. 48; Terrace 1968a, p. 267, fig. 4.

32
Statue of Wepwawet-em-hat

From Asyut tomb 14
First Intermediate Period, Dynasty 10 or 11
Wood
Height 112 cm., width 23.1 cm., depth 71.1 cm.
Emily Esther Sears Fund, 1904 (04.1780)

Wepwawet-em-hat stands in the traditional left-foot-forward pose of an Egyptian male figure in this wooden statue from his tomb. He wears a short, curled wig and a tight-fitting thigh-length kilt that has been plastered and white-washed. The walking stick and scepter that he carries were made separately and inserted into his left and right hand respectively. The statue's owner is identified on the rectangular base as "the Revered One, Wepwawet-em-hat."

Wepwawet-em-hat's statue was discovered in 1903 by Chassinat and Palanque inside an unplundered rock-cut tomb in the First Intermediate Period-Middle Kingdom necropolis at Asyut.[1] The tomb's contents[2] are typical of the First Intermediate Period/Dynasty 11; they are comparable, for instance, to those of the tomb of Gemeniemhat at Sakkara, dated to the reign of the Dynasty 10 king Merikare.[3] Asyut nomarchs supported the Herakleopolitan regime dur-

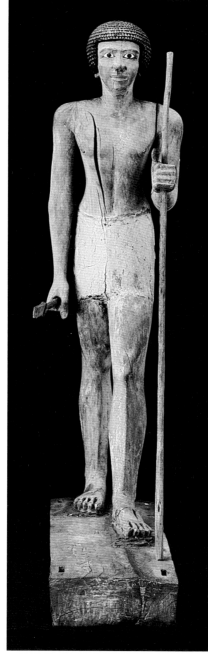

32

ing Dynasty 10, and in all likelihood the tomb of Wepwawet-em-hat may be attributed to this time. Wepwawet-em-hat's name, one of the more common ones at Asyut, incorporates the name of the city's main god, Wepwawet.[4]

Wepwawet-em-hat's face and body are rendered with sensitivity and skill, and the statue ranks among the finest of the wooden statues of the First Intermediate Period. Stylistically, it is strikingly similar to the statue of Nakhti in the Louvre.[5] On both, alabaster and schist eyes are inlaid beneath heavy, slightly arched brows, and pronounced cheekbones lend an angular quality to the face. This angularity is echoed in the ridge designating the collarbone.

Wepwawet-em-hat's trim torso is bisected above the waist by a deep depression extending from mid-chest to navel. The nipples were made separately and inserted, a technique used on wooden statues of the Old Kingdom.[6] Tangs attach arms and feet to the torso and legs, and additional tangs at the bottom of the feet fit into corresponding sockets on the base.[7] The base is pierced by rectangular slots extending in a right angle from each corner out the corresponding side. Ropes may have been threaded through these slots and looped over a carrying pole to facilitate the transport of this fragile statue from workshop to tomb.[8] Alternatively, the slots may have secured it to the floor of a shrine or a sledge.[9]

The youthfully trim striding male is the most common type of wooden statue known from the Old Kingdom and First Intermediate Period. Sometimes it was accompanied by an apparently more mature depiction of the same owner, typically displaying a fleshier torso, longer and fuller kilt, and wearing no wig.[10] These representations of the deceased, commonly placed in the burial chamber near the coffin, embodied the *ka*, namely the vital life force of their owners, which was kept alive, theoretically, by means of regular donations of food and drink from *ka*-priests.

RF

1. The tomb bears number 14 and is one of some 26 tombs of that time period excavated by that mission; see Chassinat and Palanque 1911, p. 164, pls. XXXIV-XXXV.
2. The tomb also contained a smaller wooden statue of a female offering bearer, a wooden model of a bull (cat. 33), a model boat, a model brewery (04.1782), a terracotta offering table and two wooden coffins. Inside the first coffin, which was inscribed for Wepwawet-em-hat, was his mummy and a small alabaster vessel. A bow and a shield handle rested on the coffin lid. The second coffin was uninscribed and contained only a few poorly preserved bones (Chassinat and Palanque 1911, pp. 164-166).
3. Gemeniemhat's tomb likewise contained wooden figures of the owner, female offering bearers, models of daily life, model boats, vessels for food, and the weaponry found in association with a wooden coffin. The tomb is dated on the basis of the cartouche of Merik inscribed on Gemeniemhat's false door stela; see Firth and 22, 27-29.
4. Beinlich 1973, cols. 491, 493.
5. Louvre E 11937, from tomb number seven at Asyut, Chassinat and Palanque 1911, p. 32 and pls. I, III-XXVIII.
6. As seen for example on Senedjem-ib Mehy from Giza, now Boston MFA
7. This was the most common method of manufacture for larger wooden statues. See, for instance, Steindorff 1946a, pl. XIV, nos. 72, 76, 78, 79, and pl. XV, nos. 75, 81, 90.
8. Women carrying a large jar in this manner may be seen, for example, in reliefs from the tomb of Queen Nofru (Boston, MFA 1973.147 and Cairo, JE 49927, illustrated in Simpson 1974b, pp. 106-107).

9. For an example of such a shrine, see Lehner and Lacovara 1985, pp. 169-174; examples of statues affixed to sledges pulled by ropes are illustrated in Eaton-Krauss 1984, pls. I, no. 58; XVI, no. 98, XVII, no. 100, and others.
10. The two types existed side by side in the Old Kingdom, in both wood and stone. The statues of Methethy now in Brooklyn (50.77, 51.1, 53.222) and Kansas City (51-1), attributed to Dynasty 5/6, are perhaps the finest of the Old Kingdom wooden examples. For a discussion of wooden statuary of the Old Kingdom, see Wood 1977.

Bibliography: Museum of Fine Arts 1905, pp. 13, 15; Porter and Moss 1934, p. 267; Chassinat and Palanque 1911, p. 164, pls. XXXIV 1-2; Smith 1942 pp. 79-80, fig. 48; Terrace 1968a, p. 267, fig. 3.

33

33
Model bull

From Asyut tomb 14 (Wepwawet-em-hat)
First Intermediate Period, Dynasty 10 or 11
Painted wood
Length 36 cm., width 12.5 cm., height 12.5 cm.
Emily Esther Sears Fund, 1904 (04.1778)

This wooden model bull was found in the burial chamber of the tomb of Wepwawet-em-hat of Asyut. It was standing against the wall with several other models: a female offering bearer similar to cat. 36, ceramic offering vessels, and a fine wooden statue of the deceased (cat. 32).[1]

The animal's sex is not clearly indicated, but its stockiness and the heavy fold of skin running from the chin down the throat suggest that it is a bull or an ox. The head and body of the animal were carved from a single piece of wood and the legs, tail, ears, and horns (now missing) were added separately. The pieces were carved in a very square fashion and filled out with plaster, which was also used to mask the joints at the shoulders and hips and probably around the base of the tail. The hooves were carved as part of the legs rather than added in plaster, and a thick tenon was left at the bottom of each hoof to attach the animal to the crude base.

Models of individual bulls are not common, though they frequently form parts of butcher scenes or ploughing scenes. Two similar animals were discovered in the tomb of Djehuty-nakht at Bersha, but as these animals were found without bases, it is possible that they formed part of the same model either as a pair of ploughing animals or as part of a cattle-counting scene similar to that found in the tomb of Meketre at Thebes.[2] This bull may represent an abbreviated version of a cattle-counting scene, or may take the place of a butcher scene, the only major type of food production otherwise missing from Wepwawet-em-hat's tomb.

CHR

1. The group was photographed *in situ* and published in Chassinat and Palanque 1911, pl. XXXIV.1.
2. The existence of a model base without figures, but with holes that seem to fit with the legs of the bulls in question, suggests the latter possibility.

Bibliography: Chassinat and Palanque 1911, pp. 164-166, pls. XXXIV.1, XXXV.3.

34
Model boat

From Asyut
First Intermediate Period, Dynasty 10 or 11
Wood
Height 34.3 cm., length 83.8 cm.
Emily Esther Sears Fund, 1904
(04.1779 a-c)

The symbolic association of the deceased with Osiris, God of the Underworld, led to re-enactments of certain events surrounding the deity's death and resurrection. According to ancient Egyptian religious beliefs, Osiris's body was taken by boat for burial at Abydos. Just as in life many Egyptians either made a pilgrimage to Abydos or sent a votive stela or both, in death they accompanied Osiris on his riverine voyage to his final resting place. Model boats would have served this purpose. The deceased is shown here in Osirian fashion – as a mummy – seated under a canopy. Behind him sits the tiller, in front stands the guide, and in the middle are those who held the ropes. A mummy and attendants are usually found on model craft of this type,[1] and we may assume that the boat on which this one was modeled had a funerary purpose. The design of the bow and the stern suggest that it was made from papyrus or at least patterned after a papyriform craft.

Boats are found in tombs primarily in the First Intermediate Period and Middle Kingdom, although examples are known both earlier and later. The Osirian cycle is only one motive for including them. Voyages are integral to Egyptian religious literature. The

34

sun traveled by boat through the Underworld by night and again across the sky by day. The deceased had several boat trips to make in the hereafter (see essay on funerary mythology). Boats may also have served a more secular purpose: Like funerary figurines and servant statues, they may have been intended to perpetuate the pleasures of this life in the next. Egyptians are frequently shown in tomb paintings on papyrus skiffs, fishing and fowling or jousting in mock battle. For extended voyages up and down the Nile, larger craft were necessary and kitchen boats came along.

Model craft of several types were found in the Theban tomb of the Dynasty 11 official Meketre,[2] and Sinuhe, the hero of a famous Middle Kingdom tale, recalls that when he made his triumphant return voyage to Egypt from the Levant, bread and beer were supplied from an accompanying boat.[3] The specific purpose of the model, therefore, would depend on the function of the boat.

DS

1. Landström 1970, p. 92, no. 284; Göttlicher and Werner 1971, pl. 50.
2. Winlock 1955; Landström 1970, pp. 78-81; Göttlicher and Werner, 1971, pl. 30; Göttlicher 1978, p. 53, no. 272b, pl. 21.
3. Simpson 1973, p. 71; Gunn 1941, p. 146.

Bibliography: New Orleans 1977, cat. 48.

35

35
Model of men butchering an ox

From Asyut tomb 7, pit 1
First Intermediate Period, Dynasty 11
Painted wood
Length 44 cm., width 42.5 cm., height
44 cm.
Emily Esther Sears Fund, 1904 (04.1781)

This model butchering scene was found in
the tomb of Nakhti at Asyut with a granary
scene, a brewing and baking shop, and two
boats. The scene includes four male figures
and a bound ox. The man bending over the
animal with a knife seems just to have cut
off its right foreleg, which a second man is
carrying away over his shoulder. A third
man, with a hole through his clenched fists,
probably held a piece of rope that bound the
other three legs of the ox; the rope is no
longer preserved. In order to hold the rope
taut, the man's right leg is raised, and
pushes against one of the ox's hind legs.[1]
The fourth man is fanning a fire in the brazier in the corner.

The men are painted red and are similarly
dressed in white kilts, the butcher having
used his to wipe the blood from his knife.
Two of the men wear short wigs, but the
other two, perhaps because they are engaged in the messiest tasks, have removed
their wigs. Their heads appear to have been
shaved and are painted yellow, the color
usually used on figures of women. Presumably this was done to indicate that the
men's scalps had not been exposed to the
sun.

Each figure was carved from a single piece

of wood except for the arms, which were
attached at the shoulders. The joins were
carefully masked with plaster. The legs of
each figure were sunk into holes in the floor
of the enclosure and the feet of all but the
butcher were added in plaster. His feet may
have been left off because they are hidden
by the ox. The eyes of each man were
painted with black and white, but there is
no indication of a mouth on any of the
figures.

The man tending the brazier holds a fan
painted yellow with black details. The brazier is red and supports a yellow bowl,
which may be filled with the animal's blood.

The ox was carefully carved; such details as
the cheek bones and the fold of skin along
the throat were carved in the wood, not added in plaster. The three remaining legs
were made from separate pieces and skillfully attached with plaster added to cover
the joins. The tail, ears, and horns were also
carved separately. The animal's mouth is
slightly open and a shallow slit in its throat
indicates the method of slaughter. Its body
has been painted red, the hooves black. The
eyes, which are open, were painted black
and white. The wound along the right shoulder has been painted red and white, perhaps to show the muscle and blood beneath. Despite the general attention to
detail, there is no apparent indication of the
sex of the animal, as is also true of the bull
from the tomb of Wepwawet-em-hat at the
same site (see cat. 33).

The right foreleg of the ox was made from
two pieces of wood joined at the ankle. It
was painted red with a black hoof. This limb

is carried over the man's shoulder in a fashion similar to that shown in butcher scenes
from Old Kingdom tombs.[2] It is attached
with a dowel held in the man's right hand.

The scene takes place inside an enclosure.
Whether this is meant to depict a building
or an open-air paddock is not clear. The
walls are painted black on the top and
outside and white on the inside. There is no
indication of a door or gateway on any of
the walls.

Models of men butchering oxen or calves
date from Dynasty 4.[3] The Old Kingdom examples are made of limestone and show
one butcher with a small animal, but later
examples, from the First Intermediate Period and early Middle Kingdom, are made of
wood and usually show more elaborate
scenes with multiple figures performing different tasks. The most famous of these,
now in New York, is the butcher shop from
the tomb of Meketre at Thebes.[4]

CHR

1. *Description de l'Egypte* 1822, pl. 45.1, 3, and 4
   show a man performing this task in a butcher
   scenes in the Asyut tomb of Hepdjefa. The
   scene is now destroyed.
2. For example the mastaba of Sekhem-ankh-
   Ptah, now in Boston (MFA 04.1760). Simpson
   1976b, pl. A, bottom register.
3. Four examples are listed in Breasted 1948, pp.
   35-36.
4. Winlock 1955, pp. 23-25; pls. 18-19.

Bibliography: Chassinat and Palanque 1911, p. 50,
pl. XV.1; Museum of Fine Arts 1905, p. 13-14 (illus.); Breasted 1948, pp. 36-37, 1, pl. 33.

Literature: Borchardt 1897, pp. 119-134; Eggebrecht 1973; Montet 1910, pp. 41-64; Breasted
1948; Winlock 1955.

36
Female offering bearer

From Asyut tomb 6
First Intermediate Period, Dynasty 10 or 11
Painted wood
Height 66 cm.
Emily Esther Sears Fund, 1904 (04.1774)

Discovered in tomb 6 at Asyut during the
excavations of Chassinat and Palanque,[1]
this female offering bearer was found under
a heap of stone that had fallen in from the
ceiling in the offering chapel.

Wooden statues of individual women bearing offerings were common components in
tombs of the First Intermediate Period and
early Middle Kingdom. Though the largest
number of published excavated pieces
comes from Asyut,[2] examples have been
found throughout Egypt at such sites as
Rifa,[3] Sakkara,[4] Beni Hasan,[5] and Thebes.[6]
The most famous examples are the two
from the Dynasty 11 Theban tomb of
Meketre.[7]

These offering bearers are often much

larger and better constructed than models of daily life found in the same tombs. They are frequently made with the same care as wooden statues of the deceased (see cat. 32). For this reason they appear to have some special significance and it has been suggested that they represent real or imaginary estates from which the deceased was entitled to draw provisions.[8] In this case they would replace similar representations of female offering bearers found on the walls of Old Kingdom mastaba tombs.

Though they often occur in pairs, such statues are frequently found singly, sometimes in the offering chapel, as was this example, sometimes in the burial chamber, as in the tomb of Wepwawet-em-hat at the same site.[9] The most frequently occurring type, of which this example is one, is clothed and striding forward, a basket balanced on her head by the left hand and a bird held in the right.[10]

The construction of this figure is somewhat unusual in that the basket and cushion on the woman's head were carved from the same piece of wood as her head and body. The arms and feet were made from separate pieces, probably attached with dowels. The joins are now completely covered with a thick layer of plaster. The curving left arm does not seem to have been jointed as is sometimes the case.[11]

The fingers of the left hand are long, like those of other figures from Asyut, and they were broken and reattached at some time, the thumb having been lost. The woman's skin was painted yellow, with black rosettes highlighting the naked breasts. This detail is common on the Asyut offering bearers. Chassinat describes it as tattooing,[12] but it seems more likely that this is either a stylized representation of the nipple, or perhaps an indication of a local use of some cosmetic such as black henna.

The face is quite flat, the nose formed mostly with plaster. The mouth is indicated by a single black line; the eyes and brows are merely painted in black and white.

The dress and hair style are both characteristic of the other Asyut offering bearers. A long white skirt is held up by a strap that runs between the breasts and over the left shoulder. The black wig is cut just below the ears at the sides and left long at the back. The figure wears a fillet around the head and two necklaces, one blue and one red. The cushion on her head is white and the basket is yellow with black details. The basket seems to be filled with flour, which is painted white.

Instead of a single bird, the woman clutches two in her right hand. They are constructed from four pieces of wood. The body and head of each is made from a separate piece, the base of the wings of a third and the tips of a fourth. The wings are joined

36

with a thick tenon that passes through the clenched right fist of the woman. Large amounts of plaster were added to mask the joins in the wood, and the birds were painted gray with white bellies. The feet, eyes, beaks, and wing tips were added in black.

The base of the statue was carved from a thick piece of wood, which was thinly plastered on the sides, with a thicker layer of plaster on the top and around the feet.

CHR

1. These statues are discussed in some detail in Vandier 1958, pp. 147-149, where he refers to the Boston statue by its earlier Egyptian Museum number (M.E. XIV). Vandier mentions only ten, but he seems to have overlooked one of the examples in tomb 7, where eight were found in various chambers.
2. Eleven statues of female offering bearers were found in the rock-cut tombs excavated by Chassinat and Palanque.
3. Petrie 1907, pl. XE.
4. Firth and Gunn 1926a, pls. 29B, 32B; Quibell and Hayter 1927, pl. XXVI.
5. See Garstang 1907.
6. Naville 1907, pl. IX; Steindorff 1896, pl. IX,2.
7. One now at the Metropolitan Museum in New York (MMA 20.3.7) the second in Cairo (JE 46735).
8. Vandier 1958, p. 147. For a discussion of Old Kingdom relief representations, see Vandier 1964, pp. 126-135.
9. Smaller statuettes of two female offering bearers attached to the same base frequently appear in tombs of this period. These are usually of cruder construction. For some examples, see Breasted 1948, p. 62.
10. Later examples frequently hold a *hes* vase in an upraised right hand. They sometimes appear naked, though many have been found with linen cloth wrapped around them.
11. The paint has cracked in other places where pieces of wood were joined.
12. Chassinat and Palanque 1911, p. 33, for a description of a similarly painted statue.

Bibliography: Chassinat and Palanque 1911, pp. 5-6; Museum of Fine Arts 1905 III, p. 14 (illus.); Breasted 1948, p. 63 no. 5; pl. 54a.

Literature: Vandier 1958, pp. 147-153.

37
Tomb group

From Mesheikh 101
First Intermediate Period
Harvard University-Museum of Fine Arts, 1912

a. Stela
   Painted limestone
   Height 71 cm., width 54 cm., depth 9.5 cm. (12.1479)
b. Coffin
   Wood
   Length 190 cm., width 43 cm., height 48.2 cm.; additional lid height 7.5 cm (12.1509)
c. Mummy
   Length 150 cm., width 35 cm., height 20 cm. (12.1518)

Mesheikh is situated on the east bank of the Nile opposite the modern town of Girga in Upper Egypt. It is part of a sequence of cemetery sites that includes Sheikh Farag and Naga-ed-Dêr.[1]

The tombs at Mesheikh are typical of those of the First Intermediate Period; they consist of a shaft and one or more burial chambers roughly cut into the rock. The elaborate superstructures and decorated chapels of the Old Kingdom are replaced by simple mud-brick constructions with roughly carved limestone stelae set in small mud brick chapels.[2]

There is no evidence that a superstructure existed over Mesheikh 101 – the hill itself may have served that purpose – but the excavators did find the remains of the mud-brick chapel and the stela in place (see below) with the offering pottery nearby. The chapel had been roughly one meter square with the stela set in the middle of the rear wall and a number of pots and jar stands set in front of it (fig. 52).[3]

Beneath the chapel a vertical shaft descended almost four meters below the surface of the hill (fig. 53). Two burial chambers led off the shaft, chamber A to the west and B to the east. Chamber A was sealed with a wall of mud brick. It was a rectangular room carved into the bedrock 245 cm. long and 95 cm. high, with a lintel made of wooden sticks and mud plaster. It contained only a rectangular box coffin, twenty-six pottery jars, six dishes, and six potstands.[4] The only other objects found in the tomb were three beads, one faience, one carnelian, and one amethyst.

This poor burial is an example of the decline in the funerary arts found in the period of instability known as the the First

Fig. 52

Intermediate Period. The simple narrow box coffin is roughly made out of irregular ''scrap'' pieces of wood plastered over in parts and painted yellow to give a uniform appearance. The coffin is inscribed in blue-green hieroglyphs with black outlines on the upper ends of the sides and down the center of the lid with offering formulae for the ''House Mistress Mer-irtyef.''

The body proved to be that of an elderly woman.[5] She does not appear to have had any special treatment other than wrapping in layers of linen of various weaves, the last layer being a fine fringed shawl. When she was unwrapped in the field, the excavators discovered she was wearing only a small strand of blue faience ring beads.

It was probably the knowledge of the poverty of the interment that caused the tomb to be spared from plundering,[6] as is usually the case with the few intact graves from the period.

PL

The stela found in the chapel of Mesheikh 101 is characteristic of the First Intermediate Period. To date, the Naga ed-Dêr First Intermediate Period cemeteries have yielded at least 135 stelae of similar palette and composition.[7]

Wadj-setji, his wife Mer-irtyef, and their two children stand beside food and drink offerings beneath a three-line offering formula. The inscription invokes Anubis and requests that all the food and drink man and wife require for a happy existence in the afterlife be provided for them. The decoration depicts these essentials in abbreviated fashion. In the Old Kingdom, a much more lavish display of Netherworld nourishment, often accompanied by scenes showing its preparation, was frequently carved and painted on tomb walls. By the First Intermediate Period, however, especially in sites outside the Memphite area, the needs are reduced to only those already-prepared victuals for which there was space on a stela.

Figures, piled offerings, and inscriptions are carved in sunk relief and painted in bright earth tones.[8] The rectangular frame, the unsupported mirror, and the names of the children (a daughter Ibu and a son In-Inheret, the latter theophoric incorporating the name of the local god of the Thinite nome) are represented in paint only.[9]

Wadj-setji and his son both wear the common male garment of their day, an above-the-knee-length kilt with a flared front. In place of the more usual sheath dress, Mer-irtyef is dressed only in a tightly wrapped skirt, her chest bare. Usually, only females of Nubian extraction (based on their dark skin color and short curled hair) of the First Intermediate Period and Dynasty 10 are so attired;[10] the fashion on this stela, therefore, may reflect Nubian influence.[11] Earlier, in the Old Kingdom, native Egyptian female servants and women performing ritual dances are occasionally shown bare chested.[12]

Wadj-setji, Mer-irtyef, and their daughter Ibu wear multi-row broad collars, the most common piece of funerary jewelry. Wadj-setji clasps a walking stick. His son's forearm is extended in a similar position, but the space beneath it is taken up not by a staff, but by the hieroglyphs of his name, now invisible except under ultra-violet light. In front of Mer-irtyef's face is a free-floating mirror, prized undoubtedly for its rejuvenative, solar significance as well as for its reflective capacity. Similar mirrors occur on approximately contemporary stelae from Naga ed-Dêr and other sites.[13]

Elongated noses, large eyes, tiny heads, broad shoulders, and high waists characterize First Intermediate Period reliefs south of the Memphite area. Nevertheless, the faintly incised vertical axis lines and horizontal guidelines intersecting strategic body parts indicate that the stela's artisans were aware of the existence of the traditional Old Kingdom canon of proportion but unfamiliar with its proper application.[14] The stela's overall sense of order is reflected in the way the neatly piled foods are visually set off from the figural area by Wadj-setji's walking stick. This organization, found on other stelae from Naga ed-Dêr as well,[15] forecasts a trend common at the end of Dynasty 11 and early Dynasty 12.[16]

At least nine other stelae, excavated in or attributed to the Naga ed-Dêr cemeteries, share aspects of overall composition, decoration and inscription with Wadj-setji's stela. They are called the ''Mer-irtyef Group,'' after the wife on the present stela.[17] Specific shared details include the costume and attitudes of the main figures, the nature and arrangement of the offerings, the form of the *dsr*-sign, and the orthography of *imy-wt*. In his recent work, Brovarski dates the Mer-irtyef Group to Dynasty 10.

RF

1. Brovarski 1980, pp. 296-317.
2. Dunham 1937, pp. 7-8. fig. 4.
3. Dunham 1937, pp. 17-18.
4. These types are typical of the First Intermediate Period (cf. Slater 1982) and include tall (Slater type A3c), squat (type A4a) and canister shaped jar stands, bag shaped jars (types S 4-6), hemispherical bowls (type D4b), platters with wide rims (type D3a), *hes* vases (type L2a), and a jar with a sharply carinated shoulder and flat bottom.
5. Madeline Hinkes, personal communication.
6. Slater 1982, pp. 291-298.
7. Brovarski 1980, cols. 307-308.
8. Following tradition, Wadj-setji and his son have red skin, black wigs, and white garments, while his wife and daughter have yellow skin, black wigs, and white garments. For additional notes on colors, see Dunham 1937, pp. 17-18. For additional notes on colors, I am

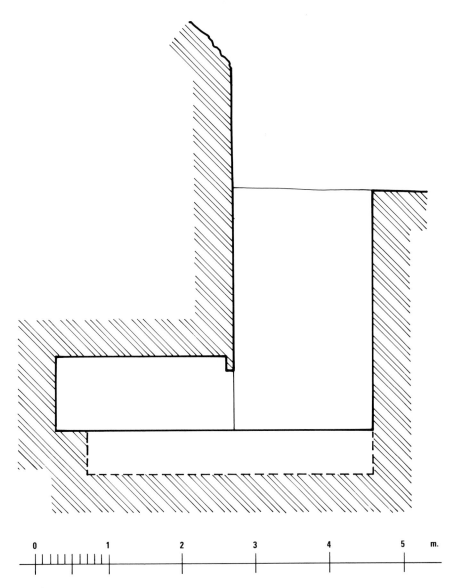

Fig. 53

grateful to Richard R. Ranta of Memphis State University.

9. Ultra-violet light greatly facilitates the reading of the son's name (Dunham 1933, pp. 39-41).
10. Fischer 1961, p. 58, note 24.
11. Brovarski unpublished.
12. Museum of Fine Arts 1987, and Nord 1981, p. 137.
13. Lilyquist 1979a, p. 74, note 880.
14. Other Naga-ed-Dêr stelae share this feature as well, as for example, MFA 25.626 and Harvard Semitic Museum 2354, illustrated in Dunham 1937, pls. VI, no. 1; VIII no. 2; and XXVIII, no 1.
15. For example, from Naga-ed-Dêr, MFA 12.1480, Cairo 43755, and Semitic Museum 2354, illustrated in Dunham 1937, pls. IV no. 2; XIX no. 1; and XXVIII no. 1.
16. For example, MMA 57.95 (time of Mentuhotep II), illustrated in Fischer 1960, pl. VII, or Louvre C2 (Year 11, Sesostris I), illustrated in Simpson 1974e, pl. 44.
17. The Mer-irtyef Group was first identified by Brovarski. For a list, see Brovarski unpublished

Bibliography: Fisher 1913, p. 21; Dunham 1937, p. 17, pl. IV; Freed 1981a, p. 73, n. 27, 35.

Literature: Dunham 1937.

38
Coffin and mummy of Pepi-seneb

From Sheikh Farag tomb 5114 C
First Intermediate Period, Dynasty 9
Wood, gesso, and linen
Coffin length 170 cm., width 51.2 cm., height 61.5 cm.; lid height 6 cm.
Harvard University-Museum of Fine Arts Expedition, 1912 (25.1512, 1513)

Descended from the coffins of the late Old Kingdom, those of the early First Intermediate Period followed much the same outward pattern.[1] They were wooden box coffins with a simple band of text around the top of the sides of the coffin and down the center of the lid. Two *wedjat* eyes on the proper left side allowed the deceased to watch the rising sun in the east. Unlike the hardwood coffins of the Old Kingdom, however, these coffins were often cheaply made of local soft woods (see cat. 37) that were veneered or even painted (see cat. 31) in imitation of finer materials. This example is covered in thin, irregular strips of cedar that have been pegged to a rough core of acacia. A liberal amount of gypsum plaster was used to fill in gaps and defects in the coffin, and the interior was plastered with the same substance and painted a yellow ochre.

The pair of *wedjat* eyes on the head end of the coffin's left side are painted black and white. The offering formulae in blue hieroglyphs record the name and titles of the deceased: "the Count, Sole Friend, and Lector Priest, Pepi-seneb." His two nicknames, Khety and Iti, are also given. The style of the hieroglyphs assigns the coffin to a group of inscriptions initially identified by Fischer and dating it to the early Herakleopolitan Period.[2]

Pepi-seneb's burial was a relatively poor one. The only grave goods included were a pile of linen on top of the coffin and a wooden walking stick beneath it. The mummy was devoid of any jewelry and swathed in layer after layer of linen until the bundle was fifty-six cm. wide.[3]

Because the mummy has not been unwrapped, the following observations are based on physical examination and on CT scans of the body. In fact, the extensive damage done to the linens by termites during burial has served to reveal many layers of linen to a considerable depth.

The bandages were made from varying widths of linen. CT scans reveal that the body was first wrapped tightly with several layers of linen bandages, possibly seven or eight according to the scale on the scan. The front of the body was then padded with

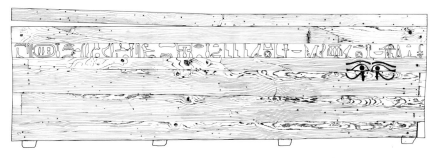

38

38

irregular wads of linen. This padding was tightly wrapped with coarsely woven linen strips, approximately nine cm. wide. After a number of such layers, a slightly less coarse fabric was used and for the upper layers a tightly woven fine fabric was substituted. The strips covering the body adjacent to the cartonnage mask were approximately ten to twelve cm. wide.

After three-quarters of the wrappings had been finished the mask was put in place and the wrapping was completed. This mask was made of cartonnage consisting of four layers of tightly woven linen, covered inside and out with gesso. The "bib" was painted white and the face painted yellow with the facial features, including eyebrows, eyes, mustache, and beard in black. Two-ply linen threads were applied to the sides and back of the mask to represent hair and were painted black. Cartonnage ears were then attached to the hair.

Approximately eight layers of fine linen were wrapped around the body after the mask was put in place. The penultimate layer was composed of twelve-cm.-wide strips wrapped from the front of the mask, around the feet and up to the back of the mask. This was anchored with a final layer of horizontally wound bandages, eight cm. wide. The mummy was lying on a large fringed sheet with the head resting on a "pillow" of folded fabric.

PL

The Mummy of Pepi-seneb

X-rays and CT scans reveal that Pepi-seneb was a man of large stature. The soft tissues of his body were not well preserved, and there was no evidence of the removal of the brain. These findings are consistent with our knowledge of mummification as

practiced during this time, when there is lit-tle evidence of elaborate embalming. The inner linen wrappings of this mummy, how-ever, have preserved the shape of the body.

A 1-cm. bone island (asymptomatic bony overgrowth) was identified in the front of the skull above the right frontal sinus.

MM

1. Lapp 1983.
2. Brovarski 1980b, col. 307.
3. The treatment of the wrappings is very similar to that of Wah excavated by the Metropolitan Museum, cf. Winlock 1940.

39
Letter to the Dead

From Naga ed-Dêr cemetery N 3500
Dynasty 6
Papyrus
Height 25.5 cm., width 15.5 cm.
Harvard University-Museum of Fine Arts Expedition, 1901-04 (47.1705)

A short letter of four vertical lines under a horizontal heading, written in black with a thick reed, appears on one side of a coarse papyrus bearing traces of an erased text. The sheet is damaged across its central axes, where it would have been folded for delivery. Syntax and paleography date the letter to Dynasty 6, a date confirmed by the name Tety-seneb, which incorporates the name of King Tety. Provenance and content indicate that the message, from an un-known writer, was intended for the dead, in this case two men. The writer directs his appeal to one of the two, and refers to both together only in descriptive phrases. Pre-sumably both men were buried in one tomb; the main addressee may have died later and so have been closer in time to the

writer. The opening words imply that an ap-peal had already been made, perhaps to the recently deceased just before his death. The absence of polite formulae indicate great familiarity, and equal status, between writer and recipient:

> Letter to Hetep-nebi (and) Teti-seneb. So then, have you seen these cries of woe, (now that) you are both here ? You are excellent, truly, but (only) for yourself here ! Heal your child ! You must seize this demon and/or demoness now. Let neither see his time. For there is no one who raises noise against the two of you here.

Only fifteen letters to the dead have sur-vived, but their range in place and date shows that they reflect a common belief

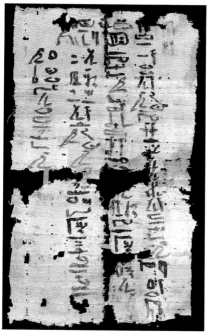

39

that ill fortune could be countered by an appeal to dead friends or family. Some letters were written on the pottery vessels used in offerings, and all were deposited at the tomb, which was perceived as the doorway between the spirit world and the living, quite literally in the false doors of the Old Kingdom (cats. 28 and 30) and later. The recurrent ''here'' in the letter denotes precisely this twilight zone where the living left food and prayers for the dead. The pleas for help form the exact mirror image of the widespread funerary prayer the ''appeal to the living'' (see essay on mortuary customs). In this letter the writer pleads with a terrible urgency ''heal your child,'' referring either to himself or to another member of the family. Disease was perceived as a hostile and personal force, to be fought by magic where medical means failed. Other letters to the dead speak of prosecuting the enemy in the legal tribunal of Osiris, but the approach of this writer is more direct, to ''seize'' the opponent. The lethal and unseen foe must not be allowed to see his ''time,'' a typically Egyptian turn of phrase to cover both the aggressor's opportunity and the victim's moment of vulnerability. To justify his appeal, the writer claims that none disturbs the tomb, peace being as important to the dead as a secure food supply. As maintainer of the cult, he feels he has a right to expect help from the deceased. These letters to the dead address not the *ka* or *ba*, but the dead man as a single individual as in life. The separate aspects of the persona clearly remain a single functioning entity, the *akh iker* ''excellent spirit,'' to which the letter alludes in ironic vein at the outset.

SQ

Bibliography: Simpson 1970, pp. 58-64; Goedicke 1972, pp. 95-98.

Literature: Grieshammer 1982, pp. 864-870; Brovarski 1982, pp. 296-317.

Middle Kingdom

40

40
Offering tray

Provenance unknown, possibly Dendera
Late First Intermediate Period to Early
Middle Kingdom
Pottery
Height 14 cm., diam. 32 cm.
Harvard University-Museum of Fine Arts
Expedition, 1907 (07.1026)

Roughly made of Nile silt, this red pottery offering tray depicts offerings of legs of beef, the head of a cow(?), and a bundle of vegetables in front of an arch roofed hut with two squat pillars flanking the entrance. Inside the hut a small bench juts out from the proper left wall; two channels or runnels start in here and were obviously impressed into the tray before the hut was added. The lintel above has since broken away. The tray upon which it sits has a raised rim and two runnels drawn out along the center to carry off libations poured on it. These ''soul houses'' are probably an elaboration of the offering basins of the Old Kingdom (see cat. 20).

Before Petrie's excavations at Rifa, few excavated examples of these objects were known. Since these trays, like the offering basins of the Old Kingdom, were meant for gifts of drink to the deceased, they had to remain exposed on the surface, and few of the humbler graves of this period had superstructures to shelter them. However, the cemetery at Rifa was situated in the outwash plain of a wadi and the graves and soul houses were soon covered with a thick layer of gravel that served to protect them from destruction.[1]

Petrie believed he could form a stylistic series of these ceramic trays that would later develop into the ''soul houses'' running from the First Intermediate Period into the Middle Kingdom;[2] however, it has now been suggested that the trays and the more elaborate ''soul houses'' are coeval, and that both belong to the Middle Kingdom.[3] This tray corresponds to Petrie's ''type A,''[4] although none of the examples from Rifa had parallel water channels as do those from Dendera[5] which may be the provenance of this piece.

PL

1. Petrie 1907, p. 14.
2. Petrie 1907, p. 14-17.
3. Niwinski 1984, pp. 806-813. This thesis, however, is not universally accepted and "early" forms are associated with First Intermediate Period cemeteries (Dorothea Arnold, personal communication).
4. Petrie 1907, pp. 16-17.
5. Petrie 1900, p. 26, pl. 19.

41

41
Soul house

From Rifa
Middle Kingdom to Second Intermediate Period
Pottery
Length 32 cm., height 36.5 cm., depth 22.5 cm.
Gift of Egyptian Research Account, 1907
(07.550)

This ceramic "soul house" from Rifa shows the development of the type from the simple hut in the center of the tray in the early examples (see cat. 40) to a model of an elaborate dwelling. This example belongs to Petrie's type E.[1] It represents a house with a columned porch such as those represented in the wooden models from the tomb of Meketre[2] and actual examples from the workmen's village at Kahun.[3] The rear wall of the structure behind the four-columned porch has a central doorway flanked by two others.

On the roof are depicted two round ventilators or *mulqafs* and between them a *satah* or an enclosed roof deck. In front of the portico a pile of food offerings is shown on the proper right, including the head of an ox, a leg of beef, loaves of bread, and bunches of vegetables. The four holes in the center were probably intended for model trees or a thatched structure surrounding the rectangular pool. A spout and runnel to carry off the libations come out from the pool.

It has been suggested that these "soul houses" develop at the same time as the simpler ceramic offering trays and served as substitute tomb chapels.[4] The presence of the runnels, however, does not support this and connects these objects with the offering trays that may indeed have been their progenitors, as Petrie initially suggested.

PL

1. Petrie 1907, p. 17.
2. Winlock 1955, pp. 17-19, pls. 9-11, figs. 56-57.
3. Badawy 1966, pp. 19-27.
4. Niwinski 1984, pp. 806-813.

Bibliography: Petrie 1907, pl. 16 A, no. 13.

42
Figures of two mourning women

Provenance unknown
Middle Kingdom, Dynasty 11
Pottery
Heights 17.5 cm. and 20 cm.
William Stevenson Smith Fund, 1983
(1983.153, 154)

Two hollow pottery statuettes of women, holding their hands to their heads in a traditional gesture of mourning, are made of a coarse-textured, straw-tempered Nile silt clay originally covered with a thin white wash. There are traces of red pigment on both figures. The left arm of the smaller figure is missing and the larger figure has been repaired. Both roughly cylindrical bodies were thrown on the wheel; the breasts, arms, and facial features were freely modeled by hand and applied to the surface. The female genitalia are crudely indicated by a rounded depression made in the damp clay before firing. The head of the large figure was wheel-made, and attached directly to the body without a neck, while that of the smaller figure was shaped by hand from a solid lump of clay.

The statuettes belong to a small group of similar painted pottery figures, all equally simply made and all representing women in a variety of mourning poses. A set of four in Brussels from Asyut[1] and a pair found in a tomb at Dendera[2] suggest that they were usually made in groups, each figure representing a different attitude of grief. These two statuettes are sufficiently distinct in style to indicate that they came from two different groups, and we have no reason to suppose that they even come from the same site, although they were purchased together. The larger of the two may be compared with a statuette in Munich, purchased by von Bissing at Arab el-Borg (near Asyut).[3] Von Bissing suggested it represented a man, taking the pointed chin as indication of a beard, but although the breasts are not shown, a deep, round depression in the region of the genitalia is like that on the smaller of the Boston figures.

During the early Middle Kingdom, figures of mourning women are common among grave goods: statuettes in painted wood were sometimes part of the equipment of model funerary boats,[4] and painted figures occur on coffins[5] and the walls of tombs. They depict mourners like those who still cry through the villages of Egypt, following the coffin, tearing their hair and garments,

42

throwing dust over their heads, and raising their arms high in the universal gesture of despair.

JB

1. Von Bissing 1931, pp. 157-160, pl. VII, 1, 2.
2. Petrie 1900, pp. 27, 65, pl. XXI, bottom left.
3. Von Bissing 1931, pl. VII, 4; Höhr-Grenzhausen, Rastel-Haus 1978, 182, p. 134.
4. Breasted 1948.
5. Garstang 1901, pl. X, E.281.

Bibliography: Museum of Fine Arts 1982-83, p. 24; Museum of Fine Arts 1987a, p. 8.

43
Tomb of Djehuty-nakht

From Deir el-Bersha tomb 10 A
Middle Kingdom, Dynasty 11

The tomb of Djehuty-nakht, nomarch of the Hare nome, is situated on the east bank of the Nile in a rocky terrace in the limestone cliffs to the north of the Wadi Der en-Nakhleh in the Gebel el-Bersha. The Harvard University-Museum of Fine Arts Expedition began excavation of this site just to the north of the modern town of Mallawi in Middle Egypt, in the spring of 1915.[1]

The excavation was particularly difficult as masses of limestone had been dislodged by earthquakes from the cliff face above, and many of the superstructures of the tombs had later been quarried away. A series of tombs stretched out along the terrace, including the famous decorated tomb of Djehuty-hotep of Dynasty 12 (cat. 47).[2] The approximate center of this group was occupied by tomb 10.

The superstructure of the tomb had been completely destroyed, but it appears to have been the standard type of early Middle Kingdom cliff tomb with an inner and outer chamber.[3] The tomb was approximately three meters wide and ten meters long. Two burial shafts were sunk into the floor of the tomb. The main shaft, A, cut down through the floor of the inner room, while a secondary shaft, B, containing the burial of an unspecified female relation, Satmeket, was found in the outer chamber.

The shaft leading to pit A was 10.56 meters deep. The fill contained numerous fragments of wooden model boats, rope, and beads, indicating the tomb had been plundered and the debris thrown back in the fill. A fragmentary unfinished statue was also found in clearing the shaft.[4] The bottom of the shaft sloped gently to the partially sealed entrance to the burial chamber. Two rough niches were visible on either side of the entrance, one containing sticks, the other containing four sealed pottery jars. The whole complex was about seven meters long and four meters wide; the burial chamber itself was only about 3.3 meters square by 2 meters tall at the rear, narrow-

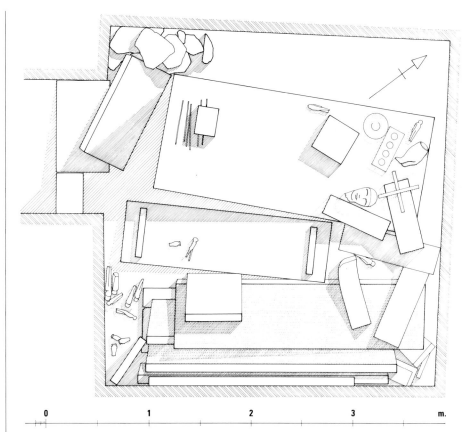

Fig. 54

ing to only 1.6 meters high at the entrance (fig. 54).

A mud-brick wall and a limestone slab partially blocked the entrance to the burial chamber. The left side of the blocking material had been been pulled down to allow access to the tomb and the interior of Djehuty-nakht's coffin. When the tomb was opened the excavators were faced with a scene of complete chaos. One set of coffins had been completely disassembled; some boards were stacked against the wall or on the floor of the burial chamber, and others had been thrown out into the pit beyond. Wooden boat models and model scenes were strewn around the chamber (see below) along with bits of mummy wrapping, fragments of jewelry, stone vessels, and other debris.

It is difficult to determine the original position of many of the objects or the exact sequence of interment and plundering. The coffins of Djehuty-nakht's wife may have been disassembled and her burial plundered when Djehuty-nakht was buried. Certainly, it would have been very difficult to fit his two large nested coffins and all the associated grave goods into the small chamber alongside the nested coffins of his wife.

The tomb was certainly robbed after the burial of Djehuty-nakht himself. It appears as though the plunderers had first tried to open the lid of the great outer coffin, but not having enough room to work in, had

then pried off the head ends of the outer and inner coffins and removed the body and other contents. The head of the nomarch was found on top of the outer coffin, along with a number of sticks, empty boxes, and the back half of a wooden mask. The torso of Djehuty-nakht's wife was found in the corner of the tomb behind her coffins; her head, legs, and arms had been ripped off by thieves in search of jewelry.

After taking what they deemed valuable, the robbers set fire to the remains of one of the mummies at the entrance to the tomb and left. Shaft B was also throughly plundered, probably soon after the burial, as was often the case.[5] However, a few fragments of a Dynasty 12 polychrome decorated coffin were found scattered just inside the tomb opening,[6] suggesting that the tomb was disturbed or lay open later in the Middle Kingdom.

PL

1. For a bibliography of earlier works on the excavation see Terrace 1967, p. 162.
2. Newberry 1893a.
3. Badawy 1966, pp. 127, 143.
4. 15-4-415; cf. Terrace 1967, p. 164, note 11.
5. Cf. Spencer 1982, pp. 76-77; Garstang 1907, pp. 91-92.
6. 21.816 and associated fragments.

Tomb Owners

The simple exterior design of his coffins and the style of their hieroglyphs make it likely that the Boston Djehuty-nakht is to be identified with either the nomarch Djehuty-nakht IV, son of Ahanakht, or with Djehuty-nakht V, the son of Nehri I; both men are known from inscriptions elsewhere at Deir el-Bersha or in the alabaster quarries at Hatnub.[7] If the latter choice is the correct one, then Djehuty-nakht, together with his brother Kay, was one of the heroes of the famous battle of Shedyetsha, probably an episode in Nebhepetre Mentuhotep's reconquest of the north.[8] Both sons of Nehri are depicted in their father's tomb at Bersha (tomb 4).[9] Both are called "eldest son," and it is possible the boys were twins or that their father had two wives. At any rate, Djehuty-nakht's mother was named Djehuty-hotep.[10]

In his coffins, Djehuty-nakht is nowhere explicitly termed nomarch, that is "Great Chief of the Hare Nome," the fifteenth Upper Egyptian province, whose capital was Khmun, the later Hermopolis and the modern El-Ashmunein, located just across the Nile from the Middle Kingdom tombs at Bersha. Instead, he is simply "Count, Controller of the Two Thrones." At Bersha "Controller of the Two Thrones" was a title of the high priest of Thoth, an office held by the nomarch.[11] In fact, in all the coffins preserved, the political title of nomarch is omitted for unknown reasons, and the rulers buried at Bersha are regularly "Count, Controller of the Two Thrones" or "Count, Controller of the Two Thrones, Overseer of Priests." Sometimes they are also "Greatest of Five" or "Great *wab* of Thoth," two other priestly titles connected with the ibis god.[12]

Djehuty-nakht's wife was also named Djehuty-nakht, "Thoth-is-Strong" or "Victorious," a seemingly martial name for a woman, but evidently not deemed so in the Hare nome.[13] The lady Djehuty-nakht receives two titles repeatedly, those of "Hereditary Princess" and "Royal Ornament." The first indicates a high rank indeed and implies that she was herself a member of the ruling family, not improbably a close relative of her husband's. The title "Royal Ornament" was commonly applied to the wives and daughters of high officials, especially in the Old Kingdom and the First Intermediate Period, as the feminine counterpart of the masculine honorific "Sole Friend." It may originally have been an actual designation of rank indicating high position at court, later becoming an indication of or claim to royal favor.[14]

The relationship of Satmeket, who was buried at the bottom of the shaft in the outer chamber of the tomb, to the two Djehuty-nakhts is uncertain. Perhaps she was a daughter. The title "Hereditary Princess" also occurs on one of the boards of her badly damaged coffins.

EB

7. Brovarski 1981, pp. 22-25.
8. See e.g., Anthes 1928, pp. 93-96; Hayes 1971, pp. 470-471; Fischer 1966; Faulkner 1944, pp. 61-63; Schenkel 1964, pp. 84-95.
9. Griffith and Newberry 1894, p. 29 and pl. 11, figs. 1-3.
10. Brovarski 1981, p. 22 and n. 107.
11. Anthes 1928, pp. 97, 107.
12. Brovarski 1981, p. 23.
13. Ranke 1935, p. 408[7].
14. Nord 1970.

Coffins

There were originally five coffins in the tomb. Djehuty-nakht had an inner and outer set of wooden box coffins, while his wife had three coffins.[15] The coffins are made of thick cedar boards with housed miter joints and were fitted together with wooden pegs, tenons and bands of copper. The bottom was rabbeted to the sides of the coffin, tied with copper bands, and secured with dowels. To the underside were attached four cross braces. The lids have two crossbraces doweled to either end on the interior side, and at each end of the lid are the remains of two cylindrical lugs used to lift the lid into position. The large outer coffin of Djehuty-nakht rested on a wooden sledge.

The coffins are finely painted,[16] but continue the design tradition developed in the First Intermediate Period (see cat. 38). The exterior is decorated only with a band of text around the top of the box and down the center of the lid, while two *wedjat* eyes are painted at the head end of the left side. It is the interior decoration of the outer coffin of Djehuty-nakht that makes it the finest of the Middle Kingdom painted coffins to survive.[17] The eastern panel shows the deceased seated before a table of offerings and attended by a priest who offers up a dish of incense. The accompanying text reads "burning incense for your *kas* twice." Behind him is an elaborately painted false door. The rest of the panel below the offering formula is taken up by a compartment list of offerings, with rows of kneeling offering bearers presenting birds, cuts of meat, jars of beer, baskets, and vessels of endless variety – all painted with the greatest care and sensitivity.

The other long side of the outer coffin is decorated with an object frieze paralleled in many coffins of the period (fig. 55).[18] These are two-dimensional representations of the objects the deceased frequently also had in his tomb. They are laid out in sequence, beginning with headrests at the head end of the coffin, a lion-headed bed, three different types of razors, including hafted razors in a case, fresh sheets, and a magic wand (see

Fig. 55

cat. 59). Next come a series of broad collars and counterpoises on caskets, weapons and staffs, a beaded kilt, bead necklaces and bracelets, an openwork fan, and a mirror in its basketwork case. Thereafter follow scribal palettes and other equipment, a beaded kilt, bracelets, *hes* vases on a table and in a shrine-shaped box, arrows and quivers, sacks of material labeled "equipment of the king," tables with offerings, ewers and basins, a cowhide shield, spearcase, and quiver of arrows, and a set of carpenter's tools. Below are incised columns of Coffin Texts.

The interior head and foot ends of the outer coffin are decorated with spells composed of large painted hieroglyphs, while additional spells from the Coffin Texts are incised below. The head end also features brightly painted vessels containing the seven sacred oils, and bags of both green and black eye paint. The lid bears two lines of ornamental hieroglyphs separated by many columns of incised Coffin Texts. The bottom of the coffin is also covered with Coffin Texts. Texts are similarly inscribed on many of the pegs joining the coffin and on the ends of the timbers. The inner coffin of Djehuty-nakht is decorated with spells from the Book of the Two Ways[19] which include a "road map" of the Underworld.

The inner, middle, and outer coffins of Djehuty-nakht's wife are similarly decorated, albeit not as fine as Djehuty-nakht's great outer coffin. None of the three coffins bears the Book of the Two Ways.

PL

15. Outer coffin of Djehuty-nakht (20.1822-6). Lid: length 263 cm., width 115 cm.; sides: length 262 cm., width 115 cm.; head end: length 100 cm., width 105 cm.; foot end: length 115 cm., width 116 cm.; bottom: length 245 cm., width 96 cm.
Inner coffin of Djehuty-nakht (21.962,963). Lid: length 224 cm., width 75.5 cm.; box: length 224.1 cm., width 80 cm., depth 75 cm. Middle Coffin of Lady Djehuty-nakht (21.964,965). Lid: length 243.5 cm., width 84 cm., depth 13.5 cm.; box: length 243 cm., width 85 cm., depth 89 cm.
Inner coffin of Lady Djehuty-nakht (21.966,967). Lid: length 205.5 cm., width 49 cm.; box: length 205.5 cm., width 56.5 cm., depth 52.5 cm. See also De Buck 1956.
16. Terrace 1967.
17. Terrace 1967.
18. Jéquier 1921.
19. Lesko 1972.

Canopic Equipment

Only one canopic jar (fig. 56) was found in the tomb, on top of Djehuty-nakht's large outer coffin.[20] Unlike earlier canopic jars, which were of simple shape and manufactured of limestone or alabaster (see cat. 10), this one is made of cartonnage, and takes the form of a human body with two feet. The top of the jar is now distorted, and only faint traces of paint remain, but slightly bent

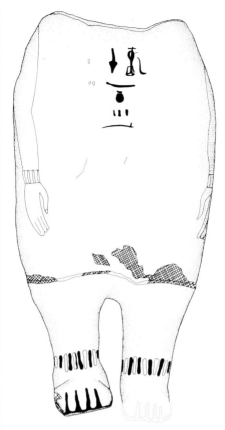

Fig. 56

arms were painted in black at the sides. Bracelets and anklets were indicated with green and black stripes, and the toes were delineated in black paint. The inscription on the front of the jar names Qebehsenuef, one of the protective Four Sons of Horus and the guardian of the intestines. Traces of the original contents, which were probably wrapped in linen, remain.

A human-headed cartonnage canopic jar lid[21] was also found in the burial chamber, at the southwest corner of the nomarch's coffin. It is greatly decayed, and the face is entirely missing, but parts of a blue wig (now faded to green) as well as a blue, red, and yellow broad collar, are visible. Human-headed lids begin to appear in the First Intermediate Period,[22] and Middle Kingdom cartonnage jars and lids have survived,[23] but cartonnage lids usually take the form of miniature mummy masks that were sometimes attached directly to the organ package.[24]

The cedar wood canopic box[25] was found in nearly forty fragments in the burial chamber west of Djehuty-nakht's large outer coffin. Parts of a second box were also found.[26] Canopic boxes, first found in Dynasty 4, were intended to house the mummified viscera, and thus their shape and decoration replicate the coffins that housed the bodies. They often contain inscriptions dedicating the deceased to the Four Sons of Horus, and in turn the protectors of the Four Sons – Isis, Nephthys, Selkit, and Neith.[27]

The canopic box of Djehuty-nakht is composed of four cedar boards on each side. Two sides also contain an inner liner of three boards, which has been pegged to the outer side. The ends of the liner sides were mitered to fit the miter housing on the unlined sides. The base is set on two runners pegged into the bottom. The lid, which was constructed of two planks secured by pegs, originally had two cross-braces on the underside that were also pegged in.

Each interior side is inscribed with six columns of incised hieroglyphs, and the underside of the lid contains five columns of cursive hieroglyphs in black paint. The texts on the interior are standard Coffin Texts for canopic boxes of the period.[28] They are surmounted by the names of the Four Sons of Horus, and are accompanied on two sides by the figures of Neith and Selkit, respectively. On the corresponding outer sides of the box, very faded inscriptions associate the name of Djehuty-nakht with each of the canopic deities. The box belonged to the wife of Djehuty-nakht, rather than to the nomarch himself.[29]

SD'A

20. 15-5-278, MFA 21.424: height 29.8 cm., diam. 17.8 cm.; see Brovarski 1978, intro. and p. 89.
21. 21.425: height 12.1 cm., diam. 7 cm.
22. Brovarski 1978, intro.
23. Hayes 1953, fig. 210.
24. Garstang 1907, p. 93, fig. 83.
25. 15-5-214, 282, 296, MFA 21.421,22; height 59.7 cm., width 54.6 cm.
26. 15-5-272, 15-5-388.
27. For general discussions of early Middle Kingdom canopic boxes, see Hayes 1953, pp. 320-323; Martin 1978, pp. 319-320; Rogouline 1965, pp. 237-254. For other Bersha canopic boxes, see Reisner 1967, pp. 377, 382-386.
28. Spells 520-523; cf. de Buck 1956, pp. 109-116.
29. *im₃ht* is written with a t replacing the usual phonetic complement ẖ.

Mummies

The mummies of both Djehuty-nakht and his wife were removed from their coffins by ancient tomb robbers, who were presumably in search of jewelry. Very little in the way of human remains was recovered by the excavators. A male head found on top of the coffin of the nomarch probably belonged to Djehuty-nakht himself.[30] The head was elaborately treated, and provides us with information concerning the mummification process at a period from which very little evidence survives (see essay on mummification). Layers of linen were molded to the skull to give it a lifelike appearance. A coarser layer at the top of the head forms a cap, much of which has decayed, revealing a great deal of well-preserved, dark brown and wavy hair. The eyebrows were painted black.

X-ray evidence indicating that this is a male skull includes the well-developed vascular grooves on the inner surface of the skull; the large, well-developed sinuses (especially the frontal); the very large and developed mastoid air cells; as well as the rugged architecture of the skull, with its strong square jaw.

CT scans of the head have revealed that the skin, nose, and lips are very well preserved, an indication of the great advances made in mummification since its first use in the Archaic Period and Old Kingdom. There was still experimentation, however, and the CT scan of the skull of Djehuty-nakht did produce one rather surprising find: the brain had been removed, a process not performed with regularity until Dynasty 18.[31] The head of Djehuty-nakht shows that the process was in an experimental stage, because the route of removal was very different from that in use during later times, namely through the nose. Holes were punched through Djehuty-nakht's maxillary sinuses, and the brain was removed through the ethmoid air cells and sphenoid sinuses. This process damaged the skull, resulting in fractures in the outer orbits of the eyes that are commonly seen in X-rays of modern boxers.

The torso of another mummy was found in the southwest corner of the burial chamber, propped against the wall.[32] It was determined to be female, on the basis of its subpubic angle (which determines the width of the pelvis), which is greater than 90 degrees, and the flaring of the right ilium (large bone of the hip).[33]

Excavation records include other references to fragmentary human remains in the tomb,[34] but the ancient plunderers did a very thorough job of destroying the bodies.

SD'A/MM

30. 15-5-279, MFA 21.11767.
31. Dawson and Gray 1968, p. ix.
32. 15-5-280.
33. Douglas Hanson, personal communication.
34. 15-5-85 (leg), 15-5-156 (hand), 15-5-618 (a few unidentified bones), and 15-5-12 (skull found just inside the entrance to the chamber).

Masks

The remains of at least two mummy masks – one of wood and the other of cartonnage – were found in the tomb. Both are typical of the late First Intermediate Period and early Middle Kingdom with high, narrow lappet wigs and long "bibs" (see cat. 46). The rear portion of the wooden mask was found on the lid of the disassembled coffins. It had been split down the middle, and the upper portion comprising the wig was painted blue-green.[35] It had a finished edge, and pegs connected it to the front of the mask. Scraps of wood with paint and gold foil seem to be from this part of the mask. It had obviously been torn to pieces to get at the gold. Fragments from the back of a similar mask were found in shaft B.[36]

Only the lower front half of the cartonnage mask survived.[37] The bib was discolored a yellowish brown with a broad collar painted in alternating bands of blue, white, green, and red, with blue teardrop pendants. The ends of the lappet wig were blue green. The face was completely destroyed except for an inlaid eye of ivory fixed in a copper setting.[38] A wooden ear painted yellow with two pegs for attachment may have belonged to this or the other mask. [39]

PL

35. 15-5-204: height 77 cm., width 35.5 cm., depth 15 cm.
36. 15-5-742: hieght 73 cm., width 25 cm., max. depth 3 cm.
37. 21.429: height (preserved) 42 cm., width 34 cm., depth 1 cm.
38. 21.471: length 4.5 cm., height 2 cm., depth 0.8 cm.
39. 15-5-15: height 5.8 cm., width 2 cm., depth 1.9 cm.

Fig. 57

Jewelry

The jewelry of the Middle Kingdom is renowned,[40] and doubtless the tomb of Djehuty-nakht contained many fine examples, which were the chief target of the tomb's plunderers. The few fragments that survive suggest that there were a large number of bracelets, anklets, and collars in gold, glazed steatite, amethyst, carnelian, shell, and faience. A number of parallels can be drawn between the bits that remain and the great jewelry finds of the Middle Kingdom.[41] Broad collar terminals and fragments of terminals, along with pieces of strung beadwork, suggest that the burial contained a number of such collars. These include a collar with blue faience hawk-headed terminals, probably the *wshn bik*, the hawk collar specified in lists of Middle Kingdom tomb equipment.[42] One or more blue beaded *wah* collars with semicircular terminals in blue faience[43] and a collar of multicolored faience beads with gold semicircular terminals and teardrop pendants would also have been included.[44]

There is also evidence for necklaces and bracelets or anklets of blue faience beads and bright blue glazed steatite beads. Very large, long, light green-blue steatite beads

may have formed a heavy collar,[45] a staff, or even a beaded kilt.[46]

A petunculus shell necklace[47] was also part of the jewelry of the tomb. A gold band .8 cm. wide with pierced, rounded ends would have been tied with a cord passed through the ends and worn as a bracelet.[48] There was also a scarab, a carnelian barrel or *swrt* bead, and a cylindrical blue glazed steatite bead on a cord (fig. 57).[49]

PL

40. Cf. Aldred 1971, pp. 87-81.
41. Aldred 1971, 130-132, 141, 145, 148; pls. 6-12, 19-47, and 73-81. Also Farag 1971.
42. Mace and Winlock 1916, p. 65.
43. 21.478a-b, length 5.6, width 2.6 cm.; cf. Aldred 1971, pl 20.
44. 21.460, 15-5-117 et al.; cf. Mace and Winlock 1916, pp. 67-68, pl. 26b.
45. 15-5-32, length 3.5 cm., diam. 1 cm.; cf. Andrews 1981, pls. 28, 46.
46. Hayes 1953, p. 309, fig. 200.
47. 15-5-194 et al.; cf. Engelbach 1923, p. 16.
48. 21.386: width .8 cm., length 6.1 cm.; cf. Wilkinson 1971, p. 64; also MMA 25.3.247 a-c.
49. Aldred 1971, pl. 21.

Models

Djehuty-nakht's burial chamber contained what is probably the largest collection of Middle Kingdom wooden models ever found, including more than fifty-five boats, at least thirty-three scenes, and a dozen or more small individual figures of offering bearers.

The original position of the models is difficult to determine because of the chaotic state of the burial chamber. Models from undisturbed graves at other sites have been found carefully positioned on top of the coffin lid and on the floor around it. The Djehuty-nakht models, on the other hand, had been flung into every part of the burial chamber, with miniature tools and containers, individual figures, and dozens of small sticklike arms littering the floor (fig. 58).

The vast majority of the models were heaped between the left side of the coffin and the west wall of the chamber. They were thrown there with no regard for their fragility, some landing on their sides, some upside down. One must assume that this was the work of robbers rather than people authorized to re-open the tomb for the second burial. It is inconceivable that priests or officials presiding over the initial burial or a subsequent interment would have treated the contents in so violent a fashion. Like the other grave goods, the models had been included for a purpose – to ensure a continued supply of goods for the spirit in the afterlife. Destruction of the models or the separation of figures from their scenes would have rendered them useless for this purpose.

In 1915, when Bersha 10A was discovered, little had been written on models, though many had been found and small groups

Fig. 58

Fig. 59

Fig. 60

Fig. 61

from other sites had been published.[50] Because of the relative lack of published comparative material, and the fragmentary condition of some of the Bersha models, it is not surprising that many of the scenes were not correctly identified at the time of their discovery. The result was that the diversity of the Djehuty-nakht collection went unacknowledged. While a few of the easily recognized scenes and boats were cited by Breasted,[51] most remain unpublished.

The quality of the Bersha models is inconsistent, ranging from the superb workmanship of the Bersha procession (see color plates) to the rough stick figures found in most of the boats and scenes. In spite of their crudeness, the tasks being performed in these scenes can usually be identified by comparison to other, more complete examples. Models from the tomb of Meket-Re, because of their detail, were invaluable in reconstructing the Bersha models.

CHR

Model Scenes

Agriculture and food preparation were among the most important activities in ancient Egypt. For this reason, they were commonly represented in the decoration of non-royal tombs, especially during the Old and New Kingdoms. Though such scenes are also found in decorated tombs of the First Intermediate Period and the early Middle Kingdom,[52] they are far more frequently preserved in the wooden tomb models that abound during these periods.

Unlike the Meket-Re scenes, which were usually provided with their own buildings, those from Bersha were assembled on rough bases made from irregularly shaped wooden planks. Slits in the long sides of many of the planks indicate that they once formed parts of boxes of mortise and tenon construction. In several cases, broken tenons are still held in place by dowels.[53] Knot holes and old dowel holes were usually plugged before new holes were drilled for the placement of figures. This can be confusing when attempting to reconstruct incomplete scenes since many of the dowels have fallen out, and it is not always clear which holes were for dowels and which were for the legs of the figures.

More than half of the scenes from Djehuty-nakht's tomb represent some aspect of food production, from ploughing the fields[54] to preparing bread and beer. The most common type of model scene – men working in a granary – is represented by no less than eight examples in Bersha 10A (fig. 59). Unlike all other scenes from this tomb, each granary scene was enclosed in a small box meant to represent a granary building with its roof removed. The corners come to peaks at the top, a typical feature of granary buildings in both models and wall paintings.[55] The walls are painted beige with a series of slanting red lines along their curved tops. There is a door painted on the outside of one wall and a t-shaped red line runs halfway up each corner.

Each granary originally included three figures: a man standing up straight, carrying a full sack of grain; a man bending over, using a pail to scoop up the grain, perhaps to measure it for counting or distribution; and a scribe squatting in one corner of the granary with a board on his knees, recording the amount of grain.

All but three of the granaries were found completely disassembled, their components scattered about the tomb. The example in fig. 59[56] was intact despite having been buried upside down at the bottom of the heap (see fig. 58).

Another very common scene – the making of bread and beer – is represented by at least three examples in Bersha 10A. The most complete includes three women and one man preparing bread and beer.[57] The women are painted yellow and wear white skirts. One woman prepares flour, a second carries a tray of loaves to the third, who squats down before a fire where the loaves are to bake.[58] The man presses mash through a sieve to make beer that will be stored in the jar in front of him.

Raising and slaughtering cattle for domestic and ritual purposes was another important aspect of food production. Considering the frequency with which one finds slaughtering scenes in Old Kingdom tomb reliefs, it is odd that there is no evidence of such a scene among the Bersha 10A models. There are, however, nine representations of another stage of meat production – the force feeding of cattle. Each of these (fig. 60)[59] represents a squatting man with his right hand extended toward a black and white spotted steer (or bull). The animal and base are carved from the same piece of wood while the man is attached to the base with a dowel. Similar figures form part of the Meket-Re stable scene.

Production of necessities other than food was also represented in model form, though such scenes are less common. The tomb of Djehuty-nakht contained two models of weavers. In one of these (fig. 61),[60] the two woman at the front are engaged in spinning. The standing woman takes flax fibers from the woman squatting behind her and spins them into linen thread against her raised knee.[61] The two women at the back are tending a loom, represented by four pegs.

A carpentry scene (fig. 62)[62] shows a man sawing boards. In more carefully made scenes, the piece of wood being sawed is lashed to a post to keep it steady.[63] Here, there is merely a post with a thin slit in the

Fig. 62

Fig. 63

Fig. 64

top for the insertion of a miniature saw that has not been found. The saw in the photograph is from Bersha 10B. Judging from the Meket-Re carpenters, the squatting man of the Bersha model was probably using an adze to even out the plank of wood in front of him. A second piece of wood, attached to the base with dowels, has a red line painted down the center in preparation for cutting.

The tomb of Djehuty-nakht also included several types of scenes not found among the Meket-Re models. One of the most unusual depicts men making bricks. Two ex-

amples of this scene were found in the tomb. Though crudely made, the scene in fig. 63[64] shows great attention to detail. Two men at one end of the scene are digging clay. One uses a hoe while the other uses his hands, perhaps to knead the clay. The base of the scene was painted black, as were the hands of the squatting figure. The two men in the center were probably originally carrying a basket of clay slung from a pole between them. The man at the front is making bricks with a wooden mold and setting them out to dry. Two rows of bricks and part of a third have been scratched into the base and painted black. The round black spots behind the man with the mold probably represent clay ready to be packed into the mold.

The final scene (fig. 64)[65] depicts a group of four marching soldiers. Two of them carry arrow or spear quivers painted to resemble cowhide. As is frequently the case in this tomb, two such scenes were found.

CHR

Model Boats

Models of boats have been found in great abundance in First Intermediate Period and early Middle Kingdom tombs. Since the Nile was the main route of transportation as well as a major source of food in the form of fish and water fowl, boats were considered necessary in the afterlife. They also played an important role in religious mythology and therefore in funerary ritual.

Two or more boats were usually included in a burial. At least one, representing the crew sailing upstream, would be placed in the tomb facing south;[66] another, its crew rowing downstream, would be placed with the bow facing north.

The Egyptians used both papyrus[67] and wood to construct river craft; model boats may be separated into two categories, according to which material is imitated. Funeral tradition seems to have required the use of "papyrus" boats for the journey to Abydos, though these boats were probably made of wood, at least in Dynastic times.[68]

Since the original papyrus craft were rafts, the bow and stern were usually pulled upright to prevent them from being swamped.[69] The model "papyrus" boats imitate this and generally have two steering oars secured to a board across the stern and supported by two stanchions. Though papyrus boats from other tombs are generally painted green, suggesting that fresh papyrus was used,[70] those from Bersha 10A are invariably yellow, suggesting the use of dried papyrus.

Model wooden boats are generally wider, with pointed bow and stern. The decks of the Bersha boats are usually painted in red and white, the red depicting the superstructure of beams and crossboards, the white

Fig. 65

showing the hatches or deck planking, or both. The stern is often higher than the bow and ends in a chock with a recess to hold the steering oar. This oar is supported by a large stanchion.

In the tomb of Djehuty-nakht, there were more than fifty-five boats. Seven of these represent papyrus boats, the rest represent wooden boats. Roughly twenty are under sail and another twenty are rowed, while six others are either poled or towed.[71] As is true of the model scenes, there are often two or more examples of each type of boat.

The funerary boat (fig. 65)[72] is typical of the papyrus boats in Bersha 10A. The bow is barrel-shaped as though many stalks of papyrus had been bound together. A rosette imitating a papyrus umbel has been attached to the end. Unlike most papyrus boats, the bow has not been bent upright. The stern section is made from a separate piece of wood. This juts forward and up and is again decorated with a rosette. The rosettes are split into pie-shaped sections painted alternately red and white. The hull is decorated with a *wedjat* eye on either side of the bow. On the deck is a small baldachin with a bier beneath. There is no evidence that there was ever a mummy on the bier.

The boat is propelled downstream by six rowers. A helmsman sits between the two stanchions just behind the baldachin. An eighth crew member stands in the prow and acts as a lookout. All eight men are painted red and wear short black wigs and white kilts.

The steering oars have been lashed to the stanchions following the example of the Meketre boats. Since this would leave no room for maneuvering the oars for effective steering, it seems likely that they were immobilized only when the boat was on a straight course. They could then be untied when the helmsman needed to use them for landing the boat or steering around a sand bar or some other obstacle.

One of the largest of the wooden boats is a traveling boat with a large cabin (fig. 66).[73] It is difficult to tell how this boat was propelled. Of the three missing crew members, the one in the bow is certainly the typical lookout who was meant to hold either a

Fig. 66

Fig. 67

Fig. 68

Fig. 69

lead line or sounding pole. The other two crew members were standing at the edge of the deck on either side of the mast. Among the Bersha models, sailing boats usually have three to five figures standing behind the mast raising the sail, while boats being rowed are usually shown with at least six kneeling or squatting figures. The existence of the mast fork, used to support the dismantled mast, suggests that the boat was not being sailed. It is possible that two

of the missing crew members were using poles to guide the ship to shore.

The cabin was built with two hinged doors and a canopy in front. Beneath this canopy a table and chest were pushed against the cabin wall to make room for the figure of the deceased and three attendants. The deceased is shown enveloped in the customary robe with only his shaved head protruding. To the side stands a fifth figure, dressed as a priest with long skirt, short-cropped hair, and yellow skin. On top of the cabin sits the helmsman.

The traveling boat may have towed a small kitchen boat (fig. 67).[74] This was provided with a cabin, various containers for food and drink, and a brazier for cooking. The cook sits fanning the fire in the bow and the helmsman sits on top of the cabin.

Boats used for fishing and fowling were also found among the Bersha models. Fig. 68[75] shows a small boat used for catching water fowl. Only one of its three crew members, the helmsman, is still in place. Two small birds crouch in the center of the deck. A second man sat behind the birds while in the bow stood a lookout. This boat may have been propelled as well as steered by the oar at the back. A similar boat with two seated figures was also found in the tomb.

Finally, a long narrow craft carries shields and a quiver of spears (fig. 69).[76] This boat is crewed by eighteen rowers (one of which is missing), a helmsman and a lookout. A long peg and a mallet on the deck were used when the boat was moored along the river's bank.

CHR

Offering Bearers

Wooden statuettes of individual female offering bearers and processions of men and women bringing gifts are common in First Intermediate Period and Middle Kingdom tombs. The statuettes of women carrying baskets on their heads (fig. 70)[77] are from the same tradition as the larger statues of striding female offering bearers discussed in cat. 36. At least eight of these figures were found in Bersha 10A, some clothed, some naked, each balancing a basket on her head with her left hand. Unlike many of the larger examples, these women carry nothing in their right hands.[78] They are also shown with their feet together rather than striding. Each figure is carved from one piece of wood with the arms and basket added. The peg legs fit into two holes in the base and the feet, when preserved, are of plaster.

Though they are roughly the same size, no two of these figures are exactly the same, showing differences in hairstyle or dress. On their heads most carry almost identical baskets whose contents are unidentifiable.

These figures are of mediocre quality, though they are more carefully made than most of the figures in the models discussed above.

A finely crafted standing figure of a woman with her arms at her sides in the traditional pose (fig. 71)[79] may depict the woman Djehuty-nakht. She is somewhat smaller than the offering bearers, but is carved with far greater care. Her lappet wig is painted black, the hair nearly reaching her waist in the back. Her face is well modeled, the brows and large eyes outlined in black while the eyes themselves are black and white. Her fingernails and toenails are white. The rest of the statuette, including the base, shows traces of yellow paint. The feet are

Fig. 70

Fig. 71

Fig. 72

partially carved from the same piece of wood as the rest of the statue, the toes having been carved from another piece attached with a dowel. A tenon at the bottom of the figure fits into the base and is held in place with a dowel on each side.

The tomb also contained a dozen well-carved male offering bearers, among which were a priest and a scribe (fig. 72).[80] None of the figures was attached to a base, and all have short-cropped hair rather than wigs. Apart from the priest, who is painted the characteristic yellow, the figures are painted red and wear white kilts.

These figures probably formed a procession of offering bearers led by the priest, with the scribe either at the beginning or the end of the procession. The quality of carving of these figures is better than that of the female offering bearers, though not as good as the standing woman just mentioned.

The prize among the models from this tomb is the Bersha procession (see color plates),[81] a piece of unrivalled quality. The missing elements of the procession have recently been discovered and, after having been displayed for many years without all of its offerings, the procession has been reconstructed. The priest leading the procession, formerly shown carrying the *hes* vase over his left shoulder and the mirror case in his right hand, now carries an incense burner in his right hand.[82] The two women in the center still carry baskets on their heads and ducks in their right hands, as is common for female offering bearers. The woman at the end of the procession, previously shown without any offerings, now carries a small chest[83] on her left shoulder and the mirror case slung over her right shoulder on a strap of linen thread.[84]

The Bersha procession, one of the finest examples of wood carving from any period in Egyptian history, exemplifies the violent disregard with which the models were treated. In fig. 73, the baskets of the women may be seen on the floor on either side of the model. According to the excavation records, the *hes* vase, one of the geese, and the mirror handle were also found in this area. Other pieces of the procession – the mirror cover, the incense burner, the second goose, and half of the painted chest held by the third woman – were scattered around the coffin.

CHR

50. The famous models from the Theban tomb of Meket-Re (Winlock 1955), the best documented to date, and the most complete set ever published, were not discovered until 1920.
51. Breasted 1948.
52. For one example, see the ploughing scene in the Theban tomb of Djar, Smith 1981, p. 155, fig. 147.
53. One tenon is still in place in the base of 21.411. The possibility that the bases might once have been attached to one another to form larger scenes is unlikely since none of the mortises can be matched up.
54. 21.408: published in Breasted 1948, p. 7, pl. 2a.
55. For other examples, see Breasted 1948, pls. 9-14.
56. 21.409: length 29 cm., width 29 cm., height 29 cm.
57. 21.886: length 28 cm., width 22 cm., height 24.3 cm.
58. See Breasted 1948, p. 39; pl. 37b.
59. 21.823: length 32 cm., width 8.5 cm., height 8 cm. See also Breasted 1948, p. 8, pl. 5a for another example from the same tomb.
60. 21.891: length 40.5 cm., width 14 cm., height 27 cm.
61. Women in similar poses may be seen in the Meket-Re weaving scene. See Winlock 1955, pls. 25-27.
62. 21.412: length 23 cm., width 18 cm., height 27.5 cm.
63. See Winlock 1955, pls. 28-29.
64. 21.411: length 54.5 cm., width 17.4 cm., height 25.5 cm. Published in Breasted 1948, p. 52, pl. 46c. Breasted seems to have been unaware of the second scene of brickmakers from the same tomb.
65. 21.803: length 39.5 cm., width 12.5 cm., height 18 cm.
66. The prevailing wind in Egypt is northerly.
67. Papyrus can grow taller than 5 m., with a base diam. 15 cm. see Landström 1970, p.17.
68. See also Landström 1970, p. 24. The cedar funerary boat of Khufu is decorated with papyrus motifs at bow and stern, see Jenkins 1980.
69. See Landström 1970, p. 18, fig. 51.
70. Landström 1970, p. 18.
71. Though most of the boats are missing some, if not all, of their original crew members and equipment, it is usually possible to determine by the number and distribution of holes in the decks whether they were being sailed or rowed.
72. 21.829: length 80 cm., width 12.5 cm., height 30.5 cm. Published in Breasted 1948, p. 68; pl. 64a.
73. 21.406: length 106 cm., width 26.5 cm., height 48 cm. Published in Breasted 1948, pp. 83-84; pl. 77a.

74. 21.494: length 55 cm., width 14 cm., height 30.5 cm. Published in Breasted 1948, p. 84, pl. 76a.
75. 21.890: length 40 cm., width 11.5 cm., height 24 cm. Breasted 1948, p. 84; pl. 77b (detail of birds).
76. 21.407: length 127 cm., width 19.5 cm., height 44.5 cm. Breasted 1948, p. 103; pl. 96a,b.
77. 21.484: base length 9 cm., width 6.7 cm., height 35 cm. 21.882: Base length 14 cm., width 8 cm., height 41 cm.
78. For other examples, see Breasted 1948, esp. pls. 52b, 53a, 55b, 58a.
79. 20.1127: base length 12.2 cm., width 7.5 cm., height 28.5 cm.
80. 21.11769: length 7 cm., width 5 cm., height 23 cm.
81. 21.326: length 66.4 cm., width 8 cm., height 41.5 cm. Published in Terrace 1968.
82. The incense burner is published in Terrace 1968, p. 19, fig. 21. For a similar model from the tomb of Meket-Re see Winlock 1955, pl. 32.
83. Only half of the box is original; the other half was reconstructed by the MFA research lab.
84. Linen thread was found in the woman's fist and at one end of the mirror case. A female offering bearer found at Deir el-Bahri carries a mirror case in a similar fashion, see Lilyquist 1979, fig. 52.

Fig. 73

Sticks and Staves

The inclusion of wooden sticks and staves in the burial reaches its zenith in the Middle Kingdom. In the Old Kingdom, walking sticks and wands as symbols of office were often depicted in relief or in the hands of statues; actual examples were occasionally included in the burial.[85] Sticks and staves along with bows and arrows become notable features of burials of the First Intermediate Period and continue on into the later Middle Kingdom.[86] More than one set can appear in a tomb; included in the burials of both women and men, they were sometimes ritually broken when deposited in the tomb.[87]

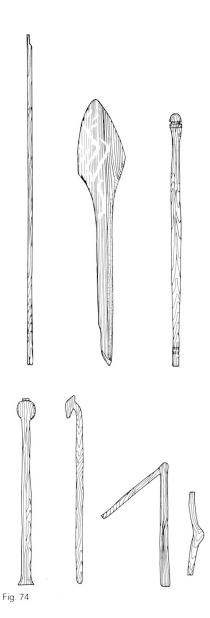

Fig. 74

The tomb of Djehuty-nakht contained well over 250 sticks and staves. Some, but not all, of these had been broken. Largely made of acacia wood, they range from twigs and branches to highly carved and finished pieces, although most are roughly carved (fig. 74). The sticks and staves found in the tomb include a wood model mace,[88] a *was* scepter,[89] a flail,[90] and the curious jointed or bent staff.[91] There were also examples of the *mdw* and *imyt-r* staffs,[92] the staff with forked bottom,[93] and the curved staff.[94]

Two large wooden oars were found, as in the tomb of Tutankamen.[95] Bows and model arrows were also found in the tomb, along with a large number of plain sticks and twigs of no certain purpose.

PL

85. See for example a *sekhem* wand from Giza 2011, MFA 37.1318, and a long staff from the same tomb, 37.1323.
86. Williams 1976.
87. Mace and Winlock 1916, pp. 76-103.
88. 21.814: length 46 cm., max. width 4.5 cm.

89. 21.440: length 48 cm., max. width 3 cm.
90. No number: length 32 cm., max. width 16 cm.
91. 21.846a-b: length 18.1 cm., 2 cm. wide, cf. Mace and Winlock 1916, pp. 78-79.
92. Eg. 21.439c: length 68 cm, width 2 cm. Cf. Fischer 1978b. pp. 5-7.
93. Fischer 1978b, pp. 17-18.
94. Fischer 1978b, pp. 7-15.
95. 15-5-743: length 71 cm., width (paddle end) 11 cm. Cf. Carter 1927, pp. 5, 32.

Miscellaneous

Two rough boxes were found on top of the coffin of Djehuty-nakht; the larger one was in pieces, while the smaller was intact, but empty. Both had originally been covered with a coat of white gesso.[96]

Fragments of a small round cake of vegetable matter were also found in the debris of the tomb. These cakes have been found in other burials of this date, placed near the head.[97]

Miniature food offerings made of cartonnage were also found in the tomb. They represent such basic food offerings as red and yellow onions, garlic, and ripe and unripe figs (fig. 75).[98] These were made either by covering a ball of linen thread with plaster, which was then painted (the onions), or by wrapping the ball of thread in a finely woven piece of cloth, which was covered with plaster and painted (the garlic). Other cartonnage offerings include a miniature duck with a ceramic core, and numerous fragmentary lotus blossoms.

Four small wooden tables were discovered in pieces around the tomb. These are roughly the same size[99] and each has either four or six dowel holes evenly distributed on the surface for the attachment of small faience vessels that were also found scattered about the tomb.[100] These may be related to the *pesesh-kef* sets found in the Old Kingdom (see cat. 11).

Scattered about the tomb were several dozen *hes* vases, ranging from a very small wooden vase covered with gold leaf[101] to a medium-size faience vase,[102] and including about two dozen alabaster vases. Most of these were found in groups of four attached in a single row to crude wooden boards with round depressions carved in the surface for the vases to stand in. One such set was found on top of the coffin.[103]

A length of linen fabric was included in the burial.[104] A fringe was attached to one side by weaving groups of five threads through the warp threads of the selvage. The warp ends of the textile were fringed by removing several weft threads. The fabric was saturated with a gummy substance, darkening the color to a red-brown. There are numerous holes in the fabric, but none appears to be the result of wear.

PL/CHR/ML

96. Mace and Winlock 1916, p. 106
97. Mace and Winlock 1916, p. 105.

98. The largest of these is 1 cm. long and .8 cm. wide.
99. 21.475: length 22.7 cm., width 16.5 cm., height 9.2 cm.
100. *Hes* vases height 7.8 cm., diam. 1.8 cm.; beakers height 3.5 cm., diam. 2.8 cm.
101. 21.379: height 3.3 cm., diam. 1.1 cm.
102. 21.456: height 15.3 cm., diam. 5.2 cm.
103. 21.897: board length 39.5 cm., width 17.5 cm., height 3.6 cm.; vase height 10 cm., diam. 6.5 cm.
104. 21.426, 15-5-101: Length 328 cm., width 110 cm. Irregularly spaced warp rep fabric; weft: 16 cm., 2 S ply, regularly spaced; warp: 28 cm., 2 S ply, occasionally doubled; fringe: 2 S ply, length 10 cm., folded in half.

Fig. 75

44
Jewelry group and mirror

From Naga ed-Dêr tomb 453b
Middle Kingdom, Dynasty 11
Amethyst, carnelian, silver, gold, bronze, ivory, faience, and glazed steatite
Various sizes
Harvard University-Museum of Fine Arts Expedition, 1921 (21.970-985, 921)

Although grave goods in the Middle Kingdom were rather meager in comparison with the lavish deposits of furniture and objects in graves of the New Kingdom, some Middle Kingdom graves did contain deposits of jewelry unequaled in quality and aesthetic appeal.[1] While many of these belonged to kings and ladies of the royal court, a few early burials of seemingly minor individuals were also endowed with remarkably sumptuous adornments. This brings to mind the lamentations of Ipuwer, probably recalling the troubled times of the First Intermediate Period, "Indeed, gold and lapis lazuli, silver and turquoise, carnelian and amethyst . . . are strung on the necks of maidservants . . . and she who had to look at her face in the water is now the owner of a mirror."[2]

One such burial was that of the estate agent Wah of late Dynasty 11, excavated at Thebes,[3] and another is this group from an otherwise simple burial in a multiple-chambered tomb from Naga ed-Dêr (fig. 76).

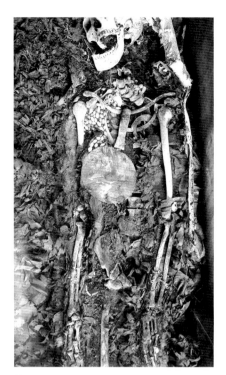

Fig. 76

The mummy was in a narrow box coffin plastered and painted with red lines to imitate wood graining. Beneath the bandages was an elaborately painted mask with a blue, red, and green broad collar and a representation of the uraeus pendant found on the neck of the mummy. Similar pendants are known from the Middle Kingdom[4] and can be considered further evidence of the usurpation of royal regalia that took place in the First Intermediate Period. It has been suggested that these uraeii may have been parts of fillets;[5] this example was clearly worn as a pendant, as reflected by its findspot and the depiction on the mask.

The filigree uraeus[6] is made of sheet silver and silver wire soldered together to form the hood and neck of the cobra. The central band forming the neck and body was incised with horizontal lines indicating the scale pattern of the snake. The ends of the wire are curled around the back in imitation of the snake's tail, and the head appears to have been broken off, as in a number of other examples, perhaps to render the serpent harmless.

Also around the neck were a series of necklaces with graduated barrel and cylindrical beads in carnelian,[7] amethyst barrel beads,[8] blue-green faience barrel beads with three cylinder beads at the ends[9] and a circular silver disk pierced in the center for stringing.[10]

Above the elbows were two armlets of carnelian, amethyst, rose quartz, and serpentine beads;[11] the one worn on the right arm had six silver amulets in the form of a bent arm.[12] On the left wrist was a bracelet of fa-

ience and carnelian beads of various shapes[13] and a string of amethyst and carnelian ring and barrel beads.[14] On the right wrist was a bracelet of faience ball beads,[15] a string of amethyst and carnelian ring beads with a large carnelian *swrt* bead in the center,[16] an amethyst scarab,[17] and a carnelian scarab.[18] On the little finger of the left hand was a green jasper scarab inscribed with the name of Mentuhotep.

Around the waist was a girdle of six bright blue-green faience amulet-beads including two crocodiles(?),[19] a Taweret bead,[20] two highly abstracted "grooved lion" beads[21] and a fancy cylinder bead.[22] These were strung along with twenty-nine carnelian ball and ring beads and nearly 600 shell beads.[23] Above the feet were two anklets with two bronze and three electrum-covered ivory claws, each strung with carnelian and amethyst ring beads.[24] These claw anklets, known from other Middle Kingdom jewelry finds, were worn by both men and women.[25]

At the breast was a mirror with a copper disk riveted to a metal tang, which was set into a cylindrical ivory handle capped by a carved blue lotus.[26]

PL

1. Cf. Aldred 1971, pp. 10-11, 13.
2. Faulkner 1972, pp. 213-221.
3. Winlock 1942, pp. 222-228.
4. Cf. Fazzini 1975, pp. 55, 135.
5. Wilkinson 1971, pp. 61-62.
6. 21.973: height 6.2 cm.
7. 21.972: length 49 cm.
8. 21.971: length 49 cm.
9. 21.970: length 60.2 cm.
10. 21.974: diam. 4.2 cm.
11. 21.975,6: length 21 cm.
12. 21.976 length 19 cm.
13. 21.978 length 29 cm.
14. 21.977 length 16 cm.
15. 21.980 length 11 cm.
16. 21.979 length 16 cm.
17. 21.982 length 2 cm.
18. 21.981 length 1.6 cm.
19. Cf. Brunton type 33 F 15, Brunton 1928, pls. 93-100.
20. Type M 2-4.
21. Type K 12.
22. Type K 3-15.
23. 21.983 length 86 cm.
24. 21.984,5 length about 15 cm.
25. Wilkinson 1971.
26. Lilyquist 1979a, p. 38, fig. 53.

Bibliography: Eaton 1941, pp. 94-98.

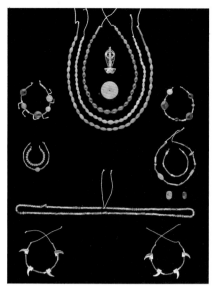

44

45
Coffin of the Lady of the House Neby

From Beni Hasan tomb 294
Middle Kingdom, Dynasty 12
Painted wood
Length 115 cm., height 75 cm., depth 61 cm.
Gift of the Beni Hasan Excavations Center, 1904 (04.2058)

Except for an elaborate doorway and eye panel on the left, or east, side of the box, the decoration of the coffin consists of hieroglyphic inscriptions at the top of each side and end, and four columns of inscription that divide the sides into panels. Two columns of hieroglyphs frame the end boards.

The inscriptions on the coffin are drawn in dark blue without outline and are framed by three lines painted alternately white, blue, white. The matting of the elaborate doorway is red, blue, green, and white. The sacred eye (see cat. 31) is black, the falcon markings blue, and the canthi in the whites of the eye red. The floor board of the coffin is missing, as are the battens that supported it.

The inscription on the east side contains

45

a prayer to Osiris for funerary offerings for Neby. The prayer on the other side is addressed to Anubis and requests a well-equipped burial. In all likelihood, Anubis was again invoked for passage to the sky in another painted line down the center of the missing lid.[1] The four columns on both sides of the coffin carry dedicatory inscriptions to the tutelary deities who protect the occupant, beginning ''One in honor with . . .'' The corners of the coffin are guarded by the four Genii of the Dead (Four Sons of Horus). Imsety and Hapy are paired on either side of the shoulders of the mummy, while Duamutef and Qebehsenuef flank the legs. Between, at the middle of the sides, are the primordial cosmic deities Shu, the god of the air, his sister-wife Tefnut, who personifies moisture, and their children the earth-god Geb and the goddess of the heavens Nut.

The doorway beneath the eye panel of the coffin served as a conduit for Neby's soul. It was customary at this time to support the mummy lying on its left side with a head-rest under the neck. This custom brought Neby's face opposite the sacred eyes (see cat. 31) at the head end of the coffin, which permitted her soul to look into the real world, in order to see the sun as it crossed the sky and even to participate in the funerary ceremonies presented at periodic intervals by her ka-priests or relatives.

The short columns of inscription on either end of the box constitute virtually identical speeches of assurance addressed to Neby by the sky-goddess Nut. As chief mourners, Nephthys and Isis traditionally guarded the funerary bed of Osiris, and Nut says, ''I have stationed Nephthys at your head for you, so that she might weep for you, so that she might spiritualize you.'' And again, at the foot end, ''I have stationed Isis at your feet for you. . . .''

The gods who appear in the texts on the coffin belong to the Osirian cycle of myth, which was successfully incorporated into the Heliopolitan pantheon presumably at the beginning of the Pyramid Age by the priests of the sun-god at Heliopolis. Originally, the Osirian and solar concepts of the hereafter were opposed. Osiris was lord of a subterranean kingdom of the dead, the realm and dominion of death,[2] while the sun-god ruled over a celestial realm where the dead person, originally the king alone, was furnished with all the necessities of life. In the course of the Old Kingdom the priests succeeded in incorporating Osiris into the Heliopolitan theology. According to the Heliopolitan tradition, Shu and Tefnut (air and moisture), the first couple to be created by the sun-god, Atem, were the parents of Geb and Nut (earth and sky). In their turn, they gave birth to a third generation of gods: Osiris, Isis, Seth, and Nephthys. Then Horus, the son of Isis, whose eyes orna-

ment the east side of the coffin, fathered the four genii Imsety, Hapy, Duamutef, Qebehsenuef.

Thus Nut plays a prominent role in Middle Kingdom coffins on two counts. First, she was mistress of the celestial hereafter, where the deceased hoped to dwell. Then too, she was the mother of Osiris and, by this period, the deceased of both sexes are identified with him. By the end of the Middle Kingdom, Nut emerged as the guardian of the lid of the coffin or the ''sky,'' as the Egyptians visualized it.[3]

Only Anubis, the canine god of cemeteries, is not incorporated into the Heliopolitan pantheon, but his association with the dead goes back to an early period, and he is the only god known in the offering formula in Dynasty IV.[4]

The coffin of Neby was excavated in the necropolis of Beni Hasan during 1902-3 or 1903-4 by John Garstang. If the evolution of the coffins found at Beni Hasan parallels that of those from Deir el-Bersha, then Neby lived during the reigns of Amenemhat II, Sesostris II, or Sesostris III.[5]

A small bronze statuette found in tomb 294 is noteworthy as an early example of the figure of a private person in metal.[6]

EB

1. Cf. Engelbach 1915, pp. 30-31; Hayes 1953, pp. 312-320.
2. Breasted 1912, pp. 143-144.
3. Hayes 1953, p. 314.
4. Barta 1968, p. 8.
5. Brovarski 1981, pp. 23-26, fig. 13.
6. Garstang 1907, pp. 142-143, fig. 141.

Bibliography: Garstang 1907, p. 223, no. 294 (x).

46
Mummy mask

From Asyut
Middle Kingdom, Dynasty 11 to Dynasty 12
Cartonnage
Height 60 cm.
Edward and Mary S. Holmes Fund, 1987
(1987.54)

Because of their fragility, relatively few Middle Kingdom masks survive. Although this mask was damaged in antiquity, the fact that it is broken in two hardly detracts from its appeal. While the bright yellow flesh tone was conventionally used in ancient Egypt to represent women, as well as young children and sometimes old men,[1] here it probably symbolized gold. The yellow of the mask's brightly painted diadem likewise stands for gold and the white substitutes for silver. The prototype of the diadem might have been inlaid with such semiprecious stones as carnelian and turquoise.[2] The full beard rendered in blue, like the eyebrows, with the bristles stippled in black,

46

lends a distinguished, if somewhat startling appearance to the face. Customarily, Egyptian men were clean shaven, only now and then sporting neat mustaches or short chin beards. The artist has taken the trouble to indicate in red the canthi and the veins in the white of the eye. He devoted less time to the decoration of the broad collar, which is partly covered by the long, black lappets of the man's wig.

In the Old Kingdom the mummy was either carefully wrapped to reproduce the form of the body (cat. 6) or covered with a plaster coating that extended over the entire body (cat. 23). The features of the face were sometimes painted on the linen.[3] By the late Old Kingdom the mummy was no longer given a lifelike appearance, and instead the body was wrapped in masses of linen sheets, bandages, and pads to round out its shape. Quite commonly, the features of the dead person were molded in the linen over the skull, covered with a thin white wash of plaster, and painted. In the course of the Herakleopolitan Period, these painted linen heads (cat. 43) evolved into separate cartonnage masks that covered the head and shoulders of the mummy, and ultimately developed in the Middle Kingdom into anthropoid inner coffins (cat. 51).

The cartonnage used for making the mummy masks consisted of layers of linen and gesso that could be molded before the plaster set. The mask was painted and, in richer burials, gilded. The Egyptian word for such a mask was swht (''eggshell'').[4]

Mummy masks very like the present one, found by the French mission at Asyut in Middle Egypt, date to shortly before or after the reunification of Egypt by Mentuhotep II.[5]

EB

1. Fischer 1963, pp. 17-22.
2. Aldred 1971, pl. 27.
3. Smith 1949, pp. 23-24.
4. Janssen 1975, p. 213.
5. Chassinat and Palanque 1911, pls. III, XXI, XXVI, XXVII.

Bibliography: Museum of Fine Arts 1986-87, p. 32.

47a

47b

47
Fragments from the tomb of Djehuty-hotep II

From Deir el-Bersha tomb 2
Middle Kingdom, Dynasty 12, reigns of
Sesostris II and Sesostris III
Harvard University-Museum of Fine Arts
Expedition

a. Wall fragment
   Height 28 cm., width 32 cm., depth 14 cm.
   (47.1659)
b. Ceiling fragment
   Height 24 cm., width 24 cm., depth 12 cm.
   (47.1660)

The rock-cut, cliff-face tomb of the Middle Kingdom reached its height of development in late Dynasty 12. Descended from the tombs of the Old Kingdom and First Intermediate Period (see cat. 43), the tombs of Dynasty 12 were strictly axial in layout. The tomb of Djehuty-hotep is a classic example of this type with a portico in front supported by two palm columns and a decorated rectangular inner room measuring approxi-

mately seven meters long and five meters wide. The decorated ceiling is flat, unlike some others of the period, which are gently arched. At the rear of the inner room a flight of low steps leads to a statue niche that could be closed by two wooden doors.[1] Outside the portico a shaft descends to a long corridor leading to a burial chamber below the niche.

Djehuty-hotep II served as nomarch of the Hare Nome (Fifteenth nome of Upper Egypt) and high priest of Thoth, the region's local god, during the reigns of Sesostris II and Sesostris III, according to inscriptions on the outer door jambs of his rock-cut tomb.[2] The latest tomb at Bersha is best known for its representation of the transport of a colossal statue from the Hatnub alabaster quarries. This scene was first copied by Banks in 1820, three years after the tomb was discovered by two English navy officers returning from Abu Simbel.[3] In 1891, Percy Newberry systematically surveyed, cleared, and published the tomb of Djehuty-hotep II, as well as others at Bersha, under the sponsorship of the Egypt Exploration Fund.[4] The Harvard University-Museum of Fine Arts Expedition re-investigated Djehuty-hotep II's tomb in 1915 and found a number of fragments, including the two featured here, that had gone unnoticed by Newberry. William Stevenson Smith placed these fragments in their context and discussed the style of the paintings in a landmark article in 1951.[5]

Painted and relief scenes cover the walls of the portico, main chamber, and shrine, and the subjects represented largely follow Old Kingdom models. The wall fragment shown here comes from the lower register of the north end of the east wall of the main chamber. It features two male attendants of the tomb owner who are the last[6] in a long procession of dignitaries of the Hare Nome.[7] Djehuty-hotep's sons lead the entourage. All the officials wear shoulder-length wigs and short, wrapped kilts. They stride to the left clasping left hand to right shoulder, a gesture of respect[8] seen as early as the Old Kingdom.[9]

Although much of the tomb is only painted, the figures and hieroglyphs in the fragment represented here were first carved in wafer-thin, unmodeled, raised relief and then painted. The artisans' true painterly genius comes through not in the precise, rather stiff, figures, but in the few preserved hieroglyphs that form part of the name and title of the last official. For example, such tiny details as whiskers and individual hairs of the ears and fur of the two rabbits are rendered with delicate, free-hand brushstrokes of reddish pink, giving them a lifelike quality. The naturalism shown in this and other scenes from the tomb rank it among the finest examples of Dynasty 12 painting.[10]

Yellow quatrefoils painted on a blue background decorated ceilings throughout the tomb.[11] Similar quatrefoils are found not only on other Middle Kingdom tomb ceilings, but also on faience vessels from Kerma.[12] It has been suggested that they represent stylized plants.[13] More elaborate examples show quatrefoils encased in squares or incorporated into complex floral and geometric motifs, the latter probably based on matting or textile prototypes.[14]

Djehuty-hotep II is known not only from his tomb, but also from at least one statue fragment found in the fill of a later temple platform at Megiddo, Israel.[15] Since nothing in Djehuty-hotep II's tomb suggests that he served outside Egypt, and since neither the statue's inscription nor its style indicates non-Egyptian manufacture, the statue may well have been made in Egypt and moved to Israel after his death.[16]

RF

1. Badawy 1966, p. 145.
2. Newberry 1893a, p. 6 and pl. V.
3. Newberry 1893a, pp. 3-4, 17-22, and passim; pls. XII and XV. For other early visitors and publications, see pp. 3-5.
4. Newberry 1893a.
5. Smith 1951, pp. 321-332.
6. Behind the rightmost figure is the traditional Egyptian border pattern of colored rectangles.
7. Smith 1951, p. 325, fig. 2 shows the block in place (no. 9). The rest of the wall is illustrated in Newberry 1893a, pl. XXIV.
8. Klebs 1922, p. 178.
9. As, for instance, in the tomb of Qar at Giza (G 7101, time of Pepy I or later), illustrated in Simpson 1976a, p. 1 and figs. 24 and 27.
10. For a fine description of the style of this tomb and comparative examples, see Smith 1951, pp. 321-332.
11. In the main chamber, a band of hieroglyphs bisected the ceiling vertically. In the portico, hieroglyphs divided the ceiling horizontally, and a black and yellow checkerboard motif filled a rectangle in the center (Newberry 1893a, p. 11 and figs. 1-2).
12. For example, from Asyut: Wilkinson 1878, pl. VIII, figs. 4 and 20; from Qau el Kebir: Petrie 1930, pl. I; Reisner 1923b, pp. 143-146 and pls. 46,2, and 47,1.
13. Smith 1957, p. 221.
14. See, for example, Blackman 1915, pls. IX and XXVIII; Wilkinson 1878, pl. VIII, figs. 4 and 20; From Qau el Kebir: Petrie 1930, pl. I; Reisner 1923b, pp. 143-146 and pls. 46,2, and 47,1; Smith 1981, pp. 210-211.
15. Chicago, O.I. A 18622. In all, fragments of four statues were found in or near the same context at Megiddo. The absence of any inscription on three, however, leaves their ownership open to question. According to Wilson, the context, Megiddo Stratum VIII, is not later than the 15th-14th century B.C. (Wilson 1941, pp. 225-226).
16. For a discussion of pieces probably taken from Egypt during the Second Intermediate Period, see Helck 1976, pp. 101-115.

48

48
Group statue of Ukh-hotep II and his family

From Meir
Middle Kingdom, Dynasty 12, reign of
Sesostris II or Sesostris III
Granite
Height 37 cm., width 38.1 cm., depth
7.6 cm.
Gift of the Egypt Exploration Fund by exchange, 1973 (1973.87)

In this granite group statue from Meir,[1] the
nomarch Ukh-hotep II stands between two
of his wives and clasps his young daughter
in front of him.[2] Ukh-hotep II wears a three-
quarter length wrapped skirt with fringed
upper border and a ''shawl'' wig, both fashionable after the beginning of Dynasty 12.[3]

His wives wear traditional sheath dresses
and the tripartite ''Hathor'' wig, typified by
bouffant lappets tapering into corkscrew
curls. Although the prototype for this hairstyle may be traced back to Early Dynastic
times, it did not become commonplace until
the reign of Sesostris II.[4]

All the figures share certain facial features;
the heavily lidded eyes, naso-labial furrows,
and large projecting ears characterize royal
and private sculpture from the reign of
Sesostris III on, although tendencies in this
direction appear in the previous reign.[5] The
group composition of the sculpture also
supports a Sesostris II-Sesostris III date,
since in the Middle Kingdom, group statuary – with the exception of offering bearers
– is uncommon prior to the middle of Dynasty XII.[6]

The figures' common back slab reaches
shoulder height. On the front an artisan has
incised the heraldic plants of Upper and
Lower Egypt, motifs traditionally associated
with royalty, and a pair of wedjat eyes.

On the basis of the identity of these figures,
W.K. Simpson attributed this statue to Meir
Tomb C 1.[7] Tomb C 1 was discovered by
Clédat in 1900; the statue was purchased in
1912 by the Walters Art Gallery, and traded
to the Museum of Fine Arts, Boston, in
1973.[8] The tomb, which was the subject of
a more complete investigation by Blackman
and Apted in 1949-50, consists of a roughly
cut portico leading into a main chamber containing niches on the side and end walls.[9]
On the basis of the orientation of the heraldic plants on the statue's back slab, Simpson suggested that it originally stood in the
south wall niche. A similar statue featuring
the same family members, now in the Cairo
Museum, probably came from a second recess in the same wall.[10]

Ukh-hotep II, nomarch of the Fourteenth
Upper Egyptian nome and overseer of
priests of Hathor, the area's primary goddess, probably held office during the reigns
of Sesostris II and Sesostris III.[11] He was a
descendant of the family of nomarchs in
power at Meir since the beginning of Dynasty 12, and was the last to rule.[12]

The lateral extension of the back slab and
its incised decoration suggest that this
piece functioned both as a statue and a
stela, an interpretation supported by the
round-top shape of the back slab on Ukh-
hotep II's companion statue in the Cairo
Museum.[13] A similarly creative and economic combination may be seen in an offering table shape decorated as a stela, dated
to the sixth year of the reign of Sesostris II.[14]

Ukh-hotep's tomb paintings display an appealing inventiveness seen, for instance, in
the style and hue of some of the fashions.[15]
This flamboyant display of artistic license is
unparalleled, and reflects a time when traditional constraints imposed by the royal
workshops no longer applied. Ukh-hotep II's
association with the cult of Hathor, goddess
of femininity and all its attributes, may have
led to the predominance of servile women
in paintings in his tomb, some of whom
wear male clothing and engage in traditional
male activities.[16] He had five wives and
seven concubines at a time when polygamy
was rare among nonroyal people in Egypt.[17]
The latter may also reflect his blatant usurpation of kingly prerogatives,[18] such as his
personal use of royal epithets and iconography. All these elements are in keeping with
a date prior to Sesostris III's widespread reforms, which subordinated provincial authority to a strong central government.[19]

RF

1. Meir, capital of the Fourteenth Upper Egyptian nome, is located on the West Bank of the Nile, 48 kilometers north of Asyut.
2. On his skirt he is identified as the "Count and Overseer of Priests, Ukh-hotep II, justified." On his left is "His wife, whom he loves, Mistress of the House, Nubkau, born of Iunet," and on his right, "His wife, whom he loves, his favorite, Mistress of the House, Khnum-hotep, born of Imu." The child's inscription reads "His daughter, whom he loves, his favorite, Nebhut-henutsen, justified."
3. Hayes 1953, p. 208.
4. Smith 1981, p. 47; Vandier 1958, p. 257.
5. Evers 1929, pp. 107-108 and pls. 64-69.
6. The unusual placement of Ukh-hotep's daughter between his feet finds a parallel in the block statue of Sesostris-Senbefny attributed on the basis of style to the reign of Sesostris III or later (Brooklyn 39.602, Fazzini 1975, p. 54).
7. Simpson 1974b, p. 103; Hayes 1953, p. 208.
8. Blackman 1914, p. 15; Simpson 1974b, p. 102.
9. Blackman and Apted 1953, pp. 13 ff. and pls. I, IV, IX-XXXII.
10. Simpson 1974b, p. 103.
11. See Fischer 1970, p. 84 for various opinions of the date of the tomb. Simpson 1974b, p. 104 supports the Sesostris II-Sesostris III attribution.
12. Blackman 1914, p. 13.
13. Simpson 1974b, p. 102, fig. 3.
14. British Museum 257, see British Museum 1913, pl. 7.
15. For example, traditionally white dresses are, on occasion painted red, green, yellow or blue (Blackman and Apted 1953, pp. 24, 27, 28, 33).
16. Blackman and Apted 1953, p. 15; Terrace and Fischer 1970, p. 81.
17. Blackman and Apted 1953, p. 13; Terrace and Fischer 1970; Simpson 1974c.
18. Terrace and Fischer 1970, p. 81. For descriptions see Blackman and Apted 1953, pp. 26-33.
19. Hayes 1971, pp. 505-506.

Bibliography: Steindorff 1946a, no. 50, pp. 28-29 and pl. XII; Simpson 1973b, pp. 48, 51; Simpson 1974c, p. 103; Simpson 1974b, pp. 100, 102-104; Needler 1981, p. 134, n. 3; Wildung 1984, pp. 162-163.

0   50   65 cm.

49

49
Fragment of offering chapel relief

From Aswan Region
Middle Kingdom, Dynasty 12, ca. 1800 B.C., reign of Amenemhat III
Limestone
Height 66.5 cm., width 66 cm.
J.H. and E.A. Payne Fund, 1971 (1971.403)

Among the fairly stereotyped formulae inscribed in the chapels of Middle Kingdom tombs are quite a few texts that provide autobiographical details about the official for whom the tomb was constructed. The fragment of relief of the overseer of fields Ankhu has a procession of offering bearers facing right in the lower register and columns of vertical texts above providing part of such an autobiographical text.[1] In ancient times the figure at the lower right was completely erased. The surface of the stone was then shaved down and a new figure, smaller and carved in a very different style than that of his fellows, replaced the original. This new figure is the one we see today, although the inscription directly above his head seems to be unaltered. The official is known through two rock-cut texts in the Aswan region[2] as well as two statues, one now lost, from the sanctuary dedicated to the deified Hekaib on Elephantine Island.[3] A block that originally extended the lower part of our scene to the left was sold at an auction in London in 1974.[4] It is likely that the official's tomb was in the vicinity of Aswan and that its location and remains of the rest of its relief may one day be found.

After various standard titles and epithets, the text relates that Ankhu served as scribe of the temple of Sesostris III and acted as henchman for the son of the king's successor, Amenemhat III, while the latter was a youth. This interesting bit of information, while not of major historical importance, is the main feature of the text. It has been pointed out by Goedicke that the signs in the text are curiously spaced; this and other details lead him to conclude that the entire text is a modern forgery.[5] This assessment has not been generally followed.[6] It seems more likely that the text has been touched up and sharpened in modern times. Indeed, the columns of texts and the vertical lines that divide the columns are sharper than the scene with the offering bearers below. It is barely possible that the procession of offering bearers is original and earlier, and that the vertical text was added later by a second hand. The principal figure of the tomb owner and figures of members of his family are lacking in the section preserved and their orientation may explain the retrograde order of the columns of texts. In some of the other texts of Ankhu (see above) he also holds the title of herald. It is conceivable that these different texts relate to more than one individual named Ankhu son of Merestekh, perhaps father and son, but it would be curious for a father and son to have mothers of the same name. The block and its history are intriguing, all the more so for raising more questions than answers, and it is probable that it will be the subject of discussion for years to come.[7]

WKS

1. Simpson 1972a, pp. 45-54.
2. Berlev 1978, p. 330; de Morgan 1894 p. 26, nos. 188, 190; Petrie 1888a, pl. VIII, nos. 175, 176; Franke 1984, Dossier 177, p. 139.

3. Habachi 1985, p. 44, no. 16, pls. 46-48, p. 166, pl. 211d; Franke 1984, Dossier 177, p. 139.
4. Christie's 1974, p. 95, pl. 24.
5. Goedicke 1975, pp. 27-30.
6. Leprohon 1983, pp. 106-107, no. 14-17; Fischer 1972, p. 23, fig. 32; Fischer 1973, p. 26, n. 55.
7. Krauss 1985, pp. 10, 195; Matzker 1986, pp. 99-100; Simpson 1984, pp. 903-906.

Literature: Simpson 1972.

50
Stela of Ameny

Probably from Abydos
Middle Kingdom, late Dynasty 12 or
slightly later
Limestone
Height 64 cm., width 49.4 cm.
Seth Sweetser Fund, 1970 (1970.630)

Ameny, a police captain, probably commissioned this limestone stela to be erected along a high terrace flanking the Osiris temple at Abydos,[1] so that he might participate in the "mysteries" of the Great God Osiris, and like him, achieve rebirth and renewal. He is shown below a three-line inscription on the left, seated beside his wife Nefer-Hathor. His parents Yot-sen and Nebu-em-mer face him over two mats piled high with food and drink offerings. In the bottom register, below Ameny, his two servants, who face to the right, bring offerings, while below his parents, his father's two servants, facing left, do likewise. Each is identified by name. The first two lines of the inscription above invoke Osiris and Wepwawet in an offering formula cut in bold, clear hieroglyphs. The third line, executed with somewhat smaller signs, lists the main male figures and their parentage. A border of rectangles encased in parallel lines frames the entire composition, and a *kheker*-frieze decorates the top.

Ameny bears the title *imy-ḫt sꜣw-prw*, literally translated as "under-supervisor of the sons of houses."[2] Based upon their contexts and representations, in the Old Kingdom these officials appear to have worked on private estates in a police-like capacity,[3] but during the Middle Kingdom, persons with the same title appear to have served as a security force on large royal projects such as quarrying expeditions.[4]

The style and format of Ameny's stela are characteristic of the end of Dynasty 12. Beginning around the reign of Sesostris III,[5] crudely carved stelae featuring many figures in repetitive passive attitudes proliferate. During the next reign,[6] a more carefully executed monument appears that is in some ways reminiscent of an earlier Dynasty 12 style.[7] The relatively few figures, including servants in "active" poses, and the care with which they are executed, suggest that Ameny's stela was made around the reign of Amenemhat III. The heavily lid-

ded eyes and articulated, open nostrils of Ameny and his family and the deeply cut outlines of all the figures find close parallels on stelae dated or datable to this time.[8]

Ameny's stela may have been one element of a stela-chapel, made up of a central section with two lateral walls. The stela's vertical format and the deliberate effort to achieve bilateral symmetry, apparent not only in the orientation of the figures, but also in the third line of the inscription, which is read from the center outward, suggests that the stela formed the central element of a stela-chapel.

Stela-chapels developed in the late Old Kingdom and proliferated in the Memphite area during the Herakleopolitan Period,[9] perhaps as an economic measure, since they condensed scenes from multi-chambered chapels onto three limestone slabs. The pre-Dynasty 12 stela-chapels characteristically feature offering bearers or scenes of food preparation flanking a false-door stela (see cat. 30). serving as the central element.[10] Later stela-chapels, attributable to Dynasty 13 or slightly earlier, feature a greater variety of scenes, including the journey to Abydos.[11] The border motif and *kheker*-frieze seen on Ameny's stela are typical of the later group.

RF

1. For a description of the probable location of the "Terrace of the Great God," see Simpson 1974a, especially pp. 9-10.
2. Fischer 1960, p. 300.
3. Yoyotte 1952, pp. 142-146.
4. Yoyotte 1952, pp. 146-148, 150.
5. For example, Manchester 3306 or British Museum 1213, illustrated in Simpson 1974a, pl. 31.
6. For example, British Museum 101 or Louvre C5, illustrated in Blackman 1935, pl. 1 and Simpson 1974a, pl. 3 respectively.
7. Freed 1976, pp. 101-102, and cf. pp. 87-91.
8. For example, BM 557, BM 247, and CG 20558, illustrated in Simpson 1974a, pl. 39.
9. Simpson 1972c, p. 8.
10. Simpson 1972c, p. 4.

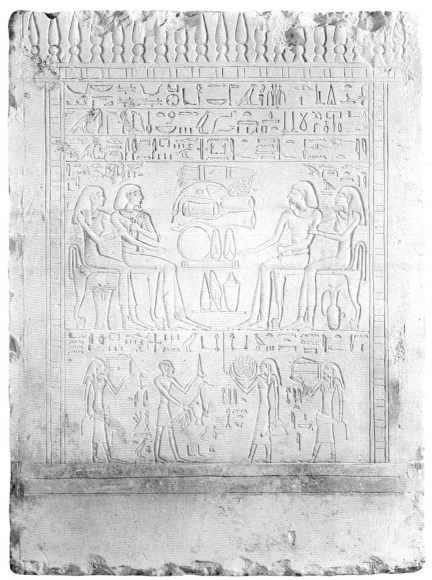

50

11. For example, Louvre C 16, C 17, C 18; and Hermitage 1063, 1064, 1075, illustrated in Simpson 1974a, pls. 70-71 and 78-79. The Hermitage stelae are datable to the reign of Khendjeder of Dynasty 13 (Lourié1935-38, p. 908).

Bibliography: Simpson 1972b, pp. 116-117; Simpson 1974b, pp. 112-114; New Orleans 1977, cat. 35.

51

51
Head end from an anthropoid coffin

Provenance unknown
Middle Kingdom, Dynasty 12 or after
Wood, cartonnage, stone, and bronze
Preserved length 78 cm., preserved width 32 cm., depth 15 cm.
Gift of Kathryn L. Maxson in memory of her father Richard E. S. Maxson, 1988 (1988.6)

This coffin was made of soft wood, probably acacia, overlaid with a layer of linen that was impregnated with gesso, and then covered with a finer gesso ground. The decorated head end of the coffin has been cut down in modern times from an entire anthropoid lid.

The coffin lid is brightly painted: the blue wig is bordered in yellow with red hatching; the banded necklace is red, yellow, black, blue, and green; and the elaborate broad collar has rows of red, green, and blue pendant beads. The face is dark green, which equates the deceased with Osiris, lord of the underworld and god of vegetation. The eyes are made of polished limestone with black painted irises and set in bronze sockets with bronze lids.

The rest of the lid would have been white.

Similar coffins occasionally have a column of text down the center of the lid giving the name and titles of the deceased and a short prayer for his sustenance in the afterlife. No trace of inscription remains on this example and in all probability it never had one.

This type of coffin illustrates the development of the anthropoid coffin that first appears in Dynasty 12.[1] The white coffin with decorated wig, face, and collar represents a bandaged body wearing a mummy mask. These early anthropoid coffins were still placed in rectangular wooden outer coffins as the bandaged mummies had been, a tradition that continued sporadically through the New Kingdom and later periods.

This example closely resembles the coffin of Userhet from Beni Hasan,[2] which has been dated to the second half of Dynasty 12.[3] However, such coffins were imitated in the Saite Period.

PL

1. Winlock 1916, pp. 47-56.
2. Garstang 1907, pp. 173-175, fig. 181.
3. Janine Bourriau, personal communication.

52
Female figurine

From Deir el-Bersha tomb 19 B
Early Middle Kingdom, late Dynasty 11 to early Dynasty 12
Wood
Height 18.6 cm.
Harvard University-Museum of Fine Arts Expedition, 1915 (20.1121)

Among the model figures found in Middle Kingdom tombs are these human figures with legs that end at the knees and are rounded off below. These figurines of women occur most frequently in faience,[1] but are also found in stone,[2] wood, and ivory.[3]

This figurine from a plundered burial shaft in tomb 19 at Bersha (Newberry Tomb 4)[4] is a particularly fine example of the genre; it is carefully carved and finished with separately carved hands and arms, one of which is now lost. The face was made of a separate piece of wood, with eyes and irises of inlaid stone. The short, curly hair is indicated by a series of little pegs that were painted black and set into drilled holes in the scalp.

It has been suggested that these figurines were "concubines" of the dead;[5] however, their occurrence in the burials of women[6] argues against this interpretation, as does the fact that these figures are occasionally shown holding infants.[7] More likely, they may symbolize fertility and rebirth,[8] as do similar representations of nude females in the New Kingdom (see cat. 74).

PL

1. Saleh and Sourouzian 1987, no. 80.
2. Cf. Hornemann 1966, no. 844.

52

3. Cf. Hayes 1953, pp. 220-221, fig. 137.
4. Griffith and Newberry 1893-94.
5. Cf. Riefstahl 1944b, p. 9.
6. Saleh and Sourouzian 1987, no. 80.
7. Cf. Hayes 1953, fig. 137.
8. Saleh and Sourouzian 1987, no. 80.

Bibliography: Terrace 1968b, pp. 18-20, fig. 18; Terrace 1968a, pp. 265-272; Smith 1960, pp. 95-97, fig. 60.

53
Human-headed canopic jar lid

From Deir el-Bersha tomb 13, Pit A
Middle Kingdom
Wood
Height 16.5 cm., diam. 15.7 cm.
Harvard University-Museum of Fine Arts Expedition, 1915 (21.498)

After the facial features of this human-headed lid were carved, the head was covered with a layer of plaster and painted. The wig is black and a black band under the chin indicates the beard. The eyes and eyebrows are outlined in black with black pupils on white. Red paint can be seen in the corner of each eye. The head is battered, with some damage to the nose. During Dynasties 9 and 10 the style of the lids of canopic jars changed from the convex disk shape of the Old Kingdom (see cat. 10) to human heads, although disk lids and cone-shaped covers continued to be used through the Middle Kingdom.[1] Examples of this new type of jar lid occur in cartonnage, pottery, wood, Egyptian alabaster, and limestone.

The jars often carried inscriptions showing that the various internal organs were placed under the protection of the Four Sons of Horus – the deities Imsety, Hapy, Duamutef, and Qebehsenuef. These gods were associated with other deities, notably the goddesses Isis, Nephthys, Neith, and Selkit.[2] Many jars of this period have arms painted or carved on the sides[3] and a cartonnage jar from Deir el-Bersha (see cat. 43) also has feet. Other jars from Bersha[4] have wooden heads on alabaster bodies with no inscriptions, although a jar in the Cairo Museum is inscribed.[5] The viscera were wrapped in linen and placed in the jars. The jars were then put into large cubical canopic chests divided into four compartments (see cat. 43). These chests were usually placed in a niche in the wall of the burial chamber.

MLB

1. Brovarski 1978, intro.
2. Hayes 1953, pp. 320-321.
3. Reisner 1967, pp. 396-397; Raisman and Martin 1984, p. 10 (no. 3), pl. 2.
4. MFA 21.949, 2807, 2811, Brovarski 1978; British Museum 30838, Ross 1931, p. 141.
5. 4994, Reisner 1967, p. 388.

Bibliography: Brovarski 1978, pp. 92-93.

53

54
Human-headed canopic jar lid

Provenance unknown
Middle Kingdom, Dynasty 12
Calcite (Egyptian alabaster)
Height 12.5 cm., diam. 5 cm.
Bequest of Mrs. Godfrey Peckitt, 1962
(Res. 1962.90)

During Dynasty 12, one of the most common materials used in making canopic jars was Egyptian alabaster. The lids of these jars were usually carved in the shape of a human head with the details of the eyes carefully painted in black.

54

Carved from a solid piece of alabaster with finely modeled features and relief lines indicating the brows, lids, and cosmetic lines, this jar lid is typical of Dynasty 12. The mouth and ears were more crudely formed; the beard, which completely obscures the chin, was indicated by drill marks on either side, its bottom shown by a horizontal line. No attempt was made to indicate the neck.

Incised lines form a sharp V down the center of the back of the headdress. The stopper at the bottom was carved with the aid of a wheel but was not hollowed. Lids made in a similar fashion may be found in Cairo.[1]

In some cases where complete sets of four jars have been discovered, the lids include one beardless and three bearded heads.[2] Though often of quite fine quality, jars and lids of the same set are frequently of different sizes and proportions.[3]

Though the Egyptian craftsmen seem to have taken care in making the burial apparatus, the embalmers were sometimes less meticulous and jars of this period have been found to contain lumps of cedar pitch mixed with mud rather than the actual viscera.[4]

CHR

1. 4059-4061, Reisner 1967, pp. 38-40, pl. XI.
2. Hayes 1953, p. 325. For another example see CG4077-4080, from Lisht and Reisner 1967, pp. 47-49, pl. XII.
3. Hayes 1953, p. 325. See for example the jars of Princess Sit-Hathor-Yunet in Hayes 1953, fig. 212, p. 324; CG 4015-18 in Reisner 1967, pp. 9-11, pl. III.
4. Hayes 1953, p. 325.

Funerary Figurines

The archaic but accurate term "funerary figurines" denotes an enormous group of objects known variously as *shabtis, shawabtis,* or *ushebtis,* depending on both the date of the particular example and the version of Chapter 6, Book of the Dead, with which the statuettes were customarily supplied.[1] The ancient Egyptians made these figurines to perform agricultural tasks required of the deceased in the Underworld. Already in Tutankhamen's burial, and especially in later tombs, several hundred were often deposited for the benefit of a single individual. Consequently, they are the most numerous of all Egyptian antiquities, with the possible exception of scarabs. They are particularly appropriate objects for the "Mummies and Magic" exhibition because the most common types were mummiform and the magical incantation from the Book of the Dead enabled them to execute the mandatory labor.

Often modest in quality, the figurines were nonetheless just as essential to the burial as the mummy, wall paintings, biographical texts, magical papyri, food offerings, models of servants, and objects of daily life. In fact, the first funerary figurines evolved shortly before the disappearance of model servants, and may be regarded as having developed out of the latter. Hybrid types – models of kitchen staff inscribed with Chapter 6 – appear sporadically in the New Kingdom,[2] indicating that the idea of "servant" was foremost in the minds of the ancient Egyptians. In contrast to the crude, mass-produced figurines of later periods, the fine modeling of early types such as cat. 56 suggests that they were important items whose magical properties were taken seriously.

A small, human-shaped wax object and model coffin from Sakkara and several similar groups from Deir el-Bahri, belonging to the family and court of Nebheptere Mentuhotep, are the prototypes of funerary figurines. They are coeval, or nearly so, dating to the Herakleopolitan Period (Dynasties 9 and 10, about 2213-2035 B.C.) and the second half of Theban Dynasty 11 (2061-1991 B.C.).[3] These figurines lack Chapter 6 of the Book of the Dead, which did not become a standard feature until Dynasty 13. Nonetheless, they are true funerary figurines. Uninscribed examples of different dates are not uncommon and still other figurines have no more than *shd Wsir* and the title and name of the deceased ("the enlightened one, the Osiris NN").

Dynasty 18 (1570-1293 B.C.) marked the period of greatest innovation in the evolution of funerary figurines. The term *shabti* was most used at this time. *Shabti*s were made of wood, stone, faience, terra-cotta, and glass. The most important development was the appearance of tools and baskets as decorative features during the reign of Thutmose IV (1419-1386 B.C.). These were fashioned separately as models or drawn on the figurines themselves.[4] They became regular features thereafter.

The finest of all funerary figurines come from Deir el-Medina, the home of the craftsmen who decorated the royal tombs in the Valley of the Kings. The term *shawabti* appears more often of these figurines than any other. Dynasty 19 examples are the most numerous, although exceptional work was also found in the Dynasties 18 and 20.

During Dynasty 19 (1293-1185 B.C.), *shabti* was again the most popular designation. *Shabti*s in the dress of the living are first found at this time. After Dynasty 19, the quality of funerary figurines declined markedly. Mold-made terra-cotta and faience examples were produced by the thousands. The orthography and epigraphy of Chapter 6 is generally wretched; often the text is incomplete. Blue faience figurines with a black fillet about the head are characteristic of the Third Intermediate Period (1070-656 B.C.), although white faience examples with details in brown or violet are also known. At this time, the *ushebti* makes its first appearance. It is the standard term for Late Period (525-343 B.C.) figurines, which are sometimes of superior quality. They are almost always made of light green, occasionally blue, faience. Mummiform in shape, these ushebtis all have false beards, a distinctive and small-blade hoe, and a small basket on the back left shoulder. On the finest examples, the proportions of the legs are particularly well rendered. The last figurines date from the Ptolemaic Period (332-31 B.C.).[5]

DBS

1 Spanel 1986.
2. Gardiner 1906; Capart 1943; Schneider 1977, pp. 216-218; 293-294.
3. Schneider 1977, I, 178.
4. Carter and Newberry 1904, pp. 45-55 and pls. 13-15; Dunham 1960, p. 120, fig. 70; Daressy 1902, p. 299, pl. 57.
5. Schneider 1977, I, pp. 338-345.

Bibliography: Capart 1943, pp. 30-34; Dunham 1960; Gardiner 1906, pp. 55-59; Hayes 1953; Schneider 1977; Spanel 1986, pp. 249-253.

55
Model coffin and *shawabti*

Provenance unknown
Late Middle Kingdom to Second Intermediate Period, late Dynasty 12 or Dynasty 13
Wood, limestone, and textile
Length 20.4 cm., height 10.8 cm., length 8.1 cm.
Hay Collection, Gift of C. Granville Way, 1872 (72.4123a-c)

55

This wooden model coffin and *shawabti* belong to a man named Intef, a name known in the Middle Kingdom.[1] The *shawabti* is summarily carved of soft wood and painted white, possibly in imitation of limestone (see cat. 56), with the details of the eyes and eyebrows indicated in black pigment. The inscription down the center reads "An offering which the king gives through Osiris to the *ka* of Intef." The *shawabti* was wrapped in linen and tied up with threads.

The model coffin copies the form of an arched lidded box coffin with rectangular ends. This type of coffin was common in the Archaic Period and in the Old Kingdom and was revived in the later Middle Kingdom.[2] The model coffin is painted white and decorated in black pigment with a pair of *wedjat* eyes and an elaborate false door that indicates a double door with the lower pivot poles exposed and a lunate window at the top. It is inscribed down the top and around the sides with offering formulae. Traces of pigment indicate that squatting figures of Isis and Nephthys were placed at the coffin's foot and head, respectively, as was common on box coffins of the period (see cat. 63). Such coffins have been found buried in sacred precincts and may have served as cenotaph burials for the deceased.[3]

PL

1. Ranke 1935, p. 36 no. 10.
2. Williams 1975-76, p. 45.
3. Hayes 1953, pp. 349-350.

56
Shawabti (funerary figurine)

From Sheikh Farag tomb 42
Late Middle Kingdom to Second Intermediate Period, late Dynasty 12 or Dynasty 13
Limestone
Height 11.9 cm.
Harvard University-Museum of Fine Arts Expedition, 1912-13 (13.3587)

The earliest funerary figurine in the exhibition, this example is exceptionally well modeled and has characteristics distinctive of both royal and private contemporary sculpture: large and flaring ears, high cheekbones, firmly set mouth, and a strong and knobby chin. The sensitive modeling and the very limited numbers of early figurines suggest that they were prized objects. Early examples frequently lack the usual inscrip-

tion from Chapter 6 of the Book of the Dead; it did not become a regular feature until the beginning of Dynasty 18. Agricultural implements did not appear until the middle of the same dynasty. As originally conceived, the tasks to be performed in the next life may have been of a general nature, not specifically agricultural, and were consequently not spelled out. Or, the labors to be performed by the figurines may have been understood by all and therefore left unwritten.

Late Middle Kingdom anepigraphic types underscore a basic problem in terminology. Neither *shabti*, *shawabti*, nor *ushebti* is appropriate (see essay on *shawabti*s). Therefore, the designation "funerary figurine," for all its antiquarian connotations, is accurate for this particular example and for general use.

DBS

56

57
Shawabti

From Semna
Middle Kingdom, Dynasty 12
Calcite (Egyptian alabaster)
Height 14.8 cm., width 4.1 cm., depth 2.9 cm.
Harvard University-Museum of Fine Arts Expedition, 1924 (24.745)

This small alabaster *shawabti* was found in debris near tomb S 537 at the site of Semna in Nubia.[1] The rock-cut tombs of cemetery 500 were originally excavated during the

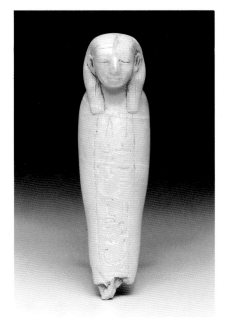

57

Middle Kingdom and Second Intermediate Period. Though they were re-used during Dynasty 18 and other tombs were excavated as well,[2] the names on this shawabti date it to the Middle Kingdom phase of the cemetery. It is also similar to a late Middle Kingdom shawabti of Heka-ib, now in the Brooklyn Museum.[3]

The facial features are well modeled with a relief line indicating the upper eyelid. The striation on the lappet wig is indicated by incised lines. The body of the shawabti is without any significant modeling though it narrows slightly at the knees. The lines indicating the column of inscription and the hieroglyphs are not particularly well carved considering the delicate treatment of the face.

Instead of the common shawabti formula or inscription, this shawabti is inscribed with a short *hetep di nesut* formula that reads "An offering that the King gives (to) the *ka* of Renes-seneb,[4] born of Iku,[5] Justified."

The piece is broken off at the bottom and there are small chips out of the nose and forehead.

CHR

1. In Dunham and Janssen 1960, p. 87, the author says that this and two other figurines may have come from S 533, a rock-cut tomb, but 537 may have been intended since the figures are placed nearer to it on map XXVII.
2. Dunham and Janssen 1960, p. 74.
3. Brooklyn Museum, L 73.2.1. On loan from the Ernest Erickson Foundation.
4. Ranke 1935, 224.1.
5. Ranke 1935, 48.10.

Bibliography: Dunham and Janssen 1960, p. 87.

58
Hippopotamus

Provenance unknown
Second Intermediate Period
Faience
Length 20.9 cm, height 10.4 cm., width 8.3 cm.
Martha A. Willcomb Fund, 1951 (51.8)

This pale green faience hippo is depicted standing with a large round belly and closed mouth. It is decorated in purple-brown manganese pigment, with a design of lotuses and marsh plants. Its provenance is not known, but it was originally brought from Egypt by Charles Hale, the American Consul General in Alexandria from 1864 to 1870.

The hippopotamus hunt is frequently depicted on the walls of Old Kingdom mastaba chapels[1] and, later, in temple decoration. As a symbol of the threatening forces of chaos, the often dangerous hippo is shown being harpooned by the king or gods to celebrate their victory over disorder, and by the deceased as a triumph over death. For this reason, these figures are usually ritually broken before being placed in the tomb; this mutilation renders them powerless as does the cutting of snakes and other potentially dangerous hieroglyphs on the coffins of the First Intermediate Period (see cat. 31). The broken legs, eyes, and ears of this example were restored for exhibition.[2]

The hippopotamus also had a more sympathetic side, and was venerated in the form of Taweret, a goddess of protection and fertility. The lotuses painted on the back and sides of the hippo symbolize creation and rebirth, as well as representing the swampy stomping ground of the creature.

The exact date of these figurines has been the subject of much debate.[3] Deposits of these figures are known from a number of sites in Lower and Upper Egypt and even in Nubia, and range in date from the Middle Kingdom to the Second Intermediate Period.[4] During the Middle Kingdom the hippopotamus was just one of a number of faience figurines that included hedgehogs, mice, cats, lions, dogs, apes, shells, and model food;[5] in the Second Intermediate Period, the hippo became larger and the other figures disappeared. The hippopotamus figures last only into Dynasty 17, when they, too, vanish,[6] perhaps to be replaced as

58

symbols of rebirth by the faience bowls of the New Kingdom, whose lotus decorative scheme matches that of these hippopotamus figures (see cat. 76).

PL

1. Klebs 1915, pp. 69-70.
2. Bothmer 1951, pp. 98-102.
3. Cf. Williams 1975-76, pp. 41-60; Lilyquist 1979b p. 27-28; Kemp and Merrillees 1980, pp. 167-168.
4. Lacovara and Markowitz (forthcoming).
5. Kemp and Merrillees 1980, pp. 160-168.
6. Saleh and Sourouzian 1987, no. 82-83.

Bibliography: Bothmer 1951, pp. 98-102; Smith 1960, pp. 98-99, fig. 62.

59
Magic wand

From Naqada
Middle Kingdom, Dynasty 13
Ivory
Length 35 cm., width 4.2 cm.
Sears Fund, 1903 (03.1703)

Common components of Middle Kingdom mortuary assemblages, carved ivory wands are known by actual examples and from representations on coffins of the period.[1] Almost always carved from the tusks of hippopotami, the wands follow the shape of the incisor. The flat bottom is usually left plain,[2] and the rounded end is often decorated with the head of a lion or leopard and followed by a procession of wild animals and monsters with protective significance.

In this example, which probably dates to the later Middle Kingdom,[3] the first figure is largely destroyed except for the upturned tail. The first complete figure, a composite feline with a lion's mane and leopard's spots, holds a knife in his front paws. It is followed by a cat and a frog, both of whom are also armed with knives. Standing behind these creatures is Taweret, a protector of women during childbirth and a popular household goddess. Taweret is typically represented with a hippo's head and body, lion's legs, and either a crocodile's tail or a complete crocodile on her back.[4]

After Taweret another composite feline stands and rests its front paws on the s_3 hieroglyph, symbol of protection.[5] The next animal, one of the most fantastic in the Egyptian menagerie, is the griffin. It has the body and tail of a leopard and the head and wings of a falcon; occasionally a human head springs from the center of its back. In spite of its fearsome appearance it seems not to have been regarded as an exclusively malevolent monster.[6] Next to last, a jackal-headed god holds a knife like all the others before him. Finally there is a walking solar disk with a uraeus and pendant *ankh*. All these bizarre figures are represented on

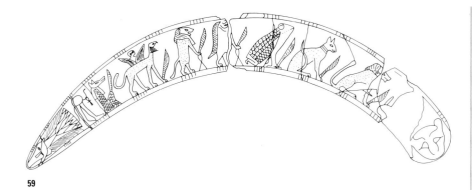

59

one or more other wands and all have apotropaic significance.[7]

The pointed end of the wand is decorated with the head of a fox, whose long ears frame a blue lotus flower; the whole composition is bordered with an incised line with groups of four perpendicular tick marks at intervals along the edges.

These wands are generally associated with beds in the *frise d'objets* on Middle Kingdom coffins.[8] It has been suggested that they were used to draw a protective circle around the bed to ward off snakes and scorpions.[9] Many of them do show marks of wear at the tips where they must have been drawn along the ground.

A number of these wands are inscribed with the phrase "Words spoken by the many amuletic figures . . . we have come that we may afford protection."[10] The wands may also have been used to protect women during childbirth,[11] and in that context, they may also have had funereal significance both for the protection of the deceased,[12] and in association with rebirth. Most of these knives appear to have been deliberately broken at the time of burial as were other votive objects, particularly during this period (see cat. 58).

PL

1. Terrace 1967, pl. 15.
2. Drenkhahn 1987, pp. 63-69.
3. Altenmüller 1986, pp. 1-27.
4. Altenmüller 1986, pp. 11-13.
5. Cf. Gardiner Sign list V 17, Gardiner 1973, p. 523.
6. Fischer 1986, pp. 13-26.
7. Altenmüller 1986.
8. Terrace 1967, pl. 15.
9. Hayes 1953, pp. 248-249.
10. Altenmüller 1986, p. 235.
11. Hayes 1953.
12. Steindorff 1946b, pp. 41-51, 106-107.

Bibliography: Steindorff 1946b, pp. 41-45, fig. 3, 106-107.

60
Mummy mask and fragments

From Sheikh Farag tomb 5202
Middle Kingdom, Dynasty 12
Cartonnage with ceramic core
Height 11.5 cm., width 9.4 cm.
Harvard University-Museum of Fine Arts Expedition, 1923 (23.1475a-c)

A head mask of cartonnage extending to the breast and shoulders was a characteristic part of the funerary equipment in burials of different social classes from the First Intermediate Period onward. After the end of the Old Kingdom, every person was allowed to achieve eternal life through identification with the god Osiris, whose death and resurrection they wanted to duplicate. Death coverings, therefore, were no longer simply an additional means to hide the decomposition of the then insufficiently mummified body (this can be seen from the examples from Giza, cats. 6 and 23). Their main aim now was to equip the deceased with divine attributes such as the long tripartite wig; the gilded or, as a substitute, yellow painted face; and the characteristic undetailed cocoon shape of the mummy, which the linen bandages formed over the body. With this divine Osirian outfit one could start the dangerous journey to the other world without fear.

Found in the debris of the Dynasty 12 tomb 5202 at Sheikh Farag in Upper Egypt, this was the mask of a woman (men's masks usually had beards). The skin and mouth are painted yellow, and the preserved right ear shows a red concentric pattern. Eyes, brows, and eyepaint are outlined in black, whereas the tripartite wig – usually blue or black – is one of the rare striped examples:[1] alternating bands of red, green, and blue are separated by narrow stripes of yellow. Comparison with other examples indicates this mask must have had a painted collar on a square breast piece, fragments of which are also preserved; in a few cases, a formula asking for offerings for the deceased was inscribed beneath the collar.[2] Such masks are known from all important First Intermediate Period and Middle Kingdom cemeteries in Egypt.[3] They were cheaply mass-produced in workshops that soon developed regional peculiarities in fabrication and design. Normally, alternating layers of linen and plaster were formed over molds with face and wig projecting. This example has a ceramic core under or between the layers; the ears were made of mud or clay, covered with plaster, and added later. On the last thick layer of plaster the paint was applied: on this piece, first yellow, then the other colors.

Members of the upper class or the royal family would normally have used more expensive materials such as gold leaf, semi-precious stones for inlay, and wood for mummiform coffins that covered head and body.[4] The best-known examples are the coffins and the famous mask of Tutankhamen dating from the New Kingdom, some 600 years later than this example. On his mask a text is incised which occurs as Spell 531 in the Coffin Texts on masks contemporary with this example from Sheikh Farag: "May you (the mask) make him (the deceased) to be a spirit, may you subdue his foes for him, may you guide him to the fair places of the realm of the dead . . . That I be one who is enduring, enduring, is what has been commanded, enduring like Re, forever."[5]

ER

1. Petrie and Mackay 1915, p. 31; Winlock 1940, pp. 253-259.
2. Andrews 1984, fig. 28.
3. E.g. Garstang 1907, pp. 172ff; Chassinat and Palanque 1911, pp. 12, 112, 177-178, pls. III, XXVI, XXVII; Petrie and Brunton 1924, p. 6, pl. XIII.
4. Hayes 1953, pp. 309-312; Mace and Winlock 1916, pp. 36-49.
5. Faulkner 1977, p. 154.

60

Second Intermediate Period

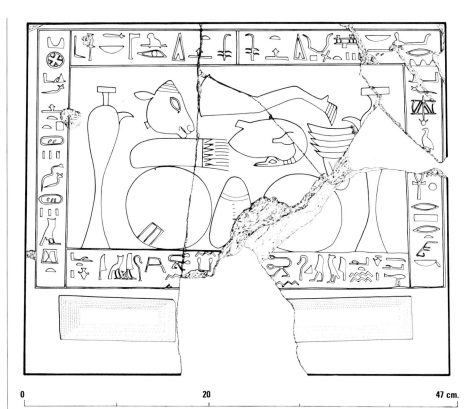

| 0 | 20 | 47 cm. |

61

61
Offering table of Iyem-iatu-ibu

From Abydos cemetery D tomb 62
Second Intermediate Period, Dynasty 13,
reign of King Sekhemra^c - Khutowi
Sobekhotep II
Limestone
Height 46 cm., width 38 cm.
Gift of Egypt Exploration Fund, 1901
(01.7303)

Part of the funerary equipment of the well-to-do Egyptian, the offering table was placed in the public area of the tomb, in front of an inscribed stela, false door, or statue, where relatives, friends, and funerary priests performed the funeral rites ensuring the immortal life of the deceased. These rites included not only material offerings of food and beverages, but also ritual recitations and magical spells.

Badly broken, the offering table reproduces the shape of the hieroglyph *hetep* ("offering") – a visual and literary allusion to its purpose. The inscriptions on the frame, beginning in the center and running to the left and right, were intended to be read by the viewer; in this way, the Egyptians believed, the food offerings would be transformed into material existence.

The basic Egyptian repast is carved rather roughly into the limestone: below are three loaves, two round and one conical; to the left and right two standing jars for water; and above the bread a cow's head and leg and a goose. Just to the right of it is a piece

of meat from the ribs of a cow, and to the left is a bundle of leeks and onions - the spicy addition to the dinner. Below these depictions are small basins and, possibly, a gutter (now destroyed), into which the funerary priest might have poured water or other liquids like wine or milk.

The inscriptions invoke the two most important gods of the realm of the dead: "Osiris, Lord of the Netherworld, that he may grant enough food to the owner of the table" and "Wepwawet, the jackal-god and mythical master of embalming, who awakens the dead to life by preparing the mummy, that he may grant the breath of life to the dead." The text on the left reads, "An offering, which the King gives, to Osiris, the Great God, Lord of Abydos, that he may give offerings and food-offerings according to requirement."[1] On the right, the text reads, "An offering, which the King gives, to Wepwawet, Lord of the Cemetery, that he may give the breath of life to your nose."

The beneficiary of these wishes is a certain Iyem-iatu-ibu (*iiw-m-i^ctw-ibw*) with the military title "Officer of the Ruler's Crew" (*ȝtw ny tt ḥkȝ*) (*itw > ȝtw*), the ruler being the King. He was leading a troop of men working on military or civilian expeditions in or outside Egypt, a kind of elite troop. Iyem-iatu-ibu ("Who comes as heart's joy") was the owner of tomb no. 62 in Cemetery D at Abydos, lying westward from the Shunet ez-Zebib. Inside his tomb, which had been reused and plundered, were an ivory shell, a fragment of an ivory inlay of a box, and an inscribed ebony fragment of a pen case,[2] together with fragments of a wooden coffin of a different owner.

Perhaps in a later stage of his life Iyem-iatu-ibu achieved the high-ranking title "Sealer of the King" at the royal court and "Chief of a Royal Department in a Temple-Area (*Imy-r₃ gs pr*)," an institution administered by the royal treasury, but working on a local level. This last title was not only on the ebony fragment of his pen case from his tomb, but also on a scarab seal and – most important – on the left side of a stela from Abydos.[3]

On the stela is depicted a certain Queen Ay, perhaps a relative of the unknown owner of the stela. We know this queen from a Dynasty 13 day-book and account-book of the royal court at Thebes, the so-called Papyrus Boulaq 18.[4] Queen Ay must be the wife of King Sekhemra^c-Khutowi Sobekhotep II, who reigned in the first half of the dynasty, only for about five years (ca. 1750 B.C.). Because Queen Ay and Iyem-iatu-ibu are mentioned on the same stela, we can conclude that he was contemporary with her and King Sobekhotep II.

Iyem-iatu-ibu was more than a warrior: as a member of the military forces, he was bestowed with a royal office. His rather poorly equipped tomb, therefore, suggests that he did not live in one of the wealthiest periods of ancient Egypt.

DF

1. To be read "*m ḥrt*," or, possibly, "*m ḥrt-hrw*" "daily"?
2. Boston MFA 01.7429.
3. Martin-von-Wagner-Museum at Würzburg, West Germany (Inv. No. H 35).
4. Scharff 1922, pp. 51-68.

Bibliography: Randall-MacIver and Mace 1902, pp. 85, 95, 100, pl. XXXIV, XLIV; Porter and Moss 1937, p. 69; Berlev 1974, pp. 26-31; Berlev 1971, p. 32ff.; Franke 1984, p. 54, no. 23.

62
Model coffin and *shawabti*

Provenance unknown
Second Intermediate Period
Wood
Length 10 cm., width 4 cm.
Hay Collection, Gift of C. Granville Way, 1872 (72.4122a-c)

This crudely carved *shawabti* and coffin are typical of the Second Intermediate Period[1] and are modeled on the provincial *rishi* type coffins of the time (see cat. 64) with their broad nemes headdresses and small faces. The *shawabti* itself is carved only cursorily; the end of the nose, the chin, and the eyes are indicated by adze strokes. The bare wood of the rough figure is covered with cursive hieroglyphs in black ink. The text is a version of the *shawabti* spell that appears on these figures in the late Middle King-

62

dom.[2] The figure was found wrapped in fairly fine linen inside the model coffin.

The coffin itself is also roughly carved in two parts. The lid is covered with adze marks roughly .7 centimeters wide. The proportions resemble those of the *rishi* coffins; a jutting chest is cut to allow the carving of the face and wig within the confines of the log itself. The coffin was covered with a wash of white pigment, and an inscription in black down the center of the lid reads, "An offering which the king gives through Osiris to the *ka* of Teti." These coffins and *shawabtis*, like those of the Middle Kingdom (cat. 55), may have been buried in sacred areas, although a number were found outside the tomb itself.[3]

PL/AMR

1. Hayes 1959, pp. 29-34.
2. Hayes 1953, pp. 350.
3. Carnarvon and Carter 1912, pp. 5, 13, pl. 43.

Literature: Brunner-Traut and Brunner 1981, pp. 266-267.

63
Coffin footboard

From Sheikh Farag tomb 5415
Second Intermediate Period to early New Kingdom
Wood
Height 28 cm., width 43 cm., depth 3.9 cm.
Harvard University-Museum of Fine Arts Expedition, 1923 (23.1476)

The goddesses Isis and Nephthys appear regularly on the footboards and headboards of coffins during the late Middle Kingdom. The coffins themselves have high arched lids with rectangular ends; the decoration is usually painted on a black background.[1] The yellow and white color scheme of this example may be a regional variation, or may be due to a slightly later date in the Second Intermediate Period.[2] It is similar to pieces known from early Dynasty 18,[3] but retains the framing bands of text characteristic of the late Middle Kingdom.

The piece is identified as a footboard because Isis and Nephthys tend to face the same direction as the mummy, which usually lies on its left side. The goddess shown here is probably Isis, who usually appears at the foot of such coffins facing right.[4] Her arms are raised in an attitude of mourning and she is drawn in the very awkward provincial style of the period. The facial features are poorly executed, as are the proportions and form of the body, with a breast protruding from beneath the arm.

The footboard is decorated in a wide range of colors. Isis is outlined in red and painted yellow, her wig is dark green blue, and her jewelry is light green. She is shown in a white sheath dress with a pattern of horizontal zig-zag lines in light green. Beneath her feet is a block border of alternating yellow and red squares framed in black. This use of color is also characteristic of the late Second Intermediate Period box coffins and *rishi* coffins from Thebes (see cat. 64).[5]

On either side of the goddess are vertical bands of solid black and strips of the open-cross pattern encountered on other coffins of the period.[6] These bands divide two panels of deep yellow and a central panel of yellow-white on each side. Each yellow panel contains part of an inscription in blue hieroglyphs.

This footboard is made of a thick plank beveled at the sides with two dowel holes to attach it to the coffin sideboards. There are also two dowel holes at both the top and bottom. The end panel of the coffin was found in a pile of debris outside of tomb 5415 at Sheikh Farag.

PL

1. Hayes 1953, pp. 347-349, fig. 228.
2. Cf. a Second Intermediate Period coffin from Abydos; Peet 1914, pp. 122-123. pl. 13/5.
3. Carnarvon and Carter 1912, pl. 60.
4. Schmidt 1919, p. 68.
5. Hayes 1953.
6. One of these *rishi* coffins is dated by a scarab of Amenhotep I. The box coffins of the period are more colorful than in the late Middle Kingdom, but Isis and Nephthys are usually no longer framed by columns of text.

63

64
Rishi coffin

Provenance unknown, probably Thebes
Second Intermediate Period, 1650-1558 B.C.
Painted wood
Length 158 cm., width 36 cm., depth 33.5 cm.
Morris and Louise Rosenthal Fund, Horace L. and Florence B. Mayer Fund, Marilyn M. Simpson Fund, William S. Smith Fund, Egyptian Special Purchase Fund, Frank B. Bemis Fund, 1987 (1987.490a,b)

The Arabic term *rishi* (feathered) is often used to describe the pattern of this type of decoration. It is possible that this type of pattern descended from the decoration of royal Middle Kingdom anthropoid coffins, of which only scant traces have survived.[1] Such an adoption of royal iconography on non-royal coffins would be paralleled by a similar borrowing that took place after the breakdown of central authority in the First Intermediate Period.[2] Added weight is given to this argument by the fact that after the beginning of the New Kingdom, the *rishi* coffin is once again restricted to royal use.[3]

This example is representative of later Second Intermediate Period coffins from Thebes. It is particularly closely related to an example discovered in the Carnarvon excavations, which has the same distinctive fields of color at the foot end.[4] Like most of these coffins, this one was carved from a single log of sycamore; the peculiar pigeon-chested form was dictated by the dimensions of the material the artisan had to work with. The face, which has been slightly restored, is painted black to indicate the equation of the deceased with Osiris. The head is covered with an adaptation of the *nemes* headdress decorated with a scale pattern, while the lappets are striped in bands of green, red, blue, and yellow, with white borders.

A beaded broad collar is painted on the chest in bands of red, blue, and greenish-brown (possibly a discolored green), with tricolor teardrop pendants in red, white, and blue. Below is a heraldic pectoral in the form of the vulture-goddess Nekhbet and the cobra-goddess Wadjet. The latter motif obviously derived from the decoration of a royal mummiform coffin.[5] The remainder of the coffin is dominated by a pair of large vulture wings in red, green, and blue, which covers the body down to the feet; a single yellow band of offering formula runs down the center. The name is omitted at the bottom of the column, as is often the case with these coffins, suggesting that they were mass-produced.

The painted decoration is confined to the lid, while the bottom half of the coffin is covered only with a layer of plaster and a

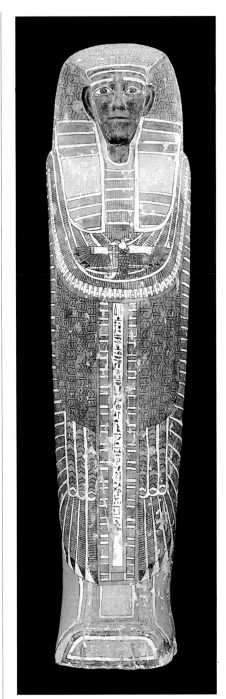

64

yellow wash. The foot end bears traces of decoration that probably would have shown Isis and Nephthys in an attitude of mourning characteristic of these coffins.[6]

PL

1. Lacovara (forthcoming).
2. Mace and Winlock 1916, p. 43.
3. Daressy 1909, pls. 3, 8, 9, 28-29.
4. Carnarvon and Carter 1912, pl. 53, 3.
5. Lacovara (forthcoming).
6. Hayes 1959, p. 31.

Literature: Hayes 1959, pp. 29-32; Winlock 1924b, pp. 217-277.

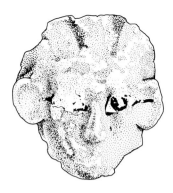

65

66

65
Face from a mummy mask

From Abydos tomb D 115[1]
New Kingdom, early to mid-Dynasty 18
Plaster
Height 6.8 cm., width 6.5 cm.
Gift of the Egypt Exploration Fund, 1901
(01.7436)

At the very beginning of Dynasty 18 a short-lived type of mummy mask appears in Upper Egyptian and Nubian cemeteries with only a few exceptions coming from elsewhere. A small face of plaster, usually not more than six to eight centimeters high, was formed in molds with a flat back and top and a half-round face sometimes including the part of the neck. In most burials only this molded face has survived due to the hardness of the plaster. Whole examples[2] and technical details on the faces prove that they were part of "normal" cartonnage headmasks as known from previous periods. An additional layer of plaster connected the face with the cartonnage mask; on this example, the front part of the headdress as well as the separately added ears are still stuck to the face; the texture from the linen layer of the cartonnage is imprinted on the back.

This mask comes from Abydos, where a relatively large number of these plaster faces have been found in early Dynasty 18 tombs.[3] The face and ears are painted yellow as a substitute for gold. The Roman nose with a definite bridge has parallels on other faces found at Abydos. The large eyes are black and white. Also black are the thin brows and cosmetic lines around the eyes; the left one runs far into the ear – probably an error of the artist, as are the two small blue stripes on the bottom of the left earlobe. As there is no beard or beard band, this piece probably belonged to a woman, as did the one from Sheikh Farag (cat. 60). The pattern of the headdress consists of red, yellow, and blue stripes running radially away from the front, thus proving that it has to be reconstructed as the royal *nemes*-headdress. After the Middle Kingdom[4] the funerary trappings of commoners were occasionally allowed to adopt royal attributes

in the hope that such a privilege would ensure an easier transition into the eternal life.

ER

1. The mask is not mentioned in Randall-MacIver and Mace 1902, p. 102.
2. Winlock 1947, fig. 14; Garstang 1907, fig. 183a.
3. Garstang 1901, p. 10f., pl. XIV; two of the faces are now in Liverpool, School of Archaeology and Oriental Studies E 5722 and E 5723, one of them in Cambridge, Fitzwilliam 134/1900.
4. Petrie 1907, pl. XB, XI.

66
Face from a mummy mask

From Rifa tomb 154
New Kingdom, early Dynasty 18
Plaster
Height 5 cm., width 4.7 cm.
Gift of the Egyptian Research Account, 1907 (07.556)

Only the molded form of this example from Rifa in Upper Egypt has survived. A bit of wood stuck to its back indicates that, unlike the other faces, it was put on a wooden mask or perhaps even on a mummiform coffin. The large eyes are painted black and white; the thin brows and the eyepaint are outlined in black. Remnants of reddish gold leaf on the face were determined by X-ray fluorescence examination to be a gold-silver alloy, which would have given its owner the color of the flesh of the immortal gods. On the front of the face is a blue stripe from the headdress; along the jawline runs the blue band of the now lost ceremonial beard, indicating that this piece once belonged to a man.

Two other examples from Rifa, now in Cambridge and Liverpool, also have blue beard bands and blue and red headdresses.[1] It may be characteristic of the molds used in Rifa workshops that none of these faces has a neck.

Plaster faces have been found mainly in Upper Egypt[2] and Nubia.[3] The fact that they have only occasionally been unearthed in northern cemeteries[4] may be due to the fact that north of Rifa only a few necropoleis of early Dynasty 18 have yet been investigated.

ER

1. Cambridge, Fitzwilliam 16/1907; Liverpool Museum 4-9-07-20; Bienkowsky and Southworth 1986, p. 86.
2. E.g. Bourriau and Millard 1971, pp. 28-57, pl. XVI.2; Downes 1974, pp. 108-109; Root 1979, p. 28.
3. Steindorff 1937, p. 73, pl. 41a; Vila 1976, pp. 151ff.; Dunham and Janssen 1960, p. 127, pl. 127D.
4. Petrie and Brunton 1924, p. 267, pl. LXIII.

Bibliography: Petrie 1907, p. 22; University College 1907, pp. 11-12.

67

Lid of an anthropoid coffin

Provenance unknown
New Kingdom, Dynasty 18
Wood
Length 146 cm., width 33 cm., foot-end depth 22.4 cm.
Egyptian Curator's Fund, 1988 (1988.1)

The anthropoid coffin, which first appears in the Middle Kingdom (see cat. 51), becomes the most common type of coffin in the New Kingdom. The coffins belonging to the Thutmoside period and later Dynasty 18 revive the black and yellow color scheme of late Middle Kingdom coffins, but add significant new decorative flourishes and more lengthy inscriptions.[1]

This piece is a fine example of its type.[2] It shows the deceased wearing a vertically striped black and yellow wig and elaborate hawk-headed broad collar in red, yellow, and blue-green. The face is yellow with black painted eyes and brows. On the chest is a careful rendering of the vulture goddess in yellow and black with her wings outstretched to protect the deceased, no doubt derived from the pectorals on Second Intermediate Period *rishi* coffins (see cat. 64).

The black resin-coated surface is divided by bands of yellow orpiment pigment, imitating mummy wrappings and inscribed with funerary texts. The central band contains a speech of the deceased, calling upon the sky goddess: "O mother Nut, spread yourself over me, placing me among the imperishable stars which are in Nun." The area which should give the name of the deceased was left blank, as in coffins of the Second Intermediate Period (see cat. 64). Around the edges of the lid are two offering formulae. The text on the proper right side calls upon Anubis and the gods of the necropolis for the standard invocation offerings for the *ka* of "Ma'a-kheru," which is probably simply the epithet "justified," rather than a name. The text running along the proper left edge calls upon Osiris and Hathor for the scent of the north wind and

67

drink from the eddy of the river, making no reference at all to the deceased and his soul. The four vertical bands on each side contain invocations by various gods, including Anubis, Geb, Duamutef, and

Dewen-'anwy. These invocations would have continued on the box of the coffin.

The head and foot ends are decorated with figures of the goddesses Nephthys and Isis, respectively, whose arms are raised in mourning. This decoration is also derived from the coffin designs of the Second Intermediate Period (see cat. 63).

The lid itself is quite narrow as are some others of the period,[3] perhaps so that it could be nested inside a middle anthropoid coffin and an outer box coffin.[4]

PL/AMR

1. Cf. Niwinski 1983, col. 435-438.
2. It was originally collected by Richard E. S. Maxson.
3. Cf. Shorter and Edwards 1938, pp. 33-34.
4. Cf. Daressy 1902. pp. 1-11, pls. 1-2.

68

68

Lotiform collar terminal

Provenance unknown
New Kingdom, late Dynasty 18 to Dynasty 19
Faience
Length 3.6 cm., width 4.8 cm., depth 0.5 cm.
Gift of C. Granville Way, 1872 (72.2647)

This faience terminal depicts a blue lotus flower (*Nymphaea coerulea-sav.*) molded in relief on the upper surface. At the rear, three small holes have been pierced through to the top for necklace strings, and a larger aperture was made at the base for the cord tie. The light blue glaze, derived primarily from copper,[1] was long used as a pigment in the manufacture of faience.

AB

Polychrome faience beads shaped like fruits (dates, grapes, mandrakes), flowers (blue and perhaps white lotus petals, cornflowers, poppy petals, daisies, lilies), and leaves (willow or perhaps palm) were strung in multiple rows for wide collars. These often ended in flower-shaped terminals (lotus or lily[2]) and were tied at the back of the neck with (red) string.[3] Complete examples have been excavated in Amarna houses[4] and the tomb of Tutankhamen.[5] They seem to have been especially popular at Amarna, where many molds for their manufacture were found.[6] Gold floral collars were also placed in royal burials at this time.[7]

The faience collars are probably simulacra or substitutes for real floral collars, known as *wah* collars, which were painstakingly pieced together from petals and leaves on a papyrus backing. These seem to have had a special relevance to funerary ritual, and we know they were worn by officiants at the funerary ceremonies for Tutankhamen.[8] A large collar was also placed at the neck of his innermost coffin, and a tiny one around the middle coffin's uraeus.[9] At about the same time the floral collar began to be shown on coffins,[10] where it soon became customary,[11] and it continued as a popular funerary motif into the Late Period.

A text on the portable chest from Tutankhamen's tomb reads, in part, "May you take the *wah*-collar of justification which was at the neck of Wen-nefer [Osiris] [so that] your limbs may become young and your heart may become strong [again] when you are assessed by the Ennead."[12] The *wah* (or *mah*) *ny maa kheru*, or "crown of justification," was an important symbol of the vindication of Osiris, and therefore the deceased, in the judgment of the afterworld.[13]

MB

1. Kaczmarczyk and Hedges 1983, p. 56.
2. The Egyptian Museum, Cairo, exhibits the eight faience necklaces from Tutankhamen's tomb. Two (948, 945) have lily terminals, one has a lotus (944), two have white-faience blocks inlaid with multicolored flowers (946, Carter 1923, p. 173, pl. 39), and three with running spirals (949, 950, 951).
3. See Carter and Mace 1923, pl. 39.
4. Frankfort and Pendlebury 1933, 18, pl. 36.1,2. Pl. 36.2 (J12833, exhibited in The Egyptian Museum, Cairo.)
5. Kacmarczyk and Hedges 1983, p. 52. Also see Needler 1966, p. 14; Eaton-Krauss 1982, pp. 234-235, no. 308; Freed 1981a, p. 45 (in color); Hayes 1959, pp. 320-321; Aldred 1971, p. 231, fig. 125 (in color).
6. Samson 1972, p. 64, pl. III; Peet and Wooley 1923, pl. 13.3.
7. "Long" cornflower, white (?) and blue lotus petals, date and mandrake shaped gold beads were found in the Royal Tomb: Martin 1974, pl. 50, no. 287. Also see Davis et al. 1910, pl. 21. A possibly complete gold collar with lotiform terminals was found in a Cypriote tomb: Marshall 1911, pp. 36-37, pl. 5, no. 581, cited by G. Martin 1974.
8. Winlock 1941, pp. 17-18, pl 6.
9. Carter 1927, pp. 129-130, 132, 136, 263-271, pls. 22, 36.
10. Davis 1910, pl. 30.
11. Desroches-Noblecourt 1976, pp. 166-167, pl. 35.
12. Courtesy L. Bell.
13. Book of the Dead, chapter 19; Jankuhn 1979, p. 764.

69

69
Wedjat eye scarab

From Deir el-Bahri
New Kingdom
Glass frit
Length 1.3 cm., width 1 cm.
Gift of the Egypt Exploration Fund, 1906
(06.2499)

On the back of this blue glass frit scarab is a *wedjat* eye in molded relief and on its base an inscribed *bolti* fish with two lotuses. Both motifs are common on Dynasty 18 scarabs and amulets,[1] often appearing in combination with royal name inscriptions,[2] as the decorative base of cowroids and scarab beetles,[3] and on the base of button seals.[4]

The combination of the sacred eye and fish with lotuses is an interesting aspect of this scarab. The *bolti*, or *Tilapia nilotica*, represents both life and fecundity;[5] when combined with the lotus, whose blossoms are literally "reborn" each morning as a result of the generative powers of the sun, it becomes a powerful symbol of rejuvenation. The lotus itself is closely associated with the god Nefertum, who is occasionally shown with the eye of Horus in his hand, an allusion to the eye offered by the son to his father Osiris.[6] Thus, the pairing of the *wedjat* eye and the *bolti* with lotuses may represent the unique relationship between the lotus, Nefertum, and the sacred eye.

YJM

1. Petrie 1925a, p. 17; Brunton and Engelbach 1927, p. 14.
2. Museum of Fine Arts 1982, p. 254.
3. Giveon 1985, no. 48245; Hayes 1959 pp. 183-184.
4. Petrie 1925, pl. XI.
5. Matouk 1976, p. 155.
6. Lurker 1980, p. 67.

70
Scarab pectoral

Provenance unknown
New Kingdom, Dynasty 19 or 20
Steatite (?)
Height 10.4 cm., width 13 cm.
Hay Collection, Gift of C. Granville Way, 1872 (72.769)

In the New Kingdom and later, the heart scarab was sometimes set into – or replaced by – a pectoral placed on the breast of the mummy, outside the bandages.[1]

This example, though missing a large fragment, is a finely detailed pectoral inscribed for the Chief Workman in the Place of Truth (the Theban necropolis), Pa-shed.[2] On the recto, the scarab beetle appears in very high relief, its back incised with the figure of the solar deity riding in a sacred barque and flanked by shrines of Upper and Lower Egypt. Below are two herons, or *benu*-birds. The *benu*, known in classical times as the phoenix, was a symbol of regeneration through its association with Re at sunrise and Osiris at sunset.[3] The scarab is flanked by the figures in somewhat lower relief of Isis and Nephthys, the sisters of Osiris, who wear tight-fitting dresses, fillets, armlets, and bracelets, and stand with upraised arms on a sacred barque. The lower half of the figure on the left has been broken away. The barque bears a *wedjat* eye beneath the feet of the remaining goddess, and rests on the base of the pectoral, which is decorated with chevrons indicating water. The scene is framed by a structure with cavetto cornice.

All of the decoration on the verso is incised, in contrast to the recto. The verso once again shows Isis and Nephthys, identified by their headdresses, seated before a large oval meant to represent the underside of the scarab, upon which a text is normally inscribed. However, here it appears as the hieroglyph for "heart," reinforcing the function of the pectoral as a heart scarab. The text is Chapter 30b from the Book of the Dead, exhorting the heart not to testify against the deceased on the day of judgment: "My heart of (my) mother, my heart of (my) mother, my heart of my forms. Do not stand against me as a witness. [Do not create] opposition in the presence of (the keeper of the balance). You are [my ka] which is in (my) body, Khnum who makes (my) limbs prosper. May you go forth to the happy place."

The pectoral has been pierced with two sets of holes at the top and back, indicating that it originally was either sewn on to the wrappings or hung around the neck.

SD'A

1. Cf. Feucht 1971; Hayes 1959, p. 420; Budge 1925, pp. 249-250, pl. XIX; Sotheby's London 1987, 53, no. 159; Bulté 1981, p. 112, and pl. IX.

2. For the name, see Ranke 1935, p. 119, no. 3.
3. For the heron or phoenix, see Houlihan 1986, pp. 13-16; Malaise 1978, p. 56 ff.; Kákosy 1982, pp. 1030-1039.

Literature: Feucht 1971.

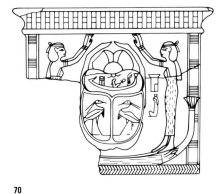

70

71
Coffin shroud

Provenance unknown
New Kingdom, late Dynasty 18 to early Dynasty 19, 1310-1275 B.C.
Painted linen
Height 32.4 cm.
William Stevenson Smith Fund, 1981
(1981.657)

This wonderfully preserved linen shroud depicts the deceased, dressed in a long kilt, broad collar, and perfumed wax cone on his wig, seated before an offering table. One hand reaches toward the offerings placed on the table, while the other grasps a linen handkerchief. The inscription above the table is very abbreviated and neglects to name the deceased, but reads ''Anubis, Lord of the Necropolis, may he grant the breathing of the (sweet) breeze of the north.''

The vivid colors were painted over a gesso ground. Scientific analysis of the pigments has revealed that the reddish color is an earth pigment colored by ferric oxide, the black is carbon black, and the blue is ''Egyptian blue,'' a pigment used extensively by the ancient Egyptians and manufactured from ground frit.[1]

The use of such linen squares as coffin shrouds was confirmed by the discovery of examples in the necropolis of Deir el-Medina, the village that housed the artisans who decorated the New Kingdom royal tombs. In the tomb of Sen-nefer, an anthropoid sarcophagus covered with a linen pall bore upon the breast, still *in situ*, a painted square, now in Cairo.[2] Many more were discovered at the site, either painted[3] or rather crudely sketched in black ink,[4] but all showing the deceased before the offering table.[5]

New Kingdom squares of painted linen, fringed on one or more sides, and decorated with scenes of worshippers before the goddess Hathor, are known from the nearby site of Deir el-Bahri.[6] However, these were apparently votive in nature, employed in the temple ceremonies devoted to that goddess.[7]

SD'A

1. Conservation report by Richard Newman, Research Laboratory, Museum of Fine Arts.
2. JE 54885, Bruyère 1929, pp. 42, 47, pl. III; Institut Français 1981, no. 38, pp. 52-53.
3. Bruyère 1926, p. 11 and 31, figs 3 and 16; Bruyère 1933, pp. 108-109, figs. 36-37.
4. Bruyère 1930, p. 87, fig. 41,1; Bruyère 1933, p. 3, fig. 1, p. 25, fig. 9; Bruyère 1934, p. 97, fig. 63; Bruyère 1939, p. 227, fig. 116.
5. See also MMA 44.2.3, Hayes 1959, p. 319, fig. 202; Ranke 1948, frontispiece, in color.
6. Naville and Hall 1913, pls. 15-16, pls. XXX, XXXI; Parlasca 1966, Taf. 54-55, pp. 153-54.
7. de Rustafjaell 1915, no. 706, p. 98 (MFA 52.28, 52.29).

Bibliography: Museum of Fine Arts 1981-82, p. 27; Museum of Fine Arts 1987, cover and pp. 46-47.

72
Counterpoise

From Semna
New Kingdom, Dynasty 18
Bronze
Height 13.8 cm., max. width 4.5 cm., depth 0.2 cm.
Harvard University-Museum of Fine Arts Expedition, 1929 (29.1199)

Originally used to keep heavy collars and necklaces from falling down the neck, the counterpoise or *menat* became an important ornament in and of itself. In the New Kingdom, *menats* were often decorated with representations of the goddess Hathor as in this example, but the association with Hathor and the deceased dates back even further. ''*Menats* of Hathor'' are given to the deceased by her priests, who ask that she grant him a ''long life and destruction of his enemies.''[1]

This example compounds three images of Hathor within the prescribed shape of the *menat*: in the center is a full figure of the

71

73
Model coffin and *shawabti*

Provenance unknown
New Kingdom, Dynasty 18
Wood
Length 32 cm., width 9 cm., depth 9 cm.
Gift of C. Granville Way, 1872 (72.4121a-c)

This miniature coffin for a *shawabti* copies a type of real coffin common during the first half of Dynasty 18[1] and descended from the anthropoid coffins of Dynasty 12 (see cat. 51). The body of the coffin is painted white to simulate the mummy bandages with a mask and collar over the body. A New Kingdom innovation is the addition of four bands of text on either side of the band of text that runs down the front of the coffin. The bands on the sides of the coffin are not inscribed in this example. The central text is a simple offering formula, written in cursive black hieroglyphs, naming Osiris.

The model is made of a soft wood, probably acacia, and is painted white with yellow bands bordered in black. The coloring of the rest of the piece is largely gone, but the wig has traces of blue pigment and the face is yellow in color. This decoration is duplicated on the *shawabti* itself, where the paint is better preserved. The facial features, the

ears, and the crossed hands are finely carved and modeled, and the paint has been carefully applied.

The *shawabti* text is inscribed in carefully incised hieroglyphs. The sculptor made two small errors, carving an owl rather than a vulture in the first line and reversing one of the baskets in the last line; otherwise the text is standard in form and content. Both the *shawabti* and the coffin belonged to an individual named Mes-nefer, a name not attested elsewhere.[2] A line of text running down the back of the *shawabti* in the gap between the end and the beginning of the *shawabti* text states, ''It is his father who caused his name to live,'' implying that Mes-nefer's father supplied this portion of his burial equipment.

Such model coffins and *shawabti*s were probably made as votive objects for burial either in the tomb or in sacred precincts (see cats. 55 and 62).

PL/AMR

1. Cf. Schmidt 1919, p. 116.
2. Ranke 1935, p. 164, lists a similar name on the pattern *ms* + adjective, Mesmen, dating from the New Kingdom.

Literature: Schneider 1977, pp. 35-36 (3.1.1.5), 38 (3.1.1.13) and 42 (3.1.1.25).

goddess holding a *was* scepter; below she appears as a cow in a papyrus skiff in a roundel, and above, she wears the vulture wig at the top of the *menat*. She wears the solar disk between two cow horns in all three representations.

The Boston *menat* was found in the fort at Semna in a building dating to Dynasty 18 below the temple built by Taharqa[2] (see cat. 107); a similar example was found in a neighboring room in the same structure.[3] Unfortunately, neither was in association with the beads from a necklace, although a similar example was recovered intact at Malkata.[4]

PL

1. Wilkinson 1971, pp. 68-69.
2. Field no. 28 -1-105 from room ''r'' in a mid-Dynasty 18 deposit in a structure beneath the Taharqa Temple; Dunham and Janssen 1960, p. 48, pl. 128a-b.
3. This example, 28 -1- 67, presumably now in Khartoum, was found in room ''m'' of the same structure and was similar to cat. 72 except that a rosette was substituted for the roundel at the bottom of the *menat*; Dunham and Janssen 1960, p. 47, pl.128 a-b.
5. Hayes 1959, p. 269.

Bibliography: Reisner 1929a, pp. 64-75, fig. 11; Dunham and Janssen, 1960, p. 48, pl. 128a-b; Holden 1982, p. 306. n. 418.

73

74

Fig. 77   Fig. 78

74
Female figure on a bed

Provenance unknown
New Kingdom, Dynasty 18
Limestone
Length 10.1 cm., width 3.5 cm., footboard
height 5.1 cm.
Hay Collection, Gift of C. Granville Way,
1872 (72.739)

A nude female figure is represented lying
on a bed with tall footboard. Though much
of the original paint is now gone, the figure
wears a black wig with red fillet, and red
broad collar, bracelets, and girdle. Her eyes
and pubic area are painted black. The bed
on which she lies was also painted black
with a red upper surface.

On the back of the headboard stands a red-
painted figure of Taweret, the hippopotamus goddess who watches over birth,
reaching forward to lean on a *sa*-sign, the hieroglyph for protection (fig. 77). Facing her
is a problematic figure, possibly the god Bes
with a tambourine. These two deities frequently occur together as protective decoration on beds. The footboard is too worn to
identify with certainty, but may include a
seated woman holding a mirror and another
object (fig. 78).

Standing figures of nude women with similar jewelry occur frequently in tomb assemblages from the late First Intermediate Period through early Dynasty 18 (see cat. 52).[1]
Variously interpreted as dolls, concubines
for the deceased, fertility figures, and
images of Isis or Hathor, their precise function is difficult to determine because their

archaeological contexts vary widely.[2]
Figures of women on beds occur more frequently in pottery[3] than in limestone.[4] Most
date to the New Kingdom, but a few are
known from the Late Period site of Naukratis.[5] The figures sometimes lie with their
heads on pillows, with both arms at their
sides, or with the right arm bent. Coiffures
and jewelry range from simple to elaborate,
and a few figures have scented wax cones
represented on their wigs. The woman is
sometimes accompanied by the figure of an
infant, generally painted at the foot of the
bed to the right of the mother.[6] She is
sometimes shown suckling the child. It is
likely that the Museum's figure once included the figure of an infant, as the woman
is placed off-center, and faint traces of black
paint remain to the right of her legs. Decorative motifs are sometimes painted on the
beds,[7] and one woman has a mirror placed
near her arm.[8]

The purpose of these figures, like that of
the earlier ones, is problematic. Some derive from tombs of children,[9] making unlikely their function as concubines. Though
their funerary nature seems undeniable,
even this has been called into question by
the finding of a number of these figures in
the debris of the workmen's village of Deir
el-Medina.[10] It seems likely that they are
meant in some way to aid the deceased in
the afterlife, whether they are substitutes
for mother or wife, or symbols of fertility.

SD'A

1. Randall-MacIver and Mace 1902, pl. 43; Peet
   1914, pl. 14; Brunton 1930, pl. 9.
2. For a discussion of the function of these
   figures, see Desroches-Noblecourt 1953 and
   Hornblower 1929.
3. Brunton and Engelbach 1927, pl. XXV, 20 and
   pl. XLVII, 10, 13; Hornblower 1929, p. 46, pl.
   VIII; Engelbach 1915, p. 19, pl. XXII,6; Petrie
   1905, pl. XL, 20; Breasted 1948, p. 96, pl. 93c.
4. Brunton and Engelbach 1927, p. 17, pl. XIII, 6;
   Hayes 1959, pp. 266 and 203, fig. 117;
   Breasted 1948, p. 96, pl. 93a.
5. Petrie 1886, pp. 40-41, pl. XIX.
6. Brunton and Engelbach 1927, pl. XLVII, 10,
   13.
7. Brunton and Engelbach 1927, pl. XIII.
8. Bruyère 1933, fig. 4.
9. Brunton and Engelbach 1927, pp. 14, 17.
10. Bruyère 1933, p. 14.

75
Funerary statuette of Pasunu

Provenance unknown
New Kingdom, late Dynasty 18 or 19
Painted limestone
Length 22 cm., width 10.8 cm., height
8.5 cm.
Samuel Putnam Avery Fund, 1971
(1971.292)

The funerary figurine of Pasunu portrays the

deceased lying on a bier, his hands flat on
his thighs in an attitude of prayer. He is
dressed in the pleated garments typical of
daily life in late Dynasty 18 and the Ramesside period, but he also wears the tripartite
wig usually seen on *shawabti*s, anthropoid
coffins, and other funerary equipment.

According to Schneider, *shawabti*s shown
in the dress of daily life (cat. 102) appear after the Amarna Period. He likens them to
the *ka*-statues of the deceased that begin to
appear during the reign of Thutmose IV. Another type of *shawabti,* showing a figure on
a bier, first appeared during the reign of
Amenhotep III.[1] In most of these examples,
the figure is mummiform and the bier is
decorated with lion-shaped legs. There is
often a *ba*-bird on either side of the mummy
or on its chest. The most famous example
of this variety was found in the tomb of
Tutankhamen.[2]

The Pasunu statuette is unusual for several
reasons. The bier is simple, though it is
clearly shown to be a platform with two
long supports rather than a large back pillar.
The figure's hands are on the thighs instead
of crossed over his chest, as is more com-

75

mon. He also wears the tripartite wig rather than the duplex wig or *perruque à ''revers''* more common for *shawabtis* with dress of daily life.

The figure is well carved; relief lines indicate the eyebrows, which extend almost to the ears, and the facial features and ears are carefully formed. The wig is striated with the lappets ending in a horizontal strip. The pleats on the sleeve and skirt front are indicated, but nothing is carved on the sides of the skirt. The garments seem to have been painted yellow, the wig was black, and the skin was red.

The inscription down the front of the skirt reads ''The Osiris, Pasunu, Justified.'' The name is not recorded in Ranke, but it seems to mean ''The Doctor.'' The mark above the name determinative is probably a gouge rather than a *t*. Below the name, where one would expect to find the hieroglyphs *mȝ*^{c}*t ḥrw*, the *mȝ*^{c}*t* has been written as a book roll. Since there are traces of paint in the inscription, it seems unlikely that it was added later.

A similar example, smaller and made of pottery rather than limestone, is in Berlin.[3] It seems likely that the MFA example originally had its own coffin.

CHR

1. Schneider 1977, pp. 161, 163.
2. Desroches-Noblecourt 1978, pl. LIV, opposite p. 259.
3. Berlin 10783, see Hornemann 1957, p. 792.

Literature: Schneider 1977.

76
Bowl

From Abydos tomb F15
New Kingdom, Dynasty 18
Faience
Height 6 cm., diam. 17.3 cm.
Gift of Egypt Exploration Fund, 1909
(09.377)

On the interior of this blue faience bowl, open and closed blue lotus flowers in black line extend from a central pool comprising a pinwheel surrounded by four concentric squares filled with black dashes. The symmetrical arrangement of the sixteen flowers extending from the sides and corners of the outer square made possible the restoration of this fragmentary bowl. Additional small lotus buds are near the rim above the flowers, which droop to the side. On the exterior, fourteen-pointed petals and sepals, alternately plain and stippled, radiate from the dark painted flat base to the dark painted flat rim.

In early to middle Dynasty 18, shallow faience bowls similar to this one reached the height of their popularity, especially in the reigns of Hatshepsut and Thutmose III

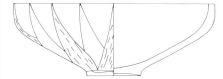

76, interior and side

(1504-1450 B.C.). They were used as votive objects in temples and shrines, particularly those dedicated to the goddess Hathor, and were included in the grave goods of private citizens. They have been found throughout Egypt at such sites as Thebes, Abydos, Sedment, Qau, Harageh, Sakkara, and Abusir, and in Nubia at Aniba, Shalfak, Buhen, and Faras.

The extraordinary variety of interior decoration includes not only the blue lotus flower (*Nymphae caerulea Savigny*) but also papyrus umbels and buds; *tilapia* fish; Hathor motifs of sistra, *menats*, and her celestial cow; small birds; and rodents.[1] No two bowls of this type are exactly alike in the specific arrangement of the elements, although occasionally the motifs and execution are sufficiently similar to suggest the same workshop.[2]

This bowl was found in one of the few Dynasty 18 tombs cleared in Cemetery F at Abydos.[3] A close parallel is one of seven faience bowls found in the lower chambers of the family tomb of Nefer-khaut at Thebes, MMA 729 in the Lower Asasif, which was cut before the end of the reign of Thutmose III.[4] Now in Cairo, this bowl was deposited with two others in the head end of the coffin of Nefer-khaut's wife Reni-nefer. Its decoration consists of a central pinwheel enclosed by two concentric squares. Both the central pool and the execution of the individual lotus flowers are close in style to the Abydos bowl but the Theban bowl differs in the addition of papyrus umbels, the position of the main floral group at the corners of the square, and in the less controlled line of the draftsman. On other faience bowls of this type that have a pinwheel in the center, surrounding motifs consist not only of floral el-

ements but also fish[5] and on one example a Hathor-headed sistrum, an ornate palmette, and the pondweed *Potamogeton lucens L.*[6]

Many of the images on the bowls are associated with rebirth. The blue lotus closes at night and opens in the morning, thus paralleling the daily cycle of the sun god Re and his rebirth.[7] The central pool, which has a wide variety of possible decoration elements – the pinwheel, checkerboard, wavy water lines, rosettes, basket-weave pattern – has been identified with the primeval waters of Nun from which life sprang and from which the sun god rises each morning.[8] The bowls are clearly associated closely with the goddess Hathor, as indicated by the Hathor images, the presence of such bowls in shrines dedicated to her, and the rare examples of prayers invoking Hathor that are inscribed on faience bowls.[9] This affiliation with Hathor can be attributed in part to her roles as necropolis deity, ''mistress of turquoise,'' ''mistress of lapis lazuli,'' and ''mistress of the malachite country,''[10] the very precious materials that the synthetic faience is meant to imitate.[11]

By far the majority of the faience bowls found in Dynasty 18 burials were empty. The fact that one bowl from Deir el-Medina tomb 1077 and other fragments from the French excavations at that site contained ''milky'' substances led to the speculation that the bowls were containers for water or milk – offerings to the goddesses Hathor, Isis, or Nut in their roles as nourishing, protective deities.[12] The bowls have also been considered drinking vessels. This idea stems primarily from the imagery of the central pool and aquatic plants,[13] but seems an unlikely possibility. Many of these faience bowls are too large and unwieldy to have functioned as drinking vessels.[14] Another suggestion is that they may have contained a solid, perfumed substance, such as ointment cones whose strong scent would have embodied certain rejuvenating processes.[15] The fact that so many of the bowls were clearly empty suggests that most of them were deposited as objects in their own right. The symbolism of rebirth in their decoration suggest that they were strictly funerary objects that never graced any table in daily life.

BAP

1. Strauss 1974, pp. 13-32.
2. Milward 1982, p. 143, cat. no. 139.
3. Ayrton and Loat 1908-1909, pp. 2-5.
4. Hayes 1935, pp. 30, 32; Porter 1986, pp. 55-58, cat. no. 2 (Cairo 65366).
5. Steindorff 1937, pl. 92, 2; Krönig 1934, fig. 20.
6. Strauss 1974, fig. 16; Keimer 1929, fig. 23.
7. Milward 1982, pp. 141-143.
8. Strauss 1974, p. 70; Fazzini 1983, cat. 35; Wildung 1980, p. 17.
9. Milward 1982, p. 141; Hayes 1935, p. 35; Porter 1986, pp. 78-79, cat. no. 8.
10. Bleeker 1973, pp. 42-45, 73.
11. Kingery and Vandiver 1986, p. 51.

12. Bruyère 1927, p. 46; Bruyère 1937, pp. 89-90; Milward 1982, pp. 141-142; Ecole du Caire 1981, p. 195.
13. Hayes 1959, p. 206.
14. Milward 1982, pp. 141-142; Winlock 1922, fig. 25; Krönig 1934, pl. 26c; Strauss 1974, fig. 7 (Bowl from Deir el Bahri, MMA 22..3.73; diameter 32 cm.).
15. Dorothea Arnold, personal communication. The Egyptological Seminar of New York, May 1987.

Literature: Krönig 1934; Strauss 1974; Milward 1982, pp. 141-145.

77

77
Amphora

From Sakkara
New Kingdom, late Dynasty 18
Calcite (Egyptian alabaster)
Height 34.8 cm., diam. 22 cm.
Acquired by exchange with Peabody Museum, 1944 (44.30)

This horizontal-handled amphora with a *wah* collar, acquired in Egypt in 1859, belongs to a class of elaborate stone vessels best known from aristocratic burials, where they held unguents (possibly perfumed).[1] These were presumably meant for use by the deceased in the afterlife. The Boston vase could have been sealed with a flat stone lid.[2] Its body shape seems to copy vases of a different material made with pointed bases; such stone amphorae are usually shown supported by a cylindrical pot stand. These stands can be carved in one piece with the body of the vase or "glued" to a protruding tang.[3] The flat base of the Boston example is unusual, but is paralleled by another vessel now in Cairo.[4] The glossy surface is also unusual,[5] and certainly not antique. As on other examples, the handles are elaborately carved with vertical ribs and horizontal grooves, and the neck is grooved.[6] Amphorae of this type are known

from the middle of Dynasty 18[7] and two examples, with slightly more elaborate handles, were found in the tomb of Tutankhamen.[8]

Lying on the shoulder is a delicate necklace, incised and probably originally picked out with blue.[9] We can see three blue-lotus flowers and four small poppy petals in the pendant. Different types of floral collars and pendants became popular vase decorations in the Amarna Period and were widely used in Dynasty 19, especially for funerary equipment. A similar pendant decorates a stone vase in Brooklyn,[10] and another in Moscow that bears the cartouche of Horemheb.[11] It may be that these are schematized versions of real necklaces, such as the two from the burial equipment of Tutankhamen, which incorporate winged scarabs with a similar band of pendant lotus flowers and poppies.[12] If this is so, they probably had a particular religious significance that is not yet understood.

MB

1. Carter 1933, pl. 78 B, p. 146; Daressy 1902, pp. 12-13, no. 24007; Bourriau 1982, no. 116, pp. 127-128. There are some dark spots inside the Boston vase, possibly from the ancient contents.
2. Davis et al 1907, pl. 29; Carter 1933, pl. 78 B.
3. Daressy 1902, pl. 4, no. 24007 - J 33779; Egyptian Museum, Cairo J 62133, from the tomb of Tutankhamen; von Bissing 1907, p. 65, pl. 4, no. 18365.
4. Von Bissing 1907, p. 87, pl. 4, no. 18452.
5. But see Daressy 1902, no. 24007.
6. Eg. Bourriau 1982, no. 116, pp. 127-8; also, Freed 1981b, p. 27, in color; von Bissing 1907, p. 70, pl. 4, no. 18379.
7. Bourriau 1982, p. 128.
8. Carter 1933, pl. 78 B (no. 552, J 62132), inscribed with the king's name. The second vase has lost its stand (no. 923, J 62133). The tomb also provided a version with two amphorae on stands, side by side, carved in a piece.
9. Brooklyn 1983, pl. 40; Carter 1933, pl. 78 B; Edwards 1976, pl. 5, no. 10.
10. Brooklyn Museum 37.386E: Brooklyn 1983, pl. 40, thought to be possibly Dynasty 18.
11. Pavlov and Matthew 1958, fig. 66. This reference courtesy of R. Holthoer.
12. Carter 1927, pl. 84 C; Edwards 1972, nos. 30, 31.

78
Situla

Provenance unknown
New Kingdom, late Dynasty 18 to Dynasty 19
Calcite (Egyptian alabaster)
Height 10.2 cm., max. diam. 6.4 cm.
William Stevenson Smith Fund, 1984 (1984.172)

Situlae in bronze, or more rarely in stone, were an important part of ancient Egyptian funerary and religious ceremonies. Tomb paintings show situlae being used to pour milk in front of the coffin as part of the fu-

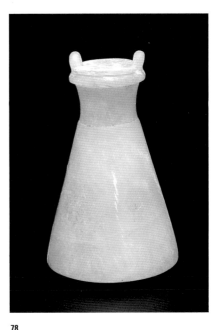

78

neral procession[1] and to offer libations to the gods or the spirits of the deceased.

Situlae appear in tomb and temple decoration at the end of Dynasty 18. Like many such early vessels, this one has a flattened bottom and a sharp, angular profile clearly copying metal prototypes; a similar example was found in the tomb of Kha[c] at Deir el-Medina.[2] It is unique in that it retains its cover, a convex disk of calcite with notches on either side. The notches allow room for two loops that would have attached a metal handle to the vessel.[3]

Actual metal situlae are much larger,[4] and this piece must have been simply a model or votive object,[5] while even smaller examples served as amulets.[6]

PL

1. Lichtheim 1947, p. 171.
2. Schiaparelli 1927, p. 110, fig. 90. Another similar piece is from Lower Nubia and now in the Cairo Museum CG 89861.
3. Cf. Schiaparelli 1927, p. 110, fig. 90.
4. Radwan 1983, pp. 147-151.
5. As in later examples, cf. Green 1987, pp. 66-115.
6. Cf. Dunham 1950b, p. 88, pl. 59c.

Literature: Lichtheim 1947, pp. 169-179.

79
Model vessels

Provenance unknown
New Kingdom
Wood
Hay Collection, Gift of C. Granville Way, 1872 (72.4267-69)

a. Height 16.7 cm., max. diam. 12.7 cm.(72.4267)
b. Height 19 cm., max. diam. 12 cm. (72.4268)
c. Height 15.8 cm., max. diam. 12 cm.(72.4269)

79a-c

Simulacra of stone vessels in Egypt date back to the Predynastic Period. During the New Kingdom such objects frequently substituted for more expensive stone grave goods. They are found in both wood and pottery and in a wide variety of shapes. Their painted surfaces indicate several types of stone, most commonly banded calcite or granite. The cylinder vase (79b), a very early type with splayed foot and conical mouth, dates to the Old Kingdom.[1] Its inclusion in New Kingdom burial equipment indicates the extreme conservatism of these ritual offerings. Covered with gesso and painted with red squiggles over a white ground to imitate red breccia, it has a flat top and two yellow bands of paint, which indicate a tied seal. The bands divide the top into four quarters, two red and two white.

More characteristic of the New Kingdom is the piriform body and flat cylindrical mouth of 79a.[2] The wood core was covered with gesso, painted yellow, and then covered with a shellac that has since yellowed. Thin black scalloped lines running obliquely down the body of the vessel indicate banded calcite. On top of the lid is an elaborate rosette of petals and lotus flowers painted in red, yellow, and blue. It is inscribed with a band of text in black pigment on the side of the vessel for the "House Mistress, Sit-amen." A blue glass vase of a similar shape now in the British Museum is dedicated to the same individual.[3]

Another New Kingdom vessel type, the one-handled "pitcher," is also represented.[4] It is also of wood covered with gesso and is painted black and white in imitation of porphyry. The color is obscured in parts by a coat of yellowed shellac. The vessel is sealed with a quartered pattern of black, yellow, white, and red bands.

PL

1. Reisner 1931, p. 175, fig. 43 no. 1.
2. Cf. Bourriau 1982, p. 81.
3. Nolte 1968, p. 151, pl. 35, 19.
4. Schulz 1987, pp. 317-318.

Literature: Schulz 1987, pp. 317-318; Lansing 1941, pp. 140-141.

80
Stela of Ahmose

Provenance unknown
New Kingdom, Dynasty 18
Limestone
Height 49.5 cm.
Egyptian Special Purchase Fund, 1981
(1981.2)

The chief of metalworkers Ahmose and the "Lady of the House" Werel, the principal beneficiaries of the offerings and formulae on this round-topped stela,[1] sit on the left side of the upper register on a high-backed chair. Ahmose wears a broad collar and a short wig that is marked by short lines around the face to indicate the striations. His kilt reaches his ankles and his left hand holds a folded cloth to his breast.

Werel is called "his sister" in the text above her, and hence is probably Ahmose's wife, since "sister" is often used to describe a wife in the New Kingdom. The fact that the sons and daughter shown in the stela are all called "his" rather than "theirs" is not necessarily an argument against this interpretation. Werel wears the typical narrow sheath dress with two wide shoulder straps partially covered by a broad collar. Her hair or wig is dressed in thick plaits, bound tightly at the bottom, and around her head is tied a fillet and a lotus bud. In her right hand she holds a blue lotus blossom flanked by two buds, while her left hand grasps Ahmose's shoulder. Both Ahmose and Werel wear on their heads the cone of scented fat or tallow customary for banquets during the New Kingdom. Beneath the chair sits a child wearing a youth-lock and sniffing a lotus. He is described as "his son, Tjer." Simpson has suggested that the names Tjer and Werel may be foreign, and perhaps indicate a foreign origin for the entire family.[2]

Facing the seated couple stands a young man with his arm extended in the gesture used while reciting the *hetep di nesut* offering formula. The caption above identifies him as a son of Ahmose named Meny and called "true of voice." He wears a short wig with no internal details, and a short kilt with a sash. His gesture extends over an offering table piled with bread, meat, vegetables, and flowers; below, lotuses have been twisted around two pots as decoration.

In the register below, five women kneel before a table of offerings, and a man sits on a low stool facing them across the table. The women are dressed like the figure of Werel in the register above. Four of them face right and hold lotus blossoms over their left shoulders; the fourth woman from the left has turned to embrace her companion and offer her a piece of fruit. The woman seated next to the table is labeled "his daughter, whom he loves, Meryt-Ptah" and the women behind her may be daughters as well, since the title may apply to all the names. The other four women are named Tinet-niwet, Nebu-em-tekhy, Sapair, and another Sapair. The man seated opposite them is called "his son, Sen-nefer," and is dressed like his father except that his kilt is only knee-length and he wears no wig.

Three lines of text give a standard offering formula in the name of Osiris, the great god, to Ahmose and Werel. The signs of this text and the register lines separating them are in sunk relief, as are all the hieroglyphs used in the captions. The texts thus contrast with the figures and offerings, which are raised. Also in raised relief are the two *wedjat* eyes flanking a *šn* and a *wsḫ* sign that fill in the rounded space at the top of the stela. This collection of symbols is not uncommon in this position.

The stela was originally completely painted, but much of the paint has faded. The background was a sandy yellow color and the flesh of both men and women was painted red. The scented cones on the heads of Ahmose and Werel and the five women in the register below are indicated only in paint. Also painted but not carved are two additional people, painted as though the carved

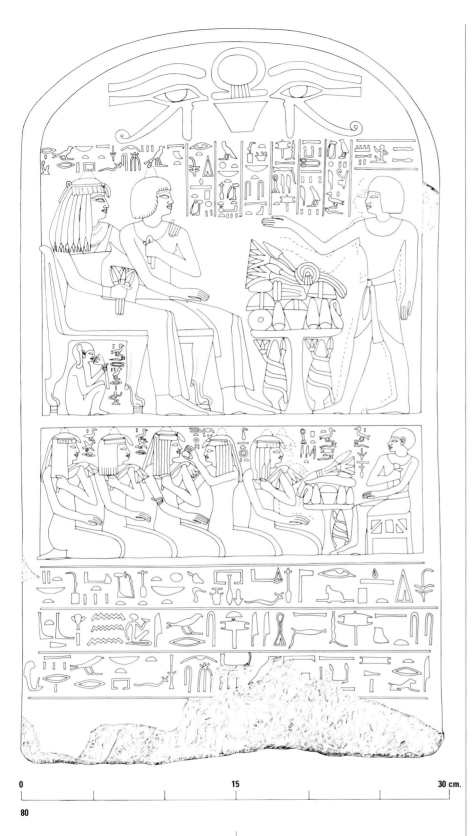

0   15   30 cm.

80

tion and there is no space in which their names could be restored on the same scale as their carved counterparts. On the other hand, they do not seem to be adjustments in paint of the figures of Meny and Meryt-Ptah, since these two figures were clearly painted as they were carved. The most likely explanation is that the painted figures represent later children added to their parents' memorial stela. The superimposition of figures at a banquet scene would be quite usual;[4] the duplication of sons reciting the offering formula before their parents is known,[5] though superimposed sons are unparalleled.

The composition of the stela and the hair and clothing styles are paralleled by several stelae of early to mid Dynasty 18.[6] The use of two names connected with the first few generations of Dynasty 18 kings (King Ahmose and his son Ahmose-Sapair) might suggest the earlier part of the range allowed by the parallels.

AMR

1. The reading of this and the other names on this stela are taken from Simpson 1985, p. 315.
2. Simpson 1985, p. 316.
3. Schäfer 1974, p. 74, cites a relief from Deir el-Bahri where this "perspective" technique was used, though he believes it to have been unintentional. The three-dimensional effect was clearly intended in some cases, however: in the tomb of Khaemwaset (Valley of the Queens no. 44) to the left of the entrance to the second corridor, a semicircular fan is carved, and on the background area between the tips of the feathers, more feathers are painted on the flat background of the sunken area, but not carved in raised relief as are the others. For a carved stela of similar date with added figures in paint, see Brunner-Traut and Brunner, 1981, p. 95 and pl. 10, no. 466.
4. Lacau 1909, 34.052 and 34.057.
5. Lacau 1909, 34.099.
6. Simpson 1985, p. 315, n. 9 and n. 10.

81

Cases with mummified pigeon or quail and duck

From Deir el-Bahri, tomb of Seniu (?)
New Kingdom, Dynasty 18, reign of Amenhotep I
Wood and linen
Acquired by exchange with the Metropolitan Museum of Art, 1937

a. Duck case
   Length 35.5 cm., duck length 17 cm. (37.552)
b. Pigeon case
   Length 17.5 cm., pigeon length 10 cm. (37.553)

Because of the importance placed on providing food offerings to sustain the deceased in the afterlife, the Egyptians supplemented offerings left at the tomb by priests and relatives with depictions of offerings in reliefs (cat. 24), model offerings (cat. 25), and prepared food. Limestone

figures overlapped them. In the upper scene the face of a second man can be seen peeping out just to the left of Meny's; his arm crosses behind Meny's and reaches out just below it, and bits of of his legs, belt, collar, and left arm survive. Another face done only in paint can be discerned just to the right of Meryt-Ptah in the register below. The scented cone on the head of this

second woman is clearly visible, as is the lotus bud over her shoulder.

The representation of perspective by carving a nearer figure or object in raised relief and painting the more distant one on a flat surface is not unknown in Egyptian art.[3] However the shadowy figures shown here were clearly not part of the original design of the stela, since they crowd the composi-

81a, b

food cases containing various types of food are known from the Old Kingdom (cat. 26). This practice continued into the New Kingdom with the deposit of wooden food cases in the tomb.[1]

These two examples were discovered in the debris of a plundered tomb by the Metropolitan Museum of Art expedition at Thebes in 1918-1919.[2] Several types of food were recovered, ranging from whole geese and ducks to cuts of beef, including a large leg and some internal organs such as the heart and liver. All of them had been carefully mummified, though not all of the original cases survived.[3]

Each of the wooden cases in the shape of dressed birds was hollowed out of two solid pieces of wood. The interior of both the upper and lower surfaces was coated with resin that extended out to the rim, originally acting to seal the two halves together,[4] along with dowels inserted into holes in the rim at both ends. The exterior was coated with a layer of plaster, bound with a linen strip, and then saturated with oil or resin. The birds, which may have been cooked, were thinly wrapped in linen that had been saturated with an oily or resinous substance, perhaps even honey, intended to enhance both the preservation and the flavor of the food.[5]

SD'A

1. Cf. those found in the tomb of Yuya and Thuya, Davis et al. 1907, pls. XXX (mummified joints) and XXXI (fowl), Quibell 1908, pp. 46-47, pls, XXII-XXIII.
2. Lansing 1920, p. 7.
3. Lansing 1920, pp. 7-8.
4. Lansing 1920, p. 8.
5. Technical information courtesy of Margaret Leveque, Research Laboratory, Museum of Fine Arts.

Bibliography: Lansing 1920, pp. 7-8; Museum of Fine Arts 1982, no. 94, pp. 111-112.

82
Gaming box for *Senet*

From Zawiyet el-Aryan, tomb Z491
New Kingdom, Dynasty 18
Faience and modern wood
Length 35.2 cm., width 11.1 cm., height 7.6 cm.
Harvard University-Museum of Fine Arts Expedition (11.3095-97)

In 1911, at Zawiyet el-Aryan, six kilometers south of Giza, the Harvard University-Museum of Fine Arts Expedition discovered a Dynasty 18 cemetery of some three hundred pit graves, largely looted. One grave contained five adults, obviously buried at different times, all with a very poor selection of grave goods. Apart from a few modest amulets and scarabs, the grave contained only two pottery vessels and the fragmentary remains of a game box, which had been placed at the head end of a simple rectangular wooden coffin bearing the skeleton of an unmummified man. The box, made of ebony wood, had green faience plaques inlaid on all sides; the top and bottom bore the familiar playing surfaces of the games *Senet* ("Passing") and Twenty Squares, a game imported from Mesopotamia. The faience playing pieces were of two types, conical and spool-shaped. The surviving die was a prismatic spindle of ivory, whose sides were marked with one, two, three, or four dots. Since many of the original faience rectangles marking the squares were lost, as were several of the pieces, it is probable that the game was buried with the dead because it was already quite old and of little further use to the living. The present box was restored in 1980 by Robert Walker of the Museum's furniture conservation staff according to the drawings in the original field notes.

Playing *Senet* and wagering on its outcome was a favorite leisuretime activity of the ancient Egyptians. The great popularity of this backgammonlike game can be measured by the enormous quantity of evidence for it that has survived from all periods of Egyptian history. Grids for the game can be seen scratched on paving stones or the roofing

82

stones of temples, where idle people must have spent hours at it. In tomb paintings or reliefs from the Old Kingdom to the Late Period, scenes of people playing *Senet* are very common and reflect the keen interest in this game on the part of many wealthy tomb owners. More than forty complete game sets and hundreds of fragments and playing pieces also survive from tombs of kings and commoners alike, indicating the great love of this game among those of all social classes, and proving that few wished to leave the world of the living without taking their game sets with them.

Although for centuries it seems to have been just a simple meaningless diversion, by Dynasty 18, probably due to the frequency with which it was buried with the dead, *Senet* was reconceptualized as a simulation of the funerary myth. It became not merely a toy with which the dead could amuse themselves throughout eternity, but a symbol of their struggle to attain immortality. According to Chapter 17 of the Book of the Dead, a deceased person could play *Senet* against his enemies in the Netherworld, and, if victorious, he could then "come forth by day as a living *ba*," joining with the sun god and achieving immortality.

From the wealth of pictorial, textual, and material evidence relating to this game, much is known about its play and meaning. The board consisted of three rows of ten squares and was conceived as a sinuous pathway of thirty steps. The pieces of the two opponents were perhaps lined up on alternating squares along the top row to start. Regulated by the moves of the dice, the players moved them forward, struggling with one another for position, until reaching the last five squares, which were usually inscribed. The fifth square from the end on traditional boards, like this one, was usually marked *nefer* ("good"). This would seem to have been the first goal of the players, and it appears as though one had to land here before going on to freedom and safety. Since the Egyptians referred to the squares on the gameboard as "houses," this square had always been known as "the good house." Curiously enough, this was the very name of the embalmer's workshop, and by Dynasty 18 some game-box makers recognized the parallel. In the later symbolic versions of the game, then, the first objective was to attain mummification. The fourth square from the end, traditionally marked X ("danger"), was in later boards conceptualized as "water" or "Nile," in which one could drown. This square, thus, apparently symbolized the journey of the dead across the Nile to the west bank prior to burial. The third square from the end, originally marked with the numeral 3, later bore images of three gods, specifically three gods of the necropolis. When a player reached this square, the Egyptians assumed he had attained burial in the tomb. The last two squares, marked with the numerals 2 and 1 respectively, were later marked with images of the gods Re and Atum, in the one, and Re-Horakhty in the other, symbolizing the union of the dead with the old sun in his transformations into the vigorous new sun as it rises at dawn. As the player carried his pieces off the board at this point, he was thought to have "come forth by day" to everlasting life.

As the attainment of the happy afterlife was the dream of every Egyptian, even the living may have played this highly symbolic version of the game for amusement in order to simulate their imagined fates. As the attainment of wealth is the primary goal in our culture, the game of Monopoly fulfills in us much the same need.

TK

Bibliography: Museum of Fine Arts 1982, pp. 266-267.

Literature: Museum of Fine Arts 1982, pp. 263-272.

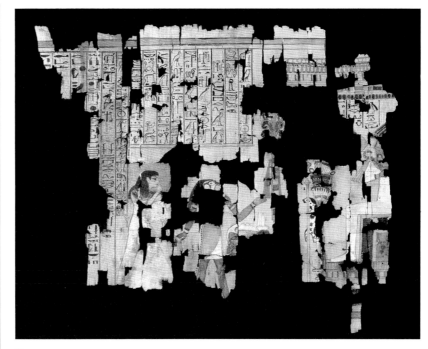

83

83
Book of the Dead scenes

Provenance unknown
New Kingdom
Papyrus
Length 40 and 49 cm., width 38 cm.
Anonymous Gift (1987.287)

Many years ago the Museum was given a box of papyrus fragments that once belonged to Battiscombe Gunn. From these fragments were reconstructed two scenes from the Book of the Dead, complete with the spells that accompany them. The scenes are skillfully painted and great care has been taken with the hieroglyphs of the main texts. The scenes are similar in style to the well known Papyrus of Ani[1] and it seems likely that they date to the same period. Unfortunately, spaces left blank for the name of the deceased were never filled in.

The weighing of the heart scene, is very similar to that in the Papyrus of Ani. The man and his wife observe as his heart is weighed against the small figure of the goddess Maat. Anubis, who checks the balance mechanism, faces a small male figure who represents the man's fate; behind him stand his two birth goddesses. Above them, on top of the scale arm, are his *ba* and a second representation of his fate.[2]

The god Thoth stands at the right recording the proceedings. The creature Ammit "the devourer," who awaits the outcome, is oddly positioned above the scale on the right, its crocodile head protruding into the columns of hieroglyphs above.

The text above this scene records the first half of Spell 30b.[3] Above the columns of

hieroglyphs a dozen seated gods and goddesses witness the judgment.

In the scene above, Horus leads the deceased into the presence of Osiris, who is enthroned beneath an elaborate booth topped by a cobra frieze (cat. 84). In front of him are a bouquet and an Anubis fetish. Between the booth and Horus an offering table is piled high with food. The complete scene would likely have shown the goddesses Isis and Nephthys behind Osiris. It may also have included small figures of the Four Sons of Horus somewhere in front of him, beneath the booth.[4] The text above Horus and the deceased is again part of Spell 30b from the Book of the Dead.

CHR

1. BM 9901, see Faulkner 1985, p. 14 (fig.)
2. See Faulkner 1985, p. 14 (fig. caption).
3. See Faulkner 1985, pp. 27-28.
4. See the scene in Faulkner 1985, pp. 34-35 (fig.)

84
Uraeus statuettes

Provenance unknown
New Kingdom, probably late Dynasty 18
Wood
Height 19 - 20.5 cm., width 4.7 - 6 cm., length (modern mount) 11.2 cm.
Hay Collection, Gift of C. Granville Way, 1872 (72.4203-4220)

Eighteen wooden uraeus statuettes of approximately the same size are similarly carved, plastered, and painted. Cobras whose colors and forms closely parallel these uraei are seen at the top of a completely preserved and beautifully executed

gilded wood canopic-shrine and its canopy belonging to King Tutankhamen[1] and found by H. Carter;[2] the wooden shrine contained the king's alabaster canopic chest. Both the shrine and canopy of Tutankhamen are protected by friezes of colorful cobras, individually modeled, mounted in a row, gessoed, and painted.[3] Although the Boston cobras vary in height, width, and state of preservation, in contrast to the uniformity of the more expertly modeled cobras of Tutankhamen's shrine, the friezes are in many ways alike: sun disks are large and circular; big heads with bulging eyes jut straight out; wide, full hoods taper to narrower bases and do not rear back; bodies and tails are not represented; each series of cobras has similar markings and coloring. Differences in quality and uniformity may reflect the differences between furnishings of royal and private tombs. The statuettes bear striking similarities in form, type, and style to the cobra friezes in painting and relief of mid to late Dynasty 18[4] and to those on Tutankhamen's shrine and canopy, suggesting they date to the time of Amenhotep III, or later in Dynasty 18;[5] their workmanship suggests that they are from a private tomb.

Each statuette is modeled from a single piece of wood,[6] and represents an aroused cobra or "Ikhet the Serpent," "protection of his (Re's) eye,"[7] at the front of a large circular sun disk (approximately one-quarter the total height and equal in width to the upper expanding hood). Thrust-out heads with large, bulging eyes are carefully carved, front and back; deep incisions are carved from the eye sockets over the jowls to the back of the upper hoods, gradually ending as the top of the hood becomes thinner and

84

narrower; rounded, triangular lines indicate closed mouths; wide, upright hoods are thicker at the top, curving slightly and tapering to their cut-off bodies; bases of the hoods are sunk into a modern plank. In profile, the ancient snakes do not rear back, but stand rigidly alert.

Traces of plaster and paint remain as follows: yellow ocher on the sun disks, tops of heads, wide bands outlining hoods, vertical ventral columns (center spine), horizontal bands marking hood sections,[8] and back of statuettes; dark blue on the heads, eye sockets, and upper section of hoods; red on the pupils of eyes and mid-section of hoods; and light blue on the lower section of hoods.

A fiercely protective symbol, always associated with royalty, divinity, or both, the uraeus or "risen" cobra appears in ancient Egyptian art from Predynastic times.[9] A frieze or series of aroused cobras is seen in its first preserved example on stone blocks atop the Dynasty 3 "Cobra Wall" of King Netjerikhet (Djoser) at Sakkara, ca. 2687-2667 B.C.[10] Carved, almost in the round, this earliest frieze no doubt symbolizes the Buto (Delta home of the cobra goddess) burial that took place in the north chapel of Djoser's funerary complex.[11] Represented two-dimensionally from the Old Kingdom onward on the *pr*-sign, ▭ "chapel" or "shrine", in the hieroglyph *t꒦yty*,[12] ▥ a vizerial title, this type of frieze appears to have architectural origins,[13] but it is not represented again on a securely dated, preserved architectural example until the New Kingdom.[14]

None of the cobras in the friezes mentioned in the above text wears a sun disk or crown on its head. A series of uraei wearing sun disks is frequently seen, however, in relief and painting from royal and private tombs of Dynasties 18 and 19. The upright cobras with sun disks are seen at the top of shrines or kiosks,[15] canopies or balduchins covering shrines,[16] and openwork biers or coffins.[17] These kiosks enclosed representations (statues) of divinities or deified royalty[18] and were often found in the decoration of private tombs. The tomb from which this example came was probably located at Thebes and belonged to a highly placed official of the New Kingdom.

In debris of the tomb of Kheruef,[19] a high official under Amenhotep III and Amenhotep IV, L. Habachi found, "14 uraei in wood painted light brown. . . . Some of these were found fixed to a piece of wood, perhaps originally fixed to the top of a shrine or a similar object."[20] An illustration displays cobras less carefully modeled and painted than those in Boston. Other wooden uraeus friezes, one in the Cairo Museum,[21] and another found in a magazine of Sety I's palace at Abydos,[22] display well-proportioned cobras wearing sun disks; but, unlike Boston's cobra frieze, their heads tilt upward and their hoods rear back.

SJ

1. Cairo CG 60686, T266, T266A; Edwards 1977, p. 153.
2. Porter and Moss 1964, pp. 573-574.
3. For excellent color photo cf. Donadoni 1972, p. 120.
4. See note 15.
5. Lilleso 1975, pp. 137-138, pl. XXII, fig. 1, p. 146, also dates two crowned, wooden uraei of approximately the same size and coloring to the late Dynasty XVIII.
6. However, 72.4204, second on the right, shows a sun disk and back of the head split off and glued back on.
7. Faulkner 1969, Utterance 221, p. 49.
8. Expanded cobra hoods display remains of painted markings characteristic of both the Middle and New Kingdom. Evers 1929, pp. 23-25.
9. Johnson 1987.
10. Porter and Moss 1978, p. 408; Lauer 1976, pl. 95.
11. Ricke 1944, p. 105, fig. 44.
12. Faulkner 1976, p. 293
13. Firth and Quibell 1935, p. 111.
14. Louvre E 17392, a large black granite cobra head and hood from Amenhotep III temple at Sanam, Upper Nubia. However, there is a wooden funerary chest belonging to *Sn*, Staatliche Museem zu Berlin (East) inv. 12708, dated by Wenig 1967, pp. 39-59, pl. I-II, to the First Intermediate Period. If this chest is of First Intermediate Period or early Middle Kingdom date, these are the earliest preserved cobras, thus far, to wear sun disks. A cobra frieze, worked as one piece whose upper part, between the heads and sun disks, has been cut away, decorates the tops of the chest. Wenig cites scholars who refer to the chest as the death bier for a child or dwarf and date it to the Graeco-Roman period, although they thought the inscription a copy from a model of the Middle Kingdom; other scholars have dated the chest to the early Middle Kingdom. Wenig suggests that the chest is a funerary shrine for food offerings and dates it to the First Intermediate Period.
15. Cairo CG 60686, T266; Donadoni 1972, p. 120; Staatliche Museen zu Berlin 12708; Wenig 1967, pp. 39-43, pls. I-II.
16. Cairo CG 60686, T266A.
17. Cairo no. TR 21/11/16/12, dated to the Late Period.
18. See Vandier 1964, p. 544 note 2 for a list of these tombs, pp. 546-552 for a description, and figs. 295-304, 306-307 for illustration.
19. Theban tomb 192.
20. Habachi 1959, p. 338, pl. IX, 4.
21. Cairo CG 26527.
22. Ghazouli 1964, p. 149, pl. XX.

85
Relief of offering bearers

Probably from Sakkara
New Kingdom, Dynasty 18
Limestone
Height 36.8 cm., width 86.7 cm., depth 7.7 cm.
Arthur Tracy Cabot Fund and Egyptian Curator's Fund, 1974 (1974.468)

Though its exact provenance is unknown, the style of this limestone relief suggests it came from the New Kingdom cemetery at Sakkara. The necropolis of Sakkara near the ancient Egyptian capital of Memphis was, along with Giza, one of the principal cemeteries of the Old Kingdom, containing some of the most famous of the decorated mastaba tombs. In the New Kingdom it again became an important necropolis, though this part of its history has never been fully documented and few of the New Kingdom tombs have been excavated. Like the tombs of the Old Kingdom, those of the New Kingdom included surface structures built of limestone blocks that were then decorated with scenes and texts.

In the nineteenth century, antiquities dealers, collectors, and travelers superficially explored the Sakkara plateau, carting away hundreds of decorated limestone blocks that are now in museums and private collections around the world. No record was made of the provenance of these blocks within the necropolis. As a result, the existence of tombs of numerous known officials of the New Kingdom can be documented, but the tombs themselves remain lost.[1]

This relief joins with a block in Copenhagen,[2] the combination of the two making it easier to identify the scene in the upper register of the Boston block. The lower register represents a line of offering bearers bringing a small oryx (judging from the straight horns), a calf, three ducks, and numerous lotus blossoms. The continuation of this register on the Copenhagen block shows more figures bearing similar offerings.

The scene above, probably the principal scene on the wall, is on a much larger scale. The main figure, probably the tomb owner or his father, is seated in a chair with lion legs. Behind the chair stands a much smaller woman, while a child wearing a long

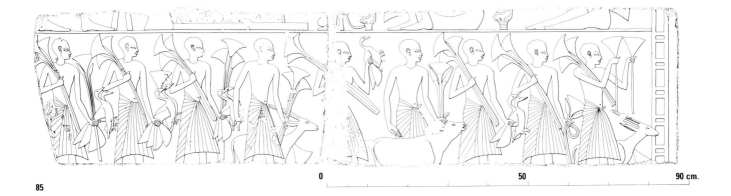

0   50   90 cm.

85

skirt or dress sits on a cushion below the chair and what appears to be a monkey stands directly before the front leg of the chair. The border decoration along the right side of the block suggests that it was at the corner of a room.

The piece is well carved with delicate modeling on the faces of the figures. A gouge in the surface of the lower left corner has been filled with plaster and carved. Traces of red paint remain on the skin of several of the offering bearers, and on the woman's feet in the register above.[3]

It has been suggested that this block and the one from Copenhagen formed part of the tomb of Amen-em-onet[4] who lived during the reign of Horemheb. While neither block joins to one of the many inscribed blocks from this tomb[5] they may form the bottom of a scene that is partially preserved on a limestone block in the Louvre.[6] This scene shows the large figure of Amen-em-onet's father Amen-mose seated before the smaller standing figure of his mother Depet.

CHR

1. See Porter and Moss 1979, pp. 701-718.
2. Copenhagen, Ny Carlsberg Glyptotek AE.I.N. 716-15. Published in Koefoed-Petersen 1956, p. 43 (52) pl. LIII.
3. It is not uncommon for women to be pink or even red in New Kingdom paintings.
4. This suggestion was made by William K. Simpson in a letter to the Museum's Collections Committee in 1974. Amen-em-onet and his wife are also known from the Theban tomb of their son Nefer-hotep. See Porter and Moss 1979, pp. 95-97.
5. For a complete bibliography of the blocks from this tomb, including the ones from Boston and Copenhagen, see Porter and Moss 1979, p. 701-702.
6. Capart 1927, pp. 42-43, pl. 59.

Bibliography: Porter and Moss 1979, p. 701.

86
North and west walls of burial chamber of Sobek-mose

From er-Rizeikat
New Kingdom, Dynasty 18, reign of Amenhotep III (ca. 1386-1349 B.C.)
North wall height 172 cm., length 31.6 cm.; west wall height 172 cm., length 21.8 cm.
Acquired by exchange with the Metropolitan Museum of Art, New York, 1954 (54.648)

These two wall comprised the north and west walls of the sandstone lining of the burial chamber of the treasury official Sobek-mose, who lived in the reign of Amenhotep III. The burial chamber was discovered in 1908 in the necropolis west of the modern village of er-Rizeikat, located between Armant and Gebelein on the west bank of the Nile. The tomb is rare example of a relief-decorated burial chamber of mid-Dynasty 18 date from a provincial cemetery in Upper Egypt. To protect the tomb from vandalism it was dismantled by Emile Baraize of the Egyptian Antiquities Organization and offered to the Metropolitan Museum for purchase.[1]

In 1911 the complete burial chamber was reassembled in the Metropolitan Museum. The north and west walls of the chamber were loaned to the Museum of Fine Arts in 1952 and were permanently transferred to Boston in 1954.[2] On display in New York are the south wall, parts of the east entrance wall, and the massive ceiling slabs reinstalled there in 1983.[3]

The blocks are decorated in sunk relief with incised hieroglyphs. Only a few traces of the original red, blue, and black paints remain. The ceiling was painted black except for the longitudinal and transverse inscribed bands, which were left unpainted, and serve as the background for the painted hieroglyphs. A *kheker* border occupies the top register of all four walls. A fourth course of undecorated blocks surely existed below the three main decorated courses since decoration almost never extended to the floor. A fourth course would have made the

original height of the chamber about 2.25 meters.[4]

Only the subterranean burial chamber of Sobek-mose is preserved; the superstructure above was never recorded. However, it has been suggested that there may have been a mud-brick chapel (perhaps topped by a small pyramid) over a shaft leading to the single subterranean chamber.[5] The chapel might have been decorated with scenes of daily life as well as views of the tomb owner and his family as suggested by a prayer inscribed on the south wall:

> he has built his funerary chapel...furnishing it with great gods and with representations of his father and his mother. It is made festive with offerings of food and with supplies that are produced in the field.[6]

Only one other decorated tomb – a Middle Kingdom painted chamber[7] – was found among the several hundred tombs in the ancient cemetery at er-Rizeikat.[8] It is also unusual when compared with the contemporary rock-cut private tombs of Thebes, approximately 25 kilometers to the north. Scenes and texts usually distributed among several rooms of the upper chambers in the Theban tombs were condensed in the burial chamber of Sobek-mose, and were restricted to abbreviated scenes of funerary rites and mortuary services.[9]

In the texts of his burial chamber Sobek-mose is most frequently called Overseer of the House of Silver, an office of the treasury. He was also known as the Overseer of the Works of the King in Upper and Lower Egypt, Overseer of All Crafts of the King, and Overseer of the Works in Southern Opet [Luxor].[10] On the south wall he is described as one who "drew forth monuments for the king of his time from the pure alabaster of Hatnub – monuments great and holy."[11] The fact that he procured stone for royal monuments suggests that he may have had access to the sandstone quarried for the temple of Luxor and exploited this source for his tomb.[12]

Although Amenhotep III is not specifically mentioned in the tomb, other evidence indi-

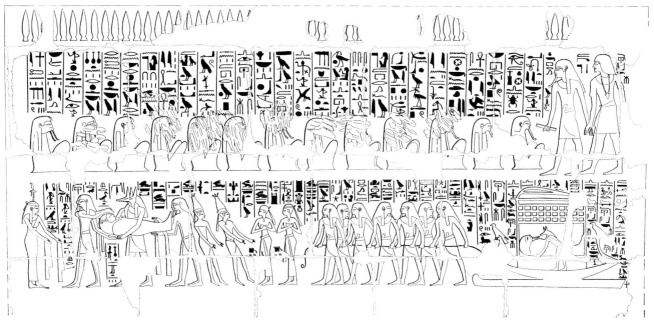

86, north wall

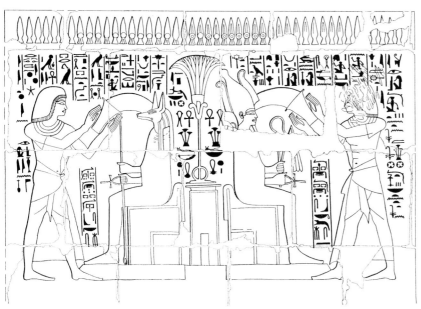

86, west wall

cates that Sobek-mose served this king. Not only is the general style of the relief comparable to that found in tombs dated to the reign of Amenhotep III, but certain phrases in the inscriptions closely parallel funerary literature of this reign.[13] The name Sobek-mose also appears on two jar labels found in the palace of Amenhotep III at Malkata,[14] and a pictorial graffito carved on the rock in Aswan depicts an Overseer of the House of Gold and Silver Sobek-mose in the act of "giving praise to the Lord of the Two Lands Nebmaatre (Amenhotep III).[15] The Sobek-mose who owned this burial chamber is probably the one referred to but we cannot be sure. Unfortunately no information about his family is included in the

tomb so that relatively little is actually known about his personal life. His titles indicate that he worked at Thebes. Since he chose to be buried in er-Rizeikat it was probably his home town. His place of origin is also suggested by his name as it incorporates the name of a crocodile god, Sobek, who was particularly associated with Sumenu, an ancient city in the vicinity of er-Rizeikat.[16]

The eastern entrance wall, which is in New York, as reconstructed by William Hayes on the basis of fragments of the door lintel and jambs, shows an abbreviated version of the rite of lustration, the first act of the offering service in preparation for the mortuary feast after the burial. The series of rituals in prep-

aration for the mortuary feast continues on the adjoining south wall. The proposed reconstruction of the north jamb includes a similar scene of ritual ablution, but preparatory instead to the burial illustrated on the north wall.

On the north wall the funeral procession and burial are depicted in the lower register. At the right the mummy is held by a priest wearing the jackal-headed mask of the divine embalmer Anubis. The mummy lies within a canopied bier mounted on a sledge and protected by birds perched on the prow and stern symbolizing Isis and Nephthys. Seven male figures representing the gods who drag the boat of Re through the regions of the night pull the bier from the embalmer's workshop to the tomb in the Western Desert. Two female priestesses, also symbolizing Isis and Nephthys,[17] precede the cortege, and two *muu* (dancing mummers) greet the approaching procession. Above is a chant that ensures that all the ways of the Underworld are open for the deceased, and that he will not encounter any obstacle. On the left the burial is represented. The pallbearers represent the Four Sons of Horus – Imsety and Hapy at the head and Duamutef and Qebehsenuef at the feet, and Anubis Khentysahnetjer ("Who is in front of the Divine Booth") and Anubis Imyut ("He who is in the bandage") at the middle. The Goddess of the West greets Sobek-mose with open arms and a speech of welcome at the west end of the wall. The upper register of the north wall shows a scene that takes place in the judgment chamber, the Hall of Justice of Chapter 125 of the Book of the Dead, which is rarely depicted on the walls of private tombs of this period and is essentially borrowed from funerary papyri.[18] On the right a god ushers Sobek-mose into the presence of twenty-four divine judges, and Sobek-mose addresses them to let them know partly that Sobek-mose:

> did not make anyone [suffer]; I did not lessen the food in the temples; I did not tamper with the food offerings of the gods; I did not take away the property of the spirits of the dead; I did not neglect the appointed dates (in regard to) choice cuts of meat. I did not oppose the god on his going-forth. I am pure.[19]

The divine judges were usually forty-two in number and have been reduced here to twenty-four shown by twelve pairs.[20] The faces of most of these figures have been deliberately defaced as has the face of Sobek-mose on the right side of the back west wall. Just when this defacement occurred is uncertain, although Hayes suggested Coptic times,[21] and a Coptic church was located near the cemetery.[22]

The west wall at the back end of the burial chamber shows Sobek-mose in the presence of the great gods of the dead, Anubis and Osiris, whom he anoints. Each ritual is accompanied by a description of the services Sobek-mose renders to the gods and the rewards he requests in return. On the right he addresses Osiris Wen-nefer "Pouring myrrh and fine oil on (your) brow, Osiris Wen-nefer, so that you may preserve my head for me, so that you may place my heart in my body for me." On the left he speaks to Anubis, Lord of Inerty (nearby Gebelein), so that Anubis "may cause me to occupy my place of everlastingness, (my) cavern of eternity, and grant that (I) go forth as a living *ba* to behold the disk of the morning sun."[23]

The south wall in New York is decorated with a male figure on the left, most probably Sobek-mose, who is performing some of the rites that precede the mortuary feast.[24] On the ceiling inscribed bands are meant to protect both the tomb owner and the burial chamber.[25]

BAP

1. Hayes 1939, p.6, p. 29, note 19; MMA 08.201.4, Metropolitan Museum of Art 1909, pp. 37-38.
2. Metropolitan Museum of Art 1911, pp. 111-112; Hayes 1959, p. 269.
3. Porter 1983.
4. Hayes 1939, p. 30, note 23.
5. Hayes 1939, pp. 6, 23.
6. Hayes 1939, p. 19; Hayes 1959, pp. 270-271; Porter 1983.
7. Hayes 1939, p. 5; Daressy 1926, p. 18.
8. Weigall 1910, pp. 296-297.
9. Hayes 1939, p. 8, p. 30, note 22; Manniche 1987, p. 30.
10. Hayes 1939, pp. 26-27, p. 36, note 193.
11. Hayes 1939, pp. 19, 27.
12. Hayes 1939, p. 23, p. 35, note 172.
13. Hayes 1939, pp. 18, 21, p. 30, note 35.
14. Hayes, 1959, pp. 248, 271.

15. Hayes, 1939, pp. 23-24.
16. Maspero 1882, p. 123; Weill 1918, p. 284; Gauthier 1928, pp. 16-17; Kuentz 1929, pp. 123, 152-153; Porter and Moss 1937, p. 161; Hayes 1939, p. 5; Gardiner 1947, pp. 20-21, 275; Yoyotte 1957, p. 87; Gardiner 1957, p. 510 (sign T1); Montet 1961, pp. 72-73; Sauneron 1968, p. 58; Bakry 1971, p. 131; Luxor 1979, p. 82; Baines and Málek 1980, p. 213; Brovarski 1984, col. 1021, note 94; Helck 1986, col. 110.
17. Munster 1968, p. 59.
18. Hayes 1939, p. 17; Seeber 1976, p. 16.
19. Hayes 1939, p. 16; Porter 1983.
20. Hayes 1939, p. 16.
21. Hayes 1939, pp. 16-17.
22. Maspero 1885, p. 186.
23. Hayes 1939, p. 20; Porter 1983.
24. E. Russman personal communication; Hayes 1959, p. 269.
25. Hayes 1939, pp. 18-20; Hayes 1959, pp. 269-272.

Literature: Hayes 1939; Hayes 1959, pp. 269-272; Smith 1960, pp. 126-128, p. 131, fig. 82

87

87
Face from a sarcophagus lid

Provenance unknown[1]
New Kingdom, Dynasty 18, reign of Amenhotep III
Granite
Height 41.5 cm., width 43.5 cm, depth 22.4 cm.
Gift of Mrs. F.E. Peabody, 1909 (09.286)

The upper portion of a granite face-mask from a mummiform sarcophagus is broken off diagonally from below the right ear to the left shoulder.[2] The chin, mouth, and lower face are lost, and the nose is damaged. Around the face is a striated wig and on the left shoulder there is a falcon-headed terminal in low relief, belonging to a broad collar on the missing portion. A hieroglyphic text, also in low relief, begins at the left shoulder and runs along the side of the lid, and the initial signs read, "*dd mdw in G[b]...*." The character of the object, the style of inscription, and the material all indicate that this mask is derived from the broken middle sarcophagus of Mery-mose, Viceroy of Kush under Amenhotep III. The

eyes are carved in the characteristic almond-shaped style of the period. Other pieces of the same sarcophagus are preserved in the British Museum and in the Louvre, but a substantial portion is completely missing.

Among the twenty-three fragments in the British Museum is one from the upper right side on which is a small part of the lappet of the wig and also the *wedjat* eye panel.[3] This piece must have belonged in very close proximity to the Boston fragment of the face-mask, although the two pieces do not actually join owing to the loss of the lower right side of the wig and face. The inscription that begins on the left shoulder of the Boston piece is continued, after an interruption caused by the missing portion, on fragments of the left-hand edge of the lid among the British Museum pieces. The original decorative scheme of the whole sarcophagus included bands of text across the cover with reliefs accompanied by longer panels of inscription, the nature of which is known from the very similar decoration applied to the inner sarcophagus of Mery-mose, which is also preserved in the British Museum.[4] The piece of the middle sarcophagus in the Louvre collection came from the upper right-hand side of the lid, and it joins certain of the British Museum fragments, but not the Boston piece.[5] The entire sarcophagus was decorated in the same fine low relief exemplified by the hieroglyphs on the fragment of the mask. Mery-mose did in fact possess three stone sarcophagi: a massive outer one of red granite, with an integral sledge-shaped base and a mummiform cover; the middle sarcophagus of gray granite, of which this face-mask is a part; and finally, a similar mummiform sarcophagus, also of gray granite.[6]

The exterior sarcophagus was found by Baraize in tomb 383 at Thebes, which was clearly the burial place of Mery-mose and must therefore have been the original provenance of the fragments of the two inner sarcophagi. The three granite sarcophagi of fine workmanship reflect the importance of their owner and the quality of his funerary equipment.

AJS

1. See Porter and Moss 1960, p. 436.
2. The term "right" and "left" are from the observer's point of view.
3. Edwards 1939, pls. XVIII-XIX.
4. Edwards 1939, pls. XVI-XVII. Other fragments of this inner sarcophagus are in collections in Vienna, Oslo, and Pague. See Komorzynski 1960, 139-40; Müller 1977, pp. 325-329; Zaba 1950, p. 509ff.
5. Varille 1947, pp. 576-70, pl. LIX.
6. Varille 1947, pp. 1-15, pls. I-XI.

88a, b, c

Fig. 79

88
Funerary cones of Mery-mose

From Thebes
New Kingdom, Late Dynasty 18, reign of
Amenhotep III
Pottery

a. Length 16.3 cm.
   Hay Collection, Gift of C. Granville Way, 1872
   (72.1810)
b. Length 14.8 cm.
   Gift of Dr. George L. Walton, 1936 (36.338)
c. Length 17.5 cm.
   Lent by William Kelly Simpson, 1972 (72.1984)

As tomb paintings and the scant archaeological evidence show, tapering lengths of
clay such as these were set in rows above
the entrance to the mud-brick superstructure of the tomb, where they were intended
to represent the ends of beams supporting
the roof (fig. 79).[1] Although they have been
found at several sites and as far afield as
Aniba in Nubia,[2] evidence indicates that the
use of such cones was restricted to the necropolis of ancient Thebes.

Funerary cones are first attested in Dynasty
11, when they are uninscribed. During the
New Kingdom it became the practice to em-
bellish their flattened, exposed ends (and,
occasionally, one or more faces of the mud
and fired-clay bricks used elsewhere in the
superstructure of the tomb) with a positive
impression, perhaps taken from a limestone
matrix,[3] containing the name(s) and title(s)
of the tomb owners; occasionally this information is supplemented by the name and title of the owner's wife and the cartouche of
the king or other member of royalty under
whom he served or in whose cult he was
active. This stamped type of funerary cone,
of which over 600 varieties are known, occurs sporadically into the Late Period.

The present cones are inscribed for "the
King's son of Kush, Mery-mose," viceroy of
Nubia under Amenhotep III,[4] from the destroyed superstructure of whose tomb[5]
they evidently originate.

CNR

1. Cf. Borchardt et al. 1934, pp. 25-35; Reeves
   and Ryan 1987, pp. 47-49.
2. Steindorff 1937, pl. 35, 1; Davies 1957,
   no. 606.
3. Cf. Davies 1957, p. vi. no. 219.
4. Davies 1957, no. 170.
5. TT 383: Porter and Moss 1960, p. 436.

Literature: Borchardt et al. 1934, pp. 25-35; Davies
1957, p. 64, n. 2; Eggebrecht 1977, cols. 857-859;
Meltzer 1974, pp. 9-12.

89
Stelophorous statue of Nen-to-waref

Provenance unknown
New Kingdom, Dynasty 18
Sandstone
Height 41 cm., width 15.2 cm.,
depth 26 cm.
Morris and Louise Rosenthal Fund, Horace
and Florence Mayer Fund, William S. Smith
Fund, Frank B. Remis Fund, 1986
(1986.747)

The stelophor or stelophorous (from Greek
stele "pillar" and phorous "bearer") statue
was an innovation of the New Kingdom.
Early in Dynasty 18 the inscription usually
began on a filling between the raised arms
of the owner and continued on his skirt.
About the time of Thutmose III the filling
was transformed into a stela resting on the
knees, as in the present instance.[1]

Here Nen-to-waref kneels and lifts his
hands in adoration, as he recites a hymn of
praise to the sun-god. His prayer is carved
on the stela that rests on his knees. The inscription is as follows:

Praising Re when he rises in the eastern
horizon of heaven by the Child of the Inner Palace and Overseer of wab priests
of Amen(?)... Nen-to-waref, justified. he
says: Greetings to you, O Harakhti, the
great god, who came into being of himself, who (illuminates) the Two Lands
with fine gold at his appearances. O He-
who-is-in-the Night-barque, permit me to
perceive your beauty in the course of
every day.

At peace with his god and himself, Nen-to-
waref serenely faces eternity. The portrait is
an idealizing one, and to a certain extent the
square face, rather wide eyes, long straight
nose, prominent cheekbones, and slightly
protruding mouth with raised corners are
features mirrored in representations of Nen-
to-waref's master, King Amenhotep II.[2]

Carved from sandstone, the statue was broken in two in antiquity and a section extending from the upper right shoulder to the
waist, along with the hands and the very
top of the stela, is missing. Since sandstone
is too rough to take paint satisfactorily, a
thin plaster or gesso coating was applied to
the stone before it was painted. Traces of
both gesso and paint are visible.

Nen-to-waref wears a plain, heavy wig, and
a long, belted skirt, whose pleated ends trail
in the dust. Beneath the linen of the skirt,
his lower legs have been modeled with considerable naturalism so that the sinews and
muscles stand out and the toes of the foot
are widely splayed.

Nen-to-waref is also known by a tomb on

89

the west bank at modern Luxor, Theban Tomb 398,[3] a granite statue once in the Varille collection,[4] and three funerary cones.[5] In the tomb and on two of the cones, he has a second name, Kamose. There is not much of a personal nature that can be said about him.[6] His title "Child of the Inner Palace" suggests he was brought up and educated at the royal court.[7] Otherwise, he functioned as Chief of the Royal *wab*-priests in the Estate of Amen, presumably in the great temple precinct at Karnak. A parallel title on the stelophor begins "Overseer of the *wab* priests ..."

A canopic jar inscribed for Kamose Nen-towaref in the Ashmolean Museum, Oxford, is now definitely known to be a forgery.[8]

EB

1. Stewart 1967, pp. 34-38.
2. Bothmer 1954, pp. 11-20; Bothmer 1975, pp. 115-118.
3. Porter and Moss 1960, pp. 443.
4. See Dewachter 1984, pp. 86-87, for thoughts on his family.
5. Davies 1957, nos. 13, 118, 119.
6. Dewachter 1984, p. 87, n. 26.
7. On the title, see Feucht 1985, pp. 38-47.
8. Whitehouse 1987, pp. 63-68.

Bibliography: Museum of Fine Arts 1986-87, p. 33.

90
Ancestor bust

Provenance unknown
New Kingdom, late Dynasty 18
Limestone
Height 23.2 cm
Loan from the Collection of Christos G. Bastis

In addition to the rituals enacted at their tombs chapels, the spirits of the dead could also receive offerings at shrines in the tombs of their descendants, at least in the New Kingdom. Excavations at the workmen's village of Deir el-Medina revealed several *ex-voto* stelae and "ancestor busts" that had fallen from niches in the walls of private houses.[1] These, together with offering tables placed in front of the niches, headrests, and wooden tags inscribed with personal names, apparently formed shrines for domestic worship.

Although the busts are generally uninscribed, the stelae and the offering tables often give formula for the deceased's *akh* or *akh of Re*.[2] *Akh*s, the effective spirits of the dead, held an important place in village life, influencing matters ranging from illness to court cases, and often receiving pleading or threatening letters from their relatives. At the household shrines, prayers and offerings were made to these spirits, a custom reflected in the admonition "Make a funerary offering to the *akh*s of our house, make an offering to the gods."[3]

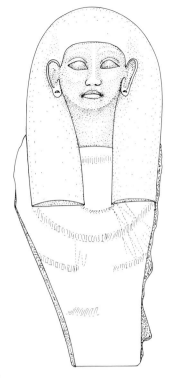

90

Such busts are known from other sites, including some tombs, where they seem to have been placed in the burial chamber rather than the chapel.[4] Bothmer has suggested on the basis of the few inscribed examples that these busts were identified with Hathor and Ptah.[5] Although none can be connected with a specific person, the parallels with the stelae mentioning the *akh*s of the deceased, occurrences of similar busts in tombs, and depictions of the busts in mortuary papyri[6] make the identification with deceased ancestors more likely.

Friedman has suggested that the form of the busts is taken from the stelophorus statues set up in niches just below the apex of pyramids at Deir el-Medina.[7] She argues that the base, so unlike a human torso, derives from the appearance of the roundtopped stela from below, with only the head appearing above it. The two types statuary appear at about the same time, however, and representations of stelophorus statues do not resemble the vignettes of ancestor busts in mortuary papyri. The amorphous torso more probably represents the shapeless form of the wrapped and deified dead characteristic of anthropoid coffins and other mummiform figures.

The ancestor bust shown here, though of unknown provenance, is similar to many from Deir el-Medina. Its finely carved head is of painted limestone, with long hair dividing over the shoulders. The torso is marked by the single line of a garment at the neck and a floral collar. The face is attractive, with large eyes and ears, perhaps the better to receive offerings and prayers. It is difficult

to determine the sex of the individual represented. Bothmer has dated this bust to late Dynasty 18, based on the use of a single cut-line to mark the inner edge of the eyelid and the resemblance of the face to those of several *shawabti*s of Tutankhamen.[8]

AMR

1. Bruyère 1939, pp. 168-174.
2. Friedman 1985, pp. 83-85.
3. Friedman 1985, p. 97.
4. Keith-Bennett 1981, pp. 43-72; esp. pp. 51-52, 59-60, and 62-63.
5. Bothmer 1987, p. 29.
6. Bruyère 1939, p. 169 fig. 65.
7. Friedman 1985, pp. 92-94, and figs. 11 and 12 on pp. 95 and 96.
8. Bothmer 1987, pp. 27 and 29.

91

91
Human-headed canopic jar of Kemes

Provenance unknown
New Kingdom, Dynasty 18
Pottery, marl clay
Height 36.5 cm., diam. 19 cm.
Hay Collection, Gift of C. Granville Way, 1872 (72.1588a,b)

This pottery canopic jar and cover were made on a wheel with the face of the lid modeled by hand. The eyes, ears, collar, and striations of the wig have been painted in black. On the front of the jar four columns of hieroglyphic signs have been painted. The text consists of the customary invocation to the goddess Nephthys to protect the deceased, the *wab* priest of Amen, Kemes, and his internal organs, which are here associated with the minor deity Duamutef.

In the course of Dynasty 18, the form of the canopic jar and the formula inscribed on each of the four jars tended to become standardized.[1] The internal organs of the deceased were linked to the Four Sons of Horus: Imsety, Hapy, Duamutef, and Qebehsenuef. Each of them in turn was associated with a specific goddess: Isis, Nephthys, Neith, and Selkit. However, the fact that the formula on this particular jar irregularly associates Nephthys and Duamutef suggests either that a mistake was made by a careless scribe or, more likely, that the standard formula had not yet become fixed at the time of this jar's manufacture.

The jars of Dynasty 18 have pronounced shoulders and are topped by human heads (see cat. 92) except for a unique set, now in the Metropolitan Museum of Art, New York, with a variety of animal heads.[2] The human heads are usually beardless. Many of the surviving jars of private individuals of this period are made of pottery, while those used in royal burials are of Egyptian alabaster or limestone.[3]

MLB

1. Sethe 1934, p. 2* Type VIII.
2. Hayes 1959, pp. 72-73, 227-228.
3. Brovarski 1978, intro.; Legrain 1904, p. 139; Legrain 1903, p. 138.

92
Human-headed canopic jar lids

Provenance unknown
New Kingdom
Pottery
Hay Collection, Gift of C. Granville Way, 1872

a. Height 12.5 cm., diam. 13 cm.; stopper 8.5 cm. (72.1570)
b. Height 12 cm., diam. 13.3 cm.; stopper 9 cm. (72.1564)
c. Height 12 cm., diam. 14 cm.; stopper 9.5 cm. (72.1565)

Like the lid of cat. 91, these canopic jar lids were wheel made. The elongated dome shape of 92a and 92b allowed the faces to be carved looking forward as in cat. 91. The hemispherical shape of 92c causes the face to tilt upward.[1] Each face was carved into the surface, 92a being quite well modeled while 92b and 92c are relatively flat. The eyes and nose and mouth of each are carved with some care, but the ears of 92a and 92c are quite crude.

The beard of 92c was added separately and the surface was covered with a red slip and burnished before the eyes and brows were painted. The surface of 92a was also covered with a red slip. The face was then painted yellow and the eyes white with black pupils. Cosmetic lines and brows and the hair line in front of the ears were also painted black. The entire wig was covered with a black resin, then it was painted with

92a, b, c

93

green and yellow stripes. The resin beneath probably accounts for the extensive flaking of the paint. The entire decorated surface was also unevenly covered with varnish, perhaps in modern times.

The surface of 92b was never slipped and the face has no paint except for the eyes. The wig is painted in two shades of blue while the collar is green and red.

CHR

1. Several similar lids are also in Boston, MFA 72.1566, 72.1567. See also Reisner 1967, p. 296, pl. XXXII.

93
Canopic jars

Provenance unknown
New Kingdom, Ramesside Period
Faience
Height 30 cm., diam. 16.2 cm.
Gift of Mrs. J.D. Cameron Bradley, 1948
(48.1286-1289)

The designs and inscriptions are painted in black on each of four blue-green faience jars, and a lotus petal ornament radiates from the mouth of the jar. A rectangular panel on the front of each depicts the deceased with arms raised in adoration of the god Osiris, who is enthroned on the left of the scene. On an altar before him rests a water pot covered by a lotus flower. Each lid represents one of the Four Sons of Horus: human-headed Imsety, baboon-headed Hapy, jackal-headed Duamutef, and hawk-headed Qebehsenuef. Similar faience jars from this period are attested in other collections.[1]

Generally canopic jars from the Ramesside period are taller and more slender than those of Dynasty 18 and are largely composed of Egyptian alabaster or limestone. Animal-headed lids become widespread from Dynasty 19 although entirely human-headed sets still persist. By this time specific organs had come to be associated with each deity: the liver with Imsety, the lungs with Hapy, the stomach with Duamutef, and the intestines with Qebehsenuef. Examination of the remains in some jars has shown that embalmers did not always strictly adhere to this formula.

MLB

1. For example Cairo 4220-4224, although the shape and design vary slightly; see Reisner 1967, pp. 155-158.

Bibliography: Brovarski 1978, pp. 163-164.

94

94
Statue of Beken-Khonsu II

Provenance unknown
New Kingdom, Dynasty 20
Black granite
Preserved height 37.5 cm., width 14 cm., depth 14 cm.
Gift by Contribution, 1907 (07.645)

This statue represents the high priest of Amen, Beken-Khonsu II, dressed in the *perruque "à revers"* and long pleated garments typical of Dynasty 20, and the leopard skin cloak of priestly office. He holds the standard of the god Amen decorated with a ram-headed protome wearing a tripartite wig and solar disk with a uraeus.

The piece is finely carved with relief lines indicating the eye lids and brows. The ears have small depressions, indicating that they were pierced. The pleating of Beken-Khonsu's garment is indicated by ridges and the leopard skin is decorated with incised rosettes and stars. A small leopard head is carved in relief at the right side of the figure's waist. The deceased's name and titles appear on the left side of the back column.

Beken-Khonsu was descended from a Theban family that included many priestly officials; he served as high priest of Amen at Karnak during the reigns of Setnakht and Ramesses III.[1] The *hetep di nesut* formula on the back column of the statue indicates that it was intended to stand in the great temple of Amen at Karnak[2] so that the deceased could continue to reap the benefits of his close association with the god. A similar statue of the same man was found in the Karnak "cachette."[3]

This statue was originally collected by Joseph Lindon Smith in Luxor;[4] nearly seventy years later, in 1974, the base of the statue was purchased in the same city.[5]

CHR/PL

1. For a genealogy see Bierbrier 1977, col. 1245-1246. See also Bell 1981, p. 55, n. 58.
2. Bell 1981, pp. 58-59.
3. Legrain 1909, pp. 27-28, pl. 24.
4. Museum of Fine Arts 1907, p. 72.
5. Bell 1974, p. 25.

95
Shawabti of Kai-neferu

From Deir el-Medina
New Kingdom, Dynasty 18, reign of Akhenaten, Smenkhkare, or Tutankhamen
Wood
Height 27.4 cm., max. width 5 cm.
Hay Collection, Gift of C. Granville Way, 1872 (72.4088)

The only known *shawabti* of the *nbt pr* ("Mistress of the House") Kai-neferu, is perhaps the most interesting of the Museum's many funerary figurines. The position of the basket – along the right upper arm – almost certainly identifies Kai-neferu as a member of the family of the Deir el-Medina workman Setau, who died during Tutankhamen's reign or perhaps earlier, in Akhenaten's,[1] and was buried in tomb

95

1352.[2] Kai-neferu's *shawabti*, like many of the others of the Setau clan, is distinctive for its excellent craftsmanship. The proportions of the figure are adroitly handled, and the facial features are especially finely modeled. The coloring is typical of Deir el-Medina funerary figurines at the end of the Eighteenth and the first half of the Nineteenth Dynasty: white body, black or blue (as here) hieroglyphs, red text-dividing lines, red face, blue wig, and polychrome necklace. The attention devoted to Deir el-Medina funerary figurines is a small, but significant, indication of the talents of the royal workman.

Setau and his extended family are depicted on a stela in the Hermitage Museum, Leningrad.[3] The *shawabtis* of several of the persons listed on the stela have been recovered, and still other *shawabtis* of persons not shown were found in Setau's tomb. Some of the *shawabtis* of two persons listed on the stela have the same basket position as Kai-neferu's.[4]

This particular configuration is extremely uncommon; it represents a very brief transitional stage in the development of *shawabti* decoration, beginning with the baskets on the front in Thutmose IV's reign and culminating with their movement to the back in Tutankhamen's. Although Kai-neferu is known only from this *shawabti* – neither from the tomb nor the stela – her place in the Setau family is quite certain by the detail of the basket. Another "Mistress of the House," Werel, is represented by three *shawabtis* in the Egyptian Museum, Turin.[5] Two of them have the same basket position as Kai-neferu's *shawabti*. Werel, too, is known neither from the tomb nor the stela, but two of her *shawabtis* have a highly unusual phrase in the text of Chapter 6 that, like the basket, appears to be unique to the Setau family.[6] By analogy with Werel, Kai-neferu was surely a relative of the Deir el-Medina workman and died sometime at the end of the Amarna Period or shortly thereafter.

Kai-neferu's *shawabti* is also quite tantalizing for the questions it poses about private religion at the end of the Amarna Period. As one scholar has noted, the texts on Setau's *shawabti* fluctuate between the old Osirian Chapter 6 and newer, Amarna texts in which the introductory phrase *shd Wsir* is omitted, as if Setau were seeking "to have the best of both worlds."[7] The coffins of two of the persons buried in his tomb bear a reference to Akhetaten, Akhenaten's capital, and have texts reflecting the beliefs of the Amarna Period.[8] However, the *shawabtis* of all the other persons, Kai-neferu included, have Chapter 6 with *shd Wsir*. Did these persons adhere to the older religion even when Akhenaten made his reforms? Or, did they perhaps acquiesce but quickly return to the early religion when Tutankhamen restored it?

DBS

1. Bogoslovski 1972, pp. 94-96; Černý 1973, pp. 50-51.
2. Bruyère 1937, pp. 95-103 and fig. 39, pl. 3.
3. Hermitage Museum 3937; Struve 1968; Bogoslovski 1972, pp. 87-96; Piotrovsky 1974, pp. 49-50 (with additional bibliography).
4. Setau, Brooklyn Museum, 48.26.2-3; see James 1974, p. 125, nos. 282-283. Luxor Museum, J. 186; see Luxor 1979, p. 103, fig. 79, no. 138. Djemera, Ashmolean Museum, Queen's College Loan 10-11, 13 and British Museum 8653 (all unpublished).
5. Inv. Nr. 2598-2600; see Fabretti et al. 1882, p. 389; Schlögl 1975; Schlögl and Sguaitamatti 1977, pl. 12.
6. For the phrase, see James 1974, pl. LXII, no. 281, 11.6-7. It also appears on the *shawabtis* of Djemera, Ashmolean Museum, Queen's College Loan 12; Metropolitan Museum of Art 66.99.85; and The Archaeological Museum, The John's Hopkins University (all unpublished); Hapi, Virginia Museum of Fine Arts, 55.8.1 (unpublished); and Werel, Egyptian Museum, Turin, 2598 and 2600 (see n. 5).
7. James 1977, p. 125.
8. Bruyère 1937, pp. 103-106 and pl. 12.

Bibliography: Luxor 1979; Bogoslovsky 1972, pp. 79-103; Bruyère1937; Černý 1973; Fabretti et al. 1882; James 1974; Piotrovsky 1974; Schlögl 1975, pp. 145-146; Schlögl and Sguaitamatti 1977; Struve 1968.

96

96
Shawabti of Tjay

From Abydos, "Hekareshu Hill"
New Kingdom, Late Dynasty 18 to early Dynasty 19
Faience
Height 21 cm.
Gift of the Egypt Exploration Fund, 1900 (00.699)

As one of the principal burial places of the dismembered Osiris, Abydos occupied a position of particular importance in the religious life of ancient Egypt. Every Egyptian's desire was to visit the god's tomb and take part in his festival, a pilgrimage that was often commemorated during the Middle Kingdom by setting up a stela or other monument at "the stairway of the Great God." The belief was that the dedicator might in this way be close to the god and partake in perpetuity of his festival offerings. As a variation on this theme, and with an essentially similar motivation, certain high-ranking individuals made a practice of depositing one or more *shawabtis* in those parts of the necropolis at Abydos (as indeed, at other localities in Egypt) that were considered to be of particular religious significance.[1] One such was "Hekareshu Hill" (so named by Petrie after the owner of the finest *shawabtis* recovered from the site) to the north of Umm el-Qa'ab.[2]

Petrie discovered the present *shawabti* during the season 1899-1900.[3] Of faience with a brilliant blue glaze, with the striations of the tripartite wig and details of the broad falcon collar picked out in black, the figure carries no implements. The standard spell from Chapter 6 of the Book of the Dead is inscribed in six horizontal bands across the front, and continues in a single vertical column down the back. The owner, the high priest of Osiris, Tjay, is evidently to be identified with the similarly titled To who flourished under Horemheb or Ramesses I and is mentioned on the dyad of Wen-nefer and Mery from Abydos.[4]

CNR

1. Cf. Schneider 1977, pp. 268 ff.
2. Cf. Kemp 1975, cols. 29-30, fig., 6
3. Petrie 1900b, pp. 32-33
4. Randall-MacIver and Mace 1902, pl. XXXVII, center; Kitchen 1980, p. 448 (no. 205). For the date of To, cf. Kitchen 1982, p. 170. For To version of the name Tjay, cf. Porter and Moss 1960, p. 38 (TT 23).

Bibliography: Porter and Moss 1960, p. 89; Randall-MacIver and Mace 1902, pp. 87 and 96, pl. XXXIX, bottom left; Kitchen 1975, p. 342, no. 140 (incomplete).

97
Shawabti of Nefer-hotep

Provenance unknown
New Kingdom, Dynasty 18
Limestone
Height 21 cm.
Edwin E. Jack Fund, 1985 (1985.707)

By the middle of Dynasty 18, the *shawabti* figure was commonly represented with hands protruding from its close-fitting shroud to clutch a wide-and a narrow-bladed hoe and one or more baskets; these latter were intended to replace those implements previously supplied separately as models.[1] Finely carved, the present *shawabti* wears a striated, tripartite wig and a broad collar. The nine horizontal bands of competently cut hieroglyphs that cover the front of the lower body carry the owner's name and title, "The Overseer of the Builders of Amen, Nefer-hotep," and a text from Chapter 6 of the Book of the Dead. The facial features are particularly well defined and perhaps represent an idealized portrait of the dead man, in all likelihood a contemporary of Amenhotep III.

CNR

1. Schneider 1977, pp. 168-169.

97

98

98
Lid of a double shawabti coffin of Nia (Iniuya) and Iuy

Probably from Sakkara
New Kingdom, late Dynasty 18
Painted limestone
Height 31 cm.
William Frances Warden Fund (1977.717)

Taking the form of two joined mummiform figures, carved in limestone and perhaps with details originally added in paint, this *shawabti*-coffin lid is inscribed in a vertical column down the front of each figure with the names of "the King's Scribe and Chief steward of Memphis, Nia (Iniuya), true of voice," and his wife, "the Mistress of the House and Songstress of Amen, Iuy." The cross-bands, which would presumably have continued on the missing coffin box, carry rituals texts beginning "Recitation" or simply "Revered before" a particular god. In the one band with sufficient space on the lid for the name of the deity, this god is identified as Anubis.

The tomb from which this item came was probably situated in the New Kingdom necropolis at Sakkara, though the precise location of the sepulcher is unknown. Several other pieces (a pyramidion, a stela, two papyrus columns, an anthropoid sarcophagus, a lintel, and various detached blocks) are associated with this monument, and supplement the basic titulary of the *shawabti*-coffin lid; they are now in Cairo, Chicago, East Berlin, and Paris.[1] The style of these pieces suggests that Nia flourished during the latter years of Dynasty 18.

Although multiple *shawabti* figures from this period are known,[2] no parallels to coffins for such pieces can be cited, nor have any *shawabti* figures of Nia or Iuy yet come to light.

CNR

1. Porter and Moss 1979, p. 707; Rammant-Peeters 1983, pp. 54-55.
2. Cf. MMA 44.4.73 Hayes 1959, p. 130, fig. 68; Leiden AST 34, AST 53, AST 68, F 1955/2.19; Schneider 1977, pls. 33-35; British Museum EA 8894.

Bibliography: Simpson 1981, pp. 325-329; Museum of Fine Arts 1987a, pp. 44-45.

99
Shawabtis of Kaha

From Deir el-Medina
New Kingdom, Dynasty 19
Limestone
Hay Collection, Gift of C. Granville Way, 1872

a. Height 22.4 cm., max. width 4.5 cm. (72.749)
b. Height 24.1 cm. max. width 4.4 cm. (72.751)

Like the *shawabti* of Kai-neferu (cat. 95), these two *shawabtis* are typical examples of the superb funerary figurines produced in late Dynasty 18 and Dynasty 19 by the royal artisans living at Deir el-Medina. Kah(a)'s title, *sdm-ᶜš m st M₃ᶜt* ("Servant in the Place of Truth"), indicates that he was one of the workmen who built the royal tombs in the Valley of the Kings. He was perhaps the son of the workman Pashedu, who lived in early Dynasty 19 and owned tombs 3 and 326 at Deir el-Medina.[1] Pashedu's wife had the

99a

very uncommon name Nedjemet-behedet, which is found on another typical Deir el-Medina figurine in Boston.[2] The workman Kaha is to be distinguished from the well-known [c]3 or hri n ist, "chief workman," Kaha, born of Huy and Tuy, who served Ramesses II in the second half of his reign and was buried in tomb 360.[3] The white limestone bodies of both *shawabti*s are well proportioned and decorated. The black hieroglyphs are confidently drawn in a style similar to that of contemporary tomb inscriptions from Deir el-Medina. The faces are painted red. No tools or baskets appear; the absence of agricultural implements is rather uncommon on Dynasty 19 figurines, but both *shawabti*s show signs of abrasion, and therefore, the tools and baskets may have been worn off.

DBS

1. Kaha is depicted in Pashedu's tomb; see Porter and Moss 1970, pp. 9-11.
2. MFA 72.755.
3. Porter and Moss 1960, pp. 424-425; Černý 1973, pp. 125, 135, 286-287, 296-297; and Janssen 1975, 600 (s.v.). To this Kaha belong four *shawabti*s in the Walters Art Gallery (22.186-188, 192); see Steindorff 1946a, p. 160 and pl. 107, nos. 720-723.

100
Shawabti

Provenance unknown
New Kingdom, Dynasty 19
Limestone
Height 15.5 cm., max. width 4.7 cm.
Hay Collection, Gift of C. Granville Way, 1872 (72.763)

This *shawabti* was standard supply, made in advance of purchase. The name of the owner is omitted both after the introductory phrase shd Wsir and at the very end, and a space is left for the name in the third line, again after the designation "Osiris." The *shawabti* is noteworthy for the *ba*-bird on the chest. As an attribute of funerary figurines, the *ba*-bird appears fashioned separately and positioned next to the model bier for one of Tutankhamen's funerary figurines.[1] The *ba*-bird does not appear on the chest of *shawabti*s, however, until Dynasty 19, and the detail of the basket on the back (see introductory essay and cat. 95) confirms this date. The outstretched bird motif is known from one of the most beautiful of all funerary figurines. An outstretched vulture, labeled Nut, appears on the faience *shawabti* of Ptah-mose, vizier and high priest of Amen during Amenhotep III's reign, and the accompanying text has an invocation to Mut, who also took the form of a vulture.[2]

During Dynasties 18 and 19, the decoration of funerary figurines sometimes copied that of coffins and sarcophagi.[3] *Shawabti*s were

100

occasionally enclosed in their own model sarcophagi;[4] various deities were invoked in separate columns of text painted along the sides;[5] and the backs were crosshatched in imitation of the bindings on the cartonnage anthropoid coffins.[6] Although the *ba*-bird is not often found on the chest of cartonnage coffins, it nonetheless has associations with the mummy and reinforces the magical significance of this anonymous *shawabti*. In illustrated papyri, it is sometimes shown hovering over the mummy.[7] The *ba*-bird was a manifestation of the personality of the deceased. Its presence here may indicate that the *shawabti* was not merely a substitute for the dead person, but a potent image in which his or her vital force was immanent.

DBS

1. Edwards 1972, cat. 10.
2. Newberry 1930-1937, pp. 343-345 and pl. 27 (CG 48406).
3. For decorative patterns on coffins and sarcophagi in general, see Schmidt 1919, and Verner 1982.
4. Newberry 1930-1937, pls. 11, 16-17, 29-30; Bogoslovsky 1972, pls. 7-8; Hamilton-Paterson and Andrews 1978, p. 181.
5. Newberry 1930-1937, pls. 15-17, 29; Bogoslovsky 1973, pls. 6-8.
6. University College, London 8825 (unpublished). For the binding on the back of a Third Intermediate Period cartonnage coffin, see Millet 1972, p. 26.
7. Andrews 1984, p. 6, fig. 3.

101
Shawabti of Ra-mose

Provenance unknown
New Kingdom, Dynasty 19
Wood
Height 20 cm.
Hay Collection, Gift of C. Granville Way, 1872 (72.4107)

Although most of its painted decoration is lost, Ra-mose's *shawabti* retains its fine modeling, which links it to the excellent figurines of early Dynasty 19. The *shawabti* rivals the best work from Deir el-Medina, which may be its provenance. All the facial details are beautifully delineated – the earlobes are even pierced. A basket no doubt was painted on the back and has now worn away. Otherwise, the *shawabti* has all the accoutrements commonly associated with funerary figurines – hoe and mattock and Chapter 6 of the Book of the Dead.

Ra-mose's *shawabti* is of a type very common in the later New Kingdom, merging two lines of thought. Although mummiform, the *shawabti* has the wig of the living. Other contemporary figurines have the dress of the living as well. The idea behind these latter types seems to have been that they were the living representatives of the dead person ready to perform the agricultural tasks described in Chapter 6. Possibly, as the dead owner rather than his representative, the *shawabti* awaited the magical gift of birth in the next life.

DBS

101

102
Shawabti

Provenance unknown
New Kingdom
Wood
Height 22.2 cm., width 6.5 cm., depth 4 cm.
Hay Collection, Gift of C. Granville Way,
1872 (72.4118)

This wooden *shawabti* is clad in the wig and
pleated garments of everyday life during the
New Kingdom from late Dynasty 18 onward.[1]
His wig, the common *perruque "à revers,"*
is carefully textured, and the pleats and
fringe of his skirt and shawl are indicated by
rounded ridges. The back of the figure has
been modeled.

The face is modeled and a small depression
in the left ear probably indicates that it was
pierced. Though the man's body is slender,
three wrinkles are carved beneath the chin,
a conventional indication of middle age. The
arms are crossed over the chest, but no
shawabti tools are indicated.

According to Schneider, this type of *shawabti*
does not appear before the Amarna period.
From the end of the New Kingdom,
*shawabti*s in everyday dress were generally
used to identify the *reis-shawabti,* who was
overseer of a group of mummiform
*shawabti*s.[2]

Though this figure has no text, the lower
half of the skirt has been left smooth, probably in anticipation of an inscription.

CHR

1. For similar examples see Schneider 1977, pls.
   30-32.
2. Schneider 1977, pp. 161-162.

Literature: Schneider 1977.

102

103

103
Shawabti of Khaemtore

From Deir el-Medina
New Kingdom, Dynasty 19
Limestone
Height 20.3 cm., max. width 7 cm.
Gift of Mary S. Ames, 1911 (11.1494)

Because the name Khaemtore is unusual,[1]
this *shawabti* likely belonged to the owner
of a statue now in the Rijksmuseum van
Oudheden in Leiden, who is identified there
as *sḏm ⁽ꜥ⁾š m st Mꜣ⁽ꜥ⁾t,* "Workman in the
Place of Truth."[2] We can therefore assign to
this *shawabti* the provenance of Deir el-Medina, the Theban village of tomb builders
and artisans who excavated and decorated
the royal burials in the Valley of the Kings.
The Khaemtore known from the Leiden
statue and several non-literary documents[3]
served Ramesses II and his successor,
Merenptah. So well-studied is Deir el-Medina that even the location of Khaemtore's
house, quite apart from his tomb, can be established with confidence.[4] Little information about Khaemtore has survived, except
for his economic transactions.

This is Khaemtore's only known *shawabti*.
The fine modeling and coloring are characteristic of Deir el-Medina work of Dynasty
19, and therefore support the equation with
the Khaemtore of the Leiden statue. Apart
from the owner's prominence, the most interesting feature of the *shawabti* is the
"wig of the living," whose significance is
discussed in connection with Ramose's
shawabti (cat. 101).

DS

1. It is not listed in Ranke 1935, the standard index of ancient Egyptian personal names.
2. Janssen 1977.
3. Janssen 1977.
4. Janssen 1977, 224, no. 24-25.

104
Shawabti of Huy

Provenance unknown
New Kingdom, Dynasties 19-20
Wood with painted gesso
Height 23.5 cm.
Hay Collection, Gift of C. Granville Way,
1872 (72.4902)

This reconstituted[1] *shawabti*, of wood covered with a layer of painted gesso, wears a
black tripartite wig and broad collar in red,
black, and green over a close-fitting white
shroud, from which braceletted hands protrude to clutch two hoes. A single water pot
is visible, slung over the left shoulder. The
lower half of the *shawabti* is inscribed with
six horizontal bands of hieroglyphs executed in black in a yellow ground, a palette
characteristic of the Ramesside period. The
text contains the owner's name, Huy (a
well-known abbreviation of Amenhotep),
and a version of the usual *shawabti* spell
from Chapter 6 of the Book of the Dead.
The man was evidently attached to a temple of the god Amen, but in what capacity is
not clear since the beginning of his title is
damaged.

CNR

1. Hatchfield 1986, pp. 93-96, no. 109.

104

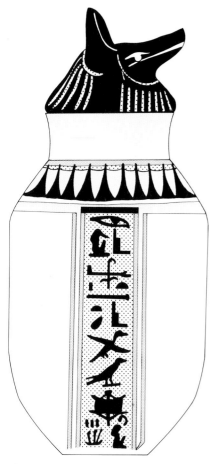

105

The pot and *shawabti*s were excavated in 1903 at the site of Abydos, the center of worship of Osiris and a revered burial ground. The tomb in which the *shawabti* pot was excavated also contained an ivory ear-stud, a ring inscribed "Horus, Lord of Heaven," and a fish-shaped dish of alabaster.[3]

SD'A

1. Randall-MacIver and Mace 1902, p. 78, pls. XLIV and LVI, 1,3,8,10,11; Ayrton, Currelly, and Weigall 1904, pls. XXII and XXIII; Reisner 1967, nos. 4239, 4240, 4241; Bourriau 1981, no. 229; Feucht 1986, no. 328. The inscriptions on most of these jars relate to *shawabti* spells (beginning "*shd*" or "*dd mdw*") rather than canopic jar texts; nearly all are from Abydos and are jackal-headed, probably representing Anubis. Other similar jars have inscriptions and lid types (i.e., the Four Sons of Horus) usually found on canopic jars; these may well be canopics rather than *shawabti* jars; cf. Randall-MacIver and Mace 1902, pl. LVI, 2, 7,13.
2. Cf. Ranke 1935, 121, no. 7.
3. Ayrton, Currelly, and Weigall 1904, p. 51 and pl. XVIII. The dish is in Boston, MFA 03.1833.

Bibliography: Ayrton, Currelly, and Weigall 1904, pl. XVIII, no. 12, and p. 51.

106, front

106, reverse

105
Shawabti jar and shawabtis

From Abydos tomb μ36
New Kingdom, Dynasty 19
Pottery
Jar height 29.5 cm.
Gift of Egypt Exploration Fund, 1903
(03.1746-1754, 1769)

This piriform pottery jar belongs to a class of objects often mistakenly identified as canopic jars because of their similar appearance. Their purpose was not to contain viscera, but to hold *shawabti* figures.[1] This jar is displayed with its original contents of nine *shawabti*s.

The jar, of Nile silt B, has a geometric decoration of black lozenges bordered in red and yellow on a white background that extends from rim to shoulder. The details on the jackal-headed stopper are painted in yellow. A vertical inscription on a yellow ground bordered in red on the front of the jar names "the Osiris, Singer of Isis, Pa-tjaw."[2]

The appealing little shawabtis found in the jar are also ceramic with painted details. At first glance, they appear to be identical, with their yellow faces, black eyes and smiling mouths, broad collars, long wigs, and vertical inscriptions. Closer inspection reveals variations in the colors, jewelry, or inscriptions on four of them.

106
Shawabti box

Provenance unknown
New Kingdom, Dynasties 19-20
Painted wood
Height 35 cm.
Morris and Louise Rosenthal Fund and Edwin E. Jack Fund, 1984 (1984.411)

During the New Kingdom, *shawabti*s were often placed in beautifully painted wooden boxes whose shape was derived from the archaic shrine of Lower Egypt.[1] Each box was divided into compartments designed to hold one or more *shawabti*s,[2] which at this period were often well-crafted and decorated (see cats. 94-105).

This double *shawabti* box is inscribed for the Constable of the Barque of Amen,[3] Pa-imi-ro-ihu, a name that survived into the Graeco-Roman period as Pelaias.[4] On two sides of the box, the deceased is represented worshiping the enthroned funerary deities Anubis, "Lord of the Necropolis" (whose double crown is awkwardly placed behind his projecting ears), and Osiris, the "Good God, Lord of Eternity." The narrow ends of the box contain representations of the human-headed Imsety and the baboon-headed Hapy, two of the Four Sons of Horus. The lids on the box would have been secured by tying rope around the projecting knobs on lid and box.

The box may have originally held three *shawabti*s, now in the Turin Museum, inscribed with the name and title of Pa-imi-ro-ihu.[5] Each of the wooden *shawabti*s is quite different in dress and appearance, unlike the mass-produced figures of later times (see cats. 127 and 130).

SD'A

1. Hayes 1959, p. 428.
2. For single *shawabti* boxes, see Hayes 1959, fig. 158, p. 263. Double boxes: see Andrews 1984, fig. 76, pp. 60-61; Hayes 1959, fig. 274, p. 429; Phillips 1948, pp. 207-212. Triple boxes: Fleming et. al. 1980, no. 43; Botti 1932, pp. 263-266; *Ägyptisches Museum Berlin* 1967, cat. 926.
3. See Legrain 1917, p. 41.
4. Cf. Ranke 1935, p. 100, no. 16.
5. Nos. 2607-2609.

107
Mirror

From Semna
New Kingdom, Dynasty 18
Bronze
Height 22.5 cm., max. width 12.2 cm.
Harvard University-Museum of Fine Arts
Expedition, 1928 (29.1197)

This mirror, excavated at the Semna fort in Lower Nubia, is of a common New Kingdom type showing a nude female with upraised arms surmounted by an open papyrus umbel. While this particular example appears to have come from a cache with another mirror and bronze vessels situated in a building below the level of the temple built later by Taharqa,[1] mirrors of this kind have been found in mid-Dynasty 18 graves in Egypt and Nubia,[2] and were probably a common grave offering.

In addition to their utilitarian value, mirrors were important as a symbol of life. In fact, the word *ankh* (''life'') is also used as a term for mirrors.[3] In capturing the image of the deceased, mirrors may have been thought to be preserves of the soul,[4] as were representations in sculpture or painting. Mirrors are shown in tomb paintings and on stelae where they are offered to or held by the deceased.[5]

This particular mirror is decorated with such regenerative symbols as the nude girl with floral collar and girdle,[6] emphasizing its magical function. However, its context and evidence of wear suggest it was used in life as well.

PL

1. Field no. 28-1-369, from room ''bn'' below the Taharqa temple in a Dynasty 18 deposit. Dunham and Janssen 1960, p. 54, pl. 128c,d.
2. Lilyquist 1982, p. 186. n. 215.
3. Erman and Grapow 1926, p. 204.
4. Lilyquist 1979a, pp. 96-99.
5. Cf. Lilyquist 1979a, figs. 118-150.
6. Wallert 1967, pp. 29-30.

Bibliography: Reisner 1929a, pp. 64-75, fig. 10; Dunham and Janssen 1960, p. 54, pl. 128c,d; Dunham 1958, pl. 70; Lilyquist 1982, p. 186, no. 215.

108
Shrine-stela and offering table of Menmaatre-emheb

From Abydos
New Kingdom, Dynasty 19
Limestone
Shrine height 55 cm.; offering table width 37 cm., depth 48.5 cm.
Gift of the Egypt Exploration Fund, 1900 (00.690-691)

This monument reproduces in limestone a wooden shrine with arched roof and high side panels. Its face carries a representation, in high raised relief, of the dedicator and his wife standing frontally, hand in hand, the man with his right foot to the fore. The incised texts that frame the composition identify them as the *wab* priest and lector priest of Osiris, Menmaatre-emheb (who is specified elsewhere on the monument as having been attached to the temple of Ramesses II at Abydos), and his wife, the ''Mistress of the House and Songstress of Isis, Weret-nofret.'' Various other individuals (including the King's Scribe and Overseer of the Double Granary, Siese),[1] some of them, evidently members of the owner's family, are represented in sunk relief on the top, side, and back panels of the monument.

The shrine and its accompanying offering table, which is roughly carved in limestone and uninscribed, were erected against the face of a stela marking the Middle Kingdom boundary of cemetery D at Abydos.[2] This stela, dedicated to Wepwawet, was subsequently usurped by Khasekhemre Neferhotep I of Dynasty 13; by the Ramesside Period it was an object of veneration in its own right. The intention of Menmaatre-emheb and of his contemporaries Amenem-onet and Hormes, who left a *shawabti*[3] and a stela, respectively, at this same spot, was twofold: to establish his presence in the following of Wepwawet, and to ensure himself and his family a share of any offerings that the boundary stela might attact.

CNR

1. Satzinger 1978, pp. 7-28, esp. pp. 24-25.
2. Randall-MacIver and Mace 1902, p. 64.
3. Randall-MacIver and Mace 1902, p. 64, pl. XXIX, center row, no. 5 (now British Museum EA 32691).

Bibliography: Porter and Moss 1937, p. 67, pl. 37; Randall-MacIver and Mace 1902, pp. 64, 71, pl. XXXVII; Hornemann 1969, p. 1177; Vandier 1958; Kitchen 1980, pp. 465-467, no. 210.

108, shrine

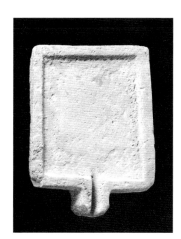

108, offering table

107

0   10   20   30   40   50   55 cm.

109

109
Funerary stela

From Sakkara
New Kingdom, Dynasty 18 or later
Limestone
Height 102.5 cm., width 51.5 cm.
Purchased from the Egyptian Antiquities
Department, 1925 (25.635)

The representation on this round-topped limestone stela is divided into two registers. At the top, a winged sun disk hovers over a scene in which the deified king Teti stands offering spouted jars to Osiris. The king wears a *nemes* headdress with uraeus and an elaborate kilt with pendant tail behind and uraeus ornament in front. He is identified as "the King of Upper and Lower Egypt, the Son of Re, Teti, the Good God and Lord of Ceremonies, given life." Before him stands the mummified figure of Osiris wearing the *atef* crown, holding a crook and flail in one hand and a longer crook in the other. He stands on a *maat*-shaped pedestal, and behind him is a tall floral motif. Over the god is the caption, "Osiris, Foremost of the West, the Great God and Lord of the Necropolis." Between the two figures is an offering table, under which are two jars with seals.

In the bottom register a man and his wife are shown, arms raised in adoration. The man wears a shoulder-length wig and a pleated kilt; rolls of flesh on his abdomen indicate a ripe old age. The woman wears a close-fitting dress worn under a long transparent garment, a full wig, a fillet, and an ointment cone with flower. At the right is a vertical text that reads, "An offering which the king gives, consisting of incense and libation, to Osiris, Foremost of the West, (and) to Anubis, Foremost of the Divine Booth, (and to) the gods who are in the necropolis, that they may give a good life to the spirit of the Osiris, the outline-draftsman Ptah-Setji, True-of-Voice." A caption above the woman identifies her as "his sister (meaning 'wife' here), the Mistress of the House, Henut-iunu."

The clothing worn by the owners of the stela, as well as the woman's hairstyle, date the stela to late Dynasty 18 or early Dynasty 19. The piece was excavated at Sakkara near the pyramid of Teti. By the New Kingdom, this general area, in particular Teti's funerary temple,[1] had become a place of pilgrimage where worshippers came and deposited tokens of their reverence toward the kings of old.[2] As the founder of Dynasty 6, Teti was especially honored, and the great number of votive objects dedicated to his memory give testimony to his enduring fame.[3]

RJL

1. Berlandini-Grenier 1976, p. 314.
2. Yoyotte 1960, p. 50.
3. Yoyotte 1958, p. 96.

Bibliography: Dunham 1935, pp. 148-149, pl. XVII, 2; Leprohon forthcoming.

110
Lintel fragment of Kha-em-was

From Heliopolis
New Kingdom, Dynasty 20
Limestone
Height 47 cm., width (decorated surface)
66 cm., thickness 15 cm.
Gift of the British School of Archaeology in
Egypt, 1912 (12.1004)

This lintel fragment was found during Petrie's excavations at Heliopolis during the winter of 1911-1912.[1] The offering scene shows the Royal Scribe, Chief Steward, Overseer of the Granaries Kha-em-was seated at the right while a *wab* priest presents him with a tray of offerings and a woman behind the priest offers a bouquet of flowering lotus.

This Kha-em-was is probably the same as the Steward Kha-em-was mentioned in the Wilbour Papyrus in connection with the mortuary temple of Ramesses III at Thebes.[2] According to Helck, the same man is mentioned in the mortuary temple itself, indicating that he held his position in the temple administration from the reign of Ramesses III into that of Ramesses V.[3]

The identity of the two people offering to Kha-em-was is more difficult to interpret. In Porter and Moss they are described as the son and daughter of the deceased,[4] but they are not specifically called "his son" or "his daughter" in the inscription above their heads. Petrie gives the priest's name as

Sary, a name attested in Ranke, but not with this peculiar spelling, which has the hieroglyph *sr* enclosed in a *hwt* sign.[5] On the other hand, the *hwt sr* is a well-known institution in Heliopolis and these hieroglyphs may be part of the priest's title. In this case, his name would be Ii.[6]

The column of hieroglyphs along the right side of the block is larger in scale than those above the figures. The text reads "to the Ka of the Songstress of Amen-Re, King of the Gods, Tjy" (or perhaps Ty).[7] This text probably does not refer to the woman depicted in the scene who is making offerings, not receiving them. Instead it probably was part of another scene, now destroyed.

The figures are in typical Ramesside dress; the men wear curve-toed sandals. The unusual chair in which Kha-em-was sits seems to be a combination of a padded folding stool[8] with a flat seat and back balanced on it. Part of the tie of Kha-em-was's skirt falls over the edge of the chair.

Immediately over the hieroglyphs at the top of the scene is a torus molding above which the surface has a slight curve suggesting a cavetto cornice. Traces of hieroglyphs at the far left of the block indicate that a second offering scene, probably the mirror image of the preserved scene, was carved on the other half of the lintel.

CHR

1. Petrie and Mackay 1915, p. 7, pl. xi (19).
2. Gardiner 1948, p. 144 §129; p. 131, §52 commentary.
3. Helck 1961, p. 242.
4. Porter and Moss 1934, p. 61.
5. Ranke 1935, p. 317.6.
6. Attested with various spellings, but not this one. Ranke 1935, pp. 7-8.
7. Ty is attested in Ranke 1935, p. 389.30, though not with this exact spelling. It may be a variation of the name Ty, Ranke 1935, p. 378.4.
8. Baker 1966, fig. 104, p. 90.

Literature: Petrie and Mackay 1915, p. 7, pl. IX (19); Porter and Moss 1934, p. 61.

111
Fragment of relief from tomb of Ptah-mose

Probably from Sakkara
New Kingdom, Dynasty 19
Limestone
Height 20.3 cm., width 15.2 cm., depth
3.8 cm.
Harvard University-Museum of Fine Arts
Expedition, 1934 (34.50)

This scene, popular in New Kingdom Theban and Memphite private tombs, depicts the tree-goddess giving reviving water to the deceased and his wife. The female form of the divinity emerges at waist height from between two branches of a leafy sycamore. She holds a vase in each hand and offers the water to Ptah-mose and his wife, who are kneeling on either side of the tree. Ptah-mose cups his palms to capture the falling stream of water. He is wearing the long, pleated skirt typical of Dynasty 19 funeral garb. His wife, coiffed with a long braided wig surmounted by an unguent cone, is dressed in a tight tunic and long, pleated cape. She holds a plant offering in her right hand and raises the left. Behind her stand two male relatives with their arms raised in adoration; both wear short, curly wigs and knee-length, pleated skirts. Behind them, two children carry floral offerings.

The tree-goddess is first seen in large garden scenes in Dynasty 18 Theban tombs. She appears among vast plantations of sycamores, phoenix and dom palms, and other species all shown in "rabbattement" and planted in rows around a large rectangular pond. These grand and gracious garden representations are no longer in vogue by Dynasty 19, and the tree-goddess scene on its own replaces them, the goddess and the life-giving water she bears personifying the garden and the cool breezes and shade it offers.[1]

This scene appears on funerary stelae, coffins, sarcophagi, cartonnages and shrouds, offering tables, papyri situlae, and *shawabti* chests, as well as on tombs walls. The tree-goddess is frequently a hypostasis of the major mother-goddesses – Nut, Hathor, and Isis – although in many funerary scenes she bears no name. The divinity is the physical synthesis of the tree and the female form in a harmonious composition. Representations differ iconographically according to period and material and show a varying juxtaposition of the two elements. They may be en-

0   50   70 cm.

110

111

tirely distinct, as on many Third Intermediate Period papyri depicting a complete female form standing in front of the tree, or totally integrated, as we see on Ptolemaic offering tables showing a stylized animated sycamore with arms opposite a female figure sprouting twigs and leaves. Most New Kingdom scenes depict the goddess as she is shown here, with a human upper body and a lower body composed of the trunk of a leafy fig-bearing sycamore, favored for its broad shade and succulent fruit. Some Memphite scenes add a palm tree as well, evoking a more complete garden.

The function of the tree-goddess is always the same: to provide food and water to the deceased in his next life. Usually the scene is inscribed with a funerary formula for drinking water in the necropolis or on the current of the river, and may contain an entire chapter – 59 or 62 – from the Book of the Dead. The scene has elements in common with other New Kingdom funerary scenes, especially that of drinking water directly from the river current.

MEL

1. For examples in Theban tombs, see Porter and Moss 1960, Appendix A, 35.

Bibliography: Los Angeles 1974; Porter and Moss 1979.

112
Coffin

From Lower Nubia
New Kingdom, Ramesside Period
Pottery
Length 39 cm., max. diam. 11 cm.
Helen and Alice Colburn Fund, 1985
(1985.808)

Ceramic anthropoid coffins were found in large numbers in Lower Nubia, no doubt necessitated by the lack of timber to produce wooden coffins. This example is less stylized than its Lower Egyptian counterparts (see cat. 113) and closely follows the standard scheme of decoration for a Ramesside coffin. The small coffin was intended for the burial of a child, a boy named Pa-nefer-neb.[1] The coffin is wheelmade of an alluvial clay, and the face and chest are part of a removable plate that allowed the introduction of the body. The head end is capped by a blue and yellow striped headdress bound by a headband of lotus petals with a pendant blue lotus flower. The face and crossed hands are painted red, and an elaborate floral collar of blue lotus petals covers the chest. Below, pairs of *wedjat* eyes, lotus flowers, and Anubis jackals flank a figure of the goddess Nut with her wings outstretched.

The lower part of the coffin is divided into only four panels; perhaps because the coffin is small, the the traditional two sets of four panels[2] were reduced. The upper

panels depict the god Osiris enthroned and the lower two show the Four Sons of Horus. The bands of hieroglyphs reproduce the binding tapes of the mummy within, and address offering formulae to "Osiris, Lord of Forever, Ruler of Eternity, Foremost of the Westerners."

This coffin was found in the spring of 1937 by Eric Stahl in a cemetery near Amada.[3] The coffin had collapsed into fragments and contained the bones of a pre-adult and some jewelry, including a scarab pectoral that was retained by the Antiquities Service.

PL

1. For another example of the name see Ranke 1935, p. 113, no. 8.
2. Cf. Schmidt 1919, pp. 125-128.
3. For other examples from Lower Nubia cf. Steindorff 1937, p. 170, pls. 39-40; and Reisner 1910, p. 166, pl. 36.

112

113
Coffin

From Tell el-Yahudiyeh
New Kingdom, Ramesside Period
Pottery
Length 200 cm., diam. 53 cm.
Gift of the Egypt Exploration Fund, 1888
(88.1041)

Ceramic coffins occur sporadically throughout Egyptian history. Pottery anthropoid coffins from the New Kingdom and later are most commonly found in Nubia, the East Delta, and the Fayum.[1] These coffins gener-

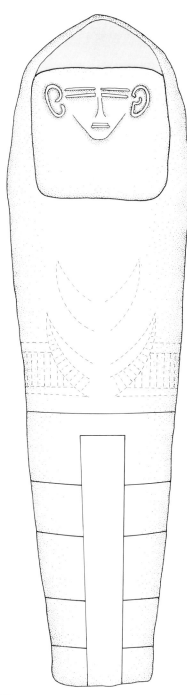

113

114

also appears to have been a central winged figure, making the decoration similar to another pottery coffin from Rikka.[3]

This coffin comes from the site of Tell el-Yahudiyeh, where a series of these coffins was excavated in a cemetery close to the ancient city. The coffins and associated grave goods had been placed in rough, mud-brick vaults and covered by a mound of rough basalt blocks and sand.[4] The cemetery had been heavily plundered and many of the coffins were badly smashed. Some of these coffins were painted in imitation of a typical Ramesside to Third Intermediate Period coffin with bands of inscription separating vignettes of the Four Sons of Horus and other gods.

Griffith, the excavator, dated the cemetery largely to Dynasty 20 by the pottery and scarabs of Ramesses III and Ramesses IV.[5] This type of coffin did persist later and undoubtedly influenced the style of the "Philistine" coffins of southern Palestine.[6]

PL

1. Kuchman 1977-1978, pp. 11-22.
2. Dorothea Arnold, personal communication.
3. Engelbach 1915, pl. 19 no. 1.
4. Griffith 1890, pp. 42-48.
5. Griffith 1890, p. 48.
6. Dothan 1982, pp. 252-288.

114
Human-headed scarab

Provenance unknown
New Kingdom
Serpentine
Length 6.4 cm., width 4.4 cm., height 3.9 cm.
Gift of Mrs. Horace L. Mayer, 1979
(1979.570)

"Heart scarabs" first appear during the Second Intermediate Period.[1] These are traditionally made of a dark green stone and are usually inscribed with a spell from the Book of the Dead, Chapter 30B[2] (see cat. 176) to prevent the heart from "speaking in opposition" (or telling the truth about the character of the deceased) in the Hall of Judgment. On some of the scarabs from the Second Intermediate Period and New Kingdom the head of the scarab beetle is replaced by a human head,[3] as in this example.

This heart scarab is carved of dark green serpentine with a human head wearing a lappet wig rising up from the front. The head occupies the center of the prothorax, which is decorated with incised dots; a series of incised lines runs down the elytra from front to back. The legs on the proper right are carefully carved and bent under the body. The underside has been largely broken away, but a fragment of preserved in-

scription identifies the owner as "the Mistress of the House, Neb(ti)."[4]

PL

1. Hayes 1953, p. 37.
2. A close parallel to this scarab in Berlin is inscribed with Chapter 6 of the Book of the Dead, "the name spell;" Wenig 1977, p. 59 no. 248, pl. 70.
3. See also Newberry 1908, p. 73, pl. 1.
4. For examples of the name, see Ranke 1935, pp. 187-188.

Literature: Malaise 1978, esp. p. 62.

ally imitate styles found in wood coffins or stone sarcophagi, and the reliance on clay may well have had to do with the scarcity of timber or the economic status of the deceased.

This example was made with a local clay, Nile silt B 1, sandy variant.[2] Such coffins were generally wheelmade as large pots in a single piece with an opening at the head to allow the insertion of the body. The opening was then covered by a faceplate on which human features were roughly modeled by hand. The painted decoration on this example has largely faded, although traces of a central band of inscription and several side bands are barely visible. There

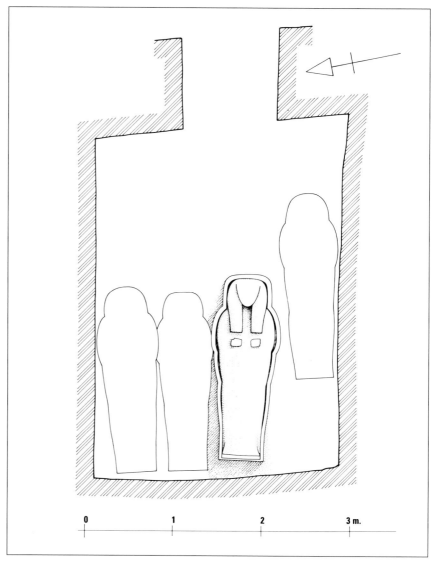

Fig.80

115
Tomb group of Henettawy

From Deir el-Bahri, tomb 60
Third Intermediate Period, Dynasty 21
Wood
Acquired by exchange with the Metropolitan
Museum of Art, 1954 (54.639, 640).

a. Outer coffin (box only)
   Length 210 cm., width 74.5 cm., height 51.5 cm.
b. Inner coffin (box and lid)
   Length 187 cm.

Deir el-Bahri tomb 60 (fig. 80) was uncovered by Herbert E. Winlock in the spring of
1924 while he was excavating for the Metropolitan Museum of Art. The tomb was excavated for the use of the family of the High
Priest of Amen Men-kheper-re of Dynasty
21, though other burials were added in the
same dynasty and the tomb was expanded
during Dynasty 23.

The original occupants of tomb 60 were
three female members of Men-kheper-re's
family. The first two burials were those of
Henettawy, daughter of Pinedjem and sister

of Men-kheper-re, and Djed-mutes-ankh,
who was probably either a wife or daughter
of the same man. The final burial was that
of Henettawy, daughter of Iset-em-akhbet
and owner of the Museum's coffins. This
Henettawy is believed to have been the
daughter of Men-kheper-re, though she
may have been his granddaughter.[1] Broken
seals of the High Priest Men-kheper-re
were found in the tomb, suggesting that
these three women were buried during his
tenure as High Priest. Some time after the
last of the women was interred, a fourth
burial was introduced into the burial chamber. The coffins were reinscribed for the deceased, a priest of Amen by the name of
Men-kheper-re (not the High Priest). Since
Men-kheper-re seemed not to be of the
same social status as the three women,
Winlock assumed that this was the first of
many intrusive burials found in the tomb.

The coffins of Henettawy are typical of the
varnished yellow wooden coffins of Dynasty 21. The group originally included outer

115b, side view

115b, top view

and inner anthropoid coffins and an anthropoid cover that lay directly over the mummy.[2] They are of particularly fine quality since, before being painted, the decoration was carved in low relief into the layer of plaster over the wood. The decoration includes vignettes of Henettawy with various gods, being judged and presented to Osiris, and making offerings to the gods.

At some time the face, hands, and hair ornaments of the inner coffin lid were ripped off for the gold that covered them. Since all three of the coffins had suffered this fate,

Winlock postulated that they were damaged during the interment of the priest Men-kheper-re. The fact that some care was taken to camouflage the robbery by covering the missing faces with linen sheeting suggested to him that the thieves were the people responsible for Men-kheper-re's burial.[3]

One fact that argues against this explanation is that the lid of Henettawy's outer coffin was missing when the tomb was discovered in 1924. At some time during or after the defacing of the coffins, the outer lid of Djed-mutes-ankh's coffin was placed on Henettawy's outer coffin box – a poor fit since Djed-mutes-ankh's coffins are much smaller than Henettawy's. The original outer lid of Henettawy seems to have been broken up by the thieves, a fragment having been found on one side of the burial chamber.[4] It seems very unlikely that the same people who took the trouble to "camouflage" the robbery by replacing the coffin lids and covering the damaged faces would have been so careless as to destroy one of the lids in the first place. A more plausible explanation is that officials discovered the robbery before or at the time of Men-kheper-re's interment, and straightened up the tomb as well as they could before adding other burials.

When the mummies from tomb 60 were unwrapped, Winlock discovered that those of the three women had been rifled. The two outer shrouds and bands of the mummies of Djed-mutes-ankh and Henettawy daughter of Pinedjem had been tucked back around the bodies while those of Henettawy daughter of Iset-em-akhbet had been sewn up the back, leading Winlock to believe that this mummy had been robbed by the embalmers before Henettawy was even buried.

As was common in Dynasty 21, the mummy of Henettawy had been stuffed with sawdust to fill it out, and glass eyes were placed in eye sockets.[5] Seven canopic packages had been put back inside the body

after mummification, four with a wax figure of one of the Four Sons of Horus (see cat. 172).[6] A heart scarab of gray feldspar (see cat. 176) was found on the mummy, but it had been disturbed and no name was inscribed on it.[7] The robbers had stolen a hawk pectoral that had been placed over the chest, its impression having been left in the resin used during the bandaging.[8] A group of amulets (see cats. 129 and 178) including three *djed* pillars, two *wedjat*-eyes and a uraeus were found in the neck area, and a scarab, a *wedjat* eye, and a square plaque were found near the wrists.[9] An iron plaque inscribed with a *wedjat* eye was also found and probably originally covered the embalmer's incision in the abdomen (see cat. 173). Between Henettawy's thighs was a papyrus with texts of the Amduat.[10] Henettawy was provided with a crude Ptah-Sokar-Osiris figure (see cat. 144) with a papyrus inside inscribed with parts of the Book of the Dead.[11] She also had two wooden *shawabti* boxes,[12] one containing seventeen *reis-shawabti*s and 172 worker *shawabti*s, the other containing twenty *reis-shawabti*s and 202 workers.[13]

CHR

1. Winlock 1942, p. 96.
2. MMA 25.3.6.
3. Winlock 1942, p. 97.
4. MMA Theban tomb card 436.
5. MMA Theban tomb card 485.
6. MMA 25.3.155A-D. For distribution see MMA Theban tomb card 487.
7. MMA 25.3.162. See MMA Theban tomb card 495.
8. Winlock 1942, pp. 113-114.
9. MMA Theban tomb card 497.
10. MMA 25.4.28.
11. Figure MMA 25.3.35; papyrus MMA 25.3.29. See MMA Theban tomb card 506.
12. MMA 25.3.19-20. See MMA Theban tomb card 500.
13. *Shawabti*s of molded green-blue faience. Height 11-12 cm.

Bibliography: Porter and Moss 1964, p. 629; Winlock 1924a, pp. 24-28; Winlock 1926, pp. 19-30; Winlock 1942, pp. 95-97, 113-116.

Literature: Chassinat 1909; Niwinski 1983, p. 116.

116
Face from anthropoid coffin

Provenance unknown
Third Intermediate Period, Dynasties 21-26
Wood
Height 23 cm., max. width 17.6 cm.
Hay Collection, Gift of C. Granville Way, 1872 (72.4735)

This finely modeled face was sculpted from a single piece of fine-grained wood. Although it is naturalistically formed from a frontal view, its back surface is a flat plane, suggesting that it was once part of another

116

object. Likely it served as the face on an anthropoid coffin. The "mask" would have been carved separately by a skilled craftsman and then pegged in place on the coffin.

A false beard, now indicated only by an empty rectangular attachment hole under the chin, suggests that the coffin was made for a man. Although beards were rarely worn in daily life, the image of the deceased on coffins was given a beard in imitation of Osiris, the King of the Gods, who was closely associated with the concept of resurrection. To be likened to Osiris was to ensure that you too would live again in the heavenly realm.

A sculpted wooden tripartite wig would have been affixed to the head by pegs. Some pegs of this type are visible on the headdress of a Late Period case in Copenhagen.[1] No doubt the hole in the rectangular block that extends from the top of the back of the Boston "mask" was intended to hold such a peg. A similar attachment piece can be seen on a face from a coffin found at the Ramesseum.[2]

The construction technique of securing the individually carved face and wig by pegs is especially prevalent from Dynasty 21 to Dynasty 26 as evidenced by coffins in the British Museum,[3] the cases of the Theban Priests of Montu,[4] as well as numerous wooden faces published by Schmidt[5] and Quibell.[6]

The surface of the face shows no traces of either paint or varnish. Although this untreated state is not the norm, it is not unique, as such fine wooden coffins as the model sarcophagus of Tutankhamen lack surface treatment.[7] Also, the wood of several coffins belonging to the Priests of Montu was left unfinished; only the wig, necklace, and inscriptions were painted. Raven has pointed out that these were the

intermediate coffins in three-case ensembles, the outer and inner coffin bearing the customary polychrome decoration.[8] Two fine examples of the natural wood finish are the cases, now in Cairo, of the priests Ankh-efen-Khonsu and Nesy-Amen.[9]

The eyes, eyebrows, and cosmetic lines of the Boston face are deeply and precisely incised to receive inlays, which are now missing. These inlays of glass, faience, or semi-precious stones would have enlivened the neutral brown surface and given the face a more naturalistic appearance. This attention to detail, along with the superior quality of the craftsmanship, demonstrates the elevated social rank of the owner of the coffin to which the face belonged.

The iconography of this type of funerary image is slow to change and consequently difficult to date. The coffin to which the face was once attached would have provided more clear-cut dating criteria. However, the Boston mask does have numerous facial features in common with Dynasty 22 royal sculpture.[10] Especially noteworthy is its strong resemblance to the head of Heka-kheper-re Sheshonk.[11] Both have full mouths with softly drilled corners, upwardly curving lower lips, high cheekbones, and similarly shaped, substantial noses. Although convincing, these similarities are not sufficient evidence to conclusively establish a specific date; they do, however, support the argument for placing this piece in the broader time range suggested by the construction technique, namely Dynasties 21 to 26.

Even though the inlays are now missing from the eyes, and numerous vertical cracks mar the surface, the high quality of this carefully sculpted and finely finished face is not diminished. The anthropoid coffin to which it was attached also must have reflected the status of the official for whom it was commissioned.

JLH

1. Koefoed-Petersen 1951, pl. XCIV. I must credit Diana Wolfe Larkin for her fine editorial assistance and creative suggestions.
2. Quibell 1898, pl. II.9, p. 11.
3. British Museum 1938, p. 49, pl. XVII.
4. Gauthier 1913.
5. Schmidt 1919, pp. 179, 188, 189.
6. Quibell 1898, pl. II.9, p. 11
7. Edwards 1976, pl. 23, cat. no. 40.
8. Raven 1981, p. 12.
9. Gauthier 1913, pp. 27, pl. III (41043), p. 74 pl. VI (41045).
10. I would like to thank Peter Lacovara for bringing this comparison to my attention.
11. Montet 1952, pl. XV.

117
Set of dummy canopic jars

Provenance unknown
Third Intermediate Period
Limestone
Average height 24.1 cm., average diam. 13.6 cm.
Hay Collection, Gift of C. Granville Way, 1872 (72.590-593)

During Dynasty 21 a change in the practice of mummification occurred: the internal organs were no longer placed in canopic jars, but were usually wrapped in linen packages, often with a wax figure representing one of the tutelary deities, the Four Sons of Horus (see cat. 172). These packages were then placed in the empty body cavity or between the legs of the mummy prior to the final wrapping. However, the innate conservatism of the ancient Egyptians prevented the total discarding of canopic jars, although these no longer had any real function. Canopic jars continued to form part of the funerary equipment of some burials, but the jars were now either dummy or too shallow to contain any human remains. This set is a fine example of the type of dummy jars in use in the Third Intermediate Period. They are each carved out of one piece of limestone, and the division between the head and body is indicated only by an incised line. The facial features are painted in black, and down the front of each jar a painted inscription names its tutelary deity; Osiris-Imsety, Osiris-Hapy, Osiris-Duamutef, and Osiris-Qebehsenuef. Similar dummy jars from this period are often uninscribed or have abbreviated texts.[1] Some stone jars have detachable heads,[2] while many wooden examples are profusely painted.[3]

MLB

1. London UC 29794-6, see Raisman and Martin 1985, pp. 28-29, pls. 10-11; Cairo 4422-4425, 4427-4430, see Reisner 1967, pp. 259-262, pls. XLVIII-IX.
2. Cairo 4398-4401, Reisner 1967, pp. 249-251, pl. XLVII.
3. British Museum EA 9562-9565.

Bibliography: Brovarski 1978, pp. 17-20.

118
Funerary stela

From Thebes
Third Intermediate Period, Dynasty 22
Painted wood
Height 24.5 cm., width 19 cm.
Sears Fund, 1904 (04.1763)

This small round-topped stela was made from a single piece of wood; covered with a layer of gesso; and painted red, blue, yellow, black, and green. Varnish survives on parts of the decoration. A woman stands on the right, arms raised, pouring a libation

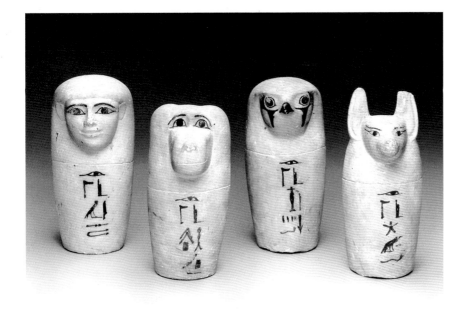

117

5. Gardiner 1944, pp. 48-50.
6. Vandier 1954, pp. 515-16; Badawy 1968, p. 415.
7. de Meulenaere 1969, pp. 96-97.

Bibliography: Leprohon forthcoming.

119
Funerary stela

Provenance unknown
Third Intermediate Period, Dynasty 22
Painted wood
Height 24.5 cm., width 20.6 cm.
Estate of Henry Williamson Haynes, Gift of
Sarah H. Blanchard, 1912 (12.590)

This round-topped stela was made from two pieces of wood joined by dowels. The wood was covered with gesso and painted blue, green, red, yellow, and black. A down-curving sign of heaven at the top is supported by *was* scepters on both sides. In the lunette two *wedjat* eyes flank a *shen* symbol, a water ripple, and an offering cup. The scene below shows a standing man with a short beard, a pleated transparent garment, a short wig with fillet, and an incense cone with attached flower. The man raises his arms in adoration and pours a libation to the sun god Re-Horakhty, who sits on a low-backed throne that rests on a *maat*-sign, the symbol of truth. Between the two figures is an offering table.

Above the man and framed at the top by a sign of heaven a vertical text reads: "Words spoken by Re-Horakhty, the Good God and Lord of Heaven, the Many-Colored of Plumage, that he may give invocation-offerings and sustenance to the Osiris, the *wab* priest of Amen Djed-Inheret."

Stelae made of wood, showing individuals praying to the sun god in the guise of Re-Horakhty, are typical of Dynasty 22 products from Thebes.[1] What makes this piece remarkable is that the symbols at the top and

118

before the seated figure of the falcon-headed sun god Re-Horakhty. She wears a long transparent robe and a broad collar, and on her head is an incense cone to which flowers have been attached. The god is crowned with the sun disk and uraeus, wears patterned mummy wrappings, and holds the crook and flail. Between the two figures is a tall offering table. In the lunette at the top of the stela, a sign of heaven curves over a winged sun disk with pendant uraei. Traditionally, one serpent wears the white crown of Upper Egypt and the other the red crown of Lower Egypt.[1] Here, unusually, both uraei wear the white crown. Two *was* scepters frame the scene – a traditional artistic device.[2]

A text over the woman reads: "Words spoken by Re-Horakhty, the Great God and Lord of Heaven, the Many-Colored of Plumage, that he may give invocation-offerings and sustenance to the Osiris, the Mistress of the House and Chantress of Amen Nes-Khonsu-pa-khered, true-of-voice, the wife of the Entrance Priest of Amen Nes-pa-her-an, true-of(-voice)."

The piece is said to be from Sheikh abd el-Qurna. Wooden stelae with such designs have a Theban origin and date to Dynasty 22.[3] In earlier periods, the deceased relied on the funerary cult of continued offerings and prayers to ensure a proper place in the hereafter, and these rituals were often shown on funerary stelae. By the Third Intermediate Period, however, a greater dependence was placed upon the efforts of the gods than on the possibly inconsistent human observances. Thus on the present stela the deceased confronts the sun god directly, associating herself with the solar cycle of birth, death, and rebirth.[4] The winged disk hovering above, representing both Re and Horus,[5] extends its protection over the whole scene.

This kind of stela may have its origins in such Ramesside "solar stelae" as the ones placed on the eastern face of the small brick pyramids of the funerary chapels at Deir el-Medina.[6] The manifestations of the sun god continued well into the Late Period at Thebes.[7]

RJL

1. Gardiner 1944, p. 48.
2. Hayes 1953, p. 285.
3. Munro 1973, pp. 6, 11.
4. Fazzini 1975, p. 107.

119

sides of the stela parallel the scene. The sign of heaven frames the other symbols, while at the center of the lunette the *shen* ring symbolizes the all-embracing circuit of the sun and may even represent the sun itself.[2] Directly beneath it, the water ripple symbolically repeats the act of libation performed by the man, while the bowl below implies an offering of incense or food,[3] thus completing the cultic act towards the god. Thus the symbols of sky, sun, and water create a microcosm of the earth, where the proper offerings and reverence to the god are observed. In addition, the sacred *wedjat* eyes of Horus represent physical prosperity and perfection,[4] themes echoed by the *was* scepters on the sides, themselves marks of well-being.[5] The hopes of the deceased for protection and continued well-being are thus represented emblematically.

RJL

1. Munro 1973, pp. 6, 11; Martin 1985, col. 3.
2. Hayes 1959, p. 161.
3. Hayes 1959, p. 161, n. 1.
4. Hart 1986, p. 93.
5. Hayes 1959, p. 91.

Bibliography: Leprohon forthcoming.

The Development of Cartonnage Cases

Throughout ancient Egyptian history, wood – both native and imported – was the preferred coffin material. The most popular alternative was cartonnage, a cheap and lightweight material that was used to fashion various funerary equipment.[1] In its original form, cartonnage was made from layers of gummed linen and plaster, but by the Ptolemaic Period "scrap paper" – in the form of unwanted papyrus documents – was commonly used instead of cloth.[2]

During the First Intermediate Period and the Middle Kingdom, cartonnage was primarily used to construct mummy masks, which were placed over the head and shoulders and represented the idealized face of the deceased adorned with a wig and collar (cat. 46).[3] The use of these masks led to the introduction of anthropoid coffins in late Dynasty 12, and some of these, too, were made of cartonnage.[4] After this initial phase, however, anthropoid coffins were generally made of wood, and throughout the New Kingdom the use of cartonnage was limited to a few objects: mummy masks, inscribed bands placed over the wrappings,[5] and the openwork covers laid over the mummy in late Dynasty 18 and the Ramesside Period.[6] By Dynasty 21 these items had virtually ceased to be used in private burials, and all the components of the coffin ensemble were made of wood.

At the beginning of Dynasty 22 there was a major change in the style of funerary equipment.[7] Wooden outer coffins continued to be used as before, but a new type of inner case was introduced, a sheath of cartonnage made in one piece and enveloping the body completely from head to foot. Such cases enjoyed great popularity throughout the ninth and eighth centuries B.C. (see cats. 120-122).

This revolution in the nature of burial equipment affected all levels of society throughout Egypt. The discovery of the royal tombs at Tanis revealed that the mummies of Dynasty 22 kings were enclosed in cartonnage cases. That of King Shoshenk II represented the mummiform body with crossed hands holding royal scepters, and was decorated with figures of deities in gold leaf.[8] The falcon head symbolized the king's role as the incarnation of Horus. Shoshenk II's silver coffin was also falcon-headed[9] – a feature apparently typical of the burials of Dynasty 22 kings.[10] Fragments of another falcon-headed cartonnage were found in the plundered sarcophagus of Osorkon II,[11] and a head in the Berlin Museum may have come from a third example.[12]

The one-piece cartonnage case was soon adopted for the burial of private individuals. This type of case appeared at Thebes about the reign of Osorkon I, quickly superseding the yellow-varnished wooden coffins that had been in use there for more than 150 years. There is no evidence of any transition period between the old and new styles of Theban burial, suggesting that the cartonnage case originated in the north of Egypt and was introduced into the Theban area only after it was fully developed.[13] Nevertheless, it is from Thebes that the largest number of cartonnages and the best-preserved specimens derive.

Although widely used in the Third Intermediate Period, cartonnage was not a mere substitute for more expensive materials. In private burials such cases were always enclosed in wooden coffins, often double and occasionally triple,[14] while the richness of the royal burials at Tanis indicates that the kings of the period had no need to practice petty economies. However, a cartonnage case could be much more quickly and easily made than a wooden coffin, and this must have been regarded as a considerable advantage. The medium of gummed linen and plaster was easy to model while soft, yet hardened to produce a tough casing. This case was made to fit very closely around the mummy, but was not actually molded around the corpse, as has sometimes been supposed.[15]

As far as can be determined from the few cartonnages that have been studied from the technical viewpoint, the following method of construction was employed at Thebes.[16] A core of mud and straw was roughly fashioned into the shape and size of the mummy and was then coated with coarse plaster. Several layers of linen soaked in gum were applied, completely covering the plastered core except for a section at the base of the feet (these layers are clearly visible at the foot of Tabes's case, cat. 121). In this way a mummiform shell of linen and plaster was built up. Such features as the wig, face, knees, and ankles were carefully modeled before the wet cloth began to harden. A long, narrow opening was left at the rear, and after the last layer of linen had been applied this rear slit was carefully opened out and the core was removed in pieces. Fragments of these mud and straw cores still adhere to the inner surfaces of some cartonnages.[17]

The faces of the Theban cases are always lifelike and well-proportioned, and precisely how this effect was achieved is still unclear. Possibly a template of wood or stone was mounted on the core before the application of the cloth, to be removed and later used again. Alternatively, the eyes, nose, and mouth may have been made in advance, applied separately, and held in place by additional layers of plaster, before the case hardened. This method is attested on some mummy masks of the Second Intermediate Period, from Mirgissa.[18]

After the removal of the core, the exterior of the cartonnage was coated with gesso, and small holes were punched in the edges of the rear flaps. The bandaged mummy was then inserted, and the rear flaps were drawn together by strings laced through the holes from head to foot. A wooden board was fitted beneath the feet and secured by wooden pegs driven through the edge of the cartonnage. In this way the mummy was sealed inside. On some examples a long strip of linen was pasted over the rear lacing, and gessoed to match the rest of the exterior.

The case, with the mummy inside, was now handed over to the draftsmen and painters to be decorated. The decoration was usually painted on the smooth gessoed surface, but the figures were sometimes modeled in slightly raised relief and then painted.[19] Gilding was often added on the face and on small elements of the design.

The subject matter of the decoration resembled that of contemporary wooden coffins; below the floral collar religious symbols and scenes usually alluded to the Osirian afterlife and the solar cycle (symbolizing resurrection after death). Solar symbolism is particularly prominent on the funerary monuments of the ninth and eighth centuries B.C. (cf. the frequent appearance of Re-Horakhty on Theban wooden stelae, in place of Osiris).[20] On the cartonnages, scarabs, beetles, winged sun disks, and images of the solar Horus occur repeatedly, while a scarab usually appears also on the top of the head.[21] Inscriptions are usually brief, consisting chiefly of standard formulae and label-texts.

The order of the designs followed fixed patterns. On the cartonnage of Shoshenk II a ram-headed falcon (representing the solar Horus) appears above figures of goddesses and other protective deities in compartments that are divided by bands of inscription. This ram-falcon sometimes appears on Theban cartonnages as part of a similar design. However, by far the most popular composition produced by Theban craftsmen showed the ram-falcon below the collar, with its wings upcurved, balanced by another falcon (with normal head) immediately below. The wings of this second bird were spread horizontally or inclined slightly downwards. The space between the two falcons was occupied by figures of the Sons of Horus in symmetrical groupings, and the area below was divided into compartments by a central inscription or an image of the Abydos fetish (see cats. 120 and 121). Many examples of this pattern are known,[22] together with numerous variations on the basic design;[23] it remained popular for about 200 years, and elements of the design were combined with new features during the stylistic transition of Dynasty 25 (see cat. 125). Cartonnages decorated with figured scenes in registers were also common in the Theban area. These usually included representations of the deceased before Re-Horakhty or Osiris, the barque of Sokar, the Hathor cow, and various demons associated with regions of the Netherworld. This design seems to have been popular mainly in early to middle Dynasty 22, when it was produced alongside the "Two Falcons" types. The concurrence of both types is conveniently illustrated by two cases in this exhibition: that of Tabes has the "Two Falcons" design, while that of her husband Nes-Ptah (cat. 170) is of the register type.

Cartonnage cases from other sites, although scarce, display distinct regional peculiarities. Third Intermediate Period examples found at el-Lahun were chiefly of linen and plaster,[24] though a layer of mud is sometimes found, in addition.[25] As at Thebes, the mummy was inserted through a vertical slit at the rear, but the faces, instead of being molded in one piece with the rest of the case, were carved separately from wood and pegged on to the front.[26] Specimens from el-Lahun and el-Hiba were more simply decorated than those from Thebes; there is usually a central inscription, above which the familiar ram-headed falcon often appears.[27] Other symbols also appear, but the areas flanking the inscription are usually white. The hands are sometimes represented in the round and sometimes merely painted, whereas at Thebes this custom disappeared at an early point (see cat. 122). Other cartonnages from Middle Egypt were more elaborately decorated, with figured scenes in registers.[28]

At Thebes the construction and design of cartonnage cases appears to have continued without major change until the end of the eighth century. During the transitional phase of the late eighth to early seventh centuries, wooden inner coffins once more replaced cartonnages at Thebes.[29] A similar transition can be observed at Akhmim at about the same time[30] and it is probable that the change occurred throughout Egypt, although definite proof is lacking. Some of the last cartonnages of this period were hybrid forms, combining traditional features with innovations. A few were made in two pieces, like wooden coffins;[31] others consisted of three pieces – front, back, and a separate pedestal that fitted on beneath the feet (possibly a legacy of the practice of using a wooden footboard to seal the cartonnage).[32] Some of these specimens were reinforced with wood, and their decoration was heavily influenced by that of the new wooden coffins.

After Dynasty 25, one-piece cartonnage cases were not used again until the Ptolemaic Period. During the last centuries of the Pharaonic era, mummy masks became fashionable once more, usually as part of a new type of covering that comprised a series of decorated plaques and a footcase, all of cartonnage (see cats. 140, 141, 150, and 151). This covering continued to be used in the Ptolemaic Period and displayed an increasing tendency to adopt Greek characteristics, which led ultimately to the appearance of cartonnage cases that represented the deceased as a living individual, dressed in contemporary Hellenistic costumes.

JHT

1. Besides mummy cases, canopic jars of cartonnage are known: Hayes 1953, pp. 320, 322, fig. 210.
2. Zauzich 1980, col. 353.
3. Examples: Chassinat and Palanque 1911, pl. 2, 3, 21, 26, 27; Hayes 1953, p. 309-310.
4. Mace and Winlock 1916, pp. 47-48, 53-54; Hayes 1953, p. 310-312.
5. E.g. Cairo CG 51010 (Yuya): Quibell 1908, p. 28-29.
6. Examples: Cairo Museum CG 51011 (Thuyu): Quibell 1908, p. 29-30; cf. Bruyère 1926, pp. 55, 176-177.
7. Taylor 1985, I, p. 132-3; Aston 1987, pp. 636-637, 641.
8. Montet 1951, p. 38-40; Brunton 1939, p. 542-544; Iskander 1940, p. 584-588 pl. LXI.
9. Montet 1951, 37-38, pl. 17-20.
10. Cf. the sarcophagus of "King" Harsiese: Hölscher 1954, p. 10, pl. 8(B) 10(D).
11. Montet 1947, pp. 39, 58.
12. Spiegelberg 1927, pp. 28-29, Abb. 2.
13. Taylor 1985, I, p. 133; Aston 1987, p. 650.
14. Boeser 1920, pp. 5-6, Taf. XIV-XV, pp. 3-5, Taf. XIV-XV, pp. 3-5, Taf. XIII.
15. Birch 1874, p. 199.
16. Quibell 1898, p. 10; Habachi 1958, p. 339; Adams 1966, pp. 55-66.
17. Adams 1966, p. 58-63, fig. 5, 7. Cf. Bolton 38.95.2 (information courtesy of Angela P. Thomas).
18. Vila 1976, p. 156.
19. Quibell 1898, p. 10.
20. Aston 1987, pp. 567-569, 573.
21. Boeser 1920, p. 4; Kueny and Yoyotte 1979, pp. 97-98.
22. Examples: Habachi 1958, XVIIIb; Dabrowska-Smektala 1963, fig. 15a, p. 29-45; Luxor 1979, p. 166-167, pl. XIV; Altenmüller 1982, Taf. 2-3.
23. Cf. Habachi 1958, pl. XVIIIb; Dabrowska-Smektala 1963, fig. 15a; Adams 1966, fig. 1.
24. Petrie 1891, p. 27.
25. Bolton 7.92.2; The presence of a mud layer was observed by the writer during a recent examination of this piece. For the inscription on the cartonnage, see Petrie 1890, pl. XXV, 7 (text).
26. Petrie 1891, pp. 26, 27-28.
27. Examples from el-Lahun: Petrie 1891, pp. 27-28; Maspero 1901, p. 191, pl. I. Specimen from el-Hiba: Botti 1958, pp. 106-107, pl. XXIX, 2. Another specimen, probably from Middle Egypt: Baqués 1971-2, pp. 242-249, pp. 242-249, fig. 8-10; Estapé 1973, pl. VII, VIII.
28. Naville 1894, p. 13, pl. VII, VIII.
29. Taylor 1984, p. 31.
30. Taylor forthcoming.
31. Examples: Louvre E 5534, Berlin 20135. For the latter, see Anthes 1943, p. 40.
32. Gauthier 1913, pp. 25, 73, 137, pl. I, II, IV, V, IX, X; Kueny and Yoyotte 1979, pp. 100-104.

Literature: Quibell 1898, p. 10; Budge 1925, pp. 221-222; Bonnet 1952, pp. 479, 480; Habachi

1958, p. 339; Adams 1966, pp. 55-66; Zauzich 1980, col. 353; Niwinski 1983, col. 446-448; Taylor 1985.

120
Coffin of Penu

Provenance unknown, but almost certainly from Thebes
Third Intermediate Period, late Dynasty 22, about 800-720 B.C.
Painted wood
Length 1.97 m.
Hay Collection, Gift of C. Granville Way, 1872 (72.4839)

According to the inscriptions on this coffin, Penu bore the priestly titles of Beloved of the God, ḥpt wdȝt of Mut, and "Opener of the Doors of Heaven" in Karnak – the latter indicating that it was his duty to open the doors of the shrine containing the god's image in the temple.[1] The texts also provide the names of Penu's father Merekhonsu, his grandfather Harsiese (both of whom were Prophets of Amen-Re), and his mother Na-ir-Bastet.

One wooden coffin and the cartonnage mummy case of Penu have come down to us, but similar ensembles that have survived complete suggest there would originally have been one or two additional coffins.[2] Penu's coffin has a finely carved face-mask of dark hard wood inserted into the lid, which is made from planks of a different timber. As is usual at this period, most of the ornamentation is painted directly on the surface of the wood. The brightly colored collar comprises a bead necklace at the throat and a series of rows of petals and flowers covering the upper breast. This bipartite collar is common on coffins of the ninth and eighth centuries B.C.[3] and is also attested in the seventh century (cat. 125).

The central inscription on the lid consists of the "offering formula" – a standard text in which the gods are petitioned to provide the deceased with necessities for the afterlife. In this example the benefits requested are food-offerings, incense, clothing, libations, oxen, and fowl. Five pairs of cross-bands divide the lid into eight compartments. In each of the first six Penu appears before a different deity: Atum, Re-Horakhty, Osiris Lord of Eternity, Osiris-Sokar, Isis, and Nephthys. In each pair of scenes Penu wears a different costume and is shown in a different attitude; in the second pair he raises his hands in adoration, and in the third pair his arms hang at his sides. The lowest compartments contain falcons representing Horus, with protective wedjat eyes between their outstretched wings. The short text bands above the scenes contain offering formulae and references to the protective function of the deities depicted.

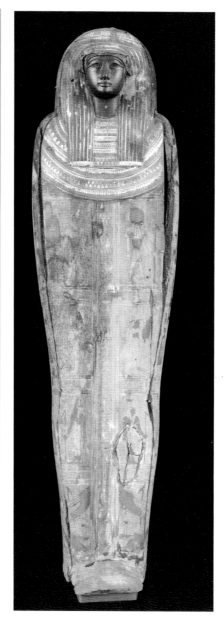

120, outer coffin

The case of the coffin is simply decorated. Around the lip runs a khekher frieze and a block border, while a simple palace-facade motif is painted around the base. Between these borders is a horizontal inscription, again consisting of an invocation to the gods on Penu's behalf.

Parallels to this coffin include specimens in Leiden[4] and Liège;[5] the latter contained a cartonnage case.[6] These can be dated approximately to the eighth century B.C.[7] Penu's coffin also displays affinities with the middle coffin of Ankh-pakhered II from the Ramesseum cemetery,[8] a piece that probably dates to about 725 B.C.[9] A few features of Ankh-pakhered's burial, however, suggest a slightly later date than that of Penu; Ankh-pakhered's mask shows the ears, which do not appear on Penu's coffin,[10] while the design of Ankh-pakhered's

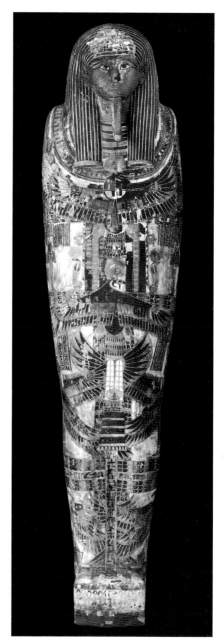

120, mummy case

inner coffin is more advanced than that of Penu's cartonnage case. An early or middle eighth century B.C. date for Penu's death and burial is therefore likely.

JHT

Mummy case of Penu

Provenance unknown, but almost certainly from Thebes
Late Dynasty 22, about 800-720 B.C.
Cartonnage
Length 180 cm.
Hay Collection, Gift of C. Granville Way, 1872 (72.4832)

Penu wears a tripartite wig without a fillet, simply striped in blue and white. The face, now damaged, was painted red, and a false beard of plastered and painted wood was attached to the chin by a tenon. The beard is of the plaited and curled type worn by the gods, and is a symbol of the new divine status that the deceased has acquired through his identification with Osiris. As on his wooden coffin, Penu wears a bead necklace and a broad garland collar composed of flowers and petals.

The design of this cartonnage is essentially the same as that of Tabes's (cat. 121), with two falcons spreading their wings across the upper body and four large compartments below, containing figures of protective deities. The two large falcons on the breast represent the solar Horus, whose epithets "The Behdetite, the Great God, Lord of Heaven, Variegated of Plumage" are inscribed in short bands at each side. Between them the Four Sons of Horus stand facing a pair of uraeus serpents. Below are figures of Isis and Nephthys, with green flesh and red dresses, extending their winged arms to protect the deceased's thighs, and accompanied by short texts in which Penu's name and titles appear. The inscriptions above the lowest compartments mention Isis and Nephthys again, indicating that the falcons at the bottom represent the same two goddesses in an alternative form.

In the center of the case, over the legs, is painted the "Abydos fetish," a religious emblem that was associated with the cult of Osiris.[11] It consists of a beehive-shaped dome surmounted by a solar disk and plumes, the whole being mounted on a pole that here serves to accommodate the offering formula. In its original form the fetish appears to have been the symbol of the nome of Abydos, and had no connection with Osiris. By the New Kingdom, however, it had come to be regarded as a "reliquary" that contained the head of the murdered god.[12] It was a very popular motif in the decoration of cartonnages in the Libyan Period (Dynasties 22 and 23) – particularly in the "Two Falcons" design, occurring on all but the earliest specimens of this layout (cat. 121).

On the wooden footboard is the galloping Apis bull with its distinctive black and white markings. This motif may have originated in the Memphite region since it does not appear in Theban funerary iconography before Dynasty 22. On many later examples the bull is shown carrying the mummy of the deceased on its back.[13] It is usually represented traveling from west to east (probably symbolizing the journey from death to a new life),[14] though occasionally it bears the mummy westward to the tomb.[15]

The designs of this case are painted in red, yellow, blue, green, and black on a white ground. A clear varnish that has since yellowed was applied over the whole surface, with the exception of a few small details such as the falcon's-heads and the plumes

of the Abydos fetish, which stand out clearly in consequence. The layout of this specimen is in several ways more advanced then that of Tabes, suggesting that it is of later date. A stylized feather motif is now used prominently for the borders, and the section between the two large falcons is arranged in a more complex manner; the triple bands of blue and red in the center of the breast, although common on cases with this design, are not found on the earliest Theban cartonnages.[16] The figures of the Sons of Horus, unlike those on Tabes's case, are depicted with arms viewed from the front – a style of representation that occurs on a "hybrid" cartonnage-coffin dating to the late Third Intermediate Period[17] and a coffin of the early seventh century B.C. in the British Museum.[18] These factors point to a date after about 800 B.C. for the burial of Penu, and this is supported by such other stylistic features as the fully frontal representation of the Abydos fetish, a distinctly unconventional form.[19]

JHT

The Mummy of Penu

X-rays and CT scans reveal that Penu was a young man at death. His body is in a poor state of preservation, and the entire thorax, abdomen, and pelvis are a jumble of bony fragments. The linen wrappings and cartonnage coffin, however, are intact, indicating that the damage occurred before final wrapping. The orbits of the eyes were filled, perhaps with wax, and artificial eyes inserted. The mummy was also provided with a metallic amulet that X-rays show to be clenched between the teeth. This amulet, which appears to be in the shape of a mouth, was probably meant to aid the deceased in regaining the power of speech in the afterlife.

MM

1. Erman and Grapow 1926, p. 164, 16; Černý 1948, p. 120.
2. New York, M.M.A. 86.1.31-4: Porter and Moss 1964, p. 676; Leiden M. 55-57: Boeser 1920, p. 5-6, Taf. XIV-XV.
3. Boeser 1920, Taf. XIII-XV; Dawson and Gray 1968, pl. Va, b, VIa, VIId.
4. M. 53: Leemans 1840, pp. 181-182.
5. Eg. 82 B: Malaise 1971, pp. 36-39, fig. 9-11.
6. Eg. 81: Malaise 1971, p. 41-42, fig. 12; de Meulenaere 1980, pp. 76-77, 79.
7. Taylor 1985 II, pp. 241-242, 257-258.
8. Berlin 20134: Anthes 1943, pp. 38-40, Taf. 7-11.
9. Taylor 1985 I, pp. 462-463; II, p. 272.
10. For the significance of this feature as a dating criterion, see Taylor 1984, p. 52.
11. Winlock 1921, p. 15-26; Otto 1975, col. 47-48.
12. Otto 1975, col. 48.
13. Kueny and Yoyotte 1979, p. 103; Andrews 1984, p. 46-47 fig. 52.
14. Quaegebeur 1983, p. 29.
15. Hamilton-Paterson and Andrews 1978, p. 78.
16. Cf. Cambridge, Fitzwilliam E.64.1896 and Hamburg C.3834: Quibell 1898, pl. XVI; Altenmüller 1982, Taf. 2-3.
17. Paris, Louvre E 5534: Boreux 1932, p. 413; Pierret 1878, p. 130-131.
18. BM 27735: Raven 1981, pl. 3.
19. Taylor 1985, I, p. 52-53, fig. 8.

Literature: Schmidt 1919, figs. 908, 956-957, 959, 1031, 1040. 1055-1057, 1059-1060, 1064, 1065, 1069, 1071; Dabrowska-Smektala 1963, pp. 23-52.

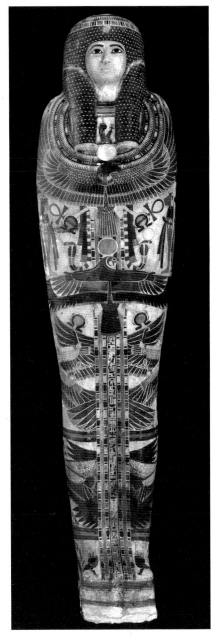

121

121
Mummy case of Tabes

Provenance unknown, but almost certainly from Thebes
Third Intermediate Period, early Dynasty 22, about 930-880 B.C.
Cartonnage
Length 167 cm.
Hay Collection, Gift of C. Granville Way, 1872 (72.4833)

This is a typical example of the one-piece cartonnage case of Dynasty 22. The central inscription reveals that the owner was the Songstress of Amen Tabes, wife of the Barber of the Estate of Amen Nes-Ptah (see cat. 170). As is the case with most coffins and cartonnages, the face-mask (here painted yellow) is a stereotype, and is in no sense a portrait of the deceased. The strands of hair composing the wig are individually delineated, each lock tipped with yellow. On the upper breast is a stylized collar composed of three rows of petals and two bands of geometrical design. Below the necklace at the throat is a small squatting image of the goddess Maat, the personification of the ideal state of cosmic order, according to ancient Egyptian beliefs. The concept of Maat also embraced the ideas of "truth" and "justice," and in the funerary iconography of the New Kingdom the goddess is usually represented in attendance when the heart of the deceased is weighed before Osiris in the Balance of Judgment. Having passed this test, the deceased is adorned by Maat with feathers (the emblem of the goddess) before passing on to eternal life. In the depiction of this episode in the papyrus of Anhai[1] an image of Maat very similar to this one is suspended around the neck of the deceased.[2] The frequent painting of this device on coffins and cartonnages of the Libyan Period (Dynasties 22 and 23)[3] probably expresses the owner's wish to pass safely through the ordeal of judgment.

The frontal decoration follows a pattern very common on the cartonnages of this period. This depiction of deities in the form of birds, or with the attributes of birds, was a prominent feature of funerary iconography in the Third Intermediate Period. Two falcons spread their wings over Tabes's body, shielding her from possible evil influences. The upper bird has the head of a ram, surmounted by a sun disk. The two falcons are not identified, but from inscriptions on similar examples it is known that they are both representations of "The Behdetite," i.e. the solar Horus (cf. cat. 120). The central inscription and lateral borders divide the rest of the surface into six compartments, the first four containing pairs of goddesses and falcons. Their wings dominate the design, forming a symmetrical, almost heraldic pattern. The symbols on the goddesses' heads identify them as Isis and Nephthys, while the falcons are named as Neith and Selkis; this quartet of powerful deities is associated with the protection of coffins and canopic containers. On parallels to Tabes's cartonnage, however, the two lower falcons are more frequently identified either as Isis and Nephthys – the Greater and Lesser Kites[4] – or as Horus of Behdet.[5] In the last two compartments, on the feet, are two of the numerous mummiform demons associated

with the gateways and halls of the Netherworld.

The emphasis of the decoration is on the magical protection of the deceased, not only in the allusions to deities whose protective role was well established in the funerary context, but also in the iconography; the sheathing of the body in wings was a motif popularized by the *rishi* coffins of Dynasty 17 and early Dynasty 18,[6] and remained (at least for royal coffins) an essential element of design as late as Dynasty 21.[7]

The inscriptions and the outlines of the designs were painted in black. The judicious use of red, green, blue, and yellow against the white background lend the piece its bold clarity. Indeed, this is one of the finest such cases, painted with great skill and care. One of several close parallels is securely dated to the reign of Osorkon I.[8] It is therefore a reasonable assumption that Tabes lived during the early years of Dynasty 22, and her cartonnage is among the earliest known examples of this type of case from Thebes.

JHT

The Mummy of Tabes

Tabes was a woman of small stature (her eyes are at the level of the chin of her cartonnage coffin). The elaborate methods of mummification practiced at the time are evident in her X-rays and scans. Her mummy is quite well preserved, and even such delicate structures as the eyes, optic nerve, and the heart could be seen. The brain was removed. Packing material was seen in the neck and throat, as well as the abdominal cavity, along with organ packages, which were not placed in canopic jars at this period (see cat. 117). Tabes was provided with several protective amulets, including a group of small ones of faience or stone, and a heart scarab (see cat. 176) set above a thin metallic winged figure. Two embalming incisions, one in the stomach region and one in the left pelvis, were covered with metallic plates (see cat. 173), but the latter was placed so carelessly that the incision is gaping open, and the amulet lies over the wrist. A package of homogeneous material, possibly sand, was placed between the legs.

No major illnesses could be identified, though Tabes appears to have suffered from dental disease. Unlike her husband, Nes-Ptah (see cat. 170), whose mummy displays degenerative changes consistent with advanced age, Tabes shows none of these changes, which leads us to conclude that she was a relatively young woman at death.

MM

1. London BM 10472.
2. Seeber 1976, p. 100, fig. 34.
3. Quibell 1898, pl. XVI; Boeser 1920, Taf. XV; Kueny and Yoyotte 1979, p. 98.
4. Quibell 1898, pl. XVI; Boeser 1920, Taf. XIII.

5. Luxor 1979, p. 167; cf. Oxford, Ashmolean 1960.1288 (unpublished).
6. Hayes 1959, pp. 29-32, 221, figs. 13-14, 131; Stadelmann-Sourouzian 1984, col. 267-269.
7. Montet 1951, p. 130-132, pl. 100-103.
8. Hamburg C.3834: Altenmüller 1982, pp. 57-58, Taf. 2-3.

Literature: Schmidt 1919, figs. 908, 956-957, 959, 1031, 1040, 1055-1057, 1059-1060, 1064, 1065, 1069, 1071; Dabrowska-Smektala 1963, pp. 23-52.

122
Mummy case of Ankh-pef-hor

Provenance unknown, but almost certainly from Thebes
Third Intermediate Period, early Dynasty 22, about 925-875 B.C.
Cartonnage
Length 179 cm.
Hay Collection, Gift of C. Granville Way, 1872 (72.4837)

During Dynasty 21 the gilding of the hands and face of the coffin was a luxury apparently reserved for members of the ruling family of the High Priests of Amen at Thebes.[1] With the introduction of new coffin styles in early Dynasty 22, gilded faces began to occur fairly frequently, even on cartonnages of those of modest rank. The owner of this case, Ankh-pef-hor, for example, seems not to have been especially important; his only recorded title is the humble "Offerer of Southern Heliopolis" (i.e., Thebes). Nevertheless, the face of his cartonnage was covered with thin gold leaf and the eyes and eyebrows were rendered more realistic by the use of inlays.

The case is decorated in a most unusual style; the scenes stand out against a dark blue background that was clearly painted after the figures had been outlined on the white gessoed surface. Apart from a few details in red, blue, and green, the figures are unpainted. Details and inscriptions were added in ink and then the front was varnished, giving most of the figures a yellowish coloring – perhaps to imitate the gilding employed on such royal cartonnages as that of Shoshenk II, which seems to have been executed chiefly in gold foil on a blue ground.[2]

A few similarly decorated cartonnages are known;[3] one, from Thebes, can be dated by external evidence to early Dynasty 22.[4] Stylistic criteria confirm this dating; the crossed hands with the curious checkered pattern, the proportions and iconography of the figures, and the style of dress worn by the deceased in the scenes are all characteristic of early Dynasty 22.[5]

The technique of adding the background color only after the scenes had been drawn made it difficult to avoid overpainting the outlines of some of the smaller and more in-

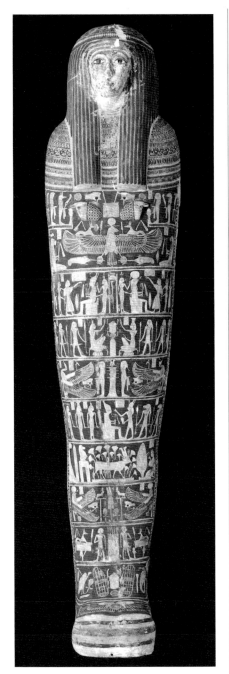

122

Nekhbet and Wadjet. Protective *wedjat* eyes, *shen* symbols, and figures of the Sons of Horus appear at each side. The area below the hands is dominated by the ram-headed falcon of Horus the Behdetite, accompanied by jackals and lion-headed mummiform deities. The eight registers below contain various scenes and symbols connected with Osirian and solar mythology. In the first register the deceased appears twice, led before the creator-god Atum on the left and before Re-Horakhty on the right. These two deities are addressed in the long inscriptions running down the sides of the cartonnage. Solar allusions continue in the second register, where Isis and Nephthys adore the rising sun in the form of a scarab beetle, and in the eighth register, which shows another scarab, here flanked by the vulture Nekhbet and the cobra Wadjet. A winged solar disk is also painted on the feet. In the fourth register, Osiris is accompanied by Isis, Nephthys, and Neith, and attended by Horus. The Osirian emblems of the *djed* pillar and the Abydos fetish (cat. 120) occupy central positions in the third and sixth registers. The fifth register contains two scenes popular in the funerary iconography of Dynasty 21, but more rarely encountered in Dynasty 22. At the left is the mountainous western slope of the Theban necropolis with an obelisk and a pylon (probably representing the facade of a tomb) before it. Emerging from the mountains, amid papyrus marshes, is a cow representing the goddess Hathor, protectress of the necropolis.[8] To the right a cow-headed goddess, standing in the branches of the sycamore trees, pours out life-giving water to the kneeling figure of Ankh-pef-hor. In Dynasty 21 parallels to this scene, the goddess is usually identified as Nut;[9] in this instance the cow's head suggests that the figure has been confused with Hathor.

JHT

The Mummy of Ankh-pef-hor

The mummy is that of a well-developed young male in a good state of preservation. The teeth are in excellent condition. The eyes are in place, and resin was poured into the orbits. Filling material was identified in the mouth, and at the base of the neck. In the center of the wrappings, just under a denser layer of linen, amulets that appear to be of wax were identified, and probably represent the Four Sons of Horus (see cat. 172).

The four chambers of the heart were particularly well seen in this mummy, and the phallus and large well-developed muscles of the thighs were well preserved. No pathological diagnoses were identifiable.

MM

1. Niwinski 1979, pp. 54-56; Niwinski 1983, col. 442.
2. Cairo JE 72196. See Iskander 1940, pp. 584, 586.
3. London BM 29577: Dawson and Gray 1968,
   p. 12, pl. VIc; Andrews 1984, p. 47, fig. 53-54; Hamburg, Mus. für Völkerunde C.4057 b: Altenmüller 1982, Taf. 2; Alexandria, number unknown: Breccia 1922, p. 166-167, fig. 74.
4. Cambridge, Fitzwilliam E.8.1896: Quibell 1898, pp. 12, 20, pl. XXVIII, XXXA. For the dating, see Kitchen 1986, pp. 566 §489, 575 §510.
5. Taylor 1985, I, pp. 317-318.
6. See above, note 4.
7. E.G. coffin of Harkhebi, Bodrhyddan Hall, Wales (unpublished).
8. Englund 1974, pp. 49-50, fig. 6.
9. Bruyère 1930a, pp. 197-198.

123
Coffin of Namenkhamen

From Thebes, Deir el-Bahri
Third Intermediate Period, Dynasty 25,
about 680 B.C.
Wood
Length 184.5 cm., max. width 50 cm., max. height 29 cm.
Gift of Egypt Exploration Fund, 1894 (94.321)

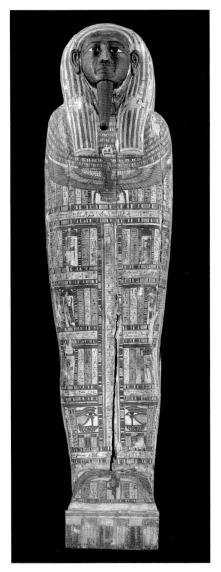

123

tricate figures (as clearly happened in many places), and it was perhaps partly for this reason that this style was soon abandoned in favor of painting the designs on a white background (cats. 121 and 170).

Ankh-pef-hor wears a striped wig with long lappets. His collar may originally have extended only as far as the row of dark blue "drop" beads (as on the specimen in Cambridge).[6] The five lower rows are painted in a different manner than the others and, unlike them, are not varnished. A similar enlargement of the collar is occasionally found on coffins of this period.[7]

Between the hands is painted a pectoral on which the names of Osiris and Isis (in cartouches) are flanked by the goddesses

This wooden anthropoid coffin is covered with a thin layer of plaster to which the decoration and inscriptions were applied. The deceased is depicted wearing a full blue and yellow striped wig with a beaded or flowered circlet around the top. A false beard attaches to the chin with a black line, indicating the way it would have been attached to the head. A broad collar covers the shoulders and upper chest, and a winged figure of the goddess Nut is painted on the breast. A band of text across the body is bordered above and below by multicolored rectangles. Under this a vertical column of text runs the length of the coffin, set off by the same multi-colored borders. Three rows of panels on either side of this text contain more texts and illustrations of Egyptian gods, notably the Four Sons of Horus. The two panels in the fourth and lowest row contain depictions of *wedjat* eyes. The goddess Isis is depicted with outstretched wings at the foot of the coffin. On the underside of the foot of the coffin the Apis bull is shown carrying off the deceased, and Nephthys is depicted on the top of the head in an attitude of mourning. Texts painted in black on alternate white and yellow backgrounds cover the sides and back. At the head of the inside of the coffin base a further text is painted.

The texts identify the owner of the coffin as the prophet of Montu Namenkhamen, son of the prophet of Amen Ankhpakhered, grandson of the vizier Ankh-Osorkon, and great-grandson of Prince Djed-Ptah-ef-ankh, who was himself himself a son of a King Osorkon and brother of a King Takelot.[1] The inscriptions clearly identify Namenkhamen as a scion of either Dynasty 22 or Dynasty 23, but the number of kings named Osorkon, three of whom had sons and successors named Takelot, makes the exact identification problematic. A comparison of the style of this coffin with similar ones in Cairo and London that date to the end of Dynasty 25[2] would fix the career of Namenkhamen to that time. Thus his ancestor would be King Osorkon III, c. 797-767 B.C. A statue in Boston of the prophet of Montu Djed-Ptah-ef-ankh, son of Ankhpakhered[3] could well belong to a brother of Namenkhamen. It is interesting to note that, when found, Namenkhamen's coffin stored extra embalming materials, and there is no indication that it was ever used for his burial.[4]

MLB

1. Bierbrier 1984, pp. 82-84.
2. Cairo 41054 and British Museum 6668.
3. MFA 1971.21 in Simpson 1977, p. 46 no. 45.
4. Naville 1893-1894, p. 7.

Bibliography: Porter and Moss 1964, pp. 649-650; Naville 1896, p. 6; Naville 1893-1894, p. 7; Bierbrier 1984, pp. 82-84.

Late Period

124

124
Ptah-Sokar-Osiris figure

Provenance unknown
Late Period
Wood with gesso and gold leaf
Height 78 cm.
Lent by Kathryn Maxson-Silberstein

The mummiform appearance and the crown of ostrich feathers, ram's horns, and solar disk are fixed attributes of this syncretistic deity. The heavy tripartite wig and the long curved beard are both emblems of divinity. Most noteworthy in this respect is the figurine's finish with gold leaf over a coating of white gesso. Gold is not just a precious material, it is a divine substance: according to the ancient Egyptians, the flesh of the gods was made of gold, and their bones of silver. Because gold does not corrode, it became a symbol of eternity and immortality. Its association with the sun and its revivifying rays also contributed to this symbolism. Thus, gold is a most fitting material for figurines of divinities, particularly for such patrons of resurrection as Ptah-Sokar-Osiris.

Though numerous Ptah-Sokar-Osiris figures have gold faces, completely gilt specimens are rather rare. A number of these were found, however, in the necropolis of the provincial town of El-Hiba[1] and roughly at-

tributed to the Saite period. Another specimen that bears the name Djedhor,[2] pointing
to a date in the Dynasty 30 or later, differs
from the El-Hiba finds in its slim proportions
and detailed decoration. The statuette that
concerns us here shares the squat outline
and the recessed eye-sockets and brows,
once inlaid, of the El-Hiba pieces.[3] The
rather flat triangular face and heavy wig suggest a date in the eighth to the sixth centuries. It seems to be altogether solid; the
wooden base (now lost) may have contained a cavity to hold the corn-mummy.

MJR

1. Botti 1958, nos. 196, 205-206, 209.
2. Florence 106 (unpublished); cf. Melbourne
   2863 (Hope 1983, 47-53, figs. 2-5): figurine
   with gold front and black back, Akhmim third
   century B.C., inscribed for Hor, son of Djedhor.
3. Botti 1958, no. 209.

Bibliography: Botti 1958; Hope 1983, 47-53.

Literature: Raven 1978-1979, pp. 251-296; Raven
1982, pp. 7-38.

125
Tomb group of Nes-mut-aat-neru

From Deir el-Bahri, temple of Hatshepsut
Third Intermediate Period, mid Dynasty 25,
about 700-675 B.C.
Gift of Egypt Exploration Fund, 1895

a. Outer coffin
   Wood
   Length 204 cm. (95.1407d)
b. Second coffin
   Wood and Plaster
   Length 186 cm. (95.1407c)
c. Inner coffin
   Plastered linen over wood
   Length 169 cm. (95.1407b)
d. Mummy
   Length 151 cm. (95.1407a)
e. Shawabti boxes
   Wood
   Height 26 cm. (95.1408, 9)

The lady Nes-mut-aat-neru was the wife of
Djedes-ief-ankh, a priest of the Theban god
Montu. By her husband's relationship to
members of the influential Besenmut family, her death can be dated fairly accurately
to the middle of Dynasty 25, about 700-675
B.C.[1] At this period many of the priests and
officials of Thebes were buried in subterranean vaults beneath the disused mortuary
temple of Queen Hatshepsut at Deir el-
Bahri.[2] Here, in 1894-95, Edouard Naville
discovered one such vault under the Hathor
chapel, which had escaped the attention of
robbers.[3] Inside, filling the narrow space almost completely, were the coffins and
funerary equipment of Nes-mut-aat-neru,
her son Djed-Djehuty-iuef-ankh,[4] and a lady
Tabek-en-khons[5] – possibly the latter's wife.[6]

The objects belonging to Nes-mut-aat-neru
constitute a typical tomb group of a member of the Theban aristocracy of this period.

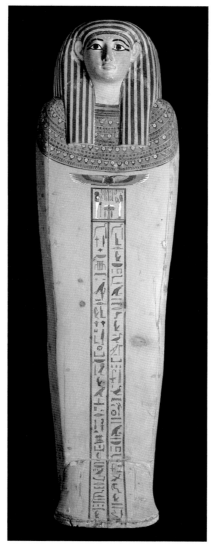

125b, lid

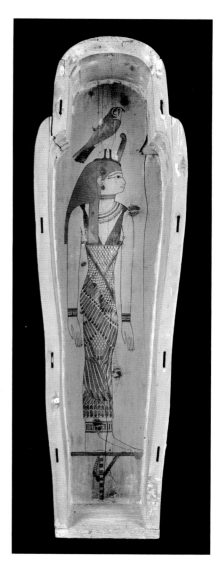

125b, interior of base

125a

125c, front

125c, back

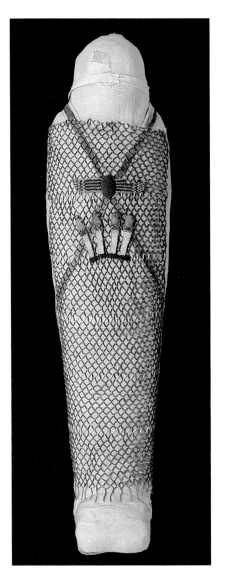

125d

The mummy was enclosed in three coffins. The outermost is rectangular, with a vaulted lid and four corner-posts. It is clearly intended as a substitute for a stone sarcophagus (not used in Theban private burials in the Third Intermediate Period) and its shape imitates that of the tomb of Osiris.[7] The undecorated sides are sycamore; the corner posts and frame an unidentified reddish wood. Naville believed that the outer coffin was taken into the tomb in pieces and assembled inside, as the entrance was too small to admit it when complete.[8] Inscribed on the posts are four standard offering formulae, addressed to Osiris, Ptah-Sokar, Re-Horakhty and Atum. Additional formulae are inscribed along the frame. The austere appearance of this coffin, with its plain panels, is unusual; the majority of specimens of this type were covered with brightly painted religious scenes and texts.[9] A black-painted wooden statuette of a jackal was placed on top of the lid at the foot end;[10] comparable figures adorned the outer coffins of Djed-Djehuty-iuef-ankh and Tabek-en-khons. Pairs of jackals were often painted on the

feet of cartonnages and anthropoid coffins in the Third Intermediate Period. These are often identified as Wepwawet,[11] but on some specimens – including Nes-mut-aat-neru's inner coffin – the name of Anubis occurs. The wooden jackal statuettes might therefore represent either of those two deities.

The second coffin is a massive anthropoid case, simply decorated but of fine workmanship. The face, wig, and collar are brightly painted on a layer of plaster. Otherwise, the lid is decorated only with a winged sun disk, a small vignette, and two columns of inscription painted directly on the smoothed surface of the wood. The base is even more sparsely adorned, with a simple offering formula painted around the exterior, and a fine profile figure of the "Goddess of the West" (a form of Hathor[12]) on the floor.

Within this case lay a third wooden coffin in the form of a mummified body standing on a pedestal and supported behind by a dorsal pillar. Its brightly colored decoration is painted on a layer of plastered linen. This type of coffin replaced the cartonnage

mummy cases of the ninth and eighth centuries B.C. Nes-mut-aat-neru's example belongs to the transitional period and in its form and decoration the influence of the old-fashioned cartonnages is still apparent. The case consists of two halves, yet when the mummy had been placed inside, the join along the edge was plastered over so that the coffin had the appearance of a one-piece cartonnage case.[13] The ram-headed falcon on the breast is clearly a legacy of the design repertoire of cartonnage (cats. 120 and 121) and was shortly superseded by a winged figure of Nut. The triple colored bands and uraeus serpents below the ram-bird are also old-fashioned elements, but the scenes of the deceased adoring Osiris at each side are relatively new. The central Abydos fetish is also a long-established motif, though the rest of the decoration, with deities in small compartments accompanied by columns of inscription, looks forward to the designs popular on seventh-century coffins. A large *djed* pillar is painted on the back of the coffin, providing symbolic support for the mummy and serving to display an inscription that records Nes-mut-aat-neru's ancestry. Among the figures and texts at the sides are two depictions of the dead lady's *ba* as a human-headed bird.

Beneath the feet of the inner coffin is an unusual depiction of the Iunmutef priest leaping over mountains, and grasping the emblems associated with certain ritual races. The galloping Apis bull (Hp) is normally pictured here (cat. 120) and it is possible that the inscription flanking the priestly figure, ''I come, I hasten (hp) to Osiris, to Busiris'' contains a punning allusion to this.[14]

The mummy was wrapped in a reddish shroud over which was placed a network of blue faience beads, extending from the shoulders to the ankles. Attached to this are a winged scarab and figures of the Sons of Horus, all composed of beads. Nes-mut-aat-neru's bead net is one of the earliest datable examples of a type of covering that was to become very popular in the centuries which followed.[15]

At this period, funerary equipment, even for wealthy individuals, was limited to the most essential items. In Nes-mut-aat-neru's case no stela or canopic jars were provided, but a collection of small mud *shawabti* figures was found, stored in two wooden boxes. The *shawabti*s, which are uninscribed, are very crudely fashioned – a type not uncommon during the later Third Intermediate Period at Thebes.[16] The boxes, with rounded ends, have a horizontal inscription around all four sides and a boat painted on the flat lid. The decoration is applied directly to the wood, as on the second coffin. In shape and

ornamentation these are typical Dynasty 25 *shawabti* boxes,[17] although a white-painted ground is more usual.[18]

JHT

The Mummy of Nes-mut-aat-neru

Nes-mut-aat-neru was a small, elderly woman who suffered from extensive dental disease, including a molar abscess extending into the jaw. Her advanced age is indicated by arthritic changes in the neck and calcifications of the cartilage of the trachea. She had suffered a broken clavicle, which had not been set, before her death. Her heart has been very well preserved, and the aorta, which is the main artery in the chest and abdomen, can be seen branching and extending into the legs. The trachea could also be identified in the CT-scans. The orbits of the eyes had been filled with what appears to be wax, and artificial eyes placed over it. The mouth, thoraco-abdominal cavity, and pelvis were filled with a loose packing material mixed with small rocks and pebbles. The four organ packages were not placed in the body cavity, but were laid on top of the thighs. The outer layers of linen appear much more dense than the inner layers, suggesting a looser wrapping or looser weave to the linen closest to the body, with finer linen employed for the outer layers.

MM

1. Taylor 1984, p. 29.
2. Vassalli 1867, pp. 143-145; Mariette 1877, p. 4-6. Coffins from these burials are published in Gauthier 1913, and Moret 1913, pp. 1-253, 270-273, 284-7, 290-312, pl. I-XXVII, XXXI-XXXII, XXXVI.
3. Naville 1895, pp. 34-35 and plan.

4. Oxford, Ashmolean 1895.153-156.
5. New York, M.M.A. 96.4.1-4.
6. Taylor 1984, p. 466.
7. Bonnet 1952, p. 666-667.
8. Naville 1894-1895, p. 35.
9. Examples: Moret 1913, pl. VI, XIII, XIV, XVIII, XIX, XXI-XXIV.
10. Naville 1894-95, p. 35.
11. Berlin 48, London BM 6684, Dublin 1881.2228 (unpublished).
12. Hornung 1983a, p. 88.
13. The true nature of this coffin has only recently come to light, and in all previous publications the piece is described as a cartonnage: Raven 1981, p. 14, pl. 5.A; Taylor 1984, p. 31.
14. Capart 1929, p. 2.
15. Aston 1987, pp. 519-523, fig. 6.
16. Aston 1987, pp. 582, 588, 589.
17. Aston 1987, pp. 594-595, 599, fig. 32.
18. Winlock 1924a, p. 30. fig. 32-34.

Bibliography: Naville 1894-1895, pp. 34-35 and plan; Naville 1898, p. 10; Naville 1900, p. 1; Capart 1929, p. 2, pl. I,2; Smith 1942, p. 1942, p. 144; Smith 1952, p. 144; Smith 1960, p. 162; Vittmann 1978, pp. 55 (q), 110 (61), Taf. 11-12; Raven 1981, pp. 14, 17, pl. 5.A, 6.B; Taylor 1984, pp. 29, 31-32.

126
Model coffin

From Abydos tomb G 57
Saite Period, probably Dynasty 26
Wood
Height 20.1 cm., width 11.4 cm., length 20.3 cm.
Gift of Egypt Exploration Fund, 1902 (02.31)

During the Ptolemaic Period, small model coffins representing the tomb of Osiris were sometimes attached to the bases of mummiform statues of that god.[1] The statues themselves frequently contained compartments that held funerary papyri, while the coffins often covered another recess in the base of the statue, which held mummified body parts, especially the penis, intestines, or heart.[2] In some cases the compartment was covered by a small Sokar falcon facing the figure of Osiris, rather than a small coffin.

The example shown here is larger than the model coffins used to cover such compartments, but it is very similar in form. Although it was not attached to an Osiride statue, it was one of four model coffins associated with four Osiride figures in a family tomb at Abydos excavated by Petrie in 1902.[3] It belonged to Iret-Horu, who bore the titles *hsk-k₃* and *imy-is*, both priestly titles in the cult of Osiris at Abydos. From the inscriptions on the coffins and other objects in the tomb, it is possible to reconstruct much of the family tree of this man, who was buried with his wife Tay-nakht (''Song-stress before the West,'' presumably a priestess in the cult of Osiris), his son Hor-maa-kheru, and his sister-in-law Meret-tefnut. Both his parents and those of his

125e

wife are known; and both fathers held the same two priestly titles held by Iret-Horu.

The tomb is beneath one of Dynasty 30 date, and Petrie suggests a Dynasty 26 date. The form of the coffin also accords well with that of full-sized coffins of Dynasty 26 (see cat. 125). Though the piece is earlier than the coffins that were used to cover receptacles attached to statuettes of Osiris, it may have served the same purpose, especially as a large quantity of wood has been cut out, albeit irregularly, from its base.

This example is more carefully made than most model coffins, and retains much of its original bright coloring. Both faces of its curved lid depict divine boats: on one side the deceased kneels in a papyrus skiff before a table of offerings and the divinities Osiris and Isis; on the other is the solar

126

Fig. 81

barque (fig. 81). A child-form of the sun god Re is seated on the prow, and seated in the barque are a hawk-headed form of Re, the god Atum in a double crown, and a lion-headed goddess – probably Tefnut. The preserved end of the lid is painted with concentric semicircles, a design often shown on the top of shrines. Beneath the semicircles, on the side of the coffin begins the inscription, which continues on all four sides: "Words spoken by (a god, possibly Osiris from the traces)(to) the *hsk-k3 imy-is* Iret-Horu, true of voice (deceased) born to the Mistress of the House, Nes-Hor, true of voice: May your head, your heart,[4] and your life be within it."

The recumbent jackal was on the coffin at the time of its discovery, according to Petrie's report; and a single falcon (though not one of those now attached to the corner-posts) is shown in the excavation photographs.[5] The four falcons currently perched on the cornerposts of the coffin are a common feature of Dynasty 26 coffins, and were apparently present on many of the model coffins found in tomb G 57. It seems likely that the better-preserved falcons of a less-well-preserved model from the same tomb were combined with the coffin of Iret-Horu before it was donated to the Museum of Fine Arts.

AMR

1. Budge 1925, pl. 25 (upper left) = (B.M. No. 18162); van Wijngaarden 1932, pl. IX, 12; also discussed in Raven 1978-79, pl. 41, no. 1.
2. Raven 1978-1979, pp. 251-296.
3. Petrie 1902, pp. 34-37 and pl. 72-76, 80.
4. Weigall 1902, p. 48, has suggested that *nw* is here a mistaken writing of the word *ib*.
5. Petrie 1902, pl. 74, 1 and 2.

127
Tomb group of the General Kheper-Re

From Giza tomb G 7757 A
Saite Period, Dynasty 26, reign of Amasis (570-526 B.C.)
Harvard University-Museum of Fine Arts Expedition (30.834, 31.812-841)

The burial of the "Military Officer" Kheper-Re[1] was excavated by George A. Reisner and the Harvard University-Museum of Fine Arts Expedition in November of 1929 as he cleared the Giza tomb G 7757 A. Kheper-Re's tomb was located directly east of the great pyramid of Khufu, on the outskirts of the mastaba field.[2] The Old Kingdom royal burial grounds in Giza and Sakkara were still considered highly desirable burial sites for the Memphite officials of this period.

The tombs of Dynasty 26 (685-525 B.C.) were designed to be unobtrusive, to deter the persistent grave robbers. The Lower Egyptian tomb of the day rarely had a super-structure,[3] consisting primarily of a deep, vertical, rock-cut shaft, up to thirty meters deep, at the bottom of which was a small burial chamber.[4] The shaft of Kheper-Re's tomb (fig. 82) was medium-sized at fourteen and one half meters deep and three meters in diameter.[5]

The tomb complex was prepared for Kheper-Re and many of his relatives. There are ten chambers in the tomb, five of which contained sarcophagi. Unfortunately, only the sarcophagus of Kheper-Re in Room X was inscribed. A wooden coffin and *shawabti*s belonging to Kheper-Re's mother, Ta-sherit-net-Isis, were found in Room III, marking her burial chamber.[6] In Room VI two stone sarcophagi were housed, along with *shawabti*s belonging to two men, Padi-Khonsu and Psamtek.[7] A number of other individuals are mentioned on *shawabti*s, but their relationship to Kheper-Re is difficult to ascertain.[8] None of these *shawabti*s appears to belong to Kheper-Re's brothers or sisters, as the parents named differ from Kheper-Re's, but one would expect to find his wife and children among them.

Kheper-Re's burial chamber, the most important in the complex, was the deepest, some 12.5 meters below the surface.[9] It was roughly rectangular, and fairly small.[10] The stone-cut room was lined with blocks that were cemented in place, a common feature of Saite tombs in Sakkara (fig. 83).[11] The large sarcophagus, which nearly filled this chamber, appears to have been hermetically sealed with wet plaster, since Reisner found fragments of plaster with impressions of the hieroglyphs from the coffin among the burial debris.[12] The limestone sarcophagus of the High Priest of Hermopolis, Ankh-Hor, was similarly sealed,[13] although it was not a common practice.

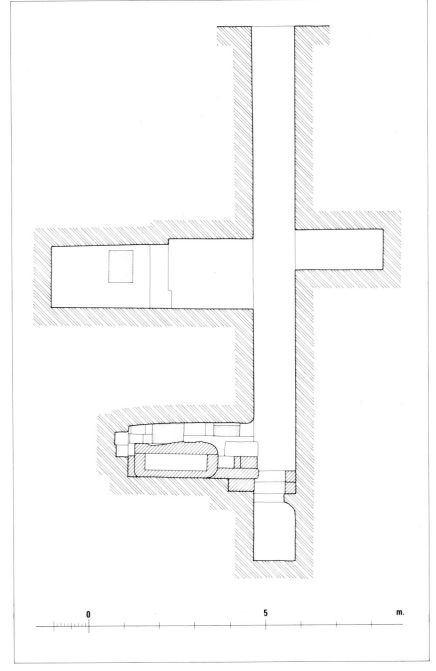

Fig. 82

When the body was interred and the sarcophagus sealed,[14] large blocking stones were cemented in place between the burial chamber and the large shaft, and associated chambers were filled with sand. In spite of such precautions, Kheper-Re's tomb, like others of this type, was robbed in antiquity. When Reisner entered the tomb he found the door blockings broken away.[15] The sarcophagus had also been entered by the thieves, but their damage was minimal. "They have entered [the sarcophagus] by breaking the underside of the head-end of the lid without otherwise damaging it."[16] Nevertheless, the sarcophagus was found in fragments; the main entry for it in the field records reports: "three baskets of

fragments of schist(?) anthropoid coffin."[17] Fortunately, this extraordinary piece could be restored.

When Reisner opened the sarcophagus, the meager remains of the body lay beneath a layer of sand and stones. "The bones are disturbed and form a shapeless mass held together with pitch in the bottom of the sarcophagus."[18] Several hard stone amulets were found in the debris in and around the coffin. The placement of various kinds of amulets on the body and among the wrappings of the mummy was one of the most characteristic funerary customs of the Saite Period (see cat. 129).[19]

Many pieces of thin sheets of gold cut into

amulet shapes were also among the remains in the coffin. This type of amulet is similar to those on the bead networks that were placed over the mummy[20] (see cat. 125d). Some of the notable shapes were: a dagger in a sheath, a quiver of arrows, and a kneeling figure of Isis.

Also among the funerary assemblage was a number of small vessels of faience, fragments of glass and alabaster pots, and many pieces of the canopic red-ware jars. No inscriptions are noted.[21] More than a hundred shawabtis were left by the robbers; no doubt they were of little or no value in antiquity.

Two of Kheper-Re's contemporaries at Sakkara, Tjai-en-nehebu and Heka-em-saf, who both served as "Chiefs of the Royal Ships" under Amasis, had more than 400 shawabtis in their tombs as well as hundreds of gold amulets, and gold toe and finger sheaths. Tjai-en-nehebu had in addition a gold mask, elaborate collars of gold and semi-precious stones, and a decorative faience bead network with gold amulets attached.[22] It is quite possible that Kheper-Re had some of these treasures in his burial chamber as well.

A total of 109[23] shawabtis were found in the tomb. Reisner found most of them among the debris of the robbers in the doorway of the burial chamber. The shawabtis in a number of Saite burials were placed in special wall niches,[24] and there is a suitable niche in the southwest wall of Kheper-Re's burial chamber.[25] The shawabtis may have originally been placed in this niche.

The shawabtis in the group vary in minor detail, size, and inscriptional style (fig. 84). All are the classic Saite style: mummiform with back pillar and small square base, molded from faience with a green-blue glaze. They wear the tripartite wig and long, narrow beard. These may be plain or marked with striations denoting locks of hair or plaiting in the beard. The length of the hair and beard varies from piece to piece; however, the beard is always equal to the length of the front lappets of the wig.[26]

The hands holding agricultural tools protrude from the cloak with arms crossed right over left.[27] The same implements are carried by all the shawabtis: the wide-bladed hoe used to mix the clay for bricks is held in the right hand and a pointed pick for opening the ground is in the left.[28] A small square seedbag suspended by either a twisted or plain cord held in the right hand is slung over the left shoulder.[29]

The execution of the facial features varies greatly from piece to piece. They may be minutely detailed, or crude and hastily rendered. However, the faint smile, a feature introduced in the Saite Period, is always visible.[30] The back pillar rises from the base to

Fig. 83

Fig. 84

the height of the bottom of the back tresses. According to Aubert, this element was inspired by the dorsal pillars and bases of statuary of the period.[31] The figure does not actually lean against the pillar, but instead appears to sink into it, so that the pillar conforms to the contours of the body.[32] It is not uncommon for Saite shawabtis of the same person to vary in size.[33]

The shawabtis of Kheper-Re vary in inscriptional styles as well. The inscriptions fall into two main categories, those with short vertical texts arranged in one to four columns down the front of the figure,[34] and those with nine to ten lines of a Saite version of the Book of the Dead.[35] In this text a new name for shawabti is introduced, "ushebti," which Schneider translates as

"one who will answer."[36] Those with this longer text occasionally have an additional vertical band of text down the back pillar.[37]

There is evidence that the Egyptians in the Saite Period intentionally produced one shawabti for every day of the year and one overseer for every ten workers; namely, 401 figures composed of 365 workers and 36 foremen (see "Funerary Figurines," p. 125). In the Saite tombs of Tjai-en-nehebu, Psamtek-mery-Ptah, and Heka-em-saf, there were exactly 401 shawabtis.[39] Aubert suggests that the type or lack of inscription might be used to differentiate the overseers from the workers.[40]

Kheper-Re's massive basalt[41] sarcophagus was found in Room X with the head oriented toward the north (fig. 85). The anthropoid sarcophagus is typical of those of the period, as it represents a mummiform figure with feet on a plinth[42] wearing a tripartite wig with lappets resting on the chest, an Osirian beard, and a wide wesekh collar. There are no indications of limbs, although Buhl notes that the slight indentations in the sides of both the lid and the base of the sarcophagus represent calves.[43]

The face represents a conventional idealized image, with no attempt at portraiture or realism. This rendering is common in the hard stone sarcophagi of the period,[44] and the bland expressionless face should be considered a deliberate style.[45]

There are two vertical lines of text below the wesekh collar, on the right and left sides of the chest, which give Kheper-Re's name and title. Behind these lines, two

more vertical columns on each side read, "Recitation: I have come that I may protect you."[46] A mummiform, human-headed Son of Horus holding a flail follows each of the vertical columns. Imsety and Duamutef are identified on the right shoulder and Hapy and Qebehsenuef are on the left. This type of formula is common on canopic jars of the period.[47] A kneeling Isis is depicted above the two sons of Horus on the right and Nephthys is found in the same position on the left shoulder. The short inscription in front of each goddess may be translated as "Recitation, the Mourner proclaims."[48]

According to the stylistic analysis of the sarcophagus, shawabtis, and tomb style, Kheper-Re can be firmly dated to Dynasty 26, specifically to the reign of Amasis. His tomb accommodated at least seven of his relatives, including his mother. His brother Psamtek-neb-peti was buried in his own tomb in Sakkara.[49]

Kheper-Re's titles, "noble," "count," and "military officer," indicate that he was a prominent member of society, and his funerary equipment further substantiates this claim. The massive basalt anthropoid sarcophagus and numerous shawabtis are not the funerary goods of the average Egyptian. Yet the fragmentary remains of gold jewelry and semi-precious stone amulets can only suggest the original splendor of the assemblage.

His military profession was his chief line of work, as the title "military officer" is the one used habitually. There was, in fact, a strong military character to this era, as numerous military men have been identified in the Sakkara necropolis. Further, Amasis, a general himself before taking the throne, maintained an army of Egyptian troops and mercenaries in Memphis.[50] Certainly Kheper-Re was an important officer in this military network.

JLH

1. The name Kheper-Re is not attested in Ranke 1935, nor is it known in the ancient historical records that are published. The coffin was dated originally to the Ptolemaic Period (Dunham 1932, p. 90; Porter and Moss 1931, p. 203).

2. Porter and Moss 1974, p. 179, plan XVIII.

3. There are very few mastabas published from Giza in Dynasty 26. One mentioned in Porter and Moss 1974, p. 296, is the stone-built mastaba of Thery, Overseer of Police. There were a series of mud-brick walls around the shaft of G 7757A, but Reisner 1929b, p. 963 does not relate them to the tomb chamber.

4. Aubert 1974, p. 226. Only a few officials from the Saite Period are known to have been buried at Giza. No doubt, Reisner's work at Giza will supply much information on this topic once it is published. Buhl 1959, p. 147, notes two sarcophagi from Giza, that of Pa-kap, with "good name" Wah-ib-Re-em-akhet #A6; and Ptah-hotep, born of Tches-herenep #K1. There are only a few shawabtis from Giza as well: see Osorkon, with "good name" Nefer-ib-Re-Sa-Neith, dating to Psamtek II (Schnei-

Fig. 85

der 1977, p. 228): Udja-Hor, the King's Herald, contemporary with Psamtek II (Aubert 1974, p. 224); the Majordomo Padepep from Giza (?) in the reign of Amasis (Aubert 1974, p. 231). The Saite tombs are far more numerous at Sakkara. For examples of shaft tombs, see excavation reports of: Tjai-en-nehebu (Barsanti 1900b, pp. 262-271); Psamtek (Barsanti 1900a, pp. 161-166); Psamtek-neb-pehti (Lepsius 1897, pp. 172-3).

5. Reisner 1929b, p. 963.

6. Ta-sherit-net-Isis is attested in Ranke 1935, 368.7, "the daughter of Isis." The *shawabti*s are object numbers 29-11-196, 197, 247; MFA 31.835. Reisner 1929b, p. 864, notes that some of her *shawabti*s were also found in the entrance hallway, Room II. A number of uninscribed *shawabti*s were "probably from Room III" as well.

7. Psamtek is attested in Ranke 1935, 136.8. *shawabti*s of Padi-Khonsu have object numbers 29-11-275, MFA 31.837-839; Psamtek's *shawabti*s are 29-11-273,-274,-315; MFA 31.836. *shawabti*s of Psamtek were found in Rooms IV and VI, which adjoin, but Reisner states that it is clear that Room VI contains

the burial of Psamtek (Reisner 1929b, p. 873.) As Psamtek is such a popular name in this period, it is not possible to ascertain whether this is the burial of Kheper-Re's father or a like-named male relative.

8. The names on the other *shawabti*s are as follows: Padi-Khonsu (29-11-275; 31. 837); T...web(?) (29-11-316); Psamtek (31.836)

9. The measurements are based on Reisner's scale drawings. See Plan A.

10. 2.6 meters long, 3.8 meters wide, and 1.6 meters deep. See Plan B.

11. Engelbach 1946, p. 235; Tjai-en-nehebu (Barsanti 1900b, figs. 1,2): Psamtek (Barsanti 1900a, fig. 3): Psamtek-neb-pehti (Lepsius 1897, Bl. 279).

12. Reisner 1929b, 29-11-61.

13. Aubert 1974, p. 236; Gabra 1959, pp. 41-52.

14. Brovarski notes that "in keeping with the archaism of the period, the Saites revived the ingenious Middle Kingdom method of lowering the heavy lid of the sarcophagus in place." (1978: Fn. 150 and references cited there: Barsanti 1900c, 283-284; Rostem 1943, pp. 351-356).

15. Reisner 1929b, p. 986.

16. Reisner 1929b, p. 986.

17. Reisner 1929b. Object Register 29-12-38. There are also other entries of fragments of the coffin: 29-12-20,-83,-215.

18. Reisner 1929b, p. 1018; The body of Tjai-en-nehebu was also heavily covered with bitumen. The coffin was filled to the brim with the substance. (Aubert 1974, p. 236).

19. Engelbach 1946, p. 238.

20. Barsanti 1900b, pp. 262-282.

21. Reisner 1929b, p. 986.

22. Björkman 1974, p. 76; Barsanti 1900b, p. 271; also Engelbach 1946, p. 274.

23. Reisner 1930. Entry 29-12-21: "98 complete (*shawabti*s) + 10 fragments + 1 (add to this 29-12-321) total 109." There is a conflicting number of *shawabti*s enumerated in the diary entries: Reisner 1929b, December entries, p. 983 ff. These entries yield a total of 183 *shawabti*s plus fragments. The *shawabti*s range in size from 10.7 cm. to 13.9 cm.

24. Barsanti 1902, pp. 209-212. In the tomb of Udja-Hor, dating to Psamtek II, were two niches, each containing 198 *shawabti*s. Drioton and Lauer 1951, pp. 469-90. Wah-ib-Re-men's tomb in Sakkara had a T-shaped niche in which two boxes of *shawabti*s were found, one with 206 and one with 200 *shawabti*s. It is also noteworthy that canopics can be found in such niches as well. (Lepsius, Text I, p. 173.) Two niches at the head end of the chamber of Psamtek-neb-pehti contained canopics.

25. The niche measures 40 cm. long, 50 cm. wide, and 70 cm. deep. The measurements of the niche are not given by Reisner; they are calculated here from the scale drawing of the tomb. See Plates I, II.

26. Schneider 1977, Wig Types 34, 36, 37, and 38.

27. Schneider 1977, Hand Positions 4 and 5.

28. Schneider 1977, Implements 8; Aubert, 1974, p. 208-9 for use and function of the implements.

29. Schneider 1977, Bag Type 26a.

30. Aubert 1974, p. 208. Brooklyn 1973, p. 35 – Bothmer notes that the smile occurs also in the sculpture of seventh century B.C.. He prefers to call it an "upward sloping mouth."

31. *Ibid.*; For the back pillar as a solar element see Schneider, 1977.I, p. 161.

32. Schneider, 1977 p. 160.

33. Aubert 1974, p. 224; Petrie 1888a, pp. 19-21, 36.

34. Aubert 1974, p. 225. He points out that the vertical inscription marks a new type of Saite *shawabti*. Further, he considers the vertical inscription a sign of the rebirth of the more ancient inscriptional styles on *shawabti*s. There are numerous text positions in the vertical style. Those with one column, framed with one column on the back pillar are Schneider, 1977. Text Position type 8b. One column framed and closed on the top are Schneider Text Position 8c. He has no categories for those with two vertical columns, framed but open on the top; two vertical columns framed; or four vertical columns framed.

35. Schneider 1977.I, p. 119, type V, VIIA, For a discussion of the development of the terms used for *shawabti*s, see Aubert 1974, p. 208; Björkman 1965, p. 32, and footnotes cited there; Schneider 1977.I, p. 139.

36. Schneider 1977.I, p. 135.

37. The horizontal inscriptions are either Schneider's Text Position 3c – "lines facing inscribed back pillar;" or 3b – "lines facing plain back pillar."

38. See Edwards 1971, p. 120 ff.; Björkman 1974, p. 76; Aubert 1974, p. 234.

39. Björkman 1974, p. 76.
40. Aubert 1974, pp. 234-235.
41. Dunham 1932, p. 90 identified the stone as slate, but Buhl 1959, p. 27, recognizes it as basalt. The case is 226 cm. long, 108 cm. at its widest point, and 79 cm. at its narrowest.
42. Buhl 1959, p. 18, notes that a plinth on which the feet are placed often continues on the back. Brovarski 1983 p. 480 notes that the position of the feet on a plinth is parallel to the contemporary painted mummiform wooden coffins.
43. Buhl 1959, p. 18. Class B sarcophagi show indications of the calves.
44. Buhl 1959. See fig. 3, type A5; fig. 7, type Ca, 4. There does appear to be a distinct difference in the softer stone sarcophagi. The white limestone head of an anthropoid sarcophagus in the Boston Museum (MFA 12.1511, see cat. 139) is an entirely different style with finely modeled features which rival the finest sculpture of the period. Also see Buhl 1959, E,a9; E,a11; E, a16; E,20; E,a25; E,b5; E,b6, and other limestone sarcophagi.
45. Buhl 1959. Some have slightly more realistic faces; see Bb, 1, fig. 6, which has naso-labial grooves and A7, fig. 5, which displays a much richer profile than normally found.
46. I would emend the text to read *ḏd mdw ii·n (i) stp·n(i) s₃ (h)r·k* This is based on *stp-s₃ hr* being translated as "protéger" (Meeks 1982, 79.2843). There is an expression *s₃w r* "To be on one's guard against" (Schneider 1977i, 90 A); however, it does not fit the context here. *Stp-s₃* plus '*r*' is not common. Also, there is *stp·i s₃ hr imsti* "I make protection over Imsety" (Budge 1974, p. 199,) Dynasty 26. See also James 1974, p. 103 *ii·n·i wn m s₃·k* "I have come that I may be your protection," Dynasty 18.
47. For the canopic jar formulas of Dynasty 26, see Sethe 1934. Type XIX.
48. One possible translation of this abbreviated text is *ḏd mdw hw(w) rmwt*. The *hw* could be an abbreviation for a number of words; however, *hww* seems to make the best sense. Faulkner 1962, p. 164 shows the same abbreviated writing of the word, with just the twisted flax and quail chick. Meeks 1981, (78.2605) lists *hww* meaning "proclaimer." The term "weeper" or "mourner," attested in Faulkner 1962, p. 149, is commonly spelled with the "*r*" first. However, there are variant writings noted by Faulkner for the weeping eye plus quail chick, as we have on the right shoulder. Here the *hw* is not written. The spelling is slightly different on the left, as the phonetic complement "*m*" is added after the weeping eye. Meeks 1980, (77.2371) attests *rmw* as "le pleurer." The expression *hww rmwt* is not common, but a similar sense is given in "The Lamentations of Isis and Nephthys:" "Your two sisters call for you in tears" (Lichtheim 1980, p. 117).
49. Psamtek-neb-pehti is attested in Ranke 1935, 136.19. For the tomb and contents, see Lepsius 1897, p. 172-173; III, BL. 279; Porter and Moss 1931, p. 146.
50. Trigger 1983, p. 281; Gardiner 1961, p. 358.

128

128
Statuette of Isis as a mourner

Provenance unknown
Saite Period, Dynasty 26
Wood, gilt, and polychrome decoration
Height 32.9 cm., base length 14.9 cm., base width 6.8 cm.
Hay Collection, Gift of C. Granville Way, 1872 (72.4127)

Throughout Egyptian history Isis and Nephthys have maintained the role of mourners. Countless funerary scenes and statuettes show these sister goddesses grieving over and protecting the deceased.

This finely featured wooden statuette depicts Isis in a classic mourning posture. The kneeling goddess sits back on her heels, her open right hand covering her mouth, her left palm down on her lap.[1] The position of the hands has been interpreted as a gesture of respect,[2] as well as an indication that the goddess is observing silence.[3] Henry Fischer notes that Isis in this pose is often referred to specifically as a *ḏryt*-mourner (the term *ḏryt* meaning literally "kite" or some other member of the falcon family).[4]

The upper and lower arms are individually carved and joined, no doubt necessitated by the complex arm position for this medium. The same construction is evident on two Dynasty 26 wooden statuettes of Isis that are in nearly identical poses.[5]

The simple tripartite wig is painted blue, but the white fillet customarily worn by these

mourners is not visible.[6] Atop the head of the goddess is her hieroglyphic symbol, a throne. The facial features are delicate and finely modeled, with eyes and eyebrows outlined in black. The gilt skin color, of which only traces remain, is typical of statuettes of this type.[7]

Although white or off-white was the conventional color worn by ancient Egyptian women in mourning, this tradition was relaxed in the late dynasties when mourners wore both red and green.[8] Here, enough paint remains to indicate that the goddess was wearing a red sheath dress. Evidence is lacking for the exact style of the garment, but no doubt it was strapless, exposing the breasts, as can be seen on images of mourners since the Old Kingdom.[9]

Sculptures of this type have been found in tombs from the Old Kingdom[10] through the Saite Period.[11] One Dynasty 26 piece found in the tomb of a man named Wah-ib-Re was located in the burial chamber itself.[12] Although the Boston piece is without provenance, it likely came from a similar funerary context.

Its style, quality, and dated parallels suggest this statuette belongs to the fine sculptural tradition of Dynasty 26.

JLH

1. For New Kingdom examples, Werbrouck 1938, fig. 66; for Ptolemaic examples in this pose, Petrie 1914, pl. XXVII, no. 150, 151; Schmidt 1919, no. 1507, 1.
2. Fischer 1976b, p. 42, through the Ptolemaic Period; I would like to thank Peter Lacovara for pointing out this reference to me.
3. Roemer-und Pelizaeus 1985, no. 170.
4. Fischer 1976b, p. 39; Bietak and Reiser-Haslauer 1982.
5. Bietak and Reiser-Haslauer 1982, abb. 86; Roemer-und Pelizaeus 1985, no. 170.
6. Fischer 1976b, p. 41.
7. Roemer-und Pelizaeus 1985, no. 170.
8. Werbrouck 1938, p. 131.
9. Fischer 1976b, fig. 10.
10. Fischer 1976b, p. 44.
11. See note 5.
12. Bietak and Reiser-Haslauer 1982, abb. 81, Room 10.2

Bibliography: New Orleans 1977, no. 18.

129
Set of amulets

From Giza tomb G 7652 A, Room IV
Late Period, Dynasty 26
Harvard University-Museum of Fine Arts Expedition, 1929

a. Carnelian
   Height 1.5 cm. (29.1239)
b. Diorite
   Length 1.2 cm. (29.1242)
c. Lapis lazuli
   Height 2.1 cm. (29.1225)

d. Lapis lazuli
   Length 2 cm. (29.1224)
e. Carnelian
   Length 2 cm.(29.1236)
f. Red jasper
   Length 2.2 cm. (29.1245)
g. Obsidian
   Length 2.1 cm. (29.1214)
h. Carnelian
   Length 1 cm. (29.1241)
i. Lapis lazuli
   Length .9 cm., height .9 cm. (29.1228)
j. Lapis lazuli
   Height 1.3 cm. (29.1231)
k. Lapis lazuli
   Height 3.1 cm. (29.1223)
l. Lapis lazuli
   Height 3.1 cm. (29.1222)
m. Lapis lazuli
   Height 3 cm. (29.1221)
n. Lapis lazuli
   Height 2.9 cm. (29.1220)
o. Lapis lazuli
   Height 1.5 cm. (29.1229)
p. Obsidian
   Length 2.1 cm. (29.1216)
q. Obsidian
   Length 1.3 cm. (29.1218)

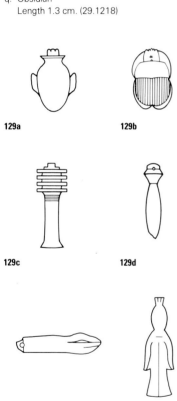

129a   129b

129c   129d

129e   129f

129g   129h

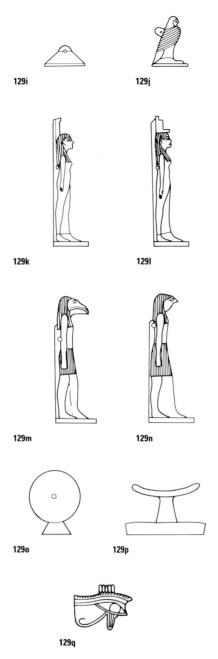

129i   129j

129k   129l

129m   129n

129o   129p

129q

Three main categories of funerary scarab amulet can be distinguished: the heart scarab, the pectoral scarab with outspread wings, and the ordinary uninscribed scarab – usually the smallest of the three.[1] The ancient Egyptians regarded the heart, rather than the brain, as the part of the body which the mind or intelligence was situated. During mummification the heart was not removed like the other internal organs, but was deliberately left inside the body, and magical precautions were taken to prevent the loss of the heart in the afterlife.

Four spells in the Book of the Dead (Chapters 26-29) ensured the heart's protection, and each was supposed to be inscribed on a heart-shaped amulet (ib) of lapis lazuli, green feldspar, or carnelian (129a).[2] Although most heart amulets are uninscribed, their purpose was clearly the same. They

are found in a wide variety of materials, the most common of which are carnelian, basalt, haematite, and glazed composition. The amulet was normally positioned on the breast, and sometimes several examples were provided for one mummy. On the breast of one found at Nebesha (see cat. 178), nine heart amulets were arranged in a row.

An example of the ordinary uninscribed scarab, 129b is made of diorite and quartz, slightly curved underneath, and is pierced from side to side to enable it to be strung on a cord or thread. Such scarabs were included among the mummy wrappings either singly or in groups,[3] and guaranteed the owner resurrection and new life. They are made from various materials, most frequently different kinds of stone.[4]

The djed pillar, which is attested at least from Dynasty 3, has been variously explained as a column of papyrus stems, a tree-trunk with looped branches, and a sheaf of bound cornstalks. Since it is a highly stylized device, it is very difficult to determine conclusively which of these interpretations is correct. Though not originally associated with Osiris, by the New Kingdom the djed pillar had come to be closely linked with the god, and its shape was reinterpreted as a representation of his backbone. The image also had connotations of stability and endurance, and it was primarily to confer these qualities on the deceased that amulets representing the djed was placed within the mummy wrappings.

Chapter 155 of the Book of the Dead, the "spell for a djed pillar of gold" was supposed to be recited over the djed amulet which was to be placed on the mummy's throat. The spell itself alluded directly to the Osirian associations of the image: "You have your backbone, O weary-hearted one, you have your vertebrae, O weary-hearted one."[5]

Two gold djed pillars (cat. 129c) were found on the neck of Tutankhamen's mummy[6] and in later burials the amulet is occasionally found in this position,[7] but is more commonly located on the breast or stomach.[8] In the Late Period several djed amulets were often provided for a single corpse and it is not uncommon to find as many as twelve laid in a row, usually in the abdominal region.[9] Djed amulets are most commonly made of glazed composition,[10] although a many are lapis lazuli.

Ancient Egyptians associated the green, fresh qualities of plants with youthfulness and new life, and the papyrus-column amulet (129d) was supposed to ensure that the deceased remained forever young and flourishing, and suffered no injury. Chapters 159 and 160 of the Book of the Dead refer to this amulet; chapter 159 is a "spell for a papyrus-column of green feldspar to be placed on the throat of the deceased."[11] Many of the surviving examples are in fact green, although they are more commonly made of glazed composition than of feldspar.[12]

Amulets representing the head and forepart of a snake (129e) prevented the owner from being bitten or devoured by the hostile serpents of the Netherworld. Chapters 33, 34, and 35 of the Book of the Dead are specifically concerned with the repulsion of serpents, but these texts are not found on the amulets themselves, despite Budge's assertion to the contrary.[13] Some of the amulets, however, bear inscriptions linking them with the uraeus that the sun-god Re wore on his forehead; this probably explains the form of the amulet, the owner invoking the aid of the god's uraeus against the serpents of the Netherworld.[14] It was clearly important for the serpent's head to be red; most examples are of carnelian, like this one, or of some other red material such as jasper.[15] It appears that the amulet was usually placed at the throat,[16] which was regarded as a particularly vulnerable part of the body.

The *tyet* (129f), one of the most common amulet types, represents a piece of cloth looped and knotted. Popularly known as the ''buckle'' or ''girdle'' of Isis, it is sometimes shown as a girdle-tie in depictions of the goddess. The name *tyet* appears to derive from *tȝyt* (''shroud'' or ''curtain''),[16] and as the device is also connected with the blood of Isis, it may have had its origin in a cloth worn between the legs of a pregnant woman to prevent unwanted bleeding, and thereby protect the child in her womb.[17]

The purpose of the amulet, and its connection to the blood of Isis, is explained in Chapter 156 of the Book of the Dead, the spell ''for a *tyet*-amulet of red jasper'': ''You have your blood, O Isis; you have your power, O Isis; you have your magic, O Isis. The amulet is a protection for this Great One, which will drive away whoever would commit a crime against him.'' The ''rubric'' of the chapter gives instructions for the correct preparation and positioning of the *tyet* amulet, adding that this will guarantee to its owner the protection of Isis.[18]

The association of the amulet with the goddess's blood accounts for the stipulation in Book of the Dead Chapter 156 that it be made of red jasper. Other red material such as carnelian and colored glass were also used, while even green and blue examples made of glazed composition are quite common. The recommended position for the tyet was on the neck, but it is more commonly encountered on the chest.[19]

Amulets in the form of the twin feathers worn as a headdress by certain gods, notably Amen and Osiris (129g), may be interpreted simply as miniature versions of the headdress intended to endow the owner with divine power. An alternative possibility, however, is that the amulets' shape derives

from that of the *pesesh-kef* (cat. 11). This was a bifurcated instrument that was probably used to support the lower jaw of the corpse at the period when embalming was in its infancy in ancient Egypt. It later came to be associated with the ''Opening of the Mouth'' ceremony, although it was probably not actually used in that ritual.[20] Nevertheless, the *pesesh-kef* occurs as an amulet and by the New Kingdom it had come to be depicted in a form virtually indistinguishable from that of the twin feathers,[21] so that it is often impossible to determine which of the two alternative interpretations should be applied to an amulet of this shape. The position of the feathers amulet, where recorded, does not help in identifying its significance; Petrie notes eight examples placed on the chest or stomach and one at the throat.[22]

The barrel-shaped bead (129h), known as a *swrt* or *swit*, was an important part of the mummy's trappings as early as the Middle Kingdom. It was worn on a necklace at the throat and is usually represented in this position on anthropoid coffins and mummy masks.[23] The bead is also shown in the object friezes of Middle Kingdom rectangular coffins, the source that provides us with its Egyptian names.

Barrel-shaped bead amulets are attested from the New Kingdom on. They are often inscribed with the name of the owner and for this reason have been dubbed ''name-beads.'' It has been supposed that the bead was intended to ensure the preservation of the deceased's name (the retention of which was important for his survival in the Netherworld),[24] but this may not have been its only function. Shorter argued that it served much the same purpose as the serpent's-head amulet (cat. 129e), since the bead occasionally carries an invocation to the eye or uraeus of Re, similar to that associated with the serpent's head.[25] Moreover, both these amulets were traditionally located on the throat and both were usually made of carnelian; hence the barrel bead, like the serpent's head, may have been intended as a protection against snake bite.

The seal amulet (129i) represents a rectangular stamp-seal with a suspension-loop and a flat, undecorated base. According to Petrie the amulet was intended to give the owner ''power over property,''[26] and some examples carry a distinguishing design on the flat surface.[27] The majority of seal amulets are made of lapis lazuli, though other materials include green feldspar, basalt, limestone, and glazed composition. These amulets were usually located on the right or left hand.

The falcon amulet (129j) has a loop at the rear to enable it to be strung on a cord or thread. It belongs to a well-known category of figurines that conferred the protection of

one of the major falcon-deities, such as Horus and Sokar. During the Late Period the falcon amulet was normally located on the chest, and examples are known in green feldspar, amethyst, lapis lazuli, and glazed composition.

Apart from having mourned Osiris and assisted in his resurrection, Nephthys played an insignificant role in funerary mythology, and she is rarely depicted or alluded to except in company with her sister Isis. Amulets representing Nephthys, however, are common from Dynasty 26, when they appear among the rows of protective deities placed on the chests of mummies.[28] Isis and Nephthys were often placed together as a pair[29] and the iconography of the two is similar. Cat. 129k shows Nephthys standing, with the hieroglyphic signs spelling her name on her head. The amulet is made of lapis lazuli, perhaps indicating that the owner was relatively wealthy, since most such figures are made of the cheaper glazed composition.[30]

Figures of Isis (129l) are attested as amulets from as early as the New Kingdom, but they were particularly common during the Late Period. The goddess is sometimes represented kneeling as a mourner for Osiris or suckling the child Horus[31] but standing figures are also extremely common. The present example is typical in showing Isis standing with one leg advanced, her arms at her sides, and wearing the hieroglyph for her name upon her head.

Between Dynasty 26 and the early Ptolemaic Period groups of figurines representing major funerary deities were among the most common amulet type. Their purpose was to endow the deceased with the protection of the gods and goddesses who were most closely associated with the Afterlife. These amulets were normally positioned in rows on the chest[32] and it is not uncommon to find two or more figures of the same deity in the wrappings of a single mummy.[33] Isis amulets are known in gold, silver, bronze, glass, lapis lazuli, and, most frequently, blue and green glazed composition.[34]

The ibis-headed Thoth (129m) is well known as the patron of learning and writing but he also played an important part in the Osirian mythology, assisting in the resurrection of Osiris and restoring the wounded eye of Horus.[35] He is therefore frequently depicted on funerary artifacts and often appears as an associate and helper of Horus. Small standing figurines of these two gods are extremely common and were usually included among the amulets representing divinities, placed on the mummy's chest in the Late Period.[36] Single Thoth amulets of this form are, however, attested as early as Dynasty 21.[37] This example shows the god standing with his left leg advanced, and wearing the kilt and tripartite wig. Lapis lazuli Thoth figurines are relatively rare; Petrie knew of only seven, as compared with 114 in glazed composition.[38] The majority of the latter were blue or green, probably in imitation of the more costly lapis lazuli.

Figurines representing Horus (129n) are among the commonest of the amulets in the form of deities, found on mummies of the Late Period. The example here, guaranteeing the protection of the god, depicts Horus in his familiar form as a falcon-headed man, standing with his left leg advanced and his arms held close to his sides. A tiny hole, pierced through the back-pillar of the figure, served to suspend it on a cord.

This specimen was found with three similar amulets, all of lapis lazuli, which represented Thoth, Isis and Nephthys. The exact positioning on the mummy was not recorded but comparison with other intact burials suggests that they would have been placed in a row on the chest.[39] Horus amulets are known in a very wide range of materials, of which the most common is glazed composition.

Cat. 129o is in the form of a disk, pierced in the center, with a trapezoidal support. Its shape is ambiguous; on the one hand it is reminiscent of the *šn* ring, a device closely associated with royalty from the Early Dynastic Period, and perhaps the origin of the king's cartouche. The *šn* appears to symbolize regeneration and protection, and this may possibly be the basic function of the amulet. Alternatively it could, as Petrie believed,[40] represent the solar disc, and in this connection it should be noted that it closely resembles the *3ht* amulet.[41] This latter represents the sun on the horizon and its purpose was to enable the deceased to see the rising sun – the giver of life and symbol of rebirth.[42] A similar significance might then be attached to the piece under discussion.

The second of the two alternative interpretations of this amulet is perhaps the more likely. The iconography, with a solid unbordered disk, conforms much more closely to the conventional Egyptian representation of the sun than to that of the *šn*, which is a hollow ring. A rare variant of the amulet adds the *atef* crown to the top of the disk[43] understandable if it represents the sun, but more unlikely to be associated with the *šn* ring.

Examples of this amulet are known in lapis lazuli and various types of stone. The recorded position is normally about the middle of the stomach, though Petrie cites two instances in which the amulet was found on the left hand.[44]

Amulets in the form of miniature headrests (129p) made their first appearance in the New Kingdom, but they do not seem to have become popular until Dynasty 26. From this time on they are quite often found within the wrappings of mummies and are usually located at the neck.

The purpose of the headrest as a funerary amulet was to guarantee the deceased sound sleep and ensure that he would not suffer the loss of his head in the Netherworld. This is made clear in Chapter 166 of the Book of the Dead, the ''chapter of the headrest,'' which specifically assures the deceased that his head will not be taken from him.

Most of the known amulets are made of haematite,[45] although this one is obsidian. The amulets are usually uninscribed, but a few examples are known that carry the text of Chapter 166 of the Book of the Dead. Cat. 129q is in the form of the eye of a falcon with its distinctive markings underneath. It represents the *wedjat*, the left eye of Horus, which was torn out by Seth in the course of their struggles over the throne of Egypt, later to be healed again and restored to its owner by the ibis-headed Thoth. According to another myth, the *wedjat* was the eye of Re, which left him and was eventually brought back by Thoth.

Both these stories contain the concept of loss or injury followed by restoration or healing. The Egyptian word *wd3t* means ''that which is whole/uninjured'' and the eye came to be regarded as a symbol of health and revitalization. For this reason the *wedjat* appeared as a protective device on coffins and other items of funerary equipment, and especially on the 'evisceration plaque placed over the mummy's embalming incision so as to magically 'heal' the wound made during the mummification process. The eye was one of the commonest types of funerary amulet and examples have been found in large quantities in cemeteries throughout Egypt. They are attested as early as the end of the Old Kingdom, but became particularly common in the Late Period.

Wedjat amulets occur in a variety of materials including gold, silver, carnelian, haematite, lapis lazuli, glazed composition, glass and wood. They were placed in various positions on the mummy, but particularly on the chest,[46] and several are frequently found on a single body.[47] This example, of obsidian, is typical of many in consisting of a small silhouette engraved of the eye and its lower markings, with the details engraved on one side. More elaborate versions of the design are also known, including *wedjat*s in rectangular frames with the background cut away, and amulets comprising four or more eyes joined together in a complex symmetrical groupings.[48]

JHT

1. Shorter 1934, p. 122.
2. Petrie 1914, p. 10.
3. Petrie 1914, pl. L, 2; pl. LI, 6-8, 10-12; Gray and Slow 1968, pp. 51, 55, pl. 79.
4. Petrie 1914, p. 23.
5. Allen 1974, p. 154.

6. Carter 1927, p. 117, pl. LXXVIII A.
7. Petrie 1914, p. 15, pl. LI, 10.
8. Barsanti 1900a, p. 162; Petrie 1914, p. 15, pl. L, 2, 3; pl. LI, 6, 8, 9, 11; pl. LII 13-15; Bietak and Reiser-Haslauer 1982, pp. 214-217, 219, Abb. 101.
9. Petrie 1914, 15, pl. L, 2, 3; pl. LI, 6, 8, 9, 11; pl. LII, 13, 14.
10. Petrie 1914, p. 15.
11. Faulkner 1985, p. 155; Allen 1974, p. 156.
12. Petrie 1914, pp. 12-13.
13. Budge 1925, p. 323; Shorter 1935, p. 174, n. 8.
14. Shorter 1935, pp. 174-175.
15. Petrie 1914, p. 26.
16. Petrie 1914, p. 26; Carter 1927, p. 117, pl. LXXVIII, B.
17. Westendorf 1980, col. 204.
18. Faulkner 1985, p. 155; Allen 1974, p. 155.
19. Petrie 1914, p. 23.
20. Van Walsem 1978-79, pp. 193-249, pl. 38 (ref. to pp. 220-270).
21. Van Walsem 1978-79, pp. 234, 236.
22. Petrie 1914, p. 16.
23. Mace and Winlock 1916, pp. 46, 62-63; Farag and Iskander 1971, p. 61, pl. XXXIX, L.
24. Petrie 1914, p. 21.
25. Shorter 1935, pp. 171-176 (esp. pp. 174-175).
26. Petrie 1914, p. 22.
27. Brunton 1948, pl. XXXIII.
28. Petrie 1914, p. 36.
29. Petrie 1914, pl. L, 3, pl. LI, 6, 8, 9, pl. LII, 13, 14.
30. Petrie 1914, p. 36.
31. Petrie 1914, p. 35.
32. Petrie 1914, p. 35.
33. Petrie 1914, pl. L, 2-3; pl. LI, 6, 8, 9, 10; Bietak and Reiser-Haslauer 1982, p. 215-217, Abb. 98, Taf. 142 B, F.
34. Petrie 1914, p. 35.
35. Bleeker 1973, pp. 131-136.
36. Petrie 1914, p. 42.
37. Montet 1951, p. 53, fig. 16, p. 78, pl. LII.
38. Petrie 1914, p. 42.
39. Petrie 1914, p. 39, pl. L, 2, 3, 5; LI, 6, 8, 9, 10; pl. LII, 13.
40. Petrie 1914, p. 17.
41. Müller-Winkler 1984, col. 578.
42. Petrie 1914, p. 17, pl. IV.
43. Petrie 1914, p. 17, pl. IV.
44. Petrie 1914, p. 17.
45. Petrie 1914, p. 15.
46. Petrie 1914, p. 33, pl. L, 2; pl. LI, 7, 8, 10, 11, 12; pl. LII, 13.
47. Petrie 1914, pl. L, 2, 3, 5; pl. LI, 6, 7, 10, 11, 12; pl. LII, 15; Gray and Slow 1968, pp. 51, 55, pl. 79; Bietak and Reiser-Haslauer 1982, pp. 214, 216, 217 218, Abb. 100, 220, Taf. 146 A-E.
48. Petrie 1914, p. 33-34, pl. XXIV-XXV.

Literature: Altenmüller 1975a; Barsanti 1900, p. 267; Bietak and Reiser-Haslauer 1982, pp. 214-217, Abb. 98,Taf. 142 B, C, 143 A,D; Bonnet 1952, p. 30; Bresciani, Pernigotti and Silvis 1977, p. 76, Tav. XXIX; Giveon 1984; Shorter 1935; Westendorf 1980; Petrie 1914, pp. 15, 17, 32-39, pls. III, IV, XXIV-XXVII; Fleming et al. 1980, p. 34, 64-65; Montet 1942, pp. 18-19, 30-32, 70-71, 82, pl. VIII, XXII, XXVII; Gray and Slow 1968, pp. 51, 55, pl. 79; Budge 1925, pp. 216-218, 306-327, 359, 362; Müller-Winkler 1984, col. 577-579; Wiedemann 1910, pp. 16-18, 27-29; Fischer 1980, cols. 686-693; Andrews 1984, p. 34, 36-37; Reisner 1907, p. 63-65, 68-89, 110, 118, pl. IV-VI, VIII, IX; Shorter 1934, p. 122; Müller-Winkler 1986 col. 824-826.

130
Shawabti of Nefer-seshem-psamtik

Provenance unknown
Late Period
Faience
Height 19 cm.
Hay Collection, Gift of C. Granville Way,
1872 (72.1675)

During the Late Period (Dynasties 26-30), *shawabti*s enjoyed a marked renaissance as their production became more and more the province of the skilled worker in faience. The present specimen, well modeled and with a good duck-egg blue glaze, wears a plain, tripartite wig and divine beard, its body wrapped in a close-fitting shroud from which the hands protrude to clutch a pick, a narrow-bladed hoe and a basket rope (the basket itself is thrown over the left shoulder). The figure has a dorsal pillar and stands upon a square base. As is usual at this date, the *shawabti* was produced in a two-piece pottery mold, and the details (including the inscription) are emphasized with a point prior to firing. Since often the artisans upon whom this task devolved were illiterate, *shawabti* texts from this period tend to be rather garbled; the present text is no exception. The owner of this figure is one Nefer-seshem-psamtik born of Semes(?), whose title is given as "Prophet of Min, Lord of Sekret." Apart from a second shawabti, also in Boston,[1] the man is unattested and his tomb unlocated. A

Lower Egyptian provenance may be suspected, however, since Sekret is presumably the same locality mentioned on two fragmentary naophorous statues of limestone recovered by Breccia from the Serapeum at Alexandria.[2]

CNR

1. MFA 72.1681.
2. Breccia 1907, pp. 64-67; Gauthier 1928, p. 67.

131
Ba bird amulet

Provenance unknown
Probably Late Period, Dynasties 26-30
Gold
Length 4.4 cm., width 2.2 cm.
Gift of F.L. Burnett, 1924 (24.117)

The three-dimensional body of this gold *ba* bird was formed by joining two thin sculpted sheets of gold, whereas the delicate outstretched wings are made from a single layer of hammered gold. The human wig, and bird's feet are clearly modeled and the feather pattern on the front and back of the wings is finely detailed.

A suspension loop on the breast indicates that this funerary amulet was meant to be sewn onto the bandages of the mummy; amulets are often found on the exterior of the wrappings on the chest.[1] *Ba* amulets adorning mummies in this fashion are found as early as Dynasty 18 in, for example, the tomb of Tutankhamen.[2] Note that in the earlier image the head is in profile, while the present example faces front. Examples from the New Kingdom and Third Intermediate Period are rare,[3] and it is not until the Saite Period that the *ba* amulet becomes a common feature in the burial assemblage. It maintains this prominent status until the end of the Ptolemaic rule.[4]

Very fine examples in solid gold are known from tombs from Dynasties 26 to 30.[5] In addition to these, there are two other types of gold *ba* amulets – the simplified flat, foil style[6] and the more ornate inlaid variety. Those inlaid with semi-precious stones have been found in burials dating to Dynasties 26-30,[7] while a fine piece in the Brooklyn Museum has been assigned a Ptolemaic date.[8]

These dated parallels suggest that this example falls within the period from Dynasties 26 to 30, an era known for its fine craftsmanship in solid amulets.[9]

JLH

1. Petrie 1890, p. 20 (tomb of Horudja in Hawara, Dynasty 30); Barsanti 1900b, p. 269 (tomb of Tjai-en-nehebu in Sakkara, Dynasty 26); Daressy 1903a, pp. 76-82 (tomb of Horkhebi in Sakkara, Dynasty 26).
2. According to Wilkinson 1971, p. 97, the earliest example of the *ba* amulet comes from the mummy of Tutankhamen. Few New Kingdom

examples have survived, although we have evidence in the form of jewelry workshop scenes in tomb paintings that *ba* amulets were made (Wilkinson 1971, p. 10). Further evidence that they were in use is offered by a bronze statuette dated to Dynasty 18, which wears a *ba* bird amulet (Cooney 1968, p. 267, fig. 11). Also, numerous *shawabti*s have *ba* birds on their chests. See, for example, Schneider 1977 (3.2.1.6, 3.2.1.14, and 3.2.1.49), all dating to early Dynasty 19.
3. For Third Intermediate Period examples, see the tombs of Hornekht and Wendebaunded in Tanis (Montet 1947, pl. 52 and Montet 1947, pl. 59). Note that these are all with the head in profile, as are those in the tomb of Tutankhamen.
4. Cooney 1968, p. 267.
5. Engelbach 1946, p. 238; Drioton and Lauer 1951, no. 52. In the tomb of Wah-ib-re-men in Sakkara, Dynasty 26, is a gold *ba* bird 1.5 cm. in height. Petrie 1890, p. 20, notes a *ba* on the chest and a *ba* bird flying "all gold and exquisitely wrought" in the tomb of Horudja, Dynasty 30. A solid gold standing *ba* amulet is in the tomb of Tjai-en-nehebu (see Maspero 1902, pl. 3). Also Vernier 1927, pl. 92, 53.375, .376, and .386 show *ba* amulets just like this piece, but they are undated. Brooklyn Museum 1983, entry 69, mentions examples in solid gold from tombs in Sakkara dating to Dynasty 27.
6. Vernier 1927, pl. LXXXVII.A; Maspero 1902, pl. IV; Effendi 1920, p. 214.
7. See note 1 above.
8. Brooklyn Museum 1983, entry 69.
9. Engelbach 1946, p. 238. For more information on gold working, see Lucas 1962, pp. 229ff.

132
Funerary stela

From Thebes
Late Period, Dynasty 25 or 26
Limestone
Height 37.8 cm., width 28 cm.
Formerly in the Spicer Collection. Egyptian Curator's Fund, 1980 (1980.166)

This round-topped limestone stela is divided into three registers. The lunette shows a sign of heaven curving over a winged sun disk with uraei; the caption, "(Long) live the Behdetite, the Lord of Heaven," appears twice. Below the lunette a man and his father, arms raised, are shown worshiping Osiris and Re, respectively. Both men wear long transparent kilts and sashes across

132

their chests; they have short hair and incense cones. The gods are wrapped in mummy bandages and sit on low-backed thrones. Osiris wears an *atef* crown and holds a flail, while the falcon-headed Re is adorned with a sun disk and holds a *was* scepter.

The lower register includes five lines of text: "An offering that the king gives (to) Osiris Foremost of the West, the Great God, the Lord of Abydos, Wen-nefer Ruler of Eternity, that he may cause the soul of the physician, the Osiris Iret-Hor-sekheru true-of-voice, son of the priest of Nemty Djed-Khonsu-iu-ankh, to go forth to heaven and (his) corpse (to go) to the Underworld, and that he may mingle with the Unwearying Stars in the sky. Iret-Hor-sekheru will never die."

The Egyptian belief that body and soul were different entities is made explicit in prayers in which the deceased was assured that his

soul would not abandon his corpse.[1] The explicit reference to the soul going up to heaven and the corpse going down to the Underworld is not unique, for the same words are sometimes found on statues[2] and sarcophagi.[3] Both of these notions are consistent with Egyptian views of the afterlife. One tradition saw the deceased going up to heaven to accompany the sun god on his journeys, while another had the dead join Osiris in his realm, the *duat*, a place not easily identified, but certainly understood as lying under the earth.[4] The reference in the text to the deceased mingling with the "Unwearying Stars," reflects another belief found in the Pyramid Texts. There the king became one of the circumpolar stars, which were regarded as symbols of permanence because they were always visible in the Egyptian sky.[5]

The motifs on the stela show remarkable unity with the text: The worship of Osiris is

a natural funerary theme, and the scene with the sun god becomes understandable when one remembers that the beliefs about the dead ascending to heaven were originally Heliopolitan traditions[6] that were eventually adopted by all Egyptians.

RJL

1. Sethe 1906, p. 114.
2. Sethe 1906, p. 481.
3. Capart 1941, p. 239.
4. Morenz 1973, pp. 204-208.
5. Spencer 1982, p. 140.
6. Morenz 1973, p. 205.

Bibliography: Leprohon forthcoming.

133
Stela of Pakhery

Provenance unknown
Late Period, Dynasty 26
Wood
Height 46 cm., width 33 cm., depth 2.5 cm.
Gift of Theodore M. Davis, 1905 (05.100)

This stela was made for Pakhery, son of the altar-keeper Disu-amen and Tadit-amenet.[1] An almost identical stela belonging to the same man was purchased in Thebes and is now in the Macclesfield collection.[2] Similar stelae in Brussels and Cairo have been dated to mid-Dynasty 26.[3]

Two pieces of wood were joined vertically to make the stela. The seam was covered with plaster on the back surface, while the front was prepared with a layer of finer plaster. The figures are white with details painted in red, against a blue background. The text has a yellow background and black hieroglyphs. Red, green, and yellow blocks border the stela.

The upper scenes show Pakhery offering to the god Re-Horakhty at the left and to Atum at the right. Below, the god Thoth brings Pakhery before Re-Horakhty, Isis, and the Four Sons of Horus. The texts consist of three offering formulae asking for favors on behalf of the deceased.[4]

CHR

1. For Pakhery and Tadit-amenet, see Ranke 1935, p. 116.17 and p. 372.21, where the spelling is slightly different.
2. David 1980, p. 62, #7; pl. 1.7. This example is stone.
3. Munro 1973, see Brussels E6253 on p. 196, fig. 18, pl. 5; Cairo A9915 on p. 202, fig. 20, pl. 5.
4. For discussion of texts see Leprohon forthcoming, MFA 05.100.

Bibliography: Leprohon forthcoming.

Literature: Munro 1973.

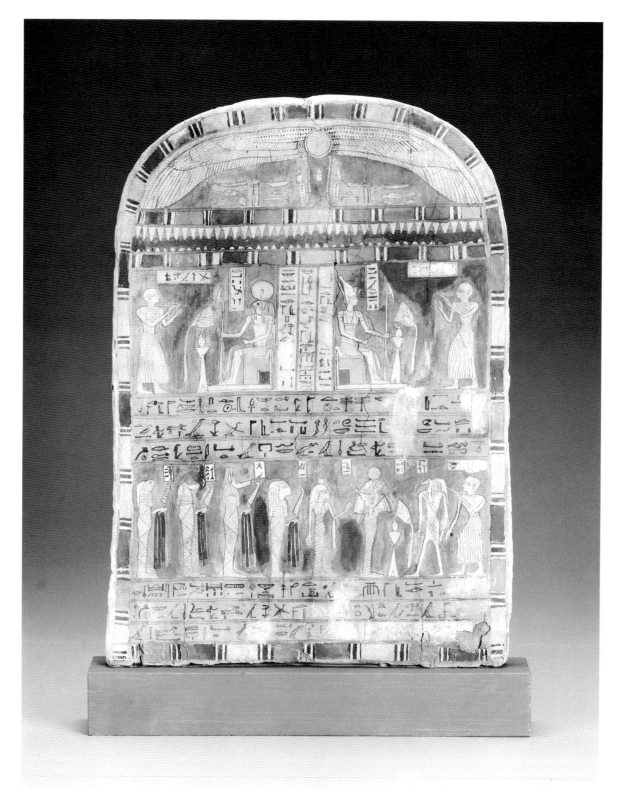

Book of the Dead

What we call the Book of the Dead was known to the ancient Egyptians as the "Utterances of Going Forth by Day," a graphic description of the literal rebirth and freedom of movement they expected its charms and magical spells to ensure. It has its origins in the Pyramid Texts of the late Old Kingdom, which were specialized for the inclusion of the kings among the gods. Few private individuals then expected an afterlife, and those that did obtained it only through close association with the king. During the Middle Kingdom, spells appropriate for non-royal persons were added, and the greatly expanded corpus, now called the Coffin Texts, was commonly inscribed inside the coffins of wealthy private individuals. This development vastly increased the numbers of people who could participate in rebirth, since the spells and relevant equipment were considered necessary to provide sufficient information to succeed in "going forth by day." By the late New Kingdom, anyone who could afford to purchase a scrap of papyrus on which a few passages were inscribed[1] could expect to participate fully. This process of increasing regularly the numbers of people with access to the Kingdom of Osiris is often referred to as the "democratization of the afterlife."

Books of the Dead appear first in Dynasty 18, usually written in hieroglyphic characters on papyrus; soon after a top register with vignettes or small illustrations of the text. These are often in color, and some copies are quite beautiful works of art.[2] Chapters also appear on cloth, leather, statuettes, boxes, etc.[3] In the Third Intermediate Period appear copies written in hieratic, the script form of hieroglyphic writing,[4] and after about 600 B.C. the vignettes move from the top of each sheet down into the text, which is written around them. The spelling, grammar, and illustration vary considerably; some copies were obviously custom-made by talented painters and learned, careful scribes. Perhaps the purchasers even chose the texts they preferred. Other copies were clearly bought "off the shelf." When these were being prepared, an artist first did the vignettes and then passed along the papyrus to a scribe who added the texts. Sometimes the scribe could not fit the whole text into the available space, and shortened or mutilated the text. In these copies, the text often does not match the vignette beside it. Also, the name of the deceased had to be inserted after purchase in a space left blank by the scribe. Corrupt and garbled texts are not uncommon, especially from later periods.

By the Late Period almost 200 spells were available for scribes to choose from. The order in which they were presented became more standardized; the current numbering system is based on the chapter order of one particularly fine example.[5]

Copies of Books of the Dead were included with the grave goods of the deceased. They were sometimes placed within the coffin in order to be handy in an emergency; in other tombs they have been found within the plinth of a statue of Ptah-Sokar-Osiris.

Chapters in the Book of the Dead provide information needed in the afterlife, primarily in the form of magical recitations to facilitate movement, passage through geographical areas, and secure the good will of the gods. Although threads of various ancient tradition and belief are interwoven, the two major ones appear to be the solar (those who proceed to heaven are associated with the sun god Re and travel across the sky with him in the sun boat for eternity) and the Osiride (those who successfully negotiate the tests of the Underworld are proclaimed "true of voice" in a trial, and enter the Kingdom of Osiris, Judge and God of the Dead). The latter tradition is the strongest, but lunar and stellar associations are included, as is a strong belief in the necessity of doing agricultural work in the fields of the Netherworld.

Because the goals are diverse, the spells contain many different ideas. Included are spells meant to be read while passing through and trying to escape hazards such as the snake Apep; charms to prevent the deceased from having to work or having to function backwards (walking upside down, eating feces, etc.); recitations to accompany rituals or even the preparations of the mummy; hymns to numerous divinities; lists of names of the inhabitants and features of the Underworld, with sample answers for trick questions that might be asked along the way; justifications of the deceased's worthiness; chants to perform while transforming into bird or animals, etc. These chapters, or utterances, are full of mythological references and details that are not always clear to us, and contain the names and attributes of hundreds of gods. They are not, however, religious by modern definitions, but are purely magical: the Egyptians believed that knowledge of the correct words and names enabled one to manipulate results in the afterlife as well as during life on earth. Thus, chapters are not technically pleas or prayers, though they are called such even by their authors, but are instead demands, proofs, and justifications designed to force the desired result. For example, one of the few to actually mention moral and ethical values, Chapter 125 suggests "what to say in order to dispose of the evil the deceased has done," clearly indicating that it was the correct words and not true repentance that absolved the evil doer. Notwithstanding the intent of this "Negative Confession," its contents (and much of Egyptian secular literature)[6] make clear that there were standards of behavior not too different from our own, and that certain crimes put one's immortality in jeopardy. Only the means of absolution differs from our own. The papyrus of Ta-Amen begins with the vignette from the "Negative Confession."

SD

1. Janssen 1975, pp. 245-246.
2. Rossiter 1979, plates.
3. Heerma van Voss 1985.
4. See the lovely Greenfield papyrus published in Budge 1912.
5. Davis 1894, reproduction of the Turin papyrus.
6. Cf. Lichtheim 1975, p. 61.

134

Book of the Dead of Ta-Amen, Chantress of Amen, Daughter of Disyast

From Sakkara
Ptolemaic Period
Papyrus
Length 28 cm., width 36.5 cm.
Gift of Martin Brimmer, 1892 (92.2582)

Although Museum records indicate that this papyrus was found in Ta-Amen's tomb, it is not identified in standard references sources. The name Ta-Amen is rather common in Dynasty 30 and later;[1] it means "She of Amen," which is quite appropriate for her position as a singer in an Amen temple.[2] Only the name of her mother is recorded.[3]

The vignettes are rather nicely drawn and neat, with typically proportioned figures for the period, on twenty rather thin sheets of papyrus now glued on linen. It is not clear whether any texts were written on the back. The vignettes are in close juxtaposition to the texts they illustrate, which are standard for the period. Ta-Amen may have selected them herself.

The judgment hall has a cornice roof, supported by papyrus columns. Seated on the left is Osiris, Judge of the Dead. His fillet, necklace, amulets, and netting are in red. Before him stand his four sons on a lotus flower, and an animal skin draped over a pole. Above, twenty-three of the traditional forty-two assessors wear the feather of truth and witness the test which Ta-Amen must pass. She kneels beseechingly before them. At the right side of the hall, the Two Truths usher Ta-Amen in. Before her is the balance, tuned and adjusted by Horus and Anubis. Her heart, in the right scale pan, must not be so laden with wrongdoing committed during her lifetime that it outweighs the feather of Truth resting in the left pan. Should her heart be so heavy with her faults that it sinks to the floor, she can expect to be devoured by the monster Ammit (part hippo, part lion, and part crocodile) who

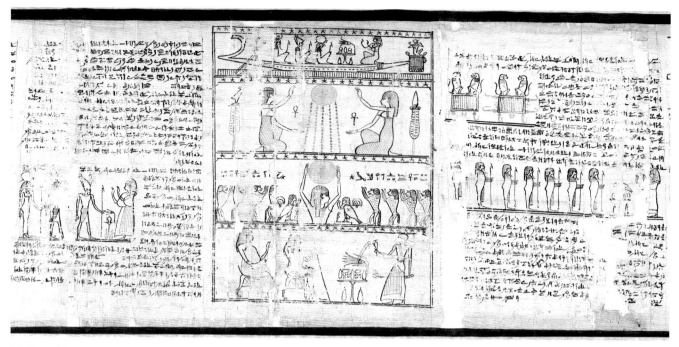

waits on a stand before Osiris. Ta-Amen, however, has nothing to be concerned about. The ibis-headed Thoth, scribe of the gods and recorder at this trial (who also appears in baboon forms on the top of the balance arm) announces in the hieroglyphic text above the scales that Ta-Amen's heart does balance, and that she is without evil. He makes a note of her innocence, dipping his pen into the inkwell of his palette. Ta-Amen is declared true of voice, and may now enter the Kingdom of Osiris. Above the scene the tone is set by a row of symbols referring to truth, weighing, fire, and the cycle of life and death that symbolizes rebirth.[4]

The text that belongs to this vignette, Spell 125, is the Negative Confession mentioned above. Although it is not present in this papyrus, it is to be assumed that Ta-Amen has access to its magic before she enters the Judgment Hall of the Two Truths. In earlier papyri, Anubis acts as the usher. In addition to recording the result of the weighing, the hieroglyphic texts above the figure give their names and titles.

This scene is the result of a conflation of several ancient traditions involving litigation and judgments in Egypt. Subsequent spells in this papyrus refer to the most prominent of these, in which Horus and his father Osiris, assisted by Thoth, are justified against their enemies, Seth and his cohort, in a trial held before Re and the Council of Heliopolis.[5] This trial itself has multiple antecedents, but its details and the personages who take part have been conflated with the Osirian judgment, creating a rich fabric.[6] The addition of this judgment concept to the mortuary literature was probably encouraged by the increasing number of ordinary Egyptians

who were able to equip themselves with the necessities for attaining an afterlife. It could have been felt that there was a need to somehow evaluate the claims of all these new candidates.

At the top of sheet 2, four baboons from the sun boat of Re sit beside two small lakes surrounded by flaming red braziers. The deceased requests their assistance in driving out her own evil and in helping her achieve entry into the afterworld with the requisite offerings. The baboons grant her request (Spell 126).[7] At the bottom, Ta-Amen stands in adoration before a heaped offering table and a row of the gods of the caverns of the Netherworld. She requests permission to pass through the gates of earth, sky, and afterworld, even as Osiris passed through, for she expects to be joined with him (Spell 127).[8]

No text appears with Book of the Dead 16 in any extant papyrus. The vignettes on sheet 3, however, are fully appropriate to the sun hymns in Spell 15, which they usually follow, and are probably not intended as a separate chapter. Above, the deceased kneels on the sun boat before three forms of the sun gods. Below, the red sun, rising between standards symbolizing east and west, is received by two goddesses, probably Isis and Nephthys.[9] Underneath, the red setting sun is adored by baboons and human-headed *ba* birds on small platforms labeled "east" and "west." The texts above read "Adoring Re when he sets in the land of the living," a euphemism for the land of the dead. At the bottom is a scene common in papyri of this period; a priest pours a libation and burns incense before two seated figures. In papyri made for men these

figures are man and woman, probably the deceased and his wife, since there seems never to be any indication that the woman is divine.[10] Since only sheet 1 of this papyrus refers to Ta-Amen with the female personal pronouns, it may be that we are here looking at Ta-Amen and her "wife."

At the beginning of sheet 4 is a chapter for going forth by day, overcoming one's enemies, and triumphing over them in the Council of the great god Osiris, a clear reference to the judgment scene and the myth of Horus and Seth. The full spell contains what is essentially a threat that if this not be permitted, the deceased will have the power of retribution (Spell 65). Spell 90 follows, protecting against the inability to speak effectively the spells contained within the papyrus. Spells 18a and 18c, in the lower half of the sheet, contain a magical insistence that the god Thoth vindicate the deceased in the presence of various councils of gods as he assisted in the vindication of Osiris against his enemies, Seth and company. The vignettes show Ta-Amen praying before the councils.[11] Full versions indicate the spell is "really excellent, (proved) millions of times."

About one third of the way down sheet 8 is Spell 19 for awarding wreaths of vindication prepared by the god Atum to Horus and by association, the deceased, for Horus's victories over his enemies. The vignette shows such a wreath, painted in red, resting on a plinth with a red door between the deceased and the god. This chapter is very typical of papyri of this period.[12]

Spells on sheet 9 ensure the opening of the mouth of Ta-Amen, so that she can speak in her own defense before the councils of the gods. The vignettes show her seated before a table of offerings. A priest performs the opening of the mouth ceremony with two implements, one ram-headed and the other an adze.[13] The rite is often shown performed on the mummy standing in front of the tomb and is intended to restore to it the faculties of communication that were enjoying during life, in fact to bring the mummy back to life (see "The Social Aspects of Death," p. 52).[14]

At the top of sheet 10, Ta-Amen offers a roll of papyrus to a god, ensuring that her name will never die; this vignette really illustrates the text of Spell 25, just below, which requests that she be remembered.[15] The text to the upper right of this scene ensures her access to magic during her passage through the Underworld (Spell 24). In the middle, Ta-Amen stands before a figure of the god Osiris, behind whom stands another god.[16] Below, she kneels in adoration, holding her heart, before two gods sitting on a plinth.[17] The text beside her reaffirms her possession of her own heart in the Netherworld, especially significant because it is the central element in the weighing scene on sheet one (Spell 26).

In the illustration beside the continuation of Spell 26 on sheet 11, the deceased stands, again holding her heart, before a figure or statue of her ba, which is shaded by a fan.[18] Below, the vignette for Spell 30 shows Ta-Amen revering a large heart scarab. To the right Spell 27 again ensures that her heart will remain with her and be loyal to her during the judgment.[19] Ta-Amen stands before a picture of the sun, in red, at the bottom of the sheet. On the other side of the sun is another large heart scarab. This vignette is attested in later periods for Spell 64,[20] but here it appears beside Spell 28, in which the deceased requests that her breast (i.e., chest) not be taken away.[21] This fear of the loss of internal organs in the chest cavity is probably related to the fear, expressed in Spell 90, of loss of coherent speech, since the heart and breast were considered to be the seats of the intellect.

Opposite the continuation of Spell 28 on sheet 12, Ta-Amen stands, holding her heart, before a table on which rests, again, her heart, this time painted in red. On a plinth facing the table rests a divine figure.[22] Spell 117, presented below, contains a charm for traversing the road in the Underworld, called Rosetau. In the accompanying scene, Ta-Amen appears before an open shrine, holding a sail that guarantees the ability to breathe in the afterlife. Sails are common motifs in the vignettes of Spells 54-56. Normally with this chapter there is an illustration of Anubis leading the deceased down a road to the tomb chapel. Spell 118 identifies the deceased with Osiris again,

and the vignette showing Ta-Amen walking away from her tomb probably belongs with the text at the bottom of the page, Spell 119, which was intended to enable the deceased to come and go freely after death.[23] Opposite Spell 119, Ta-Amen bows before a shrine with an open door, which may be intended to contain an image of Osiris.[24]

Only the last portion of Spell 127 appears on sheet 13, reiterating the triumph of Ta-Amen and the opening of the gates barring her from eternity. Spell 128 is a hymn in honor of Osiris, accompanied by an illustration showing Ta-Amen adoring a scene in which Horus offers life to his father Osiris. Behind Osiris stands the wife and mother par excellence, Isis. The hymn identifies Ta-Amen with Horus, victorious in the tribunal and savior of his father. Although it is a bit unusual for the spell, the vignette is very appropriate.[25]

On sheet 14, Ta-Amen punts a boats containing the sun god and a phoenix toward the eastern shore of the river on which stands a figure of Osiris and a djed pillar.[26] The incomplete text ensures that she can enter the sun god's boat and traverse the heavens daily with him. The missing first part, a justification for her request, states that the deceased has already ferried the phoenix to the east and Osiris to Busiris (Spell 129). Below, Ta-Amen kneels in prayer before before the falcon-headed Re, seated within his red disk. "May the heavens open! May earth open! May the east and west open...for Re when he goes forth from the horizon," she chants in this long prayer during which the deceased reiterates her identity with Re and Osiris (Spell 130).[27]

At the conclusion of Spell 130 in sheet 16 the text, in order to reinforce its power and authenticity, says that a copy of it had been found in a palace of a king "just as though (it had been) found in a mountain cavern," and that this was the very spell which Horus used for his father Osiris. Next appears the title "Spell for proceeding to heaven at the side of Re," with a vignette showing the papyrus' owner standing beneath the hieroglyphic sign for heaven before a sun with streaming rays "(I am) Re who shines in the night," she proclaims (Spell 131).

On sheet 17, an illustration of Ta-Amen standing before a small house entrance accompanies a recitation enabling her to "turn around (to) see his (sic!) house (in the necropolis)" (Spell 132).[28] The following chapter, 133, and those subsequent to it are without vignettes, probably so that more texts can be be included. Spell 133 is called a spell for making the spirit worthy and contains mythological references and glorifications of Re and Osiris.

One might have expected Chapter 1 to come at the beginning rather than at the end of the papyrus, and indeed many exam-

ples of this period follow a standard order of presentation. Nonetheless, only on sheet 18 do we find the title of the whole Book of the Dead: "Beginning of the utterances of going forth by day...to be said on the day of burial..." Later, Ta-Amen recalls her own burial ceremony ("The priest invokes for me my coffin and I hear (the reading of) my offering list"). She also describes being in the presence of the gods after death and exults in her newfound life ("I take whatever shape I want, wherever I wish to be").

Spell 2, a chapter for "going forth by day and living after death" concludes "he (sic!) goes forth by day to do whatever he wants on earth among the living." Spell 4 is a spell to enable Ta-Amen to "traverse all the roads in heaven and on earth." Spell 5 protects her from having to work in the afterlife and is reinforced by Spell 6, which ensures that a shawabti figure will perform any work required of Ta-Amen. Spell 7 provides her with the magic she needs to successfully negotiate the dreaded snake Apep, prominent in mythology as an enemy of the sun god.[29]

In Spell 10, a spell for "going forth in truth," the deceased says "I am equipped with millions of magic spells. I eat with my mouth, I excrete with my anus, for really I am a god, Lord of the Underworld." The Egyptian fear of reversals of role and function in the afterlife is quite evident here, where the spell magically provides assurance that the natural order of things will not be changed after death.[30] In the next chapter (Spell 12) is mentioned the balance of Re "in which he weighs truth every day," a clear reference to the earliest of the myths of litigation and judgment that later developed into the weighing scene. There follows a recitation for permitting freedom of movement after death (Spell 13). At the end of it are instructions for use use: "Recite over a pill from the 'life-is-therein' plant and put it at the right ear of the blessed one; on the burial day put another pill in the linen wrappings (of the mummy) on which the name has been written." A spell for keeping the gods from being angry at Ta-Amen follows (Spell 14), and the papyrus ends with a short hymn to Atum, the sun as it sets in the west (Spell 15i).[31]

SD

1. Lieblein 1871, no. 1311 and Lieblein 1892, p. 893 no. 2385; Porter and Moss 1978, p. 505; Porter and Moss 1979, pp. 746, 748; Porter and Moss 1981, pp. 812, 817, 969; Ranke 1935, pp. 357, 10.
2. Desroches-Noblecourt 1986, pp. 195-196; Gitton 1976, pp. 34 ff.; Sauneron 1957, p. 67.
3. Paralleled in Ranke 1935, p. 397, 19.
4. The scene bears a very close resemblance in many small details to that in Louvre 3079, the Persian Ptolemaic papyrus of Dd-hr (Davis 1894, pl. XXXVIII).
5. Re is even present in the Osirian judgment scene in BM 10471/11 (Faulkner 1985, p. 28).

6. Griffiths 1960, pp. 54 ff.; Drioton 1949; Spiegel 1935; see Seeber 1978 for additional bibliography.
7. Davis 1894, Turin papyrus, pl. LIL 3079, pl. XX. For the baboons' hymn to the sun god in the morning, see Parker *et al.* 1979, pp. 37 ff.; Doll 1978, pp. 17 ff.; Zandee 1960, p. 272.
8. Davis 1894, Turin, pl. LI.
9. Naville 1886, pl. XXI.
10. Faulkner 1985, pp. 42-43; Davis 1894, Turin, pl. VI; Allen 1960, pl. XIII.
11. Davis 1894, L. 3079, pl. vi, Turin, pl. XI-XIII. For the enemies, see Zandee 1960, pp. 217-224.
12. Davis 1894, L 3079, pl. VII
13. Davis 1894, L 3079, pl. VII; Faulkner 1985, p. 53.
14. Papyrus of Hunefer in Rossiter 1979, p. 85.
15. Faulkner 1985, p. 52; Davis 1894, Turin, pl. XV
16. This also illustrates B.D. 25; cf. Naville 1886, pl. XXXVI, Ax.
17. Davis 1894, Turin, pl. XV; Faulkner 1985, p. 53.
18. Davis 1894, Turin, pl. XV; Faulkner 1985, p. 52.
19. Davis 1894, Turin, pl. XVI; Faulkner 1985, p. 53. B.D. 30, represented in the vignette, is one of the spells engraved on popular amuletic heart scarabs (cf. cats. 176 and 177), albeit 30A and 30B are more common.
20. Doll 1978, pp. 314-316.
21. For an example of the physical juxtaposition of the two chapters in a papyrus that otherwise follows the standardized order of presentation, see Allen 1960, pl. XIX.
22. The usual vignette for this period; cf. Faulkner 1985, Allen 1960, pl. XVIII.
23. Davis 1894, Turin, pl. XLIV; Faulkner 1985, p. 114.
24. Naville 1886, pl. CXXX, Pj.
25. Cf. Allen 1960, pl. XXXVI.
26. For the Djed pillar, see cat. 129, Davis 1894, Turin, pl. XXXVII and LII; Faulkner 1985, pp. 120-121.
27. This illustration is found in other papyri in connection with Spells 131 and 133 (Allen 1960, pl. XXXVII; Davis 1894, Turin, pl. LIV).
28. Allen 1960, pl. XXXVIII; Davis 1894, Turin, pl. LIV.
29. For Apep, see Bonnet 1952, pp. 51-54; Piankoff 1954, pp. 137 ff.; Hornung 1982, pp. 158 ff.
30. Zandee 1960, pp. 73-78.
31. Allen 1974, pp. 15-16.

135

135
Figures of the Four Sons of Horus

Provenance unknown
Late Period, Dynasty 25 or later
Faience
Height 7.2-7.4 cm.
Gift of Mrs. S.D. Warren, 1894 (94.255-58)

Protective amulets of deities, particularly the canopic deities, were often placed within the wrappings of Egyptian mummies (cat. 172). In Dynasty 25, figures of these deities were sometimes sewn onto the outside of the mummies, or incorporated into beadnets, as can be seen on the mummy of Nes-mut-aat-neru (cat. 125). These four examples were rather crudely composed in blue-green faience. The figures are represented as mummiform,

with wigs whose lappets extend over the shoulders. Small holes in the heads and feet indicate that they were sewn onto the mummy.[1]

SD'A

1. For similar examples, see Randall-MacIver and Mace 1902, pl. LII; Andrews 1984, figs. 27, 37; Bietak and Reiser-Haslauer 1982, taf. 140-141.

136

136
Winged scarab

Provenance unknown
Late Period, Dynasty 25 or later
Faience
Width 17.5 cm.
Hay Collection, Gift of C. Granville Way, 1872 (72.3019)

Molded in a material identified as glassy faience[1] with surface details emphasized with a point, this flattened and rather schematically modeled scarab is a good example of the funerary jewelry that was mass-produced during the first millennium B.C. A series of holes in the edges of the scarab and

its separately formed wings were employed to incorporate the amulet into a bead-work shroud[2] or to attach it directly to the mummy bandages. Unlike the earlier heart scarabs, the base is uninscribed, and its amuletic effectiveness rests solely upon its form.

CNR

1. Kaczmarczyk and Hedges 1983, pp. 212-214
2. Cf., for example, Schmidt 1919, p. 176, fig. 972; p. 178, fig. 992; Dawson and Gray 1968, pl. VII, c, 25 (EA 6669)

Bibliography: Hay 1869, p. 100, no. 865.

137
Canopic jars of Horemakhet

From Giza tomb 7524A
Late Period
Calcite
Height 21.5 cm., diam. 11.5 cm.
Harvard University-Museum of Fine Arts Expedition, (29.1133-36a,b)

Toward the end of Dynasty 25 the use of canopic jars to preserve the internal organs of the deceased after mummification was revived. At the same time a more elaborate prayer formula was developed, varying only according to the son of Horus to which the jar was dedicated.[1] This standard set of prayers was inscribed on jars from late Dynasty 25 to the end of the Pharaonic Period, so jars of the Late Dynastic Period are easily identified. The set exhibited here is made of yellowish white calcite interbedded with a layer of soft white aragonite.

The various heads are not carefully carved,

the features only summarily indicated and the throat covered by the wig, in the style of this period. Sets of jars with the various animal heads or with only human heads are both attested at this time. The jars themselves are ovoid;[2] their surfaces are not highly polished, and are even pitted in places. The bottoms of the jars are very roughly pecked out. The inscriptions name the owner of this set of jars as Horemakhet, son of Hebedru (his mother). The name of his father is not given, and no titles of the owner are indicated. These jars contain the dried residue of unguents. The internal organs were usually wrapped in linen and put in such jars, which were then filled with unguents.

MLB

1. Sethe 1934, pp. 12*-15*, Type XIX.
2. Reisner 1899, pp. 70-71.

Bibliography: Brovarski 1978, pp. 151-162.

138
Fragment of funerary relief

Provenance unknown
Late Period, Dynasty 30, fourth century B.C.
Limestone
Height 33 cm., width 15 cm.
Egyptian Curator's Fund, 1976 (1976.140)

The material, the use of raised relief, and the scale all suggest that this limestone relief fragment was part of the decoration of a tomb, rather than a temple wall or a naos. To judge from the horizontal lines at top and bottom, the relief represents the full height of a register, in which a woman faces left, before a boxlike structure slightly taller than she. Her head is thrown back, and her raised arms are bent at the elbows, so that

the forearms seem to rest against the side of the structure. Her body is rendered in profile, the far shoulder concealed. The far arm appears to be higher than the near arm, their apparent asymmetry a conventional device used to show them both, and to make the gesture explicit. In each clenched fist, the woman holds the end of a long, thin, curved object, which appears to arise from (or end at) the top of her head.

As is the case with most two-dimensional representations of Egyptian women, the far foot of this figure is slightly advanced. On her near foot, the toes (somewhat obscured by surface abrasion) are rather summarily indicated. Like the structure before her, she stands, not on the base line of the register, but on some kind of low platform. Though flat for most of its preserved length, the upper surface of this footing begins to rise just behind the woman's near heel, in a shallow curve that seems to flatten at the right edge of the fragment. Above this curve, a second appears to begin at the same spot behind the woman's heel. It rises more steeply; at the point where it is broken by the edge of the stone, it is already higher than the hem of dress, and its angle of ascent seems to be increasing.

The date of this relief is fairly clear, although it must be postulated almost entirely on the style of the woman's figure. As Spiegelberg recognized in his original publication of the fragment sixty years ago, it is a product of the Late Period.[1] The rather thick female body, with its heavy breast and thighs, and the prominent, slightly pointed buttock, derives from a figure type of Dynasty 26.[2] But the bulging abdomen, in which the navel is shown as a large, shallow dish, encircled by a ring of flesh, is a later development. It is a

138

mannerism characteristic of Dynasty 30 and the Ptolemaic Period, which is sometimes mistakenly ascribed to Greek influence.[3] As Spiegelberg observed, the details of the anatomical rendering here closely parallel the treatment of the female figures on a Dynasty 30 relief from the Memphite tomb of Nefer-seshem-Psamtik, now in Cairo.[4] The two reliefs would seem to be very close, in both time and place.

The face is lean, and sober in expression. There is nothing of the smiling plumpness of the faces on the Nefer-seshem-Psamtik reliefs and most other reliefs of the fourth century B.C. This may be partly because the sculptor was not entirely comfortable placing a face at such an angle to the body: he has shown a certain awkwardness in aligning forehead and chin. But he has also distinguished the face by giving it extended cosmetic eyebrow and eyelid lines, which lend the features a formality rare for mere mortals in this period. It is a distinctly archaizing touch; together with the enigmatic quality of the woman's gesture, it probably explains why Spiegelberg, despite his recognition of its resemblance to the style of the Nefer-seshem-Psamtik reliefs, assigned this fragment to the more overtly archaizing period of Dynasty 26.[5]

Spiegelberg interpreted the two curved lines as stylized strands of hair, which the woman pulls or tears in a gesture of mourning. The surface in front of her is the wall of a tomb or a shrine, and the scene from

137

which the fragment was broken must have represented the funeral procession or final rites of the owner of the tomb.[6]

Many details of the fragment seem to support this interpretation, although what has so far been published of fourth-century tomb reliefs (a rather neglected subject)[7] yields remarkably little in the way of explicitly funerary motifs. That they did exist is demonstrated by the tomb of Petosiris at Tuna el Gebel, where the inner chapel is largely devoted to scenes of funeral and funerary cult.[8] While no scenes or poses there can be compared with this relief, the conservative, archaizing style of Petosiris's funerary reliefs – as compared with other subjects in the outer chapel, or even on the dados of the inner rooms[9] – demonstrates the survival of an old Egyptian tendency to render funerary subjects in a deliberately old-fashioned or antique way. This tendency may well explain the archaizing formality of the face on the relief fragment here.

If the woman is a mourner, the curved lines behind her feet might be the rising hills of a desert necropolis or, more likely, the upturned front of a shrine bark or the sledge on which it was towed to the necropolis.[10] The box is the shrine or bier containing the coffin and mummy. Though usually shown with the architectural details and decoration of a shrine, this could be represented as a simple box.[11] In tomb paintings of late Dynasty 18, with their elaborate representations of the burial rites, full of lively and poignant details, the bier was often represented on its way to the tomb, accompanied by sorrowing women of the household. In at least one case, a daughter stands before the bier very much as the figure stands, though without her gesture of hands and hair.[12] Representations of this kind served as models for the archaizing tomb reliefs of Dynasties 25 and 26.[13] They, in turn, would have been the forerunners of a relief like this.[14]

Nonetheless, questions remain. There is no denying that the two strands of hair, if that is what they are, have been shown in a surprisingly schematic manner. The Egyptians were usually very careful in depicting hair, which not only indicated social status, but had symbolic meanings as well.[15] For renderings as unrealistic as this, it is necessary to turn to depictions of certain gods of the Afterworld, who are shown grasping long, thin, curved strand of their hair, thrown forward in a gesture of mourning.[16]

However, tugging at the hair, or yanking it out, is not at all common in Egyptian representations of human mourners. Men do seem to be shown tearing their hair on at least one Old Kingdom example,[17] but there is little or no evidence of women doing so in any period. Dynasty 18 tomb paintings show them tossing their disheveled locks,[18] or casting dirt on their heads,[19] and these gestures are repeated in Dynasty 26 revivals of mourning scenes.[20] It may be significant that Herodotus, while noting that bereaved men did not cut their hair,[21] and that grieving women plastered mud on their heads and faces,[22] makes no reference to mourners tearing their hair. The representation on this fragment remains enigmatic, therefore, and its true interpretation is likely still to be elucidated.

ERR

1. Spiegelberg 1928.
2. James and Davies 1983, p. 54, fig 60.
3. Smith 1981, p. 416.
4. Saleh and Sourouzian 1987, no. 258.
5. Spiegelberg 1928, p. 104.
6. Spiegelberg 1928, pp. 102, 104.
7. Smith 1981, pp. 418-420; but see now Leahy 1985, p. 128, n. 31.
8. Porter and Moss 1934, pp. 169-174.
9. Lefebvre 1923, cf. pls. 28-30, 41, 49, 52 with pls. 35, 38, 46.
10. Davies 1925, pl. 25.
11. Lhote 1954, pl. 15.
12. Davies 1925, pl. 25.
13. Müller 1975, p. 134, figs 11-28, especially figs. 25, 26; Brooklyn 1956, pls. 58-59.
14. Cf. Smith 1981, p. 419.
15. Derchain 1975.
16. Piankoff 1954, pls. 12, 13; cf. Hornung 1972, p. 328.
17. Werbrouck 1938, fig. 1.
18. Mekhitarian 1954, p. 45.
19. Davies 1925, pl. 21; Lhote 1954, pl. 22.
20. Müller 1975, figs. 25, 26; Brooklyn 1956, pl. 59.
21. Herodotus II, 36; Lloyd 1976, pp. 152-154.
22. Herodotus II, 85; Lloyd 1976, pp. 351-352.

Bibliography: Sotheby 1976, lot 48; Spiegelberg 1928.

Ptolemaic Period

139

139
Mask from a mummiform sarcophagus

Provenance unknown
Ptolemaic Period, about 200 B.C.
Limestone
Height 48 cm., width 51 cm.
Purchased from the Egyptian Antiquities
Service, 1912 (12.1511)

This fragment of a limestone sarcophagus
consists essentially of a mask with a plain
enveloping wig, broken off at the level of
the neck. The face has been carved with
some care, particularly around the eyes and
mouth. No beard is indicated and the chin is
raised from the neck, showing that the
piece is certainly not of Delta origin, where
a flatter style of mask was in vogue.[1] The
sarcophagus belongs to a class that evolved
in Dynasty 30, and continued in use well
into the Ptolemaic Period. Some dated examples were found by Petrie in Cemetery G
at Abydos,[2] belonging to Dynasty 30, and
later sarcophagi of the same type are recorded from Qau and Akhmim.[3] They usually bear inscriptions down the front in vertical columns, and additional decoration could
be provided at the sides in the form of representations of the Four Sons of Horus or
other funerary deities.[4] Large *wesekh*-col-
lars with falcon-headed terminals are also a
feature of certain examples of this type of
sarcophagus. Many uninscribed sarcophagi
of this shape and material are known; they
may be unfinished, or the painted decoration has not survived.[5]

AJS

1. Buhl 1959, pp. 196-215.
2. Petrie 1902, pp. 34ff., pls. 75, 79, 7.
3. Buhl 1959, nos. Ea20, Eb6, Eb22, Fb3.
4. Buhl 1959, nos. Eb6, Eb9, Eb15, Eb20.
5. Note the faded painted inscription on Buhl
   1959, No. E b 22.

140
Mummy trappings

Provenance unknown
Ptolemaic Period
Polychrome and gilt cartonnage
Gift of Horace L. Mayer, 1959 (59.1071)

a. Pectoral
   Length 28.2 cm., width 13.1 cm., depth .2 cm.
b. Apron
   Length 33.6 cm., width 14 cm., depth .2 cm.
c. Sandal with yellow and green stripes
   Length 23 cm., max. width 8.4 cm., depth .015
   cm.
d. Sandal with yellow and black stripes
   Length 23.9 cm., max. width 7.7 cm.; depth
   .30 cm.

Cartonnage is a layering of linen that has
been soaked in a thin adhesive solution. After being molded into the desired form, the
composite then dries and hardens. Waste
papyrus was sometimes substituted for
linen in the Ptolemaic Period, beginning in
the reign of Ptolemy II. In the process, important classical documents were often in-
advertently preserved.[1]

In pharaonic times cartonnage cases were
made as one-piece mummiform shells that
enveloped the entire body. This type of
case lasted for several hundred years, until
the early Ptolemaic Period.[2] At this stage a
dramatic change in the cartonnage style can
be observed. In place of the solid case, the
new form was composed of four to six individual sections of brightly painted cartonnage that were sewn onto the shroud of the
mummy and held in place by retaining bandages.[3] Clearly there was a practical advantage to this innovation, as the pieces of
cartonnage would fit any size mummy, and
could be mass-produced. Some evidence
suggests that this trend actually had its origins as early as Dynasty 26;[4] however, it is
primarily the Ptolemaic mummies that exhibit this unique cartonnage design.

The basic components of this type of
cartonnage are: the mask, covering the face
and head; the pectoral, frequently decorated with a *wesekh* collar; the apron laying
over the legs; and the boot enclosing the
feet and ankles. Two additional pieces may
be found that cover the rib cage and
stomach.[5]

This ensemble of cartonnage sections is obviously incomplete, as the mask and boot
are missing. These were the most fragile elements of the cartonnage grouping, be-

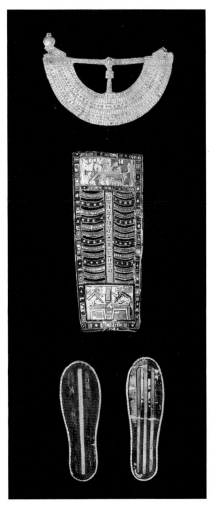

140

cause of their molded shape. Three additional sets of cartonnage in Boston are missing these same two portions.[6]

The pieces that comprise this group are the pectoral, the apron, and sandal soles. The gilt pectoral bears a six-stranded *wesekh* collar with two large falcon terminals. The falcon on the right is missing its head. An image of a *djed* shaped counterpoise, used to balance the weight of a necklace, is suspended from a loop at the back of the necklace.[7]

The long rectangular apron is finely detailed, with much of the gilding still intact. There are short horizontal pierced slits in rows down both sides of the leg cover. This decorative technique is not common, but can be attributed to the Ptolemaic Period.[8]

At the top of the apron is a classic scene from the funerary ritual, depicting Anubis performing rites over the mummy, which lies on a lion-shaped funerary bed (see cat. 171), as the mourners Isis and Nephthys look on protectively. At the bottom of the apron is another image of Anubis, this time as a jackal resting on top of a shrine. The short vertical registers above the heads of the gods, which normally contain their names, are blank. This may indicate that these pieces were hastily produced in quantity, a possibility also suggested by some sections of cartonnage that have been found in which there are blank spaces in the inscriptions where the names of the deceased were to be inserted.[9]

The two sandal soles are not part of the exterior cartonnage ensemble; they were likely found inside the boot bandaged on the feet of the mummy.[10] One sole is clearly longer and thicker than the other, and is painted with different colored stripes. This difference may also be attributed to mass-production.

A black painted vertical inscription that runs down the center of the apron identifies the deceased as Keru born of Im-hotep,[11] and records a typical request to the great god for offerings.

JLH

1. Engelbach 1946, p. 237; Andrews 1984, p. 27 cites 305 B.C.
2. Niwinski 1983, p. 448, states that the one-piece case began in Dynasty 22.
3. Dawson 1929, p. 188; David 1979, p. 85, fig. 3-4 shows bandages in pl. over the cartonnage sections.
4. Niwinski 1983, p. 458, fn. 81; Bietak and Reiser-Haslauer 1982, abb. 94 depicts a Dynasty 26 mummy with the cartonnage sections on it.
5. For discussion about these component parts of Ptolemaic cartonnage see: David 1979, pp. 36-37; Dawson 1929, p. 189; Dawson and Gray 1968, p. 24, fn. 7; Elliot-Smith and Dawson, 1924, p. 143; Engelbach 1946, p. 237; Gray 1966, p. 19; Niwinski 1983, pp. 458-459; Peet 1914, p. 92 (He notes six pieces of cartonnage, whereas all the above references

identify four); Scott 1986, pp. 160-161 (he notes six pieces as well).
6. MFA 57.765-766 (see also Schmidt 1919, no. 1415, 1416, 1418, 1506).
7. For this attachment of counterpoise, Saleh and Sourouzian 1987, no. 114.
8. Niwinski 1983, footnote 83.
9. Peet 1914, p. 92.
10. Bietak and Reiser-Haslauer 1982, p. 214; David 1979, fig. 16, p. 92 depicts similar sandal soles.
11. Meeks 1982 (130.79.1338) notes that *ms n* is translated as "né de" whereas *mst n* is "née de." The fact that the verb "born of" is written *mst* instead of *ms* likely indicates that the preceding name is feminine. The name Keru is not attested in Ranke 1935, however a feminine name Kerut is known from a recent excavation in the Asasif in the Theban Necropolis, which dates from Dynasty 30 through the Ptolemaic Period (Bietak and Reiser-Haslauer 1982, p. 281). It is possible that our writing Keru is a variant spelling of that known feminine name. The name Im-hotep may be the name of the mother or the father, as Im-hotep may be an alternate writing of the feminine name Im-hotepet attested in Ranke 1935 in the Greek Period.

141a

141b

141
Mummy trappings

Provenance unknown
Ptolemaic to Roman Periods
Polychrome cartonnage
Hay Collection, Gift of C. Granville Way (unaccessioned)

a. Ba bird
   Length 40 cm., height 29 cm.
b. Scarab
   Length 45 cm., height 13 cm.

Images of winged scarabs protecting the mummy or *ba* birds hovering over it are common funerary symbols relating to rebirth and eternal life. Throughout Egyptian history these images have been created in a variety of forms and materials, from bead-work and finely wrought gold to simple painted examples on cartonnage.

This *ba* bird and scarab are made out of flat polychrome cartonnage panels, and represent the final stage in the long evolution of pharaonic funerary trappings. The cartonnage mummiform cases of pharaonic times had evolved, by the Ptolemaic Period, into several separate units of cartonnage sewn to the exterior of the mummy bandages (see cat. 140). Aside from the three-dimensional mask and foot covering, each piece of cartonnage was a flat, polychrome panel. These lay over the chest, abdomen, and legs. Although the border of the *wesekh* collar lying on the chest was curved along the bottom edge, the other panels were basically rectangular. However, in a few cases the rectilinear confines were abandoned and the cartonnage panels were cut in the shape of protective deities or symbols. The image could be partially cut out, like the scarab on the mummy of a Djed-hor,[1] or completely cut out, like the *ba* bird on the chest of a female mummy dating to the second century A.D.[2] The *ba* bird and scarab appear to have been completely cut out.

The human-headed *ba* bird is crowned with a sun disk and has large outstretched wings. The details of the individual feathers are outlined in black over the brightly painted body and wings. The bird clasps in its feet two large feathers, symbols of Maat, the goddess of truth and order.

The top portion of the slender feathers is missing, no doubt owing to their precarious position above the wing tops. About five centimeters of the end of the bird's left wing are also missing. One reason for this is the manner in which the bird was attached to the mummy bandages: threads on the underside of the cartonnage on the end of the right wing indicate that the wing tips were attachment points. These areas could easily be broken off when the cartonnage was removed from the body. Note that the same attachment point, namely the edges of the wings, are missing from the scarab as well.

The winged scarab is executed in much the same way as the *ba* bird. It is carefully drawn, with each anatomical feature – clypeus, prothorax, elytra and legs – detailed in black. The ends of the fragile and unsupported front and back legs are now missing. The wing span is forty-five centimeters, which approximates the original measurements of the *ba* bird.

Both objects are predominately light and dark khaki, with some bright green, blue, and orange. The clear pink used for the face of the *ba* bird is not in keeping with the pharaonic artistic canon of yellow for women's skin and reddish-brown for men's, and the overall coloring is more in keeping with the Ptolemaic and Roman palette.[3] The *ba* bird and the scarab doubtless came from the same artistic workshop, and perhaps the same cartonnage ensemble, as is evidenced by such similarities in style, size, and coloring.

Large winged images such as these are commonly found on the chest or the abdomen; both placements can be verified in the cartonnage panels,[4] as well as in the earlier Saite beadwork.[5] Assuming that the two cartonnage pieces in Boston were originally placed on the same mummy, their combined height would have exceeded forty-two centimeters, and they would have covered much of the mummy's chest and abdomen.

Pieces of cartonnage sewn on the mummy in the Ptolemaic and Roman Periods often served as replacements for the full-size polychrome coffins. Further, the individual cut-out images, such as the *ba* bird and scarab from Boston, can be viewed as substitutes for more expensive gold amulets, or the beaded images that were popular in the Saite Period.

JLH

1. Dawson and Gray 1968, pl. 12c; for other examples, Schmidt 1919, p. 241, fig. 1412; p. 242, fig. 1416; p. 244, fig. 1417.
2. British Museum no. 6707 (reference provided by Peter Lacovara); other illustrations, Dawson and Gray 1968, pl. 12c; Schmidt 1919, fig. 1416, 1506-1508. Personal correspondence from Carol Andrews also notes that "a crude example is part of the molded cartonnage coffin EA 29590 from Akhmim, 21nd century A.D.
3. Zaloscer 1961.
4. For scarabs on cartonnage worn above the *wesekh* collar, Gray 1966, pl. 29.1; Dawson and Gray 1968, pl. 12a; for scarabs on cartonnage worn over the abdomen, Elliot-Smith and Dawson 1924, frontispiece; Dawson and Gray 1968, pl. 12b; for *ba* bird on cartonnage above the *wesekh* collar, Schmidt 1919, p. 242, fig. 1416.
5. For winged scarabs on bead networks at chest level, Gray 1966, pl. 14.2, 16.2, 19.2; Schmidt 1919, p. 189. fig. 1035; for scarabs on bead networks with *ba* bird at chest, Gray 1966, pl. 24.2; the same on the abdomen, Gray 1966, pl. 24.4, pl. 29.2

142a, obverse

142b, obverse

142a, reverse

142b, reverse

142
Coins

From a burial in the forecourt of Mycerinus's Pyramid Temple at Giza Harvard University-Museum of Fine Arts Expedition, 1911

a. Imitation Athenian tetradrachm
Probably mined in Egypt about 390-350 B.C.
Silver
Weight 16.6 g., diam. 2.4 cm. (11.826)
b. Ptolemaic coin
Minted at Alexandria, probably under Ptolemy I, Soter, 305-283 B.C.
Bronze
Weight 17.52 g., diam. 2.9 cm. (11.827)

The obverse of 142a bears the head of Athena wearing an Athenian helmet with a horsehair plume. On the bowl of the helmet are three upright olive leaves and a palmette spray. Athena wears disk earrings and two necklaces. On the reverse within a rounded incuse is an owl, a crescent moon and an olive spray. The Greek inscription "Athe" asserts an Athenian origin. A mark, perhaps for centering, appears in front of the owl. The edge is deformed by two or three chisel cuts, probably made by a prudent recipient to determine the quality of the metal.

One of the first coins to become widely known in the Eastern Mediterranean was the tetradrachm of Athens. It became such a generally accepted medium of exchange, used particularly for the payment of merce-

nary troops, that when coins began to be minted in Egypt in the fifth century, the form and weight of the Athenian coin was copied exactly.[1] Dies for minting Athenian coins have, in fact, been found in Egypt.[2]

This piece betrays itself as an ancient forgery through its generally clumsy style, visible particularly at the base of the helmet's crest, and because of its rounded border ridge, which takes the place of the square Athenian incuse reverse.[3] The design adheres closely to the archaic designs of the fifth century, but eye is seen in profile, as on Athenian production of the fourth century.

Coins were put in the mouths of the deceased in the Greek world to serve as "Charon's Fee": that is, to pay the boatman of the Underworld for passage across the Styx. Around 400 B.C. the Athenian writer of comedies Aristophanes mentions a fee of two obols, but the usual fee seems to have been an obol.[4] This tetradrachm, equivalent to twenty-four obols, represents quite a lavish payment, which may reflect either the absence of small change in Egypt at this time or, perhaps, a sense of distance from the entrance to the Underworld; according to Strabo, a place like Hermione, deemed to be located close to Hades, required no fee at all.[5] A number of Greek and Egyptian coins were discovered in a cache of Ptolemaic burials within the forecourt of the Mycerinus Pyramid Temple at Giza, one still held in the hand of a mummy.[6]

The obverse of 142b bears the laureate head of Zeus in a dotted border. On the reverse, an eagle holds a thunderbolt in his talons. The Greek inscription reads "of King Ptolemy." Two illegible monograms, possibly alpha pi and epsilon pi, appear in front of the eagle.

This type of coin was introduced under the first Ptolemy after his assumption of the royal title in 305 B.C. The eagle and the thunderbolt were not only the attributes of Zeus but also served as Ptolemy's personal coat of arms. The type continued to be minted for centuries, but stylistically, this example seems early. The damaged monograms[7] also suggest this chronology.

The practice of placing a coin in the mouth of the deceased became particularly common in the Greek world during the Hellenistic period. This relatively low-value bronze is typical of the denominations used.

JH

1. Kraay 1976, p. 73, fig. 204.
2. Vermeule 1954, pp. 10ff.
3. Cornelius Vermeule independently came to the view that the coin is an imitation.
4. Aristophanes 1961, lines 140, 270; cited in Kurtz and Boardman 1971, p. 211; see also pp. 163, 166, 204, 216, 331.
5. Strabo 1927, vol. 4, p. 171; Kurtz and Boardman 1971, p. 211.
6. Reisner 1931, p. 20.
7. Compare Svoronos 1908, no. 292, pl. X, 12; Kromann and Mørkholm 1977, no. 83-84.

143
Canopic chest

Provenance unknown
Ptolemaic Period (332-331 B.C.)
Wood
Height   cm.
Purchase of W.T. Ready through M.S. Prichard, 1898 (98.1128)

This wooden box represents a typically Egyptian shrine or *naos*, with its protruding base, tapering walls, and cavetto cornice. The flat lid is guarded by the figurine of a mummified falcon with feather headdress – a characteristic depiction of Sokar, patron god of the Memphite necropolis, who is often shown in this position on the roof of the tomb of Osiris. Thus, the shrine is associated with the famous Osireion. The foot of the walls is protected by a continuous enclosure rendered by the panelled *serekh* pattern. Four rows of squatting gods form an inner precinct. Above, all four walls comprise a figured scene framed by another *naos* motif; this is surmounted by a winged sun disk and two antithetic griffins, likewise solar symbols. The scene of the front depicts the bolted double doors of the sanctuary, flanked by Anubis and Horus. The two side-walls show falcon-headed Horus ador-

143

ing the mummiform Sons of Horus: human-headed Imsety and baboon-headed Hapy on the left, jackal-headed Duamutef and falcon-headed Qebehsenef on the right. The scene on the rear wall represents the *djed* pillar of Osiris flanked by the kneeling Nephthys and Isis.

Boxes like this one have been recovered from a number of tombs of late date. The painted decoration usually comprises the Four Sons of Horus, in conjunction with various symbols of Osiris (*djed*, head on shrine) and Isis (*tyet*, uraeus, winged goddess), whereas the front shows a marked predilection for the door motif. Since the Sons of

Horus were associated with the viscera, this decoration strongly suggests that such objects served as canopic chests. This is corroborated by those rare finds where the contents of the boxes were still intact. In a number of instances these consisted of packages with the embalmed entrails of the deceased; in other cases, bags of salt or potsherds were found, apparently placed there in imitation of the proper custom.

These boxes are among the last known evidence of the age-old tradition of removing the viscera during mummification, a custom first observed in the burial of queen Hetepheres, mother of Khufu (2606-2583

B.C.). Usually the separately embalmed entrails were deposited in boxes or in four vases (the canopic jars), but from the reign of Ramesses V onward (1145-1141) these packages were also restored to the abdominal cavity or deposited between the legs of the mummy. Thus, the Late Dynastic canopic chests represent a revival of the ancient customs, a tendency most characteristic of the time. Occasionally, boxes of the types concerned here have been dated as early as Dynasties 21-26.[1] In fact, they are much later, Dynasty 30 to Ptolemaic, as is demonstrated by their achaeological context and by the style of their decorations. In this respect, one may point to the details like the two griffins[2] or the triangular garments of the mummiform deities[3] depicted on the Boston specimen. A date around 300 B.C. is most probable.

MJR

1. Dobrowolska 1970a, pp. 45-62.
2. Cf. stela Cairo CG 22084: Kamal 1904-1905, pl. XXVI; Barta 1973-1974, 347 no. 33; Munro 1973, p. 257.
3. Munro 1973, p. 180.

Literature: Dobrowolska 1970a; Dobrowolska 1970b; Bruwier forthcoming.

144
Ptah-Sokar-Osiris figure

Provenance unknown
Ptolemaic Period (332-31 B.C.)
Wood
Height 80 cm.
Museum of Fine Arts (03.1625a-d)

This mummiform wooden figurine depicts the god of resurrection, Ptah-Sokar-Osiris. The mummiform body is a well-known characteristic of Osiris, whereas the tall feather-crown is usually associated with the other two gods constituting the syncretistic unity concerned, the Memphite deities Ptah and Sokaris. The god is standing on a long rectangular base decorated with a painted frieze symbolizing "all life and dominion." The texts on the statue comprise a hymn to the patron of resurrection, who is equated with the deceased, a man named Hapy-meneh, the son of Padimahes.

Similar statues have been found in numerous private tombs dating to the later periods of Egyptian history. Yet this burial custom, like so many others of the same period, ultimately derived from traditions established long before, in the royal tombs of the New Kingdom. King Amenhotep II (1453-1419 B.C.) was the first pharaoh whose tomb equipment comprised a hollow mummiform statuette containing a rolled-up funerary papyrus. Such "papyrus-sheaths" became common in private tombs of Dynasty 21 (from 1070 B.C. on). They enveloped either a Book of the Dead manuscript or a so-

144, front

144, back

called Amduat papyrus. At first, these figurines were polychrome and shaped like the god Osiris; thus, the precious guidebooks to the hereafter were put in the protection of the Ruler of the Dead himself. Later, black statues became popular, often with feathered headdresses like the specimen here. This funerary custom gradually died down about 900 B.C., when solid statuettes became fashionable.

With the Egyptian "renaissance" of Dynasty 25 (from about 750 B.C. on), the ancient tradition became associated with new religious ideas. Instead of a papyrus roll, the mummiform statues now contained a miniature mummy made of clay and grains of barley (see cat. 211). This is another symbol of new life well-known from the royal tombs of the New Kingdom, where Osiris-shaped seed-beds of barley were deposited in order to ensure the king's resurrection. Similar "corn-mummies" were manufactured in the Ptolemaic period during elaborate temple rituals in the month Khoiak (see cat. 212). The Ptah-Sokar-Osiris figures express the same symbolism, now for the benefit of the private tomb-owner. Often they were made in two halves, hollowed out just like a coffin to contain the corn-mummy. On other types a miniature sarcophagus is fixed on the protruding base in front of the statues. This "burial-place of Osiris" is then protected by a wooden image of a falcon mummy, a depiction of the god Sokaris as patron of the necropolis. The hymn inscribed on the statues explicitly equates the fate of Osiris and that of the deceased.

MJR

Literature: Raven 1978-1979, pp. 251-296; Raven 1982, pp. 7-38.

145
Fragmentary ivy wreath

Provenance unknown
Hellenistic, fourth to first centuries B.C.
Gilded bronze with clay berries
Length of largest leaf 5.1 cm.
Gift of H.P. Kidder, 1881 (81.333)

In Greek custom, wreaths were frequently placed in tombs, probably reflecting the practice of adorning the dead for the funeral.[1] Wreaths of pure gold might be used, as they were in several tombs of northern Greece.[2] Gilded bronze wreaths were, of course, economical substitutes for pure gold. Gilded wreaths have been found in Egypt, placed on the shoulders of Hadra vases.[3] This example might have come from Crete,[4] but the provenance is uncertain, and an origin in Egypt, where such wreaths are definitely known, also seems possible. The preserved wreaths from Egypt seem to be laurel, but ivy, sacred to

145

the god Dionysos and, as an evergreen plant in the Mediterranean, a symbol of eternity, would be just as appropriate; ivy is frequently used in the decoration of Hadra vases.[5]

JH

1. On wreaths in a funerary setting, see Kurtz and Boardman 1971, pp. 101, 141, 144, 152, 163, 165, 207, 209f, 212, and 247.
2. Yalouris *et al.* 1980, nos. 60 and 173, pls. 11 and 36.
3. Breccia 1912, pl. 37, n. 47; Guerrini 1964, pl. 6, D19; Enklaar 1985, p. 110, n.26.
4. Comstock and Vermeule 1971, no. 253.
5. Enklaar 1985, figs. 5h, 6g-i, 7e, 8c, 10e, 12c, 15h-j, 16a, 17p, and 19e.

146
Jewelry

a. Ring
   Possibly from Damanhur
   Ptolemaic Period
   Gold and emerald
   Length 35 cm., max. diam. 29 cm.
   Edwin E. Jack Fund, 1963 (63.1247)
b. Pair of bracelets
   Provenance unknown
   Late Hellenistic or early Roman Imperial, around 40-20 B.C.
   Gold, pearls, and emeralds
   Max. diam. 6.1 cm. and 6.2 cm., height 6.4 cm.
   Classical Department Exchange Fund, 1981 (1981.287,288)

The setting of this ring is composed of two gold serpents intertwined around a central oval bezel with a raised beaded border. A large plano-convex emerald is set in the center of the piece, which is said to come from Damanhur in the Nile Delta.

The decorative elements of the ring, although popular throughout the Hellenistic world,[1] are rich in Egyptian funerary symbolism. Emeralds are frequently shown in jewelry on the encaustic mummy portraits of the era (see cat. 159), their green color undoubtedly associated with Osiris and rebirth.[2]

The snake itself is associated both with the creator god Atum (see cat. 196), as a celestial being[3] in Egyptian religion and in the Graeco-Egyptian cult of Isis-Demeter.[4]

PL

Each of the bracelets is composed of a band studded with two rows of pearls that is hinged to a complex cluster of ornament. Its central unit is made up of a large chalice surrounded by a pair of snakes coiling around pearl-studded discs. An oblong emerald decorates the wall of the chalice and a round emerald is suspended below it. The bearded snakes are crowned with a pearl. At either side of the central unit and above the large chalice, a framed emerald is surmounted by a small chalice and a pearl, and

below it hangs and ivy leaf and a pearl.

The bracelets are splendid examples of the rich polychromatic effects characteristic of the late Hellenistic period. Individual units of the composition are drawn clearly and boldly, but these building blocks are clustered and superimposed loosely and opulently.

A close parallel for the central symbol is found in coinage of the second half of the first century B.C. On on silver cistophoric medallions minted under Mark Antony in Asia Minor in 39 B.C.,[5] and on quinarii minted at Rome under Augustus in 29-26 B.C.[6] a pair of snakes are knotted together below and rise up on either side of a basket (rather than a chalice). In these numismatic compositions, a small figure stands on top of the basket: either Victory, the god Dionysos or the bust of Antony's wife Octavia. The basket and the snakes form the cista mystica, connected with the worship of Dionysos. Dionysiac imagery continues on the obverse of the cistophoric medallions, which are circled with an ivy wreath, and the same Dionysiac allusions reappear on the bracelets, which are embellished with ivy leaves.

Such bracelets could well have appeared in a tomb in the Delta of Egypt; where the snakes and emeralds would have had additional funerary significance (see above). Indeed, such snake bracelets are often depicted as being worn by the deceased on mummy shrouds of the Roman Period in Egypt.[7]

JH

146a

1. Cf. Hoffmann 1963.
2. Morenz 1962, p. 5.
3. Kákosy 1981.
4. Cf. Wildung and Grimm 1978, no. 151.
5. Grueber 1910, nos. 133-137, pp. 502-503, pl. 114; for a splendid example with Octavia, Vermeule 1981, p. 18.
6. Mattingly 1923, p. 105, no. 647, pls. 15 and 20; Sutherland 1984, p. 61, no. 276; Sutherland 1987, p. 12, fig. 5b.
7. Cf. Parlasca 1966, pl. 60/61.

Bibliography: Hoffmann 1963, p. 110; Deppert-Lippitz 1985, pl. 32; Herrmann 1987, pp. 78-79.

147
Offering table

From Dendera
Ptolemaic Period (332-331 B.C.)
Sandstone
Height 26 cm., width 26 cm.
Gift of Egypt Exploration Fund, 1898
(98.1057)

Offering tables were common features in the superstructures of Egyptian tombs dating from the Old Kingdom through the end of the Roman Period. They were either square or rectangular; a spout projecting from their top or bottom edges allowed poured offerings to run off them. The traditional shapes of a funerary stela (usually a round-topped rectangle) and the offering table, both important tomb furnishings, are combined in this piece, since a spout is carved within its rounded top. In all other ways, the piece is decorated like a traditional offering table of its period. The uninscribed table has some typical gifts of food and drink carved on its surface to help sustain the tomb owner(s) in the afterlife. Two oval loaves of bread appear on top of the table. Beneath them is a deeply cut, square basin to hold both the cool water shown pouring from the tall jars beside it and the drink offerings that would actually be poured upon the table. The decoration is completed by two tall stalks of lotus buds and blossoms on the outer side of each jar. Traces of the white paint which once filled the incised outlines of the decoration can still be seen. While there is chipping at its edges and the bottom left surface is damaged, the overall condition of this offering table is good.[1]

Because they were decorated with images of food and beverages, offering tables could magically ensure that the deceased would never lack for food and drink in the afterlife. Many were also inscribed with a standardized prayer to further guarantee their effectiveness in magically providing nourishment for the dead.

The decoration of this table is typical of the Ptolemaic and Roman Periods.[2] The loaves of bread and tall jars, which traditionally contain cool water, are very common.

147

The deeply carved basin into which the two jars are pouring water is less typical.[3] Carved inside the top edge of this basin are four steps rising slightly from left to right. These steps probably indicate that this basin represents a reservoir or a temple's sacred lake, emphasizing the idea that the offering table's owner will have an abundance of cool water in his or her afterlife. Tall lotus blossoms complete the decoration. Because the lotus grows in water, the Egyptians linked it with ideas of creation and the giving of life.[4] This made it a popular decoration for offering tables especially during the later periods of Egyptian history.

During the Late Period, the most important part of the ongoing rituals performed for the dead at their tombs was the giving of drink offerings. This is reflected in the decoration of the offering table with its water-grown lotus blossoms, cool water jars and reservoir (or sacred lake).

JY

1. Petrie 1900a, pl. 25A.
2. For example Cairo Museum CGC 23.193 and CGC 23.190, in Kamal 1941, p. 136-137, pl. 49.
3. For example Pushkin Museum of Fine Arts I. 1.a5344 (4137) and 1.a.5347 (4095), in Hodjash 1982, 154 and 155, pp. 217, 219, 221.
4. Drioton 1941, p. 81.

148
Ba bird statuettes

Provenance unknown
Probably Ptolemaic Period
Wood
Hay Collection, Gift of C. Granville Way, 1872

a. Height 10.2 cm., base length 9.8 cm., width 4 cm. (72.4178)
b. Height 10.2 cm., base length 9.5 cm., width 4 cm. (72.4179)

These two statuettes of *ba* birds, like most of their genre, are made of soft wood and brightly painted. Typically the sculptures are crude and hastily executed, possibly indicating that they were mass produced.

Each of the birds and its thin rectangular base is carved from one solid piece of wood. The decorated wings, legs, and talons are clearly formed. The human face shows some modeling, while the eyes and eyebrows are simply outlined in black paint. A black *djed* amulet is painted on the neck of 148b,[1] while a *wesekh* adorns 148a.[2]

A hole or peg in the center of the bottom of the base of 148b indicates the manner in which these images were affixed to other wooden objects.[3] Some New Kingdom two-dimensional representations show the *ba* birds on furniture and standards,[4] and some

148a

148b

While many examples of this type of sculpture exist, aside from those associated with the above mentioned Ptolemaic stelae, few have a provenance, making them extremely difficult to date. It is most probable that they are from the Ptolemaic Period.

JLH

1. Bonnet 1952, p. 76, fig. 23, Berlin 4679 shows a *ba* bird with similar *djed* amulet.
2. Annecy 1984, no. 281, shows a *ba* bird with a *wesekh* collar.
3. Annecy 1984, p. 132, no. 281, describes a "trou de fixation au centre de la base."
4. Baud and Drioton 1928, fig. 12, Dynasty 19, Kákosy 1980, p. 48ff.
5. Annecy 1984, p. 132.
6. Munro 1973, p. 243 BM 54343 from Thebes dated 3rd-2nd c. B.C.
7. See Gray and Slow 1968, p. 46, no. 66.
8. Cooney 1968, p. 267. However, wooden examples such as those mentioned in note 4, above, must have existed since New Kingdom times, but have not survived. Also, note the small stone amulet of a *ba* bird in Hornemann 1966, no. 1305 dated to the New Kingdom.
9. Edwards 1976, p. 23, no. 40.
10. Cooney 1968, p. 267, notes that the Meroitic examples "rank among the world's worst sculptures."

Bibliography: New Orleans 1977, no. 86.

149

"Hadra vase": cinerary urn in the form of a three-handled water jar (hydria)

Probably made in Crete
Hellenistic, about 250-220 B.C.
Height 34.3 cm.
Egyptian Curator's Fund in Memory of Felicia Kutten, 1985 (1985.864)

Hundreds of ceramic hydriai of this general form and decoration have been found in the cemeteries around Alexandria, including a funerary area near the village of Hadra, from which the group takes its name. Burial of cremated remains in a hydria is an old Greek custom, and these vases probably enclosed the ashes of Greeks, who began migrating to Egypt in great numbers after its conquest by Alexander the Great. Hydriai of this kind were produced from about 280 to 180 B.C. The custom, therefore, ends not long after the resurgence of native Egyptian culture in the late third century B.C.[1]

Many Hadra vases have also been found in traditionally Greek territories, particularly Attica, Euboia, Crete and Cyprus. It has been shown that the clay for most of the Egyptian examples comes from Crete. the increasing quantity of sherds of Hadra vases found on Crete has made it clear that the island must have been the center of production.[2]

This example is typical of the Laurel Workshop, by far the largest to produce Hadra vases. The shop takes it name from the lau-rel wreath that is almost invariably painted on the neck of the hydria.[3] On this piece, another wreath is framed by "wave" or "running spiral" patterns on the front of the body. Two broad bands of color flanked by lines set off the zone of the horizontal handles. The handles, in turn, are segregated by vertical laurel branches, which lack a central stem and are framed by lines. A ten-petalled palmette springing from scrolls hangs below the vertical handle at the rear. A ring of slip encircles the base of the neck and the top of the shoulder. The top of the rim and the foot are covered with slip.

The anonymous painter of this vase, who produced an almost identical hydria preserved in Alexandria,[4] was a bold, though run-of-the-mill, decorator. He paid little at-

149, front view

149, side view

scholars suggest that these Late Period *ba* birds were placed on shrines or coffins.[5]

One certain function of these sculptures is afforded by a group of Ptolemaic tomb stelae with small staircase supports, on whose summits the *ba* bird sculptures remain affixed.[6] No doubt, as with an example from Liverpool, many such wooden stelae exist from which the precarious *ba* sculpture has fallen.[7]

Examples of the *ba* bird as a sculpture in the round, made in wood or stone, are not common before Dynasty 26.[8] The fine wooden *ba* bird from the tomb of Tutankhamen is likely one of the earliest of its type.[9] Most commonly the *ba*-bird sculptures are found from the Saite Period through the second century A.D., with the latest examples deriving from the Meroitic culture.[10]

tention to detail; no ornament is used at the center of the wreaths, his hanging palmette and running spirals are very sketchy, and his horizontal bands of color are very loosely brushed. His interest was in creating bold tonal effects; unusually broad areas of color are juxtaposed with the plain background.

Hadra vases were probably made for funerary purposes, and their simple ornamentation is understandable in this context.[5] The endemic laurel wreath suggests either the embellishment of the dead for their funeral or the status of the deceased as heroes, who were typically honored with wreaths. The symbolic meaning of the wreaths was occasionally reinforced by the presence of a bronze wreath placed on the shoulder of a Hydra vases.[6] The hydria form, a water jar, was also especially relevant for funerary purposes. In Greek tradition, the dead were notoriously thirsty, and an important first step in a successful passage through Hades was a drink from the River of Lethe or the Lake of Memory.[7]

JH

1. For the most comprehensive presentation of Hadra vases, see Enklaar 1985, pp. 106-151; Enklaar 1986, pp. 41-65.
2. For Cretan connections, see Callaghan 1980, pp. 33-47; Callaghan 1981, pp. 35-85; Callaghan 1985; Enklaar 1986, pp. 41-42.
3. Enklaar 1985, pp. 110f., 117f., fig. 1a.
4. Guerrini 1964, D5, pl. 5.
5. Enklaar 1985, pp. 109f.
6. For bronze wreaths on the shoulder of Hadra vases, see Breccia 1912, pl. 37, n. 47; Guerrini 1964, pl. 6, D19; Enklaar 1985, p. 110, note 26.
7. On hydriai and wreaths in a funerary setting, see Kurtz and Boardman 1971, pp. 101, 141, 144, 152, 163, 165, 207, 209f.

Roman Period

150

150
Mummy mask

From the Fayum
Roman Period, late first century B.C. to early first century A.D.
Gilded cartonnage
Height 50 cm., width 29 cm.
Gift of the Egypt Exploration Fund, 1902
(02.827)

The preservation of the head was a primary concern in mummification. The three-dimensional mask, popular from the Middle Kingdom on, not only provided protection for the facial features, but could also substitute for the head in the event of loss. Masks of beaten gold, like the funerary mask of Tutankhamen, were provided for royalty. The use of gold may have been a prerogative of the wealthy, but it may also have had its origin in the idea that the flesh of the sun-god, with whom the deceased aspired to be united, was believed to be overlaid with pure gold and his headdress made of lapis lazuli.[1]

The features of this gilded, cartonnage mask are broadly rendered, and the ears are flattened into a hieroglyphic form. The eyebrows create an almost uninterrupted, sweeping line, arching slightly above the large eyes. The shape of the lips barely serves to differentiate the mouth. The hair above the forehead is arranged in a frieze of fringe with up-turned curls at the ends.

The vertical locks of the massive wig, of "lapis-lazuli" blue, are punctuated by cylindrical, gold beads.[2] The shimmering cascade of blue and gold was held in place by a red fillet. The fillet, tied at the back in a large knot,[3] is decorated at the sides with gilded, stucco studs, and has a gilded, stucco *wedjat* eye in the center. The front of the wig is divided into two large section which fall over each breast. The ends of these lappets are decorated with symmetrical images of Sokar, the god of the necropolis of Sakkara, depicted as a hawk with outstretched wings.

Between the two lappets is a gilded chest ornament, an abbreviated *wesekh* or broad collar. The raised relief features a heart amulet in the center, which is surrounded by geometrically rendered lotus blossoms and rosettes. The sides and bottom edges of the breastplate are filled with a checker (basket) pattern in red, green, blue, and white (see the filler pattern on the upper side of the footcase of cat. 156). The left and right *wedjat* eyes at each lower corner complement the amulet attached to the middle of the headband.

LC

1. In a description of the wondrous birth of the first three kings of the solar-oriented Dynasty 5 (Papyrus Westcar), the triplets are delivered with ''limbs overlaid with gold'' each wearing a ''headdress of true lapis lazuli'' (Lichtheim 1973, pp. 218-219).
2. For a modern reproduction of a similar wig dating from the Middle Kingdom see Aldred 1971, cover, pl. 39 and p. 193, no. 39.
3. The knot, although complicated, does not form the shape of the amuletic design discussed in Dolzani 1967, p. 99.

Bibliography: Grimm 1974, pp. 101, 117 and pl. 3 no. 3; Simpson 1977, pp. 50 and 69.

151
Mummy mask

From El-Hiba
Roman Period, late first century B.C. to early first century A.D.
Gilded cartonnage
Height 46.55 cm., width 32 cm.
Gift of the Egypt Exploration Fund, 1903 (03.1859)

This mask is similar to cat. 150, although slightly less elaborate in decoration. It would have been placed over the linen wrapping of the head of the deceased. Additional cartonnage trappings may also have embellished the wrapped body (see cat. 140).

The top of the head is encircled by a red cord that supports six gold beads and a *wedjat* eye in relief. The headdress is delineated by vertical stripes of blue and gold bordered with red. The sides and bottom of the mask are decorated with a representation of a beadwork net with alternating rows of blue and green barrel beads joined by round gold beads in relief. The gold beads and the relief decoration in the collar were modeled in the gesso ground layer and covered with gold leaf .01-.09 mm. thick. The

151

gold has been partly eaten away, especially in thin areas, by insects attracted to the glue used to apply the gold and gesso.

Such masks were undoubtedly mass-produced; they were made over a three-dimensional form by building up numerous layers of coarsely woven linen, stiffened with animal glue. This linen substrate was smoothed with a layer of fine white gesso made from chalk and animal glue or gum. Gold leaf was applied to this ground and burnished. Red ocher, Egyptian blue (a calcium-copper silicate), a green glass frit of similar composition, carbon black, and chalk white were used in a water-based medium to complete the design.

The mask was excavated in the great Late Period necropolis at El-Hiba[1] at the apex of the Delta.

PL/PH

1. Griffith 1903, pp. 1-3.

152
Mask of a woman

From Middle Egypt
Roman Period, mid first century A.D.
Plaster
Height 24.5 cm., width 17 cm.
Acquired by exchange from the Metropolitan Museum of Art (54.638)

The gently modeled and elegantly outlined face is idealized in the Ptolemaic manner. The loose complexity of the elaborate hairstyle, however, is fully Graeco-Roman. The hair is parted in the center and combed back in wavy undulations. Long corkscrew curls fall in two tiers behind the ears, and a pair of S-curve locks descends in front of them. Short corkscrew curls border the

face. The freely rendered wreath, characteristic of Middle Egyptian masks, resembles a wreath of woven papyrus more than a wreath of flowers.

Such plaster masks, known from Ptolemaic times on, were made separately and fastened to the mummy case or cartonnage. The face was cast in a mold, and the neck and hair were later modeled free-hand over the linen wrappings. A clear joint follows the jaw-line and passes behind the ears. The top of the head behind the wreath is smooth. The hair is painted black while the flesh and the wreath retain traces of pink coloring.

Ptolemaic masks remained anchored in Egyptian tradition and showed only marginal Graeco-Roman influence. With the Roman conquest in the later first century B.C., however, pan-Mediterranean fashions were taken up overtly even in the popular craft of mummy masks. By the standards of Greece or Italy, the faces of these masks showed very little individuality, but accoutrements and hairstyles were rendered in the richly illusionistic manner of this example.

Initially in this classicizing movement, female hair was simply parted and combed back, and a row of tight curls bordered the face, much as in the upper part of this head. The fashion seems to blend the hair styles of Cleopatra or Livia, known from coinage. In the second quarter of the first century, the portraits of Agrippina were taken up in Egypt, and a long corkscrew curl was let down behind the ear. This innovation seems to have opened the door to a rich local development; corkscrew curls proliferated on the heads of the ladies of Middle Egypt throughout the rest of the century

152

and into the second. This extravagance was clearly inspired by the ''Lybian locks,'' the masses of corkscrew curls that covered the ears and neck, known from the portraits of Ptolemaic queens.[1] Wigs with fine corkscrew curls represent a related phenomenon that can be traced well back into Pharaonic times.

JH

1. Kyrieleis 1975, pls. 100, 2, 3, 6; 101; 103-105, 108, 1, 2. On the initial phases of this development in lower Egypt, see Grimm 1974, pp. 49-51, pls. 11-15

Literature: Lythgoe 1910, p. 68, illus. p. 67, middle; Parlasca 1966, p. 238, no. 194; Grimm 1974, p. 76, pl. 68, 3; Museum of Fine Arts 1976, no. 29.

153
Funerary shroud

Said to be from Akhmim
Roman Period, third quarter of the first century A.D.[1]
Linen
Height 115 cm., width 88.5 cm.
Martha A. Wilcomb Fund, 1950 (50.650)

This full-length painted linen shroud, now missing its lower end, would have enveloped a mummified body, the painterly portrait head positioned directly over the mummy's face. The scarab beetle that now appears to be suspended above the head would have been at the back of her head,[2] its outstretched wings encircling and protecting it. The rows of deities on either side of the main figure (right side preserved) would have been at right angles to it, along the sides of the wrapped body.

The deceased is depicted in a posthumous role. Her regalia is identical to that of both Osiris, King of the Dead (shown in the upper right register), and Sokar, whose figure (now missing, with only the lower leg visible) we know from parallel examples appeared in the upper left register. Her clenched hands protrude from the shroud and she holds in them (in the reverse order of the Osiris figure) the symbols of kingly power: crook and flail. Flanking her head are the tutelary deities who protect a king: the goddesses Nekhbet and Edjo in the form of winged cobras, each wearing the crown of her respective domain (Upper and Lower Egypt).

Although the attributes of her costume are undeniably royal, the deceased may not here be emulating the funerary god Osiris,[3] but the sun-god Re. The scarab beetle whose wings enfolded the deceased's head is the young form of the sun-god, Khepri. In a famous representation of the Fourth Dynasty pharaoh Chephren, the wings of the falcon-god Horus embrace the king's head.[4] The intent of the iconography is to assimilate the two images, Horus and the king, and to sig-

153

nify ''the god manifest in the person of the king.''[5] The intent here may be the same: to identify the deceased with the reborn sun-god.

The imagery that decorates the body field appears to imitate the horizontal registers of the painted, wrapped bodies of red-shrouded and of stuccoed portrait mummies.[6] The upper scene depicts a mummy on the back of a lion (bed) flanked by human-headed *ba* (soul) birds. Above the mummy is the sun, whose energizing rays revivify the lifeless corpse. The scene below also depicts a mummified body on a lion bed. A masked, jackal-headed priest, in imitation of the mortuary god Anubis, performs a funerary ritual to rejuvenate the limbs of the deceased.[7] At the head and foot of the funerary bed the goddesses Isis and Nephthys hold a canopy above the scene. The awkward representation of the far lappets of the goddesses' wigs make it appear as though they are wearing ceremo-

nial beards, and their identifying head-dresses are somewhat garbled. The disparity in artistic skill between the rendition of the portrait head and that of the mythological characters on the body field suggest that the two were executed by different artists. Perhaps the shroud was ''ready-made'' and the portrait head commissioned at greater expense.[8]

The deities arranged in horizontal registers at either side of the main figure (and beneath the enthroned figures of Osiris and Sokar) depict (at right) Re-Horakhty, and the tree goddess offering cool water to a human-headed *ba* bird. The registers at left are broken off. There would have been a striding figure to complement that of Re-Horakhty, and across from the tree goddess is a scene depicting the young Horus child hidden by his mother Isis amidst the rushes of Chemmis. None of the vertical bands was ever inscribed.

The shroud was said to have been purchased at Akhmim. There are no similarly decorated pieces from the site; although it may well have been discovered in a cemetery there, typological factors suggest a Lower Egyptian provenance, possibly Sakkara.[9]

LHC

1. On the basis of the hairstyle and on stylistic grounds, the portrait should be dated to the early Flavian period (A.D. 69-80) (Parlasca 1977, p. 29).
2. For an explanation of the similar position of a vulture above the head of a woman on a painted shroud in the collection of the Museum of Art and Archaeology, University of Missouri, see Parlasca 1963; there also "the relationship between decoration and definition of purpose was clearer when the shroud still enclosed the actual mummy and the painting was not flattened out."
3. Parlasca 1966, p. 181.
4. Egyptian Museum, Cairo CG 14.
5. Terrace and Fischer 1970, p. 41.
6. Compare the treatment of the body field with that of the red-shrouded mummy of "Artemidorus" (British Museum Inv. No. 21810) or the gilded stucco mummy in the Egyptian Museum, Cairo CG 33216.
7. Ritner 1985, pp. 149-155, associates this scene with the moon and rebirth.
8. Hermann 1962, p. 76, notes that "painted shrouds were the mass-produced products of the funerary industry" and likened the commercial production of such shrouds to the stocks of prefabricated Books of the Dead and the funerary stelae that were personalized by the addition of the name or likeness of the deceased.
9. Parlasca 1966, pp. 42-43, 181-182, n. 188.

Bibliography: Parlasca 1977, p. 29 and pl. 61 no. 1, (includes full bibliography to publication date); Museum of Fine Arts 1978, no. 5 and color plate 5.

154
Painted funerary shroud

Provenance unknown
Roman Period, late second century A.D.
Tempera on linen
Height 90.5 cm., width 4.7 cm. (assembled fragments)
Gift of the class of the Museum of Fine Arts, Mrs. Arthur L. Devens, Chairman (54.993)

Painted in tempera (watercolor) on linen, this funerary shroud, like cat. 153, was used to wrap the mummy. Consisting of at least three noncontiguous pieces of linen, the shroud has been restored.[1] When received by the Museum in 1954, its various fragments had been incorrectly assembled and crudely mounted.

The portrait depicts a woman with large, dark eyes and dark hair arranged in waves with a row of ringlets along the forehead and in front of her ears. Her hairdress has been said to reflect "Roman fashions of the reigns of Tiberius and Caligula (A.D. 14-43),"[2] and W. S. Smith compared it to the coiffure shown in the first century A.D. linen

154

portrait of a woman known as "Aline."[3] On the basis of various discrepancies between the curls of the Boston hairstyle – which reach almost to the woman's neck – and those seen in first century styles, however, Parlasca dates the Boston hairstyle to the late Antonine or early Severan Period (A.D. 161-211),[4] although by so doing he admits that the portrait must stand stylistically,

"above the average of the portraits of its time."[5]

The woman's jewelry includes drop earrings, a necklace of purplish and green barrel-shaped beads, twisted gold bracelets, and, on her left hand, two rings, one of gold, the second a round blue stone (lapis lazuli) set in a gold bezel. The features of the woman's face are crisply defined by deep philtrum lines, pursed lips, and a sharply protruding chin.

The body field is divided into two horizontal registers depicting funerary scenes in predominant colors of red, green, black, and blue. In the uppermost register, beneath the image of a winged scarab beetle (compare cat. 153) the plump figures of the goddesses Isis and Nephthys greet their brother Osiris and pour libations to him onto offering tables, whose supports are shaped like lotus blossoms. At ankle height in front of the figure of Osiris a demotic inscription gives the date "regnal year 11, third month of summer (*šmw*), day 14."[6] Behind the figure of Nephthys (at left) and written at right angles to the figure (this section of the shroud was probably folded to cover the left side of the mummy) is a lengthy demotic inscription, in a clear hand, citing the name and parentage of the deceased, as well as adding that the previously mentioned date refers to the date of her burial. The woman's name, Ta-sherit-wedja-Hor, is preceded by the epithet "the Hathor," a feminine counterpart to the masculine form "the Osiris" meaning "the deceased," the goddess Hathor being assimilated at this time with Isis.[7] The woman's name, and those of her male relatives, are native Egyptian in origin and her husband served as a priest of Serapis and of Wepwawet, a funerary deity associated with the city of Asyut. Although the woman may have been a fully acculturated member of "the ruling class of foreigners,"[8] the onomastics, the profession of her family, and the purely Egyptian iconography of the body field decoration suggest that she may have belonged to the upper classes of the native Egyptian society.

The second register depicts the falcon-headed god Horus and the jackal-headed funerary god Anubis in a posture evocative of a motif symbolizing the binding of the two heraldic plants of Upper and Lower Egypt. In this scene, however, there is but one plant, a lotus, a symbol of resurrection.[9] Balanced and raised upon the lotus blossom, like the sun-god Nefertum,[10] is a mummified body, presumably a model for the deceased. Above this mummified figure a third demotic inscription, in a slightly more cursive hand than above, repeats the name and parentage of the deceased and the date of burial. Whereas the vertical bands accompanying the pictorial scenes that were intended for hieroglyphic inscriptions were left blank, these cursive notes in the native script may have served the purpose of a "mummy ticket"[11] providing practical instructions between funerary priests and cemetery officials.

At the bottom edge of the shroud are depicted the sandalled feet of the deceased (see cat. 157). Surrounding both feet is a scene that appears upside-down on the flattened shroud, but would have covered the upper part of the vertical foot covering, facing the gaze of the deceased. Between the feet a goddess stands upon a lotus column and offers cool water from a vase held in each hand to a human-headed *ba* bird atop a lotus column at the outer side of each foot. The bottom of the shroud, like the top, is stained with funerary resins.

Although we are informed of the exact day, month, and year of burial, the name of the regnant emperor is lacking. On paleographic grounds, Malinine initially dated the demotic inscriptions to the late first century B.C. as he "observed several signs suggestive of Ptolemaic forms."[12] Richard Parker,[13] Erich Luddeckens,[14] and most recently, Richard Jasnow[15] have, however, seen no sufficient grounds for dating the inscriptions paleographically to before the first century A.D. On stylistic grounds and on the basis of the hairstyle, the portrait has been dated to the late Antonine Period (A.D. 161-192), and the burial date, presumably at some time after the actual date of death and preparation of the body, would then refer to the year A.D. 202-203, the eleventh year of the reign of Septimius Severus.[16]

LHC

1. Parlasca 1977, p. 66, no. 392. The top and sides of the shroud have been cut in recent times and the portrait lacks the shoulder area. The pieces were restored and remounted by John Finlayson, museum restorer.
2. Vermeule 1972, fig. 46.
3. Smith 1960, p. 188.
4. Parlasca 1966, p. 187.
5. Parlasca 1966, p. 187.
6. The translations of the demotic inscriptions are based on the unpublished work (1955-57) of Richard A. Parker. I thank my colleague Richard Jasnow for reviewing the reading of these texts.
7. Parlasca 1966, p. 161
8. Morgan 1976, p. 36, cat. no. 48.
9. Brunner-Traut 1980, col. 1094. For a similar design see the triple lotus lamp from the tomb of Tutankhamen in Edwards 1976, pl. 10, cat. no. 14, p. 122, cat. no. 14.
10. Compare the head of Tutankhamen upon a lotus blossom in imitation of the birth of the sun-god, in Edwards 1976, pl. 1, cat. no. 1, p. 99, cat. no. 1. The image embodies a desire expressed in Spell 81, 81 B of the Book of the Dead to assume the form of the lotus, although probably envisioned here as a single entity with the god, Nefertum (Allen 1974, p. 70).
11. That inscriptions on outer bandages could substitute for "mummy tickets" see Quaegebeur 1978, p. 235. For the dual religious and practical functions of the inscriptions see Quaegebuer 1978, pp. 236-239.

12. Parlasca 1966, p. 187.
13. Letter to William Stevenson Smith, May 21, 1957).
14. Parlasca 1966, p. 187.
15. Personal communication, August 31, 1987.
16. Parlasca 1966, p. 187.

Bibliography: Parlasca 1977, p. 66, pl. 96, no. 3; Morgan 1976, cat. no. 48; Museum of Fine Arts 1955.

Roman Portrait Mummies

Popular in Egypt from the first to the fourth centuries A.D., portrait mummies incorporated elements from the Greek artistic tradition. As an alternative to a modeled cartonnage or stucco funerary mask, a realistic portrait executed in encaustic (colored beeswax) or tempera (watercolor) on a sheet of linen or a wooden panel, was placed over the face of the deceased and consolidated into the mummy bandages. The earliest of these portraits were commissioned as easel paintings and displayed in the home (presumably with a cultic purpose), as is known from the recovery of a panel portrait still within its wooden frame[1] and from the customary angling of the upper corners of panels[2] (see cat. 155) before they were put to this final funerary use.

The first scientifically documented excavation of "portrait mummies" was conducted in the shadow of the Middle Kingdom pyramid of Amenemhat III, to the north of the vast mortuary complex known to ancient historians as "the Labyrinth," where Roman Egyptians of the ancient town of Arsinoe buried their dead. This entire Fayum province was allotted in 1887 as an archaeological concession to Sir W.M. Flinders Petrie, the British Egyptologist who pioneered the use of modern archaeological field methods. For two seasons, in the winter of 1888 and again in 1910-11,[3] in the Roman Period cemetery named for the nearby village of Hawara, Petrie uncovered a great number of intact mummies with portrait faces. These were not the first mummies with painted portraits to come from Egypt, but his scientifically organized and documented discoveries provided the archaeological evidence to authenticate and date the isolated examples that had been acquired earlier by travelers.

In most cases, portrait mummies were found buried in the open ground without "chapel, monument or tablet over them."[4] The usual method of burial was rather haphazard: as many as sixteen mummies, presumed to come all from the same family, were buried in a common grave, some damaged while being lowered into a pit.[5] From this evidence, Petrie conjectured that portrait mummies were kept in the home until a group of them could be gathered for a final interment.[6]

The occurrence of portrait mummies buried together with wedge-faced, rhombic-wrapped mummies or mummies with gilded cartonnage headpieces points to the wide range of choice within the mummification industry. It also helps to cross-date specific examples.

X-rays have corroborated Petrie's statemen (based on some examples that he unwrapped for examination) that these portrait mummies were wrapped without the inclusion of "rings, ornaments, papyri or amulets."[7] The only object found in more than one portrait mummy is a hard, leather (or metal) disk placed under the tongue (see cat. 174).[8] Whether this object was added for aesthetic reasons by the embalmer or to aid in the religious ritual of the "opening of the mouth" (see cat. 11) has not been determined.

The hairstyles, jewelry, and clothing depicted in "mummy portraits" provide us with a glimpse into the everyday lives of Egyptians in the Roman Period. Changes in style, based on fashions at the royal court, also serve to date the portraits. The relative quality of portraits has also been used as an indication of date, as the portraits of poorer quality are more likely to have been painted in the last half of the third or in the fourth century A.D., when the economy had begun to deteriorate. Successful attempts have also been made to group portraits according to schools of painters and even to identify individual artistic hands.[9]

Although the individual portraits appeal to our modern aesthetic, they are only one element of the overall design of the rest of the body, which is "descended from different types among the earlier mummies."[10] Although they have been found in the greatest concentration in the Fayum, particularly at the site of Hawara and in and around Er-Rubayat, portraits have been recovered from Sakkara to Nubia.[11] Their funerary use underscores the value of the portrait mummies for sociological and religious studies: the products of the Hellenized cultural milieu of the Fayum, they nevertheless fulfilled the requirements of the native Egyptian funerary tradition.

LHC

1. Petrie 1889, p. 10, pl XII.
2. Petrie 1911, pp. 7-8.
3. The work of these seasons is published in Petrie 1889 and Petrie 1911. Color photographs appear in Petrie 1913.
4. Petrie 1911, p. 2.
5. Petrie 1899, p. 15.
6. Petrie 1899, p. 15; Petrie 1911, pp. 2-3.
7. Petrie 1889, p. 20.
8. Gray and Slow 1968, p. 32; Cuenca 1978, pp. 61, 75 n. 2.
9. Thompson 1982, pp. 16-23.
10. Edgar 1905a, p. XII.
11. For the history of the recovery of portrait mummies, Parlasca 1966, pp. 18-58.

Bibliography: Edgar 1905; Parlasca 1966; Petrie 1889; Petrie 1911; Thompson 1982.

155
Portrait mummy of a man

From Hawara
Roman Period, A.D. 150-175
Encaustic on wood over linen
Height 167 cm., width 35 cm.
Gift of the Egyptian Research Account, 1911 (11.2891)

The larger of the two intact portrait mummies in Boston is that of an adult male. The mummy is wrapped in layers of natural linen tapes that form three vertical rows of a diamond or rhombus pattern. The rhombi are approximately three levels deep with one additional cross layer. In the center of each rhombus is a decorative square of dark linen.

The feet are wrapped in the same pattern and the central vertical row continues up from a rhombus positioned squarely between the two feet. The sides, top, and back of the head are enclosed within a plain, coarse sheet of linen. Another plain sheet envelops the mummy from the back and covers the shoulders, the length of the sides, and the bottom of the feet.

Funerary resins have discolored the linen of the foot cover, along the left side of the portrait frame, and all down the left side of the body.[1] The soil and small rocks that adhere to the wrappings, especially at the knee level, are the result of the mummy having been buried in a shallow grave dug directly in the sand.[2]

The wooden panel on which the portrait is painted was rounded at the upper corners and positioned on a base of flattened cloths which form a padding above the face of the treated mummy. The tightness with which the successive layers of bandages were bound around the edges of the panel, to form an octagonal frame, produced "a cumulative pressure on the edge of the picture"[3] resulting in the splitting of the panel. Both the padding and the prefatory rounding of the top of the panel can be seen in this example because the portrait has separated from the wrappings.

The portrait, in encaustic (colored wax) on a thin wood panel, depicts an adult male with face and torso turned slightly to the left. The man has dark, curly hair, arched, bushy brows, and a thick, curly beard. His exposed, rounded chin is encircled by a tuft of hair curving down from beneath his lower lip. His moustache is thin. The man's wide eyes are fringed by dark eyelashes. A touch of white at the end of his long nose makes it appear somewhat bulbous. His lower lip is full.

The man is clothed in a white *chiton* and wears a mantle draped over his left shoulder. The gray background shows evidence of fading along the sides where the panel had been covered by the bandages of the

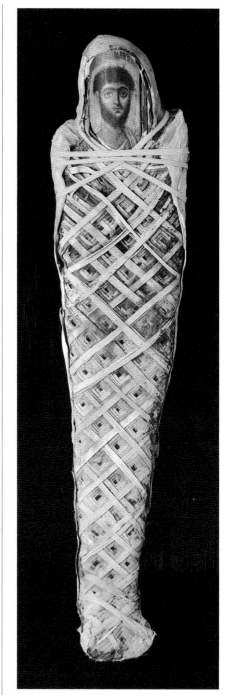

155

octagonal frame. Due to the man's hairstyle, which reminded Petrie of the emperor Lucius Verus (A.D. 161-169),[4] and to the use of reflective light in the technique of the painting, this portrait has been dated to about A.D. 200.[5]

This mummy was found buried together with a female mummy,[6] which is now in Brussels.[7] Tucked under the tapes of the portrait frame of the female mummy was a papyrus referring to an account dated to the reign of Hadrian (A.D. 127).[8] It was undoubtedly the hairstyle of the woman, however, that led Parlasca to assign the female mummy to the reign of Trajan, thus creating a dilemma: the only example of which he was aware in which mummies found buried together (the Brussels female and the Boston male) were separated by a span of more than fifty years.[9]

In an effort to resolve this conflict, and perhaps persuaded by Petrie's suggestion of a date of about A.D. 180 for the mummy,[10] Parlasca redated the Brussels portrait to the early Antonine Period.[11] The similarity of the wrappings to those of a mummy with a Trajan Period portrait[12] and the horse-shoe shaped, stucco frame that surrounds the portrait of the Brussels mummy, which is not attested at Hawara after the second century A.D.,[13] indicate a date for the manufacture of the female mummy in the second quarter of the second century.

The body wrappings of the Boston mummy offer little help in dating it. The rhombic wrappings are somewhat carelessly executed; there are no gilt buttons or strips of buttons at the chest or ankles. The square of darkened linen at the center of each rhombus, however, produces a pattern that is seen on mummies from the middle of the first to the middle of the second centuries A.D. And, although no trace of it remains, Petrie states that the Boston mummy was originally equipped with a cartonnage footcase.[14] These factors suggest a date somewhat earlier (A.D. 150–175) and more compatible with the date of the female mummy with which it was found.[15]

LHC

Mummy

The mummy, placed on two thin lengths of wood that run the entire length of the body, down both legs, is that of a poorly preserved young man who had thick calluses on the bottoms of his feet. The brain was no longer removed during mummification in this period, and residual brain contents were identified. Though there was no embalming incision, the viscera were not present, suggesting that a purging method of mummification had been employed (see "Mummification in Ancient Egypt," p. 14).

A benign bony tumor of the lower spine was identified. This tumor would be painful, and, in a modern patient, would be relieved by aspirin or surgically removed.

MM

1. The damage caused by funerary resins in general is described in Petrie 1911, p. 6.
2. The conditions of burial, "in shallow graves; often dug out in the open ground, or in the masses of rock chips which covered the surface" is described in Petrie et al. 1898, p. 20.
3. Petrie et al. 1898.
4. Petrie 1911, pp. 13–14.
5. Parlasca 1977, p. 63.
6. Petrie 1911, p. 11.
7. In the collection of the Musées Royaux d'Art et d'Histoire in Brussels (Inv. E. 4857). For a description of the portrait, see Parlasca 1969, p. 64.
8. Petrie 1911, p. 23 C.
9. Parlasca 1966, p. 52, p. 101.
10. Petrie 1911, p. 14.
11. Although the Brussels mummy is referred to in the entry for the Boston mummy as "la mummia di epoca traianea" (Parlasca 1977, p. 63), the portrait is described under its own entry as more or less contemporary with Manchester Museum Inv. 2266 which Parlasca dates "alla prima eta antoniana" (Parlasca 1969, p. 64). The gap of a quarter century between the two dates may be explained, not by redating the portrait, but by assuming that the individual died and the mummy was manufactured, with the Trajanic portrait and Hadrianic papyrus included within its wrappings, twenty-five years or so after the portrait was commissioned.
12. Cairo, CG 33.222. Parlasca 1977, p. 34.
13. Parlasca 1977, no. 366, p. 59.
14. Petrie 1911, pl. 26, no. 19. The ditto marks beneath "gilt" under the heading "Footcase" may, however, have been an error.
15. Parlasca 1966, p. 53.

Bibliography: Petrie 1911, pp. 10, 11, 13 14; pl. VII A, no. 19; pl. XXVI, no. 19; Smith 1960, p. 186; Parlasca 1966, pp. 52, 101, 251; Parlasca 1977, p. 63; pl. 93 no. 2; Thompson 1976, p. 6, fig. 2.

156
Portrait mummy of a youth

From Hawara
Roman Period, about A.D. 50
Wood and linen
Height 11.3 cm.
Gift of the Egypt Exploration Fund, 1911 (11.2892)

The portrait of this youth was painted on a wooden panel, suggesting that the deceased was old enough for the family to have commissioned a formal sitting, before an untimely death. Portraits of very young children (pre-adolescents) were more commonly painted directed onto a square of linen or onto the funerary shroud that covered the mummy.

The mummy is wrapped in a pattern similar to that of cat. 155. The natural linen tapes form vertical rows of diamonds the length of the body. The rhombi are approximately three levels deep with one additional cross layer. Gilded stucco studs were inserted at the base of the rhombi. The regularity of the pattern of studs above the footcase, and the precision of the center row of rhombi, indicate that rhombi-wrapped mummies may have been wrapped from the feet up.

Tapes across the chest secure a single cartonnage strip or band, to which are attached nine gilded stucco studs. A similar band of gilded studs was probably inserted above the foot casing. A plain sheet of linen envelops the mummy from the back, covering the sides, the back of the head, and the lower third of the underside of the footcase.

A cartonnage footcase (see cat. 157) was positioned over a base of mud and straw

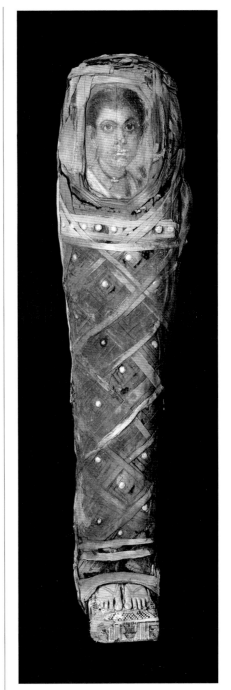

156

plastered over the wrapped feet and held in place by the rhombi wrappings that cover the ankles. The casing is made of a thin plaster coating over the coarse linen (as can be seen where the casing is broken open along the edges). The plaster was painted in bright colors, mostly pink, red, and green with touches of gold.

The upper side of the footcase depicts the feet of the deceased in three-dimensional relief. The feet are pink with gilded toes and the sandals are gilded. A multicolored checker pattern surrounds the red undersides of the sandals. The sides of the footcase are decorated with a stripe border and pink rosettes. The front edge of the footcase contains a central lotus flower with buds (a symbol of resurrection)[1] and a protective *wedjat* eye at each side.

On the underside of the footcase are the outlines of the soles of the sandals. Within these outlines are representations of bound figures. The figures represent the enemies of the deceased, personifying the Egyptian sentiment, "May your enemies be beneath your sandals."[2] The blue band above them, which ends in down-turned corners and is covered with white stars, is the Egyptian hieroglyph for "sky," and indicates that this is to be viewed in a cosmic sense, as an expression of the Egyptian desire for world order over the forces of chaos (see cat. 157).

The portrait is executed in encaustic (colored wax) on a panel board. The pudgy face of the youth is accentuated by the circular, protruding chin, and the round, dark eyes. The face is almost fully frontal, with a slight twist of the torso to the left.

The youth's dark hair is combed close to the scalp and above the ears; a small group of curls falls slightly forward in the middle of the forehead. A thin braid at each side is pulled back across the sides. A wisp of dark hair beneath the right ear may represent the sidelock of the god Horus as a youth.

The deceased wears a low-cut white *chiton*. A gold tubular pendant on a knotted, black cord functioned as a locket or case for a protective charm. A magical spell, to protect the wearer from disease or evil, was inscribed on a small bit of precious metal that was then rolled up and placed inside the case. Such protective amulets "often accompanied the wearer to the grave, whence archaeologists have retrieved them over the years."[3] The lips of the youth were covered with a layer of gilding, perhaps, as indicated by Spells 21 to 23 from the Book of the Dead, to ensure the power of speech in the afterlife.

Sexing mummies has always been a difficult problem. Archaeologists have often discovered the bodies of men in coffins intended for women, and vice versa.[4] The age and sex determinations for the subjects of mummy portraits has also presented difficulties, particularly with the very young and the very old. Although the subject of this portrait has always been considered a young girl, several factors indicate that the individual in the portrait may, in fact, be a young boy. The style of the portrait is very similar to representations of young boys (mostly from the fourth century A.D.)[5] who are identified as acolytes of the Isis cult.[6] They wear white *chitons* (a color preferred for male garments), no earrings[7] or other jewelry but the phylactery or amulet case on a black cord, and have their hair styled over the right ear with the sidelock of youth.

LHC

Mummy

During mummification, the body was placed on a length of wood, which was left inside the wrappings. The mummy is that of a young child demonstrating numerous growth arrest lines, especially near the epiphyses (growth plate) of the knee, suggesting a chronic illness prior to death. The mummy is in a poor state of preservation, reflecting the decline of the mummification process during the Roman Period. The chest and abdominal cavities are severely compressed. There are numerous disarticulations, and a badly fractured cranial vault and base of the skull. The arms of the mummy, which would normally have been placed on the thighs, are behind the body.

MM

1. Brunner-Traut 1979, 1980, p. 1094.
2. Rühlmann 1971, pp. 61-84.
3. Kotansky 1983, p. 169.
4. X-rays of a portrait mummy in a South African collection showed the mummy to be that of a woman, whereas the portrait attached to the mummy is that of "a bearded and moustachioed man" (Thompson 1982, p. 14), certainly "a clear-cut case where the portrait and its mummy are unrelated" (Thompson 1982, p. 15).
5. See, for example, the numerous illustrations of this type in Parlasca 1980, pp. 53-54 and 62-67.
6. Von Gonzenbach 1957.
7. The statement in Parlasca 1969, p. 42, that the individual is depicted wearing earrings, is incorrect. I thank Peter Lacovara, Museum of Fine Arts, Boston, for confirming this detail for me.

Bibliography: Petrie 1911, p. 4; pl. VI A, No. 30, and pl. XXVI; Smith 1960, p. 186; Parlasca 1969, pp. 42-43, pl. 16, no. 2.

157
Footcase

Provenance unknown
Roman Period, second half of the first century A.D.
Cartonnage
Height 19 cm., width 20.3 cm.
Arthur Mason Knapp Fund, 1971 (1971.217)

Thin, bootlike coverings of cartonnage often encased the wrapped feet of Roman mummies.[1] On the upper part of these casings, sandalled or bare feet were depicted in paint or modeled in stucco and painted. Although most examples show the feet painted in a light pink flesh tone, some examples show the feet completely gilded or, as here, with gilt toenails. The representation of feet in a permanent material ensured the deceased's ability to stand upright, and to come and go in the Netherworld.

Amuletic designs decorated the front edge and sides of these footcases. The most common design to appear on the front edge is a lotus blossom and buds flanked by pro-

157, top

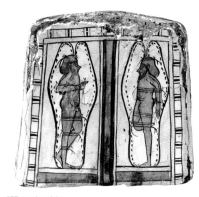

157, underside

tective *wedjat* eyes (as on the front edge of the footcase of cat. 156). The decorative motif most common on side panels (shown here both on the sides and front edge panel) is a geometric rosette bordered by vertical stripes.

The stitched and joined soles of the deceased's sandals are depicted on the underside of this footcase. Bound within the outline of each sandal sole is a representation of one of the traditional enemies of the state of Egypt. Although the hair and clothing styles that originally helped to differentiate the figures have been abandoned, the figure on the underside of the right foot depicts a brown-skinned Nubian, that on the left shows a pink-skinned Asiatic. This motif, the trampling of enemies underfoot, was traditionally employed only for the king, but was put to use during the Roman Period as a powerful magical spell for vindication in the Netherworld.

The democratization of this idea need not be seen as "a curious and somewhat illogical survival"[2] of a royal motif, if we consider that the concept of the "king triumphant" may always have contained more than a strictly political or military significance.[3] Just as the sun-god rose victorious in his daily and cyclical battle against the forces of the Underworld, the reassuring image of pharaoh smiting the mortal enemies of the state symbolized the successful and permanent establishment of the cosmic order over chaos. The focal point of the design was not the bellicose deed, but the serenity that results from decisive victory.[4] For an individual, assimilated in death with the king and the sun-god, the motif of the enemy figures securely bound and subjugated, embodied, not a morbid fascination with earthly revenge, but the hope for, and the attainment of, eternal peace.

LHC

1. Petrie 1889, p. 14, note, acknowledged that "some purists may object to the use of this word for any material not of the pulpy nature of paper (carton); but as the pulped material is always covered with stucco, and this stucco imperceptibly varies in thickness up to a massive layer, it is hardly possible to limit cartonnage so as not to include layers of papyrus or of canvas covered with stucco, which is here the material." These footcases were added to rhombic-wrapped (see cat. 156) and red-shrouded portrait mummies, as well as with mummies having cartonnage masks.
2. Simpson 1972b, p. 120.
3. Wildung 1975, col. 15. The statement that "die apotropäische Wirkung des Bildtypus. . . geht über den politischen Bereich hinaus und umfasst auch den Schutz gegen die chaotischen Mächte der Unterwelt" yet acknowledges a distinction between the two motifs which, it could be argued, may not have been distinguished in antiquity.
4. Goff 1979, p. 173.

Bibliography: Simpson 1973b, pp. 50-54; Simpson 1972b, pp. 120, 122, nos. 9 and 9a and illustration; Museum of Fine Arts 1977, cat. 27, p. 21; Museum of Fine Arts 1987, pp. 74-75.

158
Coffin footboard

Provenance unknown
Roman Period, late first century A.D.
Wood
Height 46.6 cm., width 63 cm.
Egyptian Special Purchase Fund, 1979
(1979.37)

The mythical murder of Osiris by his evil brother Seth ended in the dismemberment of his body and the scattering of its parts throughout the land of Egypt. His grieving sister and widow Isis dutifully collected the pieces and prepared the body of Osiris for a proper mummification and burial. The solar god Re sent his son, the jackal-headed Anubis,[1] to perform the burial rites of Osiris. The ritual performed by Anubis resulted in the rejuvenation of the limbs of Osiris and culminated in his resurrection.

The scene depicted in tempera (watercolor) on this wooden footboard, one of the most commonly illustrated scenes on Roman mummies (see cat. 153), recreates the mummification ritual of the god Osiris for the benefit of the deceased. At either end of the bed on which the prepared mummy lies, mourning women represent the goddess Isis and her sister, Nephthys. Attending to the mummiform body is Anubis. With

158

one hand over the body, he holds in his other hand a vessel containing funerary oils or possibly Nile water. A lunar interpretation of this scene, which likens the body of Osiris to the regenerating moon, has recently been proposed,[2] and the swastika beneath the mummy's head, an element borrowed from Indian symbolism, complements the image of cosmic and cyclical perfection. The solar aspects of this late representation are nevertheless evidenced by the choice of the color red for the mummy bandages, the color of the rising and setting sun.[3]

In each of the upper corners of the scene is a vertical line of hieroglyphic text. It is tempting to say that the texts are illegible and the artists who wrote them no longer understand their meaning,[4] but the word for "Osiris" (*Wsr*) appears at the top of the right-hand column and a phrase that might stand for the initial invocation of a standard funerary formula (*htp di nswt*) may be represented in the left hand column. Illiteracy and a late date are not synonymous, neither should a cryptic text be judged corrupt. The figures are, however, crudely rendered: the proportions are inaccurate and paint is carelessly splashed outside black outlines.

The mummy depicted on the footcase is wrapped in rhombic bandages (see cats. 155 and 156), with inserts of gilded buttons, a design that is familiar to us from contemporary Roman mummies of the late first century A.D.; it can be compared to an almost identical representation of a mummiform body on a bier in the (Tegran) tomb at Alexandria,[5] dated to no earlier than the last half of the first century A.D. Strokes of paint that extend beyond the outline of the goddesses' long, loose hair, like the bristled back of the hackled cat, are common on fe-

male figures of similarly dated funerary shrouds and coffins.[6]

LHC

1. Grenier 1977, p. 17.
2. Ritner 1985, pp. 149-155, pls. XV-XVI.
3. The solar symbolism of contemporary red-shrouded portrait mummies was examined by the author in a paper presented at the annual meeting of the American Research Center in Egypt. Cleveland, Ohio, April 28, 1984 and pursued in a forthcoming doctoral dissertation, "Portrait Mummies from Roman Egypt." in connection with this research, the author wishes to thank David A. Silverman and acknowledge a debt to Professor Edward F. Wente.
4. Museum of Fine Arts 1979, p. 22.
5. Grimm 1974, pl. 127, fig. 2 (photo of the tomb painting).
6. Parlasca 1966, pl. 60, figs. 1 and 2; funerary representations of the goddess Nut, Grimm 1974, pls. 138-139.

Bibliography: Museum of Fine Arts 1979, p.22; Grenier 1977, p. 17; Grimm 1974, pl. 127 fig. 2; Parlasca 1966, pl. 60, figs. 1 and 2; Museum of Fine Arts 1987, p. 98.

159
Fragmentary mummy portrait of a woman

Said to be from Er-Rubayat
Roman Period, about A.D. 100
Paint on wood
Height 30.1 cm., width 7.8 cm.
Cheney and Everett Funds, 1893 (93.1451)

Mummy portraits were almost unknown in Europe and North America until 1889, when Viennese art dealer Theodor Graf organized a traveling exhibition of almost one hundred portraits.[1] The portraits were mostly from

159

the cemetery of Er-Rubayat in the north-eastern Fayum. A number of portraits in American collections, like this example,[2] were purchased from the exhibit.

Only the center of the wooden panel is preserved, although more is missing from the right side than from the left. The face is almost fully frontal, but the torso is turned to the left. The loss of the left side of the panel, which shaves the profile of her left cheek, may account for the elongated aspect of the young woman's face. Her feathered brows arch slightly above liquid, light brown eyes. Her upper lip is shaped like a cupid's bow, her lower lip is full, and at the corners of her mouth are creases of an impish smile. Her small, pointed chin has a dimpled cleft in the center. Her cheeks are blushed.

A layer of corkscrew curls frames the forehead. Behind them, dark brown hair is swept up into a bun held in place by a band. The hairstyle helps to date the portrait to the late Flavian or early Trajan period.

The woman is dressed in purple *chiton* and matching purple *himation* that drapes over her left shoulder. Peeking from the lower left corner of the neckline of her *chiton* is a bit of white trim.

The loss of the side sections prevents us from knowing what sort of earrings the woman surely wore. Of the two choker-style necklaces, the upper consists of gold balls or rings connected by gold bar spacers, and the lower is of uncut emeralds threaded onto a gold chain.[3] Emeralds, which occur naturally in prismatic hexagons, were mined in the Red Sea hills, 250 km. southeast of present-day Luxor.[4] Although they "have been prospected in modern times,"[5] no stones of commercial quality have been found in the Roman mines mentioned by Strabo and Pliny.

LHC

1. For the circumstances of the recovery of portraits at Er-Rubayat see Parlasca 1966, pp. 23-27 or Thompson 1982, pp. 3-5.
2. According to Dunham 1958, p. 19, a "fine painted mummy portrait" from the Graf collection (probably 93.1450) was the very first purchase made by the Trustees of the Museum of Fine Arts, Boston, to enhance the collection of the Egyptian Department. Ebers 1893, p. 36, no. 79 (a) lists this fragmentary portrait (93.1451) as having been acquired at the same time.
3. "Raw emeralds. . .threaded on loosely linked chains" were popular at Pompeii according to Higgins 1980, p. 174.
4. Higgins 1980, p. 38.
5. Murray 1925, p. 144.

Bibliography: Ebers 1893, p. 36, no. 79(a); Buberl 1922, p. 57, no. 79; Dunham 1958, p. 19; Smith 1960, p. 186, fig. 130; Parlasca 1966, p. 246 no. 79(a); Parlasca 1969, p. 48, pl. 19 no. 4.

160
Portrait of a man

From Er-Rubayat
Roman Period, about A.D. 170
Encaustic on wood
Height 44 cm., width 19 cm.
Gift of the Egypt Exploration Fund, 1902
(02.825)

This portrait depicts a middle-aged man turned slightly to the left. His dark, wavy hair is long and falls in a wispy fringe over his forehead in a style popular during the Antonine period. His scraggly beard is especially thin along his cheeks. His moustache curves downward around full lips. Thick, bushy, eyebrows arch slightly and meet above the bridge of a thin, aquiline nose. Fleshy pouches beneath his round, dark eyes accentuate his long, gaunt face. The man wears a white *chiton* with a low, draped neckline, and a gray mantle over his left shoulder. The background is gray.

The colors of the painting are obscured as if the panel had been coated with a layer of hot wax in an emergency effort to preserve them, a technique devised by Petrie at the Hawara excavation site, and considered by him to have been a success,[1] although he could not predicted the long-term effect of a yellowed wax build-up.[2] Textile fragments adhere to the panel at the bottom, along the lower sides, and at the top left corner. These bits of linen and resin are the remains of the bandages that once held the portrait panel firmly over the face of the wrapped mummy. The oblique angle of the linen traces at the lower left corner indicates that this panel may have been set into a rhombic wrapped design with an octagonal opening or frame for the portrait.[3] The panel was structurally damaged by wood-boring insects.[4]

LHC

1. Petrie 1889, p. 19.
2. Thompson 1982, p. 13, describes the condition of the portrait in Toronto, "obscured by a thick 'protective' coat of varnish or (probably) wax, that over the years has turned from transparent to a clouded mud-brown."
3. See the octagonal design of the bandages framing the portraits of the complete portrait mummies (cats. 155 and 156).
4. Petrie 1911, p. 6, refers to them as "white ants," a common European designation for "termites."

Bibliography: Grenfell 1901, p. 7; Dunham 1958, p. 13, fig. 8; Smith 1960, p. 186, fig. 132; Parlasca 1966, p. 24; Parlasca 1977, p. 50, pl. 80, no. 2.

160

161
Funerary crown

Provenance unknown
Roman Period, said to be from the fourth
century A.D.
Papyrus
Height 9 cm., diam. 20 cm.
Anonymous Gift, 1950 (50.3788)

Although crowns played a part in Greek and
Roman ritual, it is not necessary to look
outside the sphere of ancient Egyptian beliefs to find an explanation for their funerary
use in an Egyptian context.[1] Spells 19 and
20 of the Book of the Dead,[2] in use from the
New Kingdom on, were to be recited as a
wreath was bound on the brow of the deceased in anticipation of the "wreath of vindication" to be awarded him in the afterlife
in the Hall of Judgment. In myth, Horus, the
son of Osiris, had vindicated his father
against the evil Seth in order to justify his
own claim to the Osirian throne. As every
Egyptian pharaoh was associated with Horus while he lived, and the god Osiris upon
his death, the cultic vindication of the god
was perpetually re-enacted. In the democratization of the Osirian cult, a crown assured
the deceased individual of a royal fate. The
role of Osiris as king of the gods was, at
times, eclipsed by that of the sun-god Re,
and this crown also acquired some solar
significance.[3]

The "wreath of vindication" was traditionally made of flowers (in the Late Period,
usually roses) or of gold. Floral wreaths,
modeled in stucco and painted, are depicted on funerary masks of the first to
fourth centuries A.D. (see cat. 165) and gilt
wreaths are common additions to mummy
portraits. This elaborate and unique crown
is fashioned of papyrus strips. In the center
front is a sheet of bronze overlaid with an
openwork weave. Bronze was used in the
manufacture of solar disks or hypocephali
(see cat. 183) that were placed under the
heads of mummies of the pharaonic period.
When newly made, reflection from the metallic strip in the middle of this crown must
have produced a bright star pattern, perhaps to simulate the rays of the sun.

LHC

161

1. Cf. Museum of Fine Arts 1976, p. 28, cat. 34.
2. Allen 1974, pp. 34-36.
3. Derchain 1955, p. 241.

Bibliography: Dunham 1950, p. 30; Museum of Fine Arts 1976, p. 28, cat. 34; Smith 1960, p. 189.

162
Funerary relief

From Oxyrhynchus
Roman Period, third century A.D.
Limestone
Height 141 cm., width 53 cm.
Edward J. and Mary S. Holmes Fund, 1972
(1972.875)

This funerary relief belongs to a unique group of approximately twenty monuments almost unknown in museums and private collections before 1969.[1] The sudden appearance of a sizeable corpus of stone sculptures might have raised the suspicion of modern manufacture, save that the type was not "in fashion" at the time the group entered the art market.[2] The sculptures, portraits of both men and women, must have belonged to the same mausoleum in the prosperous, provincial Roman Egyptian town of Oxyrhynchus (present-day El-Behnasa, 330 km. south of Alexandria).[3]

Like the other examples of this type, this figure was carved in such high relief as to be almost considered sculpture in the round, and was originally engaged within an architectural niche. Most of these stelae in museum collections are incomplete (some have been sawed into two or more pieces),[4] having been removed from their sculptural settings for ease of transport by the local inhabitants who discovered them.[5]

The soft and crumbly local limestone required a coating of gesso before the artists could individualize the characteristics of face and costume. Most of the details of portraiture are now lacking due to the loss of the bright colors that would have softened the coarse contours of the bodies, which are often anatomically inaccurately portrayed.[6]

The hair, dress, and jewelry of the unidentified woman[7] are typical of wealthy matrons of Roman Egypt. Her earrings are of the bar-pendant variety, one of three styles that Petrie identified from the mummy portraits he discovered at Hawara.[8] This three-pearl style usually accompanied "overloaded necklaces"[9] and, although changes in earring styles were not strictly chronological,[10] this bar-pendant style is seen on portraits of women into the fourth century A.D.[11]

Although the long, knotted gown has been seen to identify its wearer as a priestess of the goddess Isis,[12] there is no identifying inscription or other evidence.[13] A thick funerary wreath drapes diagonally from the left shoulder, across the torso. It is paralleled by

162

a sash decorated with various crown, star, and moon motifs worn by a headless statue in the Berlin Museum.[14] The men depicted in these stelae usually carry a garland of similar type in one hand (for the significance of funerary wreaths and crowns, see cat. 161).

The woman's left arm is crooked at the elbow and her left hand is held close to her body. In her left hand, she holds a vessel, perhaps "a small bowl full of sacred Nile water,"[15] although the more common attribute is a container for incense.[16] Her right arm hangs down at her side. Her right hand "may have held a sistrum or rattle"[17] (of three inscribed Ptolemaic statues of women wearing this tripartite garment, "all three bear the title *ihyt*, "player of the sistrum").[18] In other examples, the right hand holds a pellet of incense about to be placed upon an altar.[19]

Oxyrhynchus has provided us with some of the earliest literary evidence for Christianity in Upper Egypt, yet these niched funerary

stelae, with Eastern Mediterranean overtones, must represent the latest transitional phase from paganism to the Late Antique.

LHC

1. Schneider 1975, p. 11.
2. See the opinion of Klaus Wessel concerning the similarly sudden appearance on the art market of a group of stelae from Antinoe (Carroll 1965, p. 92).
3. Schneider 1975, p. 11.
4. Schneider 1975, p. 10, cat. 96.
5. Schneider 1982, p. 40.
6. Schneider 1975, p. 11.
7. Schneider 1975, p. 11.
8. Petrie 1889, p. 19; Petrie 1911, p. 11.
9. Petrie 1889, p. 19.
10. Edgar 1905a, pp. 229-230.
11. Parlasca 1980, pl. 154, no. 4 dated (p.66) to "il tardo terzo venticinquennio del IV sec."
12. Museum of Fine Arts 1976, p. 27.
13. Bianchi 1980, p. 19.
14. Kákosy 1983.
15. Museum of Fine Arts 1976, p. 27.
16. Schneider 1982, p. 42, no. 34; pp. 44-45, nos. 38-39.
17. Museum of Fine Arts 1976, p. 27.
18. Bianchi 1980, p. 18.
19. Schneider 1982, p. 42 no. 34; pp. 44-45, nos. 38-39.

Bibliography: Museum of Fine Arts 1976, p. 27; Museum of Fine Arts 1987a, pp. 78-79, p. 109; Parlasca 1978, 119 (165) pl. 41.

163
Stela of Herakleides

From Kom Abu Billo
Roman Period, about third century A.D.
Limestone
Height 33.3 cm.
William K. and Marilyn Simpson Fund, 1984
(1984.256)

In Graeco-Roman times, Kom Abu Billo served as the cemetery for the town of Terenuthis, a flourishing center for the trade in natron and salt situated some forty miles northwest of Cairo.[1] It is today best known for the hundreds of funerary stelae found there, which, like the burials they mark,[2] display an interesting blend of Egyptian and Hellenistic themes.[3] Two main types of Kom Abu Billo stelae may be distinguished: those in which the deceased is represented standing, offering upon a horned altar, or with his hands raised in the *orans* position; and those, like the present piece, in which the owner is shown reclining upon a couch. The deceased, wearing *chiton* and *himation*, lies upon a raised and heavily cushioned couch, his left hand clasping a small garland and his right extending a single-handled, stemmed cup. Before him is the Anubis dog, couchant upon a bracket, his head turned to face the spectator. In front of the couch are arranged a sheaf of wheat, an amphora upon its stand, a ladle, a cup, and a tripod table upon which rests a shallow bowl. The entire composition is framed by two

163

164

columns topped by debased palm-leaf capitals, originally surmounted by a gabled pediment that is now damaged. Two lines of Greek lightly incised between deep guidelines at the foot of the stela give the owner's name: Herakleides, "devoted to his brothers, fond of his children [. . .]" The stelae from Kom Abu Billo were mass produced in limestone, as here, and occasionally in gypsum,[4] and were originally built into arched niches in the gaudily painted mud-brick tomb superstructures; the tombs themselves took a number of varied forms.[5] Though difficult to date precisely, stelae of this type appear to have been in use for more than two hundred years, from the first to the third century A.D. or later.[6] By far the greater number were executed in sunk relief; raised relief, as here, is encountered far less frequently, and may well indicate the superior social standing of its owner.

CNR

1. Griffiths 1985, col. 424.
2. Cf. el-Nassery and Wagner 1978, pp. 231-235.
3. Dentzer 1978, pp. 63-82, esp. pp. 65-68. At other sites: Parlasca 1975, pp. 303-314.
4. El-Nassery and Wagner 1978, p. 234.
5. El-Nassery and Wagner 1978, pp. 231-233, fig. 2; Hooper 1961, pp. 2-3, pls. 1-4.
6. Cf. Parlasca 1970, pp. 173-198, esp. pp. 181-189; el-Nassery and Wagner 1978, p. 234.

Bibliography: Museum of Fine Arts 1987b, pp. 82-83.

Literature: Abd el-Hafeez and Abd el-Al 1985, pp. 42-43; Abd el-Al, Grenier, and Wagner 1985.

164
Mask

Provenance unknown
Roman Period
Gilded Plaster
Height 19 cm., width 16.5 cm.
Edward J. and Mary S. Holmes Fund
(1977.175)

Plaster funerary masks were pressed from molds and the gender-specific details that individualized the faces were added separately so that both male and female masks could be mass-produced from the same, basic form.[1] Composed of multiple, intricately rendered spirals, the hair, moustache, and beard of this mask are more sophisticated in execution than those on most stucco masks[2] – even the curls of the elaborate coiffures of women were usually rendered as stuccoed donuts – and the hair appears to have been part of the original, and perhaps unique, mold form.

The naturalistic quality of this mask is further enhanced by the eyes, crafted of calcite and painted glass, with pupils "of obsidian set in gold casings."[3] A dot of red lead in the inner corner of each eye adds anatomical precision.[4] The eyelashes are formed from the serrated edges of the copper eyelids. Since masks were produced with gaping holes where the eyes should be, it was left to the discretion of the patron to choose the material of which they would be made. The options ranged from painted stucco plugs, to miniature works of the jeweler's art such as these liquid and lifelike examples.[5]

Although most plaster masks were painted in realistic colors, at least one-third of all plaster masks were gilded.[6] The amount and quality of the gold applied varied from the spare use on ornamental details to completely gilded masks like this one. The decision, while primarily a matter of means, was no doubt influenced by religious convictions (cat. 150).[7]

This thick plaster mask exhibits none of the surface pitting that is seen on many similar examples. Perhaps the "thin layer of brown clay, which served as a ground for the gold leaf"[8] is of more permanent material than the structural plaster behind it. The brown slip must also have substituted for the ground of red or yellowish-brown paint that was the customary undercoating for gilded plaster masks.[9] The touches of red paint at the nostrils may be a carry-over from the usual red underpainting, or may be reminiscent of the "gaudily painted nostrils"[10] on the cartonnage mummies from Akhmim.

The date of this mask is problematic. It has been dated to the early third century A.D. and the beard and hairstyle have been seen to be influenced by those "made popular by the Emperor Hadrian (A.D. 117-138)."[11] Abundant hair and heavy beards were popular in ancient Egypt, however, from the Ptolemaic Period on[12] and male hairstyles are an even less secure criterion for dating than the more distinctive hairstyles of women.[13] Stylistically, the Boston head, which must have broken from a plaster headrest that fit over the head and bust of a wrapped mummy, seems most closely paralleled by the faces of cartonnage busts from the first century A.D.[14] The sensitive modeling of the facial structure, particularly around the eyes, and the attention to detail in the eyes themselves, suggest a Roman interest in naturalism. The smooth planes of the cheeks and forehead, however, preserve "the idealizing traditions of Egyptian funerary art."[15]

LHC

1. Root 1979, p. 46.
2. For a similar treatment of the hair cf. Grimm 1974, pl. 26 no. 3 (Brooklyn Museum Inv. 62.2)
3. Museum of Fine Arts 1987, p. 80. For inlaid glass eyes see Lucas 1962, pp. 98-127. The eyes of the Boston mask fall into Lucas's Class III (pp. 120-121), a category based on a technique of manufacture, not materials or a system of chronology. Class III eyes always differentiate the iris.
4. Root 1979, p. 24, notes that Egyptian painters are known to have incorrectly employed "traces of red paint to represent carbuncles on both the outer as well as the inner canthi of the eyes," a convention that "is not chronologically diagnostic."
5. Root 1979, pp. 8, 32.
6. Grimm 1974, p. 21.
7. Grimm 1974, p. 51.
8. Museum of Fine Arts 1987a, p. 80.
9. Grimm 1974, p. 21.
10. Root 1979, p. 24.
11. Museum of Fine Arts 1987a, p. 80.
12. Bothmer 1960, p. 174; Edgar 1905, p. 228, where he notes the presence of beards on men depicted on Ptolemaic tombstones and "on a few first century masks."
13. Bothmer 1960, p. 174, has even suggested that the tendency of classical archaeologists to compare the characteristics (eyes, hair, and beards) of Egyptian and Roman portrait heads serves no purpose in dating at all. For difficulties in assigning dates to the variation in hairstyles worn by women in Roman Egypt see Root 1979, pp. 42-43.
14. Compare Grimm 1974, pl. 5, no. 1, (East Berlin, Äg. Inv. 11741); pl. 6 (West Berlin, Äg. Inv. 11414); and pl. 7, no. 1 (formerly in the collection of Sir J. Epstein).
15. Museum of Fine Arts 1987a, p. 80.

Bibliography: Museum of Fine Arts 1987a, pp. 80-81, 109; Museum of Fine Arts, 1976-1977, p. 41.

165
Funerary shroud and mask

From Thebes, near Deir el-Bahri
Roman Period, fourth century A.D.
Linen and stucco
Height 93.5 cm.
Gift of the Egypt Exploration Fund, 1897 (97.1100)

In the 1894-1895 season, from a mound of limestone chips that covered the middle platform before the Anubis chapel on the northern side of the mortuary temple of Queen Hatshepsut, Edouard Naville excavated mummies of men, women, and children (fig. 86).[1] They were completely swathed in linen, but on the front of each a stuccoed and painted bust piece had been sewn. The top of the abbreviated shroud was pressed into a mold to produce the effect of a three-dimensional plaster mask,[2] the traditional funerary head covering in Middle Egypt. The neck, shoulder area, and clothed upper figure, including the arms and hands, however, continued along the flat shroud in an unbroken, painted line from the three-dimensional stucco face. At the lower edge, beneath the painted bust, a squared register depicts a mythological scene.

Naville, who had uncovered similarly decorated mummies in the previous season, referred to them as Coptic mummies as they were found buried beneath the Coptic monastery for which modern Deir el-Bahri is named. He conjectured that the mummies were "of Christians, and probably of some dignitaries of the convent."[3] In 1923-1924, continuing the excavation of the Hatshepsut complex for The Metropolitan Museum of Art, H.E. Winlock unearthed several more examples of this type. Although he characterized them somewhat unfairly as "atrocities of hideousness," Winlock correctly identified one of the female mummy shrouds as belonging, not to one of the earliest members of the Coptic (Christian) faith, but rather, to a "bedizened granddaughter of the days of paganism."[4]

The decoration of these mummies is consistent with native Egyptian funerary beliefs of the Roman era. Whereas Naville interpreted the objects held in the deceased's two hands as "a glass and the other an ear of corn, evidently the two Christian symbols of bread and wine,"[5] the objects can be identified as *canthari*[6] perhaps to hold sacred Nile water and as floral funerary garlands or wreaths (see cat. 161). The lower register contains traditional Egyptian emblems of resurrection: lotus blossoms and the barque of the funerary god Sokar. Sokar may here be identified with the sun-god Re.[7] The *henu* barque[8] is flanked by jackals,[9] poised upon their haunches, the guardians of the gateways to the Underworld.

The jackals, carrying the "key" to Hades[10] about their necks, provide a *terminus post quem* for these shrouds, as the motif is not attested before the twelfth regnal year of the emperor Trajan (A.D. 109).[11] Although the jeweled floral crowns and round faces of the shrouds bear a striking stylistic resemblance to attributes of the famous roundel or tondo portrait of the Emperor Septimius Severus and his family (dated to circa A.D. 200),[12] The exaggerated, marionette-like features and the doughy, stuccoed additions indicate a later date. On the basis of their stratigraphy, and their resemblance to various related finds, in particular a mummy ticket dated to "the second year of the Emperor Probus, that is A.D. 278" and scattered coins dating to the reigns of Diocletian (A.D. 284-305) and Constantius (A.D. 337-361),[13] found at the burial site of similarly decorated mummies excavated in the area around Medinet Habu, these Theban, stuccoed shrouds have been dated to the fourth century A.D.

LHC

1. Naville 1895, p. 33, pl. II.
2. Grimm 1974, p. 95.
3. Naville 1894, p. 4.
4. Winlock 1924a, pp. 32-33.
5. Naville 1894, p. 4.
6. Thompson 1982, p. 23, no. 40.
7. Grimm 1974, p. 123; for the solar aspects of Sokar, see Brovarski 1984, col. 1061.
8. For a description of the barque of Sokar, see Brovarski 1984, cols. 1066-67.
9. Parlasca 1966, p. 209, the position of these jackals does not satisfy the requirements of the Ritual of Embalming (Sauneron 1952b, p. 54 n. 3) as the scene on these abbreviated shrouds would not be at the prescribed position at the feet of the mummy.
10. Morenz 1975, p. 516.
11. Parlasca 1966, pp. 163-164.
12. For a photo of the Berlin tondo, see Thompson 1982, fig. 46.
13. These mummies were buried either in crudely made coffins of unbaked clay or directly in the sand. As these burials "cut into the foundations of destroyed domed tombs" of the third century (Hölscher 1954, p. 44), they must post-date these structures.

Bibliography: Smith 1960, pp. 189-190, fig. 131; Museum of Fine Arts 1976, p. 200, cat. 234; Morgan 1976, no. 111, fig. 31.

Literature: Grimm 1974, pp. 36, 95, 123, 143, pl. 112 no. 2; Brooklyn Museum 1941, pp. 16-17, pl. 9; Parlasca 1966, p. 291 no. 2, p. 208; Bonner 1941-42, p. 91.

Fig. 86

165

166, detail

166
Child's tunic

From Egypt
Coptic Period, sixth or seventh century A.D.
Length (hem to hem) 88 cm., width (sleeve to sleeve) 89.5 cm.
Warp: undyed wool, S-spun, ca. 16 warps per cm.
Weft: plain weave (with predominant weft); undyed wool, s-spun, about 30 wefts per cm.
Tapestry weave: purple, orange and undyed wool, about 56 wefts per cm.
Dovetailing, flying shuttle (tapestry area), soumak (plain-weave area)
Gift of Denman W. Ross, 1896 (96.121)

With the spread of Christianity in Egypt, mummification was gradually discontinued, and the dead were buried fully clothed or wrapped in various weavings.[1] The dryness of the Egyptian desert preserved thousands of textiles used for burial purposes in the Early Christian Period. These weavings, known as Coptic, frequently reflect the taste of the late Roman and Early Christian Periods in the Mediterranean world (about A.D. 300-700).[2] This small woolen garment, made for a child, is a well preserved example. It is woven in one piece, and the front and back are sewn together at the sides (fig. 87). The neck is slit along the warp from sleeve to sleeve. Two decorative bands, or clavi, extend from shoulder to hem at front and back; similar bands decorate the sleeves. A large leaf on each shoulder and a pair of smaller leaves near the hem on each side are typical of garment decorations discovered in Egypt and of tunics depicted in Mediterranean art of this period.[3]

With the exception of minor details in the center of the large leaves, all the ornaments are woven in purple, a color frequently employed in monochrome Coptic tapestries. The design in the clavi is composed of an undulating branch with leaves stemming alternately from its two sides. Three-dot triangles flank the branch and decorate the areas between the leaves. The large leaves are bordered by a repeating semi-circular motif; in its center adjacent orange circles frame a small cross. This seems to be a stylized version of the vine leaves frequently depicted in purple tapestries of various designs discovered in Egypt. More naturalistic versions of this motif occur in roundels and in semi-circular or triangular units framing square panels.[4]

Purple tapestries of this type were produced in the Mediterranean over a long period,[5] probably from the third to around the sixth century. The highly stylized versions of the vine motif on the shoulders of this tunic may indicate a late stage of development within the purple group. Furthermore, the use of wool throughout the garment is unusual; the more naturalistic versions were frequently woven into linen tunics.

LA-M

1. For later mummy portraits indicating that mummification continued to the fourth century, Thompson 1982, pp. 52-61; Shore 1962, pp. 45-46.
2. Trilling 1980, pp. 18-19; Kelsey Museum of Archaeology 1980, pp. 15-16.

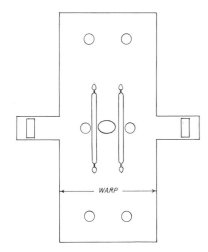

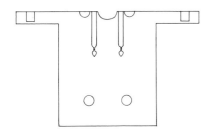

Fig. 87

3. For the general layout of Coptic and Mediterranean tunics, Baginski and Tidhar 1980, pp. 10-11; Thompson 1971, pp. 2-5, fig. 1. For children's tunics of this type, du Bourguet 1964, p. 185, no. E1; p. 275, no. F74; Kendrick 1921, p. 22, no. 334, pl. XIII. For representations of figures dressed in tunics of this type, Bianchi Bandinelli 1971, p. 95, fig. 86, 87.

4. Wulff and Volbach 1926, p. 38, pl. 68, no. 9131; Nauerth 1986, pp. 42-43; Egger 1867, pls. 10-11; Trilling 1982, p. 70, no. 63, p. 82, no. 85; p. 83, nos. 87, 88; Kendrick 1920, p. 107, no. 217, pl. 32

5. For stylistic developments of these purple tapestries, Trilling 1982, pp. 104-108. For the use of wool in later tunics, Kendrick 1920, pp. 28-29.

167
Child's garment

From Egypt
Coptic Period, sixth or seventh century A.D.
Length (shoulder to hem) 66.2 cm., width (sleeve to sleeve) 60 cm.
Warp: undyed linen, about 12 warps per cm., S-spun.
Weft: plain weave: undyed linen, about 13 wefts per cm.
Tapestry weave: red, pink, green, dark and light blue, yellow, light brown wool, about 42 wefts per cm. S-spun.
Eccentric weave, slit
Gift of Denman W. Ross, 1915 (15.701)

Woven in linen tabby, this Coptic garment continues the traditional clothing material in dynastic Egypt.[1] Unlike the straight-sided tunic with shoulder and sleeve bands that

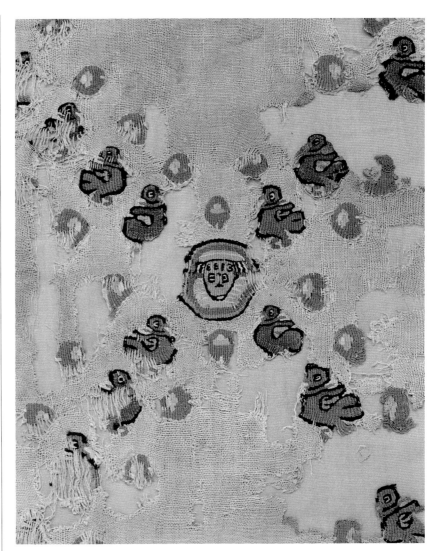

167, detail

was common the antique and Early Christian periods, this garment is bell-shaped. It also differs from many others of this period in that the warp extends from hem to hem rather than from sleeve to sleeve (see cat. 166). Tapestry ornaments composing two diagonal lines intersect at the waist, extending from the shoulders to the area above the hem at both front and back. A horizontal line at the lower edge forms the third side of a triangle that echoes the shape of the garment and repeats the triangle above the waist. The diagonals are composed of rows of parallel heart-shaped leaves flanking a row of ducks. The ducks are alternately blue and green, articulated by yellow and red; the leaves are red with pink and beige details. At the junction of the diagonals on both front and back is a medallion; one encloses a human or animal face, and the other a duck resembling those in the diagonals rows. The medallion enclosing the face likely marks the front side, since it is unique on the garment. Brocaded blue bands frame the neck and sleeves.[2] Heart-shaped leaves were frequently used

with ducks or birds on polychrome Coptic textiles, as they could be combined to form various designs.[3] Rows of disconnected heart-shaped units also occur in garments worn by female saints in the nave mosaics of Sant'Apollinare Nuovo in Ravenna (about A.D. 568). Similarly, the bird motif occurs in the apse mosaic of San Vitale, where a court lady wears a garment decorated with dispersed birds or ducks (about A.D. 547), and in garments depicted in the Sassanian reliefs of Taq-i-Bustan.[4]

Diagonals that intersect to form lozenges occur in Egyptian and Sassanian silks as well as in late Roman and early Byzantine mosaics. Since this garment was woven in one piece from one hem to the other, it seems clear that the weaver duplicated the x-shaped design from the front and the back of the garment, thus creating between the two intersecting units a lozenge comparable to those in the silks and the mosaics.[5]

LA-M

1. Hall 1986, p. 9; Riefstahl 1944a, p. 1.
2. For a similar type of garment made for a child,

du Bourguet 1964, p. 318, no. F191. For a brocaded neck band of this type, Wulff and
Volbach 1926, p. 69, pl. 89, no. 11453.

3. For heart-shaped leaves in Coptic textiles, du
Bourguet 1964, p. 231, no. E116; pp. 232-233,
nos. E117-118: Kendrick 1921, p. 24, pl.
18; p. 23,pl. 15; Wulff and Volbach 1926, p. 115,
pl. 114, no. 9102. For the use of this motif in
Coptic textiles, Kitzinger 1948, pp. 30-32.

4. Deichmann 1958, pls. 128-132, 366; Graber
1967, p. 154, fig. 166. For the motif of dispersed birds in Sassanian garments, Herzfeld
1920, pl. 63.

5. For the lozenge design in silks, Falke 1913, vol.
1, fig. 65; for a comparable design in late antique and early Byzantine mosaics, Levi 1971,
vol. 2, pl. 74; Bovino 1956, 13. For lozenges
composed of heart-shaped motifs, Ackerman
pp. 698-699.

168
Stela

From Esna
Coptic Period, seventh or eighth century A.D.
Limestone
Height 58.5 cm., width 43 cm.
Sears Fund, 1904 (04.1845)

Although Coptic art generally avoids pharaonic conventions, numerous ancient Egyptian influences persist. On stelae, architectural and animal motifs are the most
common examples. In the Dynastic Period,
such elements as the palace facade and the
mastaba niche were integral to the design
of stelae. Coptic monuments borrow a complex arrangement of architectural fixtures
from temples at Bagawat, Sohag, and elsewhere.[1] These stelae are economic substitutes for tomb chapels.[2] The architectural
designs may symbolize paradise; the heraldic animals certainly do.

This is one of two similar stelae in Boston[3]
that belong to a group from Esna and other
Upper Egyptian sites distinctive for their intricate architectural elements, symbolic animals, and flat, unmodeled surfaces. The
bird (probably an eagle, but sometimes said
to be a phoenix or ba bird) with the bulla,
which is an especially popular symbol on
Coptic stelae and textiles,[4] may represent
resurrection. The pair of peacocks under the
pediments are tokens of immortality and
paradise.[5] The pilasters surmounted by
arches recall a similar motif on other stelae
that also represent the gates of paradise.[6]
The characteristically flat surface may be a
coincidence of preservation: the stelae
were originally covered with paint or
painted plaster, which was modeled. The
coloring has completely fallen off all but a
few examples.[7]

DBS

168

1. Badawy 1945, p. 19, fig. 13; Badawy 1978, p.
98, fig. 2.64.

2. See Badawy 1945, 1978, pp. 101, 210-215;
Cramer 1957. For analogous stelae in the Cop-
tic Museum, Cairo, see Crum 1902, pls. 45-46.
(CG 8662, 8665, 8668, 8671, 8672).

3. The other is 04.1847; see Brooklyn Museum
1941, p. 23, cat. 38; Cramer 1957, pp. 5-6 and
pl. 3, no. 5.

4. E.g. Crum 1903; Zuntz 1932, pp. 33-34; Wessel 1963, pp. 116 and 209, fig. 85 and pl. 17;
Badawy 1978, pp. 218-219, 302-303.

5. Lother 1929; Stier 1938, p. 1420.

6. Drioton 1943, pp. 75-77.

7. Crum 1902, pp. 125-126, 130, 134, 138-140
and pls. 33-34, 37-38, 46-47 (CG 8591, 8593,
8596-8597, 8644, 8646, 8668, 8670, 8675,
8678); Cramer 1957, pp. 13 and 15, no. 24
and 28.

169a, front

169a, back

169
Reliquary cross and reverse
of reliquary cross

a. From Syria-Palestine
Ninth to tenth centuries A.D.
Brass
Height 11.3 cm., width 5.4 cm., diam. 1.1 cm.
Gift of Mr. and Mrs. Cornelius Vermeule III,
1961 (61.1092)

b. From Naga ed-Dêr
Ninth to tenth centuries A.D.
Brass
Height 8.7 cm., width 5.7 cm., diam. 5 cm.
Harvard University-Museum of Fine Arts
Expedition, 1947 (1987.286)

Made to contain relics[1] and suspended from chains around the neck, encolpia of this type are preserved in large quantity. Both the fragmentary example, found in an undatable Coptic tomb at Naga ed-Dêr, and the complete pectoral cross shown here are decorated in relief. These crosses with slightly flaring arms comprise two valves fastened with a clasp at the bottom and a hinge at the top to which a suspension loop is attached. The Crucifixion on the front shows a bearded Christ with closed eyes and head inclined to the left wearing a colobium (a long sleeveless tunic). At the top are chased and punched symbols of Sol and Luna. The inscription on the horizontal bar may be translated "Jesus Christ Victor." The Virgin (left) and Saint John (right), both have large heads and abbreviated bodies.

The back shows the Virgin Orans wearing a tunic and maphorion superimposed on a finely hatched mandorla. The four ends of the cross have medallions with frontal busts of the Evangelists holding closed books with covers decorated with punched designs.[2]

The iconography of these crosses relates them to several enamels dated recently to the ninth and tenth centuries.[3] The representation of a dead Christ on the cross, with bent head and closed eyes, which first appears on an icon at Mount Sinai dated to the eighth century, is common on icons and manuscripts of the ninth century;[4] As these crosses have been excavated throughout Asia Minor, Egypt, and Europe, it seems likely that they were made in the Holy Land (Syria-Palestine) as souvenirs for pilgrims.[5]

NN

1. Originally they were thought to be *staurotecae* (see King 1928, pp. 193-198), but sufficient evidence that they held parts of the True Cross and not simply relics of saints is lacking. See Frolow 1961, p. 323.
2. One of these crosses in Athens (Stathatos 1957, no. 62) identifies the Evangelists as: (above) M for Matthew; (below) M for Mark; (left) L for Luke; and (right) J for John.
3. Including the Beresford Hope Cross in London, the reliquary cross of Pope Pascal I (817-24) in the Vatican, and the Fieschi-Morgan reliquary of the True Cross in New York. See New York 1984, p. 124; Kartsonis 1982; Buckton 1982, pp. 35-36.
4. See Hausherr 1963; Weitzmann 1976, no. B36, B50; New York 1984, p. 124.
5. See von Barany-Oberschall 1953, pp. 210-212; Bank 1980, pp. 108-109.

Mummification

170
Mummy case of Nes-Ptah

Provenance unknown, but almost certainly from Thebes
Early Dynasty 22, c. 930-880 B.C.
Cartonnage
Length 205 cm.
Hay Collection, Gift of C. Granville Way, 1872 (72.4838)

Both Nes-Ptah, the owner of this cartonnage, and his father Pen-renen-utet were barbers in the temple of Amen at Thebes, a duty that involved regularly shaving the heads of all priests and officiants to ensure their ritual purity in the god's dwelling place. It is reasonably certain that this is the same Nes-Ptah who is mentioned as the husband of Tabes on her cartonnage (cat. 121), and the couple was probably buried together in some now unidentifiable sepulcher in the Theban necropolis.

A curious funerary practice of Dynasty 22 was the anointing of the cartonnage or mummy wrappings[1] and occasionally the coffin[2] with a resinous libation that has turned black in the course of the centuries. The circumstance was commented on by G. d'Athanasi as early as 1836,[3] and a number of later writers have also mentioned examples.[4] At first glance the application of this coating seems surprising, since it obscures the carefully painted scenes and texts of the cartonnages. Although this would not have nullified the efficacy of the paintings as magical aids to the deceased,[5] it seems likely that the resinous substance was originally transparent and that the ancient Egyptians did not anticipate the chemical changes that caused the darkening.

The anointing of mummies and coffins with a resinous substance is attested in burials from the Old Kingdom to Dynasty 19[6] but it is unknown in Dynasty 21 and its reintroduction toward the end of the tenth century B.C. was perhaps connected with the change in burial customs that occurred at that time. The coffins of Nestanebashru,[7] which were probably prepared in early Dynasty 22, present the earliest instance of this treatment in the Third Intermediate Period.[8] During Dynasty 22 many cartonnages were treated in this way, including that of Tabes, which has, however, been cleaned by the Museum of Fine Arts Research Laboratory. On some examples the front is completely covered with the substance,[9] while on others, such as Nes-Ptah's, only part of the surface is affected.[10] The rear is usually clean and the manner in which the liquid has run down the sides indicates that the cartonnage was anointed while in a recumbent position – probably when lying in its coffin (streaks of the black substance can be observed on the inner walls of some coffins of this period).[11] In some cases so much

170

liquid was used that the cartonnage became stuck to the floor of the coffin.[12]

The pouring of this libation must have formed part of the funeral ceremonies immediately before the interment, but its precise significance is unknown, as is the exact chemical composition of the liquid used. In a few cases where the cartonnage was anointed particularly thoroughly, care was taken to leave the face mask clean.[13] The practice was abandoned about the time that cartonnages fell out of use, the latest examples dating to around the end of the eighth century.[14]

In spite of the opaque libation, some of the decoration of Nes-Ptah's cartonnage can still be made out. While the "Two Falcons" design is found on his wife's case, Nes-Ptah's is decorated with a series of horizontal registers. Above the first is a large deity with outspread wings mostly obscured, and below this is a scene that probably showed Nes-Ptah being led into the presence of Osiris and his company after successfully passing the test of the judgment – a theme that is known from other cartonnages of the same type.[15] Nes-Ptah's figure is visible on the left side of the case and parts of the figures of two goddesses can be seen at the right. Then comes another winged figure representing "The Behdetite," and a scene in which Nes-Ptah (at right) makes an offering before a divine emblem (probably either the Abydos fetish or the barque of Sokar) that is mounted on a dais with carrying poles. Below a group of divine standards at the left, a pair of winged serpents flank a divine image, now lost, while over the feet a winged scarab beetle is flanked by mummiform deities.

As on Tabes's cartonnage, the figures and scenes were painted in bright colors. A clear varnish, now turned yellow, was applied to these, while the white ground color was left untouched to provide a contrast. A number of other cartonnages are known, which show such close affinity with that of Nes-Ptah in the layout of the designs and the style of the painting that it is probable that all of them were produced by the same group of craftsmen.[16] One of these is dated to the reign of Osorkon I,[17] thus agreeing with the date suggested above for Tabes. As with Ankh-pef-hor's cartonnage (cat. 122), the style and costume of the human figures support an early Dynasty 22 date, while the rather small face mask and high domed wig of Nes-Ptah's cartonnage also seem to be characteristic of this early period.[18]

JHT

The Mummy of Nes-Ptah

Nes-Ptah was a small man who, unlike his wife Tabes, died at an advanced age. This is indicated by moderate osteoporosis and degenerative changes in his bones, including a spinal fracture. He also had extensive hardening of the arteries in a pattern suggestive of diabetes mellitus. There is also evidence of chronic dental disease.

Nes-Ptah was more carefully mummified than Tabes, though she was provided with more amulets. His brain had been removed and linen-packing introduced into the cranium. A great deal of molten resin had been poured into his chest and abdominal cavities, and packages containing the mummified viscera are embedded in this hardened resin. His arms and legs were separately wrapped, and his phallus was wrapped

around a reed. A package of homogeneous material, probably sand, was placed between his legs. Like Tabes, the two sites of his embalming incisions were covered with metal plaques.

MM

1. Cf. Manchester 5053a (early Dynasty 22): David 1979, p.5.
2. Leiden M.17: Schmidt 1919, fig. 955; Leiden M.62, London BM 29578, Sheffield J.93.I283 (unpublished).
3. d'Athanasi 1836, p. 124-125.
4. Birch 1850, p. 274; Carter and Mace 1901, p. 144; Anthes 1943, p. 35; Dawson and Gray 1968, pp. 12, 19, pl. VId, Xa; Gray and Slow 1968, pp. 35-36, pl. 50; Becker-Colonna 1979, p. 95, Taf. V.
5. Edwards 1986, p. 214.
6. Lucas 1962, pp. 312-316.
7. Cairo CG 61033
8. Daressy 1909, pp. 196-200, pl. LVII.
9. Dawson and Gray 1968, pl. VId, Xa; Gray and Slow 1968, pl. 50; Becker-Colonna 1979, Taf. V.
10. Dolzani 1969, p. 260-262, fig. 11-12; cf. Sheffield J.93.1283 (unpublished).
11. London BM 24906.
12. Dawson and Gray 1968, p, 12, n. 2; Becker-Colonna 1979, p. 95.
13. Becker-Colonna 1979, p. 95, Taf. V; Malaise 1971, p. 41, fig. 12; cf. also Paris, Louvre, no number, cartonnage of the Lady of the House *Hr* (unpublished).
14. Birch 1850, p. 273-275; Anthes 1943, p. 35. For the dating of these pieces, see Taylor 1985, I, pp. 82, 462.
15. Dawson and Gray 1968, pl. Va; Allen 1923, p. 13.
16. Examples include Philadelphia E.14344 (unpublished), London BM 22939 and Toronto 910.10: Dawson and Gray 1968, p. 8, pl. Va; Millet 1972, pp. 18-27.
17. Berlin 7325: Königliche Museen zu Berlin 1899, pp. 235-237.
18. Cf. Hamburg C.3834 (temp. Osorkon I): Altenmüller 1982, pp. 57-58, fig. 7, Taf. 2-3.

171
Embalming table

Provenance unknown
Saite Period, Dynasty 26
Wood
Length 171 cm., height 32 cm., width 42 cm.
Lent by Peter Diem

Lion-headed beds or tables used for embalming appear as early as the Archaic period[1] and the use of the lion as a symbol of resurrection in the Heliopolitan mythology has been noted in this context.[2] There may, in fact, be two types of such beds used, one for the actual embalming process and another with a more symbolic role. Rough wooden tables have been found in embalmer's caches[3] and stone examples at Sakkara,[4] Thebes,[5] and at Memphis for the Apis bulls.[6] A fragmentary calcite table inscribed for a New Kingdom official also appears to have come from Memphis.[7]

Wooden lion-headed beds are shown on coffins of the Middle Kingdom[8] and in New Kingdom tomb paintings.[9] Actual specimens

were found in Tutankhamen's tomb;[10] fragments of another were found in the tomb of Horemheb along with a calcite example.[11] A number of elaborate painted wooden beds with lion's heads and legs date to the Roman Period.[12] These are usually combined with catafalques and acted as biers to carry the body to the tomb.

This example consists of a four-piece frame in which the shorter rails are butted against the longer rails and fastened with bronze corner brackets. On the front brackets are modeled two lions heads, while the rear fittings contain sockets for the addition of the high curving tail shown on the representations of these beds (see fig. 5). The legs are socketed into oval surrounds that form the bottoms of these fittings. Like most Egyptian furniture legs, they are carved to imitate the fore and hind legs of the animal. Each support is composed of a pair of legs that stand together on a conical pad. The surface of the table is made of four rough planks that are joined together and to the frame by dowels. Faint traces of a column of inscription in light green pigment run down the center of the bed.

This bed is similar to one in the Metropolitan Museum of Art[13] that was excavated in an embalmer's cache at the Asasif and is now thought to date to the Saite Period. The working surface of both these pieces is made of rough, inferior wood that would not be easily damaged during the embalming process.

PL

1. Moret and Abou-Ghazi 1978, p. 42.
2. Needler 1963, pp. 4-5.
3. Winlock 1922.
4. Moret and Abou-Ghazi 1978; see also Saleh and Sourouzian 1987, no. 18, the latter is more likely New Kingdom than Archaic.
5. Winlock 1930.
6. Dimick 1959, pp. 75-79.
7. Habachi 1967.
8. Terrace 1967, pl. 15.

171

9. Klebs 1934, p. 140, fig. 88.
10. Carter and Mace 1923, pp. 112-113, pl. 17.
11. Davis et al. 1912, pp. 100-103, pls. 78 and 81.
12. Needler 1963, see also Rhind 1862, pp. 89-90 and frontispiece.
13. Metropolitan Museum of Art, MMA 30.3.45.

172
Figures of the Four Sons of Horus

Provenance unknown
Dynasty 21 or 22
Wax
Height 7.7-9.5 cm.
Hay Collection, Gift of C. Granville Way, 1872 (72.4782-84, 4788)

In Dynasty 21, the practice of placing the internal organs in canopic jars was discontinued (see cat. 117). The viscera were instead packaged separately in linen and replaced in the body. In order to continue receiving the protection of the Four Sons of Horus, the deceased were often provided with a set of wax amulets representing these deities.[1] Perhaps because of its unique physical properties, wax seems to have had a magical significance for the ancient Egyptians, who employed it in the mummification process (see cat. 120) as well as for making amuletic objects.[2]

The wax Four Sons of Horus are represented as mummiform, wearing long wigs. Complete sets of the Sons of Horus were not always provided for the mummy; sometimes there were duplications or omissions of a particular deity. The set assembled here probably did not originally belong together, as the color and manufacturing technique differ among the figures. Two of them are modeled completely from wax. The human-headed Imsety and the jackal-headed Duamutef, however, are molded with wax surrounding a core of Nile mud.

SD'A

1. See Raven 1983, p. 15, esp. note 122 and pls. 2-5; Andrews 1984, p. 22, fig. 22; Williams 1918, pp. 273-74, no. 16; Ziegelmayer 1985, Abb. 14-16; Hayes 1959, pp. 424-425; Dawson and Gray 1968, no. 33; Harris and Weeks 1973, p. 49.
2. See the extensive discussion in Raven 1983.

172

173
Plaque with engraved *wedjat* eye

Provenance unknown
Third Intermediate Period or later
Lead and tin[1]
Height 8.4 cm., width 9 cm.
Hay Collection, Gift of C. Granville Way, 1872 (72.4465)

Plaques of metal, gilded wood, or wax were often placed over the embalmer's incisions

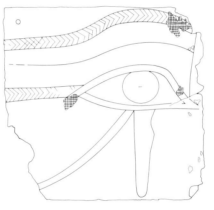

173

after the mummification process was complete.[2] Such plaques were typically decorated with the protective *wedjat* eye. This example bears an incised *wedjat* eye, as well as traces of the original linen and tissues to which the plaque adhered.

X-rays have revealed the presence of metal plaques in several of the Museum's mummies (see cats. 121 and 170). Occasionally, the incisions were sewn shut, but that of the mummy Tabes was left gaping open, and her plaque was carelessly placed over her wrist (see cat. 121).

SD'A

1. Analysis by Suzanne Gänsicke of the Research Laboratory.
2. Andrews 1984, fig. 19, p. 22; Dawson and Gray 1968, nos. 15, 16, 18, 22.

174

174
Tongue plate

From Hawara
Roman Period
Gold
Length 4 cm., width 2.7 cm.
Gift of Egyptian Research Account, 1911 (11.2890)

Egyptian mummies were sometimes provided with such accoutrements as artificial eyes (see cat. 120) and finger stalls or caps (see cat. 175) in order to make them appear as lifelike as possible, and to aid in regaining their faculties in the afterlife. In the Roman Period, roughly rectangular tongue plates of gold were placed in the mouth[1] or over the lips.[2] These plates were probably intended to aid the deceased in regaining the power

175

of speech (see "The Social Aspects of Death," p. 52), and to speak with a tongue of gold at his or her judgment before Osiris.[3]

This example was among many found by Petrie at Hawara, the Roman period site from which cats. 155 and 156 were excavated.

SD'A

1. Liverpool 13.10.1911.25, Gray and Slow 1968, p. 28, fig. 41; Petrie 1912, p. 36; Pettigrew 1834, p. 63.
2. Edinburgh 1911.210.1, Gray 1966, p. 3, note 6; Leiden 2, Gray 1966, p. 3, pl. XXIV.2 (Dynasty 26).
3. Aldred, personal communication quoted in Gray and Slow 1968, p. 32.

Bibliography: Petrie 1912, pl. XXXVI, 12.

175
Finger caps

From Giza tomb G 7540 T
Saite Period, Dynasty 26
Gold
Length of each 1.1 cm.
Harvard University-Museum of Fine Arts Expedition, 1929 (29.1441a-j)

After mummification, but before bandaging, gold was sometimes applied directly to the body. In the Graeco-Roman period, the face, chest, and nails were decorated with gold leaf,[1] and Pettigrew noted examples of extensive gilding throughout the body.[2]

These ten finger caps were excavated in Room I of Giza tomb G 7540 T, a four-chambered tomb dating to Dynasty 26. Within this room were found three wooden sarcophagi in a very disturbed state; the finger caps were not found on a mummy, but in the debris of the chamber.

Gold stalls for fingers and toes are known from burials of the New Kingdom and later; these covered the entire digit and had the nail delineated. Examples were recovered from the tomb of Tutankhamen[3] and from the royal burials of Dynasty 21 at Tanis.[4] The practice continued in the Nubian royal burials of Dynasty 25 and later.[5] The small finger caps of later times cover just the nail, and are made of thin gold, foil or leaf.

The gold applied to the body associated the deceased with the sun-god, whose flesh was thought to be of gold (see cat. 150). The magical properties of the substance are noted in a funerary text: "O undead! You have just received your golden fingerstalls and your fingers are covered with gold, your nails with electrum! The radiation of Light reaches you, she who is truly the divine body of Osiris. Gold will illumine your face in the world between, you will breathe because of gold, you will come forth because of gold."[6]

SD'A

1. Andrews 1984, p. 23, fig. 22.
2. Pettigrew 1834, pp. 63-64.
3. Carter 1927, pp. 129-130.
4. Montet 1951, p. 73, pl. XLVI.
5. Dunham 1955, pl. CXXI, A.
6. Goyon 1972a, p. 70 (English translation in Jacq 1985, p. 57).

176
Heart scarabs

Provenance unknown
Gift of Mrs. Horace L. Mayer

a. Late Period
   Serpentine(?)
   Length 5 cm. (1974.566)

b. Third Intermediate Period to Saite Period
   Brown stone
   Length 4.3 cm., width 3.3 cm. (1979.560)

After the body was mummified, the heart remained in the chest cavity, and near it was set a heart scarab. The heart scarab was a stone image of the scarab beetle, with Spell 30 from the Book of the Dead inscribed upon its flat underside (fig. 88). The instructions at the beginning of this spell state that the scarab should be made of *nmhf* stone (perhaps green jasper, though a wide variety of stones were used in practice[1]), set in gold, and either placed within the heart or suspended from a silver chain around the neck.

The spell was designed to prevent the heart from testifying against its owner during the weighing of the heart before the divine judges. The text reads: "O heart of my mother! O heart of my mother! O my heart of my coming into being! Do not stand against me as a witness. Do not contradict me with the judges. Do not act against me with the gods. Do not be my enemy in the presence of the guardian of the balance. You are my soul which is in my body, which unites and makes whole my limbs. Go forth to happiness, transport us there. Do not make my name stink in the entourage of the one who created mankind. Stand up for happiness. Hear the joy of the judgment. Do

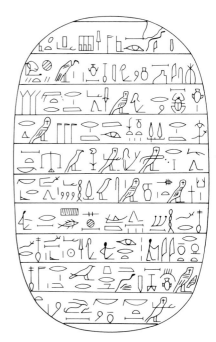

Fig. 88

176a

176b

not speak lies beside the great god. See, you will be selected to exist."

After death, the deceased traveled the Underworld until he reached the Hall of Judgment. There his heart and its scarab were put in one pan of a balance; an emblem of Maat, the goddess of truth and justice, was placed in the other. If the heart was judged virtuous, the deceased would be admitted into the realm of the resurrected dead, as one "true of voice" or "justified" in the Hall of Judgment. If the heart failed the test, the deceased would be consumed by Ammit, the crocodile-lion-hippopotamus monster who waited by the balance, and die a second, permanent death.

In depictions of this judgment, it is unclear whether a guilty heart was heavier or lighter than a virtuous one, since the vignettes invariably show the scales in balance. Clère has suggested that the balance was achieved when the heart was "empty of faults," and thus that a light heart was desired.[2] Harris, on the contrary, believes that the invariable choice of heavy stone for the material of heart scarabs implies that virtues were thought to weigh heavy.[3] If this is the correct interpretation, the heart scarab may have had a more practical function in addition to its magical properties, since the added weight of the stone scarab and its gold

mounting might compensate for a lack of virtue.

The scarab beetle was a potent symbol of resurrection. The beetle lays its eggs in a ball of dung and nutrients that it pushes along as it crawls. Eventually, the eggs hatch and young scarabs emerge from this ball, an apparent resurrection. The dung ball was also equated with the sun, which dies every night and is reborn every morning.

The green heart scarab (176a) is the more carefully made of the two examples. It belonged to a Director of Estates, Padi-Isis, the son of a woman named Inu. Its text is carved in ten evenly spaced horizontal registers, with surprisingly detailed hieroglyphs, despite its tiny scale. Traces of gold remain in the gap between the legs and the base, and on the upper surfaces of the middle legs on either side. However, the fine details indicated in the carving of the beetle make it unlikely that the entire scarab was covered in gold.

The second scarab (176b) belonged to Padi-Amen-nesut-tawy, the son of the third prophet of Amen-Re king of the gods, Hor, and a woman named Nes-Mut. The sculptor seems to have been uneasy about the length of the text; he has dispensed with register lines in order to save space and compressed the hieroglyphs as much as possible in the top half of the scarab, while the lower part is more generously spaced. The beetle itself is well modeled and polished, of hard brown stone. Although the head is carved in fine detail, the legs are only sketchily indicated, and there are no traces of gold.

AMR

1. Harris 1961, pp. 113-114.
2. Clère 1931, 430-431.
3. Harris 1961, p. 115.

177
Pesesh-kef amulets

First Intermediate Period
Harvard University-Museum of Fine Arts Expedition

a. From Mesheikh
   Gilded bronze
   Length 3.7 cm. (12.1264)

b. From Sheikh Farag
   Gilded silver
   Length 2.8 cm. (13.3920)

These tiny fragmentary metal objects represent a rare type of amulet known from tombs of the late Old Kingdom and First Intermediate Period. Complete amulets include a head, probably female, and usually with a long wig, and a flat blade split into two upward-curling points at the base. In some cases, such as 177b, the two parts were of different materials, and attached by

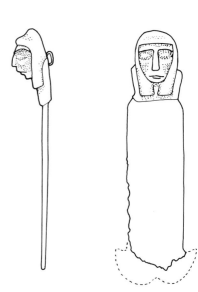

177a

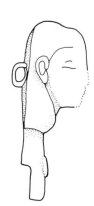

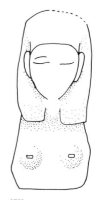

177b

two rivets. The blade almost certainly represents a *pesesh-kef*, an instrument used in funerary rituals (see cats. 3 and 11). The exact purpose of the *pesesh-kef* is unknown, so it is difficult to determine the significance of the amulet.

Only five such amulets have been published,[1] dating from late Dynasty 6 through Dynasty 11. Where details of the provenance are known, they seem to have come from burials of women, one a princess of Dynasty 11. They were often made of valuable materials, such as gold, silver, carnelian, and in at least one case, meteoric iron. The amulets were originally worn on the mummy; one example was found on a cord around a woman's neck. On the same cord were three button-shaped seal amulets (see cat. 29), three amulets associated with Hathor, and several beads.

The recent rediscovery and identification of these *pesesh-kef* amulets[2] suggests that such amulets may be considerably less rare than was hitherto believed.

AMR

1. Brunton 1935, pp. 213-217; van Walsem 1979, pp. 236-237 notes that he can add no examples to this corpus.

178
Funerary amulets

From Tell Nebesha
Late Period, Dynasties 26-30
Lengths .5-7.6 cm.
Gift of Egypt Exploration Fund, 1887
(87.671)

The cemetery of Tell Nebesha was excavated by Petrie in 1886. The majority of the tombs had been plundered, but four undisturbed mummies were found in one tomb in the southeastern part of the cemetery.[1] The bodies lay side by side in a single burial chamber but, as all the wooden objects in the tomb had disintegrated, the identities of the dead could not be determined. For the same reason the burials can be dated only approximately, to between Dynasty 26 and the beginning of the Ptolemaic Period. Petrie dated the tomb to the Persian Period,[2] although his reasons are not clear.

The value of the discovery lay in the fact that each mummy had a complete set of amulets, whose position Petrie recorded as accurately as possible.[3] Although thousands of amulets have been discovered in Egyptian tombs, precise information on their distribution is rarely available in excavators' reports.

Between the New Kingdom and Dynasty 30, amulets were usually positioned on the body according to their different magical functions, and the position of the main types remained essentially unchanged.[4] In the Ptolemaic Period, however, orderly distribution gave way to the random scattering of amulets within the wrapping.[5] The layouts of the amulets on the four Nebesha mummies follow a broadly consistent pattern, although there were many minor variations.

The set displayed here came from the first mummy, which lay on the right side of the chamber. The first two amulets to be encountered were the *menat* counterpoise, placed at the back of the neck, and the serpent's head, at the throat. The latter is unusual in that it is made of agate; carnelian was the common material.[6]

As was often the case, the upper torso received the greatest concentration of amulets. Here the right side had only a lapis lazuli frog, whereas on the left breast were a "square" (usually associated with a mason's level), nine heart amulets in a row, and the "papyrus scepter" depicted on a rectangular tablet.[7] The hearts were made of such stones as basalt, obsidian, limestone, and lapis lazuli. It is unusual to find so

many examples of this amulet on a single mummy, although four hearts were found on one of the other Nebesha bodies.[8]

Near the heart itself was another group of amulets: beneath the mason's level and square (which also occur in this area on Nebesha mummy 'B' and on that of Djedhor from Abydos)[9] lay a large scarab with six small ones, again in a variety of stones. While it is common to find several scarabs on a single body,[10] the juxtaposition of one large example with several smaller ones seems to be characteristic of the burials at Nebesha.[11]

The well-known amulets representing major divinities were absent from this mummy. Instead, aligned across the stomach were two *wedjat* eyes, four *djed* pillars, and two *tyet*s; about the navel were two basalt solar disks. A little further down was an amulet described by Petrie as a "square pendant,"[12] which has not been definitely identified.

The other main group lay on the pelvis. Here were situated the "papyrus scepter," two different forms of the twin feathers (all more commonly located on the chest), four *wedjat* eyes and the "two fingers" amulets. This last, which was probably associated with the embalming incision, was appropriately located on the left side of the pelvis.[13] A single *wedjat* eye of jasper lay between the thighs. In addition to the amulets, several small strips of gold foil were found, apparently on the breast. The significance of these is unknown. The mummy's arms had no amulets but, as on body "B," a string of small beads was place around the right wrist.

JHT

1. Petrie 1888b, p. 22, pl. XVI (tomb 23).
2. Petrie 1888b, p. 18.
3. Petrie 1888b, pp. 22-23; Petrie 1914, pl. LI, 11-12; pl. LII, 13-14.
4. Shorter 1931, p. 313; Shorter 1934, p. 121-122; Shorter 1935, p. 171.
5. Shorter 1931, p. 313; Shorter 1934, p. 121-122; Shorter 1935, p. 171.
6. Petrie 1914, pp. 25-26 (97).
7. Petrie 1914, p. 13 (21).
8. Petrie 1888b, p. 23 (B).
9. Petrie 1888b, p. 23; Petrie 1914, pl. LI (10, 12).
10. Petrie 1914, pl. L-LI (1-5, 7, 8, 10).
11. Cf. mummy "B": Petrie 1888b, p. 23.
12. Petrie 1888b, p. 23.
13. Shorter 1931, p. 312; Shorter 1934, p. 123; Shorter 1935, pp. 173-174.

Bibliography: Petrie 1888b, p. 22-23; Petrie 1914, pl. LI (11).

Literature: Reisner 1907; Wiedemann 1910; Petrie 1914; Budge 1925; Bonnet 1952, pp. 26-31; Klasens 1975, cols. 232-236.

179
Headrest amulet

Provenance unknown
Early Ptolemaic Period, about
third century B.C.
Haematite
Height 2 cm., length 3 cm., width 1.1 cm.
John Rodocanachi Fund 1976 (1976.128)

The headrest (*wrs*) of stone or wood was a common item of furniture in ancient Egypt. The Egyptians normally slept on their sides, and the headrest's curved upper section raised the head above the bed. Headrests were frequently buried with the dead, notably in the Old and Middle Kingdoms, and are often found inside the coffin, under the mummy's head. In this context the headrest was placed so as to support the side of the head at eye-level, thereby aligning the face with the all important "eye-panel" on the side of the coffin.[1] The headrest frequently appeared among the friezes of funerary gifts painted on the northern wall above the mummy's head in Middle Kingdom coffins.[2]

The purpose of burying headrests with the dead was originally purely practical: to support the head, and promote sound sleep. Later, as their function became more symbolic, small amulets of the same form placed within the mummy wrappings gradually took the place of real headrests.

The later, magical function of the headrest amulet is explained in Chapter 166 of the Book of the Dead, the "Chapter of the Headrest;" the headrest first raises the dead person from his horizontal position to enjoy eternal life and, more importantly, prevents the cutting off and loss of his head, one of the numerous unpleasant fates that might befall those who were unprepared for the hazards of the Netherworld. The decapitation recalls the dismembering of Osiris by Seth. Osiris's head, however, was restored to him and so the dead person, through his desire to avoid decapitation, assimilates himself to Osiris. This idea is also expressed in Chapter 43 of the Book of the Dead.

One of the earliest datable headrest amulets was found on the mummy of Tutankhamen and is unusual in that it is made of

179

iron.[3] Headrests of iron ore were also provided for king Hekakheperre Shoshenk II and prince Hornakht, buried at Tanis in Dynasty 22.[4] The majority of headrest amulets, however, come from private burials of the Late Period and are made of haematite. On this specimen the support for the curved rest consists of a large block rather than a column, a form attested for amulets at least as early as Dynasty 22.[5] It is made of haematite but is unusual in that it bears an inscription. The roughly incised text begins on the curved rest, and continues on the sides of the support and base. The last two lines are inscribed on the under surface of the base. The text is based on Chapter 166 of the Book of the Dead, and reads: "May the pigeons awaken you when you are asleep. May they awaken your head at the horizon. Raise yourself (for) you have overthrown your enemies. You are triumphant over what was done against you. It is commanded that action be taken against those who acted against you. You are Horus, protector of his father, Osiris, Overseer of the Granary Penu, justified. You cut off the heads of your enemies; your head shall never be taken away from you. Behold, the Osiris, Overseer of the Granary Penu cuts off the heads of his enemies. His head shall never be taken away from him." This seems to be a late version of the spell[6] and omits several phrases found in the New Kingdom Book of the Dead papyri, notably the reference to Ptah overthrowing the enemies of the deceased.[7]

JHT

1. Chassinat and Palanque 1911, p. 110, pl. XXI, 2-3.
2. Jéquier 1921, pp. 235-238.
3. Carter 1927, pp. 109-110, pl. LXXVII B.
4. Montet 1942, pp. 49, 50, figs. 37, 74, pls. X, XVI; Montet 1951, p. 50, pl. XXXIII.
5. See note 4.
6. A close parallel to this version is found on another headrest amulet, London BM 20647: Budge 1925, pp. 310-311.
7. Allen 1974, p. 162; Faulkner 1985, p. 161.

Bibliography: Price 1897, p. 190.

Literature: Reisner 1907, pp. 68-73, 110, pls. IV, VIII; Wiedemann 1910, pp. 27-29; Petrie 1914, p. 15, pl. III; Budge 1925, pp. 310-311; Bonnet 1952, p. 30; Klasens 1975; col. 233; Fischer 1980, cols. 686-693.

180
Pectoral

Said to be from Deir el-Bahri
Dynasties 19-20
Faience
Height 9.1 cm.
Gift of Miss Nina H. Burnham, 1956 (56.315)

Unlike many earlier and more spectacular examples, this blue faience pectoral, formerly in the Hilton Price collection, is purely

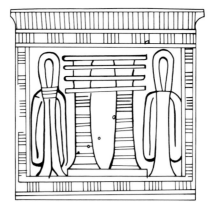

180, front

180, back

funerary in character. Decorated on its outer face with two conjoined *djed* pillars flanked by *tyet*-knots in black, the whole is contained within a border of rectangles and surmounted by a cornice. The reverse of the piece, again executed in black and surrounded by a similar border, carries a representation of the deceased, kneeling, his right arm raised and his left holding an incense burner; the reading of his name, written above, is not clear. Before and facing him, on a pedestal, squats the dog-headed Anubis, clutching an *ankh*. The pectoral is pierced with fourteen holes, two groups of three from top to top rear and a row of eight from bottom to bottom rear; the former will perhaps have been employed for suspending the ornament from the neck of the mummy and the latter for the attachment of drop pendants, rather than for sewing directly on to the mummy bandages.

CNR

Literature: Feucht 1982, cols. 922-923.

181
Inscribed mummy bandage

Provenance unknown
Ptolemaic Period
Linen
Length 239 cm., width 10 cm.
Gift of Horace L. Mayer, 1959 (59.1070)

The linen bandages that enclosed a mummy often substituted for expensive papyrus rolls as writing surfaces for funerary spells in the later periods of Egyptian history.[1] The present bandage, almost eight feet in length, contains a variant of the text and vignettes of Book of the Dead Spell 17,[2] here entitled "Spells for descending into the tribunal of Osiris."[3] The bandage is incomplete, as the torn left edge indicates; comparison with other copies of the spell indicate as many as two full columns may be missing.[4] Although signs are occasionally deformed by blotting[5] owing to the inherent difficulty of writing on linen, the text is written in standard late hieratic, with individual signs[6] and spellings[7] characteristic of the Graeco-Roman eras. Traces of resin used in mummification stain portions of the bandage in columns 2, 3, and 9-12, and the vignette above column 7. From eleven notations in the text,[8] it appears that the bandage was inscribed for the mummy of a certain Hep-meneh ("The youthful Apis"), born of the woman Ta-sherit-en-ta-kerit(?) ("The daughter of the shrine?").[9] No professional titles accompany the name of Hep-meneh, nor is his father ever named.

The scribe has divided his text into twelve columns of unequal length, often further divided into subcolumns of half lines after several initial lines of full length.[10] These divisions must reflect only spatial considerations, for they do not correspond to either sections or verses of the spells. The inscription begins at the far right with the standard epithets of Hep-meneh "the deceased, born of Ta-sherit-en-ta-kerit(?), the deceased." The absence of the owner's name suggests that the epithet applies either to the image of the deceased immediately above the text or to the mummy itself. Spell 17, said to be recited by the deceased, is one of the most important chapters in the Book of the Dead. Often the first spell copied on papyrus rolls, it is one of only three spells found in every extant copy of the Book of the Dead.[11] The chapter, which derives from Coffin Text spell 335,[12] identifies the deceased with the forms of the creator deity and provides didactic glosses on the nature of the sun-god, the gods of his entourage, and the geography of the Underworld and its demons. The glosses, introduced by phrases translated "Who is he?", "What is it?", or "Otherwise said," are often obscure, and have been the subject of detailed study.[13] The vignettes above the first eight columns on the bandage are di-

181, columns 1-3

rectly adapted from traditional illustrations associated with Spell 17.[14] From the right, Hep-meneh is shown holding a staff and wreath of justification. Next he is shown seated in a pavilion flanked by two symbols of the west (the land of the dead), while his *ba*-spirit, wearing the *ankh*-sign of life, stands before a barque bearing the standard of the ram-headed sun-god. Above columns 2-4 appear the double lions of the horizon, symbolizing ''yesterday and today;'' the solar phoenix, and the corpse upon a bier (with bags of entrails sketched as if stick figures)[15] protected by Isis as a hawk; two fecundity figures representing the lakes of natron and truth; guardians and Underworld gates surmounted by feathers of truth and the Eye of Horus; Hep-meneh offering to the celestial cow, a canopic chest with jars of the Four Sons of Horus; genii before an enthroned Underworld lord; and the sun-god as a cat slaughtering the demon Apep before a persea tree. Finally, above columns 5-8, scenes of adoration of the solar barque alternate with scenes of worship of Osiris, and the vignettes conclude with images of the sky-goddess Nut stretched over the solar scarab, a lion guardian of Re and Osiris, and the seated figures of Isis and Nephthys.

RKR

1. Caminos 1982, pp. 145-155; van Voss 1974, pp. 335-338.
2. For the text of this spell, Naville 1886, vol. 1, pp. 23-30; vol. 2, pp. 29-74; Budge 1960, pp. 376-401; for translations, Allen 1974, pp. 26-32; Faulkner 1985, pp. 44-50.
3. This title is not typical of Book of the Dead Spell 17, but serves as the heading of Spells 1, 124, and 127.
4. The text now stops at *ky dd mds rn-f*, (Naville, vol. 2, p. 64, end of §80), and thus lacks ten pages of Naville's transcription, which correspond roughly to two columns elsewhere on this bandage.
5. E.g. *in* (''by'') in col. 1/2, and *kmȝ* (''create'') in 1/9 (For column numbering, see note 10.)
6. E.g. the writing of the number 7 in columns 7/6 and 8/7, which corresponds to the forms in Möller 1912, p. 59, no. 620, and the Demotic form in Erichsen 1954, p. 698.
7. E.g. the writing of Nun ''abyss'' (col. 1/3) with the seated child; Erman and Grapow 1971, p. 214. Note also the use of *iw* for *r* throughout.
8. Only the mother's name appears in col. 1/1; both names occur in cols. 3/6-7, 5/5-6, 6/2, 6/6, 6/7 (mother's name abbreviated), 11/2

(partially under resin, 11/11-12, 12/2 (partially under resin), 12/3-4 (partially under resin), and 12/9-10 (partially under resin).

9. For the names, Ranke 1935, p. 237, 13-14, p. 370. The reading of the final element of the mother's name is questionable due to blotting which renders *k, hr* and even *p* identical; it may well be *hryt.*
10. Thus col. 1 contains four complete lines and two subcolumns of three lines each; col. 3 contains five full lines with two subcolumns of three lines each; col. 4 contains five full lines and two subcolumns of two lines each; col. 7 contains five lines, then two subcolumns of two and one line; col. 9 contains three lines, then two subcolumns of four lines each; col. 11 contains three lines, then two subcolumns of eight lines each. Within this note the lines of each subcolumn are numbered consecutively rather than labeled by ''a'' or ''b.''
11. Heerma Van Voss 1986, cols. 641-643; Faulkner 1985, p. 14.
12. Faulkner 1973, pp. 260-269.
13. See the sources listed in Faulkner 1973, p. 262, n. 1
14. Naville 1886, pp. 27-30.
15. Naville 1886, p. 28, § A.g.

182
Three embalming pots

From Giza
Late Saite or Persian Period, about 575-400 B.C.
Pottery
Harvard University-Museum of Fine Arts Expedition, 1925

a. Height 13 cm., width 14.6 cm. (25.1515)
b. Height 10.5 cm., width 12 cm. (25.1516)
c. Height 8.5 cm., width 12 cm. (25.1517)

These three squat jars with rim and instep foot, wheel made from a coarse marl clay, tempered with straw, and decorated over the surface with a white wash, come from an embalmer's cache discovered by Reisner at Giza. The surface of each has been left clean at a broad horizontal patch to highlight a short line of text. The script is the early form of demotic, as used for everyday documents in the seventh to fourth centuries B.C. The use of a white slip over the surface indicates a date at the end of the Saite Pe-

182

riod or later, as supported by parallels of the pottery type in a Sakkara embalmer's cache of that time.

Since the pots look alike, the contents had to be conspicuously labeled to avoid confusion. Therefore each bears a short text beginning with the words *ta pekheret*[1] "the prescription," followed by a different phrase in all three. A "prescription" might be magical or medical, but always contained more than one item and was intended to alter the condition of the person taking it. From the Late Period on, "applying prescriptions" meant "embalming" in the specialized context of mummification, and the embalmer's workshop could be called the "place of applying prescriptions." The embalmer himself is sometimes designated as the "physician," and clearly there was no division between medicine for the dead, medicine for the living, and magic. The ingredients of the relevant "prescriptions" were those materials used to treat the corpse before burial. In the label on the first pot, the prescription is for "cleansing," while the third probably refers to natron (*hesmen*), the principal desiccating agent in mummification.

In the Late Period, mummification increased sharply. The new scale of activity might be just the sort of pressure to prompt the appearance in embalming of humble utensils, such as these earthenware pots with their texts in the nonpriestly demotic script. The cults of the time included not only the worship connected to the Giza Pyramids and Sphinx, but also animal necropoleis for icheumon and ibis. Procedure would not have differed materially between embalming people and embalming animals, and these embalming pots could have served in either.

SQ

1. Smith 1987, pp. 69-70.

183
Hypocephalus

From Abydos, tomb of Djed-hor
Late Period, Dynasty 30
Bronze
Diam. 17.1 cm.
Gift of the Egypt Exploration Fund, 1902 (02.766)

The ancient Egyptians' concern for the protection of the head in the afterlife is reflected in several spells of the Book of the Dead, as well as the headrests and headrest amulets provided for the deceased. The hypocephalus, placed under the head of the mummy during the Late and Ptolemaic periods,[1] was inscribed with Spell 162 of the Book of the Dead, the "spell for providing heat under the head" of the deceased.[2] This spell was to be put "into writing on a new sheet of papyrus placed under

183

her head. (Then) much heat will envelop her like one who is upon earth."[3] Most hypocephali were manufactured of stuccoed linen, and more rarely of papyrus or bronze.[4]

This hypocephalus was found under the head of the mummy of the wife of Djed-hor, a priest of Hathor, whose family tomb was excavated by Petrie in 1902.[5] Bronze hypocephali were also found with two other mummies in the tomb, including that of Djed-hor himself. Varga has pointed out that the use of hypocephali was not widespread, but seems to have been concentrated in priestly families of Upper Egypt.[6]

Standard scenes are portrayed on each hypocephalus, although the number of scenes varies. The decoration of this hypocephalus was incised and filled with white pigment. In the top register, the cow-goddess Hathor, here associated with Ihet, the celestial mother-goddess, appears as the central element. She is flanked by the Four Sons of Horus and a goddess who usually possesses a head in the shape of a *wedjat* eye and holds a lotus flower, both attributes that are missing here. At the far left is a seated figure, part bird and part man, of the god Min. The register below features the seated, youthful sun-god. He is flanked by the solar boat, upon which stands the ram-headed Amen-Re, accompanied by Isis and Nephthys, and the moon-boat, upon which rests a seated baboon representing Thoth. On the other side, two additional registers

contain two baboons adoring a four-headed Amen-Re; boats with Sokar-Re and a scarab; and a figure, shown as two-headed on most other examples, that holds an Anubis standard. Each of these scenes expresses, through different aspects of Egyptian mythology, the idea of resurrection and the triumph of life over death.[7]

SD'A

1. For a discussion of possible antecedents, see Varga 1961, p. 239.
2. Allen 1974, p. 157.
3. Allen 1974, p. 157.
4. For examples, see Daressy 1903a, nos. 9443-9449, pl. XIII; Museo Civico Archeologico di Bologna 1982, p. 141; Ägyptisches Museum Berlin 1967, nos. 881-883; Birch 1883-84; Kákosy and Roccati 1985, pp. 87, fig. 24, and p. 123.
5. Petrie 1902, pp. 33-39, 49-51, pls. LXXVI-LXXVII.
6. See the extensive discussion in Varga 1961, esp. pp. 241-242.
7. For discussion of the symbolism, see Varga 1968, pp. 11-12.

Bibliography: Petrie 1902, pl. LXXIX, no. 4; pl. LXXVII, p. 50.

Literature: Varga 1961; Varga 1968; Bonnet 1952, pp. 389-390; Budge 1925, pp. 476-478.

184
Mummy labels

Roman Period, 31 B.C. - A.D. 395
Sears Fund, 1904

a. Mummy label of the Lady Takhenmet
   Possibly from Medinet Habu (?)
   Height 10.2 cm, width 4 cm. (04.1770)
b. Mummy label of the Lady Senkollanthes
   Possibly from Akhmim
   Height 9 cm., width 4 cm. (04.1771)

In Roman Egypt, labels were attached to the mummy by means of a string through a hole drilled in the rectangular wooden tag, which had been cut at two corners. The text of 184a is inscribed directly on both sides of the wood, without any white surfacing. Most such texts were written lengthwise facing the hole, but this one runs across the width in the manner of a miniature funerary stela. The inscription had both the immediate practical function of identifying the deceased and the long-term goal of recording the name for eternity. Thus it served more as a modern tombstone than as a funerary stela, which ensured food for the afterlife.

Even the brief prayer found on most tags (184b) is omitted from this example; the text reads simply "Takhenmet, daughter of Petarsomtheus son of Pathothes the scribe(?), the temple servant. Year 11, month 1 of Inundation, day 19, of Caesar. She was brought to Djeme. Her salvation occurred. She went to her fathers in Year 9, month 3 of Spring, day 10 of Caesar. The years of her life were 75, and she was temple servant for 45 years."

The laconic statistical information is typical of mummy-labels and the reason for their value to modern research. Takhenmet's label presents several unusual features, foremost among them two dates, those of death and burial. The lapse of a year and four months between the two dates is paralleled elsewhere, but difficult to explain; mummification itself would not have taken more the seventy days, and even a long journey from the unnamed place of death to Djeme (Medinet Habu, on the West Bank at Thebes) would not account for more than a few months. Presumably the mummy was kept by the family to ease the passage of departure from this world. To avoid even a passing reference to death, the text uses the euphemism "she went to her father," i.e. to the family grave. When she died at the age of seventy-five, she had already served as "servant," probably in the cult of a god, for forty-five years. Such details are rare on mummy labels. A final curiosity is the parentage of Takhenmet; instead of giving both parents, as we might expect, the father and paternal grandfather are cited, and the mother omitted. There is no obvious reason, but it lends immediacy to the phrase "went to her fathers."

The four-line text of 184b is written on one

184a, b

side only, in black with a reed pen, and runs across the tag from right to left away from the hole. The first one and a half lines contain the standard short prayer for an afterlife with Osiris, and are written in a less cursive style close to hieratic. The remainder of the text is purely demotic in form, and reads, "May her soul (*ba*) live before Osiris, Foremost of the West, the Great God, Lord of Abydos. Senkollanthes the daughter of Kollanthes, her mother being Takhomia. She died at the age of 83 (or 53 ?)."

Kollanthes was a minor deity attested only in the vicinity of Akmim, suggesting that the label came from that area. Senkollanthes itself means simply "the daughter of Kollanthes;" it refers in this case both to the lady's human father and to the deity acting as patron of the family. The necropolis of Akhmim has proved the richest source of surviving mummy labels, most dating to the second and third centuries A.D. Many labels bear inscriptions in Greek, then the official language of Egypt, and some carry the same text twice, once in Greek and again in Egyptian. Some Greek versions of the prayer for an afterlife render "her *ba*" more directly as "she," and there also occurs the translation *eidolon* ("image"). The *ba* represents the power of the deceased to move about freely, and it figures in Egyptian art as a human-headed bird. It is less closely related to the ability of the deceased to consume food, and is therefore appropriate to mummy labels, since existence rather than nourishment is the key concept. Conversely, funerary stelae, with their magically eternal supply of food, are intended for the *ka* of the deceased and do not mention the *ba*.

SQ

Literature: Quaegebeur 1978, pp. 232-259; Quaegebeur 1980, pp. 216-217.

185
Anubis statuette

Provenance unknown
Dynasty 22 to Roman Period, (946 B.C.-A.D. 395)
Wood with stucco and paint
Height 17.8 cm., width 36.1 cm.
Hay Collection, Gift of C. Granville Way, 1872 (72.4173a,b)

Anubis, Master of the Secrets, Protector of the Necropolis, Guide through the Judgment of the Dead and Overseer of Funerary Offerings,[1] is often shown in the form of a recumbent black jackal. Because of his importance in protecting the dead and helping them achieve a good afterlife, statuettes of Anubis were used to adorn the tops of wooden funerary shrines[2] and coffins.[3]

This statuette of Anubis is typical of such figures.[4] The jackal's body is thin; his front paws stretch out before him. The hind legs are folded under his body, their raised haunches underscoring the jackal's sleekness. The upraised, pointed ears enhance the general sense of alertness. The very top of the ears have broken off, as has the bottom rear edge of his left leg; otherwise the general condition of the figure is good. A hole has been drilled on the bottom of the figure between the two hind legs where the figure was pegged to the top of a coffin or shrine.

The wooden form of the jackal was stuccoed and then painted in black, red, and white, adding to its sense of animation. The body is painted black, the traditional color for Anubis. The red band, its edge falling down the front of his chest, is typically found on such figures. The eyes are unpainted except for a large red dot in their center. The ears are also enlivened by a slash of red running the length of their interior. Interestingly, while the animal is nicely carved, the paint appears hasty and crude in its application and has flaked off in several places.

As protector of the dead, Anubis ("He who is over the Mysteries") understood and guarded the secret rites of successful mummification and revivification. In this

185

role, he is shown resting on a chest that contained the texts sacred to these rituals. This is probably the original source for figures of Anubis which, when placed on chests or coffins, evoked his role as protector of the dead. The statuette's alert pose, with head raised and ears cocked, presents the image of just such an attentive guardian.

JY

1. Altenmüller 1972, pp. 328-329.
2. For example Cairo Museum JE 61444 in Saleh and Sourouzian 1987, no. 185.
3. Niwinski 1983, p. 449.
4. For example Ägyptologischen Instituts der Universität Heidelberg Inv. 190, in Feucht 1986, pp. 133-134, no. 298.

Literature: Altenmüller 1972, pp. 327-333; Feucht 1986; Niwinski 1983, pp. 434-468; Saleh and Sourouzian 1987.

0   25 cm.

186

186
Stela

From Dendera
Ptolemaic Period (332-31 B.C.)
Sandstone
Height 35 cm., width 22 cm.
Gift of Egypt Exploration Fund, 1898
(98.1054)

This round-topped funerary stela was found in a Ptolemaic Period burial chamber resting against a wall. A deep recess cut into the wall directly above it contained the mummy.[1] The proximity of the stela to the body indicates its importance in ensuring the owner's well-being in the afterlife.

The stela's placement,[2] form, and decoration[3] are typical of the Late Period. The uppermost section is decorated with a winged sun disk. Its central area is filled with a scene showing the jackal-headed funerary god Anubis embalming a mummy. Below, a two-line inscription in demotic, a late form of cursive Egyptian, reads: "Before Osiris, Pakhoumis-Iowa (?) son of Pakhoumis.[4]

The central scene showing Anubis embalming a mummy, a process he is credited with inventing, is a common one. It decorated temples,[5] tombs[6] and painted coffins,[7] as well as numerous other funerary stelae.[8] The mummy resting on a lion-shaped bier probably represents the god of the dead, Osiris, as well as the owner of the stela, who hopes to be reborn as Osiris himself was reborn.

In these scenes, Anubis usually holds a small jar as he engages in one of the many mummification rituals. This stela is unusual in that Anubis appears to be holding a looped bandage whose edges fall below his clenched fist. Bandages are, of course, an important part of mummification and Anubis is often shown holding them in other types of scenes.

The decoration of the stela, although simple, provides all that is needed. The central scene guarantees the successful afterlife of the owner whose identity is preserved for eternity through the presence of his name in the inscription.

JY

1. Petrie 1900a, p. 31, pl. XXVA, XXVB.
2. Martin 1985, col. 1.
3. For example CG 22.050 in Kamal 1905, pl. XV.
4. "m-bȝḥ Wsir P₃-ꜥḥm-Iowa s₃ P₃-ꜥḥm" The name P₃-ꜥḥm and its variants can be found in Luddeckens 1980, I, p. 166ff. I am indebted to Dr. E. Cruz-Uribe for his reading of this inscription and suggestions concerning the name Pakhoumis-Iowa (?), which is otherwise unattested.
5. For example in the Temple of Hibis, Winlock 1941, III, pl. 3.
6. For example the Tomb of Sennedjem in Western Thebes (T.T. 1) in Lange 1939, p. 117.
7. For example Cairo Museum JE 27302 in Saleh and Sourouzian 1987, no. 216.
8. For example Ny Carlsburg Glyptotek AEIN 824, Koefoed-Petersen 1948, p. 54, no. 71, pl. 71.

Animal Mummies

Mummification in ancient Egypt was not limited to human beings. Many species of animals were mummified, some as elaborately as humans. These animals were not pets (though domestic animals were occasionally mummified and placed in tombs) or sources of food for the afterlife, but were sacred animals that were buried in temple precincts.

Animal cults existed as early as the Predynastic Period. On Archaic period documents such as the Narmer palette, animal standards are shown carried in procession. The standards represented local districts, and animal cults probably began as manifestations of regional symbols; the animals themselves were a focus of religious devotion. With the establishment of a strong central government, however, many of the animal gods became national deities, anthropomorphic in form, or retaining only an animal head on a human body. The animal associated with a particular deity was not worshipped, but viewed as a representative of that deity, embodying certain characteristics of the god.

As early as the New Kingdom, and reaching fanatical heights in the Late and Graeco-Roman periods, animals were raised in temple precincts, in some cases sacrificed, offered as temple votives, and buried in great subterranean galleries. At first, a single animal was chosen to represent the god. Such was the case in the cult of the Apis bull at Memphis, one of the most ancient animal cults.[1] The Apis bull was sacred to the god Ptah, the creator-god of Memphis. Not just any bull was acceptable; the priests of the god searched the countryside until they found a bull with specific markings that the Apis must have. The finding of a new Apis was the cause of great rejoicing, and was accompanied with great ceremony and fertility rituals.[2] The bull was placed in a special enclosure to live a life of luxury:

"For these hallowed beings pass their lives in consecrated enclosures, where many prominent men attend on them, serving them the most sumptuous foods. . . They are ever treating their charges to warm baths, anointing them with the most luxurious unguents, burning all sorts of fragrant incense before them, and providing them with the most lavish bedding and with goodly ornaments. They are very solicitous that their beasts may obtain sexual gratification as nature demands; besides this, for each of the animals they keep the most handsome females of the same species, which they call its concubines, and these too they attend with the greatest care and expense. And whenever any one of these divine animals dies, they lament its passing in the same way as those who have lost a beloved child; and they bury it not merely to the best of their ability, but at an expense far exceeding the value of their property."[3]

Upon its death, the Apis was mummified with the same process used on humans, including the removal of the brain and viscera. From the New Kingdom through late Roman times, the Apis bulls were buried at Sakkara in huge sacophagi in vast underground galleries known as the Serapeum. They were provided with all the accoutrements of human burials, including canopic jars and shawabtis, the latter with human mummiform bodies and bulls' heads.[4]

In the Late Period and later, the raising and mummification of sacred animals in temple precincts was not limited to one representative animal. Rather, large numbers of a species were kept, sacrificed at a young age, mummified (gutted and thinly wrapped in elaborate patterns), and offered in the temples by pious pilgrims as a substitute for more expensive bronze votives (see cats. 194 and 195). When a sufficient number had collected in the temple, the animal mummies would be buried by the priests in sacred animal necropoleis, which are scattered throughout Egypt.[5] Animals mummified included ibises and falcons, cats and dogs, rams, crocodiles, and even fish, snakes, and shrews.

The animal cults of the later periods were extensively documented by visitors to Egypt, but were not always viewed seriously or with comprehension. A text in Clement of Alexandria's *Paedagogus* describes an Egyptian temple thus:

> The temples sparkle with gold, silver and mat gold and flash with colored stones from India and Ethiopia. The sanctuaries are overshadowed by cloths studded with gold. If, however, you enter the enclosure, hastening towards the sight of the almighty, and look for the statue residing in the temple and if a *pastophoros* or another celebrant, after having solemnly looked round the sanctuary, singing a song in the language of the Egyptians, draws back the curtain a little to show the god, he will make us laugh aloud about the object of worship. For we shall not find the god for whom we have been looking inside, the god towards whom we have hastened, but a cat or crocodile or a native snake or a similar animal, which should not be in a temple, but in a cleft or a den or on a dung heap. The god of the Egyptians appears on a purple couch as a wallowing animal."[6]

Animal mummification, like the mummification of humans, declined with the rise of Christianity. The cult of the Apis bull was the last to survive, until an edict of the Emperor Honorius banning sanctuaries for pagan use caused the destruction of the Serapeum in the fourth century A.D.[7] Thus ended one of the most mysterious and misunderstood Egyptian funerary practices.

SD'A

1. For a discussion of the Apis bull, see Vercoutter 1972.
2. Diodorus 1985, p. 110.
3. Diodorus 1985, pp. 109-110.
4. Vercoutter 1972, p. 343.
5. For a list of the most important sites, see Kessler 1985b, pp. 579-580.
6. Translation in Smelik 1979, pp. 225-226.
7. Adams 1984, p. 54.

Literature: Kessler 1985b; Vercoutter 1972.

187
Baboon coffin

Provenance unknown
Late Period
Wood
Height 27.5 cm.
Gift of Theodore M. Davis, 1905 (05.96)

This coffin, in the shape of a baboon (*Papio hamadryas*) squatting upon its haunches, with its paws resting upon upon its knees, is carved in wood, has inlaid eyes of lime set in blue glass, and originally possessed a surface covering of linen and painted gesso. The head was painted blue and the face gilded, while the fur decoration of the cape-like coat was green detailed in black. A broad collar, in red and gold, originally decorated the breast. The rear of the figure displays a vertical, white-painted rectangular slot some 26 cm. high, 7 cm. wide and 6.3 cm. deep, intended to accommodate a tightly wrapped mummy.

Like the ibis, the baboon was sacred to Thoth, and was worshipped in the temple precincts as the incarnation of the god. Extinct in Egypt itself for several centuries, baboons had to be imported from equatorial Africa and, for practical purposes, the smaller cercopithecine monkey was frequently substituted. Baboon cemeteries have been found in several parts of Egypt, notably in the Wadi Gubbanet el-Girud at Thebes,[1] at Tuna el-Gebel[2] and at Sakkara;[3] excavation at the latter site has revealed that as many as 400 baboons were buried during the Ptolemaic Period in rock-cut galleries on two levels. The boxed and plaster-encased creatures were sealed into their recesses with a slab inscribed with the date of burial and the name.[4] A close parallel to the Boston coffin, in the British Museum, is said to come from Akhmim.[5]

Several mummified baboons were discovered by Theodore M. Davis in tomb KV 51 in the Valley of the Kings in 1905.[6] However, like the famed baboon buried with Maatkare Mutemhet in the Deir el-Bahri royal cache,[7] these particular creatures may have been interred less as offerings to the god than as favored royal pets.[8]

CNR

1. Porter and Moss 1964, p. 593; Lortet and Gaillard 1909, pp. 7-21.
2. Kessler 1985a, cols. 797-804.
3. Porter and Moss 1981, pp. 826-827.
4. Smith 1974, pp. 41-43.

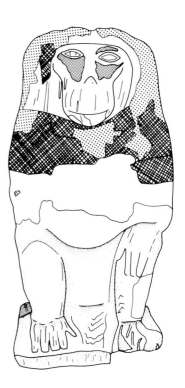

187

	blue pigment
	gold leaf
	gesso
	linen
	wood

5. British Museum EA 20869.
6. Davis et al. 1908, pp. 17-18; Reeves (forthcoming), pp. 170, 305.
7. Harris and Weeks 1973, pp. 53, 173-175; Yoyotte 1972 pp. 41-42.
8. But cf. Lortet and Gaillard 1909, p. 2.

188
Ibis mummy

From Abydos
Roman period
Linen
Length 40 cm., width 13 cm.
Gift of Egypt Exploration Fund through Prof. Thomas Whitemore, 1914 (Res. 14.34)

The ibis most often portrayed in Egyptian art is the sacred ibis, characterized by a long curved bill, white plumage, and black neck, legs, and wing tips.[1] It was found in Egypt as recently as 1850, but is extinct there today.

The ibis, along with the baboon, was associated with the god Thoth, god of wisdom and learning. He appears at the judgment of the deceased as an ibis-headed god who records the results of the weighing of the heart (see cat. 134). Though the ibis cult may have had its origins as early as Dynasty 19, most papyri mentioning the cults date to the second century B.C.[2] Diodorus, writing in the first century B.C., records the extent of the veneration of the ibis in the Graeco-Roman period. Anyone who killed an ibis, accidentally or not, was put to death:

> The people rush to the spot and dispose of the offender in fearful measure, sometimes without a hearing. And through fear of these consequences, anyone who sees one of these animals that had died draws afar back and cries out with horror, bewailing the deceased and calling to witness that he had found it already dead.[3]

Sacred ibises were raised in temple precincts at Thoth's cult centers throughout Egypt, and were mummified and interred on a large scale, especially at the sites of Sakkara, Tuna el-Gebel (the necropolis of Hermopolis Magna, the city of Thoth), Abydos, and Kom Ombo.[4] At Sakkara, vast underground galleries have been discovered north and south of the Dynasty 30 temple of Nectanebo II.[5] An estimated half million ibises were deposited there, at a rate of 10,000 birds per year. Ceremonies to bury the birds probably took place once a year. Each ibis was mummified, sealed in a pottery jar that held one or more mummies, and laid in rows in the galleries. Occasionally, particularly at sites other than Sakkara, ibis mummies were placed in ibis-shaped coffins, or in wood or stone sarcophagi.[6] At the site of Tuna el-Gebel, where both ibises and baboons were interred, there were numerous large niches to contain coffins or jars. In some galleries,

188

there were rows of eight coffins, a symbolic reference to the ancient name of the town of Hermopolis, the number eight. It was believed in early times to be the home of eight deities who created the world.[7]

Much of our knowledge of the temple administration concerning the ibis cult derives from demotic ostraca from the site of Sakkara[8] and from Greek and demotic ostraca from Kom Ombo.[9] This information is supplemented by the archaeological remains, both of the ibises themselves, and of an embalming workshop and offices found at Tuna el-Gebel.[10]

This ibis mummy, with its alternately light and dark chevron-shaped wrappings, is from the 1914 excavations of the Egypt Exploration Fund at Abydos.[11] The cemetery consisted of ninety-three jars of unbaked clay, sealed with unbaked bricks, that had originally stood in the open, seemingly without plan. In all, 1500 birds were recovered, each jar containing up to 100 mummies. The excavator commented upon the wonderful variety of geometric wrappings used in the mummification of these birds, and noted that more than sixty different types of wrappings were observed.

An X-ray and CT scan of this mummy shows an intact ibis. It has been gutted and thinly wrapped, its neck doubled back upon itself, and a wad of linen placed between the two segments of the neck for support. Several other, unprovenanced ibis mummies in the Museum's collection were found not to contain complete birds.

SD'A

1. For the sacred ibis, see Houlihan 1986, pp. 28-30.
2. Smelik 1979, p. 227, and no. 8.
3. Diodorus 1985, p. 108.
4. For a list of sites, see Zivie 1980, p. 118.
5. See Emery 1965, esp. pl. V, and Emery 1966, pl. II.
6. National Museum of Antiquities at Leiden 1987, no. 163, pp. 126-127.
7. Spencer 1982, p. 208.
8. Ray 1976.
9. Smelik 1979, p. 234.
10. Gabra 1939, p. 491.
11. Loat 1914, p. 40, pl. IV.

Literature: Smelik 1979; Lortet and Gaillard 1902; Zivie 1980, pp. 115-121; Gaillard and Daressy 1905; Ray 1976.

189
Cat mummy

Provenance unknown
Late or Ptolemaic Period
Length 51 cm., max. width 15 cm., max. depth 10 cm.
Hay Collection, Gift of C. Granville Way, 1872 (72.4903)

Surely mummified animals rank for the public among the most astonishing ''objects'' or socio-religious facts of ancient Egypt; but mummies of cats are moreover especially fascinating because they associate two archetypical and almost mythical features in our modern minds: the mummy, with all its patent associations, and the cat, an animal with rich symbolic meanings, which incurs passionate love or hatred.

Nevertheless, the mummification of cats is

tory of religions. Besides the studies of the mummies kept in museums, the rediscovery of the cat necropolis of the Bubasteion in Memphis (Sakkara) by a French mission resulted in the cleaning of rooms and shafts full of mummies more or less preserved (as well as a lot of bones), in spite of all the previous plunderings that scattered so many specimens all over the world. They form important material for the research in this peculiar field where so many questions are still waiting for appropriate answers.[4]

A-PZ

1. Kessler 1985b, pp. 571-587.
2. Te Velde 1982a, pp. 129-137.
3. Lortet and Gaillard 1909, p. 21 ff.; Armitage and Clutton-Brock 1981, pp. 185 ff.
4. Zivie 1983a, pp. 37-44; Zivie 1983b, pp. 40-56. Cat mummies and bones are studied by Léonard Ginsburg (Muséum d' Histoire Naturelle, Paris), from the paleo-zoological point of view.

not to be distinguished from the mummification of other animals, even if some particular features are associated with it. In both cases the aim is indeed to conserve for eternity the specimens (no matter how numerous they are), and not only one among them (the Apis bull, for example) of a species which is the container or at least a tangible and preferential shape (sometime among others) of a particular deity. In other words, the animal is not really sacred in itself, but it partakes of sacredness because it partakes of divinity.[1]

Of course, the cat was an appreciated animal insofar as it was the protector of the houses and granaries against pests, but it also became, very early, a figure of the goddess Bastet (Bubastis in Greek), who was at first a lioness and then cat deity (or more often provided with a female body and a cat's head) and who was a representation of the violent and angry goddess after she was pacified.[2] For all these practical and mythical reasons, cats were honored in the domestic frame as pets (a well-attested fact), but also a huge number of them seem to have been fed and, when dead, buried in the precincts of the temples of the goddess. In this respect the main place was in Bubastis (nowadays Tell Basta) in Lower Egypt. But mummies (and bones) of cats were also discovered in several other sites, often by thousands of specimens, and especially at Memphis (in the neighborhood of the Bubasteion of Sakkara) and in the Stabl 'Antar, near Beni Hasan.

The development of the cult of the gods through animal shapes (and not strictly speaking the cult of the animals) became more important in the Third Intermediate Period and mainly with the Saite and Late Periods. The cat is not an exception in this respect, but it seems that the majority of feline mummies that we know date mainly

from the Ptolemaic Period (332-31 B.C.) and a little bit later.

It could be the case of this mummy, as its aspect suggests. Cat mummies have indeed different aspects according to the time, the place, and also the means of the men who dedicated them. Here we have a fairly well preserved specimen, which was never opened. The linen pieces in which it is wrapped are themselves covered by thin, dark and light bandages, so that a geometrical decoration is created with a subtle pattern of two-tone squares.

X-ray examination shows that the animal is here more or less intact, but its position is not really natural: it is extended and its forelegs are pressed against the body so that the skeleton is slightly upset. As a rule the mummies are those of the common domestic (or half-domestic) cat of the time, the *Felis sylvestris libyca*, but other species, even wild, could also be mummified in some cases.[3] Furthermore, all kinds of processes can be observed in the mummification itself. Sometimes it was realized carefully and even, under the linen, the hair of the animal can be preserved (often yellow-red); but it can also happen that a "cat mummy" contains only a leg, or even some heterogeneous bones. It was indeed necessary to ensure an adequate "production" facing the number of pilgrims and dedicators who belonged to all levels of the society.

The most beautiful cat mummies, but also some poorer and even the newborn kittens, could be put in wooden or stone coffins, more or less elaborate, with geometric or animal shapes. Perhaps it was the case with this specimen.

Nowadays the mummified cats are a subject of renewed interest on the part of scholars, zoologists (or paleo-zoologists) as well as Egyptologists or specialists in his-

190
Kitten mummy

Provenance unknown
Late or Ptolemaic Period
Linen
Length 20.5 cm., width 4.5 cm., max. depth 6 cm.
Hay Collection, Gift of C. Granville Way, 1872 (72.4904)

By itself this mummy is not very different from the previous one (except of course for its size) and it has, very likely, the same provenance. The pieces of linen that cover it are also carefully arranged and leave on the front a kind of window that lets appear some thinner bandages organized into two-tone squares. Also noteworthy are the eyes and the ears, which are made of linen in order to give the mummy the look of a real cat's head.

According to the size of the mummy, we can guess that the animal under the wrappings is not an adult, but a kitten. The fact is confirmed by X-ray examination. And indeed the mummies and the bones found in the cat necropolis (for example at Sakkara), as well as the samples kept in museums, show that many young, and even baby animals, were mummified and dedicated like the adults, if not more. So numerous are they, in fact, that we can doubt whether they always died naturally. Perhaps some of them were indeed killed in a ritual way (by strangulation more likely than by drowning); the examination of skeletons can bring some evidence in that respect.[1] This fact seems to be in contradiction to the veneration in which the cats were held in ancient Egypt (and especially during the Late and Ptolemaic periods), as well as many other animals connected with gods or goddesses; and to kill a cat, even unintention-

190

This bronze figurine is too small to have held even a kitten and must have come from the top of a rectangular bronze animal coffin (see cats. 194-196). The cat is hollow cast, with details of the face and ears engraved on the head and a lotus garland hanging from the neck.[5] In place of the more common aegis or *wedjat* eye pendant[6] is a fish pendant.

The cat is seated with its tail curled forward; its expression is alert. Both ears are pierced, probably for gold earrings. Because the provenance of almost all of these coffins is unknown, determining their date and even authenticity is often very difficult.

PL

1. Cf. Gaillard and Daressy 1905, pp. 132-135, pl. 57 and 59; cf. also BMFA 03.1816, the head from a wooden cat coffin found at el-Hiba.
2. Scott 1958, pp. 1-7.
3. Roeder 1956, pp. 346-351.
4. Scott 1958.
5. Scott 1958.
6. Roeder 1956a.

191

ally, could indeed be punished with death.[2] But surely these kittens were put to death only in the precinct of the sanctuaries by priests entitled to act in such a way.

A-PZ

1. Armitage and Clutton-Brock 1981, 193-196; X-rays of cat mummies in the MFA have revealed separations of bones of the neck, indicating that strangulation occurred.
2. Herodotus 1985, p. 65-67; Diodorus 1985.

191
Cat

Provenance unknown
Saite Period, Dynasty 26 or later
Bronze
Height 15.9 cm., width 6 cm., length 10.2 cm.
Gift of Miss Lucy T. Aldrich, 1953 (53.2385)

Mummies of cats were occasionally buried in cat-shaped wood[1] or bronze[2] coffins or in long rectangular bronze boxes surmounted by figures of cats.[3] These vary in quality from quite rough to beautifully made and adorned with gold jewelry.[4]

192
Crocodile mummy

Provenance unknown
Ptolemaic or Roman period
Linen
Length 50 cm., width 12 cm.
Hay Collection, Gift of C. Granville Way, 1872 (72.4905)

Crocodiles, which were numerous in Nile waters, were from very early times both feared for their ferocity and revered; they were associated with the god Sobek, who had major cult centers in the Fayum and at Kom Ombo.[1] Sobek was a fertility god, later seen as a creator-god and associated with Re.

Diodorus Siculus relates that Menes, the first king of Egypt, established the city of Crocodilopolis in the Fayum after having been pursued by his own hunting dogs to Lake Moeris, where he miraculously was rescued by a crocodile, which ferried him to the other side.[2] Crocodile cemeteries are known from sites in the Fayum[3] and Kom Ombo, where they are presently displayed in a chamber of the Graeco-Roman temple. At Tebtunis, a vast crocodile cemetery with an estimated 2,000 mummies has been excavated.[4] These were not the burials of the sacred temple animal (see essay on animal mummies), but seem to have been buried by pilgrims to the temple. The simple, shallow graves were dug in the sand, and "family groups" of crocodiles were generally interred together. The small "baby" crocodiles were usually fakes that contained one small crocodile bone embedded in straw. Some burials even contained eggs.[5] The mummies were elaborately wrapped in hundreds of yards of linen arranged in geometric patterns. In some cases, long sheets of old papyrus documents were used as a base layer for the wrapping of the head.[6]

This example was given to the Museum in 1872 with a group of 120 animal mummies

192

of various types. The elaborate wrappings, particularly of the eyes and long tail, give it a lifelike appearance. An X-ray of the mummy indicates that it does indeed contain the complete, though greatly compressed, body of a young crocodile.[7]

SD'A

1. For Sobek, see Brovarski 1984.
2. Diodorus 1985, pp. 115-116.
3. Brovarski 1984, p. 1015.
4. Bagnani 1952, p. 77.
5. Bagnani 1952, p. 77.
6. Bagnani 1952, p. 78.
7. Richard Meadow, personal communication. For other examples of crocodile mummies, see Gaillard and Daressy 1905, pls. XXXII and XLVIII, National Museum of Antiquities at Leiden 1987, no. 164, p. 127.

Literature: Kákosy 1979, Bagnani 1952.

193
Ram mummy

Provenance unknown
Ptolemaic or Roman period
Linen
Length 28 cm., width 14 cm.
Hay Collection, Gift of C. Granville Way, 1872 (72.4906)

The ram was associated with several deities, but foremost with Amen and Khnum, the creator god who produced the human race on the potter's wheel. In the Graeco-Roman period, documents record that two oracles were delivered by lambs, and in each case, the king ordered the deceased lamb to be mummified as a god.[1]

Khnum's two main cult centers were at Esna and Elephantine. A cemetery of sacred rams was excavated in Elephantine in 1907-1908, and dates to the Roman period.[2] A chamber in which the embalming of the rams took place was also found. The cemetery consisted of sandstone sarcophagi, only one of which was inscribed, placed under a brick floor. Each ram was buried in a cartonnage coffin.[3] Other ram burials are known from Tihna, Tebtunis, and Mendes.[4]

This mummy, like the crocodile mummy (cat. 192), is from a large unprovenanced collection given to the Museum in 1872. Though it is missing the horns found on other examples,[5] it has floppy linen ears, and its eyes are indicated by a circle of black paint. Some of the wrappings have decayed, but their original beauty is indicated by the chevron-shaped linen bands below the head. X-rays show a complete skeleton of a young, perhaps newborn, bovid with legs drawn underneath the body.[6]

SD'A

1. Kákosy 1981, pp. 142-143.
2. Ricke 1960, pp. 33-35, taf. 22.
3. See Kákosy 1981, p. 150 and figs. 1-3.
4. Kessler 1985b, p. 579.

193

5. Gaillard and Daressy 1905, 29.669, p. 100, pl. XLI.
6. Richard Meadow, personal communication.

194
Figure of an ichneumon

Provenance unknown
Late Period
Bronze
Length 4.5 cm. width 2.5 cm.
Gift of Mr. and Mrs. deForest Thomson, 1918 (18.581)

The ichneumon, or mongoose, is often confused in Egyptian art with the shrew-mouse, which is similar in appearance. The shrew is a nocturnal animal, with small eyes that appear almost blind. The ichneumon, however, is active during the day and has larger eyes. According to Brunner-Traut, both of these animals were sacred to the sun-god Horus, and represented two aspects of the god, those of day and night.[1]

The ichneumon was associated with other cults as well, including that of the goddess Wadjet of Buto. Known as the "beast of Atum," it was revered because it killed and ate snakes. According to Diodorus, the ichneumon was also treasured for its ability to search out the brood of the crocodile and crush its eggs:

> And it performs this deed with diligence and enthusiasm, though it derives no benefit for itself therefrom. If the ichneumon did not behave in this way, the great swarms of reptiles hatching out would make the river unapproachable. But the ichneumons also kill the

194

crocodiles themselves in an extraordinary manner which is quite hard to believe: for they hide in the mud at the time when these monsters are sleeping on the shore, and when they yawn, down they leap through their mouths and descend into the interior of their bodies; then quickly gnawing through their bellies, they escape unscathed, and this causes the immediate death of their victims.[2]

Ichneumons were mummified; a mixed cemetery of cats and ichneumons was discovered at Bubastis.[3] At the site of Naukratis, Petrie found a hoard of bronze figures, probably temple offerings, that included cobras, lizards, eels, and ichneumons, along with bronzes of various deities. One of the ichneumons was hollow and contained bones of the animal.[4] Ichneumon figures in bronze, with or without bones inserted into their bases, are quite common, and usually show the animal in a striding position.[5] Ichneumon bones have also been found inside hollow bronze statuettes of the goddess Wadjet.[6]

This example shows a striding ichneumon in solid bronze. The base is hollow and may hold animal bones, though X-rays have been inconclusive.

SD'A

1. See Brunner-Traut 1965.
2. Diodorus 1985, p. 113.
3. Naville 1891, p. 53.
4. Petrie 1886, p. 41.
5. Roeder 1937, pp. 56-58, taf. 34; Roeder 1956, pp. 380-383; Emery 1971, pl. IX,2; University of Delaware 1987, no. 8, p. 35; National Museum of Antiquities at Leiden 1987, no. 158, l6. Bothmer 1949, p. 121.

Literature: Brunner-Traut 1965.

196

195

195
Falcon coffin

Provenance unknown
Late Period
Bronze
Length 11.7 cm., height 14.3 cm.
Accessioned from an unknown source, 1987 (1987.285)

Egypt is the home of many different types of falcons that can still be seen circling its skies today.[1] A majestic-looking bird of prey, the falcon soars at great heights. It is not surprising, then, that the falcon was identified from the beginning of pharaonic times with the sun-god Horus, whom the living king embodied. Some other gods, such as Re-Horakhty, Montu, and Sokar, appeared as falcons or falcon-headed men.

The Horus falcon was characterized in Egyptian art by a hooked bill, dark wings and back, white underside, and distinct black facial markings that comprised the "eye of Horus," or *wedjat*. Because its portrayal was very stylized, it is impossible to identify with certainty which of the falcon species it represents.

Falcon cults were scattered throughout Egypt, and Horus had many local cults.[2] In the Late and Graeco-Roman periods, falcons were mummified by the thousands and buried in the sacred animal necropoleis, sometimes with other birds or animals, at sites including Buto, Kom Ombo, Abydos, Sakkara, and Giza.[3] The mummies, which were not always those of complete birds, were tightly wrapped and sometimes provided with cartonnage masks in the form of falcon's heads, or buried in coffins.[4]

In the Late Period, bronze boxes surmounted by figures of falcons were also used to house falcon mummies.[5] On the Museum's example there are remains of a thin sheet of metal that sealed one end of the hollow box base after the contents were inserted. The mummy was removed at some point. The bronze falcon is well executed, with the feathering clearly indicated. The falcon wears the double crown of Upper and Lower Egypt. An inscription at the front of the base is very worn, but

seems to refer to "Horus of Pe" (Buto).

SD'A

1. For a discussion of falcons, see Houlihan 1986, pp. 46-49.
2. Altenmüller 1975d, pp. 94-95.
3. Altenmüller 1975d, p. 95. For a discussion of mummification of falcons, see Lortet and Gaillard 1902, pp. 18-21.
4. National Museum of Antiquities at Leiden 1987, no. 162, p. 126; Gaillard and Daressy 1905, pls. XLIII-XLV and LX-LXIII.
5. Ägyptisches Museum Berlin 1967, nos. 843 and 849; Merhav et al. 1981, no. 121, p. 156; Emery 1971, pl. IX.

196
Serpent coffin

Provenance unknown
Late Dynastic to Ptolemaic periods, 712-30 B.C.
Bronze
Length 55 cm., width 3.8 cm., max. height 14 cm.
William Stevenson Smith Fund, 1986 (1986.239)

In the later periods of Egyptian history, mummies of animals sacred to particular deities were frequently offered as gifts in temples and other sacred precincts. These mummified animals included not only cats, dogs, and ibises but also fish, snakes, and insects. Sometimes the animals were wrapped in linen or placed in containers of pottery, wood, stone, or metal. These varied in quality from simple pots and roughly carved boxes to small masterpieces of bronze sculpture.

The eel was sacred to the creator god Atum of Heliopolis,[1] and numbers of eels and snakes must have been offered to the temple in that city. This particularly fine example combines both elverine and reptilian features; the god has the long, undulating body of an eel and the hood of a cobra. He is shown with the divine beard and wears a *nemes* headcloth surmounted by a double crown. The head is supported by a prop hidden by the hood and the whole figure rests on a hollow rectangular box made to contain an eel or a serpent.[2] A similar coffin now in Cambridge bears a dedicatory inscription and can be dated to the fifth or fourth century B.C.[3]

PL

1. Mysliwiec 1981.
2. Cf. Müller 1964, p. 107, pl. A 153.
3. Fitzwilliam Museum E. 354.1932.

Literature: Roeder 1956, pp. 393-396; Daressy 1906, nos. 38702, 38703, p. 180.

Osiris

197
Statuette of Osiris (upper portion)

From Giza
Dynasty 26
Green schist (?)
Height 55 cm.
Harvard University-Museum of Fine Arts
Expedition, 1929 (29.1131)

This very conventional statue depicts Osiris in his standard attire: the close-fitting shroud, the scepter and flagellum in his hands, the broad collar (five regular rows of beads, ending with drop-shaped beads), and the *atef* crown (consisting of the Upper Egyptian crown flanked by two high feathers) protected by the royal uraeus, ready to spit fire against the enemies of the god or king.

The main interest of the piece lies in its technical perfection: schist, often chosen by the artists of the Saite Period, allows subtle modeling and faultless polishing. The calm, nearly smiling expression of the face, characteristic of the major Dynasty 26 monuments, reflects the endeavor to imitate the statuary of the Old Kingdom. The reverence for the remote period is also marked by the construction of numerous nobles' tombs in the ancient cemeteries of Giza and Sakkara. Lower Egyptian society of the time was prosperous, and private individuals could afford to dedicate monuments of great value. This one, found in the fill of a tomb-shaft in Giza, was offered by an otherwise unknown official, the "royal acquaintance" Ptah-irdis, son of Wepwawet-em-saf, whose tomb might have been located near the Giza sphinx.

The text on the back pillar (fig. 89), though broken, clearly states what Ptah-irdis was expecting in return from the god: "May you give me bread, beer and every good thing, may you rescue me against any evil, may you make me powerful in...." Credited with the introduction of agriculture into Egypt at the dawn of history, Osiris, frequently styled "father of grain," was believed to control the annual cycle of vegetation growth by releasing the flood of inundation; therefore, it was believed that he could ensure the material survival of the dead.

His spiritual part as well was essential. Before being admitted in his realm, the dead had to undergo judgment before a law-court, and to prove that his life had always been in accordance with Maat, the principle of universal harmony (symbolized by a feather, similar to those flanking the *atef* crown). In the back-pillar text, Osiris is styled "Creator of Maat," since, as presiding judge, he ultimately decided whether the dead was to be admitted to eternal life. The benign expression on the god's face

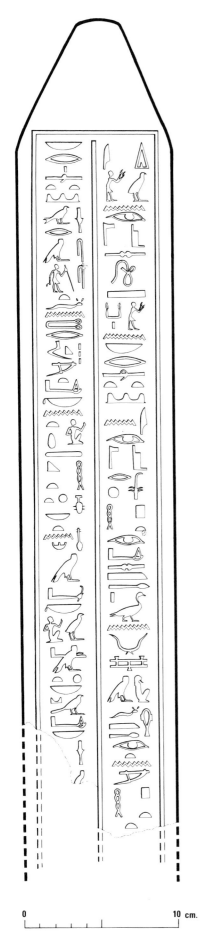

0   10 cm.

Fig. 89

197

could then be viewed as a token of his benevolence to the dead.

LP

Bibliography: Haynes 1984, p. 39, fig. 7. Dunham 1931, p. 26; Smith 1946, p. 156; Bothmer 1960, p. 48-9, 57-58; Porter and Moss 1974, pp. 204, 291.

198
Statuette of Osiris

Provenance unknown
Third Intermediate Period
Bronze
Height 25.5 cm., width 6.7 cm.
Bequest of Charles H. Parker, 1908 (08.260)

This exquisite bronze shows the god in the canonical attitude. A pair of twisted ram's horns added to the *atef* crown alludes to the affinities between Osiris and the ram. This animal was a symbol of authority and dignity – a ram is used as hieroglyph for the word *shefyt*, ("power, respect") – and the twisted horns were frequently attached to royal crowns. Besides, the ram, as a fecundity figure, seems connected to Osirian resurrection: during some late rituals, figures of the god had to be wrapped in a ram's skin, in order to revive the god and ensure the annual growth of vegetation.

The quality and refinement of technique are striking in the careful execution of such paraphernalia as the handles of the scepter and flagellum, the armlets, the feathers of the *atef* crown and the body of the uraeus-snake; the beard-braiding is delicately incised. The broad collar, with three rows of cylindrical beads and the one formed of drop-shaped pendants, is inlaid with precious metal; only on the finest bronzes is the counterpoise at the back designed with equal care. The calm, round face with its inlaid eyes, straight nose, and everted lips is a true portrait in accordance with the canons of the time.

Such a fine piece of work can only have come from a palace workshop: the position and length of the *heka* scepter confirms the Lower Egyptian origin. The high quality suggests that the object, once fastened by its

198

199

prong to a wooden base, either by itself or as part of a group, was dedicated by a very high-ranking or even royal person.

LP

Literature: Roeder 1937, especially pp. 22-25, 88-92; Roeder 1956, pp. 133-194.

199
Statuette of Osiris

From Gemaiyemi
Late Period
Steatite (?)
Height 14.5 cm., width 4 cm.
Gift of the Egyptian Exploration Fund, 1886 (87.675)

This very traditional, Lower Egyptian figure of Osiris is probably made of steatite, a

cheap and soft stone rather common in Upper Egyptian Eastern deserts. This material, sometimes called soapstone, was used for small, modest objects. It could be heated to obtain a kind of glazing, or coated with precious metals. Traces of gilding on the current example explain the rather crude style, the only roughly delineated features, and the body left unpolished to ensure a better coating.

The statue comes from Gemaiyemi, near the site of the ancient city of Buto, one of the oldest and most prestigious religious centers of the northeastern Delta. Found in the precinct of a temple, maybe dedicated to the god Ptah, this statue is a good example of the minor objects from chapels housing a secondary cult at that time. Each temple included one or more rooms devoted to various forms and rites of Osiris. Thus, col-

lections of cheap ex-votos dedicated to the god by pious votaries multiplied throughout the period. Among the mass production of poor bronze figurines, our monument, modest as it may look today, nevertheless should have been made conspicuous by the glittering of its gilding. As such, it seems to have been preserved, along with valuable bronze objects, from an older sanctuary as a deposit, to be buried under the precinct wall rebuilt in the Late Period.

LP

Bibliography: Griffith 1888, pp. 42-44.

Literature: Fuchs 1984, 1271-1274.

200
Osiris figure group

Provenance unknown, possibly from Thebes
Late New Kingdom
Steatite
Height 15.5 cm.
Gift of Theodore M. Davis, 1905 (05.91)

Carved out of a block of steatite (see cat. 199), this monument may look rather conventional in its iconography; what makes it unusual is its triplication of one and the same figure. Its technique is rather good, as indicated by the careful carving of the three faces, each one slightly different from the other. The attempt to avoid monotony in spite of repetition, a constant feature of Egyptian art throughout history, appears as well in the height of the figurines, almost imperceptibly decreasing from right to left.

From the Late New Kingdom on were found only a few groups of from two to five Osirian figures. Most of these objects are either cheap bronze or ceramic amulets, small enough to be placed on a mummy. The fact that larger ex-votos belonging to this type were often hastily made up by putting together several ready-made figurines differing in shape and size indicates a limited production. The exceptional technique of this triad makes it a rather valuable ex-voto.

The relative scarcity of similar groups in museum collections suggests the limited success of this type. Its precise meaning remains unclear: a plausible explanation is that they were intended to insist on the plural, i.e., infinite power of the god. When linked to particular sites, they might indicate the number of different forms of the god worshipped in local sanctuaries.

LP

200

201, scepter

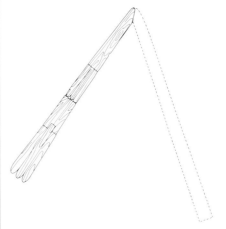

201, flagellum

201
Heka scepter and flagellum

Provenance unknown, possibly from Gurna
Dynasty 18
Wood
Scepter length 31.5 cm.
Flagellum length 35.2 cm.
Sears Fund, 1903 (03.1644 and 03.1645)

The *heka* scepter (or crook) and the flagellum (similar to a flywhisk), along with the crown of the mummiform god, were venerated among Osirian relics in the Ptolemaic

Period as organic parts of the divine body. The *heka* scepter, an emblem of power resembling of a bishop's crook, is usually short-handled on monuments from the Theban area; in the hieroglyphic script, its phonetic value is *heka*, meaning "rule" or "ruler." The flagellum consisted of three strings of truncated cones, cylindrical beads, and drop-shaped pendants (the general outlines of which are grooves in the wood) hanging from a handle (now lost).

The flat back of the flagellum and the tenon in the lower part of the crook handle ind-

icate that both objects, once painted or maybe gilded, were held by a cult-statue – either Osiris himself or the Osirian representation of a dead pharaoh receiving a funerary cult in western Thebes. In the canonical Upper Egyptian iconography, the scepter is held in the left hand, the flagellum in the right, the wrists are crossed on the chest, right over left. Few such wooden objects are preserved. Although the material is modest, the fine, careful carving reflects the importance of these attributes and testifies to the high technical standards of the statue to which they once belonged.

Whether borrowed from the rather obscure Lower Egyptian god Anedjti or directly from the royal paraphernalia (they appeared, along with the *atef* crown (see cat. 197), among the ritual panoply of Narmer the first king of Egypt), the Osirian *heka* scepter and flagellum seem inherited from a prehistoric pastoral society: the crook would have been reserved for the tribal chief, whereas the flagellum might well be a mere shepherd's whip. Throughout Egyptian history, they remained insignia of the Osirian kingship, alluding both to his beneficent authority over the kingdom of Egypt during his terrestrial life and to his prominence in the realm of the dead, reflected in his name Kheny-imentiu, "Foremost of the Westerners."

LP

Literature: Fischer 1976a, pp. 516-517; Griffiths 1981, col. 628; Martin 1979, pp. 821-823.

202
Isis suckling Horus

Provenance unknown
Late Period
Bronze
Height 27 cm., width 6.4 cm.
Unaccessioned

Among Late Period bronze figurines, Isis suckling Horus ("Isis lactans") is one of the most common types, and foreshadowed the popularity of the Isis cult that invaded the Roman world a few centuries later. Dressed in the traditional Egyptian tight-fitting robe, the goddess is depicted in the stereotyped attitude of suckling: with her right hand she offers her left breast to Horus. The baby is nude, his head shaven except for the "childhood-lock" on the right temple. Isis's vulture-cap, as well as the curled, New Kingdom fashioned wig, are usually worn by the goddess Mut, whose name simply means "mother," and are thus intended to emphasize the motherhood of Isis. The cow horns and solar disk belong to Hathor, whose motherly aspect is particularly relevant here.

After the murder and dismemberment of Osiris by Seth, Isis collected and reassem-

202

bled her husband's body and magically restored his sexual and generative power. Thus Horus could be conceived even after his father's death, as the legitimate heir to Osiris's kingdom: the iconography of the uraeus on the child's forehead is regal. The problem of royal succession is one of the main issues of the Osirian myth, and the divine suckling had, at first, an exclusively royal meaning. The goddess's milk was needed to ensure the king's rebirth as full king, either in the Netherworld after his death, or on the earth, each time the power was transmitted or renewed (namely on coronation and jubilees). But from the Late Period on, the general "democratization" of divine or royal events accounts for the popularity of such representations. The object was intended as an *ex-voto*, to be placed in a major sanctuary.

The fine workmanship of this piece – such details as the child's lock and collar and the wig are carefully indicated by fine incisions – along with such original features as the Mut head-gear, point to a workshop of high standard, presumably situated near or in the capital.

LP

Literature: Schenkel 1983, p. 340; Müller 1963, pp. 7-38.

203

203
Statuette of Amen-nakht holding a statue of Osiris

Provenance unknown
Late New Kingdom
Painted limestone
Height 16.5 cm.
Gift of Horace L. Mayer, 1957 (1957.410)

Amen-nakht wears a long tunic with fan-shaped sleeves, and a long skirt with trapezoid front; the wig, with rows of curls roughly indicated by an incised check-pattern, seems to belong to the rather elaborate type called the "double-wig." The body is entirely covered with texts, two columns on each shoulder, one on each side, seven lines on the back. The Osirian figure is crudely carved; contrary to the canonical position, the flagellum is held in the left hand, and the *heka* scepter in the right.

The Ramesside era, undoubtedly pointed to by the attire, witnessed the growing popularity of such figures holding gods' statues, showing the physical proximity of the pious votary to the divinity. Presumably funerary, the monument presents the main figures of the Osirian myth: Osiris as a mummiform figure, and his sisters Isis and Nephthys as mourners. The goddesses, schematically painted in black, seem two over-sized hieroglyphs, on the front of the garment. Nephthys has faded away, but on the right, Isis is still visible, the throne (hieroglyphic sign of her name) on her head, one hand to her forehead and the other raised to protect

her brother and husband. The back text, now lost, begins with an invocation, most probably to Osiris himself. The statuette's over-inscribed body recalls the funerary figurines (*shawabti*s).

The divine figures, schematically delineated, strongly contrast to Amen-nakht in his most elegant attire, his lips, eyelids, and wig carefully rendered. Such details as the armlet on the left wrist, or the two folds painted on the neck must be meant to bring a refined touch. On the other hand, the body as a whole looks deformed because of the over-sized head and eyes. This obviously unique object was designed for or even by Amen-nakht; his function and titles are unknown, but the monument suggests his social status must have been modest.

LP

204
Funerary stela

From Dendera
Ptolemaic Period
Sandstone
Height 47 cm.
Gift of the Egyptian Exploration Fund, 1898 (98.1055)

Remarkably sober in design, this monument features a line of hieroglyphic text giving a name, "The Falcon Pabek," and the representation of a mummy, wearing a stucco

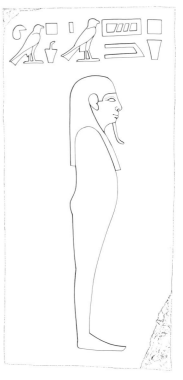

0   25 cm.

204

mask with the traditional tripartite wig. Note that, unlike the human beings, but like statues, the mummified body is shown entirely in profile. This slab was standing against the back wall of a collective tomb-chamber, beneath a recess containing several mummies. Like a label, it was intended to identify its owner among the dozen occupants of the tomb, and was placed exactly under his head.

The quality of the carving suggests that highly trained carvers, in Dendera for the extensive decoration work in the great Hathor temple at that time, occasionally worked on private order. Though humble in itself, the stela belongs to an original series of funerary documents, mainly from Dendera, where the dead is called "The Falcon NN" (e.g., Pakhem, Coptic Pachomius, a rather popular name from that time on) instead of the usual "Osiris NN." Such formulae show that, even if the popularity of Osiris was far from receding, the funerary beliefs of Graeco-Roman Egypt had become multiform: for instance, some deceased women were referred to as "The Hathor NN." The identification of the dead with the falcon deity is not a new idea: the funerary corpus known as the Coffin Texts (before 2000 B.C.) already contain "spells for assuming the form of a divine falcon." Osiris himself, when identified with the god Sokar, is frequently shown falcon-headed on the late reliefs and minor funerary objects. The word here, *Pakhem*, applied originally only to the mummified falcon, but then came to mean "idol, divine statue" in general. Thus the dead sought identification with the very principle of divinity, not only with specifically funerary gods.

This particular development in Dendera was obviously influenced by the local cult: the worship of the falcon was a main feature of this center (a necropolis of sacred falcons was also excavated by Petrie). The deceased's name itself, Pabek, means "The Falcon": thus the devotion of the stela owner to the sacred animal is expressed twice.

LP

Literature: Petrie 1900a, pp. 31-32, 55, pl. XXV B; Spiegelberg 1927, pp. 27-34; Hermann 1964, pp. 39-44; Altenmüller 1975b, pp. 55-56.

205

205
Fragment of offering stela

Provenance unknown
Saite Period, probably about 600 B.C.
Basalt
Preserved height 28 cm., width 29.5 cm., depth 6.5 cm.
Sears Fund, 1904 (04.1850)

The decoration on this basalt stela has been carefully carved in low relief, and traces of red, blue, and white paint remain on the surface. The scene depicts a man with his arms raised in prayer before the mummified form of Osiris. The man is painted red and wears a cone and fillet on his head. The single strap over his right shoulder is typical of men's garments on stelae of the same period.

The god's mummy wrappings are painted with red checks and he wears a collar over his shoulders. The *menat* of this collar hangs down his back and shows traces of red paint. Osiris holds a flail and a long staff that seems to be a cross between the crook and *was*-scepter that he usually holds. The faces of both figures are slightly modeled and have been carved with care.

Surrounding this scene is the curving figure of the goddess Nut, who is painted blue. Over her back a winged disk with two uraeus cobras echoes the curved top of the stela. The feathers are blue with red tips. The sun disk itself is carved in sunk relief because it is surrounded by the wings,

which are raised relief. A raised border has been left around the edge of the stela.

This stela is similar to a group that Munro dates to the middle of the Saite Period, many of which were found at Abydos.[1]

CHR

1. Munro 1973, pp. 286-300, pls. 37-43. Especially pl. 37, #135, now in Cairo JE 18520.

206
Architectural tondo of Osiris in hydria

From near Mallawi
Roman Imperial Period, second century A.D.
Limestone
Max. diam. 98 cm.
Gift of Paul E. Manheim, 1970 (1970.243)

The principal image of this unusual composition is popularly, but erroneously, labeled "Canopus," a putative deity of like name allegedly associated with the Delta site of Canopus, east of Alexandria. The alternate suggestion that pharaonic "Canopic jars," vessels with human or theriomorphic heads as stoppers in which selected organs of the deceased were placed, served as the visual antecedents can be likewise dismissed.

The component elements of this figure are a body in the form of a hydria, or water jar, to the neck of which is attached a human, male head. The vessel is decorated with somewhat effaced relief, and the head is

206

complex thematic conceit that is implied in the raised-relief decoration which characterizes these vessels. That decoration, here fowl and altar in association with a child god, can be associated with water, both as a source of life after death and the means by which the faithful might conquer death. The body of Osiris becomes merged with water so that both effectively become one. Consequently the hydria was never intended to hold water. Each jar could serve not only as a cult vessel for Osiris, which could be carried in procession with veiled hands, but could also function as one of the forms in which Osiris himself could be worshipped. Smaller images might also serve the needs of individuals tombs.

The tondo form of the Boston example is unique; it may have adorned the wall of either a tomb or a temple. The bland idealizing features of the face of Osiris cannot be used as a dating criterion, but the correspondences between this figure and others from excavated contexts strongly suggest a second century A.D. date.

RB

Literature: Stricker 1943; Schneider and Raven 1981; Wild 1981; Weber 1911; Beinlich 1984; Fouquet 1973; Bianchi forthcoming.

Fig. 90

207
Cup

From Abydos, tomb of Djer
Saite Period, Dynasty 26
Pottery
Height 6 cm., max. diam. 7 cm.
Gift of Egypt Exploration Fund, 1901
(01.8517)

Perhaps as early as the New Kingdom, the tomb of King Djer of Dynasty 1 at Abydos

---

covered with a *nemes*, or royal headcloth. Its lappets, decorated with vertical rather than horizontal stripes, are typical of the rendering of such headdresses in the Roman Imperial Period. Set into the *nemes* and projecting beyond the frame of the tondo is a crown consisting of two ostrich feathers, a sun disk, and the horns of a sheep. Although such an attribute may be associated with either Osiris or with Sarapis during the Roman Imperial Period, the figure here is unequivocally intended to represent Osiris, who, unlike Sarapis, is invariably clean shaven. The origin and development of this particular manifestation is debated, particularly since the earliest dated examples of this motif occur on Roman coins of the second half of the first century A.D.

These water vessels develop from a fundamentally pharaonic concept embodied by a select group of relief representations in the central room of the East Osiris Chapel on the roof of the Temple of Hathor at Dendera. These reliefs represent the various nome deities of Egypt, each bringing a "reliquary vessel," for want of a better term, which metaphysically contains that part of the body of Osiris associated with the nome, which personified, bears it. Such vessels are to be understood in terms of the Memphite theology and relate to the rites of fertility associated with Osiris. The older Egyptian antecedents from which this particular visual expression evolved remain to be identified. It has been suggested that the correspondences between aspects of the Memphite theology and of the rituals associated with the "reliquaries" at Dendera point to a Saite origin for the motif, but this suggestion cannot be verified. Until additional data is forthcoming, one ought to regard such representations in the round as exclusively Roman phenomena. It is equally clear that codified theology and a degree of standardization of such images were rapidly developed throughout Egypt in the course of the late first century A.D. and immediately transported and adopted in this thoroughly Egyptian form in Italy, where the image enjoyed great popularity in the second century A.D. This phenomenon would seem to indicate a highly organized theological administration that enabled an Egyptian synod of sorts to communicate directly with a branch of the Imperial court in Rome.

Such images, which can now be properly termed "Osiris in hydria," revolve around a (see cat. 4) became identified as the burial place of the god Osiris.[1] By the Saite Period the tomb became a major focus for the cult of Osiris; votive offerings were brought by the thousands and deposited in the area of the Dynasty 1 royal necropolis.

By far the most common gifts left by the pilgrims were small, roughly made pottery cups. The fragments of these that litter the site (fig. 90) have given it its modern name Umm el-Ga'ab, or "mother of pots." This example was recovered from the tomb by Petrie and is typical of the myriad vessels that exist in great heaps around the tomb. It has an incurved rim and rounded body with a short, narrow stump base. The vessel was wheelmade with a string-cut base of a Nile silt C fabric and finished off with a plain wet smoothed surface.[2] Examples of this type of libation cup have been found at tombs and temples throughout Egypt and in Nubia[3] and can be dated to the Saite Period.[4]

PL

1. Petrie 1901a, p. 8.
2. Dorothea Arnold, personal communication.
3. Cf. Dunham 1955, fig. 108 (18-4-14).

208
Lepidotus fish

From Mesheikh
Saite Period, Dynasty 26
Bronze
Length 23 cm., width 9 cm., width 3 cm.
Harvard University-Museum of Fine Arts Expedition, 1912 (12.1218)

The Lepidotus fish, *Barbus binni*, is probably to be associated with the *bwt* fish.[1] This freshwater fish is distinguished by its large scales and barblike dorsal fin. It was one of the fish proscribed in the Egyptian diet, because of its association with Osiris.[2]

A number of Lepidotos mummies and pisciform coffins and votive figurines are known from caches in sacred areas.[3] This example came from an area at Mesheikh where a number of bronze and wood representations of the Lepidotus fish were found.[4]

This bronze fish was hollow cast with carefully modeled fins and scales. The eyes are clear glass mounted in round raised sockets with a gesso backing and painted irises. A hole at the bottom was originally attached to a tang that would have connected the fish to a metal or wood base.

PL

1. Gamer-Wallert 1970, pp. 95-98.
2. Darby, Ghalioungui, and Grivetti 1977, pp. 380-387.
3. Cf. Werbrouck 1940. pp. 199-201, fig. 2.
4. MFA 12.1218-1221.

Bibliography: Museum of Fine Arts 1937, no. 58.

208

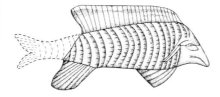

209

209
Oxyrhynchus fish

Provenance unknown
New Kingdom
Frit
Preserved length 6 cm., height 3.5 cm., depth .4 cm.
Anonymous loan

The Oxyrhynchus fish, *Mormyrus kannume*, was the most revered of Egyptian fishes. Aelian related that, "whenever fish are netted, they search the nets in case this famous fish has fallen in without their noticing it. And they would rather catch nothing at all than than have the largest catch which included this fish."[1] The Oxyrhynchus fish has a distinctive downcurving snout and dorsal ridge and in spite of the taboos recorded, it is shown being caught for food.[2]

The fish was worshipped at the site of Behnesa and associated with the god Seth. It was also believed to have swallowed the phallus of the dismembered Osiris.[3]

A large number of bronze examples, often shown with an elaborate crown, are known from the Saite and Late Dynastic Periods.[4] This example in light blue glass frit is paralleled by a fragmentary piece in dark blue glass of an Oxyrhynchus fish from a New Kingdom grave at Abydos now in the Museum of Fine Arts.[5] It is difficult to judge whether the flat frit example was originally an inlay part of some piece of funeral furniture or an independent amulet included in the burial.

PL

1. Darby, Ghalioungui, and Grivetti 1977, pp. 387-389.
2. Darby, Ghalioungui, and Grivetti 1977, pp. 387-389.
3. Gamer-Wallert, 1970. pp. 91-95.

4. Crawford 1987. pp. 25-6, fig. 5.
5. MFA 02.821

210

210
Funerary figure

Provenance unknown
New Kingdom
Wood
Height 28.3 cm.
Hay Collection, Gift of C. Granville Way, 1872 (72.4901)

Traces of painted gesso coating show that the white coloring of the body was originally alleviated by a broad collar in red and blue and by what appears to have been a vertical column of hieroglyphs in black down the front; the wig, with its parted fringe, was painted black and the face red, perhaps with the eyes outlined in black. A rectangular hole in the top of the head was intended to receive the tenon of a separately carved head ornament, apparently the *shuty* or double plumes[1]. The figure is attached to a solid, rectangular base with sloping front by means of a simple mortise and tenon joint held in position by a transverse dowel. The base itself was originally painted yellow.

This figure is related to the Ptah-Sokar-Osiris type of funerary image,[2] a blanket designation that in fact covers two distinct classes of representation: polychrome or resin-coated statuettes of Osiris – which frequently contain a rolled funerary papyrus either within the body of the figure itself or within the base – and similarly decorated statuettes of the syncretistic deity Ptah-Sokar-Osiris, occasionally solid but more often containing a miniature "corn mummy" (cats. 211 and 212) symbolizing the dead man's hope for resurrection. The Osirid type, of which this figure is a particularly well-carved example, ranges in date from Dynasty 18 to Dynasty 22 and later, when it was superseded by the Ptah-Sokar-Osiris figure (cats. 124 and 144), which survives well into the Ptolemaic Period.

CNR

1. Cf. Hay 1869, p. 48, no. 426.
2. Raven 1978-79, pp. 251-296; Taylor (forthcoming).

Bibliography: Hay 1869, p. 48, no. 426.

211
Corn-Mummy

Provenance unknown
Late or Ptolemaic Period
Linen and mud over a core of sand and grain
Height 12.2 cm.
Hay Collection, Gift of C. Granville Way, 1872 (72.4829)

Though partially obscured by its linen wrappings, this mummiform figure represents the god Osiris, who wears a tall crown and beard and holds the crook and flail. Manufactured of Nile mud over a core of sand mixed with grains of barley and wheat, such objects are known as "corn-mummies." The grains of corn contained in the figures are significant primarily as symbols of regeneration and resurrection, thus associating them with Osiris in his funerary role, rather than for their value as food.[1] Corn-mummies have their origin in the "Osiris beds" of the New Kingdom, found in burials in the Valley of the Kings.[2] The beds consisted of an Osiris-shaped frame covered with earth in which seeds of barley were ritually sown and germinated.

While the Osiris beds seem to have been a royal prerogative, small corn-mummies such as this one were often placed in the cavities of Ptah-Sokar-Osiris figures (see cat. 144) deposited in private tombs in the Late and Ptolemaic periods. Corn-mummies changed greatly in form and function, but their use continued through the Ptolemaic period (see cat. 212).

SD'A

211

1. See the comprehensive study, Raven 1982, p. 32.
2. Raven 1982, pp. 12-16.
3. Raven 1978-1979, pp. 286-287.

Literature: Raven 1982, pp. 7-34.

212
Corn-Mummy

Provenance unknown
Ptolemaic or Roman Period
Linen and mud over a core of sand and grain
Height 34 cm.
Hay Collection, Gift of C. Granville Way, 1872 (unaccessioned)

This corn-mummy, like the smaller one (see cat. 211), is composed of mud-coated linen wrappings over a filling of sand and grains of wheat or barley.[1] Its mummiform shape is intended to represent the god Osiris, who wears a tall crown and holds the crook and flail.

Unlike the smaller corn-mummy, which was probably placed in the cavity of a Ptah-Sokar-Osiris figure, this later example may have been manufactured as a part of a temple ritual celebrating the resurrection of

Osiris.[2] According to a text preserved in the Dendera Temple,[3] Osiris-shaped figures of earth and seeds were created in order to germinate the seeds, then wrapped as mummies, placed in coffins, and buried. Many of the extant corn-mummies are ithyphallic, an attribute indicated on this example by a slot in the figure where an erect phallus would have been inserted. Also missing is the wax mask covering the face and head commonly found on corn-mummies.

Five corn-mummies of this type were discovered in the Museum's collection of animal mummies, which were acquired in 1872 and are unprovenanced. Raven has noted an association between corn-mummies and animal mummies, which were also manufactured in temple precincts and ritually buried.[4]

SD'A

1. Confirmed by X-ray, which shows a homogeneous filling material interspersed with a few larger granules.
2. Raven 1982, pp. 27-29.
3. Porter and Moss 1939, p. 97; for discussion, see Raven 1982, pp. 28-29.
4. Raven 1982, p. 29.

212

Modern Radiographic Evaluation of Egyptian Mummies

In 1983, the Museum of Fine Arts, Boston, and the Brigham and Women's Hospital, Boston, undertook a collaborative project. This project, which took four years to complete, used the latest noninvasive medical imaging techniques to examine the Museum's collection of human and animal Egyptian mummies.

Mummification, as practiced in ancient Egypt, preserved the body's soft tissues (skin, hair, muscles, organs, and nerves) as well as its skeletal elements. These preserved tissues carry with them a history written over the course of their owner's life and closed at the time of death. After death the body underwent the elaborate process of mummification, a process that reflected ancient Egyptian beliefs and customs. The use of medical technology enabled us to become privy to both the medical and cultural information within these time capsules from the ancient past, information that lay beneath hundreds of yards of linen wrappings and cartonnage coffins.

Although modern medical imaging makes use of a variety of tools including sound waves and magnets, X-rays remain the cornerstone of the science. We were not the first to use X-rays to penetrate the mummies' secrets. The Egyptologist W.M.F. Petrie X-rayed mummies in 1898, just three years after Roentgen's historic discovery of this type of radiation. Many of the mummies in the Museum's collection were X-rayed in 1930, although at that time they were only X-rayed in one projection, whereas we X-rayed them in two. We also studied the mummies using computed tomography , or CT scanning, a technique unknown at that time. In this technique a beam of X-rays is passed through an object at different angles and measured at the far side of the object by detectors. This information is sent to a computer, which then reconstructs an image of the object by solving a series of complex mathematical equations.

CT scanners examine objects slice by slice and display each slice on a high-resolution, black-and-white TV screen. These images can then be transferred to film and viewed with a light box, as are conventional X-rays. The radiologist determines how thick the slices will be (1-10 mm.), how long the computer will take to examine each slice (2-10 seconds) and how many slices will be taken (in the case of the mummies, enough slices were taken to cover the entire body).

To help visualize what a CT scanner does, it may be helpful to think of a loaf of raisin bread. The scanner examines the loaf (patient or mummy) slice by slice and displays the slice on a screen from the perspective of one looking down on the slice from above, revealing the precise location of every raisin. The ability to eliminate super-impositions of overlying structures is one of CT's great advantages over conventional film techniques. Another is its ability to detect and display much smaller differences in density between internal structures than conventional X-rays. Like conventional film X-rays, CT is noninvasive and nondestructive.

The use of CT in examining the Museum's collection has revealed a great deal of information about the mummies not visualized on standard X-rays. Diseases were identified and practices of mummification documented that could not be seen otherwise. The results of this study have been reported elsewhere.[1]

Three representative CT scans are shown here. Remember, these are thin X-ray slices of a mummy with the mummy's top at the top of the picture. Dense structures such as bone are shown in white, whereas structures that are not dense, like air, are black. Structures of intermediate density are seen in various shades of gray.

A new technique allows a computer to take many adjacent CT slices and construct a three-dimensional image of an internal structure. This technique has many uses, but it is most commonly used by doctors in the design of custom artificial joints and in the surgical reconstruction of bones, especially those of the face. The mummy of Tabes (cat. no. 121, see color plates section) has been reconstructed using CT data. Although standard CT examination provided a great deal of information of anatomic and Egyptological interest, it did not reveal how the mummy looked. Here through the power of the computer we can look upon the features of Tabes, features that have been hidden from view for thousands of years.

MM

1. Marx and D'Auria 1986, pp. 321-330; Marx and D'Auria 1988, p. 150.

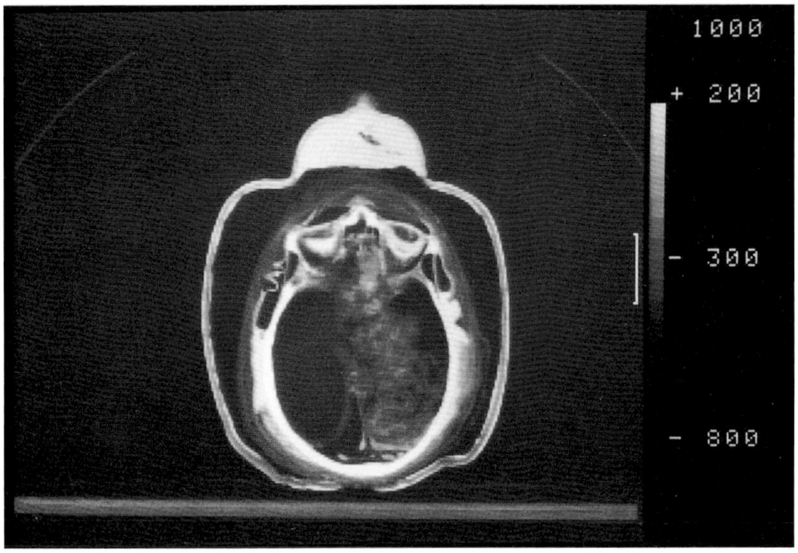

Fig. 91. CT scan through head of mummy at level of eyes. Dense structure surrounding head of mummy is cartonnage. Note defect in cartonnage in center at back of head and dense mummy mask in front of head. Eyes appear as shrunken white cup-shaped structures on top of image. Linen had been introduced through the nasal cavity, seen between eyes, and had fallen to one side of the skull. The brain had been removed.

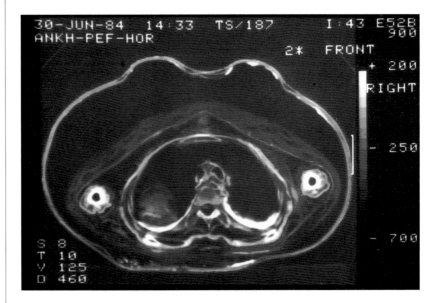

Fig. 92. CT scan of mummy through chest at level of heart. The two white rounded structures on either side of the mummy are the mummy's arms. Note the four collapsed chambers of the heart seen just in front of the spine. A circular low-density object in front of the breast bone is a wax figure placed over the heart.

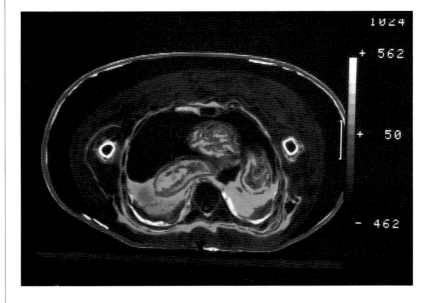

Fig. 93. CT scan of mummy through abdomen. The arms of this mummy again can be seen as white circles on either side of the abdomen. The three irregularly shaped objects within the abdominal cavity are organ packages that were replaced after mummification. The dense white material on either side of the spine is hardened resin.

Bibliography

Abbreviations

ASAE	*Annales du Service des Antiquités de l'Egypte*
BES	*Bulletin of the Egyptological Seminar*
BIFAO	*Bulletin de l'Institut Français d'Archéologie Orientale du Caire*
BiOr	*Bibliotheca Orientalis*
BMFA	*Bulletin of the Museum of Fine Arts, Boston*
BMMA	*Bulletin of the Metropolitan Museum of Art*
BSFE	*Bulletin de la Société Française d'Egyptologie*
CdE	*Chronique d'Egypte*
CG	*Catalogue Général des Antiquités Egyptiennes du Musée du Caire*
FIFAO	*Fouilles de l'Institut Français d'Archéologie Orientale du Caire*
GM	*Göttinger Miszellen*
JAC	*Jahrbuch für Antike und Christentum*
JAIC	*Journal of the American Institute for Conservation*
JARCE	*Journal of the American Research Center in Egypt*
JAS	*Journal of Archaeological Science*
JEA	*Journal of Egyptian Archaeology*
JEOL	*Jaarbricht van het Vooraziatisch-Egyptisch Genootschap (Gezelschap) "Ex Oriente Lux"*
JHS	*Journal of Hellenic Studies*
JNES	*Journal of Near Eastern Studies*
JSSEA	*Journal of the Society for the Study of Egyptian Antiquities*
LÄ	*Lexikon der Ägyptologie*, Wiesbaden
MDAIK	*Mitteilungen der Deutschen Archäologischen Instituts*
MDOG	*Mitteilungen der Deutschen Orientgesellschaft.*
MIFAO	*Mémoires de l'Institut Français d'Archéologie Orientale du Caire*
MIO	*Mitteilungen des Instituts für Orientforschung*
MJK	*Münchner Jahrbuch der bildenden Kunst*
MMA	Metropolitan Museum of Art, New York
MMJ	*Metropolitan Museum Journal*
NARCE	*Newsletter of the American Research Center in Egypt*
OMRO	*Oudheidkundige Mededelingen uit het Rijksmuseum van Oudheden te Leiden*
RA	*Revue Archéologique*
RdE	*Revue d'Egyptologie*
SAK	*Studien zur altägyptischen Kultur*
ZÄS	*Zeitschrift für Ägyptische Sprache und Altertumskunde*

Abd el-Al, Grenier, and Wagner 1985
Abd el-Hafeez Abd el-Al, J.-C. Grenier and G. Wagner. *Stèles funéraires de Kom Abu Bellou.* Paris, 1985.

Ackerman 1967
P. Ackerman. "Textiles through the Sassanian Period," in A.U. Pope, ed., *A Survey of Persian Art from Prehistoric Times to the Present* (reprinting). London, 1967.

Adams 1966
C.V.A. Adams. "The manufacture of ancient Egyptian cartonnage cases," *Smithsonian Journal of History* 1, no. 3 (Autumn 1966).

Adams 1984
B. Adams. *Egyptian Mummies.* Aylesbury, 1984.

Ägyptisches Museum Berlin 1967
Ägyptisches Museum, Staatliche Museen (West Berlin) *Ägyptisches Museum.* Berlin, 1967.

Aldred 1968
C. Aldred. *Akhenaten*, Pharaoh of Egypt: A New Study. London, 1968.

Aldred 1971
C. Aldred. *Jewels of the Pharaohs.* London, New York, and Washington, 1971.

Allen 1923
T.G. Allen. *The Art Institute of Chicago, A Handbook of the Egyptian Collection.* Chicago, 1923.

Allen 1950
T.G. Allen. *Occurrences of Pyramid Texts* (Studies in Ancient Oriental Civilization 27). Chicago, 1950.

Allen 1960
T.G. Allen. *The Egyptian Book of the Dead Documents in the Oriental Institute Museum at the University of Chicago.* Chicago, 1960.

Allen 1974
T.G. Allen. *The Book of the Dead or Going Forth by Day.* Chicago, 1974.

Allen 1984
J.P. Allen. *The Inflection of the Verb in the Pyramid Texts* (Biblioteca Aegyptia 2). Malibu, 1984.

Allen 1986
J.P. Allen. "The Pyramid Texts of Queens *Jpwt* and *Wdbt-n.(j),"* *JARCE* 23 (1986).

Altenmüller 1972
H. Altenmüller. "Anubis," *LÄ* I (1972) cols. 327-333.

Altenmüller 1975a
H. Altenmüller, "Djed-Pfeiler," *LÄ* I (1975), cols. 1100-1105.

Altenmüller 1975b
H. Altenmüller. "Achom," *LÄ* I (1972), cols. 55-56.

Altenmüller 1975c
H. Altenmüller. "Bestattungsritual," *LÄ* I (1975), cols. 745-765.

Altenmüller 1975d
H. Altenmüller. "Falke," *LÄ* II (1975), cols. 93-97.

Altenmüller 1982
H. Altenmüller. *Grab und Totenreich der Alten Ägypter*, 2nd ed. Hamburg, 1982.

Altenmüller 1986
H. Altenmüller. "Ein Zaubermesser des Mittleren Reiches," *SAK* 13 (1986) pp. 1-27.

Andrews 1981
C. Andrews. *Catalogue of Egyptian Antiquities in the British Museum 6: Jewellery I.* London, 1981.

Andrews 1984
C. Andrews. *Egyptian Mummies.* Cambridge, Mass., 1984.

Annecy 1984
Annecy, Museé-château Chambéry, museé d'art et d'histoire Aix-les-Bains, museé archéologique. *Collections égyptiennes*. Paris, 1984.

Anthes 1928
R. Anthes. *Die Felseninschriften von Hatnub*, Untersuchungen zur Geschichte und Altertumskunde Ägyptens, vol. 9. Leipzig, 1928.

Anthes 1943
R. Anthes. "Die Deutschen Grabungen auf der Westseite von Theben in den Jahren 1911 und 1913," *MDAIK* 12 (1943).

Anthes 1959
R. Anthes. *Mit Rahineh 1955*. Philadelphia, 1959.

Ariés 1974
P. Ariés. *Western Attitudes toward Death*. Baltimore and London, 1974.

Aristophanes 1961
Aristophanes. *The Frogs*, B. Rogers, trans. New York, 1961.

Armitage and Clutton-Brock 1981
P.L. Armitage and J. Clutton-Brock. "A Radiological and Histological Investigation into the Mummification of Cats from Ancient Egypt," *JAS* 8 (1981), pp. 185 ff.

Assmann 1975a
J. Assmann. "Ewigkeit, Buch vom Durchwandelnder." *LÄ* II (1975), cols. 54-55.

Assmann 1975b
J. Assmann. *Aegyptische Hymnen und Gebete*. Zurich and Munich, 1975.

Assmann 1987
J. Assmann. "Hierotaxis: Textkonstitution und Bildprogram in der altägyptischen Kunst und Literatur," in *Form und Mass: Beiträge zur Literatur, Sprache und Kunst des alten Ägypten, Ägypten und Altes Testament 12*. Wiesbaden, 1987.

Aston 1987
D.A. Aston. *Tomb Groups from the End of the New Kingdom to the Beginning of the Saite Period*. Birmingham, 1987.

Aubert 1974
J.F. and L. Aubert. *Statuettes Egyptiennes: Chouabtis, Ouchebtis*. Paris, 1974.

Ayrton, Currelly, and Weigall 1904
E.R. Ayrton, C.T. Currelly, and A.E.P. Weigall. *Abydos III*. London, 1904.

Ayrton and Loat 1908-09
E.R. Ayrton and W.L.S. Loat, "Excavations at Abydos," in *The Egypt Exploration Fund Archaeological Report 1908-1909*.

Ayrton and Loat 1911
E.R. Ayrton and W.L.S. Loat. *Pre-dynastic Cemetery at el Mahasna*. London, 1911.

Badawy 1945
A. Badawy. "La stèle funéraire copte à motif architectural," *Bulletin de la Société d'Archéologie Copte* 11 (1945), pp. 1-25.

Badawy 1966
A. Badawy. *A History of Egyptian Architecture: The First Intermediate Period, the Middle Kingdom and the Second Intermediate Period*. Berkeley, 1966.

Badawy 1968
A. Badawy. *A History of Egyptian Architecture: The Empire*. Berkeley, 1968.

Badawy 1978
A. Badawy. *Coptic Art and Archaeology: The Art of the Christian Egyptians from the Late Antique to the Middle Ages*. Cambridge, Mass., 1978.

Baginski and Tidhar 1980
A. Baginski and A. Tidhar. *Textiles from Egypt, 4th-13th Centuries C.E.* Jerusalem, 1980.

Bagnani 1952
G. Bagnani. "The Great Egyptian Crocodile Mystery," *Archaeology* 5 (1952), pp. 76-78.

Baines and Málek 1980
J. Baines and J. Málek, *Atlas of Ancient Egypt* (reprinted 1982). New York, 1980.

Baker 1966
H.S. Baker. *Furniture in the Ancient World: Origins and Evolution 3100-475 B.C.* New York, 1966.

Bakry 1971
H.S.K. Bakry. "The Discovery of a Temple of Sobk in Upper Egypt (1966-1969)," *MDAIK* 27 (1971) pp. 131-146.

Bank 1980
A. Bank. "Trois Croix Byzantines du Musée d'Art et d'Histoire de Genève," *Genava* 28 (1980).

Baqués Estapé 1971-1972
L. Baqués Estapé. "Catalogo inventario de las piezas Egicias del Museo Episcopal de Vic," *Ampurias*. (1971-72).

Baqués Estapé 1973
L. Baqués Estapé. *Boletin Informativo del Instituto de Prehistoria y Arqueologia de la Diputacion Peovincial de Barcelona* 10-12, (1973).

Barsanti 1900a
M.A. Barsanti. "Les Tombeaux de Psammétique et de Sétariban: Rapport sur la découverte," *ASAE* I (1900).

Barsanti 1900b
M.A. Barsanti. "Tombeau de Zannehibou," *ASAE* I (1900).

Barsanti 1900c
M.A. Barsanti. "Note sur le procédé qui servait à descendre sur la cuve le gros couvercle du Sarcophage en calcaire," *ASAE* I (1900).

Barsanti 1902
M.A. Barsanti. "Découverte de puits d'Ouazhouru," *ASAE* III (1902).

Barta 1963
W. Barta. *Die altägyptische Opferliste von der Frühzeit bis zur griechisch-römischen Epoche*. Berlin, 1963.

Barta 1968
W. Barta. *Aufbau und Bedeutung der altägyptischen Opferformel* (Ägyptologische Forschungen 24). Glückstadt, 1968.

Barta 1973-1974
W. Barta. "Der Greif als bildhafter Ausdruck einer altägyptischen Religionsvorstellung," *JEOL* 23 (1973-1974).

Barta 1981
W. Barta. *Die Bedeutung der Pyramidentexte für den verstorbenen König*. (Münchner Ägyptologische Studien 39). Wiesbaden, 1981.

Bates 1907
O. Bates. "Sculptures from the Excavations at Gizeh, 1905-1906," *BMFA* 5, No. 26 (June, 1907).

Baud and Drioton 1928
M. Baud and E. Drioton. "Tombes thébaines; Nécropole de Dirâ Abû'n-Naga," (*MIFAO* 57,2). Cairo, 1928.

Bauman 1960
B. Bauman. "The Botanical Aspects of Ancient Egyptian Embalming and Burial," *Economic Botany* 14 (1960), pp. 37-55.

Baumgartel 1955
E.J. Baumgartel. *The Cultures of Prehistoric Egypt* 1, 2nd rev. ed. London, 1955.

Baumgartel 1960
E. J. Baumgartel. *The Cultures of Prehistoric Egypt* 2. London, 1960.

Baumgartel 1970
E.J. Baumgartel. *Petrie's Naqada Excavation: a Supplement*. London, 1970.

Becker-Colonna 1979
A.L. Becker-Colonna. "Myths and Symbols in a Cartonnage Coffin of the XXI Dynasty from the Sutro Collection of San Francisco State University," Acts, First International Congress of Egyptology. Berlin, 1979, pp. 95-101.

Beinlich 1973
H. Beinlich. "Assiut," *LÄ* I (1973), cols. 489-495.

Beinlich 1984
H. Beinlich. *Die 'Osirisreliquien' – Motiv der Körperzergliederung in der altägyptischen Religion*. Wiesbaden, 1984.

Bell 1974
L. Bell. "Discoveries at Dira Abu el-Naga 1974," *NARCE* 91 (Fall 1974), pp. 24-25.

Bell 1981
L. Bell. "Dira Abu el-Naga: The Monuments of the Ramesside High Priests of Amun and Some Related Officials," *MDAIK* 37 (1981), pp. 51-62.

Berlandini-Grenier 1976
J. Berlandini-Grenier, "Varia Memphitica I (I)," *BIFAO* 76 (1976), pp. 301-316.

Berlev 1971
O.D. Berlev. "Les Prétendus 'Citadins' au Moyen Empire," *RdE* 23 (1971).

Berlev 1974
O.D. Berlev. "Stela Vjurcburgskogo Universitetskogo Muzeja," *Palestinskij Sbornik*, 25 (88) (1974), pp. 26-31.

Berlev 1978
O. Berlev. *Obscestvennye otnosenija v Egipte epochi srednego carstva. Social'nyi sloj "Carskich hmww."* Moscow 1978.

Bianchi 1980
R.S. Bianchi. "Not the Isis Knot," *BES* 2 (1980).

Bianchi forthcoming
R.S. Bianchi. *Cleopatra's Egypt: Art of the Ptolemies 305-30 B.C.* In press.

Bianchi Bandinelli 1971
R. Bianchi Bandinelli. *Rome: The Late Empire, Roman Art A.D. 200-400*. New York, 1971.

Bienkowsky and Southworth 1986
P. Bienkowsky and E. Southworth. *Egyptian Antiquities in the Liverpool Museum I. A List of the Provenanced Objects*. Warminster, 1986.

Bierbrier 1977
M.L. Bierbrier. "Hoherpriester des Amun," *LÄ* II (1977), cols. 1241-1249.

Bierbrier 1984
M.L. Bierbrier. "Two Confusing Coffins," *JEA* 70 (1984), pp. 82-86.

Bietak 1979
M. Bietak. "Urban Archaeology and the 'Town Problem' in Ancient Egypt," in K.R. Weeks, ed., *Egyptology and the Social Sciences*. Cairo, 1979, pp. 97-144.

Bietak and Reiser-Haslauer 1978
M. Bietak and E. Reiser-Haslauer. *Das Grab des 'Ankh-Hor, Obersthofmeister der Gottesgemahlin Nitokris* I. Wien, 1978.

Bietak and Reiser-Haslauer 1982
M. Bietak and E. Reiser-Haslauer, *Das Grab des 'Ankh-Hor, Obersthofmeister der Gottesgemahlin Nitokris* II. Wien, 1982.

Birch 1850
J. Birch. "Notes upon a mummy of the age of the XXVI Egyptian Dynasty," *The Archaeological Journal* 7 (1850), pp. 273-280.

Birch 1874
J. Birch. *Transactions of the Royal Society of Literature,* 2nd series, 10 (1874).

Birch 1883-1884
S. Birch in *Proceedings of the Society of Biblical Archaeology* VI (1883-84), pp. 37-40, 52, 106-107, 129-131, 170-173, 185-187.

Björkman 1971
G. Björkman. *A Selection of the Objects in the Smith Collection of Egyptian Antiquities at the Linköping Museum.* Stockholm, 1971.

Björkman 1974
G. Björkman. "A Funerary Statuette of Hekaemsaf, Chief of the Royal Ships in the Saitic Period," *BOREAS* 6 (1974), pp. 71-80.

Blackman 1912
A.M. Blackman. "The Significance of Incense and Libations in Funerary and Temple Rituals," *ZÄS* 50 (1912).

Blackman 1913
A.M. Blackman. *Hieroglyphic Texts from Egyptian Stelae in the British Museum* IV. London, 1913.

Blackman 1914
A.M. Blackman. *The Rock Tombs of Meir* I. London, 1914.

Blackman 1915
A.M. Blackman. *The Rock Tombs of Meir* III. London, 1915.

Blackman 1916
A.M. Blackman. "The Ka-House and the Serdab," *JEA* 3 (1916).

Blackman 1935
A.M. Blackman. "The Stela of Nebipusenwosret: British Museum #101," *JEA* 21 (1935).

Blackman and Apted 1953
A.M. Blackman and M. Apted. *The Rock Tombs of Meir* VI. London, 1953.

Bleeker 1973
C. Bleeker. *Hathor and Thoth.* Leiden, 1973.

Boeser 1920
P.A.A. Boeser. *Beschreibung der Aegyptischen Sammlung des Niederländischen Reichsmuseums der Altertümer in Leiden. Mumiensärge des Neuen Reiches,* 4th series. The Hague, 1920.

Bogoslovsky 1972
E. Bogoslovsky. "Pamyatniki i Dokumenty iz Der-el'-Medina, Khranyashchiesya v Muzeyakh USSR," *Vestnik Drevnei Istorii* (1), pp. 79-103.

Bonner 1941-1942
C. Bonner. *Proceedings of the American Philological Society* 85 (1941/42).

Bonnet 1952
H. Bonnet. *Reallexikon der Ägyptischen Religionsgeschichte.* Berlin, 1952.

Borchardt 1897
L. Borchardt. "Die Dienerstatuen aus den Gräbern des Alten Reiches," *ZÄS* 35 (1897).

Borchardt 1907
L. Borchardt. *Das Grabdenkmal des Königs Neuser-re'.* Leipzig, 1907.

Borchardt 1911
L. Borchardt. *Statuen und Statuetten von Königen und Privatleuten* I (CG). Berlin, 1911.

Borchardt 1913
L. Borchardt. *Das Grabdenkmal des Königs Sahure'* II. Berlin, 1913.

Borchardt et al. 1934
L. Borchardt, O. Königsberger, and H. Ricke. "Friesziegel in Grabbauten," *ZÄS* 70 (1934), pp. 25-35.

Boreux 1932
C. Boreux. *Musée du Louvre. Antiquités Egyptiennes. Catalogue-Guide Sommaire* 2. Paris, 1932.

Bothmer 1949
B.V. Bothmer. "Statuettes of W₃d t as Ichneumon Coffins," *JNES* 8 (1949), pp. 121-123.

Bothmer 1951
B.V. Bothmer. "A Hippopotamus Statuette of the Middle Kingdom," *BMFA* 49 no. 278 (December 1951), pp. 98-102.

Bothmer 1954
B.V. Bothmer. "Membra Dispersa: King Amenhotep II Making an Offering," *BMFA* 52 (1954), pp. 11-20.

Bothmer 1960
B.V. Bothmer. *Egyptian Sculpture of the Late Period 700 B.C. to A.D. 100.* New York, 1960.

Bothmer 1975
B.V. Bothmer. "A Contemporary of King Amenhotep II at Karnak," *Karnak V, 1970-1972.* Cairo, 1975.

Bothmer 1987
B.V. Bothmer. "Ancestral Bust," in E.S. Hall, ed., *Antiquities from the Collection of Christos G. Bastis.* Mainz, 1987, pp. 24-29.

Botti 1932
G. Botti. "Il Cafan N. 1969 des Museo Civico di Bologna," in *Studies Presented to F. Ll. Griffith.* London, 1932.

Botti 1958
G. Botti. *Le casse di mummie e i sarcofagi da el Hibeh nel Museo Egizio di Firenze.* Florence, 1958.

Bourriau 1981
J. Bourriau. *Umm el Ga'ab: Pottery from the Nile Valley Before the Arab Conquest.* Cambridge, England, 1981.

Bourriau 1982
J. Bourriau in *Egypt's Golden Age.* Boston, 1982, no. 116, pp. 127-128.

Bourriau and Millard 1971
J. Bourriau and A. Millard. "The Excavation of Sawâma in 1914 by G.A. Wainwright and T. Whittemore," *JEA* 57 (1971), pp. 28-57.

Bovino 1956
G. Bovino. *Ravenna Mosaics.* Greenwich, Conn., 1956.

Breasted 1912
J.H. Breasted. *Development of Religion and Thought in Ancient Egypt.* New York, 1912.

Breasted 1948
J.H. Breasted, Jr. *Egyptian Servant Statues.* Washington, 1948.

Breccia 1907
E. Breccia. "Les Fouilles dans le Sérapeum d'Alexandrie en 1905-1906," *ASAE* 8 (1907).

Breccia 1912
E. Breccia. *Le necropoli di Sciatbi.* Alexandria, 1912.

Breccia 1922
E. Breccia. *Alexandrea ad Aegyptum. A Guide to the Ancient and Modern Town, and to its Graeco-Roman Museum.* Bergamo, 1922.

Bresciani et al. 1977
E. Bresciani, S. Pernigotti and M.P. Giangeri Silvis. *La Tomba di Ciennehebu, Capo della Flotta del Re.* Pisa, 1977.

British Museum 1913
Hieroglyphic Texts from Egyptian Stelae, &c. in the British Museum, Part IV. London, 1913.

British Museum 1938
British Museum. *A Handbook to the Egyptian Mummies and Coffins Exhibited in the British Museum.* London, 1938.

British School 1934
British School of Archaeology in Egypt and the Egyptian Research Account, *Report of the Lth Year.* London, 1934.

Brooklyn Museum 1941
The Brooklyn Museum, *Pagan and Christian Egypt.* Brooklyn, 1941.

Brooklyn Museum 1956
Brooklyn Museum. *Five Years of Collecting Egyptian Art: 1951-1956.* Brooklyn, 1956.

Brooklyn Museum 1960
Brooklyn Museum. *Egyptian Sculpture of the Late Period 700 B.C. to A.D. 100.* New York, 1960.

Brooklyn Museum 1983
Brooklyn Museum. Japan 1983-1984, *Neferut net Kemit: Egyptian Art from the Brooklyn Museum.* Tokyo, 1983.

Brovarski 1978
E. Brovarski. *Canopics* (Corpus Antiquitatum Aegyptiacarum, Museum of Fine Arts, Boston, fasc. 1). Mainz, 1978.

Brovarski 1980
E. Brovarski. "Naga ed-Dêr," *LÄ* IV (1980), cols. 296-317.

Brovarski 1981
E. Brovarski. "Ahanakht of Bersheh and the Hare Nome in the First Intermediate Period and Middle Kingdom," in W. K. Simpson and W. M. Davis, eds., *Studies in Ancient Egypt, the Aegean, and the Sudan: Essays in Honor of Dows Dunham.* Boston, 1981.

Brovarski 1982
E. Brovarski, "Lexicographical Studies in Egyptian Pottery" in Peter Lacovara ed., *Ancient Egyptian Ceramics: Colloquium on Ancient Egyptian Ceramics II.* Boston, 1982.

Brovarski 1983
E. Brovarski. "Sarkophag," *LÄ* V (1983) cols. 471-484.

Brovarski 1984a
E. Brovarski. "Serdab," *LÄ* V (1984), cols. 874-879.

Brovarski 1984b
E. Brovarski. "Sobek," *LÄ* V (1984) cols. 995-1031.

Brovarski 1984c
E. Brovarski. "Sokar," *LÄ* V (1984), col. 1061.

Brovarski n.d.
E. Brovarski. "Inscribed Material of the First Intermediate Period from Naga ed-Dêr" (Dissertation, University of Chicago).

Brunner 1977
H. Brunner. "Herz," *LÄ* II (1977), cols. 1158-1168.

Brunner-Traut 1965
E. Brunner-Traut. "Spitzmaus und Ichneumon als Tiere des Sonnengottes," *Nachrichten der Akademie der Wissenschaften in Göttingen* I Philologisch-Historische Klasse no. 7 (1965), pp. 123-163.

Brunner-Traut 1977
E. Brunner-Traut. "Ichneumon," *LÄ* III (1977), cols. 122-123.

Brunner-Traut 1979
E. Brunner-Traut. "Lotos," *LÄ* III (1979), cols. 1091-1096.

Brunner-Traut and Brunner 1981
E. Brunner-Traut and H. Brunner. *Die Ägyptische Sammlung der Universität Tübingen.* Mainz am Rhein, 1981.

Brunton 1927
G. Brunton. *Qau and Badari* I. London, 1927.

Brunton 1928
G. Brunton. *Qau and Badari* II. London, 1928.

Brunton 1930
G. Brunton. *Qau and Badari* III. London, 1930.

Brunton 1935
G. Brunton. "'Pesesh-kef' Amulets," *ASAE* 35 (1935), pp. 212-217.

Brunton 1937
G. Brunton. *Mostagedda and the Tasian Culture.* London, 1937.

Brunton 1939
G. Brunton. "Some Notes on the Burial of Shashanq Heqa-Kheper-Re," *ASAE* 39 (1939), pp. 541-547.

Brunton 1948
G. Brunton. *Matmar.* London, 1948.

Brunton and Caton-Thompson 1928
G. Brunton and G. Caton-Thompson. *The Badarian Civilisation and Predynastic Remains Near Badari.* London, 1928.

Brunton and Engelbach 1927
G. Brunton and R. Engelbach. *Gurob.* London, 1927.

Bruwier forthcoming
M.-C. Bruwier, forthcoming publication.

Bruyère 1926
B. Bruyère. *Rapport sur les fouilles de Deir el Médineh (1924-1925) (FIFAO* 3, 3). Cairo, 1926.

Bruyère 1927
B. Bruyère. *Rapport sur les fouilles de Deir el Médineh (1926) (FIFAO* 4, 3). Cairo, 1927.

Bruyère 1929
B. Bruyère. *Rapport sur les fouilles de Deir el Médineh (1928) (FIFAO* 6, 2). Cairo, 1929.

Bruyère 1930a
B. Bruyère. *Rapport sur les fouilles de Deir el Médineh (1929) (FIFAO* 7, 2). Cairo, 1930.

Bruyère 1930b
B. Bruyère. *Mert Seger à Deir el Médineh* II. Cairo, 1930.

Bruyère 1933
B. Bruyère. *Rapport sur les fouilles de Deir el Médineh (1930) (FIFAO* 8, 3). Cairo, 1933.

Bruyère 1934
B. Bruyère. *Rapport sur les fouilles de Deir el Médineh (1931-32) (FIFAO* 10,1). Cairo, 1934.

Bruyère 1937
B. Bruyère. *Rapport sur les fouilles de Deir el Médineh (1933-34) (FIFAO* 14). Cairo, 1937.

Bruyère 1939
B. Bruyère. *Rapport sur les fouilles de Deir el Médineh (1934-35) (FIFAO* 16). Cairo, 1939.

Buberl 1922
P. Buberl. *Die griechisch-ägyptischen Mumienbildnisse der Sammlung Theodor Graf.* Vienna, 1922.

Buckton 1982
D. Buckton. "The Oppenheim or Fieschi-Morgan Reliquary in New York, and the Antecedents of Middle Byzantine Enamel," *Eighth Annual Byzantine Studies Conference, Abstracts.* Chicago, 1982, pp. 35-36.

Budge 1910
E.A.W. Budge. *Facsimiles of Egyptian Hieratic Papyri in the British Museum* 1. London, 1910.

Budge 1912
E.A.W. Budge. *The Greenfield Papyrus in the British Museum.* London, 1912.

Budge 1925
E.A.W. Budge. *The Mummy: A Handbook of Egyptian Funerary Archaeology.* Cambridge, 1925.

Budge 1960
E.A.W. Budge. *The Book of the Dead.* New York, 1960.

Budge 1974
E.A.W. Budge. *The Mummy.* A facsimile of the 2nd ed. New York, 1974.

Buhl 1959
M.L. Buhl. *The Late Egyptian Anthropoid Stone Sarcophagi.* Copenhagen, 1959.

Bulté 1981
J. Bulté. *Catalogue des Collections Égyptiennes du Musée National de Ceramique à Sèvres.* Paris, 1981.

Butzer 1976
K. Butzer. *Early Hydraulic Civilization in Egypt.* Chicago, 1976.

Callaghan 1980
P.J. Callaghan. *Annual of the British School at Athens* 75 (1980).

Callaghan 1981
P.J. Callaghan. *Annual of the British School at Athens* 76 (1981).

Callaghan 1985
P.J. Callaghan. *Annual of the British School at Athens* 80 (1985).

Caminos 1982
R.A. Caminos. "The Rendells Mummy Bandages," *JEA* 68 (1982).

Capart 1927
J. Capart. *Documents pour Servir à l'Etude de l'Art Egyptien* I. Paris, 1927.

Capart 1929
J. Capart. "Un Hieroglyphe Mysterieux," *Kêmi* 2 (1929).

Capart 1934
J. Capart. *Bulletin des Musées royaux d'art et d'histoire* 20 (1934), pp. 243-251.

Capart 1941
J. Capart. Review of A. Hermann, *Die Stelen der thebanischen Felsgräber der 18. Dynastie* in *CdE* 16 (1941), pp. 237-239.

Capart 1943a
J. Capart. "Pour esquiver la corvée agricole," *CdE* 18 (1943), pp. 30-34.

Capart 1943b
J. Capart. "A propos du cercueil d'argent du roi Chechonq," *CdE* 18 (1943), pp. 191-198.

Carnarvon and Carter 1912
Earl of Carnarvon and H. Carter. *Five Years' Explorations at Thebes.* London, New York, Toronto, and Melbourne, 1912.

Carroll 1965
J. Carroll. *Coptic Art,* S. Hatton, trans. New York, 1965.

Carter 1901
H. Carter. "Report on Tomb-Pit Opened on the 26th January 1901 in the Valley of the Tombs of the Kings," *ASAE* 2 (1901), pp. 144-145.

Carter and Newberry 1904
H. Carter and P. Newberry. *The Tomb of Thoutmosis IV* (CG). Westminster, 1904.

Carter and Mace 1923
H. Carter and A. C. Mace. *The Tomb of Tut-ankh-Amen* 1. London, 1923.

Carter 1927
H. Carter. *The Tomb of Tut-ankh-Amen* 2. New York, 1927.

Carter 1933
H. Carter. *The Tomb of Tut-ankh-Amen* 3. London, 1933.

Castillos 1977
J.J. Castillos. "An Analysis of the Tombs in Cemeteries 1300 and 1400-1500 at Armant," *JSSEA* VII (2) (1977), pp. 4-23.

Castillos 1978
J.J. Castillos. "An Analysis of the Predynastic Cemeteries E and U and the First Dynasty Cemetery S at Abydos," *JSSEA* VIII (3) (1978), pp. 86-98.

Castillos 1979
J.J. Castillos. "An Analysis of the Tombs in the Predynastic Cemetery N7000 at Naga-ed-Dêr" *JSSEA* X (1) (1979), pp. 21-38.

Černý 1948
J. Černý. "Note on $^c{}_3$wy-pt shrine," *JEA* 34 (1948).

Černý 1973
J. Černý. *A Community of Workmen at Thebes in the Ramesside Period* (Bibliothèque d'Etude, 50). Cairo, 1973.

Chassinat 1909
E. Chassinat. *La Seconde Trouvaille de Deir el-Bahari* (CG). Cairo, 1909.

Chassinat and Palanque 1911
E. Chassinat and C. Palanque. *Une Campagne de Fouilles dans la Nécropole d'Assiout.* Cairo, 1911.

Cherpion 1980
N. Cherpion. "Le mastaba de Khabausokar (MM A2): problèmes de chronologie," *Orientalia Lovaniensia Periodica* 11 (1980), pp. 79-90.

Christie's 1974
Christie's. *Primitive Art and Antiques.* London, April 30-May 1, 1974.

Classical Department 1977
Classical Department, Museum of Fine Arts Boston. *Romans and Barbarians.* Boston, 1977.

Clère 1931
J. J. Clère. "Un Passage de la Stèle du Général Antef," *BIFAO* 30 (1931), pp. 425-447.

Comstock and Vermeule 1971
M. Comstock and C. Vermeule. *Greek, Etruscan and Roman Bronzes in the Museum of Fine Arts, Boston.* Boston, 1971.

Cooney 1968
J. D. Cooney. "Siren and Ba, Birds of a Feather," *Bulletin of the Cleveland Museum of Art* 55,8 (1968), pp. 262-271.

Cramer 1957
M. Cramer. *Archäologische und epigraphische Klassifikation koptischer Denkmäler des Metropolitan Museum of Art, New York und des Museum of Fine Arts, Boston, Mass.* Wiesbaden, 1957.

Crawford 1987
J.S. Crawford. *Ancient Art at the University of Delaware.* Newark, Delaware, 1987.

Crum 1902
W. E. Crum. *Coptic Monuments* (CG). Cairo, 1902.

Cuenca 1978
E.L. Cuenca, *Radiological Examination of the Egyptian Mummies of the Archaeological Museum of Madrid, Monografias Arqueologicas* 5. Madrid, 1978.

Dabrowska-Smektala 1963
E. Dabrowska-Smektala, "Trumna Drewniana i Kartonaz odzwiernego domu Amona" 𓈖𓇋𓈖𓉐 Rocznik Muzeum Narodowego w Warszawie 7 (1963).

Darby, Ghalioungui, and Grivetti 1977
W.J. Darby, P. Ghalioungui, and L. Grivetti. Food: The Gift of Osiris. New York, 1977.

Daressy 1902
G. Daressy. Fouilles de la Vallée des Rois (CG). Cairo, 1902.

Daressy 1903a
G. Daressy. "Tombe de Hor-kheb," ASAE 4 (1903) pp. 76-82.

Daressy 1903b
G. Daressy. Textes et Dessins Magiques (CG). Cairo, 1903.

Daressy 1906
G. Daressy. Statues de Divinités I (CG). Cairo, 1906.

Daressy 1909
G. Daressy. Cercueils des Cachettes Royales (CG). Cairo, 1909.

Daressy 1926
G. Daressy. "Le Voyage d'inspection de M. Grébaut en 1889," ASAE 26 (1926), pp. 1-22.

d'Athanasi 1836
G. d'Athanasi. A Brief Account of the Researches and Discoveries in Upper Egypt, made under the direction of Henry Salt, Esq. London, 1836.

David 1979
A. R. David. The Manchester Museum Mummy Project. Manchester, 1979.

David 1980
A. R. David. The Macclesfield Collection of Egyptian Antiquities. Warminster, 1980.

David 1982
A.R. David. The Ancient Egyptians: Religious Beliefs and Practices. London, 1982.

David and Tapp 1984
A.R. David and E. Tapp, eds. Evidence Embalmed. Manchester, 1984.

Davies 1925
N. de G. Davies. The Tomb of Two Sculptors at Thebes. New York, 1925.

Davies 1943
N. de G. Davies. The Tomb of Rekh-mi-Rē at Thebes. New York, 1943.

Davies 1957
N. de G. Davies. A Corpus of Inscribed Egyptian Funerary Cones, ed. M. F. L. Macadam. Oxford, 1957.

Davis 1894
C.H.S. Davis. The Egyptian Book of the Dead. New York, 1894.

Davis et al. 1907
T.M. Davis, G. Maspero, P.E. Newberry. The Tomb of Iouiya and Touiyou. London, 1907.

Davis et al. 1908
T. M. Davis, G. Maspero, E. Ayrton, G. Daressy. The Tomb of Siphtah; The Monkey Tomb and the Gold Tomb. London, 1908.

Davis et al. 1910
T. M. Davis, G. Maspero, E. Ayrton, G. Daressy. The Tomb of Queen Tiyi. London, 1910.

Davis et al. 1912
T. M. Davis, G. Maspero, and G. Daressy. The Tombs of Haramhabi and Touatankhamanou. London, 1912.

Dawson 1929
W.R. Dawson. "A Note of the Egyptian Mummies in the Castle Museum, Norwich," JEA 15 (1929), pp. 186-189.

Dawson 1934
W.R. Dawson. "Pettigrew's Demonstrations upon Mummies," JEA 20 (1934), pp. 170-182.

Dawson and Gray 1968
W.R. Dawson and P.H.K. Gray. Catalogue of Egyptian Antiquities in the British Museum I: Mummies and Human Remains. London, 1968.

de Buck 1939
A. de Buck. De Godsdienstige Opvattinmg van den Slaap (Mededelingen en Verhandelingen Ex Oriente Lux no. 4). Leiden, 1939.

de Buck 1956
A. de Buck. The Egyptian Coffin Texts VI. Chicago, 1956.

de Meulenaere 1969
H. de Meulenaere. "Les steles de Nag el-Hassaia," MDAIK 25 (1969), pp. 90-97.

de Meulenaere 1980
H. de Meulenaere. La Collection Egyptienne. Les Etapes marquantes de son Développement. Brussels, 1980.

de Morgan 1894
J. de Morgan. Catalogue des Monuments et Inscriptions de l'Egypte antique, Tome 1: De la frontière de Nubie à Kom Ombos. Vienna, 1894.

de Morgan 1895
J. de Morgan. Fouilles à Dahchour Mars-Juin 1894. Vienna, 1895.

de Rustafjaell 1915
de Rustafjaell. Catalogue of the Interesting and Valuable Egyptian Collection formed by Mr. Robert de Rustafjaell. New York, 1915.

Deichmann 1958
F. Deichmann. Frühchristliche Bauten und Mosaiken von Ravenna. Baden Baden, 1958.

Demaree 1983
R.J. Demaree. The ȝḫ iḳr n Rˁ-Stelae. On Ancestor Worship in Ancient Egypt. Leiden, 1983.

Dentzer 1978
J.N. Dentzer. "Reliefs du Banquet dans la Moitié Orientale de l'Empire Romain: Iconographie Hellénistique et Traditions Locales," RA (1978), pp. 63-82.

Deppert-Lippitz 1985
B. Deppert-Lippitz. Griechischer Goldschmuck. Mainz am Rhein, 1985.

Derchain 1955
P. Derchain. "La couronne de la justification," CdE 30 (1955), p. 241.

Derchain 1975
P. Derchain. "La perruque et le cristal," SAK 2 (1975), pp. 55-74.

Description de l'Egypte 1822
Description de l'Egypte IV, 2nd ed. Paris, 1822.

Desroches-Noblecourt 1953
C. Desroches-Noblecourt. "'Concubines du Mort' et Mères de Famille au Moyen Empire," BIFAO 53 (1953), pp. 7-47.

Desroches-Noblecourt 1976
C. Desroches-Noblecourt. Ramsès le grand. Paris, 1976.

Desroches-Noblecourt 1978
C. Desroches-Noblecourt. The Life and Death of a Pharaoh: Tutankhamen. Boston, 1978.

Desroches-Noblecourt 1986
C. Desroches-Noblecourt. La femme au temps des pharaons. Paris, 1986.

Dewachter 1984
M. Dewachter. "Les Premiers Fils Royals d'Amon," RdE 35 (1984), pp. 86-87.

Diodorus 1985
Diodorus on Egypt, Edwin Murphy, trans. Jefferson, N.C., 1985.

Dobrowolska 1970a
K. Dobrowolska. "Trzy skrzynki kanopskie z Muzeow Narodowych w Warszawie i w Krakowie," Rocznik Muszeum Norodowego w Warszawie 14 (1970), pp. 45-62.

Dobrowolska 1970b
K. Dobrowolska. "Génèse et évolution des boîtes à vases-canopes," Etudes et Travaux 4 (1970). pp. 73-85.

Doll 1978
S. Doll. The Texts and Decoration on the Napatan Sarcophagi of Anlamani and Aspelta. Ann Arbor, 1978.

Dolzani 1967
C. Dolzani. "Alcuni Oggetti Egiziani di Raccolte Private di Trieste," in Sergio Donadoni, Sabatino Moscati, and Massimo Pallottino, eds., Studi in Onore di Giuseppe Botti, Orientis Antiqui Collectio VI. Rome, 1967.

Dolzani 1969
C. Dolzani, "Sarcophago Egiziano con mummia del Civico Museo di Storia Naturale di Trieste," Atti del Museo Civico di Storia Naturale di Trieste 26 (1969), pp. 249-275.

Donadoni 1972
S. Donadoni. Newsweek/Great Museums of the World. Egyptian Museum, Cairo. New York, 1972.

Dothan 1982
T. Dothan. The Philistines and their Material Culture. Jerusalem, 1982.

Downes 1974
D. Downes. The Excavations at Esna 1905-1906. Warminster, 1974.

Drenkhahn 1987
R. Drenkhahn. Elfenbein im Alten Ägypten. Hannover, 1987.

Drioton 1941
E. Drioton. "Un autel du culte héliopolitan," Miscellanea Gregoriana (1941), pp. 73-81.

Drioton 1943
E. Drioton. "Portes de l'Hadès et portes du Paradis," Bulletin de la Société d'Archéologie Copte (1943), pp. 59-78.

Drioton 1949
E. Drioton. Le Jugement des Ames dans l'Ancienne Egypte. Cairo, 1949.

Drioton and Lauer 1951
E. Drioton and J-P. Lauer. "Fouilles a Saqqarah: Les tombes jumelées de Neferibrê-Sa-Neith et de Ouahibrê-Men," ASAE 51 (1951), pp. 469-490.

du Bourguet 1964
P. du Bourguet. Musée national du Louvre: Catalogue des étoffes coptes 1. Paris, 1964.

Duell et al. 1938
P. Duell et al. The Mastaba of Mereruka. Chicago, 1938.

Dunham 1931
D. Dunham. "The Late Egyptian Gallery Rearranged," BMFA 29 (1931), p. 26.

Dunham 1932
D. Dunham. "Fourth Egyptian Study Room Opened," *BMFA* 30 (1932), pp. 89-90.

Dunham 1933
D. Dunham. "Experiments with Photography in Ultra-violet Light," *BMFA* 31 (1933), pp. 39-41.

Dunham 1935
D. Dunham. "Four New Kingdom Monuments in the Museum of Fine Arts, Boston," *JEA* 21 (1935), pp. 148-149.

Dunham 1937
D. Dunham. *Naga-ed-Dêr Stelae of the First Intermediate Period.* Boston, 1937.

Dunham 1950a
D. Dunham, in Museum of Fine Arts, Boston, *Annual Report* 1950, p. 30.

Dunham 1950b
D. Dunham. *The Royal Cemeteries of Kush I: El Kurru.* Cambridge, 1950.

Dunham 1955
D. Dunham. *The Royal Cemeteries of Kush II: Nuri.* Boston, 1955.

Dunham 1958
D. Dunham. *The Egyptian Department and Its Excavations.* Boston, 1958.

Dunham and Janssen 1960
D. Dunham and J. Janssen. *Second Cataract Forts I: Semna Kumma.* Boston, 1960.

Dunham and Simpson 1974
D. Dunham and W.K. Simpson. *The Mastaba of Queen Mersyankh III.* Boston, 1974.

Dunham 1978
D. Dunham. *Zawiyet el-Aryan: The Cemeteries Adjacent to the Layer Pyramid.* Boston, 1978.

Eaton 1941
E.S. Eaton. "A Group of Middle Kingdom Jewellery," *BMFA* 39 (1941), pp. 94-98.

Eaton-Krauss 1976
M. Eaton-Krauss. "Two Representations of Black-Skinned Statues in Ancient Egyptian Painting," *JARCE* 13 (1976).

Eaton-Krauss 1982
M. Eaton-Krauss in *Egypt's Golden Age.* Boston, 1982, pp. 234-235.

Eaton-Krauss 1984
M. Eaton-Krauss. *The Representations of Statuary in Private Tombs of the Old Kingdom.* Wiesbaden, 1984.

Ebers 1893
G. Ebers, ed. *The Graf Catalogue of Unique Ancient Greek Portraits 2000 Years Old Recently Discovered and Now on View in Old Vienna, Midway Plaisance at the World's Columbian Exposition, Chicago.* Vienna, 1893.

Ecole du Caire 1981
Ecole du Caire (IFAO). *Un Siècle de Fouilles Françaises en Egypte 1880-1980.* Cairo, 1981.

Edgar 1905a
C.C. Edgar in "On the Dating of the Fayum Portraits," *JHS* 25 (1905).

Edgar 1905b
C.C. Edgar. *Graeco-Egyptian Coffins, Masks, and Portraits* (CG). Cairo, 1905.

Edwards 1939
I.E.S. Edwards. *Hieroglyphic Texts from Egyptian Stelae* VIII. London, 1939.

Edwards 1971
I.E.S. Edwards. "A Bill of Sale for a Set of Ushabtis," *JEA* 57 (1971), pp. 120-124.

Edwards 1972
I.E.S. Edwards. *Treasures of Tutankhamun.* London, 1972.

Edwards 1976
I.E.S. Edwards. *Treasures of Tutankhamun.* New York, 1976.

Edwards 1977
I.E.S. Edwards. *Tutankhamun: His Tomb and Its Treasures.* New York, 1977.

Edwards 1986
I.E.S. Edwards. *The Pyramids of Egypt,* rev. ed. Harmondsworth, 1986.

Effendi 1920
M.C. Effendi. "Fouilles dans la Nécropole de Saqqarah," *ASAE* 19 (1920), pp. 208-215.

Eggebrecht 1973
A. Eggebrecht. "Schlachtungsbräuche im Alten Ägypten und ihre Wiedergabe im Flachbild bis zum Ende des Mittleren Reiches," (Dissertation). Munich, 1973.

Eggebrecht 1977
A. Eggebrecht. "Grabkegel," *LÄ* II (1977), cols. 857-859.

Egger 1967
G. Egger. *Koptische Textilien.* Vienna, 1967.

Elliot-Smith and Dawson 1924
G. Elliot-Smith and W.R. Dawson. *Egyptian Mummies.* London, 1924.

El-Nassery and Wagner 1978
A.A. el-Nassery and G. Wagner. "Nouvelles stèles de Kom Abu Bellou," *BIFAO* 78/1 (1978), pp. 231-235.

Emery 1961
W.B. Emery. *Archaic Egypt.* Baltimore, 1961.

Emery 1965
W.B. Emery. "Preliminary Report on the Excavations at North Saqqara 1964-5," *JEA* 51 (1965), pp. 3-8.

Emery 1966
W.B. Emery. "Preliminary Report on the Excavations at North Saqqara 1965-6," *JEA* 52 (1966), pp. 3-8.

Emery 1971
W.B. Emery. "Preliminary Report on the Excavations at North Saqqara, 1969-70," *JEA* 57 (1971), pp. 3-13.

Engelbach 1915
R. Engelbach. *Riqqeh and Memphis* VI. London, 1915.

Engelbach 1923
R. Engelbach. *Harageh.* London, 1923.

Engelbach 1946
R. Engelbach. *Introduction to Archaeology.* Cairo, 1946.

Engelbach and Derry 1942
R. Engelbach and D.E. Derry. "Mummification," *ASAE* 41 (1942), pp. 233-265.

Englund 1974
G. Englund. *Boreas* 6: *From the Gustavianum Collections in Uppsala, 1974.* Uppsala, 1974.

Englund 1978
G. Englund. *Akh - une notion religieuse dans l'Egypte pharaonique.* Uppsala, 1978.

Enklaar 1985
A. Enklaar. "Chronologie et Peintres des Hydries de Hadra," *Bulletin Antieke Beschaving* 60 (1985), pp. 106-151.

Erichsen 1954
Erichsen. *Demotisches Glossar.* Copenhagen, 1954.

Erman 1896
A. Erman. "Dispute of a Man with his Ba," *Gespräch eines Lebensmüden mit seiner Seele.* Berlin, 1896.

Erman 1971
A. Erman. *Life in Ancient Egypt,* H. Tirard, trans. New York, 1971.

Erman and Grapow 1926
A. Erman and H. Grapow. *Wörterbuch der Ägyptischen Sprache* I. Leipzig, 1926.

Erman and Grapow 1971
A. Erman and H. Grapow. *Wörterbuch der aegyptischen Sprache,* II. Berlin, 1971.

Evers 1929
H.G. Evers. *Staat aus dem Stein: Denkmäler, Geschichte und Bedeutung der Ägyptischen Plastik während des Mittleren Reiches* I-II. Munich, 1929.

Fabretti et al. 1882
A. Fabretti et al. *Regio Museo di Torino. Catalogo dei Museidi Antichita e Degli Ogetti d'arte Raccolti nelle Gallerie e Biblioteche del Regno* I. Turin, 1882.

Falke 1913
O. von Falke. *Kunstgeschichte der Seidenweberei.* Berlin, 1913.

Farag and Iskander 1971
N. Farag and Z. Iskander. *The Discovery of Nefruptah.* Cairo, 1971.

Faulkner 1944
R.O. Faulkner. "The Rebellion in the Hare Nome," *JEA* 30 (1944).

Faulkner 1962
R.O. Faulkner. *A Concise Dictionary of Middle Egyptian.* Oxford, 1962.

Faulkner 1969
R.O. Faulkner. *The Ancient Egyptian Pyramid Texts.* Oxford, 1969.

Faulkner 1972
R.O. Faulkner in *The Literature of Ancient Egypt,* William Kelly Simpson, ed. New Haven, 1972.

Faulkner 1973
R.O. Faulkner. *The Ancient Egyptian Coffin Texts* 1. Warminster, 1973.

Faulkner 1976
R.O. Faulkner. *A Concise Dictionary of Middle Egyptian.* Oxford, 1976.

Faulkner 1977
R.O. Faulkner. *The Ancient Egyptian Coffin Texts* 2. Warminster, 1977.

Faulkner 1978
R.O. Faulkner. *The Ancient Egyptian Coffin Texts* 3. Warminster, 1978.

Faulkner 1985
R.O. Faulkner, trans. *The Ancient Egyptian Book of the Dead,* C. Andrews, ed. New York, 1985.

Fazzini 1975
R. Fazzini. *Images of Eternity: Egyptian Art from Berkeley and Brooklyn.* Brooklyn, 1975.

Feucht 1971
E. Feucht. *Pektorale Nichtköniglicher Personen,* Ägyptologische Abhandlungen Bd. 22. Wiesbaden, 1971.

Feucht 1982
E. Feucht. "Pektorale," *LÄ* IV (1982), cols. 922-923.

Feucht 1985
E. Feucht in *Pharaonic Egypt: the Bible and Christianity,* Sarah Israelit Groll, ed. Jerusalem, 1985.

Feucht 1986
E. Feucht. *Vom Nil zum Neckar.* Berlin and Heidelberg, 1986.

Firth 1913
C.M. Firth. *Excavations at Saqqara (1911-12): The Tomb of Hesy.* Cairo, 1913.

Firth and Gunn 1926a
C.M. Firth and B. Gunn. *Excavations at Saqqara: Teti Pyramid Cemeteries* I: Text. Cairo, 1926.

Firth and Gunn 1926b
C.M. Firth and B. Gunn. *Excavations at Saqqara: Teti Pyramid Cemeteries* II: Plates. Cairo, 1926.

Firth and Quibell 1935
C.M. Firth and J.E. Quibell. *Excavations at Saqqara: The Step Pyramid,* 2 vols. Cairo, 1935.

Fischer 1960a
H. Fischer. "Old Kingdom Inscriptions in the Yale Gallery," *MIO* 7 (1960).

Fischer 1960b
H. Fischer. "The Inscription of IN-IT.F, Born of TFI," *JNES* 19 (1960), pp. 258-268.

Fischer 1961
H.G. Fischer. "The Nubian Mercenaries of Gebelein during the First Intermediate Period," *Kush* 9 (1961), pp. 44-80.

Fischer 1963
H.G. Fischer. "Varia Aegyptiaca," *JARCE* 2 (1963), pp. 17-22.

Fischer 1966
H.G. Fischer. Review of *Frühmittelägyptische Studien,* by Wolfgang Helck, in *BiOr* 23 (1966), p. 29.

Fischer 1970
H.G. Fischer. "Group Statue of Ukh-hotep," in *Treasures of Egyptian Art from the Cairo Museum,* E.L.B. Terrace and H.G. Fischer, ed. Boston, 1970.

Fischer 1972
H.G. Fischer. "Some Emblematic Uses of Hieroglyphs with Particular Reference to an Archaic Ritual Vessel," *MMJ* 5 (1972).

Fischer 1973
H.G. Fischer. "An Eleventh Dynasty Couple Holding the Sign of Life," *ZÄS* 100 (1973).

Fischer 1976a
H.G. Fischer. "Geissel," *LÄ* II (1976), cols. 516-517.

Fischer 1976b
H.G. Fischer. "Representations of *Dryt*-mourners in the Old Kingdom," in *MMA Egyptian Studies 1. Varia.* New York, 1976, pp. 29-50.

Fischer 1978a
H.G. Fischer. "Five Inscriptions of the Old Kingdom," *ZÄS* 105 (1978), pp. 42-59.

Fischer 1978b
H.G. Fischer. "Notes on Sticks and Staves in Ancient Egypt," *MMJ* 13 (1978), pp. 5-32.

Fischer 1979a
H.G. Fischer. "Kopfstütze," in *LÄ* III (1979), cols. 686-693.

Fischer 1979b
H.G. Fischer. *Ancient Egyptian Calligraphy.* New York, 1979.

Fischer 1980
H.G. Fischer. "Kopfstütze," *LÄ* III (1980), cols. 686-693.

Fischer 1986
H.G. Fischer. "The Ancient Egyptian Attitude to the Monstrous," in *Monsters and Demons in the Ancient and Medieval Worlds: Papers presented in honor of Edith Porada,* A.E. Farkas, P.O. Harper and E.B. Harrison, eds. Mainz, 1986, pp. 13-26.

Fisher 1913
C. Fisher. "The Harvard University-Museum of Fine Arts Egyptian Expedition. Work of 1912 at Gizeh and Mesheikh," *BMFA* XI (1913), pp. 18-22.

Fleming et al. 1980
Fleming et al. *The Egyptian Mummy: Secrets and Science.* Philadelphia, 1980.

Fouquet 1973
A. Fouquet. "Quelques Representations d'Osiris-Canope au Musée du Louvre," *BIFAO* 73 (1973), pp. 61-69.

Franke 1984
D. Franke. *Personendaten aus dem Mittleren Reich, Dossier 1-796* (Ägyptologische Abhandlungen 41). Wiesbaden, 1984.

Frankfort 1941
H. Frankfort. "The Origin of Monumental Architecture in Egypt," *American Journal of Semitic Languages* 58/4 (1941), pp. 329-358.

Frankfort 1944
H. Frankfort. "A Note on the Lady of Birth," *JNES* 3 (1944), pp. 198-200.

Frankfort and Pendlebury 1933
H. Frankfort and J. Pendlebury. *The City of Akhenaten* 2. London, 1933.

Fraser 1902
G. Fraser. "The Early Tombs at Tehne," *ASAE* 3 (1902), pp. 67-76 and 122-130.

Freed 1976
R. Freed. "Representation and Style of Dated Private Stelae of Dynasty XII" (M.A. thesis, New York University, 1976).

Freed 1981a
R. Freed. "A Private Stela from Naga ed-Dêr and Relief Style of the Reign of Amenemhet I," in *Studies in Honor of Dows Dunham on the Occasion of his 90th Birthday, June 1, 1980,* W.K. Simpson and W. Davis, eds. Boston, 1981, pp. 68-76.

Freed 1981b
R. Freed. *Egypt's Golden Age: A Picture Book.* Boston, 1981.

Friedman 1984
F. Friedman. "The Root Meaning of *ȝḫ,*" *Serapis* 8 (1984), pp. 39-46.

Friedman 1985
F. Friedman. "On the Meaning of Some Anthropoid Busts from Deir el-Medina," *JEA* 71 (1985), pp. 82-97.

Friedman 1986
F. Friedman. "*ȝḫ* in the Amarna Period," *JARCE* 23 (1986), pp. 99-106.

Frolow 1961
A. Frolow. "Le Culte de la Relique de la Vraie Croix à la Fin du VIe - et au Début du VIIe Siècles," *Byzantinoslavica* 12, (1961), pp. 320-339.

Fuchs 1984
R. Fuchs. "Steatite," *LÄ* V (1984), cols. 1271-1274.

Gabra 1939
S. Gabra. "Fouilles de l'Université 'Fouad el Awal,' à Touna el-Gebel (Hermopolis Ouest)," *ASAE* 39 (1939), pp. 483-496.

Gabra 1941
S. Gabra. *Rapport sur les fouilles d' Hermoupolis Ouest (Touna el-Gebel).* Cairo, 1941.

Gabra 1959
S. Gabra. "Les recherches archéologiques de l'Université égyptienne a Tounah-el-Gebel, nécropole d'Hermopolis," *BSFE* 30 (1959), pp. 41-52.

Gaillard and Daressy 1905
C. Gaillard and G. Daressy. *La Faune Momifée de l'antique Egypte* (CG). Cairo, 1905.

Gamer-Wallert 1970
I. Gamer-Wallert. *Fische und Fischkulte im alten Ägypten.* Wiesbaden, 1970.

Gamer-Wallert 1975
I. Gamer-Wallert. "Fische, Religiös," *LÄ* (1975), pp. 228-234.

Gardiner 1906
A.H. Gardiner. "A Statuette of the High Priest of Memphis Ptahmose," *ZÄS* 43 (1906), pp. 55-59.

Gardiner 1935a
A.H. Gardiner. *Hieratic Papyri from the British Museum,* third series. London, 1935.

Gardiner 1935b
A.H. Gardiner. *The Attitude of the Ancient Egyptians to Death and the Dead.* Cambridge, 1935.

Gardiner 1944
A.H. Gardiner. "Horus the Behdetite," *JEA* 30 (1944), pp. 23-60.

Gardiner 1947
A.H. Gardiner. *Ancient Egyptian Onomastica. Text* 2. Oxford, 1947.

Gardiner 1948
A.H. Gardiner. *The Wilbour Papyrus* II. Oxford, 1948.

Gardiner 1957
A.H. Gardiner. *Egyptian Grammar,* 3rd ed. Oxford, 1957.

Gardiner 1961
A.H. Gardiner. *Egypt of the Pharaohs.* New York, 1961.

Gardiner 1973
A.H. Gardiner. *Egyptian Grammar,* reprint of the 3rd. ed. Oxford, 1973.

Garner 1979
R. Garner. "Experimental Mummification," in *Manchester Museum Mummy Project,* A.R. David, ed. Manchester, 1979.

Garstang 1901
J.A. Garstang. *El Arabah. A Cemetery of the Middle Kingdom.* London, 1901.

Garstang 1907
J.A. Garstang. *The Burial Customs of the Ancient Egyptians.* London, 1907.

Gauthier 1913
H. Gauthier. *Cercueils Anthropoïdes des Prêtres de Montou* (CG). Cairo, 1913.

Gauthier 1928
H. Gauthier. *Dictionnaire des noms géographiques contenus dans les textes hiéroglyphiques V.* Cairo, 1928.

Ghazi 1980
D. Abou-Ghazi. *Denkmäler des Alten Reiches* III. Altars and Offering Tables. Fasc. 2: Nos. 57024-57049 (CG). Cairo, 1980.

Ghazouli 1964
E. Ghazouli. "The Palace and Magazines Attached to the Temple of Sety I at Abydos and the Facade of this Temple," *ASAE* 58 (1964).

Gitton 1976
A. Gitton. "Le rôle de la femme dans le clergé d'Amon à la 18e dynastie," *BSFE* 75 (1976), pp. 31-46.

Giveon 1984
R. Giveon. "Skarabäus," *LÄ* V (1984), cols. 968-981.

Giveon 1985
R. Giveon. *Egyptian Scarabs from Western Asia from the Collections of the British Museum*. Göttingen, 1985.

Goedicke 1958
H. Goedicke. "Ein Verehrer des Weisen *Ddfḥr* aus dem späten alten Reich," *ASAE* 55 (1958).

Goedicke 1966
H. Goedicke. "Die Laufbahn des *Mtn*," *MDAIK* 21 (1966).

Goedicke 1972
H. Goedicke. "The Letter to the Dead, Nag' ed-Deir N 3500," *JEA* 58 (1972), pp. 95-98.

Goedicke 1975
H. Goedicke. "Remarks about a Recent Acquisition," *GM* 17 (1975).

Goff 1979
B. Goff. *Symbols of Ancient Egypt in the Late Period,* (Religion and Society 13, Leo Laeyendecker and Jacques Waardenburg eds.). The Hague, 1979.

Göttlicher and Werner 1971
A. Göttlicher and W. Werner. *Schiffsmodelle im alten Aegypten*. Wiesbaden, 1971.

Göttlicher 1978
A. Göttlicher. *Materialen für ein Corpus der Schiffsmodelle im Altertum*. Mainz am Rhein, 1978.

Goyon 1972a
J.-C. Goyon. *Rituels Funéraires de l'Ancienne Egypte*. Paris, 1972.

Goyon 1972b
J.-C. Goyon. "La littérature tardive," in *Textes et langages de l'Egypte pharaonique* III (Bibliothèque d'étude 64). Cairo, 1972.

Grabar 1967
A. Grabar. *The Golden Age of Justinian: from the death of Theodosius to the Rise of Islam*. New York, 1967.

Graefe 1985
E. Graefe. "Talfest," *LÄ* VI (1985), cols. 187-189.

Gray 1966
P.H.K. Gray. "Radiological Aspects of the Mummies of Ancient Egyptians in the Rijksmuseum van Oudheden, Leiden," *OMRO* 47 (1966), pp. 1-30.

Gray and Slow 1968
P.H.K. Gray and D. Slow. *Egyptian Mummies in the City of Liverpool Museums*. Liverpool, 1968.

Green 1987
C.I. Green. *The Temple Furniture from the Sacred Animal Necropolis at North Saqqara*. London, 1987.

Grenfell 1901
B.P. Grenfell and A.S. Hunt. "Graeco-Roman Branch" in *Archaeological Report 1900-01*. F.Ll. Griffith, ed., London, 1901, p. 7.

Grenier 1977
J.-C. Grenier. *Anubis alexandrin et romain*. Leiden, 1977.

Gressmann 1918
H. Gressmann. *Vom reichen Mann und armen Lazarus* (Abhandlungen der Berliner Akademie der Wissenschaften, phil. hist. Klasse 1918, 7). Berlin, 1918.

Grieshammer 1974
R. Grieshammer. "Briefe an Tote," *LÄ* I (1974), cols. 864-870.

Griffith 1888
F.Ll. Griffith, in W.M.F. Petrie, *Nebesheh and Defenneh*. London, 1888, pp. 42-44.

Griffith 1889
F.Ll. Griffith. *The Inscriptions of Siût abd Der Rîfeh*. London, 1889.

Griffith 1890
F.Ll. Griffith. *The Antiquities of Tell El Yahudiyeh*. London, 1890.

Griffith 1894
F.Ll. Griffith. *Egypt Exploration Fund Archaeological Report (1893-4)*. London, 1894.

Griffith 1903
F.Ll. Griffith. *Egypt Exploration Fund Archaeological Report 1902-1903*. London, 1903, pp. 1-3.

Griffith and Newberry 1894
F.Ll. Griffith and P.E. Newberry. *El Bersheh* II. London, 1894.

Griffiths 1960
J.G. Griffiths. *The Conflict of Horus and Seth*. Liverpool, 1960.

Griffiths 1980
J.G. Griffiths. *The Origins of Osiris and his Cult* (Studies in the History of Religions XL). Leiden, 1980.

Griffiths 1981
J.G. Griffiths. "Osiris," *LÄ* IV (1981), cols. 623-633.

Griffiths 1985
J.G. Griffiths. "Terenuthis," *LÄ* VI (1985), col. 424.

Grimm 1974
G. Grimm. *Die römischen Mumienmasken aus Ägypten*. Wiesbaden, 1974.

Grueber 1910
H.A. Grueber. *Coins of the Roman Republic in the British Museum* 2. London, 1910.

Guerrini 1964
L. Guerrini. *Vasi di Hadra- Studi miscellanei* 8. Rome, 1964.

Gunn 1941
B. Gunn. "Notes on Egyptian Lexicography," *JEA* 27 (1941), p. 146.

Habachi 1958
L. Habachi. "Clearance of the Tomb of Kheruef at Thebes 1957-58," *ASAE* 55 (1958).

Habachi 1967
L. Habachi. "An embalming bed of Amenhotep, Steward of Memphis under Amenhotep III," *MDAIK* 22 (1967), pp. 42-47.

Habachi 1985
L. Habachi. *Elephantine IV: The Sanctuary of Heqaib,* Archäologische Veröffentlichung 33. Mainz am Rhein, 1985.

Hall 1981
R. Hall. "Fishing Net Dresses in the Petrie Museum," *GM* 42 (1981), pp. 37-43.

Hall 1986
R. Hall. *Egyptian Textiles*. Aylesbury, 1986.

Hamilton-Paterson and Andrews 1978
J. Hamilton-Paterson and C. Andrews. *Mummies: Death and Life in Ancient Egypt*. Harmondsworth, 1978.

Harris 1961
J.R. Harris. *Lexicographical Studies in Ancient Egyptian Minerals*. Berlin, 1961.

Harris and Weeks 1973
J.E. Harris and K.R. Weeks. *X-Raying the Pharaohs*. New York and London, 1973.

Hart 1986
G. Hart. *A Dictionary of Egyptian Gods and Goddesses*. London, 1986.

Harvey 1987
S. Harvey. "Predynastic Egyptian Pottery in the Collections of Yale University" (Undergraduate thesis, Yale University, 1987).

Hassan 1932
S. Hassan. *Excavations at Giza 1929-1930*. Oxford, 1932.

Hassan 1950
S. Hassan. *Excavations at Giza* VI.3, 1934-1935. Cairo, 1950.

Hatchfield 1986
P. Hatchfield. "Note on a Fill Material for Water Sensitive Objects," *JAIC* 25 (1986), pp. 93-96.

Hausherr 1963
R. Hausherr. *Der tote Christus am Kreuz*. Bonn, 1963.

Hawass 1979
Z. Hawass. "Preliminary Report on the Excavations of Kom Abou Billou," *SAK* 7 (1979), pp. 75-88.

Hay 1869
J. Hay. *Catalogue of the Collection of Egyptian Antiquities belonging to the late Robert Hay, Esq., of Linplum*. London, 1869.

Hayes 1935
W. Hayes. "The Tomb of Nefer-Khewet and his Family," in *BMMA Egyptian Supplements* (November 1935), pp. 17-36.

Hayes 1939
W.C. Hayes. *The Burial Chamber of the Treasurer Sobk-mose from er Rizeikat*. New York, 1939.

Hayes 1953
W.C. Hayes. *The Scepter of Egypt* I. New York, 1953.

Hayes 1959
W.C. Hayes. *The Scepter of Egypt* II. New York, 1959.

Hayes 1971
W.C. Hayes. "The Middle Kingdom in Egypt: Internal History from the Rise of the Heracleopolitans to the Death of Ammenemes III," in *The Cambridge Ancient History* I.2A, 3rd ed., I.E.S. Edwards, C.J. Gadd, N.G.L. Hammond, eds. Cambridge, 1971, pp. 464-531.

Haynes 1984
J. Haynes. *Padihershef: The Egyptian Mummy*. Springfield, Mass., 1984.

Heerma van Voss 1974
M. Heerma van Voss. "Een Dodendoek als Dodenboek," *Phoenix* 20 (1974), pp. 335-338.

Heerma van Voss 1985
M. Heerma van Voss. "Totenbuch," *LÄ* VI (1985), cols. 641-645.

Helck 1961
W. Helck. *Materialien zur Wirtschaftsgeschichte des Neuen Reiches* I. Wiesbaden, 1961.

Helck 1967
W. Helck. "Einige Bemerkungen zum Mundöffnungsritual," *MDAIK* 22 (1967), pp. 27-41.

Helck 1976
W. Helck. "Ägyptische Statuen im Ausland-Ein Chronologisches Problem," *Ugarit-Forschungen* 8 (1976), pp. 101-115.

Helck 1986
W. Helck. "Sumenu," *LÄ* 6 (1986), col. 110.

Heritage Plantation 1979
Heritage Plantation of Sandwich. *Three American Museums and Egypt.* Sandwich, Mass., 1979.

Hermann 1962
A. Hermann. "Ägyptologische Marginalen zur spätantiken Ikonographie," *JAC* 5 (1962).

Hermann 1964
A. Hermann. "Das Werden zu einem Falken," *JAC* 7 (1964), pp. 39-44.

Herodotus 1972
Herodotus II
See Lloyd 1976.

Herrmann 1987
J. Herrmann in *Art for Boston, a Decade of Acquisitions under the Directorship of Jan Fontein.* Boston, 1987, pp. 78-79.

Herzfeld 1920
E.E. Herzfeld. *Am Tor von Asien: Felsdenkmäler aus Irans Heldenzeit.* Berlin, 1920.

Hester 1976
T.R. Hester. "Functional Analysis of Ancient Egyptian Chipped Stone Tools: The Potential for Future Research," *Journal of Field Archaeology* 3 (1976), pp. 346-351.

Higgins 1980
R. Higgins. *Greek and Roman Jewellery.* Berkeley, 1980.

Hodjash 1982
S. Hodjash, O. Berlev. *The Egyptian Reliefs and Stelae in the Pushkin Museum of Fine Arts.* Leningrad, 1982.

Hoffman 1963
H. Hoffman. "Gold Finger Ring with Emerald," *BMFA* 61, no. 325 (1963), p. 110.

Hoffman 1979
M. Hoffman. *Egypt Before the Pharaohs.* New York, 1979.

Holden 1982
L. Holden in *Egypt's Golden Age.* Boston, 1982.

Hölscher 1954
U. Hölscher. *The Excavation of Medinet Habu* V. *Post-Ramessid Remains.* Chicago, 1954.

Hooper 1961
F.A. Hooper. *Funerary Stelae from Kom Abou Billou.* Ann Arbor, 1961.

Hope 1983
C. Hope. "A Head of Nefertiti and a Figure of Ptah-Sokar-Osiris in the National Gallery of Victoria," *Art Bulletin of Victoria* 29 (1983), pp. 47-62.

Höhr-Grenzhausen and Rastel-Haus 1978
Höhr-Grenzhausen and Rastel-Haus 1978. *Meisterwerke Altägyptischer Keramik.* Höhr-Grenzhausen, 1978.

Hornblower 1929
G.D. Hornblower. "Predynastic Figures of Women and their Successors," *JEA* 15 (1929), pp. 29-47.

Hornemann 1951
B. Hornemann. *Types of Ancient Egyptian Statuary* I. Copenhagen, 1951.

Hornemann 1957
B. Hornemann. *Types of Ancient Egyptian Statuary* II-III. Copenhagen, 1957.

Hornemann 1966
B. Hornemann. *Types of Ancient Egyptian Statuary* IV-V. Copenhagen, 1966.

Hornemann 1969
B. Hornemann. *Types of Ancient Egyptian Statuary* VI-VII. Copenhagen, 1969.

Hornung 1963
E. Hornung. *Das Amduat. Die Schrift des verborgenen Raumes* I: Text, II: Übersetzung und Kommentar. Wiesbaden, 1963.

Hornung 1968
E. Hornung. *Altägyptische Höllenvorstellungen* (Abhandlungen der Sächsischen Akademie der Wissenschaften zu Leipzig, Phil. hist. Klasse 59,3). Berlin, 1968.

Hornung 1972
E. Hornung. *Ägyptische Unterweltsbucher.* Zurich and Munich, 1972.

Hornung 1979
E. Hornung. *Das Buch von den Pforten des Jenseits* I: Text (Aegyptiaca Helvetica 7). Geneva, 1979.

Hornung 1980
E. Hornung. *Das Buch von den Pforten des Jenseits* II: Übersetzung und Kommentar (Aegyptiaca Helvetica 8). Geneva, 1980 (1984).

Hornung 1982
E. Hornung. *Conceptions of God in Ancient Egypt: The One and the Many,* J. Baines, trans. Ithaca, 1982.

Hornung 1983a
E. Hornung. *Tal der Könige. Die Ruhestatte der Pharaonen,* 2nd ed. Zurich and Munich, 1983.

Hornung 1983b
E. Hornung. "Vom Sinn der Mumifizierung," *Die Welt des Orients* 14 (1983), pp. 167-175.

Hornung 1984
E. Hornung. "Fisch und Vögel. Zur altaegyptischen Sicht des Menschen," *Eranosjahrbuch* 52 (1984), pp. 455-496.

Houlihan 1986
P.F. Houlihan. *The Birds of Ancient Egypt.* Warminster, 1986.

Institut Français 1981
Centenaire de l'Institut Français d'Archéologie Orientale. Cairo, 1981.

Iskander 1940
Z. Iskander. "Cleaning, Preservation, and Restoration of the Silver Coffin and Cartonnage of Shashanq," *ASAE* 40 (1940).

Iskander 1980
Z. Iskander. "Mummification in Ancient Egypt: Development, History, and Techniques," in *An X-Ray Atlas of the Royal Mummies,* J.E. Harris and E.F. Wente, eds. Chicago, 1980.

Iskander and Shaheen 1964
Z. Iskander and A. Shaheen. "Temporary Stuffing Materials used in the Process of Mummification in Ancient Egypt," *ASAE* 58 (1964), pp. 197-208.

Jacq 1985
C. Jacq. *Egyptian Magic.* Warminster, 1985.

James 1962
T.G.H. James. *The Hekanakht Papers and Other Early Middle Kingdom Documents.* New York, 1962.

James 1974
T.G.H. James. *A Corpus of Hieroglyphic Inscriptions in the Brooklyn Museum I: From Dynasty 1 to the end of Dynasty 18.* Brooklyn, 1974.

James and Davies 1983
T.G.H. James and W.V. Davies. *Egyptian Sculpture.* London, 1983.

Jankuhn 1979
D. Jankuhn. "Kranz der Rechtfertigung." *LÄ* 3 (1979), col. 764.

Janssen 1975
J.J. Janssen. *Commodity Prices from the Ramesside Period: An Economic Study of the Village of Necropolis Workmen at Thebes.* Leiden, 1975.

Janssen 1977
J.J. Janssen. "Kha'emtore, a Well-to-Do Workman," *OMRO* 58 (1977), pp. 221-232.

Jenkins 1980
N. Jenkins. *The Boat Beneath the Pyramid.* London, 1980.

Jéquier 1921
G. Jéquier. *Les Frises d'Objets des Sarcophages du Moyen Empire.* Cairo, 1921.

Jéquier 1929
G. Jéquier. *Tombeaux de particuliers contemporains de Pepi II.* Cairo, 1929.

Jéquier 1933
G. Jéquier. *Deux Pyramides du Moyen Empire.* Cairo, 1933.

Johnson 1987
S.B. Johnson. *The Cobra Goddess of Ancient Egypt: History of the Uraeus Serpent Symbol* I. London, 1987.

Junker 1929
H. Junker. *Giza* I. Vienna and Leipzig, 1929.

Junker 1938
H. Junker. *Giza* III. Vienna and Leipzig, 1938.

Junker 1940
H. Junker. *Giza* IV. Vienna, 1940.

Junker 1944
H. Junker. *Giza* VII. Vienna and Leipzig, 1944.

Junker 1955
H. Junker. *Giza* XII. Vienna, 1955.

Kaczmarczyk and Hedges 1983
A. Kaczmarczyk and R.E.M. Hedges. *Ancient Egyptian Faience.* Warminster, 1983.

Kaiser 1957
W. Kaiser. "Zur inneren Chronologie der Naqadakultur," *Archaeologica Geographica* 6 (1957), pp. 69-77.

Kaiser 1964
W. Kaiser. "Einige Bermerkungen zur Ägyptischen Frühzeit. III," *ZÄS* 91 (1964), pp. 86-125.

Kaiser 1967
W. Kaiser. *Ägyptisches Museum Berlin.* Berlin, 1967.

Kákosy 1979
L. Kákosy. "Krokodilskulte," *LÄ* III (1979), cols. 801-811.

Kákosy 1980
L. Kákosy. "A Memphite Triad," *JEA* 66 (1980), pp. 48-53.

Kákosy 1981
L. Kákosy. "The Astral Snakes of the Nile," *MDAIK* 37 (1981), pp. 255-260.

Kákosy 1982
L. Kákosy. "Phönix," in *LÄ* IV (1982), cols. 1030-1039.

Kákosy 1983
L. Kákosy. "Die Kronen im spätägyptischen Totenglauben," in *Aegyptiaca Treverensia* 2, *Das Römisch-Byzantinische Ägypten,* Günter Grimm, Heinz Heinen, and Erich Winter, eds. Mainz am Rhein, 1983, pp. 57-60.

Kákosy and Roccati 1985
L. Kákosy and A. Roccati. *La Magia in Egitto di tempi dei faraoni.* Modena, 1985.

Kamal 1904-1905
A. Kamal. *Stèles ptolemaiques et romaines* (CG). Cairo, 1904-1905.

Kamal 1909
A. Kamal. *Tables d'Offrandes* (CG). Cairo, 1909.

Kanawati 1984
N. Kanawati. *Excavations at Saqqara* I: *North-West of Teti's Pyramid.* Sydney, 1984.

Kantor 1974
H.J. Kantor. "Aegypten," in *Frühe Stufen der Kunst* (Propyläen Kunstgeschichte 13), M. Mellink and J. Filip, eds. Berlin, 1974.

Kartsonis 1982
A. Kartsonis. "Anastasis, the Making of an Image," (Dissertation, New York University, New York, 1982).

Keimer 1929
L. Keimer. "Nouvelles Recherches au sujet du *Potamogeton Lucens L.* dans l'Egypte ancienne," *Revue de l'Egypte ancienne* 2 (1929), pp. 210-253.

Keith-Bennett 1981
J.L. Keith-Bennett. "Anthropoid Busts II: Not from Deir el Medineh Alone," *BES* 3 (1981), pp. 43-72.

Kelley 1974
A.L. Kelley. "Reserve Heads: A Review of the Evidence for their Placement and Function in Old Kingdom Tombs," *Newsletter of the Society for the Study of Egyptian Antiquities* 5.1 (September 1974).

Kelsey Museum 1980
Kelsey Museum of Archaeology. *The Art of the Ancient Weaver: Textiles from Egypt (4th-12th century A.D.).* Ann Arbor, 1980.

Kemp 1968
B.J. Kemp. "Merimda and the Theory of House Burial in Prehistoric Egypt," *CdE* 43 (1968), pp. 22-33.

Kemp 1975
B.J. Kemp. "Abydos," *LÄ* I (1975), cols. 28-41.

Kemp 1967
B.J. Kemp. "The Egyptian 1st Dynasty Royal Cemetery," *Antiquity* 41 (1967), pp. 22-32.

Kemp and Merrillees 1980
B.J. Kemp and R.S. Merrillees. *Minoan Pottery in Second Millennium Egypt.* Mainz, 1980.

Kendrick 1920
A.F. Kendrick. *Catalogue of Textiles from Burying Grounds in Egypt* 1. London, 1920.

Kendrick 1921
A.F. Kendrick. *Catalogue of Textiles from Burying Grounds in Egypt* 2. London, 1921.

Kendrick 1922
A.F. Kendrick. *Catalogue of Textiles from Burying Grounds in Egypt* 3. London, 1922.

Kessler 1985a
D. Kessler. "Tuna el Gebel," *LÄ* VI (1985), cols. 797-804.

Kessler 1985b
D. Kessler. "Tierkult," *LÄ* VI (1985), cols. 571-587.

Killen 1980
G. Killen. *Ancient Egyptian Furniture* I. Warminster, 1980.

King 1928
E.S. King. "The Date and Provenance of a Bronze Reliquary Cross in the Museo Cristiano," *Pontificia accademia romana du archeologia, Memorie* II 5 (1928), pp. 193-205.

Kingery and Vandiver 1986
W.D. Kingery and P.B. Vandiver. *Ceramic Masterpieces: Art, Structure, and Technology.* New York, 1986.

Kitchen 1975
K.A. Kitchen. *Ramesside Inscriptions, Historical and Biographical* I, fasc. 7 and 8. (Oxford, 1975).

Kitchen 1979
K.A. Kitchen. *Ramesside Inscriptions, Historical and Biographical* II. Oxford, 1979.

Kitchen 1980
K.A. Kitchen. *Ramesside Inscriptions, Historical and Biographical* III. Oxford, 1980.

Kitchen 1982
K.A. Kitchen. *Pharaoh Triumphant. The Life and Times of Ramesses II, King of Egypt.* Warminster, 1982.

Kitchen 1986
K.A. Kitchen. *The Third Intermediate Period in Egypt (1100-650 B.C.),* 2nd ed. with supplement. Warminster, 1986.

Kitzinger 1948
E. Kitzinger. "The Horse and Lion Tapestry," *Dumbarton Oaks Papers* 3 (1948), pp. 1-59.

Klasens 1975
A. Klasens. "Amulett," *LÄ* I (1975), cols. 232-236.

Klebs 1915
L. Klebs. *Die Reliefs des alten Reiches* (Abhandlungen der Heidelberger Akademie der Wissenschaften 3). Heidelberg, 1915.

Klebs 1922
L. Klebs. *Die Reliefs und Malereien des mittleren Reiches.* Heidelberg, 1922.

Klebs 1934
L. Klebs. *Die Reliefs und Malereien des neuen Reiches.* Heidelberg, 1934.

Knudsen 1987
J. Knudsen. "A Question of Paint: An Investigation into Traces of Paint on the Reserve Head from the Tomb of Ka-nofer," paper presented at the Annual Meeting of the ARCE, April 24, 1987.

Koefoed-Petersen 1948
O. Koefoed-Petersen. *Les stèles égyptiennes.* Copenhagen, 1948.

Koefoed-Petersen 1951
O. Koefoed-Petersen. *Catalogue des Sarcophages et Cercueils Egyptiens.* Copenhagen, 1951.

Koefoed-Petersen 1956
O. Koefoed-Petersen. *Catalogue des bas-reliefs et peintures égyptiens.* Copenhagen, 1956.

Komorzynski 1960
E. Komorzynski. "Ein Bruchstück vom inneren Sarkophag des Prinzen Meri-mes in Wien," in *Archiv für Orientforschung* 19 (1959-1960), pp. 139-140.

Königliche Museen zu Berlin 1899
Königliche Museen zu Berlin. *Ausführliches Verzeichnis der Aegyptischen Altertümer und Gipsabgüsse,* 2nd edition. Berlin, 1899.

Kotansky 1983
R. Kotansky. "A Silver Phylactery for Pain," *The J. Paul Getty Museum Journal* 2 (1983), p. 169.

Kraay 1976
C. Kraay. *Archaic and Classical Greek Coins.* London, 1976.

Krauss 1985
R. Krauss. *Sothis-und Monddaten* (Hildesheimer Archäologische Beiträge 20). Hildesheim, 1985.

Kristensen 1926
W.B. Kristensen. *Het Leven uit den Dood.* Haarlem, 1926.

Kromann and Mørkholm 1977
A. Kromann and O. Mørkholm. *Sylloge Nummorum Graecorum, 40: Egypt: the Ptolemies.* Copenhagen, 1977.

Krönig 1934
W. Krönig. "Ägyptische Fayence-Schalen des Neuen Reiches," *MDAIK* 5 (1934), pp. 144-167.

Kuchman 1977-1978
L. Kuchman. "Egyptian Clay Anthropoid Coffins," *Serapis* 4 (1977-1978).

Kuentz 1929
C. Kuentz. "Quelques monuments du culte de Sobk," *BIFAO* 28 (1929), pp. 113-171.

Kueny and Yoyotte 1979
G. Kueny and J. Yoyotte. *Grenoble, Musée des Beaux-Arts. Collection Egyptienne.* Paris, 1979.

Kurtz and Boardman 1971
D. Kurtz and J. Boardman. *Greek Burial Customs.* Ithaca, 1971.

Kyrieleis 1975
H. Kyrieleis. *Bildnisse der Ptolemäer.* Berlin, 1975.

Lacau 1914
P. Lacau. "Supressions et modifications de signes dans les textes funéraires," *ZÄS* 51 (1914), pp. 1-64.

Lacau 1909
P. Lacau. *Stèles du Nouvel Empire* 1 (CG). Cairo, 1909.

Lacovara forthcoming
P. Lacovara. "An Inlaid Pectoral of the Middle Kingdom," *BMFA* (forthcoming).

Lacovara and Markowitz forthcoming
P. Lacovara and Y. Markowitz. "Faience Figurines in Boston," (forthcoming).

Lacovara and Wojcik forthcoming
P. Lacovara and C. Wojcik, eds., *G. A. Reisner, Archaeological Fieldwork* (forthcoming).

Landström 1970
B. Landström. *Ships of the Pharaohs: 4000 Years of Egyptian Shipbuilding.* Garden City, N.Y., 1970.

Lane 1871
E. Lane. *The Manners and Customs of the Modern Egyptians* 2. London, 1871.

Lange 1939
K. Lange. *Ägyptische Kunst.* Zurich, 1939.

Lansing 1920
A. Lansing. "Excavations at Thebes 1918-19," *BMMA* Egyptian Supplements (December 1920), pp. 4-11.

Lansing 1941
A. Lansing. "Imitation Stone Vessels of the XVIII Dynasty," *BMMA* 36, no. 1 (January 1941).

Lapp 1983
G. Lapp. "Sarg des AR und MR," *LÄ* V (1983), cols. 430-434.

Lapp 1986
G. Lapp. *Die Opferformel des Alten Reiches.* Mainz, 1986.

Lauer 1976
J.-P. Lauer. *Saqqara: The Royal Cemetery of Memphis; Excavations and Discoveries since 1850* (English trans.). London, 1976.

Lauer and Derry 1935
J.-P. Lauer and D.E. Derry. "Découverte à Saqqarah d'une partie de la momie du roi Zoser," *ASAE* 35 (1935), pp. 25-30.

Leahy 1985
L.M. Leahy. "A Saite Lintel Reunited," *JEA* 71 (1985), pp. 122-128.

Leek 1969
F. Leek. "The Problem of Brain Removal during Embalming by the Ancient Egyptians," *JEA* 55 (1969), pp. 112-116.

Leemans 1840
C. Leemans. *Description raisonnée des monumens Egyptiens du Musée d'Antiquités des Pays-Bas, à Leide.* Leiden, 1840.

Lefebvre 1923
G. Lefebvre. *Le Tombeau de Petosiris* 3: *Vocabulaire et Planches*. Cairo, 1923.

Legrain 1903
G. Legrain. "Fragments de Canopes," *ASAE* 4 (1903), pp. 138-149.

Legrain 1904
G. Legrain. "Seconde Note sur des Fragments de Canopes," *ASAE* 5 (1904), pp. 139-141.

Legrain 1909
G. Legrain. *Statues et Statuettes des Rois et de Particuliers* II (CG). Cairo, 1909.

Legrain 1917
G. Legrain. "Le Logement et Transport des Barques,Sacrées et des Statues des dieux dans quelques temples égyptiens," *BIFAO* 13 (1917), pp. 1-76.

Lehner and Lacovara 1985
M. Lehner and P. Lacovara. "An Enigmatic Object Explained," *JEA* 71 (1985), pp. 169-174.

Leprohon 1983
R.J. Leprohon. "Intef III and Amenemhet III at Elephantine," *The Ancient World: Egyptological Miscellanies* 6 (1983).

Leprohon 1985
R.J. Leprohon. *Stelae I: The Early Dynastic Period to the Late Middle Kingdom* (Corpus Antiquitatum Aegyptiacarum, Museum of Fine Arts, Boston, fasc. 2). Mainz am Rhein, 1985.

Leprohon forthcoming
R.J. Leprohon. *Stelae II: The New Kingdom to the Coptic Period* (Corpus Antiquitatum Aegyptiacarum, Museum of Fine Arts, Boston, fasc. 3). Mainz am Rhein, in press.

Lepsius 1849-1856
K.R. Lepsius. *Denkmäler aus Aegypten und Aethiopien,* 12 vols. Berlin, 1849-1856.

Lepsius 1897
K.R. Lepsius. *Denkmäler aus Aegypten und Aethiopien. Erster Textband Unteraegypten und Memphis.* Leipzig, 1897.

Lesko 1971-1972
L. Lesko. "The Field of Hetep in Egyptian Coffin Texts," *JARCE* 9 (1971-72), pp. 89-101.

Lesko 1972
L. Lesko. *The Ancient Egyptian Book of Two Ways.* Berkeley, 1972.

Levi 1971
D. Levi. *Antioch Mosaic Pavements.* Rome, 1971.

Lhote 1954
A. Lhote. *Les Chefs-d'Oeuvre de la Peinture Egyptienne.* Paris, 1954.

Lichtheim 1947
M. Lichtheim. "Oriental Institute Museum Notes, situla no. 11395 and some remarks on Egyptian situlae," *JNES* 6 (1947).

Lichtheim 1973
M. Lichtheim. *Ancient Egyptian Literature, A Book of Readings* 1: *The Old and Middle Kingdoms.* Berkeley, 1973.

Lichtheim 1975
M. Lichtheim. *Ancient Egyptian Literature. A Book of Readings* 1 (paperback edition). Berkeley, 1975.

Lichtheim 1976
M. Lichtheim. *Ancient Egyptian Literature. A Book of Readings* 2: *The New Kingdom.* Berkeley, 1976.

Lichtheim 1980
M. Lichtheim. *Ancient Egyptian Literature. A Book of Readings* 3: *The Late Period.* Berkeley, 1980.

Lieblein 1871
J. Lieblein. *Dictionnaire de Noms Hiéroglyphiques en Ordre Généalogique et Alphabétique.* Leipzig, 1871.

Lieblein 1892
J. Lieblein. *Dictionnaire de Noms Hiéroglyphiques en Ordre Généalogique et Alphabétique, Supplement.* Leipzig, 1892.

Lilleso 1975
E.K. Lilleso. "Two Wooden Uraei," *JEA* 61 (1975), pp. 137-146.

Lilyquist 1979a
C. Lilyquist. *Ancient Egyptian Mirrors from the Earliest Times through the Middle Kingdom.* Munich and Berlin, 1979.

Lilyquist 1979b
C. Lilyquist. "A Note on the Date of Senebtisi and other Middle Kingdom Groups," *Serapis* 5, no. 1 (1979).

Lilyquist 1982
C. Lilyquist in *Egypt's Golden Age.* Boston, 1982.

Lloyd 1976
A.B. Lloyd. *Herodotus Book II: Commentary 1-98.* Leiden, 1976.

Loat 1914
W.L.S. Loat. "The Ibis Cemetery at Abydos," *JEA* 1 (1914), p. 40.

Lortet and Gaillard 1902
L.C. Lortet and C. Gaillard. "Recherches sur les momies d'animaux de l'ancienne Egypte II: Sur les oiseaux momifés," *ASAE* 3 (1902), pp. 18-21.

Lortet and Gaillard 1907
L.C. Lortet and C. Gaillard. "La faune momifiée de l'antique Égypte," *Archives du Musée d'Histoire naturelle de Lyon* 9, 2 ser. (1907).

Lortet and Gaillard 1909
L.C. Lortet and C. Gaillard. "La faune momifiée de l'antique Égypte," *Archives du Musée d'Histoire naturelle de Lyon* 10, 2 ser. (1909).

Los Angeles 1974
Age of the Pharaohs: Catalogue of an exhibition at the Los Angeles County Museum of Art, April 4-June 16, 1974.

Lother 1929
H. Lother. *Der Pfau in der altchristlichen Kunst.* Leipzig, 1929.

Lourié 1935
I. Lourié. "Trois Pseudo-Stèles du Musée de L'Ermitage," *Mélanges Maspero* I (*MIFAO* 66). Cairo, 1935.

Lucas 1932
A. Lucas. "The Use of Natron in Mummification," *JEA* 18 (1932), pp. 125-140.

Lucas 1962
A. Lucas. *Ancient Egyptian Materials and Industries,* 4th ed., rev. and enlarged by J.R. Harris. London, 1962.

Luddeckens 1980
E. Luddeckens. *Demotisches Namenbuch* I. Wiesbaden, 1980.

Lurker 1980
M. Lurker. *The Gods and Symbols of Ancient Egypt.* London, 1980.

Luxor 1979
The Luxor Museum of Ancient Egyptian Art Catalogue. Cairo, 1979.

Lythgoe 1910
A.M. Lythgoe. "Graeco-Egyptian Portraits," *BMMA* 5 (1910), pp. 67-72.

Lythgoe and Dunham 1965
A.M. Lythgoe and D. Dunham. *The Predynastic Cemetery N 7000, Naga ed-Dêr Part IV.* Berkeley, 1965.

Lythgoe and Ransom 1916
A.M. Lythgoe and C.L. Ransom. *The Tomb of Perneb.* New York, 1916.

Mace and Winlock 1916
A.C. Mace and H.E. Winlock. *The Tomb of Senebtisi at Lisht.* New York, 1916.

Malaise 1971
M. Malaise. *Antiquités Egyptiennes et verres du Proche-Orient ancien des Musées Curtius et du Verre à Liège.* Liège, 1971.

Malaise 1978
M. Malaise. *Les scarabées de coeur dans l'Egypte ancienne.* Brussels, 1978.

Manniche 1987
L. Manniche. *City of the Dead—Thebes in Egypt.* London, 1987.

Mariette 1877
A. Mariette. *Deir-el-Bahari: Documents Topographiques, Historiques, et Ethnographiques.* Leipzig, 1877.

Marshall 1911
F. Marshall. *Catalogue of the Jewellery, Greek Etruscan and Roman, in the Departments of Antiquities, British Museum.* London, 1911.

Martin 1974
G. Martin. *The Royal Tomb at El-'Amarna* 1. London, 1974.

Martin 1978
K. Martin. "Kanopenkesten," *LÄ* III (1978), pp. 319-320.

Martin 1979
K. Martin. "Krummstab," *LÄ* III (1979), cols. 821-823.

Martin 1985
K. Martin. "Stele," *LÄ* IV (1985), cols. 1-6.

Marx and D'Auria 1986
M. Marx and S.H. D'Auria. "CT Examination of Eleven Egyptian Mummies," *Radiographics* 6 (1986), pp. 321-330.

Marx and D'Auria 1988
M. Marx and S.H. D'Auria. "Three-Dimensional Reconstructions of an Ancient Human Egyptian Mummy," *American Journal of Roentgenology* 150 (January 1988), pp. 147-149.

Maspero 1882
G. Maspero. "Notes sur quelques points de grammaire et d'histoire (suite)," *ZÄS* 20 (1882), pp. 120-135.

Maspero 1885
G. Maspero. "Trois années de fouilles dans les tombeaux de Thèbes et de Memphis," *MIFAO* 1881-84. 2. fascicle. Paris, 1885.

Maspero 1901
G. Maspero. "Un Cercueil du Fayoum," *ASAE* 2 (1901), p. 191, pl. I.

Maspero 1902
G. Maspero. "Fouilles de la pyramide d'Ounas. IX. Sur les bijoux d'Epoque Saite trouvés a Sakkarah," *ASAE* 3 (1902), pp. 1-9.

Massoulard 1936
E. Massoulard. "Lances fourchues et *Peseshkaf.* A propos de deux acquisitions récentes du Musée du Louvre," *RdE* 2 (1936), pp. 135-163.

Matouk 1976
F. Matouk. *Corpus du Scarabée Egyptien* 2. Beirut, 1976.

Mattingly 1923
H. Mattingly. *Coins of the Roman Empire in the British Museum* I. London, 1923.

Matzker 1986
I. Matzker. *Die letzten Könige der 12. Dynastie.* Frankfurt am Main, 1986.

Meeks 1980
D. Meeks. *Année Lexicographique* I. Paris, 1980.

Meeks 1981
D. Meeks. *Année Lexicographique* II. Paris, 1981.

Meeks 1982
D. Meeks. *Année Lexicographique* III. Paris, 1982.

Mekhitarian 1954
A. Mekhitarian. *Egyptian Painting.* New York, 1954.

Mellink and Filip 1974
M. Mellink and J. Filip, eds. *Frühe Stufen der Kunst* (Propyläen Kunstgeschichte 13). Berlin, 1974.

Meltzer 1974
E.S. Meltzer. "A Funerary Cone by Merimose, Viceroy of Kush," *Newsletter of the Society for the Study of Egyptian Antiquities* 5.2 (December 1974), pp. 9-12.

Merhav et al. 1981
R. Merhav et al. *A Glimpse into the Past: The Joseph Ternbach Collection.* The Israel Museum, Jerusalem, 1981.

Merrillees 1974
R.S. Merrillees. "Ancient Egypt's Silent Majority" in *Trade and Transcendence in the Bronze Age Levant.* Goteborg, 1974, pp. 14-41.

Metropolitan Museum of Art 1909
Metropolitan Museum of Art. "Egyptian Art—Results of Exploration and Excavation Purchases," *BMMA* 4 (1909), pp. 37-38.

Metropolitan Museum of Art 1911
Metropolitan Museum of Art. *A Handbook of the Egyptian Rooms* (rep. 1913 and 1922). New York, 1911.

Metropolitan Museum of Art 1933
Metropolitan Museum of Art. "The Egyptian Expedition's Excavations at Lisht," *BMMA* Section 2 (1933), pp. 9-28.

Michalowski 1968
K. Michalowski. *Art of Ancient Egypt.* New York, 1968.

Millet 1972
N.B. Millet. "An Old Mortality: An Egyptian Coffin of the XXnd (*sic*) Dynasty," *Rotunda* 5.2 (1972), pp. 18-27.

Millet 1981
N.B. Millet. "The Reserve Heads of the Old Kingdom," in *Studies in Ancient Egypt, the Aegean, and the Sudan. Essays in honor of Dows Dunham on the occasion of his 90th birthday, June 1, 1980,* William Kelly Simpson and Whitney M. Davis, eds. Boston, 1981.

Milward 1982
A.J. Milward. "Faience Vessels: Bowls," in *Egypt's Golden Age.* Boston, 1982, pp. 141-145.

Möller 1912
G. Möller. *Hieratische Paläographie* 3. Leipzig, 1912.

Mond and Myers 1937
R. Mond and O.H. Myers. *Cemeteries of Armant I and II.* London, 1937.

Montet 1910
P. Montet. "Les Scènes de Boucherie dans les Tombes de l'Ancien Empire," *BIFAO* 7 (1910), pp. 41-64.

Montet 1942
P. Montet. "La Nécropole des Rois Tanites," *Kêmi* 9 (1942).

Montet 1947
P. Montet. *La Nécropole Royale de Tanis* I. *Les Constructions et le Tombeau d'Osorkon II à Tanis.* Paris, 1947.

Montet 1951
P. Montet. *La Nécropole Royale de Tanis* II. *Les Constructions et le Tombeau de Psousennes.* Paris, 1951.

Montet 1952
P. Montet. *Les Engimes de Tanis.* Paris, 1952.

Montet 1961
P. Montet. *Géographie de l'Egypte ancienne, 2. To-Chema, La haute Egypte.* Paris, 1961.

Montet 1981
P. Montet. *Everyday Life in Egypt in the Days of Ramesses the Great.* Philadelphia, 1981.

Morenz 1962
S. Morenz. "The Role of Color in Ancient Egypt," *Palette* 11 (Autumn 1962), pp. 3-9.

Morenz 1964
S. Morenz. *Gott und Mensch im alten Aegypten.* Leipzig, 1964.

Morenz 1965
S. Morenz. "Ägyptischer Totenglaube im Rahmen der Struktur ägyptischer Religion," *Eranos-jahrbuch* 34, 1965 (1967), pp. 399-445.

Morenz 1975
S. Morenz. "Anubis mit dem Schlussel," in *Religion und Geschichte des alten Ägypten,* E. Blumenthal, S. Herrman, and A. Onasch, eds. Cologne, 1975.

Morenz 1973
S. Morenz. *Egyptian Religion,* A.E. Keep, trans. London, 1973.

Moret 1913
A. Moret. *Sarcophages de l'Epoque Bubastite à l'Epoque Saite.* Cairo, 1913.

Moret 1978
A. Moret. *Denkmäler des Alten Reiches* III: *Autels, bassins et tables d'offrandes* fasc. 1: Nos. 57001-57023, rev. and ed. by Dia Abou Ghazi (CG). Cairo, 1978.

Moret 1980
A. Moret. *Denkmäler des Alten Reiches* III: *Autels, bassins et tables d'offrandes* fasc. 2: Nos. 57024-57049, rev. by Dia Abou Ghazi (CG). Cairo, 1980.

Morgan 1976
S.K. Morgan. *Ancient Mediterranean.* Brockton, 1976.

Mostafa 1982
M. Mostafa. *Untersuchungen zu Opfertafeln im Alten Reich.* Hildesheim, 1982.

Moussa and Altenmüller 1971
A. Moussa and H. Altenmüller. *The Tomb of Nefer and Kahay.* Mainz am Rhein, 1971.

Moussa and Junge 1975
A. Moussa and F. Junge. *Two Tombs of Craftsmen.* Mainz am Rhein, 1975.

Mueller 1972
D. Mueller. "An Early Egyptian Guide to the Hereafter," *JEA* 58 (1972), pp. 99-125.

Müller 1963
H.W. Müller. "Isis mit dem Horuskinde," *MJK* 14 (1963), pp. 7-38.

Müller 1964
H.W. Müller. *Ägyptische Kunstwerke, Kleinfunde und Glas in der Sammlung E. und M. Kofler-Truniger, Luzern.* Berlin, 1964.

Müller 1975
H.W. Müller. "Der Stadtfurst von Theban' Montemhet," *MJK* 3. F. 26 (1975), pp. 7-35.

Müller 1977
I. Müller. "Der Vizekönig Merimose" in *Ägypten and Kusch,* E. Endesfelder, K.-H. Priese, W.-F. Rineke and S. Wenig, eds. Berlin, 1977.

Müller 1932
M. Müller. *Die Liebesposie der alten Ägypter.* Leipzig, 1932.

Müller-Winkler 1984
C. Müller-Winkler. "Schen-Ring," *LÄ* V (1984), cols. 577-579.

Müller-Winkler 1986
C. Müller-Winkler. "Udjatauge," *LÄ* VI (1986), cols. 824-826.

Munro 1973
P. Munro. *Die spätägyptischen Totenstelen.* Glückstadt, 1973.

Munster 1968
M. Munster. *Untersuchungen zur Göttin Isis vom Alten Reich bis zum Ende des Neuen Reiches.* Berlin, 1968.

Murray 1925
W. Murray. "The Roman Roads and Stations in the Eastern Desert," *JEA* 11 (1925), pp. 138-150.

Museo Civico Archeologico di Bologna 1982
Il Museo Civico Archeologico di Bologna. Bologna, 1982.

Museum of Fine Arts 1905
Museum of Fine Arts, Boston. "The Exhibition of Recent Acquisitions of the Egyptian Department," *BMFA* III (April, 1905), pp. 13-15.

Museum of Fine Arts 1907
Museum of Fine Arts, Boston. "Objects Newly Installed," *BMFA* V, no. 30 (1907), p. 72.

Museum of Fine Arts 1913
Museum of Fine Arts, Boston. "New Acquisitions of the Egyptian Department," *BMFA* XIV (1913), pp. 53-66.

Museum of Fine Arts 1937
Museum of Fine Arts, Buffalo. *Master Bronzes.* Buffalo, 1937.

Museum of Fine Arts 1955
Museum of Fine Arts, Boston. *Calendar,* April 1955.

Museum of Fine Arts 1976
Museum of Fine Arts, Boston. *Romans and Barbarians.* Boston, 1976.

Museum of Fine Arts 1976-77
Museum of Fine Arts, Boston. *The Museum Year: 1976-77.* Boston, 1977.

Museum of Fine Arts 1978
Museum of Fine Arts, Boston. *Human Figures in Fine Arts.* Tokyo-Kyoto-Nagoya, Japan, April-October 1978.

Museum of Fine Arts 1979
Museum of Fine Arts, Boston. "Egyptian and Ancient Near Eastern Art," *The Museum Year: 1978-79* (1979).

Museum of Fine Arts 1980-81
Museum of Fine Arts, Boston. *One Hundred Sixth Annual Report.* Boston, 1981.

Museum of Fine Arts 1981-82
Museum of Fine Arts, Boston. *The Museum Year: 1981-82.* Boston, 1982.

Museum of Fine Arts 1982
Museum of Fine Arts, Boston. *Egypt's Golden Age: the Art of Living in the New Kingdom, 1558-1085 B.C.* Boston, 1982.

Museum of Fine Arts 1982-83
Museum of Fine Arts, Boston. *The Museum Year: 1982-1983*. Boston, 1983.

Museum of Fine Arts 1986-87
Museum of Fine Arts, Boston. *The Museum Year: 1986-1987*. Boston, 1987.

Museum of Fine Arts 1987a
Museum of Fine Arts. *A Table of Offerings*. Boston, 1987.

Museum of Fine Arts 1987b
Museum of Fine Arts. *Art for Boston, a Decade of Acquisitions under the Directorship of Jan Fontein*. Boston, 1987.

Myers 1933
O.H. Myers. "Two Prehistoric Objects," *JEA* 19 (1933), p. 55.

Myers 1937
O.H. Myers. "Stone Objects," in R. Mond and O.H. Myers, *Cemeteries of Armant I*. London, 1937.

Mysliwiec 1981
K. Mysliwiec. "Aal oder Schlange? – Atum oder Meresger?" *MDAIK* 37 (1981), pp. 377-382.

Nauerth 1986
C. Nauerth. *Koptische Stoffe*. Frankfurt am Main, 1986.

National Museum of Antiquities at Leiden 1987
National Museum of Antiquities at Leiden. Leiden, 1987.

Naville 1886
E. Naville. *Das Ägyptische Totenbuch der XVIII. bis XX. Dynastie* 1. Berlin, 1886.

Naville 1891
E. Naville. *Bubastis*. London, 1891.

Naville 1893-94
E. Naville. "Work at the Temple of Deir el-Bahari," *Egypt Exploration Fund Archaeological Report*. London, 1893-94, pp. 1-7.

Naville 1894
E. Naville. *Ahnas el Medineh (Heracleopolis Magna)*. London, 1894.

Naville 1894-95
E. Naville. "The Excavations at Deir el-Bahari During the Winter, 1894-95," *Egypt Exploration Fund Archaeological Report*. London, 1894-95, pp. 33-37.

Naville 1896
E. Naville. *The Temple of Deir el-Bahari* II. London, 1896.

Naville 1898
E. Naville. *The Temple of Deir el-Bahari* III. London, 1898.

Naville 1900
E. Naville. *The Temple of Deir el-Bahari* IV. London, 1900.

Naville 1907
E. Naville. *The XIth Dynasty Temple at Deir el-Bahari* I. London, 1907.

Naville 1913
E. Naville, ed. *Denkmäler aus Aegypten und Aethiopien herausgegeben und erläutert von Richard Lepsius: Ergänzungsband*. Leipzig, 1913.

Naville and Hall 1913
E. Naville and H.R. Hall. *The XIth Dynasty Temple at Deir el-Bahari* III. London, 1913.

Needler 1963
W. Needler. *An Egyptian Funerary Bed of the Roman Period in the Royal Ontario Museum* (Occasional Paper 6). Toronto, 1963.

Needler 1966
W. Needler. *Jewellery of the Ancient Near East*. Toronto, 1966.

Needler 1981
W. Needler. "A Wooden Statuette of the Late Middle Kingdom," in *Studies in Honor of Dows Dunham*, W.K. Simpson and W.M. Davis, eds. Boston, 1981, pp. 132-136.

Needler 1984
W. Needler. *Predynastic and Archaic Egypt in the Brooklyn Museum*. Brooklyn, 1984.

New Orleans 1977
New Orleans. *Eye for Eye: Egyptian Images and Inscriptions*. New Orleans, 1977.

Newberry 1893a
P.E. Newberry. *El Bersheh* I: *The Tomb of Tehutihetep*. London, 1893.

Newberry 1893b
P.E. Newberry. *Beni Hasan* I. London, 1893.

Newberry 1908
P.E. Newberry. *Scarabs*. London, 1908.

Newberry 1913
P.E. Newberry. "Some Cults of Prehistoric Egypt," *Annals of Archaeology and Anthropology* V (1913), pp. 132-142.

Newberry 1930-1937
P.E. Newberry. *Funerary Statuettes and Model Sarcophagi* (CG). Cairo, 1930-1937.

New York 1984
The Treasury of San Marco, Venice. Metropolitan Museum of Art, N. Y., 1984.

Niwinski 1979
A. Niwinski. "Problems in the Chronology and Genealogy of the XXIst Dynasty: New Proposals for their Interpretation," *JARCE* 16 (1979), pp. 49-68.

Niwinski 1983
A. Niwinski. "Sarg NR-SpZt," *LÄ* V (1983), cols. 434-468.

Niwinski 1984
V. Niwinski. "Seelenhaus," *LÄ* V (1984), cols. 806-813.

Nolte 1968
B. Nolte. *Die Glasgefässe im alten Ägypten*. Berlin, 1968.

Nord 1970
D. Nord. "HKRT NSWT = 'King's Concubine'?" *Serapis* 2 (1970), pp. 1-6.

Nord 1981
D. Nord. "The Term hnr: 'Harem' or 'Musical Performer'? in W.K. Simpson and W. Davis, eds, *Studies in Honor of Dows Dunham*. Boston, 1981, pp. 137-145.

O'Connor 1972
D. O'Connor. "A Regional Population in Egypt to circa 600 B.C.," in B. Spooner, ed., *Population Growth: Anthropological Implications*. Cambridge, 1972, pp. 78-100.

O'Connor 1974
D. O'Connor. "Political Systems and Archaeological Data in Egypt: 2600 - 1780 B.C.," *World Archaeology* 6 (1974), pp. 15-37.

O'Connor 1979
D. O'Connor. "Abydos: The University Museum-Yale University Expedition," *Expedition* 21 no. 2 (1979), pp. 48-49.

Ogden 1982
J. Ogden. *Jewellery of the Ancient World*. New York, 1982.

Otto 1960
E. Otto. *Das Ägyptische Mundöffnungsritual. Teil II: Kommentar* (Ägyptologische Abhandlungen 3). Wiesbaden, 1960.

Otto 1975
E. Otto. "Abydos-Fetisch," *LÄ* I (1975), cols. 47-48.

Parker et al. 1979
R. Parker, J. Leclant, and J.-C. Goyon. *The Edifice of Taharqa by the Sacred Lake of Karnak*. Providence, 1979.

Parlasca 1963
K. Parlasca. "A Painted Egyptian Mummy Shroud of the Roman Period," *Archaeology* 16 no. 4 (Winter 1963), p. 266.

Parlasca 1966
K. Parlasca. *Mumienporträts und verwandte Denkmäler*. Wiesbaden, 1966.

Parlasca 1969
K. Parlasca. *Ritratti di Mummie* I (Repertorio d'Arte dell'Egitto Greco-Romano, Series B, A. Adriani, ed.). Palermo, 1969.

Parlasca 1970
K. Parlasca. "Zur Stellung der Terenuthis-Stelen-eine Gruppe römischer Grabreliefs aus Ägypten in Berlin," *MDAIK* 26 (1970).

Parlasca 1975
K. Parlasca. "Hellenistische Grabreliefs aus Ägypten," *MDAIK* 31 (1975).

Parlasca 1977
K. Parlasca. *Ritratti di Mummie* 2, (Repertorio d'Arte dell'Egitto Greco-Roman Series B, A. Adriani, ed.). Rome, 1977.

Parlasca 1978
K. Parlasca. "Der Übergang von der spätrömischen zur frühkoptischen Kunst im Lichte der Grabreliefs von Oxyrhynchus," *Enchoria* 8 (Sonderband 1978).

Parlasca 1980
K. Parlasca. *Ritratti di Mummie* 3, (Repertorio d'Arte dell'Egitto Greco-Roman Series B, A. Adriani, ed.). Rome, 1980.

Pavlov and Matthew 1958
V.V. Pavlov and M.E. Matthew. *Monuments of Ancient Egyptian Art in the Museums of the Soviet Union*. Moscow, 1958.

Peet 1914
T.E. Peet. *Cemeteries of Abydos Part II, 1911-12*. London, 1914.

Peet and Woolley 1923
T.E. Peet and L. Woolley. *The City of Akhenaten* 1. London, 1923.

Petrie 1886
W.M.F. Petrie. *Naukratis* I, 1884-85. London, 1886.

Petrie 1888a
W.M.F. Petrie. *A Season in Egypt: 1887*. London, 1888.

Petrie 1888b
W.M.F. Petrie. *Nebesheh (Am) and Defenneh (Taphanhes)*. London, 1888.

Petrie 1889
W.M.F. Petrie. *Hawara, Biahmu, and Arsinoe*. London, 1889.

Petrie 1890
W.M.F. Petrie. *Kahun, Gurob, and Hawara*. London, 1890.

Petrie 1891
W.M.F. Petrie. *Illahun, Kahun, and Gurob*. London, 1891.

Petrie 1892
W.M.F. Petrie. *Medum*. London, 1892.

Petrie 1896
W.M.F. Petrie. *Naqada and Ballas*. London, 1896.

Petrie 1900a
W.M.F. Petrie. *Dendereh*. London, 1900.

Petrie 1900b
W.M.F. Petrie. *The Royal Tombs of the First Dynasty* I. London, 1900.

Petrie 1901a
W.M.F. Petrie. *The Royal Tombs of the Earliest Dynasties* II. London, 1901.

Petrie 1901b
W.M.F. Petrie. *Diospolis Parva: The Cemeteries of Abadiyeh and Hu*. London, 1901.

Petrie 1902
W.M.F. Petrie. *Abydos I*. London, 1902.

Petrie 1905
W.M.F. Petrie. *Ehnasya*. London, 1905.

Petrie 1907
W.M.F. Petrie. *Gizeh and Rifeh*. London, 1907.

Petrie 1909
W.M.F. Petrie. *Qurna*. London, 1909.

Petrie 1911
W.M.F. Petrie. *Roman Portraits and Memphis* IV. London, 1911.

Petrie 1912
W.M.F. Petrie. *The Labyrinth, Gerzeh, and Mazghuneh*. London, 1912.

Petrie 1913
W.M.F. Petrie. *The Hawara Portfolio: Paintings from the Roman Age*. London, 1913.

Petrie 1914
W.M.F. Petrie. *Amulets*. London, 1914.

Petrie 1920
W.M.F. Petrie. *Prehistoric Egypt*. London, 1920.

Petrie 1925a
W.M.F. Petrie. *Buttons and Design Scarabs*. London, 1925.

Petrie 1925b
W.M.F. Petrie. *Tombs of the Courtiers and Oxyrhynkhos*. London, 1925.

Petrie 1930
W.M.F. Petrie. *Antaeopolis*. London, 1930.

Petrie and Brunton 1924
W.M.F. Petrie and G. Brunton. *Sedment I*. London, 1924.

Petrie and Mackay 1915
W.M.F. Petrie and E. Mackay. *Heliopolis, Kafr Ammar and Shurafa*. London, 1915.

Pettigrew 1834
T.J. Pettigrew. *A History of Egyptian Mummies*. London, 1834, reprinted Los Angeles, 1983.

Phillips 1948
D.W. Phillips. "A Sculptor's Shawabty Box," *BMMA* 6 (March, 1948), pp. 207-212.

Piankoff 1954
A. Piankoff. *The Tomb of Ramesses* VI. New York, 1954

Piankoff 1955
A. Piankoff. *The Shrines of Tut-ankh-amon* (Bollingen Series XL, Egyptian Religious Texts and Representations, 2). New York, 1955.

Piankoff 1957
A. Piankoff. *Mythological Papyri* (Bollingen Series XL, Egyptian Religious Texts and Representations 3). New York, 1977.

Piankoff 1964
A. Piankoff. "Quel est le 'Livre' appelé 𓏞𓆓𓏏𓏲𓏛𓂝 *BIFAO* 62 (1964), pp. 147-149.

Piankoff 1968
A. Piankoff. *The Pyramid of Unas* (Bollingen Series XL, Egyptian Religious Texts and Representations, 5). Princeton, 1968.

Pierret 1878
P. Pierret. *Recueil d'inscriptions inédites du Musée Egyptien du Louvre* vol. 2. Paris, 1878.

Piotrovsky 1974
B. Piotrovsky. *Egyptian Antiquities in the Hermitage Museum, Leningrad*. Leningrad, 1974.

Porter 1983
B.A. Porter. "Burial Chamber of the Treasurer Sobekmose," Information panel text, Metropolitan Museum of Art, 1983.

Porter 1986
B.A. Porter. "Egyptian Decorated Faience Bowls of Early Dynasty 18 from Thebes from the Excavations of The Metropolitan Museum of Art and Lord Carnarvon and Howard Carter," (Master's thesis, Columbia University, New York, 1986).

Porter and Moss 1931
B. Porter and R. Moss. *Topographical Bibliography of Ancient Egyptian Hieroglyphic Texts, Reliefs, and Paintings* III: *Memphis*. Oxford, 1931.

Porter and Moss 1934
B. Porter and R. Moss. *Topographical Bibliography of Ancient Egyptian Hieroglyphic Texts, Reliefs, and Paintings* IV: *Lower and Middle Egypt*. Oxford, 1934.

Porter and Moss 1937
B. Porter and R. Moss. *Topographical Bibliography of Ancient Egyptian Hieroglyphic Texts, Reliefs, and Paintings* V: *Upper Egypt: Sites*. Oxford, 1937.

Porter and Moss 1939
B. Porter and R. Moss. *Topographical Bibliography of Ancient Egyptian Hieroglyphic Texts, Reliefs, and Paintings* VI: *Upper Egypt: Chief Temples*. Oxford, 1939.

Porter and Moss 1960
B. Porter and R. Moss. *Topographical Bibliography of Ancient Egyptian Hieroglyphic Texts, Reliefs, and Paintings* I: *The Theban Necropolis* pt. 1: *Private Tombs,* 2nd edition, revised and augmented. Oxford, 1960.

Porter and Moss 1964
B. Porter and R. Moss. *Topographical Bibliography of Ancient Egyptian Hieroglyphic Texts, Reliefs, and Paintings* I: *The Theban Necropolis* pt. 2: 2nd ed., rev. and aug. Oxford, 1964.

Porter and Moss 1974
B. Porter and R. Moss. *Topographical Bibliography of Ancient Egyptian Hieroglyphic Texts, Reliefs, and Paintings* III: *Memphis* pt. 1: *Abû Rawâsh to Abûsir,* 2nd ed., rev. and aug. by J. Málek. Oxford, 1974.

Porter and Moss 1978
B. Porter and R. Moss. *Topographical Bibliography of Ancient Egyptian Hieroglyphic Texts, Reliefs, and Paintings* III. *Memphis* pt. 2.1: *Saqqâra to Dahshûr,* 2nd ed., rev. and aug. by J. Málek. Oxford, 1978.

Porter and Moss 1979
B. Porter and R. Moss. *Topographical Bibliography of Ancient Egyptian Hieroglyphic Texts, Reliefs, and Paintings* III. *Memphis* pt. 2.2: *Saqqâra to Dahshûr,* 2nd ed., rev. and aug. by J. Málek. Oxford, 1979.

Porter and Moss 1981
B. Porter and R. Moss. *Topographical Bibliography of Ancient Egyptian Hieroglyphic Texts, Reliefs, and Paintings* III. *Memphis* pt. 2.3: *Saqqâra to Dahshûr,* 2nd ed., rev. and aug. by J. Málek. Oxford, 1981.

Posener 1981
G. Posener. "Les 'afarit' dans l'ancienne Egypte," *MDAIK* 37 (1981), pp. 393-401.

Posener-Kriéger 1976
P. Posener-Kriéger. *Les Archives du temple funéraire de Neferirkare-Kakai* (Bibliothèque d'Etude 65). Cairo, 1976.

Posener-Kriéger 1977
P. Posener-Kriéger. "Les Mesures des Etoffes à l'Ancien Empire," *RdE* 29 (1977), pp. 86-96.

Posener-Kriéger and de Cenival 1968
P. Posener-Kriéger and J.-L. de Cenival. *The Abu Sir Papyri* (Hieratic Papyri in the British Museum, Fifth Series). London, 1968.

Price 1897
A Catalogue of the Egyptian Antiquities in the Possession of F.G. Hilton Price. London, 1897.

Prominska 1986
E. Prominska. "Ancient Egyptian Traditions of Artificial Mummification in the Christian Period in Egypt," in *Science in Egyptology*, A.R. David, ed. Manchester, 1986, pp. 113-122.

Quaegebeur 1978
J. Quaegebeur. "Mummy Labels: An Orientation," in *Texts Grecs, Démotiques et Bilingues* (Papyrologica Lugduno-Batava 19), E. Boswinkel, P.W. Pestman, eds. Leiden, 1978.

Quaegebeur 1980
J. Quaegebeur. "Mumienetiketten," *LÄ* IV (1980), cols. 216-217.

Quaegebeur 1983
J. Quaegebeur. "Apis et la Menat," *BSFE* 98 (October 1983).

Quibell 1898
J.E. Quibell. *The Ramesseum and Tomb of Ptah-Hetep*. London, 1898.

Quibell 1908
J.E. Quibell. *Tomb of Yuaa and Thuiu* (CG). Cairo, 1908.

Quibell 1909
J.E. Quibell. *Excavations at Saqqara (1907-1908)*. Cairo, 1909.

Quibell 1923
J.E. Quibell. *Excavations at Saqqara (1912-1914): Archaic Mastabas*. Cairo, 1923.

Quibell and Hayter 1927
J.E. Quibell and A.G.K. Hayter. *Excavations at Saqqara: Teti Pyramid, North Side*. Cairo, 1927.

Radwan 1983
A. Radwan. *Die Kupfer-und Bronzegfässe Ägyptens*. Munich, 1983.

Raisman and Martin 1984
V. Raisman and G.T. Martin. *Canopic Equipment in the Petrie Collection*. Warminster, 1984.

Rammant-Peeters 1983
A. Rammant-Peeters. *Les pyramidions égyptiens du Nouvel Empire*. Louvain, 1983.

Randall-MacIver and Mace 1902
D. Randall-MacIver and A.C. Mace. *El Amrah and Abydos (1899-1901)* (Egypt Exploration Fund, Monograph 23). London, 1902.

Ranke 1935
H. Ranke. *Die Ägyptischen Personennamen* I. Glückstadt, 1935.

Ranke 1948
H. Ranke. *Meisterwerke der Ägyptischen Kunst.* Basel, 1948.

Raven 1978-1979
M.J. Raven. "Papyrus-Sheaths and Ptah-Sokar-Osiris Statues," *OMRO* 59-60 (1978-79), pp. 251-296.

Raven 1981
M.J. Raven. "On some coffins of the Besenmut Family," *OMRO* 62 (1981), pp. 1-7.

Raven 1982
M.J. Raven. "Corn Mummies," *OMRO* 63 (1982), pp. 7-34.

Raven 1983
M.J. Raven. "Wax in Egyptian Magic and Symbolism," *OMRO* 64 (1983), pp. 7-47.

Ray 1976
J.D. Ray. *The Archive of Hor.* London, 1976.

Reeves forthcoming
C.N. Reeves. *Valley of the Kings: The Decline of a Royal Necropolis.* London, forthcoming.

Reeves and Ryan 1987
C.N. Reeves and D.P. Ryan. "Inscribed Egyptian Funerary Cones In Situ: An Early Observation by Henry Salt," *Varia Aegyptiaca* 3 (1987), pp. 47-49.

Reisner 1899
G.A. Reisner. "The Date of Canopic Jars of the Gizeh Museum," *ZÄS* 37 (1899), pp. 61-72.

Reisner 1907
G.A. Reisner. *Amulets* (CG). Cairo, 1907.

Reisner 1910
G.A. Reisner. *The Archaeological Survey of Lower Nubia, Report for 1907-1908.* Cairo, 1910.

Reisner 1913
G.A. Reisner. "New Acquisitions of the Egyptian Department: A Family of Builders of the Sixth Dynasty," *BMFA* 11 (November 1913), pp. 53-66.

Reisner 1923a
G.A. Reisner. *Excavations at Kerma* I-III (Harvard African Studies V). Cambridge, 1923.

Reisner 1923b
G.A. Reisner. *Excavations at Kerma* IV-V (Harvard African Studies VI). Cambridge, 1923.

Reisner 1929a
G.A. Reisner. "Ancient Egyptian Forts at Semna and Uronarti," *BMFA* 27 (October, 1929).

Reisner 1929b
G.A. Reisner. MSS, Diary, Giza 1929, March 4-December 4, 1929. Object Register, Giza, 29-4-241 to 29-11-289.

Reisner 1930
G.A. Reisner. Object Register, Giza, 29-11-390 to 30-1-99. 1929-1930.

Reisner 1931
G.A. Reisner. *Mycerinus.* Cambridge, 1931.

Reisner 1932a
G.A. Reisner. *A Provincial Cemetery of the Pyramid Age: Naga ed-Dêr* III. Oxford, 1932.

Reisner 1932b
G.A. Reisner. "The Position of Early Grave Stelae," in *Studies Presented to F.Ll. Griffith,* S.R.K. Glanville, ed. London, 1932, pp. 324-331.

Reisner 1936
G.A. Reisner. *The Development of the Egyptian Tomb Down to the Accession of Cheops.* Cambridge, Mass., 1936.

Reisner 1942
G.A. Reisner. *A History of the Giza Necropolis* I. Cambridge, Mass., 1942.

Reisner 1967
G.A. Reisner. *Canopics* (CG). Cairo, 1967.

Reisner unpublished
G.A. Reisner. "A History of the Giza Necropolis 1.2." Department of Egyptian and Ancient Near Eastern Art, Museum of Fine Arts, Boston.

Reisner and Smith 1955
G.A. Reisner and W.S. Smith. *A History of the Giza Necropolis* II. Cambridge, Mass., 1955.

Rhind 1862
A.H. Rhind. *Thebes: Its Tombs and their Tenants, Ancient and Present.* London, 1862.

Ricke 1944
H. Ricke. *Bemerkungen zur ägyptischen Baukunst des Alten Reiches* (Beiträge zur ägyptischen Bauforschung und Altertumskunde IV). Zurich, 1944.

Ricke 1950
H. Ricke. *Bemerkungen zur ägyptischen Baukunst des Alten Reiches* (Beiträge zur ägyptischen Bauforschung und Altertumskunde, V, II). Zurich, 1950.

Ricke 1960
H. Ricke. *Die Tempel Nektanebos' II. in Elephantine und ihre Erweiterungen* (Beiträge zur ägyptischen Bauforschung und Altertumskunde VI). Zurich, 1960.

Ridley 1973
R.T. Ridley. *The Unification of Egypt.* Deception Bay, 1973.

Riefstahl 1944a
E. Riefstahl. *Patterned Textiles in Pharaonic Egypt.* Brooklyn, 1944.

Riefstahl 1944b
E. Riefstahl. "Doll, Queen or Goddess?" *Brooklyn Museum Journal 1943-1944* (1944).

Ritner 1985
R.K. Ritner. "Anubis and the Lunar Disc," *JEA* 71 (1985), pp. 149-155.

Roeder 1937
G. Roeder. *Ägyptische Bronzewerke.* Gluckstadt, Hamburg, and New York, 1937.

Roeder 1956
G. Roeder, *Ägyptische Bronzefiguren.* Berlin, 1956.

Roehrig 1976
C.H. Roehrig. "First Intermediate Period Seal-Amulets." (Master's thesis, Bryn Mawr College, 1976.)

Roemer- und Pelizaeus-Museum 1985
Roemer- und Pelizaeus-Museum Hildesheim, *Nofret - Die Schöne. Die Frau im Alten Ägypten.* Hildesheim, 1985.

Rogouline 1965
Mlle. Rogouline. "Evolution des réceptacles à canopes," *BIFAO* 63 (1965), pp. 237-254.

Root 1979
M.C. Root. *Faces of Immortality. Egyptian Mummies, Masks, Painted Portraits, and Canopic Jars in the Kelsey Museum of Archaeology.* Ann Arbor, 1979.

Ross 1931
E.D. Ross. *The Art of Egypt through the Ages.* London, 1931.

Rossiter 1979
E. Rossiter. *The Book of the Dead: Papyri of Ani, Hunefer, Anha.* Geneva, 1979.

Rössler-Köhler 1980
U. Rössler-Köhler. "Jenseitsvorstellungen," *LÄ* III (1980), cols. 252-267.

Rostem 1943
O.R. Rostem. "Note on the Method of Lowering the Lid of the Sarcophagus in a Saite Tomb of Saqqara," *ASAE* 43 (1943), pp. 351-356.

Roth forthcoming
A.M. Roth. "The Distribution of the Old Kingdom Title Hntj-š," *SAK (Proceedings of the 4th International Congress of Egyptology, 1985),* in press.

Rühlmann 1971
G. Rühlmann. "Deine Feinde fallen unter deine Sohlen, Bemerkungen zu einen altorientalischen Machtsymbol," *Wissenschaftliche Zeitschrift der Martin-Luther-Universität,* Gesellschafts- und sprachwissenschaftliche Reihe, Halle-Wittenberg XX G, H. 2 (1971), pp. 61-84.

Saad 1945-1947
Z. Saad. *Royal Excavations at Helwan.* Cairo, 1945-1947.

Sakkara 1938
The Sakkara Expedition. *The Mastaba of Mereruka* 2. Chicago, 1938.

Saleh and Sourouzian 1987
M. Saleh and H. Sourouzian. *Official Catalogue: The Egyptian Museum Cairo.* Mainz, 1987.

Samson 1972
J. Samson. *Amarna.* Warminster, 1972.

Satzinger 1978
H. Satzinger. "Der Leiter des Speicherwesens Si-êse Sohn des Qeni und seine Wiener Statue," *Jahrbuch der Kunsthistorisches Sammlungen in Wien* 74 (1978).

Sauneron 1952a
S. Sauneron, ed. *Rituel de l'embaumement.* Cairo, 1952.

Sauneron 1952b
S. Sauneron. "Note sur une Bandelette Decorée," *BIFAO* 51 (1952).

Sauneron 1957
S. Sauneron. *Les prêtres de l'ancienne Egypte.* Paris, 1957.

Sauneron 1968
S. Sauneron. "Quelques Monuments de Soumenou au Musée de Brooklyn," *Kêmi* 18 (1968), pp. 57-78.

Schäfer 1906
H. Schäfer. "Die Entstehung einiger Mumienamulette," *ZÄS* 43 (1906), pp. 66-70.

Schäfer 1932
H. Schäfer. "Djed-Pfeiler, Lebenszeichen, Osiris, Isis," in *Studies presented to F. Ll. Griffith,* S.R.K. Glanville, ed. London, 1932, pp. 424-443.

Schäfer 1974
H. Schäfer. *Principles of Egyptian Art,* J. Baines, trans. Oxford, 1974.

Scharff 1922
A. Scharff. "Ein Rechnungsbuch des königlichen Hofes aus der 13. Dynastie," *ZÄS* 57 (1922), pp. 51-68.

Scharff 1931
A. Scharff. *Altertümer der Vor-und Frühzeit Ägyptens* 1. Berlin, 1931.

Schenkel 1962
W. Schenkel. *Frühmittelägyptische Studien.* Bonn, 1962.

Schenkel 1983
W. Schenkel. "Säugen," *LÄ* V (1983), cols. 339-342.

Schiaparelli 1927
E. Schiaparelli. *La tomba intatta dell' architetto Cha.* Turin, 1927.

Schlögl 1975
H. Schlögl. "Eine Uschebti der Ramessidenzeit," *Oriens Antiquus* 14 (1975), pp. 145-146.

Schlögl and Sguaitamatti 1977
H. Schlögl and M. Sguaitamatti. *Arbeiter des Jenseits* (Zürcher Archäologischer Hefte 2). Zurich, 1977.

Schmidt 1919
V. Schmidt. *Sarkofager, Mumiekister, og Mumiehylstre I Det Gamle Aegypted. Typologisk Atlas.* Copenhagen, 1919.

Schneider 1975
H.D. Schneider. "Provincial Roman Art from El Behnasa," *Verlenging Antieke Beschaving* 50.1 (1975).

Schneider 1977
H.D. Schneider. *Shabtis: An Introduction to the History of Ancient Egyptian Funerary Statuettes with a Catalogue of the Collection of Shabtis in the National Museum of Antiquities at Leiden,* 3 vols. Leiden, 1977.

Schneider 1982
H.D. Schneider. *Beelden van Behnasa.* Zutphen, 1982.

Schneider and Raven 1981
H.D. Schneider and M.J. Raven. *Die Egyptische Oudheid.* Gravenhage, 1981.

Schott 1945
S. Schott. *Mythe und Mythenbildung im alten Ägypten* (Untersuchungen zur Geschichte und Altertumskunde Ägyptens 15). Leipzig, 1945.

Schulz 1987
R. Schulz in *Ägyptens Aufstieg zur Weltmacht,* A. Eggebrecht, ed. Mainz, 1987.

Scott 1958
N.E. Scott. "The Cat of Bastet," *BMMA* (Summer 1958).

Scott 1986
G. Scott. *Ancient Egyptian Art at Yale.* New Haven, 1986.

Seeber 1976
C. Seeber. *Untersuchungen zur Darstellung des Totengerichts im Alten Ägypten.* Munich and Berlin, 1976.

Seeber 1978
C. Seeber. "Jenseitsgericht," *LÄ* III (1978), cols. 249-252.

Sethe 1906
K. Sethe. *Urkunden der 18. Dynastie* 1. Leipzig, 1906.

Sethe 1908-1922
K. Sethe. *Die Altägyptischen Pyramidentexte,* 4 vols. Leipzig, 1908-1922.

Sethe 1933
K. Sethe. *Urkunden des Alten Reiches I,* 2nd ed. Leipzig, 1933.

Sethe 1934
K. Sethe. "Zur Geschichte der Einbalsamierung bei den Ägyptern und einiger damit verbundener Bräuche," *Sitzungsberichte der Preussichen Akademie der Wissenschaften Phil-Hist. Klasse* 13 (1934), pp. 12*-15*.

Settgast 1963
J. Settgast. *Untersuchungen zu altägyptischen Bestattungsdarstellungen.* Glückstadt, 1963.

Shore 1962
A.F. Shore. *Portrait Painting from Roman Egypt.* London, 1962.

Shore and Smith 1956
A.F. Shore and H.S. Smith. "A Demotic Embalmer's Agreement," *Acta Orientalia* 25 (1956), pp. 277-294.

Shorter 1931
A.W. Shorter. "The Study of Egyptian Funerary Amulets," *CdE* 6 (1931).

Shorter 1934
A.W. Shorter in *Bucheum I,* R. Mond and O.H. Myers. London, 1934.

Shorter 1935
A.W. Shorter. "Notes on some Funerary Amulets," *JEA* 21 (1935), pp. 171-176.

Shorter and Edwards 1938
A.W. Shorter and I.E.S. Edwards. *A Handbook of Egyptian Mummies and Coffins Exhibited in the British Museum.* London, 1938.

Simpson 1970
W.K. Simpson. "A Late Old Kingdom Letter to the Dead from Nag' ed-Deir N 3500," *JEA* 56 (1970), pp. 58-64.

Simpson 1972a
W.K. Simpson. "A Tomb Chapel Relief of the Reign of Amunemhet III and Some Observations of the Length of the Reign of Sesostris III," *CdE* 47 (1972).

Simpson 1972b
W.K. Simpson. "Acquisitions in Egyptian and Ancient Near Eastern Art in the Boston Museum of Fine Arts, 1970-71," *Connoisseur* 179, no. 720 (1972), pp. 113-122.

Simpson 1972c
W.K. Simpson. "Two Egyptian Bas Reliefs of the Late Old Kingdom," *Bulletin of the North Carolina Museum of Art* 11 (1972), pp. 3-13.

Simpson 1973a
W.K. Simpson. *The Literature of Ancient Egypt: An Anthology of Stories, Instructions, and Poetry,* 2nd ed. New Haven and London, 1973.

Simpson 1973b
W.K. Simpson. "Ptolemaic-Roman Cartonnage Footcases with Prisoner Bound and Tied," *ZÄS* 100 (1973), pp. 50-54.

Simpson 1973c
W.K. Simpson in *The Museum Year: 1972-73, Museum of Fine Arts, Boston.* Boston, 1973, pp. 47-51.

Simpson 1974a
W.K. Simpson. *The Terrace of the Great God at Abydos: The Offering Chapels of Dynasties 12 and 13.* New Haven and Philadelphia, 1974.

Simpson 1974b
W.K. Simpson. "The Middle Kingdom in Egypt: Some Recent Acquisitions," *BMFA* 72 (1974).

Simpson 1974c
W.K. Simpson. "Polygamy in Egypt in the Middle Kingdom?" *JEA* 60 (1974), pp. 100-105.

Simpson 1976a
W.K. Simpson. *The Mastabas of Qar and Idu.* Boston, 1976.

Simpson 1976b
W.K. Simpson. *The Offering Chapel of Sekhem-ankh-Ptah in the Museum of Fine Arts, Boston.* Boston, 1976.

Simpson 1977
W.K. Simpson. *The Face of Egypt: Permanence and Change in Egyptian Art.* Katonah, New York, 1977.

Simpson 1981
W.K. Simpson. "A Shawabti Box Lid of the Chief Steward Nia (Iniuya) Acquired by General Jean-Joseph Tarayre," *Bulletin de Centaire* (Supp. *BIFAO* 1981), pp. 325-329.

Simpson 1984
W.K. Simpson. "Sesostris III," *LÄ* V (1984), cols. 903-906.

Simpson 1985
W.K. Simpson. "A Stela of the Chief Coppersmith Ahmose," in F. Geus and F. Thill, eds., *Mélanges offerts à Jean Vercoutter.* Paris, 1985.

Slater 1982
R.A. Slater. *The Archaeology of Dendereh in the First Intermediate Period.* Ann Arbor, 1982.

Slugett 1980
J. Slugett. "Mummification in Ancient Egypt," *MASCA Journal* 1 (Supplement, 1980), pp. 163-167.

Smelik 1979
K.A.D. Smelik. "The Cult of the Ibis in the Graeco-Roman Period," in *Studies in Hellenistic Religions.* Leiden, 1979, pp. 225-243.

Smith 1935
W.S. Smith. "The Old Kingdom Linen List," *ZÄS* 71 (1935), pp. 134-149.

Smith 1942
W.S. Smith. *Ancient Egypt as represented in the Museum of Fine Arts, Boston.* Boston, 1942.

Smith 1946a
W.S. Smith. *Ancient Egypt as represented in the Museum of Fine Arts, Boston.* Boston, 1946.

Smith 1946b
W.S. Smith. *A History of Egyptian Sculpture and Painting in the Old Kingdom.* London, 1946.

Smith 1949
W.S. Smith. *A History of Egyptian Sculpture and Painting in the Old Kingdom* 2nd ed. London, 1949.

Smith 1951
W.S. Smith. "Paintings of the Egyptian Middle Kingdom at Bersheh," *AJA* 55 (1951), pp. 321-332.

Smith 1952
W.S. Smith. *Ancient Egypt as represented in the Museum of Fine Arts, Boston.* Boston, 1952.

Smith 1957
W.S. Smith. "Painting in the Assiut Tomb of Hepzefa," *MDAIK* 15 (1957).

Smith 1958
W.S. Smith. *The Art and Architecture of Ancient Egypt.* Baltimore, 1958.

Smith 1960
W.S. Smith. *Ancient Egypt as represented in the Museum of Fine Arts, Boston.* Boston, 1960.

Smith 1981
W.S. Smith. *The Art and Architecture of Ancient Egypt,* rev. by W.K. Simpson. Harmondsworth, 1981.

Smith 1974
H.S. Smith. *A Visit to Ancient Egypt. Life at Memphis and Saqqara (c. 500-530 B.C.).* Warminster, 1974.

Smith 1987
M. Smith. *Catalogue of Demotic Papyri in the British Museum III: The Mortuary Texts of Papyrus BM 10507.* London, 1987, pp. 69-70.

Sotheby 1976
Sotheby Parke Bernet. *Antiquities and Islamic Works of Art, May 8, 1976.* New York, 1976.

Sotheby's London 1987
Sotheby's London, Sale Catalogue for 13 and 14 July 1987. London, 1987.

Spanel 1986
D.B. Spanel. "Notes on the Terminology for Funerary Figurines," *SAK* 13 (1986), pp. 249-253.

Spencer 1982
A.J. Spencer. *Death in Ancient Egypt.* Harmondsworth and New York, 1982.

Spiegel 1935
J. Spiegel. *Die Idee vom Totengericht in der ägyptischen Religion.* Glückstadt, 1935.

Spiegel 1971
J. Spiegel. *Die Auferstehungsritual der Unas-Pyramide.* Wiesbaden, 1971.

Spiegelberg 1927
W. Spiegelberg. "Die Falkenbezeichnung des Verstorbenen in der Spätzeit," *ZÄS* 62 (1927), pp. 27-34.

Spiegelberg 1928
W. Spiegelberg. "Sitzungen der Kunstwissenschaftlichen Gesellschaft München 1927-28," Sitzung am 6. Dezember 1928, *Münchner Jahrbuch der Bildenden Kunst* N.F. 6 (1929), pp. 102-105.

Stadelmann 1981
R. Stadelmann. "Die ḫntyw-š der Königsbezirk š n pr-ᶜₐ und die Namen der Grabanlagen der Frühzeit," *Bulletin du centenaire, BIFAO* 81 Supplement (1981), pp. 153-164.

Stadelmann-Sourouzian 1984
H. Stadelmann-Sourouzian. "Rischi-Sarg," *LÄ* V (1984), cols. 267-269.

Staehlin 1966
E. Staehlin. *Untersuchungen zur ägyptischen Tracht in Alten Reich.* Berlin, 1966.

Stathatos 1957
Collection Hélène Stathatos, Les objets byzantins et post-byzantins. Limoges, 1957.

Steier 1938
A. Steier. "Pfau," *Paulys Real-Encyclopädie der classischen Altertumswissenschaft,* Bd. 19., Stuttgart, 1938, cols. 1414-1421.

Steindorff 1896
G. Steindorff. *Grabfunde des Mittleren Reichs in den Königlichen Museen zu Berlin* 1 (Mitteilungen aus den Orientalischen Sammlungen VIII). Berlin, 1896.

Steindorff 1901
G. Steindorff. *Grabfunde des Mittleren Reichs in den Königlichen Museen zu Berlin* 2. Berlin, 1901.

Steindorff 1913
G. Steindorff. *Das Grab Des Ti.* Leipzig, 1913.

Steindorff 1937
G. Steindorff. *Aniba* 2 (Service des Antiquités de l'Egypte, Mission Archéologique de Nubie 1929-1934). Glückstadt, Hamburg, New York, 1937.

Steindorff 1946a
G. Steindorff. *Catalogue of the Egyptian Sculpture in the Walters Art Gallery.* Baltimore, 1946.

Steindorff 1946b
G. Steindorff. "The Magical Knives of the Middle Kingdom," *Journal of the Walters Art Gallery* 9 (1946), pp. 41-51, 106-107.

Stewart 1967
H.M. Stewart. "Stelophorous Statuettes in the British Museum," *JEA* 53 (1967).

Strabo 1927
Strabo. *Geography,* H. Jones, trans. Loeb Classical Library. Cambridge, Mass., 1927.

Strauss 1974
E.C. Strauss. *Die Nunschale. Eine Gefässgruppe des Neuen Reiches.* Munich and Berlin, 1974.

Stricker 1943
B.H. Stricker. "Een egyptisch cultusbeeld uit grieksch-romeinschen Tijd." *OMRO* 24 (1943), pp. 1-10.

Strouhal 1986
E. Strouhal in *Science in Egyptology,* A.R. David, ed. Manchester, 1986.

Strudwick 1981
N. Strudwick. *The Administration of Egypt in the Old Kingdom.* London, 1981.

Struve 1968
V.V. Struve. *Etyudy po istorii severnogo Prichernomor'ya Kavakazai Sredney Azil.* Leningrad, 1968.

Sutherland 1984
C.H.V. Sutherland, ed., *The Roman Imperial Coinage* I. London, 1984.

Sutherland 1987
C.H.V. Sutherland. *Roman History and Coinage.* Oxford, 1987.

Svoronos 1908
J.N. Svoronos. *Die Münzen der Ptolemaeer.* Athens, 1908.

Taylor 1984
J.H. Taylor. "A Priestly Family of the 25th Dynasty," *CdE* 59 (1984), pp. 55-71.

Taylor 1985
J.H. Taylor. *The Development of Theban Coffins during the Third Intermediate Period: A Typological Study* (Dissertation, University of Birmingham, 1985).

Taylor, forthcoming
J.H. Taylor. "Some Late Coffins from Akhmim."

Taylor forthcoming b
J.H. Taylor. "Egypt, Ancient: Funerary Art." *The Dictionary of Art* (forthcoming).

Tefnin 1984
R. Tefnin. "Discours et iconicité dans l'Art égyptien," *GM* 79 (1984), pp. 55-71.

Terrace 1967
E.L.B. Terrace. *Egyptian Paintings of the Middle Kingdom: the Tomb of Djehuti-nekht.* New York, 1967.

Terrace 1968a
E.L.B. Terrace. "An Age of Reflection: The Egyptian Middle Kingdom in Boston," *Connoisseur* (August 1968), pp. 265-272.

Terrace 1968b
E.L.B. Terrace. "The Entourage of an Egyptian Governor," *BMFA* 66, no. 343 (1968).

Terrace and Fischer 1970
E.L.B. Terrace and H.G. Fischer. *Treasures of Egyptian Art from the Cairo Museum.* London, 1970.

Te Velde 1967
H. te Velde. *Seth, God of Confusion.* Leiden, 1967.

Te Velde 1982a
H. te Velde. "The Cat as Sacred Animal of the Goddess Mut," in *Studies in Egyptian Religion Dedicated to Professor Jan Zandee.* Leiden, 1982.

Te Velde 1982b
H. te Velde. "Commemoration in Ancient Egypt," in *Visible Religion: Annual for Religious Iconography I: Commemorative Figures.* Leiden, 1982.

Theodorides 1971
A. Theodorides. "The Concept of Law in Ancient Egypt," in *The Legacy of Egypt,* 2nd ed., J.R. Harris, ed. Oxford, 1971.

Thompson 1971
D.L. Thompson. *Coptic Textiles in the Brooklyn Museum.* Brooklyn, 1971.

Thompson 1976
D.L. Thompson. *The Artists of the Mummy Portraits.* Malibu, 1976.

Thompson 1982
D.L. Thompson. *Mummy Portraits in the J. Paul Getty Museum.* Malibu, 1982.

Trigger et al. 1983
B. Trigger, B.J. Kemp, D. O'Connor, and A.B. Lloyd. *Ancient Egypt: A Social History.* Cambridge, 1986.

Trilling 1982
J. Trilling. *The Roman Heritage: Textiles from Egypt and the Eastern Mediterranean.* Washington, D.C., 1982.

Tufnell and Ward 1966
O. Tufnell and W.A. Ward. "Relations between Byblos, Egypt, and Mesopotamia at the End of the Third Millennium B.C. A Study of the Montet Jar," *Syria* 43 (1966).

Tyler and Griffith 1894
J.J. Tyler and F. Ll. Griffith. *The Tomb of Paheri.* London, 1894.

Ucko and Hodges 1963
P.J. Ucko and H.W.M. Hodges. "Some Pre-Dynastic Egyptian Figurines: Problems of Authenticity," *Journal of the Warburg and Courtauld Institutes* 26 (1963), pp. 205-222.

Ucko 1968
P.J. Ucko. *Anthropomorphic Figurines.* London, 1968.

University College 1907
University College, London. *Catalogue of Egyptian Antiquities Found by Prof. Flinders Petrie and Students at Gizeh and Rifeh. 1907.* London, 1907.

University of Delaware 1987
University of Delaware. *Ancient Art at the University of Delaware.* Newark, 1987.

University of Pennsylvania 1980
University of Pennsylvania. *The Egyptian Mummy. Secrets and Science.* Philadelphia, 1980.

Van Baaren 1964
T. Van Baaren. *Menschen wie wir. Religion und Kult der schriftlosen Volker.* Gütersloh, 1904.

Van Walsem 1978-1979
R. van Walsem. "The *psš-kf*: an Investigation of an Ancient Egyptian Funerary Instrument," *OMRO* 59 (1978-1979), pp. 193-249.

van Wijngaarden 1932
W.D. van Wijngaarden. *Beschreibung der Aegyptischen Sammlung des niederländischen Reichsmuseums der Altertümer in Leiden* XIV: *Grabtafeln und Osirisfiguren.* The Hague, 1932.

Vandier 1950
J. Vandier. *Moʿalla: la Tombe d' Ankhtify et la tombe de Sebekhotep.* Cairo, 1950.

Vandier 1954
J. Vandier. *Manuel d'archéologie égyptienne* II. Paris, 1954.

Vandier 1958
J. Vandier. *Manuel d'archéologie égyptienne* III. Paris, 1958.

Vandier 1964
J. Vandier. *Manuel d'archéologie égyptienne* IV. Paris, 1964.

Varga 1961
E. Varga. "Les Travaux Preliminaires de la Monographie sur les Hypocephales," *Acta Orientalia* XII (1961), pp. 235-247.

Varga 1968
E. Varga. "Le fragment d'un hypocephale egyptien," *Bulletin du Musée Hongrois des Beaux-Arts* 31 (1968), pp. 3-15.

Varille 1941
A. Varille. "Le Tombeau Thébain de Vice-Roi de Nubie Merimes," *ASAE* 40 (1941), pp. 567-570.

Varille 1947
A. Varille. "Les Trois Sarcophages du Fils Royal Merimes," *ASAE* 45 (1947), pp. 1-15.

Vassalli 1867
L. Vassalli. *I Monumenti Istorici Egizi il Museo e gli scavi d'antichita esequiti per ordini de S.A. il Vicere Ismail Pascia. Notizia Sommaria.* Milan, 1867.

Vercoutter 1972
J. Vercoutter. "Apis," *LÄ* I (1972), cols. 338-350.

Vercoutter 1976
J. Vercoutter. *Mirgissa* III. *Les Nécropoles.* Paris, 1976.

Vermeule 1954
C.C. Vermeule. *Some Notes on Ancient Dies and Coining Methods.* London, 1954.

Vermeule 1972
C.C. Vermeule. *Greek and Roman Portraits: 470 B.C.-A.D. 500.* Boston, 1972.

Verner 1982
M. Verner. *Altägyptische Särge in den Museen und Sammlungen der Tschechoslowakei* (Corpus Antiquatatum Aegyptiacarum). Prague, 1982.

Vernier 1927
E. Vernier. *Bijoux et orfèvreries,* 2 vols. (CG). Cairo, 1927.

Vila 1976
A. Vila. "Les Masques funéraires," in J. Vercoutter, *Mirgissa* III: *Les Nécropoles.* Paris, 1976, pp. 151ff.

Vittmann 1978
G. Vittmann. *Priester und Beamte im Theben der Spätzeit* (Beitrage zur Ägyptologie, Band 1). Vienna, 1978.

von Barany-Oberschall 1953
M. von Barany-Oberschall. "Byzantinische Pektoralkreuze aus Ungarischen Funden." *Forschungen zur Kunstgeschichte und Christlichen Archäologie* 2 (1953).

von Bissing 1907
F.W. von Bissing. *Steingefässe* (CG). Vienna, 1907.

von Bissing 1931-1932
F.W. von Bissing. *Archiv für Orientforschung* VII (1931-2).

von Gonzenbach 1957
V. von Gonzenbach. *Untersuchungen zu den Knabenweihen im Isiskult der römschen Kaiserzeit.* Bonn, 1957.

Wallert 1967
I. Wallert. *Der Verzierte Löffel.* Wiesbaden, 1967.

Ward 1970
W.A. Ward. "The Origin of Egyptian design-amulets," *JEA* 56 (1970), pp. 65-80.

Ward 1978
W.A. Ward. *Studies on Scarab Seals: Pre-12th Dynasty Scarab Amulets.* Warminster, 1978.

Weber 1911
W. Weber. "Zwei Formen des Osiris," *Untersuchungen zur aegyptisch-griechischen Religion.* Heidelberg, 1911, pp. 29-48.

Weigall 1902
A.E. Weigall. "The Inscriptions," in W.M.F. Petrie, *Abydos* I. London, 1902.

Weigall 1910
A.E. Weigall. *A Guide to the Antiquities of Upper Egypt from Abydos to the Sudan Frontier.* New York, 1910.

Weill 1918
R. Weill. *La fin du moyen empire égyptien – Etude sur les monuments et l'histoire de la periode comprise entre la XIIe et la XVIIIe dynastie* 1. Paris, 1918.

Weitzmann 1976
K. Weitzmann. *The Monastery of Saint Catherine at Mount Sinai: the Icons* I: *From the Sixth to the Tenth Century.* Princeton, 1976.

Wendorf 1968
Fred Wendorf. "Site 117: A Nubian Final Paleolithic Graveyard Near Gebel Sahaba, Sudan," in Fred Wendorf, ed., *The Prehistory of Nubia* 2. Dallas, 1968, pp. 954-995.

Wenig 1967
S. Wenig. "Ein Kasten für Opferspeisen aus dem Mittleren Reich," *Forschungen und Berichte* 8 (1967).

Wenig 1977
S. Wenig. *Ägyptische Altertümer.* Dresden, 1977.

Wenke 1980
R.J. Wenke. *Patterns in Prehistory.* New York, 1980.

Werbrouck 1938
M. Werbrouck. *Les Plureuses dans l'Egypte Ancienne.* Brussels, 1938.

Werbrouck 1940
M. Werbrouck. "Princesse Egyptienne," *CdE* 15 (1940), pp. 197-204.

Wessel 1963
K. Wessel. *Koptische Kunst: Die spätantike in Ägypten.* Recklinghausen, 1963.

Westendorf 1970
W. Westendorf. "Beiträge aus und zu den medizinischen Texten," *ZÄS* 96 (1970), pp. 145-151.

Westendorf 1980
W. Westendorf. "Isisknoten," *LÄ* 3 (1980), col. 204.

Whitehouse 1987
H. Whitehouse. "A Forgery Exposed," *Discussions in Egyptology* 9 (1987), pp. 63-68.

Wiebach 1981
S. Wiebach. *Die ägyptische Scheintür.* Hamburg, 1981.

Wiedemann 1910
Wiedemann. "Die Amulette der Alten Aegypter," *Der Alten Orient* 12.1. Leipzig, 1910.

Wild 1966
H. Wild. *Le Tombeau de Ti* III. Cairo, 1966.

Wild 1981
R.A. Wild. *Water in the Cultic Worship of Isis and Sarapis.* Leiden, 1981.

Wildung 1975
D. Wildung. "Erschlagen der Feinde," *LÄ* 2 (1975), cols. 14-17.

Wildung 1980
D. Wildung. *Fünf Jahre: Die Neuerwerbungen der Staatlichen Sammlung Ägyptischer Kunst Munchen 1976-1980.* Mainz, 1980.

Wildung 1984
D. Wildung. *Sesostris und Amenemhet. Ägypten im Mittleren Reich.* Munich, 1984.

Wildung and Grimm 1978
D. Wildung and G. Grimm. *Götter Pharaonen.* Mainz, 1978.

Wilkinson 1878
J.G. Wilkinson. *The Manners and Customs of the Ancient Egyptians* I. London, 1878.

Wilkinson 1971
A. Wilkinson. *Ancient Egyptian Jewellery.* London, 1971.

Williams 1918
C.R. Williams. "The Egyptian Collection in the Museum of Art at Cleveland, Ohio," *JEA* 5 (1918), pp. 272-285.

Williams 1975-76
B. Williams. "The Date of Senebtisi at Lisht," *Serapis* 3 (1975-76).

Wilson 1941
J. Wilson. "The Egyptian Middle Kingdom at Megiddo," *AJSL* 58 (1941).

Wilson 1944
J.A. Wilson. "Funeral Services of the Egyptian Old Kingdom," *JNES* 3 (1944), pp. 201-218.

Winlock 1916
H.E. Winlock. *The Tomb of Senebtisi at Lisht.* New York, 1916.

Winlock 1921
H.E. Winlock. *Bas-Reliefs from the temple of Rameses I at Abydos* (M.M.A. Papers, Vol. I, pt. I). New York, 1921.

Winlock 1922
H.E. Winlock. "The Egyptian Expedition 1921-1922: Excavations at Thebes," *BMMA Egyptian Supplement* (December, 1922), pp. 19-48.

Winlock 1924a
H.E. Winlock. "The Museum's Excavations at Thebes," *BMMA* 19 (The Egyptian Expedition 1924-25), pt. 2 (Dec. 1924), pp. 5-33.

Winlock 1924b
H.E. Winlock. "The Tombs of the Kings of the Seventeenth Dynasty at Thebes," *JEA* 10 (1924), pp. 217-277.

Winlock 1926
H.E. Winlock. "The Museum's Expedition at Thebes," *BMMA* 21 (The Egyptian Expedition 1925-26), pt. 2 (March 1926), pp. 5-32.

Winlock 1930
H.E. Winlock. "A Late Dynastic Embalmer's Table," *ASAE* 30 (1930), pp. 102-104.

Winlock 1940
H.E. Winlock. "The Mummy of Wah Unwrapped," *BMMA* 35 (December 1940), pp. 253-259.

Winlock 1941
H.E. Winlock. *Materials Used at the Embalming of King Tut-'Ankh-Amun.* New York, 1941.

Winlock et al. 1941
H.E. Winlock et. al. *The Temple of Hibis in the El Khargheh Oasis.* New York, 1941.

Winlock 1942
H.E. Winlock. *Excavations at Deir el-Bahri 1911-1931.* New York, 1942.

Winlock 1947
H.E. Winlock. *The Rise and Fall of the Middle Kingdom in Thebes.* New York, 1947.

Winlock 1955
H.E. Winlock. *Models of Daily Life in Ancient Egypt.* Cambridge, Mass., 1955.

Wirz 1982
G. Wirz. *Tod und Vergänglichkeit. Ein Beitrag zur Geisteshaltung der Ägypter von Ptahhotep bis Antef.* Saint Augustin, 1982.

Wood 1977
W. Wood. *Early Wooden Tomb Sculpture in Ancient Egypt* (Dissertation, Case Western Reserve, 1977).

Wulff and Volbach 1926
O. Wulff and W. Volbach. *Spätantike und koptische Stoffe aus ägyptischen Grabfunden in den Staatlichen Museen Kaiser-Friedrich-Museum.* Berlin, 1926.

Yalouris et al. 1980
N. Yalouris, M. Andronikos, K. Rhomiopoulou, A. Herrmann, C. Vermeule. *The Search for Alexander.* Boston, 1980.

Yoyotte 1952
J. Yoyotte. "Un Corps de police de l'Egypte pharaonique," *RdE* 9 (1952).

Yoyotte 1957
J. Yoyotte. "Le Soukhos de la Maréotide et d'Autres Cultes Régionaux du Dieu-crocodile d'Après les Cylindres du Moyen Empire," *BIFAO* 56 (1957), pp. 81-95.

Yoyotte 1958
J. Yoyotte. "A propos de la parenté féminine du roi Téti (VIè dynastie), *BIFAO* 57 (1958), pp. 91-98.

Yoyotte 1960
J. Yoyotte. "Les pélerinages dans l'Egypte ancienne." *Sources Orientales* 3 (Paris, 1960), pp. 17-74.

Yoyotte 1972
J. Yoyotte. "Les Adoratrices de la IIIe Periode Intermediaire. A Propos d'un Chef d'Oeuvre Rapporte par Champollion," *BSFE* 64 (1972), pp. 31-52.

Zaba 1950
Z. Zaba. "Un Nouveau fragment du sarcophage de Merymôsé," *ASAE* 50 (1947), pp. 509-514.

Žabkar 1968
L. Žabkar. "A Study of the Ba Concept in Ancient Egyptian Texts," (Studies in Ancient Oriental Civilization #34). Chicago, 1968.

Žabkar 1973
L. Žabkar. "Ba," *LÄ* I (1973), cols. 588-590.

Zaloscer 1961
H. Zaloscer. *Porträts aus dem Wüstensand: Die Mumienbildnisse aus der Oase Fayum.* Wien, 1961.

Zandee 1960
J. Zandee. *Death as an Enemy According to Ancient Egyptian Conceptions.* Leiden, 1960.

Zandee 1969
J. Zandee. "The Book of Gates," in *Liber Amicorum. Studies presented to Prof. Dr. C.J. Bleeker* (Studies in the History of Religions. Supplements to Numan XVII). Leiden, 1969, pp. 282-324.

Zauzich 1978
K-T. Zauzich. "Kartonage," *LÄ* III (1978), col. 353.

Ziegelmayer 1985
G. Ziegelmayer. *Münchner Mumien.* Munich, 1985.

Zivie 1976
C.M. Zivie. "Gisa," *LÄ* II (1976), cols. 602-614.

Zivie 1980
A.-P. Zivie. "Ibis," *LÄ* III (1977), cols. 115-121.

Zivie 1983a
A.-P. Zivie. "Les tombes de la falaise du Bubasteion à Saqqara," *Le Courrier du CNRS* 49, (1983), pp. 37-44.

Zivie 1983b
A.-P. Zivie. "Trois saisons à Saqqarah: les tombeaux du Bubasteion," *BSFE* 98, (1983), pp. 40-56.

Zuntz 1932
D. Zuntz. "Koptische Grabstelen. Ihre zeitliche und örtliche Einordnung," *MDAIK* 2 (1932), pp. 22-38.

Errata

The following are corrections for typographical errors in *Mummies and Magic: The Funerary Arts of Ancient Egypt.*

P. 9, Chronology: The dates for Dynasty 24 should be 760-685 B.C.

P. 26, note 2: "pp. 14-141" should read "pp. 14-41."

P. 49, last line: "Otto 1980" should read "Otto 1960."

P. 59, note 15: "Altenmüller 1975" should read "Altenmüller 1975c."

P. 72, notes 1, 3, 13: "Trigger 1986" should read "Trigger et al. 1986."

P. 73, notes 1, 3, 4, 15, 16: "van Walsem 1978" should read "van Walsem 1978-79."

P. 73, note 18: "Petrie 1898" should read "Petrie 1901b."

P. 74, note 1: "Fischer 1979a" should read "Fischer 1979b."

P. 74, notes 3, 4: "Petrie 1901" should read "Petrie 1901a."

P. 74, note 8: "Petrie 1925a" should read "Petrie 1925b."

P. 78, entry 8, note 2: "Fischer 1979" should read "Fischer 1979a."

P. 78, entry 8, Literature: "Reisner 1923" should read "Reisner 1923b."

P. 79, note 3: "Wente and Simpson 1972" should read "Wente and Simpson 1973a."

P. 79, note 5: "Reisner 1923" should read "Reisner 1923b."

P. 79, Literature: "Riefstahl 1944" should read "Riefstahl 1944a."

P. 83, entry 13, note 19: "Lucas and Harris 1962" should read "Lucas 1962."

P. 87, entry 14, note 6: "Smith 1947" should read "Smith 1946b."

P. 87, entry 15, note 1: "Riefstahl 1944" should read "Riefstahl 1944a."

P. 91, entry 21, Bibliography and Literature: "Smith 1947" should read "Smith 1946b."

P. 92, entry 23, col. 2, line 22: "no traces of the skeleton remained" should read "excavation photographs clearly show that there was a skeleton beneath the plaster layer."

P. 98, entry 29, Bibliography: "Reisner 1932" should read "Reisner 1932a."

P. 98, entry 30, col. 2, line 9: after "remainder" insert "in raised relief."

P. 99, entry 30, Bibliography: "Simpson 1972i" should read "Simpson 1972c."

P. 100, entry 32, note 3: "Merik" should read "Merikare"; "Firth and 22, 27-29" should read "Firth and Gunn 1926a, pp. 52-54; Firth and Gunn 1926b, pls. 22, 27-29."

P. 100, entry 32, note 6: insert "13.3466, Smith 1946b, pl. 23 a-b" after "MFA."

P. 101, entry 34, note 3: "Simpson 1973" should read "Simpson 1973a."

P. 103, entry 36, note 4: "Firth and Gunn 1926a" should read "Firth and Gunn 1926b."

P. 103, entry 36, Bibliography: "Museum of Fine Arts 1905 III" should read "Museum of Fine Arts 1905."

P. 105, entry 37, note 12: omit "Museum of Fine Arts 1987, and."

P. 105, entry 37, note 16: "Simpson 1974e" should read "Simpson 1974a."

P. 106, entry 38, note 2: "Brovarski 1980b" should read "Brovarski 1980."

P. 107, entry 39, Literature: "Grieshammer 1982" should read "Grieshammer 1974"; "Brovarski 1982" should read "Brovarski 1980."

P. 108, entry 40, note 5: "Petrie 1900" should read "Petrie 1900a."

P. 109, entry 42, note 2: "Petrie 1900" should read "Petrie 1900a."

P. 110, note 8: "Schenkel 1964" should read "Schenkel 1962."

P. 112, note 41: "Farag 1971" should read "Farag and Iskander 1971."

P. 116, notes 81, 82: "Terrace 1968" should read "Terrace 1968b."

P. 116, note 84: "Lilyquist 1979" should read "Lilyquist 1979a."

P. 122, entry 48, Bibliography: "Simpson 1973b" should read "Simpson 1973c."

P. 123, entry 49, Literature: "Simpson 1972" should read "Simpson 1972a."

P. 123, entry 50, note 2: "Fischer 1960" should read "Fischer 1960a."

P. 124, entry 51, col. 1, line 2: "Middle Kingdom, Dynasty 12 or after" should read "Saite Period."

P. 124, entry 52, note 4: "Griffith and Newberry 1893-94" should read "Griffith and Newberry 1894, p. 29."

P. 126, essay, note 2: "Capart 1943" should read "Capart 1943a"; "Schneider 1977" should read "Schneider 1977, I,."

P. 126, essay, note 4 and Bibliography: "Dunham 1960" should read "Smith 1960."

P. 128, entry 59, note 11: insert ", p. 249" after "Hayes 1953."

P. 131, entry 63, note 5: "Hayes 1953" should read "Hayes 1959, pp. 30-32."

P. 132, entry 65, line 47: "After the Middle Kingdom" should read "From the Middle Kingdom on,."

P. 134, entry 68, note 5: "Kacmarczyk" should read "Kaczmarczyk"; "Freed 1981a" should read "Freed 1981b."

P. 134, entry 68, note 6: "Wooley" should read "Woolley."

P. 134, entry 69, note 4: "Petrie 1925" should read "Petrie 1925a."

P. 135, entry 71, note 4: "Bruyère 1930" should read "Bruyère 1930a."

P. 135, entry 71, Bibliography: "Museum of Fine Arts 1987" should read "Museum of Fine Arts 1987a."

P. 138, entry 76, note 8: "Fazzini 1983" should read "Brooklyn Museum 1983."

P. 144, entry 84, note 20: "Habachi 1959" should read "Habachi 1958."

P. 147, entry 86, note 16: "Brovarski 1984" should read "Brovarski 1984b."

P. 147, entry 87, note 5: "Varille 1947" should read "Varille 1941."

P. 148, entry 89, col. 2, line 11: *"phorous"* should read *"phoros."*

P. 152, entry 95, notes 1, 3: "Bogoslovski" should read "Bogoslovsky."

P. 152, entry 95, Bibliography: "Bibliography" should read "Literature."

P. 152, entry 96, Bibliography: "Porter and Moss 1960" should read "Porter and Moss 1937."

P. 154, entry 99, note 1: "Porter and Moss 1970" should read "Porter and Moss 1960."

P. 154, entry 100, note 5: "Bogoslovsky 1973" should read "Bogoslovsky 1972."

P. 160, entry 111, Bibliography: "Porter and Moss 1979" should read "Porter and Moss 1978, p. 572."

P. 163, entry 115, Literature: "p. 116" should read "cols. 441-444."

P. 164, entry 117, note 1: "Raisman and Martin 1985" should read "Raisman and Martin 1984."

P. 167, essay, note 27: "Baqués 1971-2" should read "Baqués Estapé 1971-72"; "Estapé 1973" should read "Baqués Estapé 1973."

P. 168, essay, Literature: "Zauzich 1980" should read "Zauzich 1978."

P. 171, entry 122, note 3: "Völkerunde" should read "Völkerkunde."

P. 171, entry 122, note 9: "Bruyère 1930a" should read "Bruyère 1930b."

P. 173, entry 124: omit the Bibliography references.

P. 175, entry 125, note 3: "Naville 1895" should read "Naville 1894-95."

P. 175, entry 125, note 6: "p. 466" should read "p. 46."

P. 175, entry 125, Bibliography: omit "p. 1942" after "Smith 1942."

P. 178, col. 3, line 21: "Psamtek-neb-peti" should read "Psamtek-neb-pehti."

P. 179, note 14: "Brovarski 1978" should read "Brovarski 1983."

P. 179, note 19: "p. 238" should read "p. 275."

P. 179, note 24: insert "1849-1856" after "Lepsius."

P. 179, note 30: "Brooklyn 1973" should read "Brooklyn Museum 1960."

P. 179, note 33: "Petrie 1888a" should read "Petrie 1888b."

P. 179, note 35: "Björkman 1965" should read "Björkman 1971."

P. 180, entry 127, note 46: "Schneider 1977i" should read "Schneider 1977.I."

P. 180, entry 127, note 48: "ḥw(w)," "ḥw," and "ḥww" should read "ḥw(w)," "ḥw," and "ḥww."

P. 180, entry 127, note 50: "Trigger 1983" should read "Trigger et al. 1983."

P. 180, entry 128, note 4: omit "Bietak and Reiser-Haslauer 1982."

P. 181, col.2, line 7: phrase should read "as the part of the body in which the mind."

P. 181, col. 3, line 23: "looped" should read "lopped."

P. 181, col. 3, line 36: "was placed within the mummy wrappings" should read "were placed within the mummy wrappings."

P. 183, col. 2, line 53: "silhouette engraved of" should read "silhouette of."

P. 183, col. 2: "groupings" should read "grouping."

P. 183, Literature: "Barsanti 1900" should read "Barsanti 1900b."

P. 184, entry 131, col. 2, last line: "solid amulets" should read "solid gold amulets."

P. 185, entry 132, col. 1, line 15: "Djed-Khonsu-iu-ankh" should read "Djed-Khonsu-iuf-ankh."

P. 190, entry 134, note 7: "pl. LIL 3079" should read "pl. LI; L 3079."

P. 191, entry 137, line 11: "Hebedru" should read "Hedebru."

P. 192, note 13: "p. 134" should read "p. 34."

P. 194, entry 140, note 1: "p. 27" should read "p. 28."

P. 194, entry 140, note 3: "p. 85" should read "p. 92."

P. 194, entry 140, note 6: "57.765-.766" should read "57.764-.766."

P. 194, entry 140, note 11: "Ranke 1935" should read "Ranke 1935, p. 9, 5."

P. 194, entry 141, col. 3, par. 5, line 4: "elythra" should read "elytra."

P. 195, entry 141, note 1: "pl. 12c" should read "pl. 12b."

P. 195, entry 141, note 2: "21nd century" should read "2nd century."

P. 195, entry 141, note 5: "Gray 1966, pl. 14.2, 16.2, 19.2" should read "pl. 24.2, 26.2, 29.2."

P. 196, entry 143, col. 2, line 4: "Qebhsenef" should read "Qebehsenuef."

P. 199, entry 147, note 2: "Kamal 1941" should read "Kamal 1909."

P. 203, entry 152, col. 1, line 2: "Lybian" should read "Libyan."

P. 206, essay, note 10: "Edgar 1905a" should read "Edgar 1905b."

P. 207, entry 155, notes 2, 3: "Petrie et al. 1898" should read "Petrie 1889."

P. 209, entry 157, Bibliography: "Museum of Fine Arts 1977" should read "Museum of Fine Arts 1976"; "Museum of Fine Arts 1987" should read "Museum of Fine Arts 1987a."

P. 209, entry 158, Bibliography: omit references to Grenier 1977, Grimm 1974, and Parlasca 1966.

P. 213, entry 163, Literature: insert "pp. 42-43" after "Abd el-Al, Grenier, and Wagner 1985."

P. 214, entry 164, note 3: "Museum of Fine Arts 1987" should read "Museum of Fine Arts 1987a."

P. 214, entry 164, note 12: "Edgar 1905" should read "Edgar 1905a."

P. 214, entry 165, note 1: "Naville 1895" should read "Naville 1894-95."

P. 214, entry 165, note 3: "Naville 1894" should read "Naville 1893-94."

P. 214, entry 165, notes 7, 8: "Brovarski 1984" should read "Brovarski 1984c."

P. 216, note 2: "Trilling 1980" should read "Trilling 1982."

P. 217, entry 166, note 4: "Egger 1867" should read "Egger 1967."

P. 218, entry 168: add "**Bibliography:** Brooklyn Museum 1941, p. 23, cat. no. 39; Cramer 1957, p. 10, cat. no. 13 and pl. 8, fig. 13; Museum of Fine Arts 1976, pp. 203-204, cat. no. 240."

P. 221, entry 171, note 6: "Dimick 1959" should read "Anthes 1959."

P. 227, entry 181, note 1: "van Voss 1974" should read "Heerma van Voss 1974."

P. 228, entry 183, note 4: "Daressy 1903a" should read "Daressy 1903b."

P. 230, entry 185, note 2: "Cairo Museum JE 61444" should read "Cairo Museum JE 6144."

P. 230, entry 186, note 5: "Winlock 1941" should read "Winlock et al. 1941."

P. 231, entry 187, note 1: "Lortet and Gaillard 1909" should read "Lortet and Gaillard 1907."

P. 234, entry 190, note 2: "Herodotus 1985, p. 65-67" should read "Herodotus II, 65-67."

P. 234, entry 191, note 6: "Roeder 1956a" should read "Roeder 1956."

P. 235, entry 192, notes 1, 3: "Brovarski 1984" should read "Brovarski 1984b."

P. 238, entry 197, Bibliography: "Smith 1946" should read "Smith 1946a."

P. 243, entry 206, Literature: insert "p. 142" after "Schneider and Raven 1981."

P. 245, entry 210, note 2: "Taylor (forthcoming)" should read "Taylor (forthcoming, b)."

Color Plates

Objects on loan to the Dallas Museum of Art

Cover Coffin panel of Satmeket
    From Bersha
    Middle Kingdom
    Wood
    See pp. 109-117

I.   False door of Sat-in-teti
    From Sakkara
    Old Kingdom
    Limestone
    Cat. no. 30

Index